# EDUCATION AND SOCIETY
## Information Processing 92

VOLUME II

# IFIP Transactions A: Computer Science and Technology

International Federation for Information Processing

Technical Committees:

SOFTWARE: THEORY AND PRACTICE (TC2)
EDUCATION (TC3)
SYSTEM MODELLING AND OPTIMIZATION (TC7)
INFORMATION SYSTEMS (TC8)
RELATIONSHIP BETWEEN COMPUTERS AND SOCIETY (TC9)
COMPUTER SYSTEMS TECHNOLOGY (TC10)
SECURITY AND PROTECTION IN INFORMATION PROCESSING SYSTEMS (TC11)
ARTIFICIAL INTELLIGENCE (TC12)
HUMAN-COMPUTER INTERACTION (TC13)
FOUNDATIONS OF COMPUTER SCIENCE (SG14)

IFIP Transactions Abstracted/Indexed in:
INSPEC Information Services

A-13

# EDUCATION AND SOCIETY
# Information Processing 92

Proceedings of the IFIP 12th World Computer Congress
Madrid, Spain, 7-11 September 1992

## VOLUME II

Edited by

ROBERT M. AIKEN
*College of Engineering*
*Temple University*
*Philadelphia, U.S.A.*

N·H

1992

NORTH-HOLLAND
AMSTERDAM • LONDON • NEW YORK • TOKYO

ELSEVIER SCIENCE PUBLISHERS B.V.
Sara Burgerhartstraat 25
P.O. Box 211, 1000 AE Amsterdam, The Netherlands

ISBN: 0 444 89748 8
ISBN Set: 0 444 89750 X
ISSN: 0926-5473



This book is printed on acid-free paper.

Printed in The Netherlands

# IFIP PRESIDENT'S INTRODUCTION

The latest of the twelve IFIP Congresses coincides with the 500th anniversary of one of the discoveries of the New World. Hardly by chance the venue of the Congress is charming Madrid, where many celebrations will commemorate an event that leads us back half a millenium in history.

This Congress is a turning point in IFIP's tradition of organizing its Congresses on a three-yearly basis. All future Congresses will be held every two years: the 13th is scheduled for 1994 in Hamburg, Germany and the 14th in Canberra, Australia.

In the last three years, our world has undergone sweeping changes. This period, falling between the 11th and the 12th IFIP Computer Congress, will have a very special place in mankind's history, not only for its political developments, but also for the enormous progress in data-processing which is to be demonstrated in Madrid.

The significant influence of the IFIP Technical Committees and Working Groups on the structure and contents of Congress' 92 made it possible for hundreds of IFIP specialists, both academics and practitioners, to consider this Congress as their own creation. At the Congress there will be many other who will come in touch with IFIP for the first time. Naturally, our hope is that they will be able identify IFIP as their own international professional organization.

At a time when many human activities rely on the use of computers, the organization of a World Computer Congress is not an ordinary endeavor. Thanks to the outstanding professionalism and rich experience of the Congress' International Program Committee, participants will have a variety of choices to explore the many tracks and trends in the domain of data-processing.

Finally, I would like to wish the Congress participants a most fruitful and enjoyable stay in Spain. I am convinced that at this most important IFIP event you will meet old friends and make many new ones.

*Academician Blagovest Sendov*
*President, International Federation for Information Processing*

# EDITOR'S FOREWORD

This Volume is Number II of the three volume set that comprises the Proceedings of the twelfth World Computer Congress (IFIP Congress 92). The papers in this volume are from Stream 4: *Informatics and Education*; Stream 5: *The Vulnerability of the Information Society* and the special symposium: *Informatics for Environmental Protection*. The volume is divided into these three sections with papers and panels listed in the order they were presented at the Congress. Invited papers have been designated as such, and unlike previous years, there were no responder replies. The theme of this conference emphasized putting theory into practice, thus many of the papers report on actual experiences.

As the world is increasingly looking to people in the informatics profession for assistance in solving (or at least working on) very complex and difficult problems it is encouraging to note that two of the six streams of this conference as well as several symposia focus on education, social and professional issues. The papers in this volume represent incisive and penetrating insights to a number of critical issues by people from around the world. Credit must be given to the Program Chair, Wilfried Brauer and his Program Committee for having the vision to highlight these topics.

After being reviewed by at least three referees, the contributed papers were selected by the Program Commitee at the end of February, 1992. The selection process was very competitive with less than one third of all submitted papers to Streams 4 and 5 accepted for publication. The quality of the papers in this volume reflects the high standards of the selection process. Moreover, these streams reflect the truly international flavor of this Congress with Streams 4 and 5 each having (co-)authors representing more than 25 different countries!

In addition to the direct and visible contributions of papers, much time and effort by many dedicated professionals was devoted to making these proceedings possible. The task of choosing the invited speakers and reviewers plus organizing the technical program was accomplished by the Program Committees. The referees (and their colleagues) did yeoman service in getting the reviews done and returned within one month! Special thanks go to Nate Hoskin, Laurie

Shteir, Judy Lennon, Elizabeth Sparkman and Gary Bredbenner who assisted me and to Inez van der Heide and Avril Hofman at North-Holland for their editorial advice. Their support was crucial in preparing this volume.

A very special thanks goes to all the authors. It was difficult for them to meet the page restrictions which were imposed. In several instances authors did not follow the typing guidelines, but I accepted the papers hoping that they will reproduce legibly. Many had to substantially alter their papers. In a few cases I allowed an extra page or two, and in three cases, for unusual circumstances, we accepted papers well beyond the limits. To all of you, and to Klaus Brunnstein, who worked with many of you (as well as me) a big THANKS.

*Robert M. Aiken*
*(Editor)*

# TABLE OF CONTENTS

## Administrative Aspects



## CAL/CML/Educational Software



## Pedagogical Aspects

**Applying Research to Support Learners – Part I**



**Applying Research to Support Learners – Part II**

**Ethics of Computing: Information Technology and Responsibility**



**Legal Aspects: Fighting Vulnerability With Law?**

## Improving IT Security and Safety



## Diminishing Vulnerability in an Artifact Society

---

* Paper not submitted

# PROGRAM COMMITTEE CHAIRMAN'S FOREWORD

Innovation cycles in computer technology are extremely short, and the research results of today will be used tomorrow in products of daily practice. It is not only the single breakthrough result which may have such an immediate effect but it is more and more also the incremental innovation, based on many research and development findings in many different areas of computer technology, communications, and electronics - contributed by people from many different countries - that drives the rapid growth of the computer industry. Communication and collaboration of people from different fields and different countries is therefore a growing need.

IFIP's World Computer Congresses are ideal platforms to meet researchers and practitioners, educators and users, leading professionals and young innovators, to discuss ideas, experiences, problems in a wide forum of people from all parts of the world and all parts of computer science and technology.

IFIP Congress 92 starts a new congress line. Congresses now take place more often, i.e. every even year: 1992 in Madrid, Spain, 1994 in Hamburg, Germany, 1996 in Canberra, Australia. The Congress structure was changed: we have 4 parallel streams for the core areas of software, hardware, theory, and education; from the many possible other areas only a few were selected for the 1992 Congress - the next Congresses will make another selection. These additional topics are presented in one (full-length) stream, two 3-day subconferences and 4 symposia. In addition to the traditional presentation of invited and submitted papers, the presentation of posters is encouraged to give more people the opportunity to participate actively in the Congress.

The program committee's composition and structure is also new. I wanted to give the people from the country in which the Congress is organized a much greater influence and I wanted a modular structure and distributed operation of the committee. This resulted in having 7 subcommittees consisting of people from several countries, but with a representative from Spain in each of them; these committees had their own way of inviting speakers and selecting the papers submitted to their respective subcommittee chairmen. The kernel program committee consisting of the subcommittee chairman and the Spanish representative plus a (varying) small number of other subcommittee members met only 3 times (in Madrid, Munich, Madrid). The subcommittees also had their additional ways and means of announcing the call for papers.

The number of submitted papers was much higher than expected on the basis of previous IFIP Congress experiences: For the streams and subconferences we received in total almost 500 submitted papers whose authors come from almost 50 countries. Several of these submissions were carefully solicited. From all the submissions 171 were accepted for presentation and publication - in addition to the 34 invited talks in the streams and subconferences plus 32 invited talks in the 4 symposia and the two keynote speeches contributed by the program committee to the opening and closing sessions. Most of these papers as well as many statements of the speakers in the 19 panel discussions are printed in the 3 proceedings volumes.

That the proceedings are published in three distinct volumes, each with another emphasis and each targeting at different groups of readers is also an innovation of this IFIP Congress. I would like to thank in particular the traditional IFIP Congress proceedings publisher, Elsevier

(North-Holland), and its excellent IFIP liaison, Mrs. Stephanie Smit for making this possible as well as for the flexibility in the cooperation with the program committee and the editors. My sincere thanks go also to the three proceedings editors who also have been very active program committee members.

I was very happy that so many prominent people have been willing to devote quite a lot of their scarce time to work intensively within the program committee. It was a great pleasure for me to work with them. In particular I would like to express my great appreciation and sincere thanks to the very efficient and reliable vice chairman Carlos Delgado Kloos as well as to the subcommittee chairmen, who had more or less to work as the chairmen of full-size conferences, and to the poster and tutorial organizer. The symposia organizers Brian Oakley, Bernard Glasson, Bernd Page and Joseph Traub managed quite independently to set up very attractive programs which on the one hand are emphasizing IFIP's concern on university - industry collaboration and on the other hand present newly developing working groups. It was very easy for me to work with them and I thank them particularly.

Special thanks are also due to the two prominent keynote speakers our committee was able to find:

Philip Kahn, Chairman of C.E.O. and President of Borland International speaks on "Software Craftsmanships in the 90's".

Pamela Mc Corduck, a world famous writer on computing and its relationship to culture and civilization, speaks on art and artificial intelligence - and her speech is also documented in these proceedings (cordial thanks for that!).

Not only the Congress program, also the Congress site will be very influential for attracting the participants from around the world. The Spanish organising committee under the chairmanship of Mrs. Rosa Alonso and with the help of the Spanish representative to the IFIP General Assembly, Angel Alvarez, did an enormous job in preparing this large Congress - many thanks and good luck to them.

Munich, May 1992

Wilfried Brauer
Program Committee Chairman

# ORGANIZING COMMITTEE CHAIRWOMAN'S FOREWORD

First of all, it is an honour for me to be able to state that the support conferred by Spain to this 12th World Computer Congress has been wholly emphasized by the personal attention given to this celebration by His Majesty and by His attendance at the Opening Ceremony.

This is the first time that this biennial broad-based Congress has been held in Spain, hosted by FESI (Federacion Espanola de Asociaciones de Informatica), the Spanish member organization of IFIP (International Federation for Information Processing). FESI is a federation of Spanish professional Associations, foundations concerned with information technology, computer science schools and national research institutions.

This 12th IFIP Congress '92 will cover the main areas of information technology applicable to both academic and industrial fields.

Under the theme, "From Research to Practice", the Congress will demonstrate the relevant role that advanced computer technology and its application play in long-term corporate benefits and show how, daily, actions are taken to increase that role.

To comply with the Congress' aims, an extensive program has been implemented. Firstly, a technical programme has been scheduled, including five parallel streams, two subconferences and four symposia. Six one-day pre-congress tutorials have been organized, an exhibition of products, scientific books and publications, and a wide range of technical visits. An excellent – and typical – social program has also been carefully prepared, full of attractive events, such as the reception and the Congress banquet.

An additional attraction to the Congress could be the celebration of EXPO '92 (Seville) and the nomination of Madrid Cultural '92 and other no less important events in the country, such as the Olympic Games in Barcelona.

It is unnecessary to say that the accomplishment and success of an event like a World Congress is the result of a group of persons working together as a team, trying to solve all the problems – big and small – in order to provide the international attendance and speakers with the best possible scenario for all the technical and social events. To face up to this challenge, there have been people working hard for a long period of time, always in pursuit of an international contribution to the progress of science and even – and why not? – looking for improvements in the quality of life of all human beings.

For all these reasons, and many others, I would like to express my most sincere thanks to all those persons without whose contribution it would not have been possible to come to a happy end.

Thanks to Mr. Brauer, Program Committee Chair, to all the members of the Committee, to the Committee of Honour, to the Spanish Authorities, to all Patrons, Institutions and, finally and most warmly, to all my colleagues and friends on the Organizing Committee as well as the FESI President, Spanish IFIP representative and to the Alcatel and Fundesco teams, whom I had the opportunity of chairing during so many hard working but wonderful days.

Rosa Alonso

# IFIP CONGRESS '92 COMMITTEES

## International Program Committee

Chair: Wilfried Brauer, Technical University of Munich, Germany
Vice Chair: Carlos Delgado Kloos, Technical University of Madrid, Spain
Past Chair: Hervé Gallaire, GSI, France
OC Chair: Rosa Alonso, Alcatel N.V.

## Subcommittees

### Stream 1: Software Development and Maintenance

Chair: A. Nico Habermann, National Science Foundation, USA
Members: P. Botella, Technical Univ. of Catalonia, Barcelona, Spain
L.M. Koroleff, Moscow State Univ., Russia
R. Kurki-Suonio, Tampere Univ. of Technology, Finland
A. Yonezawa, Univ. of Tokyo, Japan

### Stream 2: Algorithms and Efficient Computation

Chair: Jan van Leeuwen, University of Utrecht, The Netherlands
Members: J. Diaz, Technical Univ. of Catalonia, Barcelona, Spain
S. Even, The Technion, Haifa, Israel
R.M. Karp, Univ. of California at Berkeley, USA

### Stream 3: From Architectures to Chips

Chair: Gerald Reijns, Delft University of Technology, The Netherlands
Members: C. Delgado Kloos, Technical University of Madrid, Spain
E. Hörbst, Siemens A.G., Munich, Germany
Y. Tohma, Tokyo Institute of Technology, Tokyo, Japan

**Stream 4: Informatics and Education**

Chair: Peter Bollerslev, Ministry of Education, Copenhagen, Denmark
Members: R. Aiken, Temple Univ., Philadelphia, PA, USA
A. Balasubrahmanian, Indira Gandhi National Open Univ., Delhi, India
I. Stanchev, Research Center for Education in Informatics, Sofia, Bulgaria
A. Vaquero, Complutense Univ., Madrid, Spain

**Stream 5: The Vulnerability of the Information Society: Social, Legal, and Security Aspects**

Chair: Klaus Brunnstein, University of Hamburg, Germany
Members: W. Caelli, Queensland Univ. of Technology, Brisbane, Australia
R. Moeller, Sears & Roebuck, Chicago, USA
J.A. Pino, Univ. of Chile, Santiago, Chile
F. Sáez-Vacas, Technical Univ. of Madrid, Spain

**Subconference 1: Expanding the Power of the Personal Computer**

Chair: Friedrich H. Vogt, University of Hamburg, Germany
Members: I. Agamirzian, FORTHINFO, St. Petersburg, Russia
C.P. Lucena, Catholic Univ., Rio de Janeiro, Brazil
R. Puigjaner, Univ. of the Balearic Islands, Palma de Mallorca, Spain
B. Robinet, IBM France, Paris, France
R. Schwartz, Borland European Technology Center, Paris, France

**Subconference 2: Enhancing the Intelligence in Information Systems**

Chair: Gordon Davis, University of Minnesoty, USA
Members: R. Benjamin, Rochester, New York, USA
J.P. Laurent, Univ. de Savoie, Chambery, France
M. Lundeberg, Stockholm School of Economics, Sweden
J. Motiwalla, National Univ. of Singapore, Singapore
A. Olivé, Techn. Univ. of Catalonia, Barcelona, Spain

**Symposium Organizers:**

**Symposium 1: Cooperative Research Programs**
Brian Oakley, Logica Cambridge Ltd., U.K.

**Symposium 2: Informatics for Environmental Protection**
Bernd Page, University of Hamburg, Germany

**Symposium 3: Encouraging Academic / Practitioner Collaboration**
Bernard Glasson, Curtin Univ. Perth, Australia

**Symposium 4: Continuous Algorithms and Complexity**
Joseph Traub, Columbia Univ., New York, NY, USA

**Spain's Organizing Committee**

Chair: Rosa Alonso, Alcatel N.V.
Members: Jose Ignacio Boixo, ALI
Miguel Angel Eced, AEIA
Jaume Argila, ATI
Nuria Castell, Technical Univ. of Catalonia
Francisco Fernández-Campón, Alcatel Standard Electrica S.A.
Manuel Gamella, FUNDESCO
Javier Leach, Complutense University of Madrid
Luis Maté, Technical Univ. of Madrid
Roberto Molero, ERITEL
Luis A. Petit, CITEMA
Ramón Puigjaner, Univ. of the Balearic Islands
Antonio San Martin, FYCSA - Alcatel

# REFEREES

## Stream 4: Information and Education

The following members of IFIP's Technical Committee on Education (TC-3) co-ordinated the review process for this stream. They were ably assisted by over 100 colleagues from around the world.

Aiken, R.
Balasubrahmanian, A.
Bollerslev, P.
Levrat, B.
Lewis, R.
Martin, D.
Stanchev, I.
Vaquero, A.S.
Wibe, J.

## Stream 5: The Vulnerability of the Information Society: Social, Legal, and Security Aspects

The members of the Program Committee were greatly assisted by the following persons with the refereeing of papers in this stream.

Bansler, J.
Bathnagar, S.C.
Beardon, C.
Berleur, J.
Bjerg, K.
Bontchev, V.W
de Greef, B.
Frerk, G.
Goossens, P.M.M.
Haddon, L.
Holvast, J.
Kolm, P.
Korpcla, M.
Larsson Tendenfors, I.
Mambray, P.
Monse, K.
van Rijn, F.
Sizer, R
Tantam, M.
Yngström, L.

# STREAM 4: INFORMATICS AND EDUCATION

**Peter Bollerslev**
**Chair**

Education and Society / R. Aiken (Editor)
Information Processing 92, Volume II
Elsevier Science Publishers B.V. (North-Holland)



# Educational telecommunications services: a case study on an integrated approach

Ferran Ruiz i Tarragó

Generalitat de Catalunya - Programa d'Informàtica Educativa, Via Laietana 64, 1r, 08003 Barcelona, Spain

## Abstract

Information and communications technology is increasingly available in primary and secondary schools. There is evidence of a strong need of integrating technical developments in curriculum development activities, school organization, teacher training and resource access. This paper deals with an approach to educational telecommunications services aiming at this integration. Simultaneous lines of action are the organization of telecommunications-based distance learning activities, the implementation of curriculum development strategies and the construction of information retrieval services, altogether with the stimulation of participation of teachers in those developments.

Keyword Codes: H.3.5; H.4.3; K.3.1
Keywords: Online Information Services; Communications Applications; Computer Uses in Education

## 1. Introduction.

In the last few years educational telecommunications have emerged as an entirely new field of educational activity and research. The quality and quantity of efforts devoted to it show that many expectations have risen in schools, universities and further education colleges, usually with the mixed aims of giving a community dimension to education and of harnessing the potential of technology for the benefit of new forms of teaching and learning.

Drawing on current experience and research, Riel <1> states that "building a community of educators is not simply a technical matter of installing computer technology. The promise of a new social organization, an electronic community, is not realized when computers are connected with modems. The evolution of local, national and international electronic communities requires attention to group organization, group dynamics and educational leadership". This paragraph expresses clearly the global complexity of innovation in this field, so educational administrations should play an important role in planning, supporting and organizing telecommunications-based distance learning activities, information retrieval services and curriculum development strategies. The role of educational administrations is particularly crucial in primary and secondary school levels, in which the success of telecommunications depends on its integration in the curriculum and school structure.

Building on these ideas, an integrated approach to educational telecommunications has been developed by the Programa d'Informàtica Educativa ("Informatics in Education Programme", hereafter called PIE) of the Department of Education of the regional government of Catalonia (Spain) with the set up in 1988 of a telematic network named XTEC (that stands for "Xarxa Telemàtica Educativa de Catalunya" or Catalunya's Educational Telematic Network). Using Whiting's words <2>, this development is aimed at giving "the types of support which can be hosted on existing telecommunications networks: 1) learner-to-learner, learner-to-tutor communications; 2) information provision and conferencing; 3) data and information base access and searching." The integrated approach we are referring to means that by network we understand the global interplay of server operation, modems and software in schools, specific services for education, and educational leadership and organizational and training support.

XTEC links all the state secondary schools in Catalonia, a growing number of primary schools, both public and private, and many institutions related with education. It is hosted by a Honeywell Bull DPS8/49 computer linked to a specific telecommunications front-end. The operating system of the host supports software packages for teleconferencing, document database management and retrieval, electronic mail, news service and file transfer of any type of computer file. In a progressive movement to more open standards some of the existing services and other new applications are at present being implemented in a UNIX environment. For further details on technical aspects see Castells <3>.

This paper considers the three main educational applications that are built upon the aforementioned set of software facilities: 1) a reference resource database, 2) a range of curriculum development activities by means of teleconferencing, and 3) an extension of the activities of in-service teacher training. Finally some further comments are made on the integrated approach to educational telecommunications.

## 2. The SINERA database of educational resources.

In an era in which societal change imposes curriculum reform and school restructuring, curriculum development needs a substantial provision of up-to-date resource materials. The teacher usually faces a real difficulty to select the most suitable materials because of the excessive flow of information -many times lacking appropriate structure-, the variety and dispersion of sources and the time constraints of education professionals. Innovative teachers often feel the need of help to cope with the great amount of information, and information technology can contribute to help them obtain the resources they need at the right moment.

In order to facilitate teachers a fast and easy access to relevant information, a specific resource database named SINERA was designed and created from the very beginning of XTEC. This database, whose name is acrostic of "System of Educational Information and Learning Resources", is actively updated with the aims of broadening its topical scope and expanding its coverage, to make it relevant to teaching and learning in almost every curriculum area. At present it has more than 12000 records.

The records stored in SINERA are meant to be used as reference information concerning a variety of types of resources. These are books, papers, journals, materials for the classroom, test items, sound and video recordings, software and databases. It also contains some descriptions of places to visit, itineraries, museums and educational institutions.

Regardless that variety of types of materials, SINERA was designed and implemented as a single database instead of creating different databases each of them containing information on an homogeneous type of resources. Technically that design relies on: 1) the capabilities of the document database management software (MISTRAL) of integrating heterogeneous types of information in a single database structure, and 2) the fact that the access to different types of resources can be made easy with a specifically designed interface. MISTRAL's query language is based on keywords and boolean operators and provides advanced search features such as relational operators and free-text search, use of thesaurus, management of the visualization formats, etc. This search facilities -available in a full-duplex access mode- require the user's acquaintance with the query language's commands of MISTRAL, specifically in what concerns command search. Because this is a real drawback for many teachers, there is a videotex access mode that implements an interface that simplifies the search process permitting even the novice to move easily and effectively within the database. The user is guided at every step having only to write in the blank areas of predefined screens. These screens allow the definition of the types of resources to be searched, broadening or limiting the search terms, selecting the educational levels for which the information is searched and the display and storage of the information retrieved.

SINERA is internally structured in 23 fields and for the user records have always the same pattern, irrespective of their source or the type of information they contain. The main fields are: type of resource; title, both Catalan and original; author's name and affiliation; publisher; name of periodical; date; language of the document; levels of the resource (whether the resource contains single identifiable resources or is part of a bigger set); characteristics (physical features that can be used for its identification in a search); location in some specific cases; standard classification code; availability; descriptors on focus (author's perspective and educational goal of the resource), subject and educational level; identifiers; abstract and data on the information provider.

The approach of building a single comprehensive resource database has proven to be useful for two main reasons. Firstly, from the managerial point of view, it facilitates the concentration of human, organizational and economic resources in a big online resource database project. Specifically it also easies the development of in-service training activities through traditional courses and, as it will be commented in section 4, through distance learning methods. The second main advantage is that teachers know that a single database contains reference information useful in many curriculum topics and types of activities with students. It would be uncomfortable for teachers to have to search several databases to find the information they need depending on the type of resource.

The SINERA database has already a reasonable size. It is planned to launch a systematic effort of promotion of its use in relationship with the educational system reform that is currently being prepared. We hope, although we still have no evidence, that this approach will motivate a broader use of project work methods and will deepen the development of information skills.

## 3. Curriculum development through teleconferencing.

One of the main goals of using information technology in education is that it can foster the formalization and communication of ideas in almost every topic or level. This type of work can be carried out in classroom settings, but the communicational dimension takes a greater role when the dialog is established beyond the school walls. Literature on this type of activities shows a growing evidence that in that case the style, precision and presentation of ideas are higher, and that the students' interest in the subject increases.

The curriculum related activities based on teleconferencing are called teledebates. They consist of the progressive construction of a database of messages by students of different schools on a given topic in a structured form, with a leader or moderator that takes the responsibility for overseeing the organization and the development of the whole process.

As a model example of structured teledebates we comment on a specific teledebate named JULIA that has established a successful pattern for this type of activities. JULIA was a teleconference developed in 1989/90 on Catalan language and literature based on a novel by a living author. The conference brought into contact the author herself, a teledebate moderator and twenty two groups of students through a carefully prepared curricular activity that lasted six weeks. Under PIE's direction a call for interested teachers was made and finally 16 had the leadership of the activity in their schools. Negotiations began on the curricular objectives of the activity and on selecting the appropriate novel, which would be compulsory reading for students of 22 selected classes of 15/16-year-old students, the calendar and pace, the initial teacher training activities and the type of work students should do. The conference was structured on seven topics, concerning the creative process, the plot and the main themes of the novel chosen for the debate.

In the six-week period of the conference the activity was made as follows. Each participant class was divided in seven groups, each one dealing with a specific topic of the debate. Every Monday a group of students downloaded the messages of the other groups working on the same topic. During the week they discussed the incoming contributions and wrote their own comments and points of view and every Friday they sent their work to the server to be downloaded the next Monday by the other participants. Half of the students had had previous experience in word processing, but none of them knew about telecommunications processes, although they mastered them easily. Technical performance of students was far more higher than teachers performance, so continued support was offered to teachers through electronic mail and some group meetings.

The agreed objectives were the following: 1) to increase the motivation for reading literature, 2) to foster group work and discussion and to deepen in literary analysis, and 3) to stimulate the development of writing skills. These objectives are not different from the strictly curricular objectives that teachers already had. Nevertheless, it was agreed that the use of telecommunications and word processing incorporated a further value in the development of information and communication skills.

This teledebate is an example that has set the pattern of other similar activities that have been developed since then. It is complex to organize: it requires a specific effort of planning, negotiation on issues such as pedagogical aims, number and level of students involved, pace and calendar, and coordination inside each school and among schools participating in it. The leadership of the PIE contributes to overcome the numerous barriers that hinder the process. More open ended types of curriculum development through teleconferencing are teledebates such as the collective construction of fictional tales based on traditional folk culture, as well as open investigations on local, geographical and social environment in the form of a collective writing process, both of them addressed to early secondary school students.

## 4. Distance in-service teacher training.

An important part of the activity of the PIE is devoted to in-service teacher training in educational uses of information technology through traditional courses. Almost 700 courses have been run in the last two academic years. This effort is coordinated with other main activities such as installation of computer equipment in schools and software development.

In order to extend the range of in-service training activities making use of the telecommunication services provided by XTEC, the PIE organized two experimental "Online In-service Teacher Training" (OITT) courses on some specific educational uses of information technology during the academic year 1990/91 <4>. The telematic network was used both as a delivery system and as the link between a physically separated instructor -who acted as a course coordinator- and the learners in a new way of interaction. This implies a change of role for the course coordinator and the learners themselves. The course coordinator is meant to act mainly as a facilitator; that is, not to be so concerned with formal teaching and course direction, but with facilitating more active and self-directed learning by the participants.

This in-service teacher training scheme would fit in the "Formal learning" taxonomy of expressed or implicit learner requirements established by Whiting <2>. That means that the learners follow a formal study that leads to an in-service teacher training certificate. Similar approaches to the use of CMC in training are described by Gray <5> using the CAUCUS computer conferencing system and by Legrottaglie and others <6>.

The in-service project started by redefining and adapting two already existing sets of course material and giving them a specific approach for distance learning supported by telematics. The courses selected and developed were "Using spreadsheets in education" and "Online information retrieval: the SINERA database". These subjects could be attractive to a wide range of teachers because their concepts and methods can be applied in a wide range of curriculum areas.

The services provided to in-service learners were: 1) a distance delivery system to download files and text materials; 2) a collaborative learning environment based on the teleconferencing facility; and 3) continued private tutorial help and guidance by means of electronic mail. The learners also received written course materials of a modular structure (made by desk-top publishing techniques), application and communications software specific to each course, and a certificate of course attendance.

The courses were structured in 7 modules of learning activities that had to be completed sequentially and finished by the student in 2 weeks. A personal project was the final part of the course that led to an in-service training certificate. A comprehensive evaluation of this project was undertaken by an external organization by means of a task force group on advanced training techniques. Its main findings <7> can be summarized as follows:

1) Students joined in motivated by the courses' self-learning approach and their interest on the telematic support methodology. The expectations generated by this approach were the main motivation and the subject matter of the courses, being important, was ranked as less motivating. This could mean that mainly innovative and information technology-prone teachers were attracted by the courses, irrespective of their previous background.

2) Students' perception of the usefulness of the telematic tools evolved during the course. At first any technical problem was discouraging but students' confidence grew continuously. Thus, they changed their mind about the value of the support and delivery system.

3) E-mail and file transfer were the tools mainly used by students: all students that finished the courses used them systematically. The individualized support and facilitating activities of the course coordinators through electronic mail was ranked as high by students.

4) On the contrary, only 45% of the students were engaged systematically in the teleconferencing activities, probably because of lack of suitable strategies of motivating action. This seems to be the main weakness of the project: course coordinators need a specific training and expertise in stimulating the participation in the group teleconferences, and that was not available in this pilot project. Additionally, teachers didn't appreciate very much the collaborative learning aspects of the teleconferencing facility.

Building on these experiences, the same courses have been launched again in the academic year 1991/92 and the overload of the coordinators has been reduced. We expect that this, jointly with the use of specific facilitation techniques such as the proposed by Davie <8>, will contribute to the understanding that in the learning process, collaborative learning can be as important as student-teacher communications.

This methodology of distance learning supported by telematics services is difficult to implement at a broad scale by many factors. One of them is that teachers are mostly used to traditional classroom instruction and do not have direct experience of alternative methods. Nevertheless, there is no doubt that a growing number of people are becoming aware of the benefits of a more flexible learning approach and that will produce an increasing demand.

## 5. Final remarks.

We want to stress that, from an educational point of view, networks are people communicating data and ideas and getting information with the use of technological systems that overcome communication barriers. Communication and delivery of information need a purpose-oriented participation of people in a common environment easy to handle and use. In the three levels of action so far explained, the most important concept is participation of people with common interests.

Participation of teachers is a key element in the development of the SINERA database. Their involvement is the starting point to generate information because they know about the educational potential of the materials and their pedagogical relevance.

Needless to mention the importance of the role that the educational administration plays in building a powerful resource database, because Catalonia, having its own language, is a "rare language area" in terms of the world's information industry. The educational system faces the influx of information in other languages. As the Finnish Palosuo <9> states "No other country is going to produce national material for us ..." and this is both applicable to the language itself and to the selection of culturally adequate educational materials. Thus, specific developments in a limited language community can't be done without leadership and participation of all sectors involved in education.

It is widely admitted that the students' development of information and communication skills will play a fundamental role in their professional and adult life. Telecommunications give a new dimension to these skills and its development requires a strong commitment both of teachers and educational authorities. The only way to overcome the barriers that make changes and curriculum innovation difficult to carry out is to work together at every level (classroom, school, district). We hope that in the near future curriculum development activities based on telematics are more self-sustained due to the growing number of people that become aware of its potential and that are willing to add the communication dimension to educational activities.

Finally, it is necessary to further explore the relationships between educational innovation, school organisation and information technology and communications. As an OTA report states <10> "Little attention has been paid to how distance learning can meet broader school reform goals, such as restructuring education and using technologies as tools for change". Integrated approaches to educational telecommunications like the one described in this paper try to contribute in this direction.

## References

1 M. Riel, "Four Models of Educational Telecommunications: Connections to the Future", Education & Computing 5 (1989) 261-274.

2 J. Whiting, "New perspectives on open and distance learning for adult audiences". In "World Yearbook of Education 1988 - Education for the New Technologies" edited by D. Harris. Kogan Page, London, 1988.

3 J. Castells, "The Educational Telematic Network of Catalonia: Functional Characteristics and Structure". Proceedings of the International Symposium "Learners and the Global Village", Jerusalem, 1989.

4 F. Ruiz, J. Vivancos, J. Baldrich, "XTEC Online In-service Teacher Training Project". In "Learning Technology in the European Communities", proceedings of the DELTA Conference on Research and Development, 1990. Kluwer Academic Publishers, 1992.

5 R. Gray, "CMC on In-Service Training". In "Mindweave - Communication, Computers and Distance Education", edited by R. Mason and A. Kaye. Pergamon Press, 1989.

6 M.C. Legrottaglie and others, "Implementation Considerations about Cooperative Learning in On-line Education". EC Newsletter, vol 2, n 3, (Sep - Dec 1990).

7 D. Cabrero, P. Martín, C. Simón, C. Viorreta, "Informe de Evaluación Externa de los Cursos con Soporte Telemático", Fundesco, Madrid, June 1991.

8 L. Davie, "Facilitation Techniques for the On-line Tutor". In "Mindweave - Communication, Computers and Distance Education", ibidem.

9 E. Palosuo, "Being a database host in a rare language area". In "Information - Knowledge - Evolution", edited by S. Koskiala and R. Launo. FID Public. 675, North-Holland, 1989.

10 L. G. Roberts (project director), "Linking for Learning - A New Course for Education". Congress of the United States - OTA, Washington, 1989.

Education and Society / R. Aiken (Editor)
Information Processing 92, Volume II
Elsevier Science Publishers B.V. (North-Holland)
1992 IFIP.

# Telematic Services in Catalan Schools: Working Environment and Achievements

Jordi Castells, Guillem Carreras, Jaume Porta, Jordi Bertran, Xavier Jordà

Programa d'Informàtica Educativa, Dept. Ensenyament, Generalitat de Catalunya. Av. Francesc Cambó, 21 4rt, 08003 Barcelona.
Email: EAVERGES@EBRUPC51.bitnet

Manel Medina and Leandro Navarro

Universitat Politècnica de Catalunya. C/. Gran Capitán, s/n. Mod. D4, 08034 Barcelona. Email: leandro@ac.upc.es

**Abstract**

This paper introduces the current status and usage of telematic services in Catalan schools. The availability of the telematic service XTEC (Catalan Educational Telematic Network) allows development of educational activities that can only be possible through the usage of telematic services.

This work includes the description of the environment and available services, as well as the activities that have been developed.

Keyword Codes: K.3.1, K.4.0, C.2.4
Keywords: Computer Uses and Education, Computers and Society, Distributed Systems.

## 1. THE EDUCATIONAL INFORMATION TECHNOLOGY PROGRAM (PIE) OF THE CATALAN GOVERNMENT

Spanish education is organised in a decentralised way, allowing many of the autonomous regional governments, amongst them Catalonia, complete responsibility for actions in this field. To scale the size of project, we have to say that the number of public schools in Catalunya is about 2000, of which 400 correspond to high school institutions, and the remaining to primary teaching.

The PIE is a service created by the Department of Education of the Catalan government, in order to introduce and improve the usage of new technology in the public- non-universitary-educational service of Catalunya. To fulfill this goal, some streams of activity were set up, and their main characteristics can be summarized as follows:

- Creation of an Information Technology classroom in all the public centers, both primary and secondary. Each of them has about 10 PC compatible computers, with HD, modem, and color screen, printers, and general purpose software: Compilers: PASCAL, LOGO, BASIC; Integrated program composed of: text editor, data base and spreadsheet; Graphic editor; Spelling checker for the

Catalan (ADHOC) and aranes (VORA) languages, both developed within the PIE, and several general purpose and computer assisted programs.

- A great number of educational centers have been equipped according to their specific requirements: CAD, office automation, text editors, robotic, computer aided laboratory, LAN, laser printers and CD-ROM.
- A special emphasis has been given to the primary education centers, which, in addition, have got color printers, and software specially tailored to the youngest users:
  Text editor: QUADERN; Relational environment: ELECTRA; Touch sensitive tablet peripheral allowing interaction with computer programs in several environments.
- The teachers have been trained in order to allow them to learn and acquire skills in use and educational application of the new information technologies. In the period 1986..1991, 886 courses have been given, representing as much as 41,167 hours of lecturing, given to 16,853 attendants.
- A network of diverse telematic services has been created, the XTEC (Catalan Educational Telematic Network), which promotes the interchange of shared information within the Catalan educational system. The service is available to the pupils as well as to the teachers, and to both the public and the private schools, assuming that they have got the adequate hardware (computers and modems), needed to access the services.

## 2. THE CURRENT XTEC ENVIRONMENT

This paper describes the XTEC environment, seen from several viewpoints: Technological, Computational (supported telematic services), Educational (promoted educational activities), and future trends from the technological and educational viewpoints.

### 2.1 XTEC technological viewpoint

The XTEC communications center is based on a BULL computer (DPS8, running the GCOS8 operating system), that offers services over the following protocols:

- Videotex CEPT1 over public data networks X.25 (IBERPAC).
- Videotex CEPT2 over ordinary phone lines.
- Distributed services over ordinary phone lines.
- Distributed services over public PSDN X.25 (X.28 access) (IBERPAC).

The educational centers choose the access mean that best suits the kind of service they want to reach, considering its physical location with respect to the main computer.

As mentioned before, all the educational centers, furnished by the PIE, are provided with a modem board, which allows them to connect the PC with the XTEC services. The software needed to access these services is freely available to all educational centers (public and private).

### 2.2 Computational view of the XTEC provided telematic services

As seen in the previous section, XTEC provides two kinds of services, depending on the access mean: Videotex or Distributed services protocols.

#### 2.2.1 Videotex accessible services

The PIE provides the same services indistinctly through both CEPT1 (as supported by the public Spanish videotex service IBERTEX), or CEPT2 (MINITEL emulated over the public telephone network). The user must have the adequate software to access the XTEC services using the intended connection mean.

The telematic services provided through videotex are the following:
**Electronic mail:** This is the only videotex service that requires user identification, due to privacy and confidentiality reasons. All the educational centers furnished by the PIE, have got their own identification, and individual users may get an independent one upon request.

The message handling service allows a user to send messages to other individual users or groups of users, who will be informed of the existence of pending messages when accesing the service.

**Bulletin board:** This videotex service acts as a public bulletin board, where any user may ask questions, and receive answers from other users. In order to speed up the access to the messages, they are ranked according to subject: information technologies, technology, hobbies, etc.

**Electronic news:** This service is like an electronic magazine, edited by the PIE. It is used to disseminate to the teachers news about the educational information technologies, and other items of general interest to teachers or pupils.

This service has a tree-like structure. Currently there are more than 1000 "living" pages, periodically updated with fresh news edited by a group of people with newspaper production background.

**Database Access:** Through the videotex it is possible to query several documental databases, of interest to teachers and pupils. All of them have been created and filled within the Catalan educational system, and are managed through the MISTRAL database software, available over GCOS8. The currently available databases are:

- SINERA. It is currently filled with more than 11,000 references to didactic resources that a teacher may need during lecturing activity. These resources range from magazine articles to educational software, including: videotapes, slides, books, etc.
- MILANYS. It was made up by pupils, and contains about 4,000 documents referring to facts and people related to Catalan history.
- FORMACIO. It provides access to all the references to courses and seminars available to teachers, promoted by the Catalan government. It is updated several times a year, and holds references to the more than 4,000 yearly offered activities.

**Inquiries:** The videotex service also provides information about the thoughts of the users on several subjects that are periodically updated. As the user answers the questions asked by the system, she/he gets information about the current status of the answers.

**Computer chatting:** This service is very well known by regular videotex users, since it allows them to interchange short messages between all the users using the service at that time.

**Studying in Catalunya:** This service has a tree-like structure, and provides updated information about all educational possibilities from the Educational department of the Catalan government. It is addressed mainly to pupils and tutoring teachers, who are able, in this way, to get information about the educational centers, offered curricula, university entrance requirements, etc.

### 2.2.2 The distributed services

The distributed services offered by XTEC are accessed through a special software (OLIMP), distributed by PIE. OLIMP adds friendliness and power to the telematic services, distributing part of them into the PCs. This distribution makes it possible to provide features above the upper threshold imposed by the videotex. The distributed services currently offered by XTEC are:

**AGORA:** This is a telematic service that provides support for a large amount of electronic conferences (public or privates), organized according to subject. Later on we will describe the educational activities supported by this service.

**HERMES:** This service allows the transfer of files between the main XTEC computer and the users. It offers an "anonymous-ftp-like" service, that supports several levels of privacy, depending on the mailbox to which the file is linked.

**2.3 The educational services of XTEC**

To our mind, XTEC is an integrated environment of communications that has to provide services of an educational character to Catalan schools. This means that for each educational service we want to provide, it is necessary to carefully analyze the telematic mean(s), that best fit into the application requirements, in order to provide the best friendliness at the lowest cost.

To interchange small amounts of information, videotex seems to be the best choice. But when it is needed to interchange large amounts of information, or executable programs, then distributed services (AGORA and/or HERMES) are needed. Very often, the same activity requires several telematic means.

In the following sections, we will introduce some examples of the activities already supported by the XTEC.

**2.3.1 Millennium game**

This game was played during the celebration of the 1,000 years of Catalan history, and its aim was to fulfill a database of cultural and historical facts (MILANYS).

This activity involved more than 1,000 pupils and teachers of primary and secondary schools. In addition to the production of entries of the database, participants asked questions about the history of Catalunya and answered questions introduced by other teams or by the jury.

The development of the game involved both videotex and duplex services.

The final result of the game was the MILANYS database, already mentioned, now accessible for consultation, and is of great help in the subject of history.

**2.3.2 The on-line conferences about literary works**

The PIE has promoted electronic conferences about literary works (novels), between teams of scholars, using the AGORA distributed service. The mechanism is the following:

- Before the start of the dialog, the pupils read the book, analyzing it from several viewpoints.
- Then, they contribute to the dialogue with their opinions.
- Whenever possible, the author comments on them.

These activities normally last about 6 weeks. Three books have been analyzed to date:

- "Julia", by Isabel-Clara Simó, who was involved in the dialogue, along with 600 pupils grouped in 21 teams belonging to 15 different schools, and generating 447 messages.
- "Tirant lo Blanc", by Joanot Martorell, with the participation of Maria Aurèlia Capmany, along with 15 teams of 11 schools that produced 402 entries.
- "La ronda del Guinardó" by Joan Marsé, with the participation of Fernando Valls, as well as 300 pupils, belonging to 10 schools, and totalling 271 messages.

**2.3.3 Automaton**

This electronic conference, addressed to teachers of the technological subjects taught in secondary education, was centered in automata. It is organized in 6 issues: Sensors, processors, controllers, documentation, activities, and curricular aspects.

The videotex electronic mail, as well as the HERMES distributed application, are also important elements allowing the communication between the participants.

**2.3.4 Penelope**

This is an electronic conference about collective literary creation, in which 26 primary schools have been involved. It simulates the journey of a character, Penelope, through several villages of the region of the schools involved. The pupils from each school have to greet her when she arrives, give her board and lodging, and describe to her the main characteristics of their town.

This activity is included in the Social sciences subject of study.

**2.3.5 The rural telematics**

The PIE gives special attention to the primary schools located in rural areas, in which the geographical isolation can be partly saved through the usage of telematics. Three telematic activities have been developed for the centers located in these zones;

- Activity with pupils: "TELENOIS". Which has been split into three items:
  · Creation of a tale, based on a fantasy object, proposed by one of the schools participating.
  · Production of pictures for the tales created by other schools, following the first activity.
  · Collection of information, pictures and social impact of Catalan popular tales and legends.
- Activity exclusively addressed to teachers: "TELEBASICA". Which is an electronic conference between teachers of those schools participating in the evaluation of this kind of activity.
- Experimental activity: "METEOROLOGIA". Which is aimed to daily collect and analyze meteorological data, from the centers involved in this activity.

**2.3.6 Remote training through telematic means**

The PIE has promoted two courses, addressed to teachers, using telematic tools to set up contact between teacher and pupil: videotex electronic mail for private dialog, AGORA to spread general information, and HERMES to allow pupils to send homework to the teachers.

So far, the courses running within this activity are: Teledocumentación (distance documentation) and Educational applications of spreadsheets.

**2.3.7 International contacts**

Telematics is the right tool to help in the communication between pupils of different countries. The PIE participates in several experiments of this kind:

- Catalunya / United Kingdom, 25 centers on each country participate in shared activities at two levels:
  · "By couples", using the UK service "Campus 2000".
  · "By groups of schools", with 5 schools in each of them, using the XTEC/Catalan service AGORA.
- Catalunya / Europe, in collaboration with a French server, located at the "Centre d'Etudes Pédagogiques de Sèvres-Paris" (center of pedagogical studies of one of the Paris universities), which provides a world wide coverage. Our students have participated in debates of diverse kinds, such as: poetry week, multilingual tales, Golf war, traditional holidays, Regional tourist leaflets, etc.
- Catalunya / USA, Activity coordinated by the private center "Project", that keeps 8 educational centers from each side in contact. They have interchanged more than 200 messages, and participated in two video-conferences, with on-line images.

**2.3.8 Guidance for University enrollment**

By the end of each academic year, the videotex based service "Questions and Answers" provides pupils and tutors a channel where questions about University enrollment may be submitted. The answer comes from the *Direcció General d'Universitats* of the Department of Education.

## 3. PLANS FOR EVOLUTION

The evolution of technology has paved the way to emerging standard platforms, now available for the implementation and provision of open and powerful educational telematic services, towards offering standard services where available, and building a distributed system covering both servers and users equipped with personal computers. This evolution is important in educational telematics as well, and in the XTEC project several actions go in this direction to allow current production and service environments take the most of these new possibilities.

Those actions are based on the following guidelines:

- Adopting the UNIX platform as main development environment. The first action has been the installation of two UNIX servers: BULL DPX 2/340 and Fujitsu S 1300.
- Adopting Local Area Network technologies for accessing both local production servers and remote locations from different machines.
- Availability of X.400 based electronic mail service (QX400), that will expand the current XTEC service in domain and functionality. This software will enable cooperation without barriers of distance, nation or organisation. The growing size of the electronic mail community and the availability of X.500 directory services suggest the introduction of this service to provide users support in locating people's addresses.
- Availability of relational databases (Oracle) to support institutional information databases and specialised educational databases. One action in this direction is the implementation of a meteorological database where pupils can store and consult data.

The system is currently composed of MSDOS personal computers and one single server machine that may be accessed via Videotex (Ibertex) or transparent access (terminal emulation). Two main obstacles are: services are *difficult to use*, and a *single centralised* server for a distributed organisation.

On one hand, *difficulty of use* is due to the complexity of remote communication (e.g. use of modems, response delays, noise, low bandwidth, unreliability), and to the complexity of interacting with command line interfaces that may be complex and very application specific. *Client programs* are used to provide users with an easy to use windows environment that interacts locally with users and translates the result to remote interactions on behalf of the user.

This has been experienced in one tele-debate service having a specially complex and specific command line interface. People had to remember a lot of specific commands and, at the same time, they had to keep a mental map of the structure of the discussion. The client program *(AGORA)* provides a menu interface with scroll windows that solves both problems.

The result is that some processing is moved to the PC, thus isolating users from communications services and applications. Following the direction stated by Open Distributed Processing research (ISO & CCITT standardisation effort), PCs and servers are nodes of a distributed processing environment where processing may be located where it is more efficient. This means that the User Interface (and parts of applications eventually) may start migrating from the server to the client, moving the communications link inside of the distributed system, farther from the user.

On the other hand, there is the need to match the present centralised service with the distributed nature of our Department. In fact there are not only organisational but also economical reasons for distributing the service into several servers located where branches *(Delegacions Territorials)* and user communities are located. This means that a natural evolution of the service would go in the direction of a distributed server system composed of several interconnected server machines situated at different locations. This step is not trivial because this needs an important technological and organisational evolution.

Thus, we have two needs of distribution: already *started*: between server and PC (client), *future*: within the server system, composed of several server nodes at different locations.

Both approaches may be supported by existing platforms for distributed applications (e.g. ANSAware) providing support for distributed systems running on UNIX and MSDOS machines: applications may be accessed remotely as if they were local (*distribution transparency*), applications may move (*migration*) from one to another node without disturbing the normal functioning, PC and UNIX applications may offer services to each other (*inter-operability*).

To summarise, the XTEC started from dumb terminals and a single proprietary server. In the present and the near future, PCs are becoming more active, and we will have a UNIX server machine providing standardised services (e.g. X.400). The future will see the integration of client and server, and the distribution of the single server into several server nodes.

## 4. PERSPECTIVES

Telematics in education appears as a fact of undoubted interest, specially in group work among people from different settings. Success of the experiences is based on planning, implementing and following actions very carefully, and the right degree of ergonomics and functionality of services and telematic activities available.

In the following years we will see an important acceleration of actions in this field, favoured by the technological evolution, and the pressure that social uses of technology will put on the educational system. In this sense, it may be advisable for educational policies from different countries to work together in a coordinated way and adopt technical and methodological standards to enable open and flexible actions, respecting and benefitting from different cultures.

## 5. REFERENCES

1 Guia dels serveis d'accés de la XTEC, April 1991.
2 ANSA Reference Manual, APM, Cambridge, 1989.
3 ISO/IEC JTC1/SC21/WG7 (ODP) Working Documents.

Education and Society / R. Aiken (Editor)
Information Processing 92, Volume II
Elsevier Science Publishers B.V. (North-Holland)



# E-mail as an educational tool in learning statistics

Benita Compostela[a] and Henk Sligte[b]

[a]Departamento de Psicologia Social, Facultad de Ciencias Politicas y Sociologia, Universidad Complutense de Madrid, Spain

[b]Center for Innovation and Co-operative Technology, Universiteit van Amsterdam, Grote Bickersstraat 72, 1013 KS Amsterdam, The Netherlands

**Abstract**

The European Schools Project (ESP) is an initiative of the Center for Innovation and Co-operative Technology at the University of Amsterdam. ESP is a network of secondary schools in various countries in- and outside of Europe, that perform collaborative distance learning projects. The projects, termed teletrips, involve various types of learning and inquiring activities. Teletrips are collaborative learning projects, designed by teachers from partner schools around a part of curriculum that is thought to be mutually relevant. Leading idea of a Teletrip is the combination of local research of pupils around a certain topic and exchange of research results with partner-schools, using a foreign language and electronic mail.

This paper reports on some of the results of the Teletrip "Statistics in Everyday Life", in which schools in the United Kingdom, Germany and Spain were involved. The project took place between autumn 1990 and spring 1991. New technologies were used in two different ways. First electronic mail was used to share information and data. In the second place appropriate software, for word processing, spreadsheet and statistical analysis, the latter specially designed for education, was used to support the local education of statistics.

This paper was co-operatively written by the authors, using ESP's telematic facilities.

Keyword Codes: K.3.0; K.3.1; C.2.0
Keywords: Computers and education, General; Computer Uses in Education; Computer-Communication Networks, General

## 1. STATISTICS AND TELETRIPS

Statistical language has become widespread. Every day we encounter statistics in the form of tables, diagrams, and in economic or electoral predictions. It's nearly impossible to open up a newspaper or to watch a reporting on television in which statistical language does not appear in any way. Only those who are acquainted with statistics will be able to judge the statistical reports in a proper way, and to discover when and where these reports are tendentious. In these days of high degrees of quantification, statistical knowledge and skills are inevitable, something education has to provide.

In traditional schools knowledge of any discipline is transferred directly, as subjects little related with real life, to be learnt by heart, while skills are directly derived, as operations to be executed in relation to the body of knowledge. Increasingly, realistic contexts are thought to be important for the educational process, in combination with work in co-operative groups and integrated use of technological applications. Computer mediated communication (CMC) is a relatively new way of achieving this combination. Instead of prescribing pupils' activities, a world is offered in which all kinds of activities become necessary to participate, including pupil-driven learning activities with regard to subject matter and skills. Conceptually seen, a comparable world to the one of LOGO is offered, in which children can perform activities, that start to resemble mathematical behaviour. With CMC meaningful activities are triggered on the basis of a seductive world, a world that consists of peers from other countries and other cultures.

The European Schools Project (ESP) is a network of secondary schools performing collaborative distance learning projects on certain parts of curriculum. The projects, termed teletrips, involve various types of learning and inquiring activities. Results of the activities are exchanged using electronic mail, and foreign language is used as a medium for the tele-conversations. The ESP, co-ordinated by the University of Amsterdam, has about 90 participating schools in 12 countries, of which 9 European, having designed about 50 teletrips for the school year 1991/1992 on a variety of subjects, in various languages (figures of October 1991).

Every year a face-to-face conference is organized to evaluate old teletrips and to design new ones. In June 1990 the 4th ESP Conference took place in Copenhagen, Denmark. During the conference it was decided to design and plan a teletrip on statistics, involving schools in the United Kingdom, Germany and Spain, countries in which statistics curriculum is similar.The project took place between autumn 1990 and spring 1991.

This paper reports on some of the results of this teletrip. Eight schools from three countries, Spain, Germany and England, have participated, producing enough variety to include in the statistical operations. The computer mediated communications have expanded the horizons of the classrooms. One of the most exciting features of the project was to get acquainted with other pupils in other countries, all working in similar ways on similar topics. Students and teachers have been very interested in co-operation on sharing data and exchanging results. All in all a real international collaborative comparative study was performed on every-day characteristics of the students' context.

The new technologies were used in two different ways. First electronic mail was used to share information and data. Secondly appropriate software, for word processing, spreadsheet and special designed statistical software (the latter by Piet van Blokland, Free University of Amsterdam), was used for the tedious and repetitive work.

## 2. OBJECTIVES OF THE TELETRIP ON STATISTICS

The teletrip was designed to support acquisition of knowledge and skills at two levels, thus anticipating the variety in prior knowledge. Both in Germany and Spain the project was done at two different levels, while the school in the United Kingdom only did the first level. The pupils were a cross section of the schools' population; some were 11, others were 18 years old.

The first level objectives were as follows. By the end of project pupils had to be able to:

- use the various types of software,
- differentiate between quantitative an qualitative variables,
- calculate mean and standard deviation in quantitative variables manually,
- calculate absolutes and relative frequencies in variables manually,
- design histograms and pie-charts,
- check their work with spreadsheet and statistical software,
- design statistical graphics with computer,
- discover the computer as an efficient tool,
- get a general impression of computer mediated communication,

- develop a feeling to be a member of the European Community.

In addition to the objectives at the first level, pupils in the second level had to be able to perform comparisons between data belonging to different groups, to calculate Pearson correlation co-efficients and to analyse for regressions.

## 3. OVERVIEW OF THE ACTIVITIES

Before beginning the actual teletrip a questionnaire was designed by the participating teachers. Every pupil filled out the questionnaire as part of a home work assignment. In addition the teachers explained the context of the work to the pupils: the work was to be done at the same time by pupils of the same age from several countries in order to make various comparisons between the countries, and to practise various ways of representing.

In several classes every pupil wrote a letter to pupils of the partner-schools. In other classes only one letter was written and sent on behalf of all pupils together. The answers to the questionnaire were written by the pupils with a word processor and saved in text-only format. Every pupil filled out a row with his or her answers. In each course a matrix was produced in which the number of rows were equal to the number of pupils in the class, and in which the columns indicated the number of the question of the questionnaire. This matrix was sent immediately to other schools involved in the teletrip. After that the teacher taught in the classroom the calculation of mean and standard deviation, and manual design of diagrams and correlation. Subsequently the work continued in the computer room where the data matrix was translated into the spreadsheet for the statistical work.

## 4. THE QUESTIONNAIRE

The questionnaire every pupil had to fill out as part of the home work assignment looked as follows.

NAME OF SCHOOL ........................
DATE ..................
1. Age (AGE)
2. Number of brothers/sisters including yourself (CHILD)
3. How much do you weigh (Kg)? (WEIGHT)
4. What is your height (cm)? (HEIGHT)
5. Do you belong to a sport club?(1=yes, 0=no) (CLUB)
6. How many hours each week do you spend on home work assignments? (HOMEWORK)
7. How many hours a week do you spend watching television? (TV)
8. Do you smoke? (1=yes, 0=no) (SMOKE)
9. On your dad's side, how many brothers and sisters are there including your dad? (DFAM)
10. On your mum's side, how many brothers and sisters including your mum?(MFAM)
11. Does your dad smoke? (DSMOKE)
12. Does your mum smoke? (MSMOKE)
13. How tall is your dad (cm)? DHEIGHT
14. How tall is your mum (cm)?MHEIGHT
15. What is your dad's weight (kg)? DWEIGHT
16. What is your mum's weight (kg)? MWEIGHT

## 5. DATA COLLECTION AND ANALYSIS

Obviously, in order to fill out the questionnaire, a number of activities had to be performed. First pupils had to ask questions to their parents. In addition they had to undertake some measuring with regard to their own characteristics, and to do some estimation. In this way data collection was situated in a real world context, appending real dimensions to the figures.
In contrast to abstract manipulations, the calculated frequencies, absolutes and relatives for the variables of the questionnaire kept on having a relation with the figures the pupils acquired. In addition, mean, mode, median, variance and standard deviation was calculated for the quantitative variables, while histograms and pie-charts were made. Linear regression, correlation coefficient, the best fitting line and a scatter plot was also done by pupils of the second level.

## 6. WORKING IN THE COMPUTER ROOM

When all the questionnaires were filled out and the pupils had learnt statistics in classroom, the work in the computer room could begin. The level of 'computer-literacy' at the side of the pupils was very different. When pupils came into the computer room for the first time for this project, minimally some of them had worked before with a computer.

First a text processor was used to write letters to colleagues in the partner-schools. The teachers gave the pupils instruction about how to use the text processor. As only a few functions were used, pupils managed to deal with the programme in one hour. In addition pupils learned to send messages by electronic mail.

Pupils made the data matrix with a word processor. Each pupil typed a row of this file including the answer to the questionnaire. The file was saved in ASCII or text-only format. After that every pupil received a copy of this file, thus getting the complete data. This data-file was sent to all schools involved in the project using electronic mail.

The atmosphere in the computer room was not competitive. Each pupil was asked to help other pupils in trouble.

## 7. SOME RESULTS OF THE STATISTICS

In this section we pass some results of the actual work as an illustration. They are not meant to give an exhaustive report on the inquiry. This can be obtained from the authors.

| 1 | 2 | 3 | 4 | 5 | 6 | 7 | 8 | 9 | 10 | 11 | 12 | 13 | 14 | 15 | 16 |
|---|---|---|---|---|---|---|---|---|---|---|---|---|---|---|---|
| 16 | 2 | 68 | 181 | 0 | 05 | 02 | 0 | 1 | 2 | 1 | 0 | 183 | 160 | 079 | 64 |
| 15 | 1 | 57 | 174 | 1 | 10 | 04 | 0 | 1 | 1 | 1 | 0 | 194 | 151 | 100 | 58 |
| 15 | 2 | 65 | 177 | 1 | 14 | 07 | 0 | 1 | 2 | 1 | 0 | 174 | 172 | 114 | 89 |
| \| | \| | \| | \| | \| | \| | \| | \| | \| | \| | \| | \| | \| | \| | \| | \| |
| 17 | 2 | 59 | 172 | 0 | 10 | 19 | 1 | 4 | 2 | 0 | 0 | 170 | 155 | 072 | 60 |
| 17 | 1 | 48 | 158 | 0 | 25 | 10 | 0 | 3 | 5 | 0 | 1 | 163 | 156 | 071 | 51 |
| 18 | 2 | 60 | 180 | 1 | 18 | 18 | 0 | 2 | 4 | 0 | 0 | 182 | 155 | 086 | 62 |

Figure 1: Example of a part of a data matrix

In the matrix above the 16 categories represent the questions of the questionnaire. So the last entry represents a pupil of 18 years old, having one brother or sister, weighing 60 Kg, 1,80 meters tall, who belongs to a sport club, spending 18 hours a week on home work, and the same amount of time on television, and who is a non-smoker. Columns 9 to 16 give a profile of the pupil's parents.

By processing the data with the spreadsheet, the mean and the standard deviation for the quantitative variables was acquired.

| Variable | Mean | Standard Deviation |
|---|---|---|
| AGE | 17,56 | 0,68 |
| CHILD | 2,57 | 0,94 |
| WEIGHT | 53,32 | 15,33 |
| HEIGHT | 160,82 | 31,42 |
| HOMEWORK | 17,82 | 5,98 |
| TV | 15,71 | 8,09 |
| DFAMILY | 3,64 | 1,63 |
| MFAMILY | 4,18 | 2,00 |
| DHEIGHT | 162,50 | 5,47 |
| MHEIGHT | 158,36 | 44,38 |
| DWEIGHT | 69,54 | 21,46 |
| MWEIGHT | 61,57 | 7,05 |

Figure 2: Mean and Standard Deviation

Also histograms and pie charts were derived, of which some follow as an illustration.

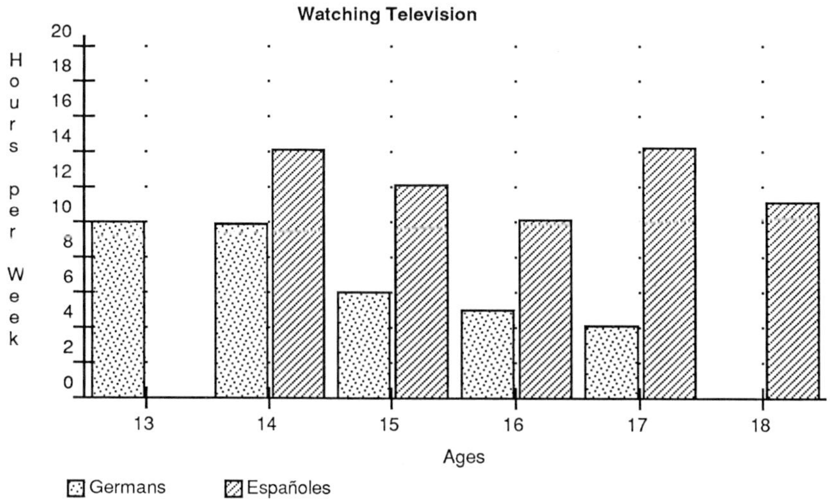


Figure 3: Histogram Television Watching

The histogram above shows that Spanish students spent more time watching TV than their German colleagues. The time German students spent behind their televisions decreases when their age increases, something that doesn't happen with Spanish students.

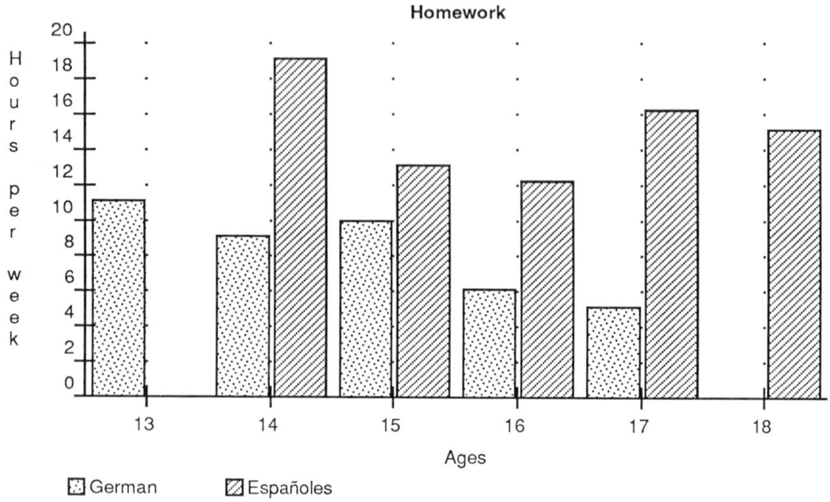


Figure 4: Histogram Homework

This histogram above shows that Spanish pupils spent more hours on their homework than German pupils and also that German students spent less time studying when their age increases. This finding in fact made the German teacher very worried.

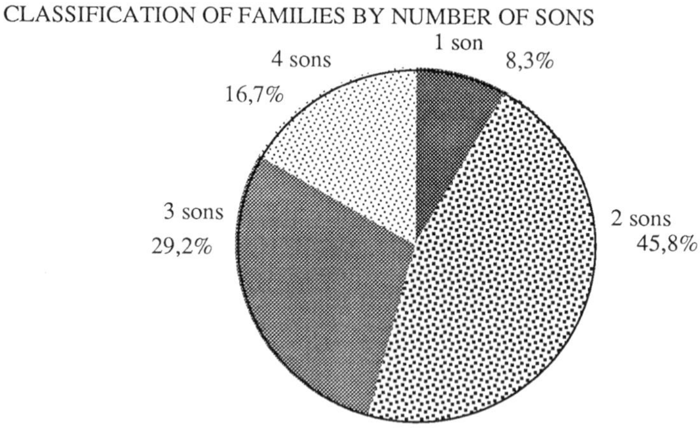


Figure 5: Pie Number of Sons

The second level in the project was devoted to more elaborate ways of analyzing the collected data. Between the variables weight and height regressions and correlations were calculated and studied. Pupils also made use of the spreadsheet to calculate the correlation coefficient and the best fitting line.

## 8. CONCLUSIONS

Under the aegis of the ESP a large number of teletrips have been performed up to now. Although electronic mail is still a primitive medium, it is suitable to be used for increasing the quality of secondary education, if some caveats are kept at the back of the mind. It is important to have a clear conceptual structure of the teletrips, a structure in which (tele)conversations are introduced as a supplement to the usual forms of instruction, in which co-operation between pupils and teachers is stimulated, both between and among themselves, and in which, more than usual, traditional boundaries between disciplines are broken down. As effects upon the increase of quality, enhanced motivation, deeper insight in the domain, better communicative foreign language use, increased intercultural consciousness, and sensitivity for the use of telematics, was observed. In the teletrip on statistics similar effects were noted by the teachers.

A teletrip is not the most easy project to organize within secondary education. The pressure of compulsory curriculum is that vigorous that only a limited period of time can be spent on tele projects. In Germany only two weeks were found, and in Spain four weeks, to be devoted to the project. Both pupils and teachers indicate that this time is too short. Pupils asked for continuation of statistical work to fully explore the possibilities of the operations upon the data. Teachers expressed their appreciation for such an attitude, but other compulsory subjects left no room for extension. Design and planning is difficult too, both locally and with the conversation partners abroad. Again the lesson tables and schedules leave little room for improvisation.

Within these constraints the participants state to have taken part in a worthwhile project. First of all the 'double' character of the teletrip was appreciated. In a natural way, not only data was exchanged, but all kinds of aspects concerning the data were discussed by pupils and teachers of the partner schools. This aspect is increasingly recognized as a major success factor for collaborative distance learning projects. Secondly, technology is integrated within the lessons, something still happening scarcely in European secondary schools. Open ended software is used as a natural extension of the more traditional educational activities. Also at the level of the teachers motivation for learning to use new tools was observed. Pupils were enthusiastic in sharing data with colleagues from abroad and in interacting, mediated by the computer. They considered this work to be a more effective tool for understanding than text books.

It was found to be important that teachers and pupils could do the work as they liked, so the rules were made to be very soft, allowing the teachers' and pupils' imagination to be present in each step. For example pupils from Instituto de Bachillerato J.L. Sampedro wrote, in addition to the e-mail, a lot of letters to German pupils by "Snail-Mail", as surface mail came to be called, because they were very interested in sending photographs of their faces. Pupils from other schools preferred to write letters with the opinions of whole group altogether. Teachers could choose software they preferred, to feel comfortable in using technology in their class. In spite of the fact that different spreadsheets were used, always each partner was capable to read the work done because of the portability created by transmission in text-only format. At the level of the technological infrastructure, provided by the European Schools Project, a special distribution list was assigned to the project. Using a certain electronic address all partners received a copy of the sent messages automatically, where this had to be done separately before.

As an overall conclusion it seems that the concept of teletrip is an asset to the secondary schools' repertoire. It provides an innovative approach to education mediated by the computer. Moreover, teletrips provide an addition to more traditional forms of education.

A more complete description of ESP and of this teletrip is obtainable from the authors.

Education and Society / R. Aiken (Editor)
Information Processing 92, Volume II
Elsevier Science Publishers B.V. (North-Holland)


# ISDN Interactive Distance Learning - A Step Closer To Near Paperless Learning Environment ?

Hock-Guan Tan

Computer Based Training Centre, Deputy Principal's Office, Ngee Ann Polytechnic, 535 Clementi Road, Singapore 2159

**Abstract**

Human resources development and high productivity of our limited resources poll are vital to our nation's economic thrust. This paper presents our use of telecommunication and computing technologies for education. It briefly describes our project on the development of ISDN(Integrated Services Digital Network) Interactive Distance Learning(IDL) and presents the results of the ISDN-IDL field trial. Our plan for a flexible access environment to render various forms of learning activities such as mastery learning, electronic coaching or consultation, electronic discussions or tutorials, electronic library services, electronic mail and bulletin boards services to learners at off-campus sites through the use of mature and emerging technologies will be put forth. The development of the project has since given rise to a notion of a near paperless learning environment. The potential benefits and long term gains of our project, difficulties encountered and potential problems will be highlighted. The paper also discusses the approach and strategies adopted for the project.

Keyword Code : K.3.1; J.0; C.2.0
Keywods : Computer Uses in Education; Computer Application, General;
Computer-Communication Networks, General;

## 1. Introduction

In Singapore, the limited workforce available and the rapidly changing demand on them require them to be trained in new areas due to changing social, economic, and technological environment. Since the workforce cannot be relieved for prolonged period and must be trained alongside their daily duty, distance learning is sought to be one of the solutions. Ngee Ann Polytechnic(NP), Singapore has been exploring off-campus computer based learning activities since early 1987. In response to the government call for distance learning as a mean to meet the aspiration of many Singaporean adults for further education in August 1991, the polytechnic embarked on a research and development program on distance learning.

The advancement in telecommunication technologies such as high speed digital networks, audio-video processing, multipoint conferencing, together with other emerging technologies in computing provide an alternate mode of delivering distance learning. Literature[1,2] show that electronic distance learning concept is feasible and it is envisaged that it will become the main force behind the development of human resource development in this decade. As Singapore has a nationwide public Integrated Digital Services Network(ISDN), it is an advantage to exploit this advanced telecommunication infrastructure for distance learning. The polytechnic's sound foundation in courseware development and that more than 40% of our students own PCs form a good base for electronic distance learning programs. The availability of ISDN PC Card and the development PC-based ISDN Visual Communication System by Singapore Telecom, Information Technology Institute and a local computer firm further mold our concept of electronic distance learning into ISDN Interactive Distance Learning(IDL) or simply ISDN-IDL.

## 2. ISDN Interactive Distance Learning

Interactive Distance Learning in our context, refers to the provision of education by electronic means using telecommunication and computing technologies, and involving two-way communication. As such, it becomes clear that the technology required for IDL would have to be able to handle information in the form of images, data and audio concurrently. Many existing distance learning practioners adopted broadcasting media such as satellites, cable TV, microwave link and broadcast TV to deliver their education programs. These technologies provide a one way communication in which the conventional telephone lines have to use to complement the learning process. The emergence of ISDN that allows simultaneous voice, data and image transmission at relatively higher speed resolve the constraints posed by existing technologies, giving rise to a more efficient mode of distance learning.

Traditional distance learning programs make use of text-based materials and occasionally supplemented by video tapes or computer based programs. Over the years, many have reported and confirmed the cost effectiveness of computer based instructional programs[3,4,5 & 6]. The evolving of hypermedia and related products added new dimensions to the development of these programs. Today, many electronic learning materials with high resolution graphics and audio capabilities are already available. Proper design of these materials will make learning much more exciting, attractive and effective. With ISDN, distance learners can dial up for such materials for individualized learning at their own convenience.

Individualized learning can be enhanced by having a Computer Managed Instruction(CMI) system to systematically control the instructional programs. Such system usually characterized by testing, diagnosis, learning prescriptions and thorough record keeping[7]. Literature shows that it is effective and gives rise to positive changes[8]. Such complete automated learning environment is appropriate for mastery learning and will be adopted in our ISDN-IDL programs. It is conceived that with ISDN, distance learners can be assessed either on-line or off-line and rendered with appropriate learning materials instantaneously. In the off-line case, learners are expected to up-load test data for diagnosis.

It is envisaged that with ISDN-IDL, distance learners will enjoy additional facilities such as electronic coaching or consultation in the form of audio-graphics conferencing[1,10] and electronic discussion or meeting through multimedia video conferencing[1].

## 3. ISDN-IDL Field Trial

In early 1991, a collaboration program between the polytechnic and Fujitsu Singapore Ltd to develop and implement a full scale ISDN-IDL by end of 1993 was launched. Both organizations had an earlier partnership in the development of a Computer Based Training(CBT) Courseware Development Methodology, CMI and Generic Graphics Library using Fujitsu's Integrated Authoring System, SchoolBox II. The project has inspired the confidence and has provided a platform for both parties to launch the second collaboration program.

Both organizations developed and tested a prototype ISDN-IDL system in September 1991. The prototype make use of two PCs, each with a ISDN PC Card installed and connected to a public switching system, Fujitsu's Fetex-150. The system software was designed to test the various options of delivering distance learning materials. These include On-line Real-time Line Holding, On-line Batch Download loading and On-line Real-time Partial Line Holding. First option provide on-line learning, i.e. the PC remain connected to the host computer via the ISDN line until the learner completed or aborted the course. The second option allows the learners to download designated courseware for off-line self-spaced learning while the third option requires learners to dial up the host computer to download a special 'key' file before s(he) could view a course. The last option provides some form of security measures for restricted learning materials. The prototype software contained a DOS Redirector function(similar to that of NetBIOS) and a Expedite File Transfer(EFT) function. Utilizing a single 'B' channel operating at 64 kbps, an hour of courseware of 1 MB in size was transferred in just over 2 minutes. Distance learners viewed the courseware via both on-line and off-line options and learning records were collected by the host computer. The use of D channel to interact with the learners while s(he) was viewing the lessons, was also tested. The experiment was satisfactory and confirmed our initial expectation of ISDN-IDL.

## 4. Notion of a Near Paperless Learning Environment

With the success of the field trial of the prototype system, a consolidation plan for ISDN-IDL was then evolved. A distributed ISDN-IDL system network architecture for the polytechnic was conceived and the operational schematic diagram is depicted in figure 1. Each host handles up to a maximum of 32 sessions concurrently. Making full use of all channels(i.e. 2 B bands at 64 kbps and 1 D band at 19.2 kbps), distance learners from off-campus sites could dial up to departments concerned to take up a distance learning course through public ISDN switch. They can also assess the host via polytechnic's fiber optics network while on campus.

The system software to be developed will include a System Manager, Data Analysis

Manager, Database Viewer and a Database Manager. System Manager will handle most of the communication functions and provide system administrator a mean to monitor and control the data flow. Besides administrating files receiving and dispatching, it will also manage call states and handle password verification. Data Analysis Manager takes cares of learner performance diagnosis and instructional prescription. The learner performance diagnosis supplies information that required for instructional prescription that specifies the instructional objectives that need to be taught to the individual learner. Database Viewer provides academic administrative functions to restricted users for students' registration, course registration, curriculum development and so on. The Database Manager provides functions for routine housekeeping jobs on all the databases. The program used by distance workstations have two main functions. One takes care of the interface between the user and ISDN API(Application Programming Interface) while the other takes care of the front end in which the learners communicate with the host computers. These include a Directory Manager that allows learners to set host number and description, a Dialer to dial to the host computer, download/upload facilities, compression/decompression facilities as well as a courseware executor for the purpose of executing courseware for viewing. With a CMI mechanism, the ISDN-IDL system provides us a mean to implement mastery learning for our distance learning courses.

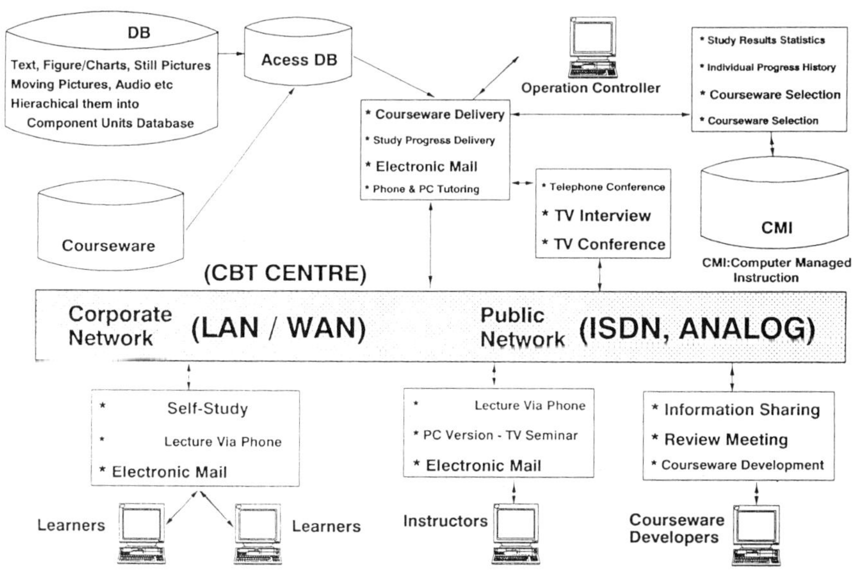


Figure 1. Operational Schematic Diagram for Distance Learning via ISDN

Our ISDN-IDL facilities will also cover multipoint conferencing with multimedia capabilities and audio-graphics conferencing that allows the display of graphic images simultaneously on all learners' screens combine with audio interactions to facilitate electronic coaching or consultation, and electronic discussions or tutorials. Other complementary facilities for electronic library services, electronic mail and bulletin boards services are also planned. The electronic library services make use of our existing library system for database browsing and can be extended to include on-line document retrieval from existing media. Electronic mail facility is needed for feedback, questions and answers, making appointment for further consultation etc. It is a much needed facility for a productive and efficient learning environment. Bulletin board services is very common and popular among active PC users, it is useful for an electronic forum type of activity and encourages learners to share information and exchange ideas. These additional facilities can also be considered for the existing full-time course and to make learning on campus more fun.

With such development underway, we envisioned a near paperless learning environment where learning could simply take place "at anytime and at anyplace". What the learners require will be a computer with ISDN adapter, optional audio and visual input devices. S(he) obviously required to register for one of our distance learning course and is a subscriber of ISDN services. Paper based materials will be reduced to bare minimum as soon as most electronic teaching and learning materials are developed. Since test can be conducted on line, exercises and assignments can be completed using word processors or graphics tools, a day which many of us would learn "near paperlessly" is inevitably near. However, it should be noted that our project is possible due to our changing social, economical, and technological environment. We also expect many possible hurdles that will be addressed in the later section. Three ISDN-IDL certificate courses are being planned. The development of curriculum and learning materials is already underway and the first trial run is expected to be in early 1993.

## 5. Potential Benefits and Long Term Gains

The ISDN-IDL project is believed to be the first in the Asia Pacific region. As education is a vital component in human resource development, it is imperative to place a high premium on education to ensure the fullest development of the new generation. While widespread use and adoption of ISDN-IDL concept are anticipated in the near future, cost will not be the critical factor relatively to the availability, speed and flexibility of the communications and standardization of systems as well as instructional resources. The concept of ISDN-IDL is pertinent to our Singapore's environment and it is expected to lead to cost saving in the long run. This saving can be in the form of reduced traveling time and cost incurred, less need of paper based materials and so on. Many other benefits of electronic distance learning[12] will also be realized in our model of ISDN-IDL.

Our project, a part of our government-led drive to exploit the existing telecommunication infrastructure for education and training sparks off a new class of professionals in academic pursuit. The expertise and experience gained by these individuals in the near future will contribute greatly to the nation's plan of becoming the first electronic country by the turn of this century. In the long run, it is anticipated that our project will lead to higher productivity of Singapore's limited resources pools in terms of human manpower, advanced technologies and other physical resources. The development and implementation of broad band ISDN in Singapore by 1986 is expected to further enhance our ISDN-IDL environment.

## 6. Our Approach and Strategies

Recognizing the potential of ISDN and emerging computing technologies and their implications to provide a more efficient mode of instructional delivery prompted us to adopt an approach to look ahead and to position ourselves for the future. We gained strong management support for ISDN-IDL and preferred a decentralized approach for fast pace development. The Deputy Principal's Office is playing the role of a coordinating body and one single strategic courseware development tool for ISDN-IDL was being endorsed.

The polytechnic adopts a strategy of keeping abreast with the changing technology, and with it, the teaching and training environment. To work with prominent industries is one of our solutions. As Fujitsu Ltd. is responsible for the supply of ISDN lines and switches in Singapore, it is naturally one of the best partners to work with. In addition, we also collaborate with local industries and institutions to develop computer based learning materials and organize activities to inculcate the necessary culture and climate for successful implementation.

## 7. Difficulties Encountered and Potential Problems

The first difficulty that we faced was lack of tools or equipment that support the necessary industrial standards in several areas of our projects. While works on tools or conversion utilities for SGML(Standard Generalized Markup Language) and CGM(Color Graphics Metafile)which will eventually form the standard for all our distance learning materials is underway, we adopt SchoolBox II Integrated Authoring System developed by Fujitsu Ltd. as the base for our development. Emerging standards such as CCITT H.261, MPEG and JPEG for video applications, MPC for multimedia applications, X.400 for email services and G4 for scanned images transmissions are also being considered.

Development of ISDN-IDL curriculum is new and the expertise available is limited. Although many junior staffs that are willing to develop ISDN-IDL, there remain a problem in motivating more senior staff to take part and to lead the projects. The phobia to adopt and accept new technologies is one of the many difficulties to overcome. Some potential problems include duplication of development efforts on courseware materials that requires proper coordination, standards and quality of learning materials that require sound quality assurance plan, reusability and maintainability of the learning materials that requires the staff to spend considerable up front time in the analysis and design stage of courseware development[13].

## 8. Conclusion

New technologies have always affected how instructional materials should be delivered. ISDN-IDL is identified as an efficient mode of delivering distance learning courses. Our plan for a ISDN-IDL system has been presented. The system will couple with a built-in CMI mechanism for mastery learning and complemented with services such as electronic conferences, electronic library services, electronic mail and bulletin boards services. With such system in mind, we plan and aim towards an electronic learning environment and to realize possibly, a near paperless learning environment. We conceived that such an environment will make learning more captivating, absorbing and effective. It provides opportunities for a greater audience and will also boost up the overall literacy level. The concept of ISDN-IDL is appropriate to our rapidly changing society and ever increasing demands of a well trained and highly flexible workforce. It also aims to exploit our existing technological infrastructure and limited resource pool to attain higher productivity.

## 9. Reference

1. Dennis R Knapczyk(1991), "A Distance-Learning Approach to In service Training", Technology Horizons in Education, Vol. 18, No., April 1991, 68-70.
2. Robert Chin(1991), "Interactive Distance Learning : Preliminary and Recommendations", A Working Paper for Ngee Ann Polytechnic-Fujitsu Singapore-Information Technology Institute Joint Development Project.
3. David Roman(1985), "Computer-Based Training Tutorials Well-Taught", Computer Decision, Vol. 10, No 18, December 1985, 82-90.
4. Larry C. Christensen(1987), "Learning Without Human Instruction", ITTE SIGs Newsletter 3, Oct/Nov/Dec 1987, 3-5.
5. Boon-Tian Tan, Yeow-Chin Yong & Hock-Guan Tan(1987), "Validation of the Effectiveness of CAI as a Form of Remediation", Proceedings of EDUCOMP '87, Kuala Lumpur, Malaysia
6. Linda R. Copper(1991), "CAI with Home-Bound Students Proves Successful in Model Program", Technology Horizons in Education, Vol. 18, No. 6, January 1991, 68-69.
7. Burke, R.L. "CAI sourcebook", Englewood Cliffs, N.J. :Prentice-HAll, 1982
8. Hofmeister, Alan and Maggs, Alex, "Microcomputer Applications in Education and Training", Holt, Renehart and Winston, 1984, 5-1 to 5-16.
9. Marcia Kirkpatrick(1991), "Coast Guard Designs its Own CBT", Technical & Skills Training, October 1991, 17-22.
10. Graham Finnie(1989), "Switching the US on to ISDN", Telecommunications, Vol. 23, No 7, July 1989, 66-69.
11. Nathan Rudyk(1991), "Make Meeting Battle-Ready with Multi-Media Software", Technical Notes, IIS Technologies, A Bell-Canada Company.
12. David Carl(1991), "Electronic Distance Learning : Positive Outweigh Negatives", Technology Horizons in Education, Vol. 18, No.10, May 1991, 67-70.
13. Hock-Guan Tan, Yeow-Chin Yong & Jessica Ng(1991), "Reusable and Maintainable Software Approach for Courseware Development", Proceedings of International Conference on Multi-Media in Education and Training, Kogakuin University, Tokyo, Japan, Sept. 13-15, 1991

Education and Society / R. Aiken (Editor)
Information Processing 92, Volume II
Elsevier Science Publishers B.V. (North-Holland)



# Where is the ELITE: Excellent Liberal I. T. Education?

Geoff Cumming

Department of Psychology, La Trobe University, Bundoora, Australia 3083

**Abstract**

This paper advocates broad changes to computer science education. First, the effectiveness of this education should be enhanced by exploitation of ideas from education, psychology and cognitive science including: detailed description of expertise, the cognitive apprenticeship model of learning, and focussing on learners' conceptual change. Second, higher general abilities should be addressed more explicitly, and examination of social and ethical aspects of computer use should receive much greater attention. Finally, liberal education for computer science students is more important than ever: most fundamentally this requires reconceptualising computer science as a discipline grounded in liberal culture. Development of a distinct discipline of computer science education is justified and necessary.

Keyword Codes: K.3.2; K.4.0; K.7.3
Keywords: Computers and Education: Computer and Information Science Education; Computers and Society: General; The Computing Profession: Testing, Certification, and Licensing

> "Computer Science students! Some may be clever, but they don't read, they can't write, they don't communicate. They're so narrow! So boorish! A job ticket—that's all they want of the university. Society, culture, argument—these might as well not exist." (Common caricature.)

> "Do the universities [via computer science] provide for society the intellectual leadership it needs or only the training it asks for?" (Dijkstra, 1989, p.1402.)

This is a deliberately tendentious and disputatious paper. I advocate changes to computer science education with the aim of increasing computing expertise, developing students' communication and other general abilities, increasing attention to social and ethical aspects, and, most fundamentally, presenting computer science to students as part of a liberal education, and as a discipline grounded in culture.

I intend my argument to cover informatics, information technology—the IT of the title—and related fields. I use the term computer science, or CS, because this is the term most often used in discussions of education in relation to IT, but I intend CS to have a very broad meaning. My discussion mainly addresses undergraduate CS degrees, but largely applies also to other CS education.

Most of my argument has some applicability to engineering, and other technologies and sciences, but it is not the purpose of this paper to examine the extent to which the argument applies to other disciplines.

I rejoice that computers offer a wealth of marvellous tools, that they allow us to think in ways probably otherwise impossible, and that they open up the intriguing challenges of cognitive science (Posner, 1990). However, even more than most other technical disciplines, CS knows about and contributes to breathtaking and dangerous changes to our world, yet offers an education that is too often merely instrumental, introverted, and technocratic. I argue first that CS learning can be improved by exploitation of the ideas of expertise, apprenticeship and conceptual change that are being studied by cognitive scientists interested in learning. The need for explicit attention to higher, general abilities grows from this, and leads on to concern about ethical and social issues. Most generally, CS students should develop a sense of cultural setting and human values: they need and deserve a liberal education.

## 1. THE DEVELOPMENT OF EXPERTISE IN COMPUTING

First, consider the development of computing abilities: psychology and cognitive science may now have useful contributions to offer. Psychologists interested in learning have, at last, moved on from trivial tasks learned by rats to study the most impressive human learning: the development of expertise. Human expertise is complex and subtle: studies show that it comprises knowledge and skills at a diversity of levels (Chi, Glaser & Farr, 1988).

### 1.1. Human expertise: Mathematics

As an example of a detailed description of expertise consider Schoenfeld's (1985) identification of four components of mathematical expertise:

(i) Resources: facts, skills, procedures, memory for particular problems.

(ii) Heuristics: not only the well-known Polya (1945) collection, but specialisations of these; 'consider a special case' would for example have different specific versions in geometry, and in various fields of algebra.

(iii) Control: the ability to manage resources, to monitor what is being done, to decide when to shift tack, to judge the prospects of some particular approach.

(iv) Beliefs: a mathematical 'world-view'; expectations as to what is required and acceptable; attitudes to various broad approaches, for example the building of a formal proof; knowledge of one's own abilities.

In the expert these components are intertwined but all identifiable. Schoenfeld presents evidence that good mathematical education needs to pay attention to all four aspects of expertise. In particular, components (ii), (iii), and (iv) are essential and need to be addressed explicitly. These components, especially (iii), are strongly related to metacognition ('thinking about thinking'), so Schoenfeld's approach accords well with current educational ideas that, first, metacognition is vital and, second, that the best way to promote it is to discuss, model and practise it explicitly.

Schoenfeld is advocating the appealing idea that we should regard learning as being progress towards expertise. Attainment of expertise may seem in practice to be too broad and distant a goal, but this approach does emphasise the importance of higher-level abilities, and of seeing the immediate learning aims in a wider and longer-term context.

### 1.2. Apprenticeship as a model of learning

Apprenticeship is the method that has evolved in many human societies as the mechanism for moving a novice towards expert status in a set of abilities important for the society.

Apprenticeship comprises a broad range of types of learning interaction between student and expert. For example the expert demonstrates an activity to the novice, who then undertakes part of the activity while the expert gives guidance. The learner works at simplified versions of a skill, and practises subcomponents of tasks. The expert evaluates the learner's performance, and guides the novice in developing the ability to evaluate his or her own performance. More and more of any task is taken on by the learner, and tasks tackled gradually increase in complexity. Most importantly, the learner is progressively expected to undertake more planning, control and evaluation.

The diversity of types of learning interaction corresponds quite closely with the diversity of components of expertise. Implicit is Schoenfeld's notion that the different components need to be addressed explicitly.

The above view of apprenticeship may be idealised, even romanticised, but is still useful. Collins, Brown, and Newman (1989) apply a 'cognitive' apprenticeship model to teaching and learning in several areas, including reading and creative writing. They give a detailed argument for the fruitfulness of the concepts of expertise and apprenticeship in a broad range of educational areas.

### 1.3. Learning as conceptual change

The other main contemporary perspective on learning that computer science should exploit is that of learning as conceptual change (West & Pines, 1985). Consider the well-known 'naive science' demonstrations: even physics graduates too often betray Aristotelian assumptions about the world when asked simple real-world questions (McCloskey, 1983). They may, for example, say that the ball whizzing around on the end of a string will spiral (!) if the string breaks. Passing physics exams does not, alas, guarantee that the conceptual understanding underlying everyday applications has been achieved.

Successful education must elicit appropriate conceptual change. This is most likely to occur if the prior erroneous conceptions are challenged directly, and the desired new conceptions identified as strikingly different. In other words, learning is not merely a journey aiming to end at Point B (the expert, or canonical conceptions), but a journey starting at Point A (the particular student's initial conception) and proceeding towards Point B. We are likely to be more successful teachers if we have some idea of A, as well as B, and—the great challenge—design the student's learning experiences with A as well as B in mind.

### 1.4. Towards a new computer science education

Computer science embraces theory, deep and complex concepts, and also a vast body of practice. It is therefore an ideal field for exploitation of the contemporary approaches to learning sketched above. Moreover, emphasis on the higher components of expertise would seem especially warranted when specific knowledge at Schoenfeld's first level has a short useful lifetime, as is the case for CS, which changes at a notoriously rapid rate.

There has been some interest in novice-expert differences (e.g. Bateson, Alexander & Murphy, 1987) and in the conceptual changes required in learning programming (e.g. Bonar & Soloway, 1985). But there has been little systematic attempt to develop the possibilities: scanning for example ACM SIGCSE publications reveals few signs that CS educators even know of the existence of the flourishing research on expertise, apprenticeship and conceptual change. Conversely, psychologists and educators have been busy applying these ideas to the teaching of science and mathematics, but have paid little attention to CS.

Good teachers of CS can retort that they have always addressed higher abilities explicitly, and have helped learners appreciate how the new conceptualisations differ from the old. They are no doubt correct, but the research referred to above gives evidence that the new approaches do offer more than a pretentious relabelling of good craft practice.

#### 1.4.1. Expertise, apprenticeship, and system development

In CS, system development is an obvious candidate for analysis in terms of the development of expertise via apprenticeship. It would be very valuable for an expert teacher of system development to attempt a detailed description of the desired expertise parallel to Schoenfeld's for mathematics.

Such a teacher would probably already be using a sequence of exercises and projects that could to some extent be described in terms of the Collins et al. (1989) cognitive apprenticeship model. It would be valuable to spell out this description in detail, to relate it to the description of target expertise, and then to look for guidance as to how the teaching approach might be improved, and how it might serve as a model for other areas in CS education.

#### 1.4.2. Conceptual change in computer science

Dijkstra (1989), for example, emphasises how challenging and deep are some of the concepts that good CS education should impart. Those who work with logic programming languages have investigated the mental models that learners may find useful in coming to terms with strange programs initially seen as declarative. Work in educational computing has studied conceptual change in children writing programs in Logo (e.g. McDougall, 1990). There would seem to be ample scope for much more extensive exploitation in CS of the notion of learning as conceptual change.

### 1.5. A discipline of computer science education

In this first section of the paper I am claiming that psychology, contemporary science education, and cognitive science offer approaches likely to increase the effectiveness with which CS courses can help students develop the desired computing expertise. It is up to CS educators to explore these approaches, and assess the extent to which my claims are justified. The time may now be ripe for concerted development of a specialist discipline of CS education.

In the next three sections I shall consider briefly three topics that are already mentioned in the best CS curricula, but that warrant more detailed and sustained attention: communication skills and other higher abilities; uncertainty and scientific method; and social and ethical issues. They may be regarded as bridging between the specifically computing matters discussed above, and the broad liberal education addressed later in this paper.

## 2. HIGHER, GENERAL ABILITIES

The expertise analysis above stresses the importance of explicit attention to higher abilities, such as those of planning, use of strategies, assessment of progress, control of resources, and knowledge of one's own capabilities. This analysis was made with reference to CS itself. In my view this list should be extended to include other higher abilities of even greater generality. I have in mind skills such as critical analysis, lucid communication, and cooperative group working. These are skills often emphasised by employers as vital for success in CS employment; they are essential if a computing professional is to communicate and work effectively with people from other disciplines, and also is to participate in development of the CS discipline itself.

On the principle, well-established by Schoenfeld and others, that the best way to develop a desired higher-level ability is to identify, describe and address it explicitly, I would advocate that these further, more general abilities should be addressed within CS courses. To the argument that pressure of essential business requires that these be left for possible coverage in non-CS courses taken by CS students, I would make two points.

First, in the main we are talking about process not content. I am not pointing to an additional body of material that must fight for space in a crammed curriculum. Rather, the question is one of methods of presentation, treatment and assessment of material already in the curriculum. Beck, Cassel, and Austing (1989) address this question and give an interesting discussion of how CS can be approached as a "core discipline of liberal arts and sciences". As a small illustration, requiring submission of a critical, analytic essay could demonstrate understanding of some CS topic area, and also some of the desired higher abilities. Requiring preparation of an essay is scarcely a revolutionary suggestion, even if alarming to many students, and possibly professors. We should do it, despite such possible alarm.

Second, the millenia-old pious hope of educators that higher skills transfer automatically has proved to be extremely shaky. Studying Latin improves your Latin, but any 'training of the mind' does not transfer by magic to other fields! If CS graduates are to be good communicators and good analytical thinkers, they need to develop and use these abilities in the context of CS; the abilities will not transfer automatically to CS if they are developed in courses in history or whatever. Recall the physics graduates who can write all the equations, but not always transfer the understanding to tell you how the ball will fly off the string.

### 2.1. Educational computing

This paper is mainly about advocacy, not implementation, but CS educators may find value in studying the research in educational computing that is investigating how computers can be used to promote the development of higher cognitive and other abilities. This research is concerned not with teaching *about* computers, but with using them to support educationally valuable activities, sometimes including programming and often requiring considerable initiative by the learner. Weir (1987) gives one notable discussion of some of this work. Most of this research has been with primary and secondary school students, but the concepts and findings are sufficiently general to warrant serious attention by those seeking to improve the effectiveness of CS education, especially when higher abilities are of particular interest.

## 3. UNCERTAINTY AND THE NATURE OF SCIENCE

My second bridging topic is uncertainty. Psychologists debate endlessly the extent to which psychology is a science, and if so why and how. My view is that a good course in experimental psychology gives a better education in science and the scientific method than do many courses in the traditional science disciplines. Partly this arises from the combination of practical work and research methods with library work and essay writing. More fundamentally it arises from the necessity in psychology to weigh uncertainty, to hypothesise, and to confront doubt and disagreement even while a beginning student.

In the traditional sciences the student often gets the impression that there is a vast body of accepted fact and theory. Way out ahead is the frontier, where research is done. But, except for the occasional 'gee-whizz' talk, research is years away, and only for special people who continue that far. Even if the 'investigative method' of teaching is used, and students are encouraged to form hypotheses, observe, and draw conclusions, there is usually an underlying correct answer, which must be obtained if full marks are to be earned.

Consider, however, just about any momentous public question concerning science. You might nominate in-vitro fertilisation, or global warming, or nuclear power, or genetic engineering. In every case there is technical uncertainty, and in addition the need to weigh social aspects and values. On both counts the traditional science student is likely to be poorly-prepared to contribute to debate. I would hope, however, that a psychology student would have had much experience grappling with partial information, and with conflicting and uncertain evidence. Consideration of social aspects is another issue—more on that below.

In my view, education in all sciences should be more like the psychology education I have sketched as an ideal. Again this is primarily a question of process rather than content: I am not asking for a unit on uncertainty to be squeezed into the physics or biology course. I am asking that any course labelled as science should be true to that name by taking training in the scientific method seriously, especially by addressing uncertainty.

You may regard this section as a detour, irrelevant to CS. You may be right: CS is argued to be more akin to mathematics and/or to engineering than to chemistry (Baldwin, 1990; Parnas, 1990). Along with Abelson and Sussman (1985, p. xvi), I would then be worried about the use of the word science in the title of the discipline. Is it there merely for reasons of claimed prestige, or does it signal the relevance of an investigative, empirical approach and the assessment of theory against observation? Denning et al. (1989), in their influential report on the Core of CS, argue that the experimental scientific method is indeed an important paradigm in CS. If, then, an ability to think about and cope with uncertainty is an important attribute in a computer scientist, it needs to be discussed in CS textbooks and fostered in CS courses.

## 4. SOCIAL AND ETHICAL IMPLICATIONS

As my third bridging topic, consider the social and ethical implications of CS. The main point to make here is that the overly-familiar cliches such as "the rate of change has never been greater, and it's still increasing", and "nothing about the future is certain, except uncertainty" remain grimly true.

We have become hardened as innumerable sci-fi predictions either become humdrum reality, or are recognised as laughably off-beam.

We cannot, however, afford to become inured to the marvel and threat of change. Remember that one night the wolf did indeed come.

The social results of the application of CS have been drastic, alarming, wondrous. Future effects will be even more so. We are immersing our world in vast irreversible experiments, the tools for which are shaped by scientists and technologists of many narrow specialisations, with computer scientists especially prominent.

### 4.1. Unprecedented questions

Consider the recent past. To what extent is instantaneous global speculative trading of currencies, equities and futures via the computer screen responsible for economic instabilities and inequities, and for social alienation? What are the social effects of the introduction of telecommunications, and automated factories in rural subsistence communities? Over the last two years we have all been gripped by our TV screens, elated and appalled by turns, as the Soviet Union and Eastern Europe have reshaped themselves momentously: How have these changes been influenced because computer technology has allowed instant knowledge around the world of what is happening, and instant influence back? These are hard questions, and they have no precedents.

### 4.2. Social effects: Further examples

Consider what might have been, and is likely next time. The development of cheap and deadly computer-controlled (Orwell would have relished the epithet 'smart') weapons, and their potential in the hands of individuals or small groups need no rehearsing here. Revelations of the extent of spying and data storage within Eastern Germany by the Stasi are astonishing and horrifying, but the damage was somewhat limited by the technology of paper and filing cabinets. Now, however, all this information could be held, and kept available for dreadfully flexible access and cross-reference, on a computer system costing no more than a luxury motor car.

Of course computers also offer many exhilarating possibilities for the future: education is one, if we can understand sufficiently well how people learn, and how computers can be used to enhance learning (e.g. Goodyear, 1991).

Sproull and Kiesler (1991) report research on the diverse and extensive effects of computer networking in organisations. Turkle (1984) gives an analysis of how individuals in various circumstances choose to use computers, and how their thinking, self-concept and social relations can be deeply influenced. People vary greatly in their choices and reactions. Turkle frequently uses the language of personality in describing how people interact with computers, and chose "The Second Self" as the title for her book. Turkle's observational work may be dated, but her main conclusion remains compelling: the computer is an artifact of great and intrusive power.

### 4.3. Choosing applications of computer science

Since the first days of fire and stone axes, technology has been available for positive or negative uses. Smulders and Wills (1985), in examining whether social implications should be the core of CS education, quote Albert Speer, Hitler's Minister of Armaments and Munitions:

> Basically, I exploited the phenomenon of the technician's often blind devotion to his task. Because of what seems to be the moral neutrality of technology, these people were without scruples about their activities. The more technical the world ... the more dangerous was this indifference of the technician to the direct consequence of his anonymous activities ... (Speer, 1970).

The stakes are now even higher. In addition, we face not the simplicity of a few Oppenheimer block-buster questions—to bomb or not to bomb—but a myriad of questions large and small to be addressed all over the world about how computer technology is to be used. We must try to foster, and fervently hope for, wisdom on the part of the computer scientists giving the crucial expert advice leading to all these decisions.

### 4.4. Reacting to social and ethical implications

CS professionals, teachers, and students can react smugly that whatever happens they are likely to be on the inside and among the winners; or they can turn away from the enormity of it all and practise what psychologists label denial; or they can recognise the issues but leave any action to others—supposed specialists in ethics, and in social applications of computers. The duty of CS teachers, however, is to recognise the very real dangers and possibilities, and the uncertainties inherent in many applications of computers, and to help their students come to a similar awareness.

Some excellent resource materials are beginning to appear, e.g. Forester (1989), and Forester and Morrison (1990), but the task remains a very great challenge. To the extent that science is seen as needing to be objective, and scientists as having low person orientation, serious engagement with the divergent, uncertain and human aspects of social implications will be difficult. Head (1979) gives a detailed analysis.

The message of HCI (human-computer interface) studies is that designing safe, effective and usable systems requires extensive knowledge of humans. This remains insufficiently recognised within CS, but the argument here goes much further.

Take this as an impassioned plea for renewed and serious attention to consideration of the social effects of computer applications. Social effects should be discussed in conjunction with the ethics of individual professionals and of business and other organisations. Every CS student should have to confront these issues in a variety of contexts. All CS academic staff should raise social implications in their teaching; every CS department should have some staff members for whom social and ethical issues are a special interest. Links with other academics interested in ethics, or in social effects of computers should be strengthened, whether these academics are in departments of philosophy, psychology, or sociology, or elsewhere.

## 5. LIBERAL EDUCATION: BEYOND THE COMPUTING

All the goals I have advocated for CS education so far in this paper—excepting possibly the exploitation of cognitive science ideas as discussed in my first section—do appear already in the most enlightened CS curricula, such as that of the expert U.S. group whose report is summarised by Turner (1991).

I wish to go further and argue that CS should be embedded within a liberal education. The necessity to develop higher, general abilities and to consider the societal setting of CS applications require not merely changes within CS course components, but consideration of the full educational experience of CS students. Before this final stage of the argument, however, I examine briefly CS students.

### 5.1. Students choosing computer science

I searched the literature, trying to find evidence relating to my opening caricature of CS students. I found surprisingly little systematic, large-scale assessment of the characteristics of CS students, or of comparisons with students choosing other disciplines and professions.

The early and influential work of Turkle (1984) includes descriptions of some CS students that are not reassuring. More than most artifacts, computers can for some students be a refuge, and a cloak for personal inadequacies.

Jackson, Holden, Locklin, and Marks (1984) studied the interests and characteristics of more than 10,000 American college students across 17 groupings of subjects. They found that CS students were the most "logical, impersonal and nonverbal".

Anderson (1990a) reports a longitudinal study of entrants to a number of professions. He found that students of engineering—of those studied, the profession probably most similar to CS—"related more easily to things than to people. ... they had the least tolerance of complexity. Questions like the impact of technology on quality of life or the environment were at best a distraction." (p. 7). If CS students are similar the caricature gains support, and the task of addressing uncertainty, and social implications becomes harder.

Matheson & Strickland (1986) give evidence that other students tend to stereotype CS students as unsociable, so some students themselves may hold my caricature.

Computer science colleagues tell me that some CS students are refugees from essay writing, and more broadly that the caricature does have some justification, but also that some students express frustration at the limited opportunities to examine societal and other liberal aspects of CS. I conclude that the caricature may slander many, but cannot be easily dismissed.

#### 5.1.1. Sex differences

The most obvious fact about choice of CS is that it is made much more frequently by men than by women. Moreover, women may be more likely to drop out than are men of equivalent qualifications and aptitude (Campbell & McCabe, 1984). A detailed investigation of CS courses and students, from the point of view of sex differences, led Kay, Lublin, Poiner, and Prosser (1989) to advocate that CS courses be made more appealing to women. To achieve this they recommend that courses should be less strongly technology-centred, and should emphasise broader problem-solving skills and communications skills. Their prescription is entirely concordant with the main thesis of this paper. One very valuable side-effect of the changes I am advocating could therefore be a reduction in the sex differences in CS participation and success.

### 5.2. Liberal education

I turn now to the final and main stage of my argument.

The fundamental assumption of all good education is that the teacher does not know the complete answer. The teacher can help the student acquire knowledge and develop skills at the various levels in the Schoenfeld list. At the higher levels however, and in relation to broader educational goals, we can merely aim to help the student develop the values, attitudes, and general abilities needed for successful functioning in situations that we cannot now foresee.

How can we do this? The best recipe anyone has offered is to aim for a broad, liberal education of the highest quality. My central thesis is that a good CS education not only should include CS components developed in the several ways advocated above, but also must be part of a general liberal education.

A liberal education is one that develops students' higher abilities, especially those of unfettered critical analysis, and gives a sense of cultural heritage, and of cultural and human values. In offering such a definition, even more than in putting forward the arguments in this paper, I am very conscious that I speak from a particular cultural background. It is especially necessary at a World Congress to acknowledge this personal perspective. I am identifying issues of world-wide significance: I can only invite readers to assess my analyses of these issues, and to present their own analyses, from their own cultural and intellectual perspectives.

#### 5.2.1. Traditional advocacy of liberal education

The stirring and eloquent arguments made regularly over the centuries and in many cultures in favour of liberal education rest partly on general considerations, and partly on factors specific to the place, culture and time. Matthew Arnold (1869/1963), for example, advocated in the broadest terms the study of "the best that is known and thought in the world" and "a free play of the mind on all subjects which it touches". He also made the argument particular to the social and religious situation of the time, and to the dangers arising from what he saw as the "rawness and provinciality of his countryman".

General arguments refer to nobility of the enlightened human condition, to human cultural development to ever-higher levels, and to the need for detached and well-informed wisdom if human affairs are to be conducted felicitously. These arguments apply with unprecedented force today. They can also be made particular to the dangers arising from information technology. Consider two illustrations in which modern communication technology is central.

### 5.3. Deep societal influences of information technology

Modern communications mean that in many countries government decisions are strongly influenced by community opinion; governments are likely to make far-seeing, enlightened decisions only to the extent that the people can, in the face of myriad crass and destructive media and commercial pressures, maintain enlightened perspectives and values. Liberal education is one of society's principal means to this end.

On the one hand mass community opinion; on the other the occasional critical decisions by key people, probably in full public view. In 1975 Australia experienced a political crisis when the Governor-General dismissed the Whitlam Government, even though that Government still maintained the confidence of the House of Representatives. Debate continues about the legality—let alone wisdom or honour—of many aspects of the affair. Probably all, or at least nearly all aspects were strictly, legalistically constitutional. But strong and sensible political conventions were openly flouted. Some analysts at the time speculated about tanks in the streets of Canberra. A significant number of Australians still had vivid memories of Germany in the 1930s, and how Hitler came to power, each step being constitutionally correct, or very nearly so. Some reported that they saw chilling parallels.

At the moment of crisis and in full view of the world Whitlam, although righteously indignant, accepted the sacking. A caretaker administration was installed and an election held. The unthinkable—such as tanks in the streets—was thought, but did not eventuate. The likely reason: the attitudes and values of Whitlam and other key players, and their knowledge of the attitudes and values of the Australian people, as developed, largely, by general liberal education.

**5.4. Computer science and liberal education**

I submit that it is not fanciful to find in these two illustrations—government by opinion poll, and political crisis—renewed reason to advocate liberal education. This is a general advocacy, and so CS students must be included. But there is a deeper reason for identifying CS students in particular: information technology plays a crucial role in my two illustrations, yet the role may be sufficiently indirect for them not to be chosen in the CS course as examples of social effects. CS students need to consider critically the interplay of technology, culture and human values more deeply than by study of a few immediate examples of social effects. Furthermore, CS students need an understanding of culture and values to give a context in which to analyse technology and its effects.

My earlier discussion advocated a broadening of approach in CS course components by giving increased attention to higher-level abilities, and to consideration of social and ethical aspects. My argument here is that such measures do not go far enough. In addition to making CS components themselves more liberal in these ways, any good CS degree must as a whole offer liberal education.

**5.5. Computer science itself as a liberal discipline?**

Am I merely asking for liberal studies in other disciplines alongside CS course components? That would be valuable but, even so, is not the ideal.

My argument so far might be caricatured thus: if liberal culture is paint, what I want is that CS components should be given a quick wash of this paint, diluted, and that CS students should as well have on the side a few dollops of the full strength paint. Intellectual culture is not, however, like that.

Geertz (1983), in the course of giving an "ethnography of modern thought" emphasised the diversity of the intellectual world-views of different disciplines. He referred to the "radical variousness of the way we think now", and argued that this variousness extends "beyond the merely professional realms of subject matter, method, technique, scholarly tradition, and the like, to the larger framework of our moral existence" (p. 161).

The conclusion I draw from Geertz is that the outcome I am seeking—the situating of CS in liberal culture—cannot be fully realised by any simple mixing of a new technical discipline with bits from traditional liberal disciplines. Instead we need to create a CS discipline that is rooted in liberal culture and heritage, but in which these enduring values are expressed through the epistemology, culture and practice of CS. I suggest this as the fundamental challenge to scholars and practitioners seeking the improvement of CS education.

I argued earlier that the time may now be ripe for the building of a discipline of CS education. I now identify a central task for this discipline as the reconceptualisation of CS itself as part of liberal culture. These developments can underpin the changes in CS education that are required to achieve the ELITE that our societies need.

## 6. COMPUTER SCIENCE EDUCATION: TOWARDS CHANGE

### 6.1. Computer science curricula at present

I can say little about the diversity of CS curricula that are at present followed in different countries. The traditional British undergraduate degree is probably too narrow to meet the demands I am making; in Australia some undergraduate CS degrees offer scope for breadth while others are almost exclusively technical in content. The traditional U.S. first degree structure would seem to come closest to meeting some of my demands, with the typical requirements for breadth. Lidtke (1990) and Turner (1991) give overviews of recent U.S. developments in CS curricula.

### 6.2. Professional societies

In many countries professional societies, many of them members of IFIP, contribute to CS education in a variety of ways: they accredit courses, specify professional and ethical standards, conduct examinations for entry to the profession, and run programmes of continuing education. They have, therefore, considerable scope to contribute to the changes I am advocating.

The Australian Computer Society, for example, is active in all four ways mentioned. Its accreditation of courses, however, is primarily in terms of their technical content; little mention is made of general educational goals, and there is no requirement for non-computing liberal education.

### 6.3. The educator: The meat in the sandwich

An OECD report points to a paradox of our time: the weakening of the humanities and social sciences just when the values conveyed and the abilities developed by them are increasingly necessary to society, especially in relation to technology. (OECD Working Paper, 1990, cited in Anderson, 1990b).

Around the world education is increasingly being pressured by governments and some employer bodies to be more instrumental towards social and economic ends, and to take a more immediately vocational approach. At the school level, Skilbeck (1990) documents these pressures. On the other hand, a recent particularly enlightened report from a Committee of the Australian Senate concludes that Australian university education tends to produce "highly trained technicians who are undereducated in the broader sense of the term" (Senate Standing Committee on Employment, Education and Training, 1990, p. xiii). That Committee would presumably be in sympathy with the argument of this paper.

There is also pressure from students seeking qualifications and skills that will be immediately useful for employment. These demands from students are especially strong in cases where students are paying large tuition fees, such as is often the case for students moving to another country for higher education. There is pressure for courses to be shortened, for summer semesters to be used, and for strong links to be built between courses and employment. The resulting developments can to some extent be healthy, but from the viewpoint of this paper there are also obvious dangers.

With pressures from governments above, and students below, the university and the profession are the meat in the sandwich. They must, however, belie the passiveness of this metaphor: they must summon strength to assert the necessity of CS education that is both excellent and liberal. They must work for achievements that would justify an honourable response to Dijkstra's challenging question quoted at the start of this paper.

**Acknowledgements**

I am very grateful for comments, on a draft of this paper, from Tony Adams, Robert Aiken, Murray Frazer, Nathan Hoskin, Judy Kay, Gerry Maynard, Anne McDougall, Liz Sonenberg, Roly Sussex, Geoff Webb, Sandra Wills, and Judith Wilson.

## 7. REFERENCES

Abelson, H., & Sussman, G. J. (1985). **Structure and interpretation of computer programs**. Cambridge, MA: MIT Press.

Anderson, D. S. (1990a). Universities and the professions. **Australian Educational Researcher, 18**, 1-15.

Anderson, D. S. (Ed.). (1990b). **Mere technicians?** AVCC Occasional Paper No. 7. Canberra: Australian Vice-Chancellors' Committee.

Arnold, M. (1963). **Culture and anarchy**. Cambridge: Cambridge University Press.

Baldwin, D. (1990). Teaching introductory computer science as the science of algorithms. **SICCSE Bulletin, 22**, 58-62.

Bateson, A. G., Alexander, R. A., & Murphy, M. D. (1987). Cognitive processing differences between novice and expert computer programmers, **International Journal of Man-Machine Studies, 26**, 649-660.

Beck, R. E., Cassel, L. N., & Austing, R. H. (1989). Computer science: A core discipline of liberal arts and sciences. **SIGCSE Bulletin, 21**, 56-60.

Bonar, J., & Soloway, E. (1985). Pre-programming knowledge: A major source of misconceptions in novices. **Human-computer interaction, 1**, 133-161.

Campbell, P., & McCabe, G. (1984). Predicting the success of freshman in a computer science major. **Communications of the ACM, 27**, 1108-1113.

Chi, M. T. H., Glaser, R., & Farr, M. J. (1988). **The nature of expertise**. Hillsdale, N. J.: Erlbaum.

Collins, A., Brown, J. S., & Newman, S. E. (1989). Cognitive apprenticeship: Teaching the crafts of reading, writing, and mathematics. In L. B. Resnick (Ed.), **Knowing, learning, and instruction: Essays in honor of Robert Glaser** (pp. 453-494). Hillsdale, N. J.: Erlbaum.

Denning, P. J., Comer, D. E., Gries, D., Mulder, M. C., Tucker, A., Turner, A. J., & Young, P. R. (1989). Computing as a discipline. **Communications of the ACM, 32**, 9-23.

Dijkstra, E. (1989). On the cruelty of really teaching computing science. **Communications of the ACM, 32**, 1398-1404.

Forester, T. (Ed.). (1989). **Computers in the human context: Information technology, productivity and people**. Oxford: Blackwell.

Forester, T., & Morrison, P. (1990). **Computer ethics: Cautionary tales and ethical dilemmas in computing**. Oxford: Blackwell.

Geertz, C. (1983). **Local knowledge: Further essays in interpretive anthropology**. New York: Basic Books.

Goodyear, P. (Ed.). (1991). **Teaching knowledge and intelligent tutoring**. Norwood, N. J.: Ablex.

Head, J. (1979). Personality and the pursuit of science. **Studies in Science Education, 6**, 23-44.

Jackson, D. N., Holden, R. R., Locklin, R. H., & Marks, E. (1984). Taxonomy of vocational interests of academic major areas. **Journal of Educational Measurement, 21**, 261-275.

Kay, J., Lublin, J., Poiner, G., & Prosser, M. (1989). Not even well begun: Women in computing courses. **Higher Education, 18**, 511-527.

Lidtke, D. K., (1990). Recent developments in computing curricula in higher education. In A. McDougall & C. Dowling (Eds.), **Computers in education** (pp. 241-246). Amsterdam: Elsevier.

Matheson, K., & Strickland, L. (1986). The stereotype of the computer scientist. **Canadian Journal of Behavioural Science, 18**, 15-24.

McCloskey, M. (1983). Intuitive physics. **Scientific American, 77**, 114-122.

McDougall, A. (1990). Children, recursion and Logo programming: An investigation of Papert's conjecture about the variability of Piagetian stages in computer-rich cultures. In A. McDougall & C. Dowling (Eds.), **Computers in education** (pp. 415-418). Amsterdam: Elsevier.

Parnas, D. L. (1990). Education for computing professionals. **Computer**, January, 17-22.

Polya, G. (1945). **How to solve it**. Princeton, N.J.: Princeton University Press.

Posner, M. I. (Ed.). (1990). **Foundations of cognitive science**. Cambridge, MA: MIT Press.

Schoenfeld, A. H. (1985). **Mathematical problem solving**. New York: Academic Press.

Senate Standing Committee on Employment, Education and Training (1990). **Priorities for reform in higher education**. Canberra: Australian Government Publishing Service.

Skilbeck, M. (1990). **Curriculum reform: An overview of trends**. Paris: OECD.

Smulders, M., & Wills, S. (1985). Are social implications the core of computer science. In A. D. Salvas (Ed.), **Communication and change** (pp. 55-57). Melbourne: Computer Education Group of Victoria.

Speer, A. (1970). **Inside the Third Reich**. London: Weidenfeld & Nicolson.

Sproull, L., & Kiesler, S. (1991). **New ways of working in the networked organization**. Cambridge, MA: MIT Press.

Turkle, S. (1984). **The second self: Computers and the human spirit**. London: Granada.

Turner, A. J. (1991). Computing curricula 1991: A summary of the ACM/IEEE-CS Joint Curriculum Task Force report. **Communications of the ACM**. **34**(6), 68-84.

Weir, S. (1987). **Cultivating minds: A Logo casebook**. New York: Harper & Row.

West, L. H. T., & Pines, A. L. (Eds.). (1985). **Cognitive structure and conceptual change**. New York: Academic Press.

Education and Society / R. Aiken (Editor)
Information Processing 92, Volume II
Elsevier Science Publishers B.V. (North-Holland)



# Mapping a Microcomputer Strategy for Informatics Education

Robert Behling and Wallace Wood

Computer Information Systems Department, Bryant College, 1150 Douglas Pike, Smithfield, RI 02917

Abstract

The pace of change in computer hardware and software, as well as the changing business organization, has placed new pressures on educational institutions. To effectively deal with these pressures, especially those associated with microcomputer technologies, requires careful and comprehensive planning. When mapping a microcomputer strategy the planning process moves from developing a vision through operational guidelines to unit plans, budgets, and training, all focused on delivering effective informatics education. The planning process is dynamic, requiring regular review and adjustments. A good mapping system will allow educational institutions to more effectively utilize their resources, as well as improve their performance in the educational marketplace.

Keyword Codes: K.3.2; K.3.1
Keywords: Computer and Information Science Education; Computer Uses in Education

## Introduction

Colleges and universities can no longer consider computers and information systems as pieces of exotic laboratory equipment, special purpose tools, or passing fads. During the past decade, advances in hardware and user-friendly software have encouraged academic administrators and faculty to expand and more fully utilize these systems. With the merging of computer, communication, and office automation technologies, educators must begin to view information as an organizational resource, and informatics education can no longer be delivered as an isolated and stand-alone discipline.

Society is becoming dominated by computers, but many schools are lagging behind in implementing technological advances [1]. Students of the future will expect and require a strong commitment to computers in the classroom. Educational institutions must address these needs by supporting faculty initiatives, providing specialized facilities, and providing adequate technical support. Educators should not become enamored with the latest state-of-the-art hardware; however, before they assess the costs associated with the entire system. Costs for all components of a software purchase, for example, include not only the software product but the associated maintenance, support, and training. These costs are on the rise, with microcomputer software showing the largest overall cost increases [2]. It is easy to fall into the trap of having a laboratory full of equipment that is under utilized because of limited availability of appropriate software.

There are numerous and powerful pressures from organizations and employers of graduates for specialized skill training that may divert attention from the more broad based educational issues [3][4]. In business, as well as educational organizations, information technology is no longer used primarily to automate paperwork. Educational institutions must provide graduates who are prepared to function in this evolving form of business organization and need to bear this in mind when planning for, acquiring, and utilizing information technology resources. It is also important to recognize that on many campuses academic and administrative computing are coming together, sharing resources and technical support staff.

## The Impact of Microcomputers

Computers, especially microcomputers, represent scary technology for administrators [5]. While the full impact of the microcomputer on the traditional information system will not be known for some time, it has been predicted that by the mid 1990's as much as 80% of corporate computing power will be on networks of personal computers. Users want flexible systems that fit their needs, and they want control. In the past microcomputers primarily supported individual work, the system of the future will take advantage of distributed technologies to support groups as well. At Case Western Reserve University, networks make it possible for students and faculty, researchers, scholars, and administrative staff to all interact and form a strategic resource for the university [6]. Projects such as ATHENA at Massachusetts Institute of Technology provide client/server software for the university environment, bringing powerful technologies to diverse groups of researchers and scholars [7].

Before mapping a microcomputer strategy can be discussed and presented, it is critical that a set of assumptions regarding microcomputers be formulated. Because the technologies are evolving so rapidly, the following assumptions focus on the organizational impact of microcomputers rather than on the specifics of hardware and software.

For the purposes of this paper, the number of important impacts of microcomputers over the past decade include:

(1) The traditional mainframe system is being replaced with end-user computing and stand-alone applications employing microcomputers.

(2) Connecting computers through communications technologies and networking software enhances the ability of individuals and groups to share data and software.

(3) Microcomputers are providing a level of user comfort not typically found with mainframe systems.

(4) There continues to be cost/benefit improvements with the introduction of more powerful microcomputer hardware.
(5) The marketplace continues to provide an increasing array of choices, both in hardware and software.
(6) There has never been a technology that has evolved as rapidly as microcomputers, and there are signs that the pace will continue.
(7) Security of data resources and software is much more difficult to control in a networked microcomputer environment.
(8) It is no longer possible for organizations or educational institutions to rely on the advice of in-house experts when acquiring microcomputer technologies.

If an analogy to sports can be drawn, not only have we changed the size of the ball, we have changed the playing field, we lack adequate officials and referees, and we are constantly referring to outdated rules when attempting to assess fouls or settle disputes. Under these conditions it is no wonder that fans become confused when they attend a game, just as educators and administrators often become confused when they receive conflicting expert advice relating to the deployment and utilization of microcomputers. The solution is to develop a more comprehensive planning process involving central administration, academic administration, and faculty and students.

## Mapping a Microcomputer Strategy

When mapping a microcomputer strategy we need to view computing and information systems as part of the organizational infrastructure, just like the library, offices, and telephones [8]. In many, if not most educational institutions, information systems and information technology is critical to the organizations survival and growth [9]. Viewing information technology as a campus-wide issue will boost efficiency and enhance competitiveness, and integrating academic and administrative planning activities will mean better systems, better services, better support, and better utilization of resources. Even though the old rules no longer apply, computer administrators, like bureaucracies, tend to hang on to the status quo [5].

Any strategy addressing the use of microcomputers in a university setting must address microcomputer laboratories. The heavy emphasis on experiential learning necessary in computer education requires a strong emphasis on the facilities used to support and augment the more traditional forms of education. If not carried out properly, the establishment of a microcomputer or end-user laboratory can have unforseen negative consequences [10]. Computer laboratory designers must keep in mind that form follows function and needs and applications must be described and defined before selecting hardware and software. It also should be noted that facilities design is a dynamic process, and decisions must be evaluated and adjusted in response to changes in the environment. The fact that a laboratory has been established is only the beginning. Administrators must recognize that they have an ongoing commitment to enhance the facility by providing current hardware and software, as well as an effective learning environment for users.

The most critical issue associated with the management and operation of computer laboratories is adequate staffing with people possessing both technical competence and communication skills [11]. Microcomputers bring more end-user computing with more limited skill users who need support. It is not generally possible for microcomputer support staff to specialize in one functional area or one software product as was found with mainframe technicians. A comprehensive staffing plan, including carefully described job descriptions, is critical to mapping a microcomputer strategy. The very nature of the specialized duties of support staff create dead-end positions with little or no room for advancement. Thus, support personnel have a high rate of turnover, are generally at the beginning of their careers, and may find it difficult to effectively interact with high-powered and demanding faculty and administrators. Also, the notion that funds are better spent on tangible goods (microcomputers and equipment) rather than software and salaries, is often in evidence. In the case of technical support the low cost provider is generally not the best, yet most acquisition/purchasing systems are fine-tuned to respond to the low bid as the most acceptable.

State of-the-art computing is becoming a priority requirement to attract and retain the best faculty and staff [8]. Although a number of universities recognize the need for computer-literate faculty, few offer opportunities for comprehensive training [1]. Training must be planned as an ongoing process, not a single event. The plan should provide resources for academic faculty and staff to learn, develop, and refine computer applications for teaching, research, and administrative activities. At many schools the payoff in terms of promotion and tenure is for research and publication, not for teaching. Administrators must also provide support to faculty for using computers to improve learning, and must include this in their faculty performance evaluations

A commitment to technology is a commitment to ongoing change, but do not expect the evolution of the organization to match the pace of technological change. Implementing any technology plan will mean an ongoing financial and strategic struggle. While this struggle may be useful to provide a forum for all of the concerned interest groups, it is critical that it be managed in such a way that special interests do not exert undue influence. There needs to be a balance between continually chasing technology and the commitment of resources to provide a stable and user friendly environment.

It is also very important for planners and administrators to understand that the economic life of microcomputer equipment is much less than assumed with mainframe equipment. Obsolete does not mean not functional, it means not adequate, and this includes both hardware and commercial software. In the twenty-first century it is predicted that desktop computers will be as powerful as today's super computers. In between we are sure to see a number of "generations" as the systems evolve.

Plans to continually replace or upgrade equipment must be included in planning documents. Just as with an automobile trip a map is necessary to guide the traveller from their starting point to their destination (See Figure 1). In the case of mapping a microcomputer strategy the way is shown through a formalized planning document that is made known throughout the organization. The strategy should be mapped in

Figure 1

Mapping a Microcomputer Strategy

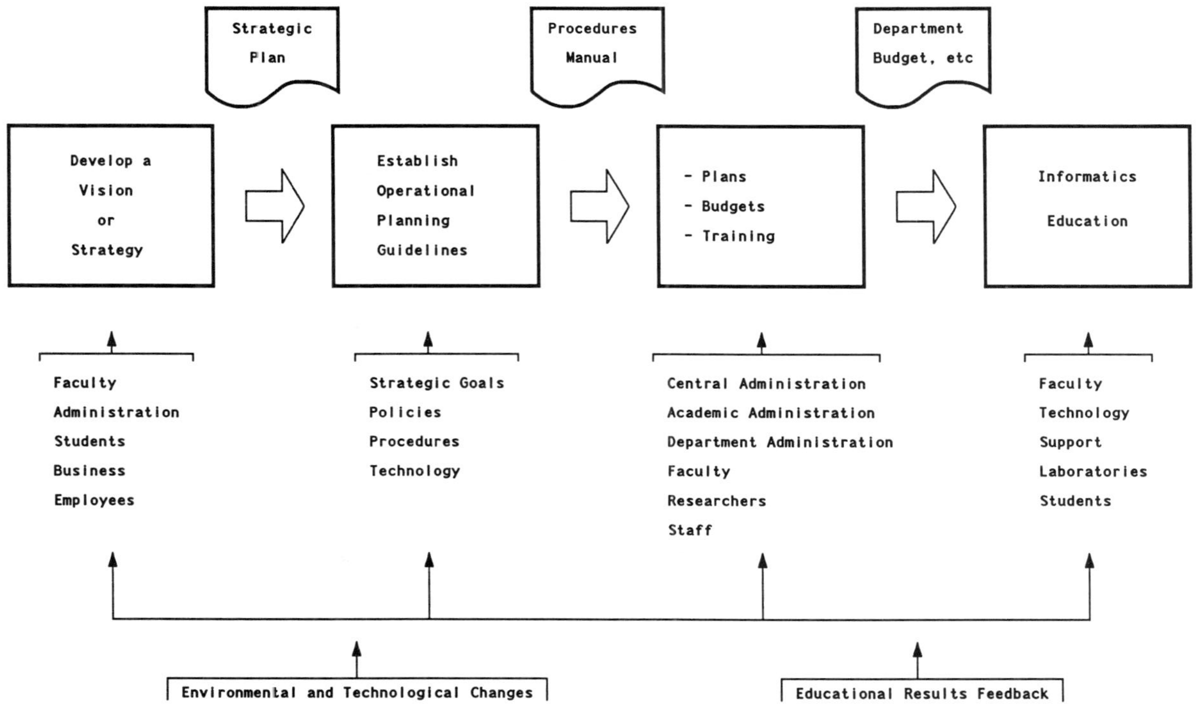

sufficient detail to allow for the development of formalized operational planning guidelines. When produced in a procedures manual the guidelines will provide both academic and administrative units adequate information to allow them to prepare their operating plans, while at the same time providing a vision for microcomputer technology beyond the current planning cycle. Each institution has a different mix of resources, academic and administrative needs, and willingness to assume risk, so each plan will be unique. The important thing is that the plan be made available in a formalized way. Once the strategic plan is developed and in place it serves to guide all resource allocation for technology expenditures. The plans, budgets, staffing, and training can then focus on delivering informatics education that is consistent with the institutional vision. Because the mapping process is a dynamic one, fine tuning and adjustments to the strategic plan, procedures manuals, and operating plans will routinely occur.

## The Costs and Benefits of Mapping a Microcomputer Strategy

Perhaps the most obvious cost is in the planning process itself. Planning is difficult and time consuming, requiring commitment from all end-user groups to work together and focus on a common vision. It is an awesome responsibility to develop a document that will guide budgets, embrace or restrict technologies, and service as diverse a group as a university population. There will be high costs in compromise, difficult choices, and conflicting perceptions of the mission of the university.

Academic institutions are committee based, and as such are generally slow to respond. They often lag one or more years behind other organizations, and additional planning may slow them down even more. It is imperative that the strategic planning not be rushed, yet is also imperative that it be completed in a reasonable planning cycle. There is a delicate balance required to give the plan a best effort and formalize a document in a reasonable time frame. Delays will cause missed opportunities, confusion, and inappropriate expenditures. Haste may provide a document that produces unacceptable results.

The benefits of mapping a microcomputer strategy must focus on selling strategic planning to all constituencies involved. That is, it must emphasize that everyone gains with more effective use of resources. Because all components of the organization are familiar with the vision (strategy), they can operationalize this in their budgets and short term planning. Their objectives will be more synchronized with the needs of the institution, their budgets will be more focused, and there will be fewer surprises as the organization evolves.

## Conclusions

These are trying times for institutions of higher learning. The fast pace of technological change, the pressure of restricted budgets and limited resources, together with a need to keep close to state-of-the-art requires much more careful planning than has been the case in the past. Without organization-wide goals and objectives that can be translated into individual functional plans and budgets, it will be impossible to effectively control the application and utilization of microcomputers. By establishing a procedure to map a microcomputer strategy for informatics education organizations can greatly improve their performance in the very competitive educational marketplace.

## Bibliography


1. Evans, S. and L. Chaney. "Provision for Faculty Microcomputer Training and Facilities at Collegiate Schools of Business, "The Journal of Computer Information Systems, Winter 1989-90, pp 22-26.

2. Hamilton, R. "Up, Up and Away: Costs hiked 40% since '84," Computerworld, Aug 31, 1987, pp 21,26.

3. Schrage, M. "Killing Thought with Spreadsheets," The Boston Sunday Globe, April 14, 1991.

4. Watson, H., D. Young, S. Miranda, B. Robichaux and R. Seerley. "Requisite Skills for New MIS Hires," Data Base, Spring 1990, pp 20-28.

5. Shurkin, J. "Computing Gets An Overhaul At Stanford University, "Personal Computing, December 1987, pp 179-185.

6. Salamone, S. "Network Innovators: Raymond Neff,"Network World, Jun 3, 1991, p 76.

7. Savage, J. "College takes cheaper road to Athena," Computerworld, Jan 28, 1991, p 37.

8. Rifken, G. "It's a computer-based contest to win the best and brightest," Computerworld, Jan 9, 1989, pp 43-45.

9. Alexander, M."College Means Business with IS," Computerworld, Jan 8, 1990, pp 55, 62-63.

10. Johnson, L. and P. Dileepan. "The Management of Microcomputer Laboratory Resources," The Journal of Computer Information Systems, Summer 1990, pp 53-56.

11. Schwartz, R. and R. Kennedy. "The Management and Mismanagement of Microlabs in Colleges of Business," Interface, Summer 1989, pp 31-35.

Education and Society / R. Aiken (Editor)
Information Processing 92, Volume II
Elsevier Science Publishers B.V. (North-Holland)


# MANAGING END-USER COMPUTING: A SYSTEMATIC VIEW

H.C.Harrison(a) and Gong Qizhong(b)

(a) Department of MIS, University College Dublin, Ireland

(b) Department of Information Management, Southwestern University of Finance & Economics, P.R. China

Keyword Codes: H.0; K.3.1; K.6.1
Keywords: Information; End-User Computing; Management

## 1. INTRODUCTION

Over the last decade, the rapid growth of the development of computer-based information systems by the users who are not programmers or system analysts, namely, End-User Computing has been one of the most significant phenomena in the computing area. End-user computing consumed 40 to 50 percent of computing resources in several companies surveyed and the number of end users is growing at a rate between 50 and 60 percent per year[1]. There is no doubt that end-user computing is becoming the dominant kind of computing.

As a result of this rapid growth, organizations are now moving into a new phase of information related management. Managers are confronted by different management problems. In fact, end-user computing makes a major transformation of the nature of managerial work and is of growing strategic importance to many organizations[2]. As a new subject, there was a great amount of research directed towards end-user computing in the 1980s. The purpose of this paper is to present a system model for the management of end-user computing. From a system viewpoint, management should be concerned with the corporate issues of strategy,structure and management processes. These issues should be systematically addressed to accommodate a new computing environment. A proper management process for end-user computing, in essence, depends on keeping the critical balance between support and control in a timely fashion.

## 2. A SYSTEM MODEL FOR END-USER COMPUTING MANAGEMENT

An organization and its management is, virtually, an open system, made up of four elements: strategy, technology, structure and the management process (figure 1). The system interacts with the environment in which it exists and must, to survive, modify itself in response to a rapidly changing environment. In the system, on the other hand, elements are interrelated and interdependent. A change in one element inevitably has effects on others[3].

The growth of end-user computing strongly implies that both environment and the technology for producing information systems are significantly changed. In the old traditional environment, the IS department controls the delivery of information and is responsible for systems design, while users are removed from the development process[4]. Now, users are much more active and even develop applications themselves with user-friendly software. In such a context, the strategy, structure and management process must change to keep the system in balance. In other words, there are at least three fundamental issues that end-user management needs to address. There should be:-

(1) an end-user computing strategy.
(2) a suitable structure.
(3) an effective management process.

From a system viewpoint, firstly, not one of these issues can be ignored. Secondly, all the three issues are closely interrelated.

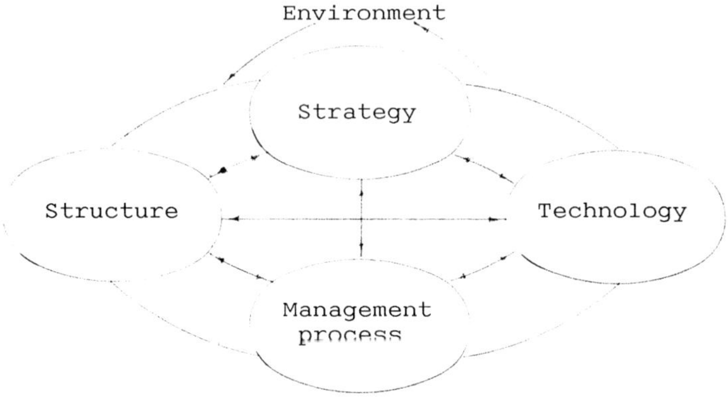


Figure 1: An organization and its management can be seen as an open system, made up of strategy, technology, structure and the management process.

## 2.1 Strategy

Most organizations have extensive information system strategic planning dealing with paperwork-oriented data processing, but little attention has been paid to the development of a strategy for end-user computing[1]. This is the main reason why these organizations can't manage end-user computing effectively.

The rapidly changing environment makes strategic planning more difficult. However, strategy is absolutely necessary. For example, if an organization plans to install a network in the future and allows users to access a corporate database, the strategy may call for a preemptive action with respect to adopting high level standard control.

In fact, strategy planning is often done on a rolling basis [5]. Such a procedure allows an organization to revise its strategic plan and maintain a degree of flexibility based on new information.

## 2.2 Structure

Although there are some arguments about what kind of structure is suitable for end-user computing, it is beyond argument that the IS department, which was designed twenty years ago to accommodate the management of central processing oriented technology, can't meet the needs of end-user computing.

Many organizations have accommodated end-user computing by establishing an information center originating from IBM (Canada) in 1976. The information center is based on a concept of providing end users with direct access to computers and information processing resources through a central facility. Hardware, software, training and consulting assist users in applying information resources to their problems.

The information center is a proven solution for supporting end-user computing. Many are very successful. However, the information center is an incomplete solution for end-user computing. There are some potential problems in information center operations[6]:

(1) The information center focuses on support, but both support and control are important to end-user computing.

(2) The information center may not even have full backing of IS departments.

(3) The information center can only react to expressed user needs, yet, many opportunities may not be recognized by technologically unsophisticated users.

(4) The information center has no authority to coordinate disagreements and conflicts of resource allocation and computing policies.

These problems have implications for a centralized structure. The structure plays a planning, monitoring, coordinating, consulting and justifying role concerning the operations of end-user computing. Before a more suitable structure is found, the IS department is in the best position to throughly understand the situation of information processing in the organization. To carry out effective management throughout an organization, the IS department will also need to have the mandate, authority and resources to accomplish it[7].

### 2.3 Management Process

What comes next is developing an effective management process carried out by a designed structure to put the strategy into action. The management process answers the questions: (1) how should the strategy be implemented? (2) when? (3) how efficiently?

The management process for end-user computing usually falls into two catagories: support and control.

#### 2.3.1 Support

It is clear that the degree of success of end users' performance is largely dependent on the support that end-users can obtain. A well-thought-out training program and a supportive environment are two main issues that are important in the support for end-user computing.

- Training

End users will develop systems well only if their computing knowledge is comprehensive enough to understand computing and its role in their applications.

Training is a critical area today. Firstly, different users need different training according to factors like education level, computing knowledge, age, the position in an organization and so on. Secondly, end-user computng technology is coming to the market in extraordinary diversity. This makes the training process more complex and expensive. Some managers attempt to control the expense through reducing training. But good managers see training as a valuable investment.

The method and content of training often vary, depending on different requirements. Training may be for a specific new package or for general understanding of information processing. Training may act as a consulting service for meeting users' requirements on an as-needed basis.

- Supportive Environment

Management should create a supportive environment, in which the end-user computing takes place, to satisfy users' needs and encourage users' motivation. Generally, end-users need management support, e.g. reward system, and technology support. The technology support includes two dimensions: the variety of support functions and the quality of support services.

In addition to training, users need guidance in chosing the proper software tool for a given application, consultation during the design of an application, as well as assistance in debugging. These support functions are often provided by information centers in many organizations.

The quality of support largely depends on information center personnel. They should have the following attributes: a good knowledge of current software packages, understanding users' business problems, good interpersonal skills, patience and enthusiasm, and service orientation. These traits are not generally found in IS staff groups[8]. In many information centers, local user experts are playing an important role. They speak their own language and make the instruction vivid with practical examples.

2.3.2. Control

The essence of the control process is to regulate the organization's activities in conformity with the strategy and objectives.

Management has come to recognize that end-user computing costs are rising too fast; poorly developed user applications are causing trouble. There is an evident need for a well-defined control process in the end-user computing area.

The most important issues with regard to the control process for end-user computing include standardization, figuring out critical systems and evaluating/justifying.

- Standardization

Hardware, software and data standards must be established to regularize activities and facilitate coordination. For example, there should be a policy to limit the number of types of personal computers to ensure that the training courses, support services and network protocols can be put in place. Software standards can make it easier to share data, documents and analyses. Otherwise, users might have to repeat an extensive learning process when they transfer to another department. Without data standards, integration between applications will be minimal and frustrating.

- Critical Systems

As users generally have not enough computing knowledge, there should be a control process to evaluate what kinds of systems end users can expect to develop efficiently and what kinds of systems do not.

Generally, the following applications, at least during the early end-user computing stage, should not be handled through end-user development[9]:

(1) Data entry involving organization files and databases.
(2) High volumes of transactions requiring processing efficiency and multiple processing steps.
(3) Applications which are sensitive to an organization.
(4) Applications requiring formal specifications and documentation.

- Evaluating/Justifying

Evaluating and justifying helps to ensure that what is intended to be accomplished is accomplished within the defined criteria.

The evaluating and justifying process for end-user computing includes the following four steps:

(1) Define success.
(2) Develop criteria, methods and procedures for evaluation.
(3) Reach an agreement with management with respect to steps 1 and 2.

(4) Implement the evaluation methods and procedures.

## 3. THE BALANCE BETWEEN SUPPORT AND CONTROL

A successful management process for end-user computing not only should include support and control, but should also keep a balance between them.

The balance is critical[10]. When control is too tight, like a monopolist approach in some organizations where IS departments attempt to maintain firm control over all end-user computing , it may restrict learning and innovation thereby creating general dissatisfaction among end users. In contrast, when control is too loose, like a laissez-faire approach in some organizations, it holds no assurance that user developed systems have a business value and have no risk to the organization.

The balance is changing over time. During the early phase of end-user computing, the emphasis of management should be placed on support to encourage users' interest, learning and involvement. Control is not an issue at this time. As the number of end users grows, however, the relative importance of control increases to minimize the risk from user developed systems. In essence,the management process is dynamic. The track of a proper management process is somewhat like the curve in figure 2.

Moreover, the balance is closely related to an organization's circumstances such as computing resources, staff behavior, the present situation of end-user computing and management style. Different organizations require a different balance according to their different circumstances.

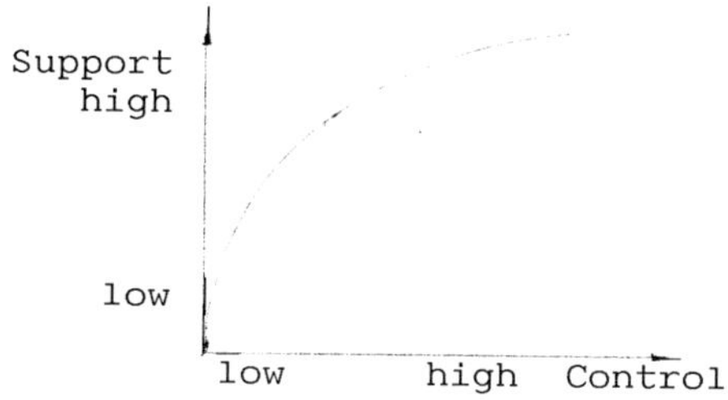


Figure 2: An effective management process lies in keeping an optimal balance between support and control in a timely fashion.

## 4. CONCLUSION

Strategy, structure and the management process are all important issues for the management of end-user computing. Only when they are addressed systematically, can end-user computing be managed effectively. Firstly, from a system viewpoint, not one of these issues can be ignored. One aspect should not be stressed to the neglect of others. Secondly, these issues are closely interrelated. The structure should reflect the strategy. Management processes should match the structure and embody the strategy. The effectiveness of the management of end-user computing largely depends upon how well these issues are coordinated.

The management process of end-user computing, in essence, is a dynamic process. The art of end-user computing management does lie in reaching an optimal balance between support and control in an appropriate manner, at appropriate time and at an appropriate place.

## REFERENCES


1) Rockart,J.F. and Flannery,L. 1983, " The Management of End User Computing," Communications of the ACM, Vol.26,No.10 (October), pp.776-784.
2) Parsons,G.L. 1983, "Information Technology: A New Competitive Weapon," Sloan Management Review, Vol.25,No.1 (Fall), pp.3-14.
3) Brown, W.B. and Moberg, D.J. 1980, Organization Theory and Management: A Macro Approach, John Wiley & Sons, New York.
4) Rivard, S. 1987, " Successful Implementation of End-User Computing," Interfaces, Vol.17,No.13(May-June), pp.25-33.
5) Glueck,W.F. and Jauch,L.R. 1984, Strategic Management and Business Policy, McGraw-Hill, Inc., New York.
6) Turban,E. 1988, Decision Support and Expert Systems: Managerial Perspectives, Macmillan Publishing Company, New York.
7) Cooper,R.B. 1988, " Review of Management Information Systems. Research: A Management Support Emphasis," Information Processing & Management, Vol.24,No.1, pp.73-102.
8) Carr,H.H. 1987, "Information Centers: The IBM Model vs. Practice," MIS Quarterly, Vol.11,No.3(September) pp.325-338.
9) Senn,J.A.1989, Analysis & Design of Information Systems, McGraw-Hill, New York.
10) Henderson, J.C. and Treacy, M.E. 1986, "Managing End-User Computing for Competitive Advantage," Sloan Management Review, Vol. 27, No.2(Winter), pp.3-14.

Education and Society / R. Aiken (Editor)
Information Processing 92, Volume II
Elsevier Science Publishers B.V. (North-Holland)




# MAGE : a methodological framework for the cooperative development of educational software

Thierry NODENOT (1)(2) and Guy GOUARDERES (1)

(1) Laboratoire API, 50 chemin des maraîchers, 31062 Toulouse, FRANCE
Tel. : (33) 62 25 88 85, Fax : (33) 62 25 88 01

(2) Laboratoire LICIAP, Université de Pau et des Pays de l'Adour, Faculté des Sciences et Techniques, 64000 Pau, FRANCE, Tel : (33) 59 80 75 64 Fax : (33) 59 80 75 90

## Abstract

The development of complex educational software requires a rational approach that looks like those that software engineers call for. We propose a methodological framework which allows a real cooperation between the two classes of users concerned about software educational engineering : the pedagogues and the software engineers. This framework is mainly based on the availability of a formal language which allows a communication between the classes of users. We present this language and we show how it can be used to implement any educational software, from their requirements to their use.

Keyword Codes : K.3.1, D.2.1, I.2.4, D.2.10

Keywords : Computer Uses in Education, Requirements/Specifications, Knowledge Representation Formalisms and Methods, Design

## 1. INTRODUCTION

Recent developments in CASE technology (Computer-Aided Software Engineering) have focused on the activities which support the development of software [1]. We can quote *requirements analysis*, *formal specification* (Abstract data types, objects), *integration*, *inter-operability*, and *controlled evolution*. Nevertheless, the large effect of such advances often fail because there is no methodology which ensures a convenient product will be available after the last stage of development.

The same problems arise in the domain of courseware engineering. Educational software becomes more and more complex and its methods of development follow the same process. The development of learning environments, complex simulations, or intelligent tutoring systems requires methods which are different from those that software engineers can use because these methods are mainly applied by pedagogues who necessarily have an educational viewpoint, but they are not purely educational because the aim is to develop a software system. *Specific engineering methods for educational software* must be proposed to the developers.

We noticed the efforts that researchers make to identify and connect the activities proposed to the pedagogues during the development of courseware [2], [3], [4], [5]. But we were surprised that the data processing aspect of such a development was taken into account only at the end of the process, or even ignored. We think that a complex courseware is the result of a narrow cooperation between a team of pedagogues and a team of software engineers : they perform a development which is both educational and data processing oriented. Their cooperation is called co-authoring.

In this paper, we particularly present the formal language used in our methodological framework. It allows pedagogues and software engineers sharing-out the responsibilities of the development of courseware. This research comes within the scope of the production of a courseware engineering system : the ICES(1) [6], [7], [8].

## 2. THE "MAGE" METHODOLOGICAL FRAMEWORK OF THE "ICES" PROJECT

The major component of a courseware engineering system (for example, the ICES) is the methodology which is proposed to the developers of educational software. The methodology is not directly manipulated by the developers, because the courseware engineering system provides them with methods and tools which automate or facilitate its use. However, the cooperation and the integrity of such methods and tools are essentially based on the underlying methodology. It ensures the compatibility between the data that the different methods and tools require or provide, and thus, it provides the framework for the integration of these methods (and tools) in a courseware engineering system. So, the characteristics of the "MAGE" methodological framework that we are going to detail, should not be misunderstood :

- it provides a "process-model" for the development of courseware. It will be hidden from the users but such a methodology is necessary to build integrated methods and tools,
- the different methods (and tools which automate them) will provide external models (which can be textual, graphical or formal) that the developers will use to describe the behaviour of the proposed courseware [9].

In particular, the language used by the developers to describe the properties of a courseware according to a particular method will be, most of the time, different from the underlying language used, at the methodological level, to integrate the different methods used in the courseware engineering system.

### 2.1. The principles of the "MAGE" methodological framework

The functioning of "MAGE" follows from four principles which allow :

- to split the process of development into a sequence of stages. We distinguish the specification, the design, the implementation, the validation, and the distribution stages. Each of this stages concerns both the pedagogues and the software engineers, because the former must design and validate the educational behaviour of the courseware, and the latter must design and validate the architectural structure of the courseware,
- to provide the developers with a model -called the spiral model- [10] which allows them to achieve the different stages of development. This model promotes prototyping as a means to understand and communicate the behaviour of a system,
- to take into account the particularities of educational software compared to classical

(1) "ICES" is an acronym for Integrated Courseware Engineering System. The French acronym for the "ICES" is "AGDI".

applications. We shall distinguish three levels of abstraction : *the pedagogic dimension* which is the set of concepts and learning objectives related to the domain in which the educational software will act, *the didactic dimension* which focuses on the different learning strategies that the pedagogues foresee to meet the educational objectives (these strategies are more or less learner controlled), *the mediatic dimension* which takes into account the interactions of the student with the educational system during the apprenticeship of the concepts modelled for the domain,

- to propose a formal language which will be used to store and share the descriptions modelled by the developers when, thanks to a convenient method, they describe the proposed courseware, or when they want to exchange informations during the development. This formal language will not be directly used by the developers because this language is at the methodological level and the users interact with tools and methods adapted to their capabilities.

We are going to focus our attention on the formal language proposed by "MAGE". For general informations about the other principles, and in order to fully understand the example that we will give in paragraph 2.4, we recommend the reader to previously refer to [11].

## 2.2. A single formal language for the whole cycle of development

During the different stages of development, the two classes of users design descriptions thanks to their particular methods and tools, but the “MAGE” methodological framework must provide means to store and share these informations between the different methods used in the courseware engineering system. We need a language which supports the integration of both the methods and the classes of users. Our major aim is to provide a language which promotes precise descriptions because this precision is necessary if we want the classes of users to communicate and to cooperate but also for the automation of the methodology.

The language we have chosen is called “Spec” [12]. We are going to detail the main characteristics of this language, its capabilities in the domain of educational engineering.

## 2.3. The main characteristics of the "Spec" language

"Spec" is a formal specification language intended to span the entire process of software development. It has been explicitly designed for large-scale applications, including parallel, distributed, and real-time systems. "Spec" is compatible with Ada and, from our point of view, it can be used to write specifications in common styles for the different types of courseware (tutorials, intelligent tutoring systems, learning environments, ...).

The language designed by V. BERZINS and LUQI has three main characteristics which has lead us to choose it for designing courseware :

- it provides means for describing *abstractions*. It has been designed to encourage designs that separate different concerns into different modules, to make review and evolution easier. It provides an inheritance mechanism that can be used for view integration and for specifying constraints to the interfaces of many modules (each one can inherit the messages, the concepts and states of another module),
- it provides a mathematical approach for organizing the mental processes of design. *Logic* is the basic tool for describing the requirements of a software system. It is easier to write a precise description of the behaviour of a system using logic than to write a program implementing the system, because logic provides more powerful primitives. The language uses second-order temporal logic, which has the familiar first-order logic as a subset (second-order temporal logic provides operators on sets, unbounded sets,

sequences, relations, ... and provides two temporal operators to talk about properties of the system that involve more than one state at a time : the operators next and previous),
- it promotes *an event model* to describe the behaviour of a software system. Four kinds of primitives are suitable : modules, messages, events and alarms. Modules can be used to model external systems such as users and peripheral hardware devices, as well as software components. The behaviour of a module is specified by describing its interface which consists of the set of stimuli recognized by the module and the associated responses (a stimulus is an event or an alarm which is associated with a module, a message, and a time).

Used in the framework of "MAGE", the "Spec" language allows the description of a courseware, for each stage of its development, and each of its levels of abstraction (pedagogic, didactic and mediatic models). The dynamics of the apprenticeship is taken into account by the event model, the levels of abstraction by the integration of "Spec" modules, and the functioning of these modules by predicates and goals using second-order logic.

## 2.4. The practical use of the "Spec" language for designing educational considerations

The "Spec" language allows to model both educational and data-processing considerations. As this language has been developed for designing software systems, we shall not describe any data processing stage, but we shall focus our attention on the stages of specification and design, from an educational viewpoint.

### *2.4.1. INITIAL AIMS FOR AN EDUCATIONAL SOFTWARE*

Here is a text that explains the initial requirements for the educational software that a team of pedagogues wants to develop :

"The aim of this educational software is to control that eleven-year-old students know the different properties of *quadrilaterals*. The system must check that the *route* proposed by the student (composed of a sequence of quadrilaterals) respects the given *order*. The orders must be adapted to the abilities of the student, and the goal is to help him *arrange* the different quadrilaterals according to their *geometrical properties* (figure 2)" :

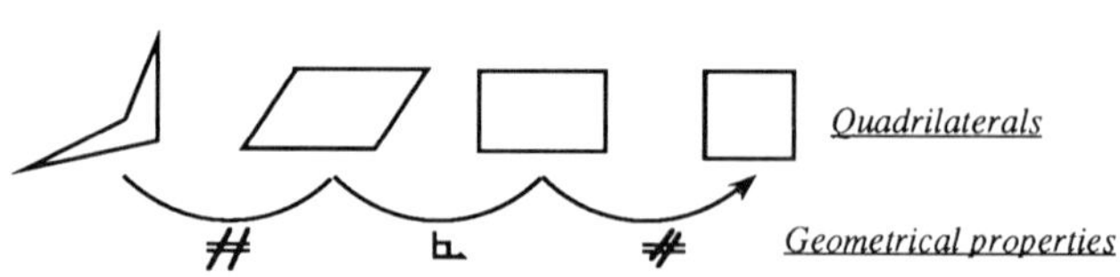


*figure 2 : an example of route*

### *2.4.2. THE SPECIFICATION STAGE FROM THE VIEWPOINT OF PEDAGOGUES*

Let us begin by the pedagogic model. The "Spec" description must detail the concepts and the goals which are connected to the domain in which the educational software will be used. From the initial aims, the pedagogues describe the concepts called quadrilateral and geometrical property, the partial ordering operator(2) (to arrange) between the different quadrilaterals : this operator considers the properties of the quadrilaterals to arrange them.

(2) The diamond and the rectangle cannot be arranged according to their geometrical properties.

Hence the "Spec" description :

```
DEFINITION Concepts-and-goals-of-the-
    pedagogic-model
-- description of a CAL concept in this courseware :
   all of them are quadrilaterals
CONCEPT  cal-concept : type
   WHERE Subtype(cal-concept, quadrilateral)
CONCEPT  quadrilateral : type
-- description of the geometrical properties of a
   quadrilateral: has-two-right-angles, has-opposite-
   sides-equal, and has-4-sides-equal
CONCEPT  has-two-right-angles(q : quadrilateral)
   VALUE (b : boolean)
CONCEPT  has-opposite-sides-equal (q :
   quadrilateral)
   VALUE (b: boolean)
...
-- description of the quadrilaterals which are known
   in the courseware : ordinary-quadrilateral,
   parallelogram, diamond, rectangle and square
CONCEPT  ordinary-quadrilateral : type
   WHERE ALL (q : ordinary-quadrilateral ::
             not(has-opposite-sides-equal(q)) and
             not(has-two-right-angles(q)))
   Subtype(ordinary-quadrilateral, quadrilateral)
CONCEPT  parallelogram : type
   WHERE ALL(p : parallelogram ::
             has-opposite-sides-equal(p))
   Subtype (parallelogram, quadrilateral)
CONCEPT  diamond : type
   WHERE ALL(d : diamond ::
             has-4-sides-equal(d))
   Subtype (diamond, quadrilateral)
...
CONCEPT  square : type
   WHERE Subtype(square, diamond)
         Subtype(square, rectangle)
-- description of the goals of the pedagogic model :
   the operator < means that c2 has all the
   properties of c1 and others.
CONCEPT  "<" (c1, c2 : cal-concept)
   VALUE (b : boolean) WHERE b <=>
             the-properties(c1) < the-
   properties(c2)
   goal("<", courseware)
CONCEPT  the-properties(c : cal-concept)
   -- this concept deals with the geometrical
   properties of quadrilaterals
END
```

The concepts of the didactic model allow the pedagogues to define the different learning strategies that they want the students to use when they learn the quadrilaterals of the pedagogic model. Here, the pedagogues describe the concepts of *route* and of *order*. A refinement of the initial aims (thanks to prototyping) can lead them to classify the orders according to the strategy of arrangement which is proposed to the student. We shall distinguish the *augmentative strategy* in which the student must add geometrical properties to discover new quadrilaterals ant the opposite strategy called a *reductive strategy* :

```
DEFINITION Concepts-of-the-didactic-model
INHERIT Concepts-and-goals-of-the-pedagogic-
   model
-- Description of the concept of route : a route is
   composed of cal-concepts which are
   quadrilaterals
CONCEPT  route : type
   WHERE needed-for(cal-concept, route)
CONCEPT  length(r : route)
   VALUE (n : nat)
-- Description of the concept of order
CONCEPT  order : type
CONCEPT  title(o : order)
         VALUE (q : question)
CONCEPT  used-strategy(o : order)
   VALUE (s : strategy)
CONCEPT  is-initial-concept(o : order)
   VALUE (c : cal-concept)
CONCEPT  is-final-concept(o : order)
   VALUE (c : cal-concept)
-- Description of the concept of strategy and of its
   instances
CONCEPT  strategy : type
   WHERE ALL(s : strategy,
             SOME(r : route) :: needed-for(r, s))
   -- the used strategy can be recognized from the
   given route
CONCEPT  augmentative : strategy
CONCEPT  reductive : strategy
END
```

*Adapting* the orders to the routes which are given by a student is a didactic goal that the pedagogues must describe now. Here, they explain what are the criteria that will lead the proposed educational software to choose one order among the others. The "Spec" description tells that "if the route given by the student matches the order, the next order (if there is one) will be more complex. On the other hand, if the route does not match the order, the next order will be simpler. The analysis of a route is achieved through a comparison between the arrangement of the quadrilaterals in the route proposed by the student and the arrangement required by the learning strategy matched to the given order. These orders and their chaining will be described during the educational design.

```
DEFINITION Didactic-goals
INHERIT concepts-and-goals-of-the-pedagogic-
    model
INHERIT concepts-of-the-didactic-model
-- The goal is to know if another order must be
   proposed to the student, and what order?
CONCEPT  other-route(r : route, o : order) VALUE
         (b : boolean)
         WHERE   b <=>
   (respect(r, used-strategy(o)) and (SOME(o' :
   order::
                                o' = follows(o)))
   or
   (not (respect(r, used-strategy(o))) and (SOME(o' :
   order :: o' = precedes(o)))
   goal(other-route, courseware)
CONCEPT  respect(r : route, s : strategy)
   VALUE   (b : boolean)
   WHERE   ALL(c1, c2 : cal-concept ::
                  precedes(c1, c2, r) =>
                                precedes(c1, c2, s)

CONCEPT  precedes(c1 c2 : cal-concept, r : route)
   VALUE  (b : boolean)
   -- true if for the given route, c1 appears before c2
CONCEPT  precedes(c1 c2 : cal-concept, s :
   strategy) VALUE  (b: boolean)
   -- true if for the strategy s, c1 must appear before
   c2
   WHERE b <=>(s = augmentative and
               the-properties(c1) < the-properties(c2))
               or (s = reductive and
               the-properties(c1) > the-properties(c2))
-- concepts which are not completely described
   during the specification stage but the informations
   which are given will do the software engineers
CONCEPT  precedes(o : order)
         VALUE(o' : order)
CONCEPT  follows(o : order)
         VALUE(o' : order)
END
```

### *2.4.3. THE DESIGN STAGE FROM THE VIEWPOINT OF PEDAGOGUES*

During this stage, the pedagogues are going to describe how the functions "precedes" and "follows" compute the next order that will be proposed to a student. They use the "Spec" language to describe the different classes of orders which are used by the educational software, and the mechanisms allowing their chaining.

This stage has enabled us to put to the fore :

- complex orders (they require that the student combines several geometrical properties), simple orders (they require that the student discovers only one geometrical property), and functions whose aim is to decompose complex orders into simpler ones,
- some mechanisms allowing the automatic generation of orders : when an order defines neither the quadrilateral the student has to discover, nor the geometrical properties he must combine, these mechanisms generate orders that progressively inform the student.

By doing this, we indirectly put to the fore some functions that the software engineers will have to design and implement (the function of decomposition, the function of generation of orders) and data (the initial order, the order which is the objective of the CAL session, the intermediate orders, ...) that the pedagogues will implement during the implementation stage.

### 3. THE AUTOMATION OF "MAGE"

The "MAGE" methodological framework is currently implemented with the support of a set of facilities providing an infrastructure for constructing Integrated Project Support Environments : PCTE (Portable Common Tool Environment) [13]. This standardized environment is particularly convenient to define the data repository which will be shared by software engineers and pedagogues. We use HP9000 workstations and the Emeraude product (which is an implementation of the PCTE interfaces) to define the part of the repository which will allow the pedagogues and the software engineers to store "Spec" descriptions. We also try to solve the problems of mapping the underlying "Spec" descriptions and the different concrete viewpoints that pedagogues will use to model these descriptions in a natural way. The works of M. RUEHER [14] for the definition of a "multi-shape" model specification suggest a promising solution to this problem.

## References


[1] J. HEWETT, T. DURHAM, Computer-Aided Software Engineering : commercial strategies, Ovum Ltd, 1987

[2] M.D. MERRILL, Prescriptions for an authoring system, Journal of computer-based instruction, vol. 14, n° 1, oct. 1986

[3] A. BORK, Suggestions for developing technology based learning material, Interactive learning international, Wiley, janv. 89

[4] DELTA, R&D in Information and Communication based learning technology, DELTA'90, juillet 1990

[5] J. SCHOENMAKER, E. NIENHUIS, J. SCHOLTEN, J. TITULAER, A Methodology for Educational Software Engineering, Computers in Education, IFIP fifth World Conference on Computers in Education (WCCE'90), juillet 1990

[6] M.N. BESSAGNET, T. NODENOT, G. GOUARDERES, J.J. RIGAL, A new approach : Courseware Engineering, Computers in Education, IFIP fifth World Conference on Computers in Education (WCCE'90), juillet 1990

[7] G. GOUARDERES, Le projet Atelier de Génie Didacticiel Intégré (AGDI), T.S.I. - Technique et Science Informatiques, Vol. 9, n°5, octobre 1990

[8] M.N. BESSAGNET, Spécification fonctionnelle d'un Atelier de Génie Didacticiel Intégré, Doctorat de l'Université Paul Sabatier, Toulouse, octobre 1991

[9] T. NODENOT, Dialogue dans un atelier de génie éducatif, 4èmes journées internationales du génie logiciel et ses applications,Toulouse, décembre 1991

[10] B.W. BOEHM, A spiral model of software development and enhancement, ACM SIGSOFT Software Engineering Notes, vol. 11, n° 4 p. 14-24, août 1986

[11] T. NODENOT, A methodology for cooperative developments of educational software, 4th International Conference on Computers And Learning (ICCAL'92), Wolfville, Nova Scotia, Canada, juin 1992

[12] V. BERZINS, LUQI, Software engineering with abstractions, Addison-Wesley publishing compagny, 1990

[13] I. CAMPBELL, Portable Common Tool Environment, Computer standards and interfaces, n°8, p. 67-74, North Holland, 1988

[14] M. RUEHER, Un modèle multiforme pour la spécification, numéro spécial Bigre+Globule sur les langages de spécification, n°55, juillet 1987

Education and Society / R. Aiken (Editor)
Information Processing 92, Volume II
Elsevier Science Publishers B.V. (North-Holland)



# A Fuzzy Logic-Based Intelligent Tutoring System (ITS)

Dr. Wes Regian[a] and Dr. Gerald Pitts[b]

[a]Air Force Armstrong Laboratory, Brooks Air Force Base, San Antonio, Texas

[b]Computer Science Department, Trinity University, 715 Stadium Drive, Campus Box 60, San Antonio, TX 78284

**Abstract**

Most current Intelligent Tutoring Systems (ITS) use rule-based inference engines in order to select a prototype remediation for students[1] . Even Though this method has shown a great accomplishment in the area of artificial intelligence, many system experts are not satisfied with the rigidity of rule-based methods. Recently, research on possibilities for assessment using computer-based apprenticeship environments has been conducted by a team at the Learning and Development Research Center, University of Pittsburgh, suggests the possibility of using fuzzy variables instead of ordinary rule-based leveling methods. This paper describes an innovative technique for using a "fuzzy relations" approach to knowledge inference. This hybrid approach to the intelligent module of the ITS should prove to be a tremendous asset for timely individualized learning. Fuzzy relations not only provide speed in decision support over rule based inference engines, but a more experienced control of learning sequence, material and remediation. Key words: I.2.1 Expert System, I.2.6 Tutor, and I.2.4 Knowledge Base.

## 1. ITS ANATOMY

In an ITS, individualized instruction is an emergent property of several interacting components. ITSs often consist of four, sometimes five, distinct components. These are the expert module, the instructional module, the student model, the interface, and often a device simulation or other instructional environment (See Figure 1.1).

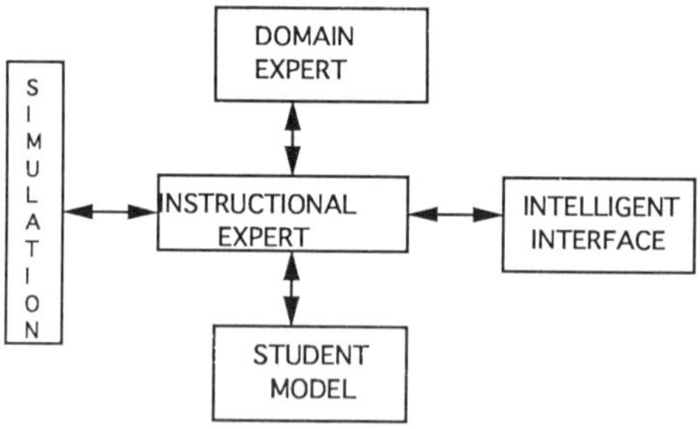


Figure 1.1

The expert module is a programmed representation of expert knowledge in the target domain (that which is being taught). It is almost identical to what is commonly known as an expert system, except in this context it is often very articulate (able to generate some form of rationale for it's actions) and capable of generating alternative solution paths (rather than a single 'best' path). The expert module brings domain knowledge to the ITS. In some useful sense, the system 'knows' how to perform the task which it is seeking to teach, and can demonstrate that knowledge.

The instructional module is a programmed representation of expert knowledge on pedagogy in the target domain. It is generally not articulate but is usually capable of generating alternative instructional approaches based on the current knowledge level of the current student. While the expert module typically derives from knowledge engineering with an expert practitioner in the target domain; the instructional module may derive from knowledge engineering with an expert instructor in the target domain (which may or may not be the same person as the expert practitioner), with a general training specialist, or both.

The student model constitutes a repository for information about each student that uses the system. It differs from the expert and instructional modules in that it is a mere shell at the beginning of an initial tutoring session, whereas the latter two are generally complete when the development of the ITS is complete. At the beginning of an initial tutoring session the student model is merely a place to store specific kinds of information about students in particular formats that will be useful for the instructional module to access. The student model is dynamically updated during tutoring sessions to maintain current information about the student such as what the student knows, what the student does not now, and misconceptions the student may have. The student model brings situational awareness to the ITS. Thus, the system 'knows' who it is teaching to, and can make informed decisions about what to teach next, and how to teach it.

The interface provides the methods by which the student interacts with the ITS. The interface may include such output methods as computer generated graphics and text, recorded video images, or speech synthesizers; and such input devices as a mouse, keyboard, touchscreen, joystick, or voice recognition system.

## 2. MODEL METHODOLOGY

Figure 2 represents a logic flow diagram of the FBITS (Fuzzy Based Intelligent Tutoring System). Lesson frames are presented to the student in both text and graphic display when appropriate, under the umbrella of "accepted learning strategies" classified by Richard S. Michalski[2].

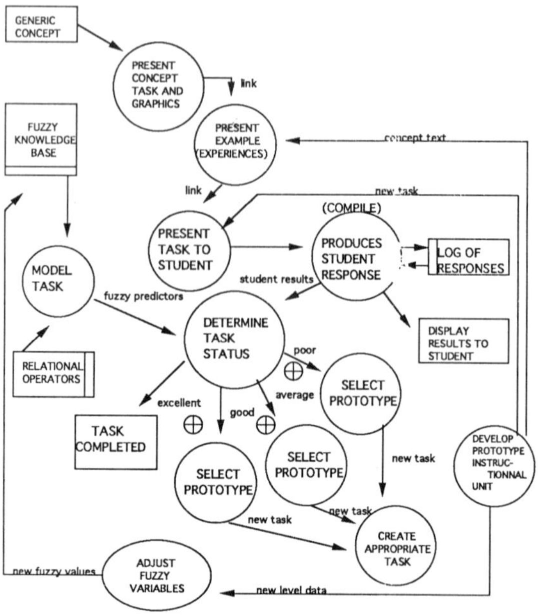


Figure 2.1

A task completion is then asked of the student for the purpose of identifying the learning status of this student as well as assessing remedial needs.

Fuzzy relation sets are formed by composition of fuzzy knowledge (provided by experts) and task result variables into fuzzy predictors. These fuzzy predictor variables are composed of length of task, task completion percentage, expected completion percentage, dynamic error detection, and completion confidence interval. The variables provide immediate inference rule selection. From the inference engine comes performance ratings and task determination. Possible ratings are :

A. Excellent - task is complete continue to next concept.
B. Good - minimum remediation prototype to be general.
C. Average - more substantial remediation prototype to be selected.
D. Poor - very substantial remediation prototypes to be selected.

Prototype remediation is further individualized by fuzzy logic mapping of individual performance data to date upon learning theory clarity to provide evidence combinations. This learning evidence indicator adjusts the prototype task (generated previously) level to fuzzy predictor tasks remediation. This remediation prototype is now an intelligently generated learning task customized to the student's needs and the learned experience of the fuzzy based intelligent agent.

Three major fuzzy value tables are utilized

1. Cognitive Ability Table (Figure 2.2).
2. Predictor Table(Figure 2.3).
3. Adjuster Table(Figure 2.4).

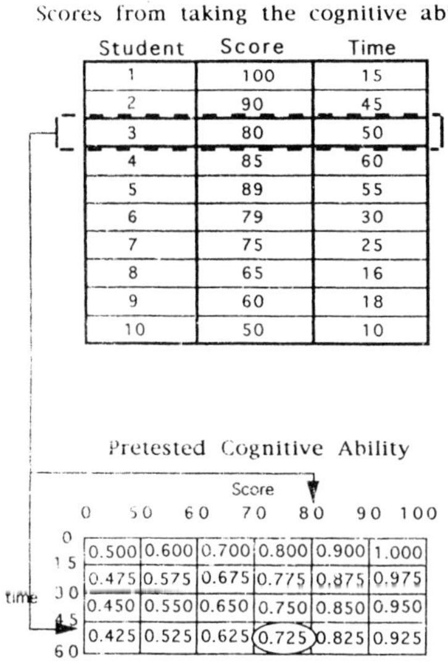


Figure 2.2 The assignment of fuzzy values according to time completion,

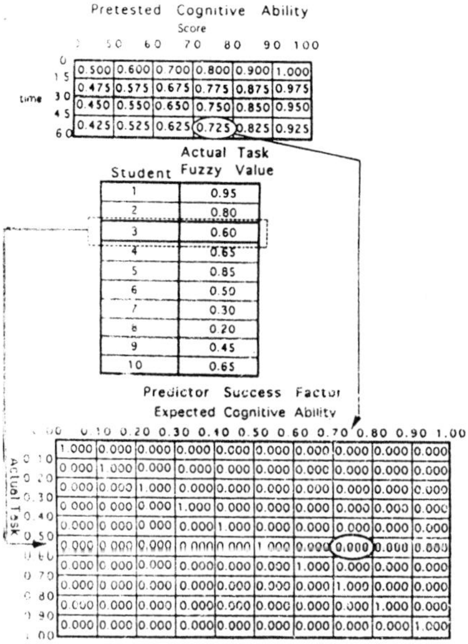


Figure 2.3: Using the actual task fuzzy scores value and the expected to determine how much confidence we have in the actual fuzzy value.

FUZZY PREDICTOR ADJUSTMENT
EXPECTED TASK COMPLETION

| CONFIDENCE | 0.10 | 0.20 | 0.30 | 0.40 | 0.50 | 0.60 | 0.70 | 0.80 | 0.90 | 1.00 |
|---|---|---|---|---|---|---|---|---|---|---|
| 0.10 | 0.010 | 0.020 | 0.030 | 0.040 | 0.050 | 0.050 | 0.040 | 0.030 | 0.020 | 0.010 |
| 0.20 | 0.009 | 0.010 | 0.020 | 0.030 | 0.040 | 0.040 | 0.030 | 0.020 | 0.010 | 0.009 |
| 0.30 | 0.008 | 0.009 | 0.010 | 0.020 | 0.030 | 0.030 | 0.020 | 0.010 | 0.009 | 0.008 |
| 0.40 | 0.007 | 0.008 | 0.009 | 0.010 | 0.020 | 0.020 | 0.010 | 0.009 | 0.008 | 0.007 |
| 0.50 | 0.006 | 0.007 | 0.008 | 0.009 | 0.010 | 0.010 | 0.009 | 0.008 | 0.007 | 0.006 |
| 0.60 | 0.005 | 0.006 | 0.007 | 0.008 | 0.009 | 0.009 | 0.008 | 0.007 | 0.006 | 0.005 |
| 0.70 | 0.004 | 0.005 | 0.006 | 0.007 | 0.008 | 0.008 | 0.007 | 0.006 | 0.005 | 0.004 |
| 0.80 | 0.003 | 0.004 | 0.005 | 0.006 | 0.007 | 0.007 | 0.006 | 0.005 | 0.004 | 0.003 |
| 0.90 | 0.002 | 0.003 | 0.004 | 0.005 | 0.006 | 0.006 | 0.005 | 0.004 | 0.003 | 0.002 |
| 1.00 | 0.001 | 0.002 | 0.003 | 0.004 | 0.005 | 0.005 | 0.004 | 0.003 | 0.002 | 0.001 |

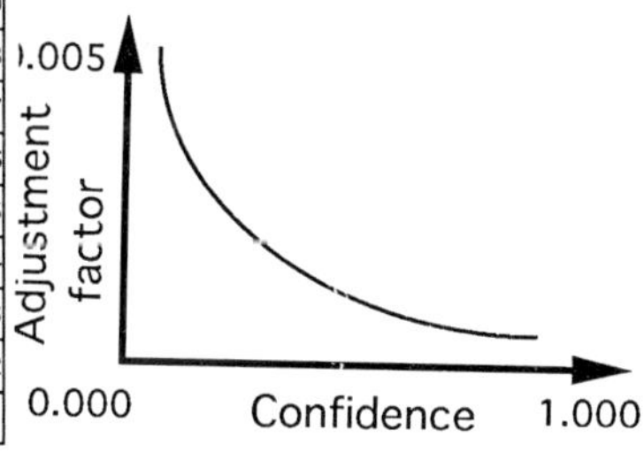


Figure 2.4: A sample of an adjuster table with the growth rate of adjustment factor with respect to confidence level.

The cognitive ability table contains the fuzzy values associated with a cognitive skill. All trainees must be pretested to measure their "raw competence level".

The predictor table consists of fuzzy confidence values that show how well the students will do on the actual task, based on their cognitive ability. The confidence values will adjust themselves if our expectation does not match task accomplishment.

The adjuster table consists of adjustment factors that increase or decrease the confidence levels in the predictor table. The values in the table are generated by an exponential distribution. The farther the prediction from the actual result, the greater the impact of the adjustment.

The test coordinator subjectively assign fuzzy values to different scores to indicate the "cognitive ability" of the student, Figure 2.2 In this sense, the greater the score, and the less time taken, the larger the fuzzy value generated Initial values are insensitive at this point, but the table will adjust itself to "learned" fuzzy values as time progresses. For convenience, a linear fuzzy value assignment is suggested. Note however, that the fuzzy values must reflect logical value assignment order. For instance, a fuzzy value of score 90 completed in 30 minutes must not be lower than a fuzzy value of a score 80 completed in 30 minutes.(See Figure 2.3)

After every student is assigned an expected fuzzy value based on his or her accomplishment on the cognitive skill test, then, he or she will attempt to do the actual task selected, by on his or her fuzzy predictor. Initially, the predictor success factor table is initialized to all zero values except at the diagonal points, because the diagonal values are the intersecting points between the expected fuzzy values and the performance fuzzy values (Reference Figure. Initially, the highest confidence that the student is going to score as predicted is assumed. Similarly, there is no confidence that a student who scores a 0.5 for his or her cognitive ability test will receive as high as 0.7 or 0.9 on his or her actual task.

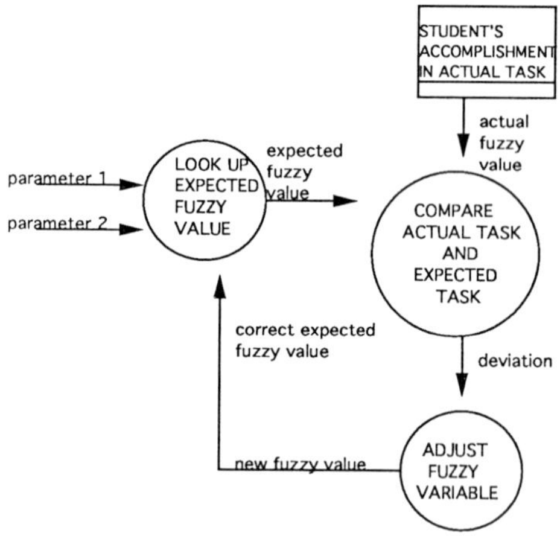


Figure 2.5: Fuzzy variable logic flowchart.

If expected fuzzy values do not match actual values, several values must be adjusted. The first correction will be made to previous confidence values. For instance, consider a student who scores 0.7 on his cognitive ability test and 0.8 on the actual task. It appears the prediction is inaccurate, therefore there is a need to increase the confidence value between 0.7 of the expected value, and 0.8 of the actual value. The model also reduces the "too much confidence" fuzzy value at that intersection. The second correction is made on the cognitive ability table. The original fuzzy values are adjusted to reflect their "soundness" with respect to the predictor table.

The predictor table values (a function of the adjuster values) are mapped by the adjustment value for confidence values. The values in the adjuster table are arranged in such a way that they are larger when the confidence values are low, and smaller when the confidence values are high (Figure 2.5). This allows the lower confidence values to grow at an increasing rate over the interval higher values. As the small fuzzy values become "hot values", the confidence in it will increase drastically as opposed to the diagonal fuzzy value we assigned a one originally. Notice that the fuzzy values in the middle of the Expected Cognitive Ability axis is assigned higher adjustment factors than those of the far left and right. This serves as a leveling factor to see the effect of applying larger values to the adjuster table.

The intersect point of two parameters in the cognitive ability table provides the index where the fuzzy value is stored. As an example, in Figure 2.2, the score of 80 and time 50 minutes are assigned the fuzzy value of 0.725.

Figure 2.3 shows how the expected fuzzy value (0.725) is used with the actual task value in order to obtain their confidence value. The confidence value at this point is 0 because of the initialization process.

Figure 2.6 shows how the confidence values change after consulting the adjuster table for the proper adjustment factor. The zero confidence level is increased by 0.030 because the expected fuzzy value does not match the attained fuzzy value. There is now some confidence that another student may hit this value again. The original expected fuzzy value is reduced because the column must sum one. The confidence value is used in the adjuster table to look up for the proper adjustment factor to use.

After several tutorial sessions, the confidence values in column eight will eventually change to the values shown in Figure 2.7. Notice that if a student scores between 71 and 80 on the cognitive ability test, he or she has the highest probability of scoring a 0.3 on his or her actual task -- the eighth column of the predictor table has the highest fuzzy value (0.310) at row 3. The fuzzy values in the cognitive ability table, in this case, do not really represent one's "smartness", but a fuzzy predictor of task completion.

The original cognitive ability table could be modified to reflect the new fuzzy values. The largest fuzzy value in the predictor table is matched with the actual task fuzzy value. This value then will replace the original value in the cognitive ability table. See Figure 2.7.

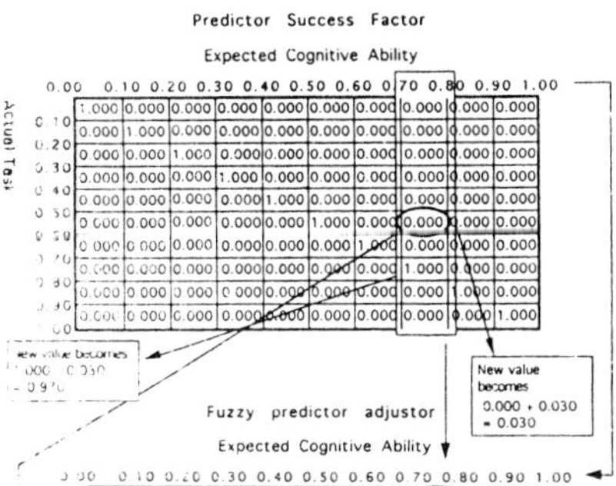


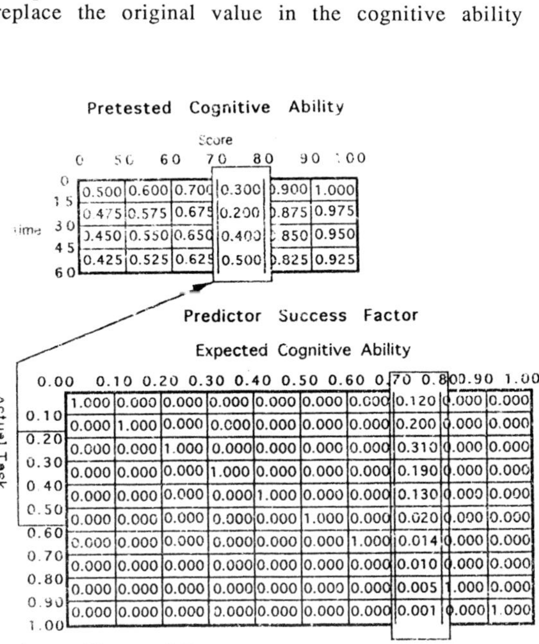


Figure 2.6 The change of confidence values in the predictor table.

Figure 2.7

## 3. IMPORTANCE TO THE AIR FORCE

Education and training are critical issues for the United States Air Force. In Air Training Command, the Air Force operates the largest education and training system in the free world. Air Training Command (ATC) offers 6,000 courses in 350 different career specialties. In addition to recruiting, ATC is responsible for military, flying, and technical education and training. In 1988, ATC trained 385,314 students at a cost of $2.8 billion, using command assets of $7.3 billion.

The Air Force training community has long seen the potential of automated instruction. Nevertheless, the Air Force has failed to capitalize on the technology it helped to create. Fewer then 5% of Air Training Commands courses are delivered via computer. The single more important reason for this failure is that there is currently no principled method of reliability developing instructionally effective automated instruction.

## 4. IMPORTANCE TO BUSINESS, INDUSTRY, AND EDUCATION

This project is as important to the United States as it is to the Air Force. Two crises that are facing the U.S. are the educational crisis (declining achievement, soaring costs) and the work-force crisis (massive changes in job-skill requirements). The education crisis can be directly addressed through basic research on how to teach, and the work-force crisis can be directly addressed through basic research on how to train.

The line between education and training is a thin one, particularly in the case of research. Most, if not all, of the fuzzy logical principles developed in this research project will be useful for automated instructional systems in any educational setting.

## 5. REFERENCES

1 Sleeman, D. H., & Brown, J. S. (Eds.) (1982). Intelligent tutoring systems. London: Academic Press.

2 Michalski, Richard (1986). Machine Learning Volume II, pp.14. Morgan Haufmann Publisher.

Education and Society / R. Aiken (Editor)
Information Processing 92, Volume II
Elsevier Science Publishers B.V. (North-Holland) 


# Takeaway Learning Resources for Information Technology Courses

Sylvia Willie

Faculty of Information Technology, Queensland University of Technology, GPO Box 2434, Brisbane, Queensland, 4001 Australia.
*Telephone*: +617 864 2641; *Fax*: +617 864 1507; *e_mail*: s.willie@qut.edu.au

**Abstract**

Study materials, including computer based materials, which are portable to the student's choice of study venue widen the scheduling options for adult students. Home computers are becoming more widespread and study materials used at home are now practical. Findings from recent research led to development of Takeaway interactive simulations linked with computer managed learning (CML) for use in those learning situations where visual representations can augment the learning process. Face to face lectures continue to be the major teaching strategy with formative CML exercises and simulations providing instructional support, feedback and reporting. The future will see greater use of Takeaway simulations and exploratory learning materials.

Keyword codes: K.3.2; I.6.3;H.1.2
Keywords: Computer and Information Science Education, Simulation and Modelling Applications, User/Machine Systems.

What, if any, are the benefits to part-time students of home computer access? How can information technology be used to increase available study hours and improve feedback for part-time students in Information Technology? Is it possible to use the technology to provide learning materials which are not merely computer driven replicas of the *book paradigm*? These are the questions which research at the Faculty of Information Technology (FIT), Queensland University of Technology (QUT), addressed during 1990. The project was funded by a Department of Employment, Education and Training (DEET) Reserve Fund Grant.

QUT specialises in preparing students for technologically based professions and the Faculty of Information Technology, comprised of schools of Computing Science and Information Systems, covers the broad spectrum of informatics professions. There is a high demand for places, even in recessionary times but a historically high student to staff ratio means teaching staff are stretched thin. This makes it difficult to provide students with useful, timely feedback on their progress.

Undergraduate subjects in the Faculty are conducted on the traditional University lines of face-to-face, on campus lectures, required texts with assigned readings and tutorial sessions.

CML exercises complement the traditional materials and provide continuing feedback to the student.

Part-time students make up about a quarter of the faculty student body. Most are full-time workers, mature adults with very busy lives of whom most have family obligations in addition to their paid employment. Time is their most precious resource and scheduling their time to enable them to meet all the obligations that study, work and a family impose is their most frustrating task. Where the student is employed in a computer field, this can be exacerbated by the scarcity of computer professionals in Australia which makes overtime work the only alternative in many organisations.

What options are available which could improve student's time for study and give more frequent as well as timely feedback within the constraints of available staff? Are there ways to use information technology to do this? Computer managed learning (CML) which focuses on maintenance of administrative records, questionbank control and delivery of randomised sets of questions to students showed potential. Note that these task are similar to those corporate computers have been efficiently handling for nearly 30 years. As Alan Kay reminded us (Kay,1990), classroom teaching is one of the few professions to show so little change in the past century.

The CML system selected in 1987 is mainframe based and does not require expensive graphics terminals. Trials began in 1988 and by 1990, 2500 students were enrolled in CML supported information technology subjects, rising to over 6000 in 1992.

In addition to the Faculty's CML facility, the University has an expanding Computer Based Education (CBE) facility which delivers interactive drill and practice and tutorials on a PC network housed in the campus library. Students can use the facility only when the library is open; however bookings for a terminal can be made in advance.

University students have been selected through the education system to be proficient at assimilating information from printed materials. Using computers as page turners can be more frustrating than enlightening to these students. This is particularly the case with part-time students who consider time their most precious resource. Where the computer based materials can be used from a variety of locations, particularly from home, they become more practical; otherwise, the student may well prefer a portable book. Takeaway computer based courseware allows students their choice of computer and location whether at home, at work or at a laboratory on campus.

## Home Computer Access

Part-time information technology students with a computer at home decrease the number of trips to campus and are able to convert the travel time to study time. Additionally the anxiety of late night travel is largely avoided, a particularly important benefit for women. Students reported that spending more of their study time at home helped keep them in touch with their families. All students reported more time spent in exploratory learning and deeper learning about computer topics when they had a readily available machine. Drop out was nil in the study sample and achievement higher than with previous groups (Willie, Moy & Knight, 1991).

Laptop based delivery mechanisms can allow the student to escape into the stacks of the library, the laboratories, to an observation site or to their own personal study space. The portability advantage of the laptop should be remembered when looking for effective ways to meet instructional objectives. These are already used for note taking at lectures and for laboratory sessions and future use will increase.

## FEEDBACK FROM STUDENTS

In early 1990 discussion groups were conducted, followed by a telephone survey of over 150 students and former students. The aim was to

1. determine the types of problems part-time students have with their studies,
2. find out what motivates them to continue in their studies,
3. ask their opinion about the various forms of computer delivered instructional materials with which they had experience.

All students, aside from a control group of 30, had taken subjects which used the FIT CML system as part of their instruction and over two-thirds had used the CBE, (91% of full-time students). The group surveyed was drawn from subjects with lecture populations of between 150 and 350. The telephone sample was weighted toward part-time students due to our project interest.

*Student Study Problems*: Time management was the major problem students encountered. This was cited by both full-time and part-time students. The younger, full-time students experienced difficulty in scheduling their papers and assignments while older, part-time students found juggling work, study and, often, family commitments their more difficult task.

*Motivations to continue:* We looked at what kept students progressing toward their degrees. Earlier work by Tinto (1975, 1982) and by Kember (1989) showed dropout was influenced by student goals and social commitments as well as academic success. Tinto's model was developed in the US residential university setting while Kember was primarily interested in problems of distance education students. QUT is a non-residential, urban campus, but many of the same conditions apply to students' attrition.

Participants in the discussion groups spontaneously cited many extrinsic and intrinsic goal and social motivators as contributing to their degree completion. A summary list was compiled from the discussions and each of the students in the telephone sample was asked which of the reasons had a bearing on their personal study.

Extrinsic motivators relating to employment showed up in three comments. The relevance of University degree to their *job prospects* and *job performance* had stronger influence on full-time students. Part-time students, already in the workforce, were nearly three times as likely as full-timers to keep studying because they *want to change careers.*

Intrinsic motivators to *finish what they started* and simply *learning for the joy of it* ranked highly with two-thirds or more of the part-time students with a slightly lower rating among the full-time students.

Social commitments such as *family moral* (55%) and *financial* (31%) support were important in keeping the full-time students studying while *company moral* and *financial* support were more important among the part-time students.

*Opinions of computer delivered methods:* Certain problems and benefits were identified in connection with computer based educational materials.As part of the survey, students were presented with opinion statements about the computer delivery method they had experienced.

TABLE 1

REASONS FOR CONTINUING TO STUDY

| | Studying Part time % | Full time % |
|---|---|---|
| Better Job Prospects | 78 | 93 |
| Perform Better in my Job | 58 | 64 |
| Want to Change Careers | 41 | 14 |
| Finish What I Started | 69 | 53 |
| I Enjoy Learning | 65 | 69 |
| Family Moral Support | 44 | 55 |
| Family Financial Support | 12 | 31 |
| Company Moral Support | 26 | 5 |
| Company Financial Support | 24 | 3 |

Eighty seven students had used CML at QUT and 121 had used CBE (some had used both). Interviewers read out the appropriate set(s) of statements which summarised the major opinions arising from the group discussions and asked the students whether they agreed or disagreed with each statement.[1]

Among both sets of users the strongest positive opinion supports the use of takeaway materials for further study. Between the two systems, the CML system was seen to be the least disadvantageous for part-time students (see Willie, 1991a, 1991b for additional information on this research).

The problems with developing interactive computer based learning resources have been well documented in the literature. The major issues are the 150 to 200 development hours per hour of student exercise and associated costs, adequacy of the testing, unwanted side effects of later modifications, the quality of the student model and concomitant design of the branching. Well designed materials are motivating to students, maintain their attention and support rapid learning; unfortunately there are too many cases where the materials do not attain these goals.

Record keeping and feedback for both student and lecturer are also important. Authoring packages do not commonly utilise relational database technology which limits reporting and information gathering capabilities to those provided in the original package or custom written for the client.

Many education needs can be met more economically with less labour intensive methods of delivery than CAL. The Royal Navy (Mizen, Marley and Moore,1990) evaluated various interactive methodologies and found that only Simulations and Drill-and-practice were economically effective when delivered by computer. Face to face and print based materials were more effective than interactive computer based Tutorials.

The Faculty of Information Technology arrived at a similar conclusion. Two areas where computer delivery can effectively meet courseware needs are -

1. Conveying basic terminology and concepts to the student. This includes the delivery of diversified examples of concepts which cannot be economically covered by face-to-face methods.

2. Illustrating advanced or difficult concepts where graphics or animation can contribute to more rapid understanding.

[1] The *strength* of their opinion was elicited by asking 'would that be moderately (dis)agree or strongly (dis)agree?' which also encouraged the students to express an opinion.

TABLE 2

OPINIONS OF COMPUTER MANAGED LEARNING

| | Weighted Agreement Ratio Used CML % |
|---|---|
| Like to take question printout home | 2.5 |
| Helps deal with large classes | 2.0 |
| Encourages keeping up with subject | 1.8 |
| Useful for Revision | 1.7 |
| 24 Hour access is useful | 1.7 |
| Helps learn through quicker feedback | 1.5 |
| Helped me get a better mark | 0.5 |
| Identifies misunderstanding or lack of knowledge | 0.1 |
| Disadvantages part-time students | -1.5 |

Computer managed learning addresses the first area. As used in the FIT it has the advantage of providing a portable learning resource at a development cost of less than 10 hours per hour of student exercise. Learning objectives can be reinforced through use of proven directed questions which lead the student to read assigned texts, develop algorithms to solve a problem, explore the nuances of database queries or any of a variety of tasks which do not require their presence at a computer terminal. CML can also be used to capture the outcome of the students' experiments with particular software in a computer laboratory. Importantly, students receive a printed record of their achievement as soon as they enter the answers, while their attention is still focused on the subject, not weeks later when assignments have been hand marked and hand recorded.

Lecturers can quickly draw on available resources to populate the questionbanks and questions are easily tested. As each question can stand on its own, complex paths through the materials don't exist. The students are issued a printed quiz which is randomly drawn from large sets of questions which cover relevant learning objectives. The lecturer's previous experience is used to distribute the emphasis among the sets of objectives represented in the questionbanks. Feedback reports provide actionable information on the degree to which their strategies are correct.

The illustration of advanced or difficult concepts is targeted with Takeaway interactive courseware, either as simulations or as exploratory learning materials (See Willie, et al. 1991a, 1991b; Knight, et al. 1991 for more complete reporting of this work.) The cost of development is 15 to 20 times higher than CML, so the decision cannot be taken lightly. However, some of these materials can be purchased or traded with other educators. Student access is provided through central distribution points or over data communications systems and site licensing or royalty free distribution is standard for materials used in this manner.

TABLE 3

OPINIONS OF COMPUTER BASED EDUCATION

| | Weighted Agreement Ratio Used CBE % |
|---|---|
| Prefer printed copy of ques/answers | 3.1 |
| Only use it for assigned exercises | 2.3 |
| Encourages keeping up w. subject | 2.0 |
| Useful for revision | 1.8 |
| Usually get a terminal when I want | 1.3 |
| Disadvantages part-time students | -0.4 |

SUMMARY

Learning materials which are portable to the student's choice of study venue are preferred by adult students and an effort must be made to provide computer delivered materials which can be used at any location. In a few years, interactive multi-media will become a broadly deliverable option. In the meantime educators in information technology should make use of the increasing availability of home computers to widen scheduling options, particularly for part-time students.

Additionally, it is important that educators not loose sight of the tasks to which computers have traditionally been very well suited ... routine maintenance of data and performance of predictable duties.

## References

Kay, Alan. 1990. 'Point of View is Worth 80 IQ Points: The User Interface as an Amplifier of Human Endeavour.' Keynote Address, IFIP Fifth World Conference on Computers in Education. Sydney.

Kember,David. 1989. 'An Illustration, with case studies, of a linear-process model of drop out from distance education,' *Distance Education*, Vol. 10, No. 2, pp. 196-211.

Knight,Elizabeth, Cristina Cifuentes and Sylvia Willie. 1991. 'Takeaway Courseware,' Conference Proceedings, Information Technology for Training and Education, 1991.pp. 72-78. Brisbane.

Mizen,Cdr AE, Cdr PE Marley and Lt Cdr G Moore. 1990. 'Computer Based Training in the Royal Navy' *Computers in Education,* McDougall and Dowling, eds. IFIP, Elsevier Science Publishers (NV) (North-Holland), 893-897.

Tinto,Vincent. 1975. 'Dropout from higher education.' *Review of Educational Research*, Vol. 45, No. 1, pp. 89-125.

1982. 'Limits of theory and practice in student attrition,' *Journal of Higher Education*, Vol. 53, No. 6, pp. 687-700.

Willie, Sylvia. 1991a. 'Research Summary, Conclusions and Recommendations.' Report 1, *Research into Improved Student Access and Completion Rates for Part-time Students in Information Technology Subjects*. Faculty of Information Technology, QUT. Brisbane.

Willie, Sylvia. 1991b. 'Perceptions of Computer Delivered Learning Materials, Particularly Among Part-time Students.' Report 3, *Research into Improved Student Access and Completion Rates for Part-time Students in Information Technology Subjects*. Faculty of Information Technology, QUT. Brisbane.

Willie, Sylvia, David Moy and Elizabeth Knight. 1991. 'Home Computer Access for Part-time Students.' Report 2, *Research into Improved Student Access and Completion Rates for Part-time Students in Information Technology Subjects*. Faculty of Information Technology, QUT. Brisbane.

Willie, Sylvia, Cristina Cifuentes and Elizabeth Knight. 1991a. 'Takeaway Courseware: What are the benefits?'. *Interactive Learning International*, Vol. 7, pp. 227-241.

Willie, Sylvia, Cristina Cifuentes and Elizabeth Knight. 1991b. 'Takeaway Courseware: An Exploration of Potential.' Report 4, *Research into Improved Student Access and Completion Rates for Part-time Students in Information Technology Subjects*. Faculty of Information Technology, QUT. Brisbane.

Education and Society / R. Aiken (Editor)
Information Processing 92, Volume II
Elsevier Science Publishers B.V. (North-Holland)


# Computer-related attitudes and self-image as a function of students' age

B. Offir and Y.J. Katz

School of Education, Bar-Ilan University, Ramat-Gan 52900, Israel

**Abstract**

Effective computer use in the classroom involves decision-making regarding the instructional process, based on an understanding of the individual's ability as well as psychological needs. In the present research a single psychological trait - self-image - was examined, regarding its relationship to computer-related attitudes at different age levels. Results of the study indicated the existence of a positive and significant relationship between self-image and computer-related attitudes. With the advance in age, increasingly more positive correlations between students' self-image and computer-related attitudes were discerned. An attempt was made to explain the results in light of the differential psychological need for independence and the corresponding levels of learning self-image which characterize students belonging to different age groups.

## 1. INTRODUCTION

Despite rapid developments in educational technology, school teaching methods remain remarkably traditional (1). There is an increasing awareness that Computer Assisted Instruction (CAI) has many advantages over traditional teaching methods regarding the fulfillment of educational goals (2-3), and therefore provides an alternative instructional method for the classroom.

However, the expectation that the computer can be utilized as an effective alternative teaching aid has thus far not materialized (4-7). There have been some suggestions as to how computers can be used with greater efficiency in the instructional process. For example, Juliff (8) indicated that improvement in color and graphics technology can increase CAI efficiency in the classroom, and Mevarech & Ben-Artzi (9) found that CAI contributes to superior achievement in mathematics, as a result of the fixed feedback given to students by the computer.

There are also psychological issues relevant to efficient CAI use. Griswold (10) and Kulik, Bangert-Drowns & Williams (11) indicated a relationship between psychological issues and effective CAI in the classroom. Katz & Offir (12) confirmed the existence of a positive relationship between the age of the students engaged in CAI and their motivational level regarding CAI. Katz & Offir (13) showed that students with a positive social image and a feeling of dissatisfaction with traditional teaching methods were positive regarding the use of computers within the framework of CAI.

The present study addressed one of the major psychological issues conceivably underlying successful CAI utilization. The central aim was to examine the relationship between self-image and computer-related attitudes of learners at differential age levels. Understanding possible connections between these two factors may be helpful in determining more effective use of CAI.

## 2. METHOD

### 2.1 Sample

The research sample consisted of 251 students at different age levels, broken down as follows: 77 nine-year-olds studying in grade 4 in elementary school; 89 thirteen-year-olds in grade 7 in junior high school; 45 eighteen-year-olds studying in grade 12 in high school; and 40 students aged 27 to 32 studying on the tertiary level.

### 2.2 Instruments

Two research instruments were used in the study. The first was a 15-item questionnaire designed to examine students' computer-related attitudes (12). The items form a general factor, computer-related attitudes, which has a latent root of unity and explains at least 10% of the variance. The reliability coefficient of the questionnaire, established by the Cronbach Alpha method, was .64. The second instrument used was the Self-Image Questionnaire designed by Ben-Ari (14). This instrument consists of 25 items and examines two self-image variables, social self-image and learning self-image. For the purpose of the present study, the 12 items examining learning self-image were used. This factor has an eigenvalue greater than 1.0 and explains more than 10% of the variance. The Alpha reliability coefficient of the learning self-image factor was .89.

### 2.3 Procedure

The two instruments were administered to the research sample during regular classes in their respective learning environments. The subjects were told that they were participating in a research study to determine how to best use computers in the learning situation.

## 3. RESULTS

A Pearson correlation analysis was computed on the data collected in the study. A significant correlational relationship was found to exist between students' computer-related attitudes and their learning self-image at all age levels.

### 3.1 Tables

Table 1
Means, standard deviations, and Pearson correlations for computer-related attitudes and learning self-image (N=251)

| Age group (years) | CRA** Mean | CRA S.D. | LSI*** Mean | LSI S.D. | Pearson corr. CRA with LSI |
|---|---|---|---|---|---|
| 9 | 50.5 | 10.8 | 38.7 | 7.3 | .43* |
| 13 | 54.9 | 10.4 | 43.6 | 9.8 | .55* |
| 18 | 60.4 | 9.1 | 52.8 | 9.2 | .89* |
| 27-32 | 61.2 | 8.9 | 53.6 | 8.4 | .90* |

* P<0.05
** computer-related attitudes
*** learning self-image

The statistically significant correlations between the two research variables increased hierarchically with an increase in students' age, the lowest correlation characterizing the nine-year-old subjects and the highest correlation typifying the 27-32 year-olds.

## 4. DISCUSSION

The results of the present study clearly indicate that age is a factor that influences the relationship between students' computer-related attitudes and learning self-image. The differential influence of age may be explained in light of previous learning experience gained by the subjects in the different age groups. Children aged nine have only three years of school experience, and because of their young age it appears that they feel dependent on the inter-personal relationship with their teachers (12) and prefer this relationship in the learning situation to more impersonal CAI learning. Thus, their computer-related attitudes are somewhat ambiguous, as is their learning self-image. The correlation between computer-oriented attitudes and learning self-image is positive and significant, but the squared correlation does not explain more than 18.49% of the variance.

The 13-year-old subjects, being at the critical developmental stage of adolescence, have a psychological need to "prove" their independence. Learning with a computer rather than being dependent on the interpersonal teacher-student relationship gives this age group the opportunity to emphasize their newly found need for independence (12); this, in turn, increases the level of computer-related attitudes as well as learning self-image. Thus, the correlation between the two research variables is positive and significant, with an increased squared correlation that explains 30.25% of the variance.

The remaining groups, namely the 18-year-olds and those between the ages of 27-32, unlike the other two groups of students, consist of adults who are well aware of their independence and have a well-established learning self-image. The fact that they utilize computers within the learning process clearly indicates their positive computer-related attitudes as well as their positive learning self-image, as topics of study at the adult age are usually a matter of preference. The fact that these subjects chose to study material taught by CAI is an additional indication of positive orientations towards this learning method. The significant and highly positive correlations between computer-related attitudes and learning self-image apparently confirm this notion as do the high percentages of variance - 79.21% and 81.00% - explained respectively by the squared correlations of the 18-year-olds and the 27-32 year-olds.

It may be concluded from the results of this study, which confirm previous research findings as well (11-13), that differential attitudinal and psychological sets characterize students at different age levels. More specifically, these sets differentially typify computer users at the elementary, secondary and tertiary educational levels. Thus, it is postulated that CAI methodology should be adapted to the different attitudinal and psychological needs of students in each age group. Instructional software compilers should take the relevant attitudinal and psychological variables into consideration when preparing educational software for different age groups, in order to contribute to CAI effectiveness.

## 5. REFERENCES


1 B. Offir & Y.J. Katz, Computer oriented attitudes as a function of risk-taking among Israeli elementary school teachers, Journal of Computer Assisted Learning, 6 (1990) 168-173.

2 E. Hoyle, Computers and education: a solution in search of a problem, In J. Megarry, D.R.F. Walker, S. Nisbet and E. Hoyle (eds.), Computers and Education, Kogan Page, London, 1983.

3 J. Megarry, Thinking, learning and educating: The role of the computer, In J. Megarry, D.R.F. Walker, S. Nisbet and E, Hoyle (eds.), Computers and Education, Kogan Page, London, 1983.

4 H.J. Becker, Using computers for instruction: The results and implications may surprise you, Educational Computing, February (1987) 149-162.

5 V.C. Cohen, A reexamination of feedback in computer-based instruction: Implications for instructional design, Educational Technology, January (1985) 33-37.

6 P. Moore, Children, teachers and computers: A joint venture in learning, Journal of Curriculum Studies 19(2) (1987) 187-190.

7 B. Offir, Interactive microfiche and computer-assisted learning, Information and Image Management, 3(1987) 47-48.

8 P. Juliff, Fundamental issues in end-user education, Education and Computing 6(1-2) (1990) 17-22.

9 Z.R. Mevarech and Ben-Artzi, Effects of CAI with fixed and adaptive feedback on children's mathematics anxiety and achievement, Journal of Experimental Education, 56(1) (1987) 42-46.

10 P.A. Griswold, Elementary school students' attitudes during two years of computer-assisted instruction, American Educational Research Journal, 21 (1984) 737-754.

11 J.A. Kulik, R.L. Bangert-Drowns and G.W. Williams, Effects of computer-based teaching on secondary school students, Journal of Educational Psychology, 75 (1983) 19-26.

12 Y.J. Katz and B. Offir, Computer-oriented attitudes as a function of age in an elementary school population, In F. Lovis and E.D. Tagg (eds.), Computers in Education, Elsevier Science Publishers, 1988.

13 Y.J. Katz and B. Offir, Computer-assisted instruction and students' social orientation, Proceedings of 5th Jerusalem Conference on Information Technology, IEEE Computer Society Press, Los Alamitos, 1990.

14 R. Ben-Ari, Satisfaction of interpersonal needs as a way of improving inter-ethnic relations in an ethnically integrated school, Unpublished doctoral dissertation, Bar-Ilan University (Hebrew), 1982.

Education and Society / R. Aiken (Editor)
Information Processing 92, Volume II
Elsevier Science Publishers B.V. (North-Holland)




# In support of children: Research on learning with computers

Laura R. Winer[a] and Marion A. Barfurth[b]

[a] Independent researcher, 4546 Kensington Ave., Montréal, Québec H4B 2W5 Canada

[b]Department of Education, Université du Québec à Hull, C.P. 1250, Succ. B, Hull, Québec J8X 3X7 Canada

**Abstract**

The Vitrine 2001 was a computer-based learning environment in which children worked on different machines doing different activities to achieve their personal learning goals. The software selection criteria are presented. Observations on what the children did are presented by kind of activity, as well as general observations on breadth and depth of interactions and unexpected uses. An important distinction emerged between software (in the technical sense) and activity (in the functional sense). The adequacy of software is a necessary but not sufficient condition for success. How, when, with whom and in what context software is used must be considered as important factors in the successful use of computers in education.

Keyword Codes: K.3.0; K.3.1
Keywords: Computers and Education, General; Computer Uses in Education

## 1. INTRODUCTION

The Vitrine 2001, a project of a Quebec government funded research and development centre, was created to study children's actions and learning in a multi-machine, multi-activity, free-choice computer-based learning environment. "Vitrine" means showcase, and the Vitrine was a showcase to try out new ideas in educational computing. "2001" was a product of circumstance; the street address of the building was 2001 St. Laurent Blvd and the futurist implications were welcome.

The research goal was to observe children working in a computer-based learning environment and learn about their likes and dislikes, their behaviour, their learning strategies, what and how they learned, sex differences, etc.. The pedagogical philosophy followed the constructivist approach, drawing on both Piagetian and Brunerian learning theories (Brown, 1985; Bruner, 1966; Harel, 1990; Papert, 1980; Piaget & Inhelder, 1969). The computers, and the software, were available for the children to accomplish their personal goals, and it was up to each child to determine what to do and how to do it.

Another important concept fundamental to this project is that of functional learning environments. The salient point of functional learning environments is that learning activities are defined as having a function or purpose *from the point of view of the child.* This concept is based on two assumptions: children are intrinsically motivated to work on tasks that are meaningful to them; and the most effective educational environment is one that provides meaningful tasks; i.e. tasks that embody some function or purpose that children understand (Newman, 1987).

An important characteristic of the Vitrine 2001 project was that intact regular class groups participated. The class is the functional unit in schools; if there is any hope of computers making real headway into the public school system, it must be both feasible and worthwhile for class-sized groups to work with them. The full-time project personnel consisted of two researchers, one animator, and one teacher seconded from a local school board.

Three class groups (from French schools) participated in the Vitrine research project during the two years it was in operation: a grade 2 class (10 girls, 9 boys, 7-8 years old), a combined grades 4/5 class (10 girls, 13 boys, 9-11 years old) and a combined grades 2/3 class (12 girls, 13 boys, 7-9 years old). The younger classes made 23 half-day visits per year to the Vitrine, the older group 16 full-day visits per year. The children were free to choose their activities and were made explicitly aware of their participation in a research project. Data were collected from numerous sources, including observation, interview and self-report forms (see Barfurth & Winer, 1991). Data were stored and analysed using a data base which permitted the systematic consultation and extraction of relevant data (Winer & Carrière, 1990, 1991).

## 2. The electronic environment: Software selection criteria

From early observations of the children working in the Vitrine, it became clear that distinguishing between *software* and the *activity* carried out with the software was very important. According to Webster's dictionary, software is "the entire set of programs, procedures, and related documentation associated with a system and especially a computer system". An activity is an "educational procedure designed to stimulate learning by firsthand experience". While educators commonly talk about using a given software program with students, this does not necessarily indicate the type of experience the students had. The specific computer program used is not the sole determining feature of the kind or quality of interaction. This diversity is almost self-evident in the case of "open" software, but it is extremely important to be sensitive to the fact that this phenomenon exists with applications and "closed" software.

The software available for the children to select from was varied on many dimensions, and the software bank was not restricted to either "educational" or "children's" software. The general criteria for software selection included the following.

•*User control.* The user has a choice of how to proceed in terms of content or difficulty.

•*Openness.* Software was considered *open* if it allowed the user to modify or add to the content or structure of the information being processed by the computer.

•The software had to be *nonviolent, nonsexist,* and *nonracist.*

•Every effort was made to have the software in French, as the *language* of the interface clearly contributed to facility of usage by the children.

•The *popularity* of different kinds of applications; for example, given the popularity of crossword puzzles, different programs for creating and solving crossword puzzles were sought.

•The *accessibility* of the software; for example, there are a number of digitilization programs available for the Macintosh. The choice was between more professional output and an easier interface—simplicity won.

•Software was sometimes chosen in order to rationalize the *resources*; for example, a high demand for text-processing meant that a text-processor was found that would run on an underutilized machine.

## 3.0 A typical day in the Vitrine

As mentioned, each class and teacher came to the Vitrine once a week for either a half or full day. The following description gives an idea of a "typical" day.

The children arrive in the morning by school bus. Each child takes his or her binder from the shelf. (Each child was given a binder at the beginning of the year to store notes, drawings, productions, disks, etc.) The two younger groups choose their activities, while the older children go to work on their projects. Some children run to their computer and start working right away; others wander around leisurely, look at what the others are doing, ask questions, give comments, etc. The children work alone, in pairs, or in small groups, as they wish. If something exciting seems to be happening somewhere, a small crowd may congregate to watch a child playing a game, to look at a drawing or a LEGO object. Breaks of about 10 minutes are imposed after each period of roughly one hour; these are used for relaxation breathing, snacking and "stretching one's legs". The younger groups fill in two "co-researcher reports" a visit, one before the break and another before leaving. The older group, which spends a full day in the Vitrine, completes three reports.

While the children are working, the class teacher is free to do whatever he or she wishes Depending on the day, the teacher may be correcting homework, reviewing class work with a child, observing the children working in the Vitrine, working with children on the computer, or even working on his or her own at a computer. The animator and Vitrine teacher are responding to questions, trying out new activities, or encouraging children in their work. The two researchers are observing the children (taking notes and photos, filling in maps) or interviewing the children or the teacher. There are occasionally other adults in the Vitrine; for example, a software evaluation project which lasted for several weeks had one person stationed at a computer working with children on a specific package.

## 4. Observations by "cluster"

In order to create a useful framework in which to look at what the children did in the Vitrine, the software has been grouped together in "clusters" or coherent units. There are clearly many different groupings possible; this one is presented for use insofar as it is functional and permits the discussion to focus on the children's activities rather than specific characteristics of different software packages. The three groups of children will be treated as one when their behaviours were similar; any notable differences are indicated

The groupings used were the following: games (including educational, simulation, arcade and adventure), graphic arts (including drawing, image digitilization, layout and animation), text processing, programming, music, and communication.

### 4.1 Games

Not surprisingly, games were a very popular activity for all groups in the Vitrine. There was a large variety of games, including educational games (for specific content or skills), baseball and chess games, simulation/games, and several arcade-type games. Many of these called upon logical thinking and planning skills, especially those which allowed the children to create their own games or extend existing ones. In addition to entertainment, the games served as learning environments, either for the context (for example, several children learned how to play baseball or chess from the games), or for more general logical and planning skills. The educational games often included content learning, most often related to language or mathematics, but sometimes related to very specific content, such as animals that live in the province of Ontario.

The children were asked to articulate, on their self-report forms and in the interviews, what they learned while playing the different games. The children indicated an awareness of the different kinds of learning occurring. The status of games was the same as the other software—they were not relegated to a secondary position—and the children's reflections on their interactions were expected to be as thoughtful as for any other type of software. There were instances, however, when the games were explicitly used for relaxation, providing a break from more "strenuous" activities. This was especially true for the older group, whose functioning was project oriented. They paced themselves, with focused work sessions relieved by relaxation interludes.

## 4.2 Graphic Arts

There was a large variety of graphic arts programs available in the Vitrine. They included programs for drawing, animation, image digitilization, and graphic layout.

*Drawing:* The most common and the most popular type of graphics arts program was drawing, and the children exploited the different programs on the different machines to advantage. The children produced different outputs (for example, illustrations, colouring books, etc.) in exploratory or self-expression contexts.

The drawings were created in different contexts for different purposes. Sylvia, a grade 3 girl, worked for several weeks on making a colouring book. A trio of boys in grades 4/5 worked on posters for nutrition week at school. In the second year of the project, there was a colour jet printer which produced very high quality printouts; this obviously was a motivator for exploring the use of colours and textures.

The children demonstrated a practical understanding of fairly sophisticated concepts, such as text and graphics mode. For example, a grade 3 girl, Rosalind, wanted to do a clock. After drawing the outline of the face, she figured out that she could go into TEXT mode and then type the numbers rather than having to draw them.

Using the drawing programs also sometimes led the children to fairly complicated interactions with the computer. For example, Rosalind also became quite expert in file management using an MS-DOS based system.

*Animation:* Graphic animation programs added another dimension to graphic arts for the children. The ability to create dynamic "drawings" allowed the children to integrate movement into their previously static graphics. Unlike activities which had a non-computer parallel (for example, drawing, playing chess or other games), animation was something which the children could create only through the computer, as tools like flip-books were not part of their environment. There were two different programs available with which the children could create animated sequences: while they were both object oriented, one offered a greater choice of tools and resources, including the possibility of integrating sound, and permitted the creation of more sophisticated sequences. Concepts which were encountered in this activity included cloning and object programming. Both programs were used by different children to create interesting and imaginative sequences. One example of the use of animation is described later in the section on "Unexpected uses".

*Digitilization:* The children had access to image scanning as well as video digitilization. These tools were adopted for different uses as the children wished. The most common use of the camera was to take photographs of classmates or objects (for example, an inflatable turtle wearing sunglasses). Two of the children participated in a project to create "instruction" cards, similar to the LEGO/Logo activity cards, for LEGO objects which they had created. The scanner was used most often by the older children who brought in handmade drawings which they wanted to use in their newspaper or for posters.

*Graphic layout:* Graphic layout refers to the design of a printed page, often integrating text and graphics. The most commonly used graphic layout program offered a high degree of structure. The children could select existing borders and images to place on a greeting card and they could insert their own text. While very popular, the limited number of graphics available meant that some children were frustrated by not being able to have the image that they wanted.

In the first year, a group of older children tried to use another program to produce posters. While they did produce a few, they found the software complicated to use and no other children were interested. Layout was then most often done by physically cutting and pasting drawings and text onto pages; the children did however pay attention to the style, font and size of the characters used.

### 4.3 Text processing

Writing was a popular activity in the Vitrine, most notably by girls, but many boys also became interested in some form of text production. The content of the children's productions varied greatly and included creative writing, letters to friends or family, poems, a class newspaper (with factual stories and "features" such as riddles). The children did not use "children's" text processing programs more than "adult" programs; the choice criteria were related more to the quality of the output than features of the programs themselves. In fact, many of the children preferred "grown up" programs with their smaller letters than large type child programs precisely because they looked more "grown up". Also, once the children had seen the quality of the laser printer, they accepted the dot matrix output somewhat grudgingly. The children often commented on the relative ease of writing with a computer: "you don't need an eraser", "you can save", "it looks neater". The children did not really exploit the editing capabilities; they did however appreciate the ease of correcting spelling mistakes, which was often done in collaboration with the teacher.

### 4.4 Programming

Programming was done either in HyperCard or a variation of Logo. Hypercard was introduced using adventure games. Children both explored existing games and created their own, either by changing the content of the cards or constructing their own stacks. This brought them in direct contact with the complex notions of stacks, individual cards, buttons and the relationships among them. The children surprised us more often than not with their mastery of these concepts; although they did not create very complicated paths through the stacks, the few children who did undertake to create their own (and these were by and large children who were not very sure of themselves or advanced in their school work) did manage their stacks quite well.

The experience of Logo programming underlined the importance of varied support systems. Children used existing examples as models and requested individual tutoring in addition to consulting reference materials. Programming was done either in screen mode (two grade 5 boys invented and programmed a game involving navigating a helicopter to arrive at a given target), or more often to control external objects, a floor turtle or LEGO objects that the children created themselves. The external objects fulfilled a very important role for both the older and younger children, as they allowed them to see the results of their commands to the computer in a tangible form. In addition, the LEGO construction activity allowed the children to create personalized environments in which to program.

### 4.5 Music

Music was present in two main forms in the Vitrine. While there were no keyboards, there was a program permitting the creation and playback of musical compositions on the Apple II GS. The program came with a bank of songs which the children played to familiarize themselves with the program; several of the children (from both age groups) went on to input songs, either reproducing popular songs or classical music which they already knew, or creating their own compositions.

LogoWriter also offers the possibility to program music, and a grade four boy devoted a significant amount of time to programming songs and sound effects to accompany his friends' LEGO amusement park. As music is programmed in LogoWriter by frequency rather than by conventional notes, this was a very challenging project, and sparked discussions on music in a different way than the children were accustomed to.

## 4.6 Communication

Six ICONs (the official educational computer of the province of Ontario) were networked together and placed in different areas of the Vitrine (3 upstairs and 3 downstairs). As well as having a variety of drawing, text processing, games, simulations, and other software, it had a communications program that permitted two or more of the machines to communicate, allowing the children to explore this facet of the technology. One of the more innovative uses of this software came from the grade 4/5 group. When one of the researchers asked Antony to get the children up from downstairs, he turned to Alice who was communicating on the messaging system and asked her to send a message to Lewis who was on the system downstairs. The children who had been downstairs came up in response to the message. The communication feature was highlighted by assigning the name of a city to each machine; the children would address each station by its city (e.g. Paris calling New York).

## 5.0 Breadth versus depth

To give an idea of the different ways individual children functioned in the Vitrine, several "extreme" cases will be presented. Some children seemed to have made a point of trying as many different things as possible. In the grade 2 class, Julia, a child described by her teacher as one who was interested by everything, tried 21 different activities in the course of her 23 visits. These ran the gamut from text processing to music, from graphic animation to LEGO/Logo, and a variety of games. Her experience would clearly be very different from one week to the next. By contrast, Oliver worked on only four activities over the course of his albeit shorter year (he arrived late and visited only 11 times)—LEGO/Logo, Mac-a-Mug, Deluxe Paint II, and Jeu de mémoire. Despite the different time frames, these different patterns of usage also reflect the children's personalities and preferences. Each child created a personal Vitrine experience.

In the combined grade 2/3 class, Beatrice, a child described by her teacher as one who did not like teamwork, tried only seven different activities in 23 visits. She effectively cut herself off from most of the group at the beginning of the year by working on her own on one of the drawing programs. However, the expertise which she thus developed was then referenced by the other children, and she was gradually drawn into the group. She ended up being the class photographer and created an album of photos taken using a digitizing program with a video camera. In contrast, Sebastian, a child described as a model student with perseverance and enthusiasm, tried 22 different activities over the same period of time. His experience was clearly very different—he took advantage of the Vitrine's variety to satisfy his curiosity whereas Beatrice used it to help overcome certain affective and social integration problems which she was experiencing in relating to the group.

The combined grade 4/5 class functioned on a project-oriented basis in the Vitrine, as encouraged by their teacher. Although their first five visits were spent in a free exploration mode, their different functioning is reflected in the generally smaller number of activities which the children tried. Some children still explored a significant variety of activities; for example, Alice and Joanne each tried 14 different activities in their 16 visits. The other extreme is however much more striking. Edgar, a child described by his teacher as a LEGO addict in real life, spent the bulk of his time working on LEGO/Logo, trying only two other activities briefly. He found a familiar and loved activity in the Vitrine, and quickly latched on to it. It is important to note that the LEGO/Logo group which formed in this class created complicated scenarios (for example, an amusement park with different rides and games, coordinated to music) which required sophisticated programming in addition to the complex objects. A similar example is Eric, who became engrossed in developing an adventure game in Hypercard; he tried only three other activities in the Vitrine.

## 6.0 Unexpected uses

Most of the ways that the children used the various software could be characterized as expected; this is in no way meant to disparage the creativity, imagination and enthusiasm which the children brought to their work. There were however, a number of instances where children used individual pieces of software in ways which we feel merit special mention. The following examples illustrate not only how imaginative children can be, but are also instructive as to how imaginative we should be in looking at the educational applications of computers.

Ernie's Big Splash is a program created by Children's Television Workshop for preschool children. Ernie (a character from Sesame Street) is in his bath and the goal is to create a path which will allow his Rubber Duckie to reach him. The path is created by the child choosing from a selection of squares, each of which has an entrance and an exit for the duck to move through as well as a graphic sequence illustrating a different kind of movement. For example, one square has an elephant which lifts the duck up with his trunk; another has a fire hydrant which lifts the duck up on a stream of water. Because the squares have their entrances and exits on different sides, the choice of squares determines the path the duck will follow. This program has attractive graphics and sound; even so, we were surprised at the interest it engendered in the grade 2 and 3 children. Upon observation and discussion with the three boys using the software, we found that they had expanded on the original idea to create a more challenging context. One "game" they played was to use the graphic sequences to make a film. They created a story linking each square together, and amused themselves by showing each other their "films". The language they used to describe their actions changed while making films—instead of talking about sending the duck to the beginning of the path, they talked about rewinding the film. Other challenges invented included filling the screen completely or making symmetrical paths for the duck to follow. These constraints changed the task into a non-trivial one for their ability level.

Another example of a child adapting software to his own interests occurred with a child from the older group. This was a child whom the teacher described as a math fanatic, so we were not surprised when Roger asked for an activity which would have something to do with math. He was encouraged to look around and see what he could find. After some time observing and trying out different programs, he settled into working with a graphics animation program. He had created a "film" in which four triangles evolved together to form a square. This was an instructive lesson for us and the teacher in how one can use open software to approach specific content in a given discipline.

## 7.0 Conclusion

There are several lessons to be learned from the experiences we observed the children having in the Vitrine. Rather than thinking in terms of the software only, we must approach the use of computers in education from the point of view of the pedagogical, human and physical context in which it will be used. While adequate software is a necessary condition for successful applications, it is not sufficient. Educational software is not a turn-key operation—you don't just hand it over to a child and expect learning to occur. How, when, with whom and in what context software is used must be considered as important factors in the successful use of computers in education.

We must also be open-minded in looking at software to be used for educational applications. Our experience showed that many worthwhile activities may be carried out with software originally designed for home or professional use. We must also develop an approach to educational computing which maximizes what is available rather than waiting for the perfect program. Computer software is a tool which it is up to us to help children use in the most appropriate and beneficial way.

But where will our ideas come from? One source which is often overlooked by educators is the children whom we are trying to help learn. By letting children play with the software without imposing unnecessary constraints we can observe ideas which may be developed into enriching activities. For example, math projects using animation, computer conferencing for geography learning as well as second language learning.

A final point to be kept in mind when thinking about computer-based activities for children is that although adults often express concern about overtaxing children's abilities by having them work in a multi-machine, multi-activity environment, we found the children to be quite adept at switching from one program, machine, and/or operating system to another. Their choice of programs was guided by their goal and practical considerations such as the availability of machines and personal preferences rather than any snob appeal of "brand names". This means that we can take advantage of all available resources to create enriching learning environments.

## 8.0 References

Barfurth, M.A. & Winer, L.R. (1991) Des outils de recherche qualitative dans les Environnements Pédagogiques Informatisés (EPI). In La Technologie Éducative à la Croisée des Disciplines. (pp. 173-79). Sainte-Foy, Québec: Télé-université.

Brown, J. S. (1985). Process Versus Product: A perspective on tools for communal and informal electronic learning. In M. Chen, & W. Paisley (Ed.), Children and Microcomputers - Research on the newest medium (pp. 248-266). Beverly Hills, CA: Sage.

Bruner, J. S. (1966). Toward a Theory of Instruction . Cambridge, MA: Harvard University Press.

Harel, I. (1990). Constructionist Learning. Cambridge, MA: MIT Media Laboratory.

Newman, D. (1987). Functional Environments for Microcomputers in Education. In R.D. Pea, & K. Sheingold (Ed.), Mirrors of Minds: Patterns of Experience in Educational Computing (pp. 57-66). Norwood, NJ: Ablex Publishing Co.

Papert, S. (1980). Mindstorms . New York: Basic Books.

Piaget, J., & Inhelder, B. (1969). The Psychology of the Child . London: Routledge & Kegan Paul.

Winer, L.R. & Carrière, M. (1991) A Qualitative Information System for Data Management. Qualitative Sociology, 14, 3/4.

Winer, L.R. & Carrière, M. (1990). The Use of a Relational Database in Qualitative Research on Educational Computing. Computers & Education,15, 1-3, 213-220.

Education and Society / R. Aiken (Editor)
Information Processing 92, Volume II
Elsevier Science Publishers B.V. (North-Holland)



# Reorganization of Management Information Education In Light of the Advent of EUC/UF

**Nam Won Suh**

College of Business Administration, Korea University
Seoul, Korea 136-701
TEL/FAX: (+82-2) 920-1157/924-7529

**ABSTRACT**

Management information education (MIE) is acutely concerned with the changing attributes of computer users in business organizations. Then, the recent arguments of End-User Computing' and 'User Friendly' amply solicit a fundamental reorganization of MIE programs. In approaching this renovation task, two unorthodox strategies, termed 'dualistic setup' and 'distributed shift' are offered, both based on the concept of 'infused application.' Also presented are viable guidelines for implementing the strategies, analyzed along both technical and social contours. Finally, a new paradigm for both information technology and MIE--'the interfacing of computer <u>onto</u> man'--is enunciated.

Keyword Codes: K.3.2;K.7.2;K.4.3
Keywords: Computer and Information Science Education; Organizations; Organizational Impacts

## 1. INTRODUCTION

Ever since the first reproducible design of the computing machine was completed, the task of expanding the number of computer users has been the most pertinent and common issue to all computer professionals. Evidently, today the growth of computer users in society is tantamount to the progress of industrialization.

Obviously, measures to realize the user expansion have taken divergent forms of ideas, schemes, and/or gadgets. Nonetheless, the most elaborate efforts involving the user expansion are represented in the two distinctive movements: End-User Computing (EUC) and 'User Friendly' (UF). Indeed, the concept of 'user' has taken a drastic turn from yesterday's 'computer buff' to today's 'novice.' Notwithstanding, EUC and UF can be taken as the most concerned ones: the former denoting the conversion of general staff personnel to 'dependable' users; the latter turning line workers to 'pseudo' users, both involved in business operations. These changing attributes of the computer user in business organizations decisively invite management information education (MIE) to undertake a massive remodeling of its programs.

This paper specifically analyzes the relevant context of EUC and UF, discusses the institutional and pedagogic circumstances, and proposes a set of strategic standpoints, and subsequent guidelines for reprogramming and implementing modern MIE. Furthermore, this paper formulates, and relies on, a set of unique concepts and assertions with reference to various research papers and a questionnaire survey undertaken for this study. Finally, a new paradigmatic view as to IT/MIE approaches is enunciated.

## 2. END-USER COMPUTING AND USER FRIENDLY EXAMINED

### 2.1 End-User Computing Recapitulated

In essence, the goal of EUC advocates lies in tearing down the traditional organizational units of data processing (DP) and/or information systems (IS). In other words, a significant portion of the tasks of DP/IS professionals in business firms is being distributed among non-DP/IS professionals in the same organization, as EUC plans are implemented. Thus, the scope of users has become diffused to include those who have previously been left out of the training program and MIE.[1] The works of programming and system analysis have become so standard and rudimentary that non DP/IS staff in business firms are led to accomplish their computerizing tasks under their own discretion.

Indeed, a substantial number of successful cases are reported in America.[2] On the other hand, it has also been discovered that actual implementation of EUC involves many obstacles ranging from the misuse of data stored in the center to the lack of documentation for individual tasks.[3] Therefore, as far as MIE is concerned, the impact of EUC poses a broader spectrum of user problems, particularly in developing countries.

### 2.2 User Friendly Reviewed

User Friendly presents a new perspective on MIE also, pertaining to 'any device or system designed to be used without extensive user training.' Practically, all UF-oriented schemes seem to have the capability to expand the number of users with no educational programs: 'the novice himself prescribes the user technology.'[4] Therefore, every business employee should be regarded as either an 'imminent' or 'eventual' user. Nevertheless, one decisive drawback of UF still exists: the performance of UF-oriented products is short of the ideal level of allowing full access to all non-DP/IS personnel for operating business systems.

### 2.3 EUC vs. UF Under Management Information Education

As indicated, EUC and UF are accepted as mutually reinforcing forces favoring the expansion of the range/type of user groups in business organizations. While EUC converts staff personnel of non-DP/IS departments to a new class of 'functional' user, UF confidently allows all employees, including line workers, access to operations systems as 'operational' users. Subsequently, MIE, and user training in particular, now encounters a complex perspective in projecting its future course. Superficially assessed, EUC demands the provision of an extensive educational program of IT to non-DP/IS professionals in the business firm. UF, in contrast, suggests the installation of a low-profile, yet, wide open program.

## 3. ATTITUDES OF BUSINESS FIRMS SURVEYED

The attitudes of business firms in regard to the advent of EUC/UF comprise an important factor in remodeling MIE. For this reason, 100 managers in Seoul, the capital city of Korea, equally divided into two groups-- DP/IS professionals and manpower specialists-- were asked to respond to a prepared questionnaire. The survey conclusions are:

(1) Both EUC and UF were acknowledged to be factors influencing the outcome of future DP/IS systems.

(2) However, EUC is barely underway, due to the ineptness and the manpower-drain effect of/in non-DP/IS units.

(3) A substantial portion of system integration projects is contracted out to outside system houses which draw only a fraction of their manpower from business institutions.

(4) EUC may limit its target to System Analysis only, apart from System Design and Programming.

(5) Expertise in the use of high-level languages no longer seems necessary. Instead, the ability to use the package-type software is unanimously encouraged.

(6) There has emerged a new class of users, designated as 'job-users,':a composite of the 'functional user per EUC' and 'job user per UF,' whom MIE has to entertain.

## 4. BACKGROUND OF MANAGEMENT INFORMATION EDUCATION

### 4.1 The Installation and Evolution of the Program

In the early 1970s the 'exotic' education program on the integrated subject of IT/management was envisaged and implemented. Korea was then on the verge of its industrialization take-off. Therefore, it was imperative that the first educational venture encountered cultural constraints:

(1) The tradition-oriented management practices of the preindustrial culture,[5]

(2) The total unawareness of computers as well as the low profile of data/information perception in society.

(3) The start of DP activities controlled by a mainframe vendor which served as the only source of IT inside the country,

(4) The non-existence of computing facilities available for training purposes,

(5) The frequent job-rotation of white-collar workers: the ineffectual cause of promoting professionalism,

(6) The total lack of experienced teaching staff on IT in educational institutions.

In order to overcome these preindustrial features in the society, a series of seminars on computer were undertaken. Information sheets were also prepared for the purpose of media/public education on machine computing. After a one-year of such ground work, the MIE project was launched as evening course in two formats: (1) a two-year degree program and (2) a one-year adult program as a subsidiary. The central theme for guiding the curriculum development was "PCS technique supplemented with modern (Western) management know-how."

Over the last two decades, MIE programs have undergone several overhauls, as the information society of the country has steadily progressed. Then, the original PCS-oriented idea became upgraded to the pioneer version of the MIS of the MBA program. At this stage, MIE far exceeds the original goal of the user expansion, incorporating a host of new application techniques for business data/information processing.

## 4.2 The Success Factors Delineated

From the two-decade MIE operation at the postgraduate level, outstanding success factors can be delineated:

(1) The Korean economy has sustained industrial growth at an appreciably high rate throughout the period.

(2) The program content was designed and occasionally revised to serve always the practical needs of particular periods of business firms.[6]

(3) The manpower and materials needed for class instruction and laboratory training were 'borrowed' from all spheres of the information industry.

(4) The central theme of the educational program has always been the 'infused application.

(5) Texts and teaching materials based on 'infused' subjects of IT/management were properly developed and published for each lecture course.

(6) The observation of a unique pedagogic guidance, to be discussed later, during class and vocational hours.

### 4.3 Recent Curriculum Reviewed

The initial program of user education for business students has steadily developed over the last two decades into a full-fledged MIS field (MIE) of the MBA program. The one-year adult program was dropped a decade after. And the admissions demand of the program still runs high. Only one third of the total applicants are admitted. Major requirements for the completion of MBA degree are:

(1) Mandatory enrollment in the three foundation courses-- Managerial Economics, Business Statistics, and Management Strategy vs. Environment.

(2) Three compulsory electives out of 5 introductory subjects-- accounting, finance, marketing, production and international management.

(3) Completion of 5 MIS option courses-- MIS Introduction, OS Basics, SE, SA & D, and Database.

(4) Submission of an MBA paper as proof of individual research on the subjects of application technology.

(5) Attendance of one non-credit laboratory course unless the student has work experience in the area of DP/IS.

### 4.4 'Infused Application' As Pedagogic Approach

The underlying theme of the program, accepted and observed by all of the participating staff, is the 'infused application.' This MIE methodology requires the upholding of a unique assertion that 'applications of IT infused into management theories, or vice versa, predominantly decide the efficiency of DP/IS systems.'

The 'infusion' theory can be substantiated by reformulating, for example, conventional organizational theories like social communication, as advanced by Chester Barnard,[7] in terms of Shannon/Wiener's communication model. As a matter of fact, the operational process of management functions are effectively explained in line with Cybernetics. Likewise, the infusion of management/IT is practical for many other subjects of MIE.[8]

## 5. NEW STRATEGIES OF MANAGEMENT INFORMATION EDUCATION

### 5.1 Basic Strategies to Reorganization

In renovating the MIE program, two basic strategies are workable: (1) the 'dualistic setup' and (2) 'the distributed shift.' The key difference of these two lies in whether the educational program under the supervision, or within the scope, of the MIS group in business schools should/not entertain the job user--the functional user and the operational user--in its reorganization scheme. In other words, if it is asserted that the education of both users has to be dealt within the realm of MIS, then the MIE program needs to be reorganized per the 'dualistic setup.' On the other hand, if it is realistic to shift the education of the job user to other MBA function areas, a reorganization based on the 'distributed shift' becomes practical.

## 5.2 Reorganization Guidelines Per 'Dualistic Setup'

Where there is a relatively short history of an educational programs for DP/IS manpower, the 'dualistic setup' is recommended. Then a set of new guidelines emerge:

(1) To open all lectures of the MIE program to all MBA students, with course revisions per the systems' requirements of business operations.

(2) To introduce a new set of problem-exercises with 'packaged software,' so that the MIS option students can also become as adept as the job user.

(3) To curtail the session-hours of High-Level Languages, and to substitute them with Automatic Programming.

(4) To place greater emphasis on the Analysis part of the SA/D course, supplemented with 'Logical' topics, 'Structured' methods, and Prototyping solutions.

(5) To replace laboratory facilities in part with devices which have capabilities like the stand-alone, LAN, and multi-media I/O.

## 5.3 Remodeling Principles Per 'Distributed Shift'

Understandably, where the MIE program has built up a strong reputation, the 'distributed shift' is suitable. Under this strategy, the department of MIE acts a coordinator for the entire MBA programs. Guideline details for implementation based on 'distributed shift' are:

(1) To specify and assign the tasks of both functional/ operational user education to each non-MIS function departments.

(2) To install an IS-oriented lecture course in each function department: AIS for Accounting, CIM for Production, Telemarketing for Marketing, EDI for Finance and/or International Business.

(3) To augment the MIS curriculum with modern topics such as Expert System, Decision Support System, WAN, LAN, OA, FA, EFT, and EDI.

(4) To upgrade the level of MIS lecture courses, covering the latest issues such as On-Line Information Services, Global Networking Systems, Object-Oriented Systems, IS prospects under Super/Note conglomerates, and Intelligent Society.

(5) To include the items (5) listed in the Guidelines of Paragraph 5.2.

## 6. CONCLUSIONS

In reality, the inception and implementation of any reorganization project of MIE are impelled by a complex set of forces surrounding the institution concerned. Yet, in this paper, the advent of EUC/UF is highlighted as the most important force.

Information technology (IT) is in essence the art of interfacing man and computer. In the past, IT has taken the position of interfacing man onto computer, clearly recognizing computer science as the starting ground. However, this paper argues that IT has now turned around to address interfacing needs in the opposite direction: the advanced IT takes the view of interfacing computer onto man. In fact, the 'about-face' interfacing provides a common premise for many latest IT movements, as denoted by such terms as *Logical, Structured, Natural,* and *Object.*

Now, the paradigmatic view of all arguments developed in this paper can be summarized: the reorganization of MIE is based on the principle of 'the interfacing of management/IT problems/solutions onto users of all categories in the business firm.' Thus, the conversion of management/business operations into *ideal computer-run systems* are greatly expedited.

## NOTES AND REFERENCES

[1] Raymond R. Panko, "Directions and Issues in End-User Computing," INFOR, Vol. 25, No. 3, August 1987, pp. 181-197.

[2] R. Ryan Nelson (ed.), End-User Computing--Concepts, Issues and Applications," John Wiley & Sons, 1`989.

[3] Gordon Davis, "Caution:User-Developed Systems Can Be Dangerous To Your Organization," Ibid, pp. 209-230.

[4] M. D. Good & Others, "Building a User-Derived Interface," Communication of ACM, Vol. 27, No. 10, October 1984, pp. 1032-1034.

[5] Nam Won Suh, "Management and Its Environment in Korea," in Management In An International Context, Harper & Row, New York, 1972.

[6] One successful case of IT education, which combines with a non-information subject is found in Paul Van Binst & Luc Wilkin, "Informatics and Human Science: A Working Synergy," Information Processing 89, the Proceeding of IFIP Congress, pp. 415-418.

[7] Chester I. Barnard, The Functions of the Executive, Harvard University Press, Twelfth Printing, 1956.

[8] For other cases of the infused management/IT models, see Nam Won Suh, Management Information: Concepts, Models, and Practices, Trade Management Co., Seoul, 1973, 1983, & 1991.

Education and Society / R. Aiken (Editor)
Information Processing 92, Volume II
Elsevier Science Publishers B.V. (North-Holland)


# A model for teaching the management of information systems & technology

C. James Bacon.

Senior Lecturer in Information Systems. University of Canterbury. Christchurch, New Zealand. Fax: +64-3-642-727. E-mail: JamesB@Accy.Canterbury.ac.nz

**Abstract**

Teaching the management of information systems & technology (IST) has become especially significant, at a time when the effective management of IST has become a critical factor in many organisations. But teaching IST management is also a challenge, in determining what to teach, and how. Given the integrating nature of the manager's role, managers and users of IST need to understand and deal with the subject of IST as an integrated whole, if their management is to be effective. Based on a survey of syllabii, texts, and users, a unifying model is presented that aims to address this challenge and this need. The model implies requisite definitions for the discipline of IST, and its management, which are developed as a foundation. A taxonomy is also developed.

Keyword Codes: K.3.2; K.4.0; K.6.0.
Keywords: Computer and Information Science Education; Computers and Society; Management of Computing and Information Systems

## 1. INTRODUCTION

Information Systems (IS) is a relatively new area of study and practice that draws on a number of disciplines [1-2]. It is also evolving and expanding. Furthermore, IS is taking on an increasingly strategic significance for the organisation. For example, a 1991 survey carried out in the United Kingdom showed that: "90 per cent of top executives perceive IT [information technology], as a strategic element in building business advantage" [3]. For this and other reasons, the effective use and management of IS/T is now every manager's responsibility. For the teacher of IS/T there is, consequently, a real challenge in assessing what to teach and how to teach it.

If the teaching of information systems and/or technology (IST) has its special challenges, so does the teaching of management, dealing as it does with the dynamic and `fuzzy' areas of cognition, behaviour, communication and organisation. In today's organisation, the manager's job is both critical and demanding. A manager must operate in an environment that is global, turbulent and highly competitive. And a manager is required to be a leader, if resources and talents are to be optimized in achieving organisational aims. This means that the teacher of management has to address the same environment and requirements, if that teaching is to be effective.

For the functional manager of IST and the business manager with IST responsibilities, there is no `silver bullet'. There is no single factor which, if properly addressed, will ensure success in using and managing IST resources. What is required is an overall, integrated view of IST and its management, so that understanding is optimised and focus given to those areas necessary. The need, therefore, is for an integrating model of IST management, complemented by a taxonomy that amplifies and supports the model. That is the aim of this paper.

## 2. APPROACH

In developing the model it was first necessary to review the background of information system/technology, and to develop foundational definitions for IST and its management. This lead to a survey of the syllabii of IST management courses in 75 IST-teaching institutions; 37 in the United States, 4 in Canada, 16 in Britain, 10 in Australia, and 8 in New Zealand. The aim of the survey was to: (a) identify those subjects that are commonly taught in such courses, and (b) identify other subjects included in innovative courses, by leading institutions focusing on IST *management*. In parallel, a survey, of 18 texts relating to IST management was undertaken, with the aim of complementing the survey of syllabii. These two surveys enabled a prototype model and taxonomy to be developed. The inter-relationships between main subject areas in the model were based on: (a) relationships filtered from the data gathering, and (b) the author's own experience in consulting practice (in London and New York), and teaching IST management for the past eight years. Thirdly, a survey of studies/surveys was undertaken, of: (a) curriculum surveys, (b) user studies, and (c) related research studies, which enabled development of the completed model (if something like this ever is completed).

The model is now being used in teaching. Based on the improved level of comment and response in class discussion, it appears that student understanding is enhanced. However, this is subjective; no formalised assessment has as yet been undertaken. The model and taxonomy are introduced at the first lecture on IST management. Both are then referred to throughout the course (including identification of specific subjects in the taxonomy for which we do not have sufficient lecture time), in communicating the context of each main subject area.

## 3. GOOD TEACHING

The management of IST is application oriented. Therefore, good teaching must also address market needs, and the practices, techniques and problems out in the field, if it is to be relevant. At the same time, good teaching at the university level provides intellectual leadership [5]. Consequently, a course of study in IST management needs to include innovative subjects and concepts, and change where necessary. The management of IST calls for new ways and new directions if its potential is to be exploited. It must not be viewed, for example, as just a `tool'. In some graduate courses the subject is taught with IST being a functional area, in others it is treated as an integral component in all aspects of the organisation [6]. In either case, it needs to have a conceptual framework, if it is to provide an effective basis for innovation and change. At present, there is no agreed, underlying structure or framework for the subject; there is no paradigm.

Simply put, good teaching is that which encourages high quality learning [7]. This is brought about by: (1) making the material stimulating, (2) using clear explanation, and (3) making it clear what has to be understood, and why. There are other attributes of good teaching. Notably, it needs to be planned in some systematic way [8]. The subjects need to link with each other according to some logical pattern and goal, and their inter-relationships need to be part of an overall scheme, for full understanding and appropriate application.

## 4. A DEFINITION FOR IST AND ITS MANAGEMENT

The study of information systems is not only concerned with information but also the effective use of information technology, be it computer hardware, software, or communications. Information technology is defined herein as follows:

> Information technology (IT), is any computer, communications, or related hardware and componentry, or any software excusive of application software, that is used in developing, processing, or delivering information systems. (Application software is the application of technology, rather than technology itself).

Information is generally the focus in IST. However, technology may be viewed as being of equal importance where the need is not so much information as such, but an enhanced means of developing, processing or delivering it. In some cases it is the use of new technology, rather than new information, that makes the difference. Thus, the area of study is not just information systems, but information technology as well. Information systems & technology, or IST, therefore appears to be the more complete term.

Previous definitions of information systems have tended to focus on the system or systems, rather than the field of study. For example: "information systems are applications of IT by individuals, organisations or society. They are used to overcome human cognitive and physical space/time limitations, improve management decision-making and control, and gain competitive advantage" (Seddon, ibid). But the *study* of IS (or IST) is not the same as an information system. Therefore, the following definition is proposed for information systems & technology (IST) as a field of study and practice:

> Information systems & technology (IST) is the field of study and practice concerned with the development, processing and delivery of information and systems in the organisational and environmental context, and the application of such information and systems, together with the technology involved.

Thus, IST is oriented to the *application* of information, information systems, and information technology.

To be of optiimal use, a definition for the management of IST should apply not only to the IST functional manager, it should also be useful to the manager of a user function with responsibilities for IST. In addition, since the organisation is dependent on IST, its senior/general management need to be involved with the overall management (or governance) of IST. Therefore, the definition should also be useful for top management in respect of their involvement in IST. Lastly, the definition should be useful for those who undertake IST management without being formally designated as managers. Examples include systems accountants, client/user representatives, project coordinators and business unit managers in a decentralised organisation.

The following definition for the management of IST is therefore proposed:

> The management of information systems technology (IST) is concerned with: (1) the effective use, coordination and support of organisational resources and activities, through (2) the planning, development and exploitation of information,

information systems, and information technology, so as to (3) optimise the fulfillment of managerial, organisational and societal aims, plans and policies.

## 5. A MODEL AND TAXONOMY

The Definition of IST Management leads to an overall conceptual model that embraces the main subject areas in teaching the management of information systems & technology. The model also endeavors to represent the inter-relationships between these main areas. Respective areas may then be presented and taught within the context of the whole. The aim is for the parts and the whole to become more meaningful, and for overall understanding to be enhanced. It is a unifying model for teaching the management of IST.

The main subject areas of the model are introduced by grouping them within three bases: (I) Management, (II) Development, and (III) Technology, as shown in Figure 1.

---

I. Management Basis

1. Foundations of IST Management.
2. Strategic IST Management.
3. Project Management.
4. Behavioral/Human Resource Management.
5. Organisational Analysis/Development
6. Operations Management.
7. Security & Control.
8. IST Evaluation & Measurement.
9. Ethical & Social Impact.
10. Functional & Business Usage.

II. Development Basis

1. Systems Development Methodology.
2. Testing, Quality Assurance and Maintenance.
3. Data & Information Architecture.
4. System Types & Related Areas.

III. Technology Basis

1. Hardware Technology
2. Software Technology.
3. Communications Technology.
4. Technology Perspectives

---

**Figure 1. The primary bases and main subject areas of IST mgt.**

Those subject areas grouped under Management Basis are essentially oriented toward the management responsibility; those under Development Basis are essentially development oriented; and those under Technology Basis are technology oriented. IST management includes the latter two groups, in spite of their orientation to something other than management, because they require some knowledge and involvement in pursuing IST management responsibilities.

A Model for teaching the management of IST is shown in Figure 2. It is a vehicle for communication, analysis and questioning within the overall framework of IST management. For example, how does Ethical and Social Impact relate to Systems Development Methodology? One answer is that, if the issue of data privacy is to be addressed, it needs to be done as part of the system development process. How does

Hardware Technology relate to Strategic Management? Part of the answer is that Hardware Technology is a means of effecting strategic plans. But there is a two-way flow, in that the management of IST also needs to be pro-active in exploiting hardware (and other) technology to achieve strategic aims.

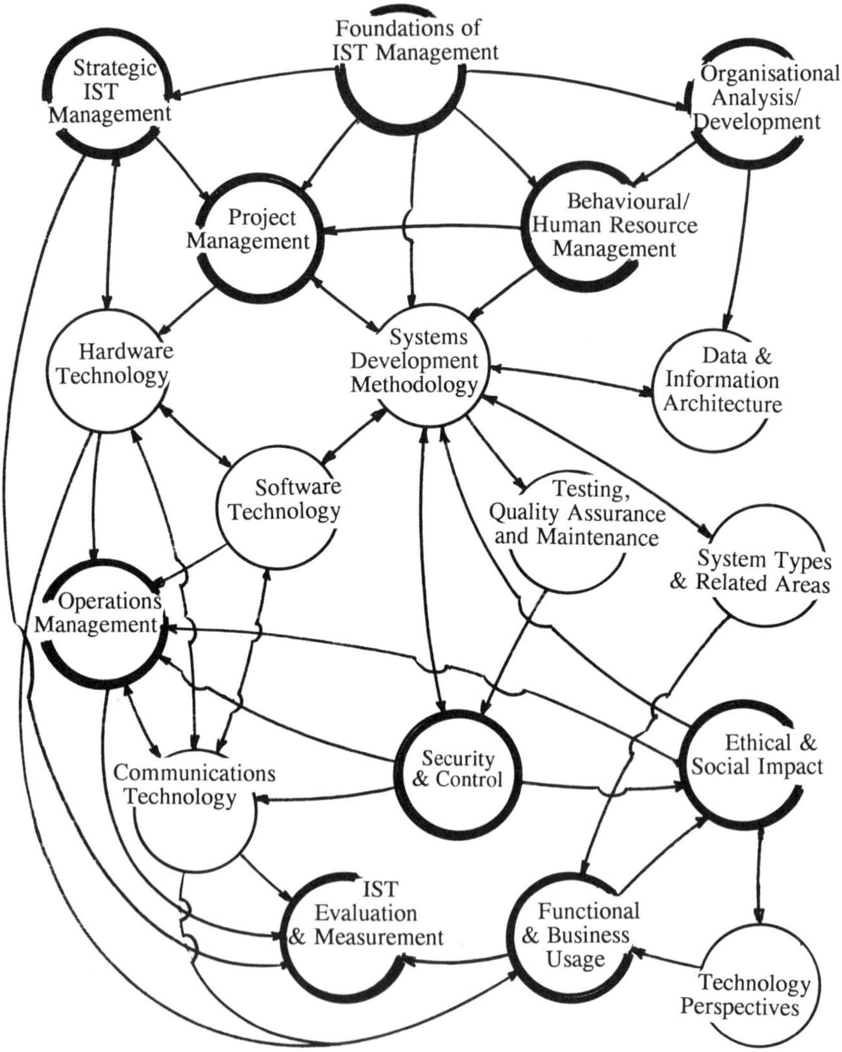


**Figure 2. A model for teaching the management of information systems & technology with management basis areas emphasised**

Owing to space limitations, the taxonomy of some 140 specific subjects based on the model is not included in this paper. It is available from the author.

The validity of the model and taxonomy depend on the degreee to which they meet the tests of comprehensiveness, parsimony, and utility [1]. But there is another criteria that needs to be added, that of viability. The model and taxonomy should therefore: (1) include everything that needs to be included, (2) include only that which should be included, (3) be practical and useful in addressing the subject of IST management, and (4) be reasonably robust in accommodating changes.

Figure 2 breaks the rules of simplicity, in that there are 18 main subject areas inter-relating with each other. However, each of these main subject areas can be separated and treated in their own sub-model. This is shown in Figure 3, using the example of the Ethical & Social Impact subject area.

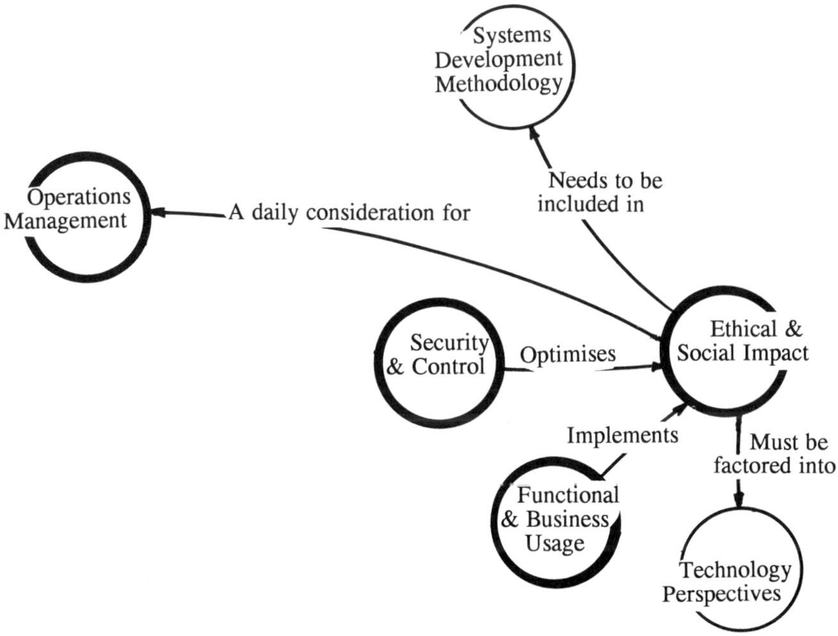


**Figure 3. Sub-model of the ethical & social impact subject area and its inter-relationship with other main subject areas**

According to the taxonomy, specific subjects included within the subject area of Ethical & Social Impact are: Professional Ethics, Data Privacy & Data Freedom, Impact of IST in the Workplace, and Impact on Lifestyles. Thus, the sub-model can be used to show that Security & Control optimises the protection of Data Privacy. In the case of Operations

Management, since it interfaces on a day-to-day basis with the workplace and external environment, it needs to consider its ethical and social impact. The subject of Functional & Business Usage relates to cases and examples of IST usage in particular functions or lines of business. Such usage represents the implementation (or avoidance), of ethical and social considerations. Lastly, ethical and social impact must or should be a factor in considering past, present, and future Technology Perspectives.

The sub-model for each main subject area is therefore a more specific vehicle for communication, analysis and questioning, within the overall framework of IST management. In the sub-model it also becomes feasible to identify the nature of the inter-relalationships between main subject areas. Thus, the overall model illustrates and provides an integrated framework for the management of information systems & technology as a whole. A sub-model for each main subject area then illustrates that area in the context of other subject areas with which it inter-relates.

## 6. CONCLUSION

Owing to space limitations, discussion of the syllabii, texts, curricula studies, industry studies and related research reports that were included in the data gathering and analysis must be brief. Some 12 curricula studies were included, covering computer science, accounting information systems, information systems, and graduate management. About 10 user surveys, in the United States and Britain, were also included. In addition, the syllabii of 75 leading institutions, and 18 textbooks relating to IST management, were included in the data gathering and analysis. These surveys and studies indicated: (a) the subjects that are commonly considered pertinent to IST management, (b) innovative subjects that need to be included, and (c) an indication of how the various subjects tie together. It is hoped that the resulting model will be of some value to colleagues searching for better ways of teaching the management of information systems & technology. As previously stated, there is insufficient space to include the supporting taxonomy. It is available from the author.

## 7. REFERENCES

1 Vogel, Douglas R and Wetherbe, James C. MIS Research: A Profile of Leading Journals and Universities, Database, Vol. 16 (1), pp. 3-14, Fall, 1984.
2 Keen, P.G.W. MIS Research: Current Status, Trends and Needs, in Information Systems Education: Recommendations and Implementation, by Buckingham, R.A. Hirschheim, R.A. Land, F.F and Tully, C.J. Cambridge University Press, 1987.
3 Management Today (U.K.), Terminal Shyness, pp. 92-93. Nov, 1991.
4 Seddon, Peter. Information Systems: Towards a Definition for the 1990s, Proceedings DBIS, 1991, Second Annual Conference on Information Systems and Database Special Interest Group, University of New South Wales, February, 1991.
5 Dijkstra, Edsgar W. On the Cruelty of Teaching Computing Science, Communications of the ACM. Vol. 32, (12), pp. 1398-1404, December, 1989.
6 Finnie, Gavin R. Teaching Computing Skills to MBAs, Interface, Vol. 12, (4), pp. 46-51, Winter, 1991.
7 Ramsden, Paul. Evaulating Teaching; Supporting Learning, Keynote Paper, Annual Conference of the Higher Education Research and Development Society of Australasia, Griffin University, Nathan, Brisbane, Australia 4111, July, 1990.
8 Gagne, Robert M., Briggs, Leslie J., and Wager, Walter W. Principles of Instructional Design, Holt, Rinehart and Winston, 1988.

Education and Society / R. Aiken (Editor)
Information Processing 92, Volume II
Elsevier Science Publishers B.V. (North-Holland)



# Academic Computing Centers as Strategic University Resources

Stephen D. Franklin

Office of Academic Computing and the Department of Information and Computer Science, University of California, Irvine, California 92717, U.S.A.

**Abstract**

This paper examines the significant and evolving role of academic computing centers in creating and maintaining computing milieux supportive of the multiple missions of contemporary universities. While such centers have often been characterized in terms of specific facilities and services, their importance and strategic value to the universities they serve are founded on their ability to identify and to deliver ever-changing, ever-growing technological capabilities to faculty, students and other academic personnel in a manner which strives to maximize the positive impact of these capabilities while minimizing any diversion of focus from primary academic missions.

Keyword Codes: K.0; K.3.m; K.6.m
Keywords: Computing Milieu, General; Computers and Education, Miscellaneous; Management of Computing and Information Systems, Miscellaneous;

## 1. INTRODUCTION

*"The Machine That Changed The World"* announces the title of a recent television series, a joint American-British-German production. It is a concise and accurate summation of the impact of *"The Computer"* on the second half of the twentieth century.

Universities have been a key developmental, proving and promulgating vehicle for this impact. As such, they often have been both instigator and early beneficiary of a growing and changing understanding of what "computing" encompasses and enables. Working together with key innovators, academic computing centers have played critical roles in broadening the availability and impact of new capabilities and in creating the environment and infrastructure which enable routine use of what was formerly "cutting-edge" and which establish the basis for further innovation.

In a field changing as rapidly as computing, the continued relevance, contributions and importance of academic computing centers are open to reexamination.

While different universities may come to different conclusions on such matters, this discussion describes the importance of academic computing centers as less dependent on specific technologies and more a reflection of the contributions such organizations can make in matching developments and trends in computing with the academic mission and environment.

## 2. STRATEGIC RESOURCES

Any discussion which claims "academic" in its name must offer at least one or two definitions early on. In the singular, "resource" means a source of expertise or information. In the singular or more usually as a plural, the word signifies a source of support, a source of wealth, or (more simply) an available means.

"Strategy" has an honorable etymology, entering English directly from the classic Greek word for (military) generalship. Its modern use makes it a "very common word" in library titles according to Melvyl, the University of California's computerized library catalog, which finds it in "over 10,000 records" of holdings published in the past 10 years.

Variously used as signifying a plan, ploy, pattern, position or perspective for achieving institutional objectives, "strategy" as a contemporary concept "draws us into some of the most fundamental issues about organizations as instruments for collective perception and action." [1, p.17]. As both concept and perspective, "strategy becomes a fundamental framework through which an organization can assert its vital continuity, while, at the same time, it forcefully facilitates its adaption to a changing environment." [2, p.6]

For this discussion, then, "strategic resources" are available means (sources of information, expertise, support) of achieving institutional objectives, objectives which might well not even be envisioned without such resources. That is, strategic resources contribute both to the definition and to the achievement of goals the institution considers essential to its mission. In this manner, strategic resources are an essential part the institution's fundamental definition and understanding of itself.

Over the past thirty years, much of the discussion of computing's organizational role and impact has addressed the relationship between computing and decision authority structures and has been expressed as "the computing and centralization debate." Examining this debate, George and King [3] argue effectively that while it's "no longer useful to talk about computing and centralization in terms that have been used in the past," the discussion has been useful and that "the most interesting 'impacts' of the technology have been to alter our views of what we are studying." Their "consolidated view" emerging from the debate recognizes the limitations of managerial intent and action, that "features of the environment such as availability of technology and expertise, social and legal structures and community opinion shape both what is possible and desirable," and that organizational history "shapes the opportunities and constraints surrounding organizational structure and the use of technology."

Our present discussion moves these insights, developed in discussing organizational decision authority structures, to consideration of academic computing centers as strategic university resources.

We examine both the organizational and technical milieux in which such centers exist including some of the principal challenges present and the opportunities that can be identified and exploited by considering academic computing centers as strategic resources. The purpose of our discussion is to shape constructive visions of "Preferred Futures for Academic Computing Centers" much as the workshops reported in [4] address similar concerns and issues for university libraries.

## 3. THE UNIVERSITY MILIEU

The dual academic missions of universities are education and research. The first represents the preservation, transmission, broadened availability, and even trusteeship of our culture's intellectual heritage. The second is the advancement, extension, innovation and enrichment of that heritage. Each is fundamental to the other and central to who we are individually and collectively. They are the university's organizational goals.

In *Academic Tribes* [5], Hazard Adams characterizes the university milieu with wry discernment:

- "The Diffusion of Academic Authority [is such that] no one has the complete power to do any given thing."
- "The Diminishment of Organizational Allegiance [is such that] the fundamental allegiance of the faculty member will be to the smallest unit to which he belongs."
- "The Protective Coloration of Eccentricity. Eccentricity is not only to be tolerated ..., it is often a positive virtue."
- "Antinomy the First. The faculty is the university; the faculty are employees of the university."

A university's single most valued asset is its faculty. Their autonomy, initiative, and individual choices in their respective areas of competence must be respected, encouraged and supported. At the same time, these individuals must also function collectively. Instruction and research responsibilities place different demands on the same faculty. Intramural ties are extremely important, most obviously so for educational cohesiveness and at the research group level, but also for interdisciplinary research. Discipline-based ties, on the other hand, are rarely localized and the world-wide academic community is famous for its long-range, long-term connections, interconnections and interdependencies.

More broadly, universities most important assets are its academic personnel: faculty, students, instructors, researchers, librarians, and other academic support staff.

In addition to funding for general programs, universities depend heavily on extramural funding for specific projects, most often research. These funds are generally the result of proposals to extramural agencies put forward by individual faculty or groups of faculty who become "Principal Investigators" (PIs) for the projects and who control the funds allocated to them. As PIs, faculty have responsibilities and concerns somewhat similar to proprietors of individual shops or businesses within the academic shopping center of the university.

## 4. THE ACADEMIC COMPUTING MILIEU

By "academic computing," we mean computing as an immediate part of the educational and research activities of the university. We exclude the use of computing in various administrative activities ranging from budget preparation to equipment purchase, payroll, business correspondence, etc. Even with such applications excluded, there are relatively few aspects of the contemporary computing capabilities that are not found in the academic computing milieu. Indeed, academic applications continue to push to their limits virtually all aspects of computing capabilities: number "crunching," "memory hog," I/O speed, file size, network bandwidth, etc..

Even a minimal list of particularly important components of the academic computing milieu shows the staggering task confronting would-be users: computer networks (local, national, and international) and networked-based services; interoperability; personal computers; the cornucopia of software ("freeware," "shareware," site/bulk licenses), workstations (including "killer micros" inexpensive systems with "supercomputer-like" performance on numerically-intensive tasks); clones, commodity components, and peripherals; security and authentication; documentation; secondary storage capabilities and capacities (pushing from gigabytes to terabytes); competing operating systems; and (possibly the most daunting aspect) jargon whose disconcertingly rapid evolution reflects the frenetically dynamic nature of computing.

Heterogeneity and connectivity (or the need for connectivity) are key characteristics of the academic computing milieu. Faculty autonomy, diverse demands of different disciplines, and the discipline-based, inter-institutional connections among faculty make heterogeneity inevitable and even essential in any university's academic computing environment. The value and importance of local and inter-institutional computer networking is evident from the leading role universities have played in developing, deploying and exploiting it.

Computer networking overcomes or mitigates spatial separation, facilitates sharing of resources, promotes and sustains interpersonal contacts. It has proven so important to the academic enterprise that it has fostered major national and international efforts to advance and support it.

Campus networking involves significant infrastructure investment for installation and operation [6]. Broader computer networking has grown from advanced research projects (ARPAnet) and networking "Because It's Time "(BITNET) to an international federation of technically independent networks (Internet). In late 1991, the United States Congress approved a five-year project to build the National Research and Education Network (NREN) as a national electronic super-highway [7].

The NREN will be significantly faster than existing networks, but many of the services it will support are already available and some are almost as ubiquitous a part of the academic computing milieu as keyboards and video display screens. For example, electronic mail or the "ftp" (file transfer protocol) program will retrieve current information on almost any aspect of networked based services. *Zen and the Art of the Internet* [8] is a good place to begin learning about and learning to use network-based and network-accessible resources.

Among the now commonplace networked-based services are electronic mail, newsgroups and bulletin boards, and interactive access to "remote" systems including logins, program execution, file access and file transfer. In many situations, the access is so transparent to the user that one may not even know what remote system(s) are involved.

So many university and research libraries (over 500, at this writing) now have their catalogs and other data available over the Internet that one needs a program ("HYTELNET") just to keep track of them and an archive query system ("archie") to locate copies of the program among the over 50 gigabytes of information at ftp archive sites allowing anonymous access.

More sophisticated and general purpose wide area information servers for "browsing through terabytes" across the network are already available (in preliminary form) and being used by academic researchers in areas as diverse as Biology, Literature, and Political Science [9].

## 5. ACADEMIC COMPUTING CENTERS

Academic computing centers have been an essential part of the academic computing milieu at most universities since the first computers arrived on their campuses. At their best, they have a long history of helping develop new uses of computing, of introducing new users to computing, of fruitful collaboration with faculty and computer vendors, of collecting and disseminating the successes and experience of others, and of being "centers" in the sense of "regions of concentration," or "points around which something is described" ("coordinating foci"), rather than "sources from which something originates."

Because academic computing centers have often been identified and have often identified themselves in terms of the (largest) systems they operate, the overwhelming growth and importance of smaller systems, ranging from personal computers through "mini-supercomputers," has seemed to some to argue that the need for academic computing centers is past. Indeed, the academic computing center as "owner" of a substantial portion of the computing equipment on campus is an arrangement that is gone or being phased out at most universities, being replaced by departmental, research group, and even individual "ownership" of most computing systems. (For our purposes, the "owner" of a computer system within the university is best understood as the the entity within a university which controls the acquisition and use of the system.)

Although the rise of personal computing has been used as an argument for the decline of academic computing centers, other developments argue for the continued importance and value to universities of academic computing centers: computer networking, large scale information storage and retrieval, and multimedia computing. All reflect the fact that separating "computing" from "networking" and "information technologies" is a distinction more arbitrary than useful.

Continuing to use "academic computing center" in this discussion serves multiple purposes. It maintains a simple name with historic roots and keeps the practice of honoring history as much as logic, just as "computer" was adopted half a century ago to designate a machine rather than a person. It also acknowledges the fact that the meaning and content of "networks" and "information technologies" have been as profoundly broadened by "computing" as they have broadened "computing." Finally, it reflects the technical perspective that the networking which is most simply viewed as connecting separate computer systems is, in fact, integrating individual components into a larger system. Indeed, the (overly imaginative) common rhetoric of "seamless, integrated computing with full interoperability" is a marketing-oriented representation of this perspective.

Given the perspective or prospect (some might say "vision") of heterogeneous, distributed, networked computing systems (and sundry "peripherals") appearing to academic users as an integrated system where various computers (including one's "own") have distinct identities when appropriate but work in conjunction with others, one is struck by how well this matches the (idealized) university, its organization and its values.

There are, however, critical areas that require attention if the potential benefits of this "fit" are to be realized. We'll discuss three of these and academic computing centers' capabilities in addressing them: academic focus, balancing change and continuity, the computing marketplace.

### 5.1 Maintaining academic focus

"Maintaining academic focus" in an academic computing operation is extremely important, but not nearly as important as maintaining it in those for whom computing is not an object of study or of operational responsibility but rather a means to an end. Potential benefits of computing to the academic enterprise are largely illusory if they are available only to individuals who divert a significant portion of their attention from their primary academic tasks.

Putting the technological capabilities and possibilities at the service of those whose principal concerns are other than computing has always been the role and strength of good academic computer centers. Doing this requires the presence within such a center of personnel attuned to the academic milieu with a range of skills, aptitudes and interests. Without such personnel working together, individuals are limited to what they can fully accomplish by themselves.

This limitation is particularly unfortunate when the individual is a faculty member or student whose talents and interests lie in work to be accomplished with the aid of computing, not in overcoming difficulties with using a computer. It is equally distressing when the individual lacks the appropriate tools (e.g., software, particular data) which exist but are not known to the individual or when the person knows of their existence but cannot access them without substantial cost or effort, effort which may help only a limited subset of those who could benefit from the tool. Common examples of this last phenomenon find many people on the same campus or, indeed, even the same department independently acquiring and installing the same software package or data.

While academic computing centers have always supported users of computing, one of the more pronounced developments in the computing milieu has been the increasing number of computer "owners." As the number of individuals, groups and departments "owning" computer systems has grown, the "work" of ownership has not disappeared even if it has not always been done adequately or, in some cases, done at all. The work of ownership includes software acquisition, configuration, and maintenance, as well as system selection, interconnection, backup, and other routine operational activities. By supporting or performing all or some of these ownership activities, academic computing centers enable academic "owners" (e.g., faculty, students) the benefits of ownership with minimal diversion of focus from their academic tasks.

## 5.2 Balancing change and continuity

No matter how great the additional capabilities, how intriguing the new possibilities and how advantageous the pricing, continuing change can engender personal and institutional stresses and, one might even say, "hysteresis." Tracking what is both current and proven is a job in itself. Assuring "backward compatibility" so that moving forward doesn't sacrifice previous work, staying with something as long as it meets one's needs, leaving something when it constrains one's work, all of these are continuing "challenges." (Some might say "problems;" others, "opportunities.")

Perhaps because they are used to being at the cutting-edge of their own disciplines, some faculty work to maintain a similar position with regard to their use of computing. Others find the pace of change in computing best handled by staying with what they first learned. This second group sees much effort and little purpose in mastering new tools (especially tools fundamentally different from ones that have proved adequate in the past) unless and until the new tools have been shown to have immediate benefits and applicability to the academic tasks at hand.

By learning with and from both types of faculty in facing the change-related "challenges" described above, academic computing centers are a logical venue for promoting and maintaining both continuity and adaptation in the academic computing milieu. Being attuned to the different and legitmate attitudes of faculty members is a special talent to be cultivated among academic computing center staff.

## 5.3 The computing marketplace

As the number of participants in the computing marketplace has grown, the advantages to be gained from experience and expertise have also grown. Clone and commodity components are more readily and inexpensively available than ever before, but *"Caveat emptor"* is still a reasonable motto when determining if different components will "plug and play" together.

Academic computing centers engage in a number of activities to enable universities to get the most from the computing marketplace. Perhaps the most fundamental is maintaining the technical competence to determine what in the marketplace works with what is already present on campus or is planned to be present. Recognizing or specifying "standards" for campus use must be coupled with actual working-systems experience.

Routine business arrangements like site, group or bulk licensing of software usually require technically competent contact points which academic computing centers provide. Such arrangements constitute one class of examples of where academic computing centers as coordinating foci allow economies of scale in selection, configuration, acquisition and operation of hardware and software. Some academic computing centers act as internal resellers or brokers of computer equipment and systems. Some simply act as acquisition or configuration consultants. In all these situations and others, academic computing center activities simplify and lessen the cost of doing business for both universities and vendors. In addition to routine business relations, "strategic partnerships" between universities and vendors are often based, in part, on academic computing center participation.

## 6. SUMMARY

Computing is essential to the academic enterprise. Within the university, as elsewhere, the understanding of what "computing" encompasses is changing. While academic computing centers can be expected to provide a smaller fraction of total computing resources than in the past, what they can be expected and challenged to provide can be of increasing importance in integrating academic computing resources, in allowing those using these resources to focus on their primary academic endeavors, in broadening the utility of these resources, and in helping shape the academic community's vision of what can be accomplished with these resources.

## 7. REFERENCES

1. Mintzberg, H. The General Strategy Concept I: Five Ps for Strategy. In G. Carrol and Vogel, D., Ed., *Organizational Approaches to Strategy*, Ballinger, Cambridge, Mass., 1987.

2. Hax, A. and Majluf, N., *The Strategy Concept and Process: A Pragmatic Approach*, Prentice Hall, Englewood Cliffs, N.J., 1991.

3. George, J. and King, J. Examining the computing and centralization debate. In *Communications of the ACM*, v. 34, no. 7 (July 1991), 63-72.

4. Dougherty, R. and Hughes, C. *Preferred Futures for Libraries: A Summary of Six Workshops with University Provosts and Library Directors*, Research Libraries Group, Inc., Mountain View, Ca., 1991.

5. Adams, H., *The Academic Tribes, 2nd ed.*, University of Illinois Press, Urbana, Ill. 1988.

6. Arms, C., Ed., *Campus Networking Strategies*, Digital Press, Bedford, Mass., 1988.

7. McClure, C., ...[et al.]. *The National Research and Education Network (NREN): Research and Policy Perspectives*, Ablex Pub, Norwood, N.J., 1991.

8. Kehoe, B., *Zen and the Art of the Internet: A Beginner's Guide to the Internet*, Brendan P. Kehoe (brendan@cs.widener.edu), Chester, Pa., 1992. (Available by anonymous ftp to ftp.cs.widener.edu).

9. Stein, R. Browsing through terabytes. In *Byte Magazine,* v. 16, no. 5 (May 1991), 157-164.

Education and Society / R. Aiken (Editor)
Information Processing 92, Volume II
Elsevier Science Publishers B.V. (North-Holland)


# Computers in the Classroom: A National Proposal

Ali Mili[a*] and Noureddine Boudriga[b]

[a] University of Tunis II, Tunisia. Currently: University of Ottawa, Department of Computer Science, Ottawa, Ont. K1N 6N5 Canada

[b] University of Tunis II, Faculty of Sciences of Tunis, Department of Mathematics, 1002 Belvedere Tunisia

**Abstract**

The Ministry of Science and Learning of Tunisia has appointed us as consultants to make a proposal for the nationwide introduction of computers in Higher Education. This paper reports on our main recommendations and conclusions.

Keyword Codes: K.3.1; K.3.2
Keywords: Computer Uses in Education; Computer and Information Science Education

## 1 HIGHER EDUCATION IN TUNISIA

Because of its cultural links with France, Tunisia has an educational system that is similar to the french system of higher education. Three premises stem from this:

- All institutions of higher education in Tunisia are under the control of a single centralized authority, namely the *Ministry of Science and Learning.* This authority defines educational programs, enforces degree requirements, and backs the worthiness of degrees within and beyond the national borders.
- The administrative unit in the Tunisian educational system is not the *university*, but rather the *faculty* [†]; Tunisia has sixty seven faculties, each defined by a specific discipline. Each faculty is headed by a *dean*, who refers to an elected body, the

*Correspondence author.

[†] The closest thing we have found to a Tunisian faculty in the north american system is the *college* within a university: the college of engineering; the college of liberal arts; the college of science, etc..

scientific council, for proposing decisions and options, and reports to the ministry for finalizing decisions and issuing decrees.

- The educational program of each institution is organized into three cycles: The first cycle is two years long and leads to a general degree, that does not train for any particular employment, but prepares for the following cycle. The second cycle is two years long and leads to the *maitrise*, which is equivalent to a north american Bachelor. Finally the third cycle leads to the *DEA* after two years (equivalent to the Master) and to the doctorate after longer terms.

Upon our appointment, we have set out to investigate the current situation of the Tunisian university system with regards to the introduction of computers and the teaching of computer related courses. To this effect, we have selected a set of about ten typical faculties, spanning a wide range of specialties, and have met with their deans and teaching staff to discuss past experiences and future prospects with computers. Our main conclusions, after this initial step, were the following.

- **Scale of Use of Computers.** In all the institutions which we have visited (ranging from Literature to Engineering to Journalism) computers were used by teaching staff and students, although to a varying extent.

- **Motivation for Introducing Computers.** More often than not, the staff we have interviewed does not seem to have a clear idea why computers were useful for their purposes. They associate the use of computers with great improvements in teacher productivity and student interest, even in cases when their past experience does not substantiate the claim.

- **On the Uses of Computers.** The use of computers as teaching aids is not widespread; even institutions which started computer aided instruction programs find, after the initial excitement period, that teachers and students lose interest.

- **Computer Science Curricula.** This is the area where the lack of planning shows its worst symptoms. Individual institutions react to the problem of introducing computer courses in their curricula in an ad-hoc fashion, without proper planning of programs and resources. Most typically, computer science courses are added as an afterthought to an existing curriculum (in the faculty's field of specialty). In addition, these courses are designed and taught by temporary instructors, who change from year to year, leaving a legacy of confusion and chaos.

After assessing the situation on the basis of our selected *sample* set of institutions, we have proceeded towards a solution in three consecutive steps.

- We have contacted the appropriate services of UNESCO (Paris) and IFIP (Geneva) in order to investigate past nationwide experiments in the introduction of computers in the classroom, and to search for premises on which experts would be unanimous [1, 2, 3, 4, 5, 6].

- We have defined a set of twenty one profiles of educational programs, ranging from Agriculture to Statistics. For each such profile, we prescribe a set of computer science courses to be taught at each of the three cycles of instruction: first cycle, second cycle, and third cycle. The computer courses proposed for each cycle are taken from a pool of thirty one courses, divided into four classes: five 100-level courses, eleven 200-level courses, nine 300-level courses and six 400-level courses.
- We have conducted a survey of all the sixty seven faculties, for the purpose of assessing the resources needed by each faculty in order to implement our computerization program. Such resources include the acquisition of equipment, the hiring of teaching staff and the training of available and interested teachers. We have assessed the cost of implementing the whole program, in terms of the resources mentioned above; and have made proposals for implementing this program over a three year period.

# 2 PREMISES OF OUR PROGRAM

In light of our contacts with UNESCO and IFIP experts, and based on our bibliographic references pertaining to the subject of computer uses in education, we have derived a number of premises, which will guide us throughout the conduct of our study. We present them below.

1. **Introducing Computers by Necessity.** If one considers past experiments, one finds that the most common disease among failed computerization efforts is that they consisted of delivering computer equipement to institutions before ensuring that the receiving institutions felt a strong need for this equipment. To steer clear of such pitfalls, one has to raise the interest of the receiving institutions long before one delivers the goods.
2. **Involve the Interested Parties.** Managers know the golden rule that, in order to gain the cooperation of subordinates, one needs to involve them in the decision process. By virtue of the same rule, we feel that it is necessary to involve the receiving institutions in the decision making that must take place in the process.
3. **Long Term Informatization.** A commonly observed pitfall among previous large scale informatization efforts is that they do not outlast the initial excitement period; students and teachers feel soon that they have done all there is to do with computers, and lose interest in the venture. In our project we must make provisions for keeping users interested, by plugging them firmly in the productive loop. Such provisions consist in particular in exporting sufficient access to the users so that they can exercise their creativity and keep making the most of the equipement and software they have.
4. **The Connection.** In order for the experiment to generate interest and encourage further participation, we feel that there must be a way for users to communicate with others who share their interests and concerns, both inside and outside of the country. Hence we must make provisions for network connection.

5. **National Human Resources.** The implementation of this project requires a great deal of coordination and monitoring, but requires in fact little scientific or technical expertise. So that the whole project can be carried out without technical help from abroad. Using national human resources carries a number of payoffs: a trivial economic payoff; a technological payoff (foster the development of national expertise); a strategic payoff (promote autonomous development).

6. **Avoid Throwing Dinars[‡] at Problems.** We make it a point of honor to make a proposal which involves as little money as possible, out of the belief that the success of such a venture has less to do with buying expensive equipment than with using and exploiting resources (human and material) in a rational fashion.

# 3 THE EDUCATIONAL PROGRAM

We have defined twenty one profiles of education. These profiles differ by the volume of computer science courses, as well as the kinds of computer science courses that must be taught in each of the cycles. Each of the sixty seven faculties of the Tunisian university system is assigned a profile. These profiles are: Agriculture; Architecture; Business Administration; Teaching, Education; Journalism; Letters and Humanities; Psychology and Linguistics; Social Sciences; Philosophy; Medical and Veterinary Sciences; Biology; Chemistry; Sciences of the Earth and Atmosphere; Mathematics; Physics; Statistics; Aeronautics; Chemical Engineering; Civil Engineering; Electrical Engineering; Mechanical Engineering.

Each profile is defined by a set of courses to be taught in the first, second, and third cycle. Each course is, in turn, defined by a course syllabus and one or more textbooks. The twenty one profiles are made up of no more than thirty one courses in total (although they are made up of three to four courses in general), which allows for some standardization, and a large potential for resource sharing.

These courses are divided into four levels: The 100-level courses are introductory courses, with no prerequisites; some of them are self-contained, in that they make up a complete training program of participants, while others form the basis for further upper level courses. The 200-level courses are end-courses for profiles which require little computing exposure and include background courses for profiles which require substantial computing exposure. The 300-level courses are reserved for profiles which require substantial computing exposure, and are usually taught in the third cycle. Also, they deal typically with advanced applications of computing to other fields: expert systems and decisions support systems (useful for management profiles), information retrieval systems (for library science, e.g.), data analysis (for statistics profiles, as well as medical sciences), operations research (for applied mathematicians and decision sciences profiles). Finally the 400-level courses include two categories: research oriented courses, treating subjects that are for the most part current research topics; application oriented courses, dealing with the use of highly specialized software packages.

[‡]The *Dinar* is the Tunisian currency, worth about a US dollar.

# 4 A PROPOSED IMPLEMENTATION

## 4.1 The Survey

We have dispatched a survey form to all sixty seven institutions across the country, and have collected the following information about each one of them:

- The number of students that are registered in the institution, distributed across the three cycles.
- The number of teachers currently working in the institution on a full-time basis, who specialize in computer science (hence are able to teach computer science courses). In the Tunisian educational system, a distinction is made between two categories of teachers: the A-rank teachers, who are responsible for giving lectures (these correspond to *Associate Professors* and *Full Professors*, in a north american context); and the B-rank teachers, who are responsible for such auxiliary tasks as teaching assistance and tutoring (these correspond, in title if not in function, to *Assistant Professors* and *Teaching Assistants* in north america).
- The number of teachers currently working in the institution on a full-time basis, who are convertible to a computing profile. We have, to this effect, defined a number of criteria to determine whether a teacher is convertible to a computing profile.
- The volume of computer equipement currently available in the institution, expressed in a uniform measure. To this effect, we have defined two standards of workstation: an A Station, which is equivalent to an IBM PC AT; and a B station, which is equivalent to a SUN workstation. Our definition of a workstation includes the hardware and software overheads required to hook it up to a network (local, national, regional).

On the basis of this information, as well as some predefined parameters (such as the number of workstation hours per lecture hour, the number of students per workstation, the ratio of teachers of each rank per student, the number of hours that computers are available for use each week, etc..), we have established the cost of the project for each faculty, and for the whole ministry. Below are details of this budget.

## 4.2 Computer Equipement

For each faculty, the number of workstations required to carry out the project is computed on the basis of the following information: the number of students in each cycle; the profile of education that we propose for the faculty; the volume of coursework included in the profile of education that we propose for the faculty, for each cycle; a predefined table indicating for each profile and each cycle within the profile whether A stations or B stations are required; such nationwide standards as, the weekly volume of availability of the computer equipment, the number of hours students must work on the computer for every class hour and the number of students sharing the same machine; and finally the number of workstations of each caliber (A and B) that the faculty already has.

We have found that the ministry needs a total of 1685 A stations, and 1062 B stations. Also, we felt that the acquisition of this number of workstations as turnkey items is quite wasteful; we made the recommendation to the ministry to negociate with manufacturers the possibility of setting up a plant that would mount the stations from some raw form (kits? VLSI boards?) and / or would provide for their maintenance. Finally, we recommended that this equipment be delivered over a period of three years, in such a way as to be always behind the demand.

## 4.3 Hiring New Faculty

The volume of teaching staff to be hired by each faculty is computed on the basis of the following information: the profile of education proposed to the faculty, as well as the number of students in each cycle of the faculty; the nationwide ratios of students per faculty, for each cycle of education and each rank of teachers.

We have found that the ministry needs to hire 77 A rank teachers and 52 B rank teachers.

## 4.4 Training Faculty

As we look at the pool of *convertible* teaching staff, and at the teaching duties that await them, we distinguish between three categories of people:

- Teachers who require only a background training in computer hardware and software to fulfill their teaching duties.
- Teachers who require some advanced training in computer science or engineering in addition to the background training in hardware and software. These would typically be teachers who come from a scientific field that is connected to computer science: mathematics, physics, logic, linguistics, etc...
- Teachers who require some advanced expertise in the use of some software product family in addition to the background training in hardware and software. These would typically come from a scientific or engineering field that makes extensive use of computers, and would have had prior experience with using computers in their work.

To cater for the need of converting these teachers, we have designed three training programs, to be offered to the teachers as intensive courses (typically summer courses, offered during the summer break).

- The *X* training program, which provides a background education in computer hardware and software, and the use of computer equipement for simple programming tasks and for the operation of applications.
- The *Y* training program, which provides some advanced education in some fundamental topics of computer science, such as computer architecture, systems programming, compiling techniques, structured programming, linear programming, operations research, optimisation, etc...

- The *Z* training program, which provides some advanced expertise in the use, operation and customization of some highly specialized software package, such as CAD packages for example.

After accounting for all the convertible teaching staff and assigning educational programs to them, we have found that the ministry needs to plan for the following needs over the next three years: 176 attendants to the X program; 67 attendants to the Y program; and 69 attendants to the Z program.

# 5 CONCLUSION

Our final report was delivered to the ministry in July 1991, and its recommendations is due to be implemented starting in 1992. Hence we have no hindsights to offer as far as the success or failure of our proposals. We do feel reasonably confident about the premises we have taken to make our decisions, however.

The cost of the whole operation is about six million dinars over three years, not including the cost of hiring teachers; this is a major exclusion indeed, but the bottleneck seems to be finding the right people rather than finding the required financial resources. If implemented as proposed, the project will have an important impact on the training of no fewer than an estimated forty thousand students year after year.

**Acknowldegement**

The authors are grateful to Professor M. Charfi, Minister of Science and Learning, for his encouragement. They are also grateful to Professor S. Belaid, *Chargé de Mission* at the Ministry, for his support, cooperation and assistance.

# References

[1] *Computers in Education.* F.B. Lovis and E.D. Tagg, editors. North Holland, 1988.

[2] *Informatics and Education.* R. Lewis and E. D. Tagg, editors. North Holland, 1988.

[3] *Computers in Education.* A. McDougall and C. Dowling, editors. North Holland, 1990.

[4] *Computers in Education.* K. Duncan, D. Harris, editors. North Holland, 1985.

[5] *Computers in Education.* R. Lewis and E.D. Tagg, editors. North Holland, 1981.

[6] *Programme Modulaire pour l'Enseignement de l'Informatique.* UNESCO, 1985.

Education and Society / R. Aiken (Editor)
Information Processing 92, Volume II
Elsevier Science Publishers B.V. (North-Holland)



# University Computer Services: A Third World Experience

Abdallah D. Abdallah and Adnan H. Yahya

Department of Electrical Engineering, Birzeit University, Birzeit-West Bank

**ABSTRACT**

This paper discusses the state of computing in Third World institutions of higher education. It gives the characteristic features of computing services, the problems they face, their possible paths of development and offers a model for computerization in a Third World university. This model is directed towards more efficient utilization of the available resources and extending services to additional sectors of the university community. It also offers a set of suggestions that can help improve university computer services. The material presented here is based on a study of the case of one of the West Bank institutions. The choice of the studied school was made to reflect the kind of issues faced by other local universities in the area of computing services. We believe that many of the issues and problems addressed here are characteristic of the situation of computing services in many Third World institutions of higher learning.

Keyword Codes: K.3.1; K.4.1; K.4.3
Keywords: Computer Uses in Education; Public Policy Issues; Organizational Impacts;

## 1. INTRODUCTION AND BACKGROUND MATERIAL:

The use of information technology is expanding in all sectors of activities in most developing nations. Computers are playing an increasingly important role in many enterprises including educational institutions. Despite the relatively large investment, computer services in developing nations do not generally meet the expectations.

Computer services in institutions of higher learning suffer from many of the problems faced in other enterprises[2,4,10]. To make our study of educational computer services in developing nations more general we surveyed these services at all educational institutions in the West Bank and selected for detailed study an institution that has an established and separately operating computer center offering services to administrative and academic users, with an outlined multi-year plan for computerization and a reasonable student enrollment and faculty numbers. While the computer services at many educational institutions may face many problems besides those discussed here due to lesser expertise or other special circumstances, we believe that the issues addressed here will be faced by most services at one stage or another.

The initial computerization plan of the selected institution were based on a projected student enrollment of 5000 and a faculty of around 300. The university has 4 colleges: science, commerce, arts and engineering, as well as a moderately sized library, a research center, several community service units and the traditional administrative units of an educational institution but no graduate programs in any discipline. The computer center has been functioning for 12 years[5]. The study of the experience of this center is vital because of the following reasons:

-The center was the first unit in the university to introduce computer equipment;

-A relatively large number of computer specialists is concentrated in the center;
-The main computing facilities are located and operated at that center;
-The center provides computing services to all sectors of the university;
-The management of the center reports directly to the highest administrative level and the services provided by the center reflect the policy and give a good indication of the direction adopted by the university administration in this field.

Through the many years of operation of the center one can detect the following:

-no substantial changes or development to the provided services and their quality have been observed. A good example is the quality of the outputs of the computer systems that are still as bad as they were ten years ago. The work of the center has been limited to maintaining the bad system without attempting to find radical solutions to the existing problems;

-at all times there has been a reasonable number of computer professionals at the center who could improve the provided services; we believe that the performance level of the center does not reflect the capabilities and potential of its staff;

-no chances have been provided to raise the technical level of the members of staff through sending them to attend specialized workshops and other forums. On the other side no sufficient incentives have been given to them. This led to the continuous leak of computer professionals from the center and to great instability in the staff;

-although the center had conducted a few training courses to the employees and academic staff of the university, the contents of these courses did not exceed the basics of DOS and word-processing, and the center's contribution to raising the general computer literacy level of the university community is minimal and not sufficient.

## 2. THE CHARACTERISTICS OF COMPUTER SERVICES:

1- From the beginning of computer introduction to the university there had been a concentration on providing computer services to the administrative sector. On the other hand there had been an almost total neglect of academic computing. There are no computing facilities dedicated to the service of academic staff and there is also a shortage in the services provided to the students. Students have no free access to university computing facilities and the services provided to them do not exceed the support for programming courses which are taken by the students of science and engineering only. The students of arts, and until this year of business, do not take any computer related courses nor have any access to computers.

There is no computer network within the university and no resource sharing between various departments. Resource sharing is a very important issue especially in small universities with limited funding[8]. The different units do not use compatible computers and/or compatible software packages. This leads to the redundancy in data storage, violation of database integrity and the repetition of the same efforts at different sites on the campus. The only transfer of data between the different university units is being accomplished through physical transfer of computer media.

2- Advanced technological means and computer accessories are not used for reasons not related to funding issues. Remote communications with computer facilities via telephone is not practiced, although the situation in the West Bank forces the university employees to stay away from work for long periods due to closures and curfews imposed by military occupying forces which makes such means of communications very important to access computer facilities.

There exists no national computer networks and the university is not connected to any external data networks. This prevents academic and administrative staff from efficiently contacting colleagues in other universities and sharing information with them. Modern software packages and programming techniques are not used.

3- The underutilization of computers. Computers work for limited hours and they are not used to full capacity even during their working hours. Full systems are completely dedicated to data input/output operations. For example a super mini was used exclusively for data entry purposes in the university library for more than one year. This is especially odd in view of the shortage in computer resources.

4- Planning for computer services is very weak. Decisions about equipment acquisition are made on the spot when a funding opportunity appears without prior analysis and planning of the real computing needs of the institution. Purchase of new equipment is made when the old equipment is about to stop operating or after it has stopped which results in operational difficulties during conversion periods.

The expectations of the administration from computerization is neither high nor ambitious. The administration is unable to evaluate the performance of the computer center on scientific basis that takes into account the returns on the large investments in computing. The limited evaluation is based on nonqualitative assessment of success and failure. This is characteristic to the situation in Third World countries.

Sometimes decisions concerning computer related activities are taken without coordination with the side responsible for providing computer services.

6- The bad quality of the computer outputs and the ignorance of the aspects of human engineering.

Our watch of the number of computer installations in the university on the one hand and the available computer services and their quality on the other shows that there has been a continuous increase in the number of computers with no considerable change in the span and quality of computer services[2]. Programs that were written 10 years ago are still in use at substantial costs despite their poor quality. Old systems are still being used and maintained despite the fact that they have been outdated a long time ago. This leads to very high operating costs. This is not justified in view of the big advances in computer technology which cause university computing facilities to become outdated rather quickly[6].

The above mentioned characteristics of the university computing services lead to the conclusion that these services are very poor, insufficient, lack good planning, unbalanced and inefficient.

## 3. THE SOURCES OF PROBLEMS IN UNIVERSITY COMPUTING:

The sources of the problems facing university computerization can be divided into two groups:

1- The first group is a product of the conditions that prevail in the occupied territories. They include the instability of the situation in the country, the short work day, the inability of the employees to reach working places as a result of the repressive measures undertaken by the occupying authorities such as closure of universities and curfews imposed on towns and villages and restrictions on movement. This results in the worsening of the work conditions and the need to put computer installation in badly prepared locations in which the requirements for proper functioning are not maintained. On the other side this limits the access to and utilization of the installations. Restrictions on money flow and taxes imposed on educational institutions make financing purchases of computer resources very difficult[2].

Although this group of problems is specific to the universities in the West Bank, some of the problems encountered here are faced by universities in some politically unstable Third World countries.

2- The second group of problems is a product of internal factors and solving them depends on the intention of the decision making bodies in the university. Here we will focus on this group of problems as they are the ones that can be solved by using the same available resources without substantial additional costs[2]. This group includes :

*a- Computer policy issues:* The absence of a clear policy for computerization. This includes the absence of a computer acquisition policy which outlines the procedures that must be followed for new equipment purchases and the absence of a comprehensive plan for computerization which takes into account the current and future needs of the different departments.

The absence of clear studies of the real needs prior to purchasing the equipment which results in the need to replace or update this equipment shortly after it has been purchased. There is no permanent supervising expert committee to set computer policies and plans for computerization, to supervise the execution of these policies and plans and to assess the work of the computer center and other units that have and use computers in the university. No special attention is given to assigning a computer professional to supervise the university computer services.

There are no sufficient incentives to attract good computer professionals and to retain them in the university. The university is unable to compete with the private sector in this respect.

*b- Computer literacy issues:* The low level of computer literacy among the decision making bodies leads to uninformed, and frequently incorrect decisions concerning the university computerization and many of the problems facing computing services can be traced to this factor.

Computer literacy of the academic staff has a great impact on the level and quality of the offered computing services[7]. This is not only because the top administration of the university is usually drawn from the faculty members. The higher the level of computer literacy of individuals the better will be the recognition of their exact real needs, as well as the more accurate will be their assessment of the offered computer services.

A survey of computer literacy was conducted among the faculty of studied university. The results point to the low level of computer literacy among the academic staff. More than 40% of the faculty members did not take any computer course or training course in computer usage. Their main source of information about computers is the media and individual efforts. Nevertheless the majority of the faculty feel that the level of computing services offered to them is very bad and insufficient. They feel that better services could be offered using the available resources. The majority feel that they need general computer education as well as computer training courses. The faculty members were not sure about their exact needs of computer services which is due to their level of computer literacy and their inability to assess the potential of computers to help them in the fields of their work and specialization. The negative evaluation of the offered services reflects a feeling that the needs of faculty members are being ignored and that nobody cares about raising their level of knowledge in computer related topics and applications rather than a reflection of the knowledge that computing services are not up to the required standards.

Raising the level of computer literacy of the faculty will help them in their daily work and will affect the level of the offered computer services:

-it will stimulate the knowledge and recognition of the importance of using computers;

-it will result in informed specific demand on specialized software packages and advanced computing facilities;

-it will affect course development to take advantage of the use of this important technology in classes[3] and will lead to offering more computer related courses which in turn raises the general level of computer literacy in the university;

-it will put pressure from the academic body on the administration to limit improper computer policies and to improve the efficiency of resource usage and consequently improve the computer services.

## 4. TOWARDS MEETING THE NEEDS IN COMPUTING SERVICES:

An institution needs to have a vision about the ultimate status of the computing services to be able to do short and long term planning and acquisition of information technology resources. We believe that these services need to cater for the immediate needs of students, faculty and administrative staff including computer literacy activities and allow for development activities in the data-processing area. They must also be able to offer services to the surrounding communities due to the important role played by educational institutions in developing nations in the process of technological development of their environment[9]. The vision must be based on realistic estimates of the student enrollment, course and program offerings and research and development activities needed for proper functioning of the institution. We believe that the following is a realistic picture of the needed computing services at a developing nation educational institution:

1- A reasonable student/computer seat (PC, terminal, Workstation) ratio. Based on a calculation of 5 hours per week per student ratio and a 40 hour week availability of computing resources the school must have a computer seat for every 8 students. Every teacher must ultimately have his own computer seat but before that and taking into account the present use of computers by teachers the number can be reduced to one seat for every 4 members for the first year climbing to one seat per teacher in 2 years. A computer pool (laboratory) can meet the faculty needs at the earlier stages[2].

2- The computers must be networked internally (within the school) and a link to the outside world must be established. Due to difficulties in connecting to global computer networks, a telephone link (not permanent) can be used to send and receive mail with the outside world. This has the advantage of encouraging communications and sharing of valuable resources between faculty members, with their students and with the outside world and the creation of well-integrated systems rather than bits and pieces of computerized components lacking a reasonable degree of cohesion. Reductions in the cost of storage media, peripheral devices and software can be achieved. The structure of the university and the flow of information will determine the proper topology for the required network which must be chosen very carefully. Access to computer facilities must be achievable from outside the campus to account for physical inaccessibility of systems for long periods.

3- Reliable and adequate support must be provided through computer center personnel and appropriate contracts with hardware and software vendors to ensure proper functioning of systems and the necessary backup facilities in cases of failures of vital systems. Major effort should be directed to grant adequate protection to users and systems including sufficient isolation of administrative files and well-defined rules of access control.

4- A mechanism is needed to guide computer systems acquisition and selection and to study the demands of various campus bodies and to choose the best alternatives to meet these demands at a reasonable cost. The body taking these decisions must have adequate knowledge about the potential and limitations of information technology and the directions of its development to be able to recommend state of the art solutions as opposed to the current practices of sticking to obsolete and unimaginative systems.

5- Computer center staff must be sufficient and qualified to provide consulting to the university community, update and administer the existing systems, conduct research and development activities to cater for the future needs of the administrative and academic units and to offer continuing education programs of different levels to present and potential users and services to the surrounding community.

6- More integration of information technology resources into the educational process is needed to improve the quality of instruction and make up for some of the lacking resources including laboratory equipment[3].

7- A forum is needed to encourage communications between the various participants of the computerization process. This can take the shape of network bulletin boards, a newsletter issued by the computer center and lecture-discussion sessions between the staff of the computer center and the university community as well as organizing local and regional conferences[1].

## 5. SUGGESTIONS AND RECOMMENDATIONS:

Improving educational computing services in developing nations can be achieved through the following:
1- A major effort to raise the level of computer literacy of all members of the university community[11]:
-for the administrative staff through a continuing process of criticism of the present state of affairs in university computing and acquainting the administration with the proper ways of effective utilization of information technology and the possible gains from improved computerization practices as compared to the major losses resulting from the continuation of the current obsolete and inefficient practices.
-for the academic staff to enlist them to fight the incorrect computing practices and press for better and more comprehensive computer services and to encourage them to introduce computers into their instructional and research activities and pass their knowledge to their students.
-for students to enable them to make better use of the available resources as early as possible in their studies and to grant them the necessary skills to face their future tasks which are very likely to involve the use of information technology products.

This activity must be accomplished through a well-designed program with the necessary budgets.
2- The adoption of well-studied computerization policies and detailed plans for the execution of these policies spanning resource acquisition, maintenance, training of users and computer professionals and implementation of computerized systems and updating the adopted plans and policies whenever needed.
3- Establishing a body to supervise the computing services, to draft and/or approve computerization plans and policies and to ensure adherence to them and their execution. A good degree of continuity must be maintained for this body by appointing it for extended periods and avoiding frequent total replacements of its membership. Membership of this body and the direct computing services administration must be entrusted to individuals knowledgeable in the field of computers and capable of understanding the potentials and limitations of information technology and utilizing state of the art solutions to meet the needs of the university.
4- Conducting studies of the level of utilization of existing computer services, exploring unused resources and employing them to meet the needs of the educational institution.
5- Granting all members of the university community more access to computer resources including documentation and extending computer services to more spheres of university activities. Encouraging more members of the university community to participate in the computerization effort by writing programs, suggesting solutions and demanding new services and establishing a mechanism to ensure good communications between users and the administration of the university computing services.
6- encouraging the sharing of resources within individual institutions and between different institutions on the local and international levels and creating the needed mechanisms to facilitate this process. This includes hook-ups to local and international networks and establishing bodies and forums to share resources and expertise[1]. This can help in ensuring backup computing facilities for emergency cases.

## 6. CONCLUSION:

We believe that the continuing discussion of the issues raised in this paper is of crucial importance for more efficient utilization of the existing computer resources and for better returns on future investments in information technology products and infrastructure and directing them to serve the developmental needs of Third World nations. The familiarity of college graduates with good models of information technology exploitation can help propagate sound computerization practices to the various sectors of the national economy. Adequate services provided to students can help their better understanding of the potential and limitations of information technology. Advanced computer services are a major component of a healthy research environment since, in addition to many other benefits, they enable easier contacts of researchers with their counterparts locally and internationally. This can play an important role in the attraction and retention of faculty members which acquires special importance due to the stiff competition for the limited number of potential faculty members who are third world countries' nationals. However, the effort needed to bring these services to an acceptable level is substantial and needs to be based on a scientific study of the matter and the possible approaches to remedy the situation.

## REFERENCES:

1. Abdallah, A. and Yahya, A.; Equity Problems in Information Technology: A Third Word Perspective; *Proceedings of the International Conference on Information Technology*, Tokyo, Japan, October 1990. Part 2, pp. 405-412.
2. Abdallah A. and Yahya, A.; Patterns of University Computing in Developing Nations: The West Bank Experience; *Third Southeastern Small College Computing Conference*, Birmingham, Alabama, U.S.A.; 10--11 November 1989.
3. Balkovich, E., Lerman, S. and Parmelee, R.; Computing in Higher Education: The Athena Experience; *Communications of the ACM*; Vol. 28, No. 11, November 1985. pp. 1214-1224
4. Bennet, J. and Kalman, R.(eds.); *Computers in Developing Nations.* North Holland Publishing Co. 1980.
5. Birzeit University Computer Committee; *A Report on University Computerization.* Birzeit University, Birzeit, West Bank, January, 1983.
6. Elizandro, D., Cagle, M. and Starks, S.; An Implementation Strategy for Academic Computing Facilities in a Small University; *Proceedings of the First Annual South Central Small College Computing Conference*, Austin, Texas,March 1990. pp. 37-46.
7. Masat, F.; *Computer Literacy in Higher Education; AAHE-ERIC/Higher Education.* Report No. 6, 1981. Washington, D.C.: American Association for Higher Education, 1981.
8. Sadowski, B.; Resource Sharing to Enhance Academic Computing. *The Journal of Computing in Small Colleges*, Vol. 5, No.1, September 1989.
9. Yahya, A.; Local Considerations in Computer Science Curricula Development; *Proceedings of the 20th Technical Symposium on Computer Science Education SIGCSE92*, St. Louis, Missouri, U.S.A.; March 1992. PP. 129-129
10. Yahya, A. and Abdallah A.; Computers in Economic Development: The West Bank Case; *Conference on Information Technology in Support of Economic Development*, Khartoum, Sudan, December 9-12, 1990
11. Yahya, A. and Abdallah A.; Some Problems of Computer Literacy in Developing Nations; *EURIT90: Third European Conference on Information Technology and Education*, Herning, Denmark, April 23-27, 1990

Education and Society / R. Aiken (Editor)
Information Processing 92, Volume II
Elsevier Science Publishers B.V. (North-Holland)


# A National Survey of the Pedagogical Uses of Informatics in French Universities

Bernard Dumont

Laboratoire d'Ingénierie Didactique, U.F. de Didactique des Disciplines
Université Paris 7, 2, place Jussieu, 75251 Paris Cedex 05, France

**Abstract**

At the request of the French Ministry of Education, we undertook a survey during the first part of 1991, to evaluate the uses of New Technologies in the French University system's preliminary 2-year diploma (DEUG)[1]. Here are the most important results about the role of Informatics in pedagogy at this particular level.

## 1. FRAMEWORK OF THE STUDY

At the request of French Ministry of Education, we undertook a survey during the first part of 1991, to evaluate the uses of New Technologies at the DEUG[2] level. New Technologies mean all information and communication technologies: video, CAL, CD-ROM, telematics, Databases,... but only if they were directly related to teaching and learning, leaving out administrative uses. Here is limited our report on Informatics, even if nowadays it is sometimes difficult to separate video from Informatics.

The Ministry of Education did not want us to study Centers for Distance Education, medical or language departments.

Our main objective was to report on:

- teaching practices, according to subject and publics,
- the sorts of products,
- the networks and the links within and between universities and or public and private partners,
- problems in creation, use and broadcasting of products,
- Needs, wishes and expectations (especially from the Ministry itself).

There was no evaluation of products or practices.

A group of six persons worked on this study. We listed the names of people we thought they are important in this domain. We met or phoned around 200 colleagues, all around France: teachers, presidents of universities or national associations, head of Informatics workshops,... We wanted direct and human contact with these persons instead of pen and paper inquiry, to go further and deeper in our analysis and to allow our colleagues to express more easily what they are living in their teaching.

## 2. ACTORS

### 2.1. Creators

The best way to characterize creators is to say they are: "few in numbers", "idealistic", "often working in small and isolated groups", but "always very motivated and even passionately dedicated to their work".

Most are in a difficult situation: they seldom receive any institutional reward in terms of career advancement. Only a few can take time from their official schedule to create. They usually don't receive any support or understanding from their own colleagues or university.

More often than not, they work in a team. One of the members must act as a "Jack of all trades": pedagogue-computer scientist, graphist, ergonome,... if they want to complete their project. The ideas come from the group, even if the final product is the work of only one of them (not necessarily a teacher). Products keep up with changes in contents and curricula, often in the area of didactics research.

Often, these creators are pioneers, rescued from different waves of fashion in the education world. In some disciplines such as Chemistry, Physics or Biology, creators are organized enough to meet in congresses or seminars to share ideas and software. Many of them would like to commercialize their products but are quite frustrated about how to do so. We have found some collaborative creation between some universities, sometimes even transdisciplinary cooperation.

### 2.2. Users

The users who are also creators are likely found in Sciences rather than in Humanities departments.

The decision to introduce New Technologies in a curriculum is sometimes a collective one from the department, especially for tutorials. There are also teachers who send their students to work with some software, even when these teachers are not directly involved in the use of that software, it being considered outside of their official duties.

### 2.3. Students

Students, in Sciences or in Humanities, are very concerned with New Technologies. In some cases, they put pressure on their teachers to use some educational software. Even if they are critical, they are also tolerant of software that may not be entertaining or friendly as the ones they are used to on a commercial basis. Students seem to work very easily with these new products and technologies. They are very motivated to use them as soon as they think they can be a help to understanding. It is important to note that student pressure has been the reason for the creation of some software. For instance, in Biology, because of a strong opposition to real experimentation on living animals, some teachers created computerized substitutions.

Among students there is a big demand for educational software: for help, for deeper understanding, for self-training.

Many of them are ready to help younger students in using New Technologies for a small payment.

### 2.4. Networks

There are several very active networks in France. Some are inside a discipline, as in Chemistry, or within a special objective, like Promosciences, for promotion of sciences for instance. Somewhat formal, these structures are playing an important role for information display and software circulation, organizing meetings, data bases, providing newspapers,... Some students' associations are also involved.

## 3. PEDAGOGICAL USES OF INFORMATICS

Several roles for Informatics were observed during the survey. The following categories are not perfectly distinct but are representative of the current situation.

### 3.1. Tutorial and self-directed learning software

These products aim to give students more responsibility and more autonomy in their learning process. In the Paris area, several thousand students use this kind of software every year, for instance in Biology and Computer Science. In the North of France, Lille University is creating tutorials on Trade, using Minitel.

### 3.2. Self-evaluation tests

Although one of the most important aspects of CAL at the beginning, self-evaluation is not very wide spread today. Nevertheless, several Parisian universities are offering such tests in Physics, Chemistry and Mathematics to first year students, with a personal diagnosis afterwards.

### 3.3. Data acquisition and processing software

This kind of product is very developed in Experimental Sciences, even if its use is sometimes controversial for young students.

Such products are available in Physics, Chemistry and Biology. The common idea is the following: an acquisition card enables the user to make experimental measurements, to store and to process them, then to draw curves, diagrams,...

Usually, teachers like these products because:

- students need to be familiar with current techniques of data acquisition and processing in real time, as used in professional laboratories,
- Teachers keep a central role during these tutorials where software has not so much pedagogical features.

### 3.4. Simulation and modeling software

These simulate phenomena that are unlikely to be observed directly and in real time by students, because of security, scale, time, cost,... Some of them, used before tutorials, are a mean of reducing breakage costs later.

Students created some of them as part of a project. Indeed, several teachers ask their students to use their knowledge in programming to build some simulations to solve problems in the discipline that could not be solved without computer.

### 3.5. Graphics, animated images and conceptualization help

All this software can be classified with the label "help for representation". In Mathematics, there are some good examples of such software[3], producing "images" on which it is easier to hypothesize.

In Chemistry, a programme for use in Crystallography is built as a help to visualize in 3D; with it it is possible to create images of crystals and to see them from any angle.

In Physics some software is organized as games to help students "conceptualize".

### 3.6. Professional and desktop software

In some cases, students must be taught how to use the professional software used in industry or research.

For instance, in History or Geography, students are to work with cartography software. They use statistical software in Literature, History, Economy, Agronomy, Biostatistics, Psychology and Geography. In Literature, lexicography software is taught as well as software for analysis and text comparison. In Musicology professional software is used.

In all Humanities Departments visited during the survey, students have to become familiar with word processors, spreadsheets and data base systems.

### 3.7. Pedagogical data bases

Professors have developed, for use in their teaching, some data bases in Humanities (for instance, lexical and literary history data bases) and in Sciences (Chemistry and Physics). Some of them are quite sophisticated, and enable students to make clear some concepts or theoretical models and to build their own representation frames.

### 3.8. Expert-systems and problem solving partners

It seems that "problem solving partners" are mostly developed in Chemistry[4]. Intelligent tutoring Systems are still the subject of research but are not really used in university teaching.

## 4. INFORMATICS CENTERS

The French national plan, "Plan Informatique pour Tous", launched in 1985, seems to get better results at the university level than at the secondary level. Maybe because of the better quality of micro-computers provided then but, above all, by the creation of "computer workshops", well supervised and run by competent people.

Some departments rely completely on these structures, asking their students to go and work there. However, there is much pressure in several universities, from some departments, to have their own rooms with their own equipment. Then the problem is often also to get competent people to help students and to maintain the computers and the software in good condition.

Self-service has many advantages for learning but leads to many problems such as piracy.

Of course, the situation is changing as quickly as hardware does: lower prices, and networking are just two of many reasons for change.

## 5. OBSTACLES

### 5.1. General obstacles

The main obstacle is time. All the colleagues met for this study complained about the lack of time to integrate correctly New Technologies in their teaching, because this sort of activity is not included in their official job description.

There is also lack of training in general for use of as well as creation of software. Many of them need some help to use these new tools in their ordinary practice.

Another problem results from the lack of pluri-annual financial support, especially for acquiring and maintaining hardware.

### 5.2. Obstacles to creation

There are only a few tools for developing educational software and they are usually too expensive for a laboratory budget. They all demand a long period of adaptation from the teacher and, anyway, they also require competence to produce a final and correct programme.

Evolution and changes in hardware add more constraints.

Qualified people to produce good software are often missing in teams that are only made up with teachers.

### 5.3. Obstacles to commercializing

Some products are sold on a ten or more basis. More of them are exchanged between colleagues, often without documentation. The French market for educational software is not flourishing, even at the secondary level. A central structure for information on existing products is missing, as is a structure for commercialize local products at a national level.

### 5.4. Obstacles to use

The main problem is "compatibility", especially with graphic cards.

## 6. THEMES OF REFLECTION

### 6.1. To face real problems

Two main problems met when students begin university studies in France could be partially solved with New Technologies: the rapidly rising number of students in first year and the failure rate after one or two years. It seems that political solutions are taking into account only square meters and number of teachers.

### 6.2. To think about deep resistance

People who use and develop educational software are too much involved in their work, convinced of their ideals and used to working with other colleagues sharing the same objectives. They sometimes forget they are isolated among many teachers who don't believe, for instance, that:

- students must learn how to manipulate software from industry or laboratories,

- New Technologies may be some help for better understanding and a better way of learning,

- computers are not supposed to replace teachers in their fundamental roles,...

Also, some teachers may think, after analyzing their teaching, that these technologies are not suited to their didactical objectives.

## 7. PROPOSALS

### 7.1. To help teachers

The real situation of colleagues must be taken into account on an official level to find a global solution to this problem. People involved in using or creating educational software must officially receive time for these activities, as well as training in methodology and didactics.

The work done by these teachers should be recognized as part of their research production and should be used for their career progression. In France, today, in most disciplines, only research in the subject is accepted, and not research in teaching the subject. This is why the problem is not only an administrative one. Teachers themselves have to change their attitudes.

### 7.2. To organize creation

A national coordination structure must help teachers to create. There is a need for "new blood", and positions must be offered at the university level, for creating and introducing New Technologies in teaching. National and regional projects should be launched to promote global planning and to find enough energy and competence to produce quality software.

### 7.3. To commercialize these new products

This is not the responsibility of teachers. They have to find a structure to help them make their complete products available, with all documentation and accessories, everywhere. There must be some incitement for use even by those who did not create the products.

## 8. TO REACT BEFORE IT IS TOO LATE

People involved in introducing New Technologies in their teaching are less and less numerous. They are getting tired and, in a few years, they will retire. It is time to go from makeshift to professional creation and commercialization, to organize training and information, to recognize the value of such research, for these people, at a personal level, and for universities, at a global level. Problems are real and crucial. They ask for realistic solutions. It is time to react.

---

[1] The full report is available at the above address.

[2] The French University system's preliminary 2-year diploma.

---

[1] The full report is available at the above address.

[2] The French University system's preliminary 2-year diploma

[3] In French they are called "imagiciels" from "images" and "logiciels".

[4] For instance, a software called "Mendeleïev" has been created on the periodical elements' board, in an American and French project, the SERAPHIM PROJECT, including an image data base on videodisk.
The French responsible is Prof. Daniel CABROL, at Nice University.

Education and Society / R. Aiken (Editor)
Information Processing 92, Volume II
Elsevier Science Publishers B.V. (North-Holland)



# Integrating Social Impact and Ethics Issues Across the Computer Science Curriculum

C. D. Martin and H.J. Holz, Electrical Engineering and Computer Science Department, The George Washington University, USA

**Abstract**

A strategy is presented for integrating social and ethical concerns into the computer science undergraduate curriculum through the four-year curriculum. Concerns related to the teaching of ethics in a technical curriculum are addressed. The proposed strategy begins with a first year Computers and Society course with a strong emphasis on ethics. followed by a series of case studies to be presented in subsequent computer science core courses, and a final social and ethical impact study to be included as part of the senior engineering project.

Keyword Codes: K.3.2, K.4.1, K.4.2
Keywords: Computer and Information Science Education, Public Policy Issues, Social Issues

## 1. INTRODUCTION

Computer technology is particularly powerful due to its potential to change how we think about ourselves as human beings, how we make decisions in governance and social policy, and how we save and pass on knowledge. There is a lack of focus in the computer field regarding the integration of social impact awareness and ethical behavior into professional practice. The challenge computer educators face is to develop strategies that will raise the awareness of students regarding ethical and moral issues related to computer technology at the same time that they are developing their technical expertise.

This challenge is particularly difficult given the traditional mindset of technically trained professionals who view social impact and ethics issues as topics auxiliary to the foundation material in computer science. This paper suggests a strategy in which the development of an ethical framework at the freshmen level followed by the integration of social impact and ethics topics throughout the curriculum is viewed as fundamental to the development of competent computer scientists. Presenting these topics in a sufficiently holistic and robust way, contrary to the way that they are now apologetically presented in most curricula, will provide a relevance to the other foundation material that will enhance technical expertise and provide a deeper educational experience for students.

> "...societal and technical aspects of computing are interdependent. Technical issues are best understood (and most effectively taught) in their social context, and the societal aspects of computing are best understood in the context of the underlying technical detail. Far from detracting from the students' learning of technical information, including societal aspects in the computer science curriculum can enhance students' learning, increase their motivation, and deepen their understanding (Miller, 1988, p 37)."

### 1.1 New CS Curriculum Standards

The computer science curriculum is at yet another crossroads with the announcement of the latest set of recommendations, *Computing Curricular 1991*, in February, 1991 by the ACM/ IEEE Computer Society Joint Curriculum Task Force. There has been much discussion regarding the necessity of preparing ethically and socially responsible computer scientists, especially in light of highly publicized computer viruses that have been the source of considerable embarrassment to the profession. To this end the task force articulated a tenth knowledge unit called Social, Ethical and Professional Issues that must now be incorporated in future computer science programs (ACM/IEEE Task Force). Of the 271 hours to be spent on computer science foundation material, it is suggested that 11 hours should be devoted to the knowledge unit on social issues (Turner, 1991). In addition, the social and professional context is viewed as one of three general principles that should frame the entire curriculum (Turner, 1991).

The Computer Science Accreditation Board (CSAB), which has accredited over 100 programs since it was established in 1984, also requires instruction in the social and ethical implications of computing as a criterion for program accreditation. The dilemma arises in implementation of the ethics and social impact strand. Should this strand be present in all computer science courses or should it be taught in a stand-alone course? The new ACM/IEEE curricular recommendations and the CSAB criteria allow the flexibility of either option as long as the material is covered.

### 1.2 Strategies for Implementing a Computers and Society Strand

Three different strategies have been suggested in the past for implementing this strand: the whole course approach, the module in every course approach (Miller, 1988), and the capstone software engineering approach (Gotterbarn, 1991). The advantage of the "whole course" approach is that it insures that ethics and social impact have at least the commitment of a certain number of credit hours in the curriculum. Such a course is usually taught by someone who is committed to and understands the importance of the material. Some question the value of lumping all of the material into one course, implying to students that it is unrelated to the rest of the curriculum. Often students resent taking such a required course since they share the view of some of the Computer Science faculty that it is a "soft" course.

As Johnson has stated, it is important not to communicate the message that "we do computer science here, and, as a separate matter, we think about ethics. The message should be that whenever you do anything, you think about the consequences at the same time (1988, p. 1)." Another problem with the "one course" approach, particularly if it is taught by one professor, is the danger that students may be left with the impression that the attitudes and ethical judgements of that professor are the right answer to the issues. This is especially true if the professor does not have a strong background in philosophy and ethics and does not make a concerted effort to show the students how to evaluate the issues from several perspectives.

The other question that arises with such a course is the placement of the course at the beginning (freshman level) or at the end (senior level) of the curriculum. The modular approach addresses the timing question, since it spreads the material across the curriculum (Miller, 1988). It also addresses the problem of having the material presented from only one point of view. Joseph Weizenbaum, professor of Computer Science at the Massachusetts Institute of Technology, favors the M. I. T. approach of including discussions of social impact and ethics in the context of other computer science courses already in the curriculum to eliminate the tendency of professors "to skip over ethical considerations with the excuse that it is taught in Ethics 101 (DeLoughry, 1989)." However, he recognizes the possibility that such material could receive short shrift in a crammed technical syllabus.

The capstone software engineering course (Gotterbarn, 1991) attempts to deal with the issue within a technical context as the students leave the curriculum. The argument in favor of this approach is that the students will then have the technical understanding to deal with the social and ethical issues and can do so within the context of their own senior project. However, if this is the only time in the curriculum in which social impact and ethics are presented, the students will tend to have only a narrow view of the issues as they relate to a particular project.

## 2. CREATING A SOCIAL AND ETHICAL CONTEXT

A combination of all three approaches should be used throughout a four year program to truly integrate the social and ethical context with the technical context. This represents a curricular commitment of about 30 hours, well beyond the 11 hours required by the new ACM/IEEE curricula, but it more completely captures the spirit of making the social and professional context part of the overall framework of computer science education. The proposed strategy incorporates all three of the approaches previously mentioned across the four year curriculum: a first year Computers and Society course with a strong emphasis on ethics, a series of case studies to be presented in all subsequent technical courses, and a final social / ethical impact analysis to be included with the senior software engineering project.

### 2.1 The Computers and Society Course

The cornerstone of the proposed approach is a required Computers and Society course given in the first year. The purpose of the Computers and Society course is to provide students with 1) an awareness of the social and ethical issues caused by computer technology, 2) the analysis skills to consider how these issues are related to subsequent comptuer courses, and 3) the decision-making tools to deal with the issues as they actually arise in their future professional careers.

### 2.2 Teaching the Ethics Component

A key consideration in integrating ethics and social impact into the curriculum is to come to grips with the issue of how best to teach and incorporate ethics topics. Basic ethical values are learned in the formative years of childhood in the home, church and school. The purpose of specific ethics education, such as computer ethics, should not be to indoctrinate the individual with new values, but to assist individuals "in clarifying and applying their ethical values as they encounter new, complex situations where it may not be obvious how ethical values may apply or where the appropriate application of one of these values may conflict with other ethical values (Parker, et al., 1988, p. 1)." Students must be made to recognize that technology is not value-free, but value-laden. "Any technological decision ...is a value-based decision that not only reflects a particular vision of society but also gives concrete form to it (Christenson, 1986)."

Computer scientists and ethicists have raised serious concerns about how to teach ethics in the computer science curriculum (Bynum, 1991; Gotterbarn, 1991; Miller, 1988; Mahowald & Mahowald, 1982). For example, to what extent do computer science students need to be grounded in "theoretical" as opposed to "practical" ethics? One view is that spending too much time on various ethical frameworks will only confuse students and lead them to believe that there is no right answer. "Not stressing philosophical theory has the advantage of not stressing the apparent lack of agreement among philosophers (Gotterbarn, 1991)." A related concern is that computer science faculty have little experience in teaching ethics. They "may fall into the trap of preaching a moral code of their own instead of raising questions, elaborating possible answers, and exploring justifications (Miller, p. 38)."

Ethics, in fact, cannot be taught; what can be taught is a framework that incorporates personal, social and professional values to be used for evaluating ethical dilemmas and making decisions. In accepting the premise that technology is value-laden, we stress the need to teach a methodology of explicit ethical analysis in all decision-making related to technology.

A preliminary core of ethical precepts has been developed by the computer professional societies in the form of ethics codes. Computer science can borrow the strategy of traditional university ethics courses to use this framework to analyze case studies (Parker, 1988; Veatch, 1977; Weiss, 1982) and readings to arrive at a deeper understanding of the issues through small group discussions.

The metaphysical framework taught is based on a set of classnotes developed by Robert Barger (1989). Barger divides metaphysical theories into four camps: idealist, realist, pragmatist, and existentialist. These four theories are presented within a cartesean coordinate space in which the student is asked to determine where his or her values fit. The framework is presented to help students understand that metaphysics differ by person and culture and to enable students to identify how their viewpoint relates to the viewpoints of others.

Four professional codes of conduct are taught using a paper (Martin & Martin, 1990) that analyzes the four codes for similarities, differences, and efficacy and presents the major themes present in all of the codes. The four ethics theories are then combined with the common themes in the codes of conduct to establish a connection between personal, theoretical and professionals considerations (Figure 1).

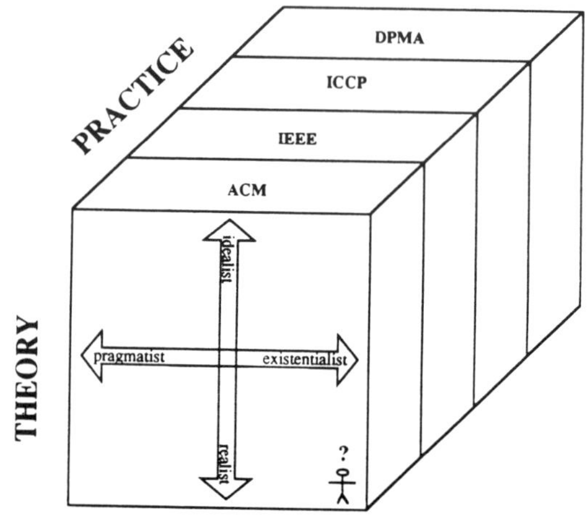


Figure 1: Relating Personal, Theoretical and Professional Ethical Considerations

The ultimate goal is to provide a personalized metaframework (Figure 2) for each student to analyze ethical questions. This framework can be updated as the ethics codes are updated in the future.

### 2.3 Teaching Social Impact Awareness

The second half of the course covers a broad spectrum of topics from the computer field. The content is not static and depends, in part, on the availability of films and guest lecturers. Examples include the role of computers in medicine, computers in the workplace, legal issues in computing, privacy and databases, computer crime, and the history of scientific methodology. Within each topic, ethical and societal issues are identified and discussed in lecture and in a weekly discussion group. Students must pick a topic for a term paper, in which they will explore the ethical and societal issues in more depth.

In addition, sometime during the semester each student must read a science fiction short story and present an ethical analysis of the technological content of the story as related to the topic of the day in their discussion group. The student then gives a written report of their analysis and the discussion group's reaction. The use of science fiction serves several purposes. In general, it is a genre which liberates the reader to explore extrapolated ethical questions, and it reminds the student that non-technical people have been considering the same issues the course addresses for quite some time, in a way that helps to legitimize the undertaking to the student.

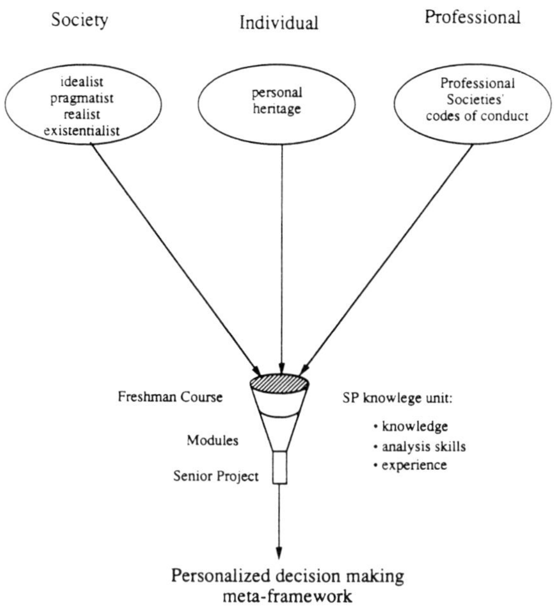


Figure 2: Developing a Meta-framework for Ethical Decision-Making

## 2.4 Social Impact Modules

Miller (1988) has suggested an excellent strategy of incorporating ethical and social impact issues into the traditional technical courses in computer science using a case study approach.

> "The idea is straightforward: the professor distributes or presents material concerning the use of computers [relevant to the particular course being studied] and then students and the professor discuss questions about the material. Cases can be fictionalized scenarios, news items, book excerpts, interviews, and the like. Ideally, the professor should encourage students to questions assumptions and to identify the values at stake in the cases. The case studies can show that technical computer science concepts are intertwined with questions society must ask and answer when people use computers (Miller, 1988, p. 39)"

Miller provides examples of case studies that could be used in traditional courses on computer programming, computer systems, computer organization, file processing, operating systems, data structures and analysis, and programming languages as well as a source list for many other case studies.

Although Miller presented an excellent strategy for incorporating the case studies into the standard curriculum in a way that would not take up in inordinate amount of time in an already crowded curriculum, what was missing was the underlying analysis framework that students would need in order to evaluate the case studies. This problem is aeeressed by providing such an analysis framework in the first year Computers and Society course. By repeatedly being confronted with case studies in courses throughout their four year program, students (and professors)will come to realize that concern about social and ethical issues is an important underlying context in their computer science education. The social and ethical strand will serve as a unifying theme across the curriculum.

### 2.5 Senior Software Engineering Project

The senior software engineering project has been traditionally required in most computer science curricula for the purpose of integrating and personalizing the technical skills which the student has been accumulating for three years. In the new ethical framework proposed in this paper, an ethics component would be added to the senior project. Under the proposed framework, the student enters the senior project with both skills and experience in making ethical and societal analysis of computer related topics.

Two new components are added to the project: an impact statement and an ethics diary. The ethics diary is kept as part of the lab log, listing ethical dilemmas that arose along the way, and the resolution of those dilemmas. (An example of an ethical dilemma might be the lack of time for the student to do adequate testing to insure reliability of the product.) The ethics diary follows the form of the scenario evaluation, in which the student compares personal responses to codes of conduct. The diary forms the basis for the impact statement. The impact statement presents an analysis of the ethical and societal implications of the product. It would discuss such things as the quality, reliability, capabilities and limitations of the product. It would also discuss the impact that the product would have on both primary and secondary users as it relates to their jobs and quality of life.

## 3. DISCUSSION

Implementation of the ideas presented in this paper requires a major commitment of effort on the part of computer science departments to integrate the social and ethical impact of computer technology across the curriculum. Such an effort is both worthwhile and necessary for the future of the computer science profession. Previous efforts to implement only one of the components discussed has resulted in a fragmented and unsatisfactory understanding of the issues on the part of students. By integrating this strand across the four years of the computer science curriculum, departments will send the message to students that ethical and social impact concerns are taken seriously. It will also send a message to future employers of their students that their students will be able to think, discuss and write about technical issues within a social and ethical context.

The most serious problem in implementing this integrated approach across the computer science curriculum is the lack of familiarity that most professors have in locating and preparing materials to deal with the social and ethical issues. What is needed at the outset of such a curricular change is for a single faculty member or committee in a computer science department to be designated to direct the effort and advise the rest of the faculty. This person or committee would be responsible for establishing the syllabus for the first year Computers and Society course, for developing an initial set of scenarios to be used by the rest of the faculty in the other computer science courses, and for establishing a format for the social and ethical impact statement to be included with the senior project. Over time the rest of the faculty would become more comfortable in dealing with the issues and developing their own scenarios as students who were prepared to analyze and discuss the issues moved through the curriculum.

### 3.1 Beyond the Computer Science Curriculum

Computer ethics education is made more complicated because there are computer users at all levels throughout our society. Twenty years ago computers were not nearly so numerous or networked together as they are today. Individuals who controlled computers functioned strictly as computer professionals or computer scientists serving other people by providing them with computer output. Now, because of the widespread use of computers, distinguishing between specialists who work only with computers and those who use them as tools for other disciplines lacks significance. "Computers have become as commonplace as telephones. The related ethical issues have thus become more democratically defined....Ethical principles applied to millions of computer users effectively become the equivalent of common law (Parker, et al., 1988. p. 3)."

This paper has presented a strategy for integrating social and ethical concerns into computer science undergraduate education throughout the four year curriculum by presenting a first year course, a series of case studies to be presented in all technical courses, and a final social and ethical analysis to be included as part of the senior software engineering project. The principles suggested here for putting technical study within the framework of social and ethical impact can be applied to all educational computer settings, and we should demonstrate a commitment to ethical behavior by providing an ethical context across computer education at all levels.

## 4. REFERENCES


ACM / IEEE Joint Curriculum Task Force. *Joint Computing Curricula 1991.* Feb. 1991

Barger, R. N. (1989). "Notes on systematic philosophies." unpublished class notes. Eastern Illinois University Charleston, Illinois 61920

Bynum, T.W. (1991). "Human values and the computer science curriculum." Proceedings of the National Conference on Computing and Values, Southern Connecticut State University, August, 1991.

Christenson, K. E. (1986). "Ethics of information technology." *The Human Edge: Information Technology and Helping People.* Geiss, Gunther and Viswanathan, Narayan (ed.). New York, NY: Haworth Press.

DeLoughry, T. J. (1988) "Failure of colleges to teach computer ethics is called oversight with potentially catastrophic consequences." *The Chronicle of Higher Education,* February 24, 1988, A15.

Gotterbarn, D. (1991). "The capstone course in computer ethics." Proceedings of the National Conference on Computing and Values, Southern Connecticut State University, August, 1991.

Johnson, D. (1988). The ethics of computing *Edutech Report, 4* (5), 1-2.

Mahowald, M.D. & Mahowald, A.P. "Should ethics be taught in a science course?" Hastings Center Report, Vol. 12, no. 4 (August, 1982), 18.

Martin, C. D. and Martin, D. H.(1990). "Professional codes of conduct and computer ethics education." *Social Science Computer Review,* Duke University Press, Spring, 1990(8:1).

Martin, C. D. and Holz, H. J.(1991). " Non-apologetic ethics education: A strategy for integrating social impact and ethics in the CS curriculum." Proceedings of the National Conference on Computers and Values, Univ. of Southern Connecticut, USA, August, 1991.

Miller, K. (1988). "Computer ethics in the curriculum." *Computer Science Education,* 1, 37-52.

Parker, D. B., Swope, S., and Baker, B. N. (1988). Ethical conflicts in information and computer science, technology and business: final report (SRI Project 2609). SRI International, 333 Ravenswood Ave., Menlo Park CA 94025.

Trauth, E. M. (1982). "The professional responsibility of the techknowledgable." *ACM Computers & Society Newsletter ,13* (1), 17-21.

Turner, A. J.(1991). "Summary of the ACM/IEEE-CS joint curriculum task force report: computing curricula, 1991." *Communications of the ACM,* June 1991, Vol. 34, No. 6., 69-84.

Veatch, R. (1977). *Case studies in medical ethics.* Cambridge, MA: Harvard University Press.

Weiss, E. (ed.) (1982). "Self assessment procedure IX: A self assessment procedure dealing with ethics in computing." *Communications of the ACM, 25*(3), 183-95.

Education and Society / R. Aiken (Editor)
Information Processing 92, Volume II
Elsevier Science Publishers B.V. (North-Holland)


# Application Oriented Informatics and Informational Disciplines: A symbiosis bridging the gap

Tom J. van Weert

School of Informatics, Faculty of Mathematics and Informatics, University of Nijmegen, PO Box 9010, 6500 GL Nijmegen, The Netherlands
E-mail: school@cs.kun.nl; fax: +31 80 55 34 50

**Abstract**

Informatics is both a fundamental and an application oriented science. Its applications are to be found everywhere in business and industry and in all kinds of other disciplines. There are four main application areas: business, (technical) processes, languages and knowledge representation. In each of these application areas there are severe problems with quality.
In "Informational Disciplines" there is a close interaction between application oriented informatics and another discipline. Information Engineers educated in these disciplines may well be able to bridge the gap between users and informaticians and help solve the application quality problem.
At Nijmegen University application oriented informatics is taught to both students of informatics and students in "informational disciplines". An extensive software house project brings these students together for professional integration of learned knowledge and skills.

Keyword Codes: J.0; K.3.0; K.3.2
Keywords: Computer Applications, General; Computers and Education, General; Computer and Information Science Education

## 1. INFORMATICS AND ITS APPLICATIONS

### 1.1 What is informatics?

What is *Informatics* or Computer Science? According to Webster's Dictionary, a science is a branch of knowledge or study, especially concerned with establishing and systematizing facts, principles, and methods, as by experiments and hypotheses.

Informatics, like physics, may be pursued as a theoretical science, but also as a science oriented towards the design of applications. According to Webster's, the whole of such applications in society constitutes a technology, in this case *informatics technology*. This technology is used in all kinds of disciplines: in the exact sciences, in medicine, in the social sciences, but also in other technologies.

Sometimes the bond between informatics and another science or technology is so close that the two melt together into an *"informational science"* or an *"information technology"*. An example of such a technology may be found in telecommunication, where traditional communication technology and informatics technology have melted together.

**1.2 Informatics technology in business and industry: technology pull**

In any organization in our industrial society we find two basic processes: the primary process, which encompasses the primary activities, e.g. production activities and the secondary process, which encompasses activities controlling and supporting the primary process, e.g. stock administration.

Introduction of computers into automation was started in the secondary process. And now computerized *information systems* are indispensable in secondary process activities. At first, economy of scale was the target, when simple administrative processes were automated. Miniaturization of computers lead to the stage of informatization where the computer reached the personal work place in the secondary process. Management Information Systems (MIS), Decision Information Systems (DIS), etc. have more or less successfully been developed to support the professional. Now we are moving into the stage of communication where an integrated work place is taking shape in the form of a personal workstation on which an intelligent information system acts as a more or less autonomous agent in a network of other information system processes.

There is a long tradition of mechanical automation of the primary process, but use of computer flexibility in primary process automation is rather novel. The first computers lacked the capacity and the power to handle the quantity of data and the necessarily complicated processing. Informatics technology applications in the primary process are now developing quickly. Computer Assisted Design (CAD), Computer Assisted Manufacturing (CAM), Computer Integrated Manufacturing (CIM), etc. based on robotics, process control and real time-applications have been developed. More and more "Embedded Software" is being build into military and consumer goods. *Technical*, process control *systems* are at now the heart of the primary process.

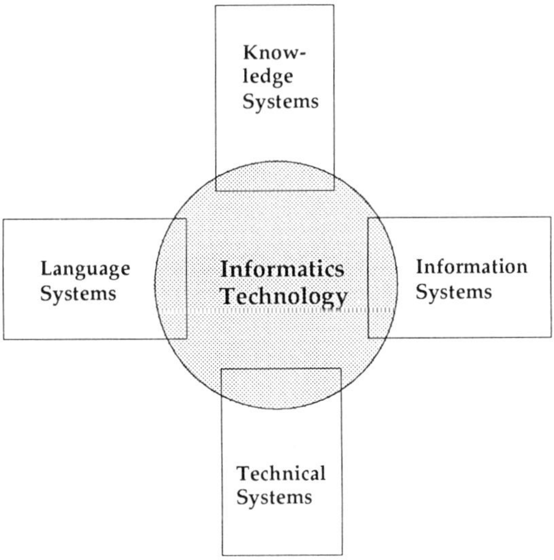


Figure 1 Four main application areas of informatics technology

The organization of production is changing. In the sixties production bureaucracies were still mass producing in their characteristic cost effective way. In the seventies, however, because of a growing demand for flexibility and quality, a change in production organization was needed. Industry is now moving towards an organizational structure consisting of market oriented business units in which primary and secondary process activities are merged. Human activities in the production process are becoming more complex and technology is used to support these activities. From this a strong pull on informatics technology results to provide an integrated, computerized work place, in which information systems and technical systems are combined and which acts as an autonomous agent in a network of integrated work places.

### 1.3 The human factor: technology push

Although much progress has been made, computers at the work place are still not really easy to work with. Humans prefer to communicate in other ways than by moving a "mouse" over icons. In order to upgrade the human-computer interface computer systems must master the understanding and speaking of natural languages. This has made natural languages an important research and application area of informatics.

To be able to understand natural language and to translate between natural languages computers need access to a vast mass of knowledge which has to be organized in a suitable way. Because of this, and other applications, knowledge representation and artificial intelligence also have become important areas of research and application within informatics.

As research [1] shows, promising developments of informatics technology may be expected in *languages systems* and *knowledge systems* in the not too far away future. These developments will provide for a technology push.

## 2. INFORMATIONAL DISCIPLINES

Applications of informatics technology are not only found in business and industry, but also in most sciences. One form of interaction between informatics technology and such other disciplines is that of use. General software tools, such as text processing tools, spread sheets, etc. are used by the professionals in the discipline. But one may also find use of more specialized applications which are aimed at a specific discipline only. All these applications are based on (combinations of) the four main application areas of informatics: information systems, technical systems, language systems and knowledge systems.

Sometimes a much stronger bond exists between a discipline and informatics. It is forged by the use of models, methods and techniques from the science of informatics in the discipline. The scientific questions addressed by an informational discipline are still questions within the domain of that discipline, but the treatment of these questions is impossible without the use of scientific elements from informatics. An informational science or *informational discipline* typically consists of three parts: elements from the discipline itself, elements from application oriented informatics and integrative elements from both.

Take the discipline of medicine as an example. Use is made of specialized medical applications of information systems for the administration of medical records, of specialized technical medical systems to pin-point radiation in the human body, of specialized medical knowledge systems to produce a medical diagnosis. Given time, language systems will allow patients to talk directly to such systems. For effective development of these specialized systems combined medical and informatics know-how is needed, embodied in *informational medicine.*

There is, however, more to an informational discipline than just the development of specialized tools: informational medicine models medical reality. To specify these models medical knowledge is required, but also concepts and methods from informatics. It is in this area of modelling that medicine and informatics integrate.

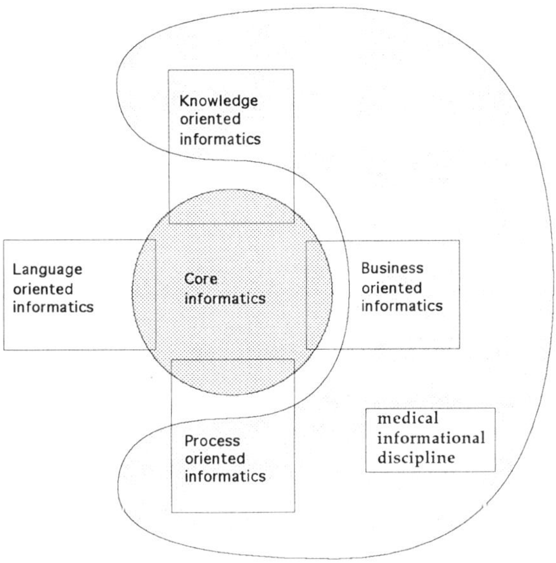


Figure 2 The medical informational discipline in relation to informatics

## 3. INFORMATION ENGINEERS: BRIDGING THE GAP

In the development of new applications of informatics *application oriented informaticians* play an important role using models, methods, techniques, etc. which are relevant to broad classes of applications. The business oriented informatician is involved in designing information systems for business and industry. The process oriented informatician is designing technical systems, the language oriented informatician language systems and the knowledge oriented informatician knowledge systems. These informaticians have only a working knowledge of the particular application area for which they are designing systems.

Applications of information technology are used by people, usually referred to as *"users"*. These users are working with specific aims within an organizational framework. In their work they need the right tools to support them, for instance tools in the form of application software running on standardized computers. These tools used to be build by informaticians, which resulted in user unfriendly behaviour. The gap between user concerns and informatics problem solving was too big: user and informatician were unable to understand each other.

Current informatics applications cover application areas so complex and are so integrated in the organization that their design and their implementation into the organization cannot be left to informaticians only. There is a need for a "*Boundary Spanner*", an expert in the application area, who also has a broad knowledge of information technology. In the design of applications such a "Boundary Spanner" is able to bridge the gap between the future users of the application and the application oriented informatician who is designing the application.

It is typical for the "Boundary Spanner" to play his or her role in the first and last phases of the software life cycle. First there is the development of a Definition of Policy. Then he or she will work in collaboration with an application oriented informatician on the Planning and the

Application Definition. Further on in the cycle criteria for acceptance are developed and the implementation of the application into the organization designed. And in the end of the software life cycle a "Boundary Spanner" will monitor application use.

A "Boundary Spanner" is concerned more with the results of informatics applications than with how to technically realize these results. Therefore the generic name of *Information Engineer* might be considered appropriate.

## 4. THE SITUATION AT NIJMEGEN UNIVERSITY

### 4.1 Informatics and informational disciplines

At Nijmegen University several informational disciplines are found in different departments. For example: Business Information Engineering, Cognition Science and Language, Speech & Informatics. But also Medical Information Engineering, Informational Physics and Informational Chemistry. These informational disciplines educate *information engineers* and their research is aimed at scientific questions for which specialized informatics models and applications have to be developed.

At Nijmegen University both fundamental and *application oriented informaticians* are educated in the Department of Informatics. Application oriented informatics deals with models, methods, techniques, etc. relevant to broad classes of applications. There is business oriented informatics and (technical) process oriented informatics. But also language oriented informatics and knowledge oriented informatics. There is an informatics core encompassing elements common for all application orientations, such as programming, software engineering and theoretical foundations of informatics.

### 4.2 University education in the Netherlands

University education has two phases. The first phase of four nominal years of study (6720 student hours of study) leads to the equivalent of a Master's degree (Doctorandus). After completion a student may find a job in business or industry. The second phase of again four nominal years of study and research work leads to a Doctor's thesis and the Doctor's degree. Only a limited number of Master's students, specifically aiming at a career in research, enters this second phase of university study. Both phases of university education are found at Nijmegen University. It is possible to get both degrees in Informatics, but also in one of the informational sciences.

In the Netherlands there are two types of institute for post-secondary informatics education: (technical) university and higher vocational education. Between the two there are clear distinctions. Where university education is aiming at the novel, at innovations, higher vocational education is aiming at the usual, the current practice in professional life.

### 4.3 University research

In the Informatics Department at the University of Nijmegen research is done in the following areas: fundamental software engineering, computer systems and technical applications (telecommunication systems, real time - systems, neural networks), theoretical informatics and computational models, information systems. The Informatics Department is cooperating in more than 15 international research projects, in some of them as main contractor.

In other departments of Nijmegen University, housing informational disciplines, informatics related research is done, for example: research on knowledge representation and knowledge systems in the Department of Psychology and the Department of Informational Medicine, research on natural language understanding and speaking in the Department of Languages and Speech, research on neural networks in the Department of Medical Physics. Some of this research is done in cooperation with the Informatics Department.

#### 4.4 Education in Application Oriented Informatics, the first phase

Education in application oriented informatics at Nijmegen University is aimed at the four main application areas of informatics. Furthermore, application oriented informaticians should have a working knowledge of the application area in which they will be realizing innovative applications. This implies that the educational programme has to have *breadth* .

In university education modelling and abstraction play an important role. To acquire the necessary skills a student has to specialize. Therefore the educational programme has to have *depth.*

Learning of knowledge and basic skills is one thing, to apply this knowledge expertly to professional problems quite another. University educates experts. This implies that professional problems have to be posed to the students to learn to *integrate* topical knowledge and basic skills into expert insight and skills.

Breadth is implemented by allowing choices. All students start with the same educational programme of core informatics. After either one year (1680 hours of study) or two years (3360 hours of study) they may choose to earn a Master's degree in fundamental informatics, application oriented informatics or in mathematical informatics. Their choice may be reinforced by choosing specific elements from another discipline (800 hours of study required). At the moment business oriented informatics and technical (process) oriented informatics are offered as specializations within application oriented informatics. A specialization in language and knowledge oriented informatics is in preparation. But after one year of study a student may also choose to earn a Master's degree in the informational disciplines Cognition Science (knowledge systems) or Language, Speech & Informatics (language systems).

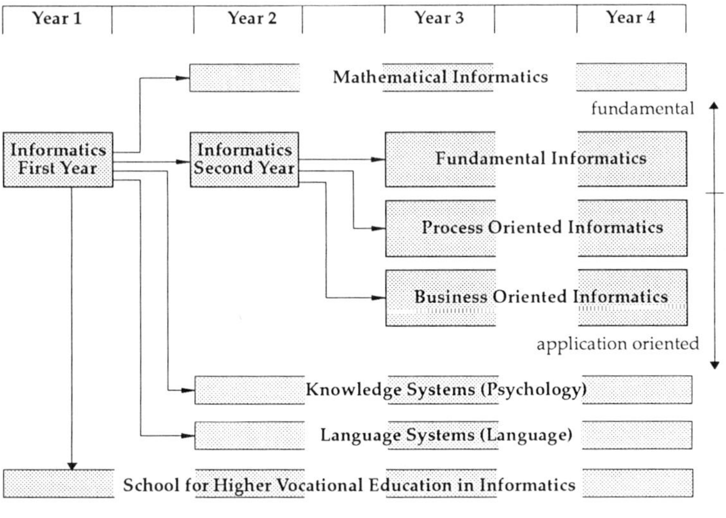


Figure 3 Breadth in informatics education

Depth is achieved through specialized topics and the Master's thesis. A student will take two specialization topics, each requiring 480 hours of study. The last part of the specialization requires professional involvement with the topic. Specialization in another discipline is also required (800 student hours of study). Finally, the student has to write a Master's thesis (840 hours of study) on a specialized topic. The thesis has to be defended in public.

Integration is achieved by a professional case study and the Master's thesis. Students in application oriented informatics will do a professional case study in which they will play a professional role in each of the phases of the software life cycle: together the students operate as a *professional software house*. Real applications have to be designed and realized including an appropriate user interface and professional documentation. These applications are build for real customers within university and cover all application areas. Students studying informational disciplines in other departments of Nijmegen University are taking part in the student software house as information engineers. Supporting the case study informatics students will also receive software engineering education; the total time spend on both will be about 1000 hours of study. Aim is to offer the students a software engineering education along the lines set out in [2] while they are working on a real problem in an integrative way. Team-work, planning, communication and presentation are learned, but also cooperation between informatician and information engineer.

When working on the Master's thesis a student has to integrate knowledge and skills to scientifically address a specific professional problem. The individual results have to be professionally presented, both in writing and in a lecture for a critical audience.

The following topics are covered in the curriculum of application oriented informatics: Mathematics (1040 hours of study), Theoretical informatics (320 hrs), Computer systems (480 hrs), Systems and organizations (160 hrs), Programming (640 hrs), Software engineering (480 hrs), Student software house (520 hrs), Societal issues and philosophy (280 hrs), specialization in application oriented informatics (2 x 480 hrs), specialization in an informational discipline (800 hrs), Master's thesis (840 hrs), free choice (160 hrs), miscellaneous (40 hrs).

### 4.5 Application Oriented Informatics education in informational disciplines

Students at Nijmegen University may follow first phase education in informatics, but also may choose to earn a Master's degree in an informational discipline. In the curicula of these informational disciplines three parts may be identified: elements from the discipline itself, elements from application oriented informatics and integrative elements in which elements from the discipline and from informatics are integrated.

About 800 hours of study in application oriented informatics will typically be found as part of these curicula. The topics covered are programming and data structures, modelling, interfacing and software engineering. For the students in informational disciplines education in these topics is in most cases offered in special courses which are provided by the Informatics Department. The treatment of the topics in these courses differs for the different application areas: business, technical, language and knowledge applications. In some informational disciplines a professional case study forms part of the software engineering education. In this case study future Information Engineers cooperate with students of application oriented informatics in a student software house and learn how to bridge the gap.

## 5. REFERENCES


[1] D. Straub & J. Wetherbe, Information technologies in the 1990's: An organizational impact perspective, Communications of the ACM (32, 11) (1989) 1328 - 1339.

[2] G. Pomberger, Software Engineering education - Adjusting our sails, in: F.Lovis, ed., Informatics at the university level: Teaching advanced subjects in the future, proceedings of the IFIP WG 3.2 working conference (Elsevier, Amsterdam, 1992), in print.

Education and Society / R. Aiken (Editor)
Information Processing 92, Volume II
Elsevier Science Publishers B.V. (North-Holland)



# Harmonising Information Technology Curricula with the Needs of Industry: An Australian Approach

Judith H. Hammond, F.A.C.S.

School of Computing Sciences, University of Technology, Sydney, P.O. Box 123, Broadway, Australia 2007

**Abstract**

This paper discusses a national Australian study, focussing on industry's assessment of its education and training needs for computing professionals for the next ten years. The study identifies the skills and knowledge required, what tasks are currently performed and the context in which these tasks are performed. The analysis, together with known technological advances, predicts tasks that will be important for the computing industry in the future. The study provides a benchmark for educators, trainers and curriculum developers to develop new curricula harmonising with industry needs.

**Keyword Codes:** K.1; K.3.2; K.7.1
**Keywords:** Computer Education, Computer Industry, Occupations

## 1. THE CHANGING EDUCATION SCENE

Information technology is now fast becoming integrated into the core of all business and industry. Government documents in many countries spell out national and global IT strategies. If these strategic plans are to succeed, it is vital that IT education and training remains relevant and that IT curricula harmonise with industry needs. Typically, educational responses (if any) to industry's criticisms of poorly trained graduating professionals have been to expand the number of subjects and courses offered, either within a computing science discipline or by proliferating courses in other disciplines. Where traditional views of computer science held sway from the 1960s to the 1980s, it is now clear that substantial changes are needed. Educational planners and curriculum developers need to devise programmes with more than an anecdotal, informal understanding of industry needs (1).

This paper discusses an Australian federal government Department of Employment, Education and Training (DEET) initiative to provide a solid base for educators and curriculum developers to better understand industry needs. Between 1988 and 1990, DEET conducted a national study on education and training needs for computing professionals (2), in terms of the content and context of current and future computing work and industry's commitment to future developments which may require redirecting educational initiatives.

## 2. AIMS OF THE STUDY

The DEET study * was initiated because of an increasing belief that the shortage of computing professionals was shifting from one of massive numbers to one of specific skills. If this was true, then it would greatly affect future government education and training policies and strategies. The DEET project was initiated to research the views of industry about its education and training needs for the next ten years, with the hope that the results would lead to more relevant curricula and more practical career path guidance.

The study concentrated on the *computing industry*, which was defined as "involved in the use of this (information) technology to achieve business objectives"(3). The definition of the *IT industry*, was defined as "involved in the design, development, manufacture and marketing of information technology" and was not addressed in the study.

The main aim of the DEET study was to provide curriculum developers with a comprehensive, detailed, authoritative analysis of the skills and knowledge which were required by computing people currently and in the future, as perceived by industry. This was achieved by identifying the current skills and theoretical knowledge required by industry and those likely to be required in the next ten years; and the skills and knowledge that education should provide to take advantage of IT developments as they emerged. Guidance was provided for curriculum developers on the range and level of skills and knowledge expected by industry of its applicants prior to entering the workforce and of its employees by way of continuing education and training.

Current training patterns, internal and external to computing organisations, were to be ascertained and the quantity, quality and content of this training reviewed. Thus curriculum developers and training providers could be provided with a benchmark for developing new programmes.

## 3. METHODOLOGY

A three phase approach provided data on present work requirements and projections of tasks for the next decade. These were an environmental scan, surveys on the current situation and a three-round Delphi future needs phase.

The environmental scan provided details about recent and impending developments in IT and the skills and training implications demanded by those developments, as seen by industry. A literature review was undertaken and two workshops, involving an expert group employed in the computing industry, was conducted. The main issues addressed were the definition of computing professional classifications, the experts' perceptions of the supply and demand for computing professionals over the next ten years, an understanding of the current scope and potential for the industry and the likely impact of technological developments on the computing industry.

The second phase consisted of surveying the current state of the industry by telephone and task analysis surveys, interviews, questionnaires, panel sessions. Current employment, education and training patterns were

---

* The author was a member of the Federal Government selected Steering Committee for this DEET study.

assessed, and data gathered on tasks which would generate task projections and training needs. The telephone survey involved over 400 computing companies in all industry sectors (totalling nearly 7000 computing personnel). It ascertained the nature of the current employment of computing people, the projected changes in demand in the near future, and the current extent of industry based training. A task analysis mail survey, listing 253 tasks was sent to 220 computing professionals in about 200 organisations selected from all industry sectors. This provided data about the tasks performed by each classification of computing professionals, the importance attached to each task, the source of training for tasks and current career paths. From this information, future requirements could be investigated.

The three round Delphi future needs phase centred on future education and training needs. It involved fifty industry and education experts reviewing the skill mix requirements, projections and other key factors uncovered in the first two phases and arriving at a consensus for the future. In the first round, the experts rated future advances in their own area of IT expertise (such as knowledge based technology, user interfaces) against the current task/skill mix of computing personnel. These mixes were modified in the second Delphi round against the technological advances likely to occur by the late 1990s. Finally, the experts stated how they saw the general nature of IT work changing in the future. The Delphi technique succeeded in establishing a consensus about technological developments and their implications for education and training, thus laying a foundation for curriculum developers to build courses more closely harmonising with future industry needs.

Finally the task data for present work requirements and projections of tasks for the next decade were subjected to a training needs assessment, with a view to enabling detailed knowledge and skill requirements to be fed into curriculum development processes.

## 4. FINDINGS

It is impossible to detail all the findings of such a comprehensive study. Some significant findings are described, focussing on industry's education and training needs in terms of the content of the current computing workforce, the context in which computing people work, and industry's corporate strategies and plans involving immediate and long-term commitment to IT.

### 4.1. Content of the current computing workforce

The study reviewed job classifications for computing occupations including those used in other studies, and by consultation with experts. The following fourteen job classifications were determined:

| | | |
|---|---|---|
| Data Processing Manager | Database Manager | Systems Manager |
| Systems Analyst | MIS Manager | Programmer |
| Systems Programmer | Computer Engineer | Computer Technician |
| Communications Specialist | Technical Support Specialist | Systems Trainer |
| Other Technical Experts | Computer Sales and Marketing | |

The next step located a cross section of computing professionals in the required occupations at a large number of sites. Most professionals were employed in medium to large organisations. Small organisations (<50 people) tended not to employ computing professionals, but used technologies that were either self-supporting or supported by contractors or similar personnel. Programmers and systems analysts dominated employment - more than 50% of all computing staff. The most rapid increases were technical support, communication specialists and system trainers.

The major employers of computer professionals were finance, property and business services (40%), followed by wholesale/retail (16%) and public administration and defence (12%). The size and types of computers used by organisations indicated that 95% of organisations used personal computers (valued at less than $Aus12,000), 64% used small mainframes ($Aus12,000 to $Aus150,000), 69% used medium computers ($Aus150,000 to $Aus1.5mill) and 19% used large computers (greater than $ Aus150,000).

The average time allocated to internal training in organisations was about 5% of a person's average working hours, and for external training was less than 4%. Tertiary qualifications were held by 48% of computing professionals, with 62% of these qualifications being in computer science. Overall, the study found that only 30% of all computing professionals held qualifications in computer science. This suggests that, when selecting new employees for computing jobs, other recruitment criteria have more importance than the knowledge gained in a computer science degree.

### 4.2. Context in which Computing People Work

The context provides a basis on which curriculum developers can integrate different types of computing work into more relevant computing curricula.

| Management Major Class of Tasks | Analyst-Programmer Major Class of Tasks | Technical and Support Major Class of Tasks | Other Major Class of Tasks |
|---|---|---|---|
| 1 project management | 5 acceptance testing | 9 network architecture management | 14 training |
| 2 departmental management | 6 application design | 10 technical support & sales | 15 marketing |
| 3 applications management | 7 project leadership | 11 service support | |
| 4 data management | 8 programming | 12 operations | |
| | | 13 user documentation | |

Figure 1. Task Groups within Major Classes of Tasks

Fig. 1 shows fifteen task groups, each one representing a logical unit of work, in terms of four major classes of tasks. They came from the 14 job classifications noted earlier and determined the work performed by people in each classification. Four major classes of tasks were determined, each one containing several task groups typifying the functions of the group.

It became clear that task groups described the work of computing people more accurately than job titles. Many task groups overlapped significantly, even though they were not associated with a particular job. For example, project management was found in several task groups. Operations was performed in most jobs, whereas other tasks, such as training, were not. Therefore, it was decide that it was more accurate and meaningful to interpret the findings in terms of task groups as logical units of work rather than job titles. This was expected to result in a more reliable interpretation of future skills and knowledge required.

The frequency with which tasks were done varied greatly between jobs. The most common task was reading periodicals, trade journals, and technical literature to keep up to date (performed by 83% of the sample), followed by determining clients/users' needs (63%), identifying problems in a system (63%), providing advice to management (63%) and assisting users (66%). The tasks computing people performed least often numbered thirteen and tended to be the mundane tasks such as designing work units (5%), writing a report on the number of service calls received (2%) and providing advice on cataloguing equipment (3%). These tasks were frequently done by specific groups, such as trainers, sales and marketing personnel and computer technicians.

An analysis of the relationship between the various major task groups and the overlap between tasks found that there was considerable overlap in the time spent on various functions. For example, data processing managers spent most of their time on operations, with departmental and project management, application design and project leadership also being important. The functions of this group were more widespread than most other job classifications. As expected, project management and departmental management had a marked correlation.

Occupational groups spent little time on just one task group. Most respondents spent some time on all task groups. For example, the mean time spent by all occupational groups was greatest for operations, programming, applications design, project leadership and project management. The least time spent was on service support, marketing and training. This highlights the varied nature of computing work and suggests that multi-skilling is common, an important factor when developing curricula to ensure a broad range of programmes and delivery systems. Generalised training programmes may be needed across several areas of the functions typically performed in one job classification. On the other hand, programmers, computer technicians and systems trainers, with more specialised jobs, may need more specific programmes.

The type of industry was not found to be important in deciding the types of computing tasks performed, whereas the size of the company was. Large firms spent far more time on project and data management. Programming was more important in small firms.

One method for identifying the context in which computing people work was by correlating age, sex and work experience with tasks done within task groups. It was confirmed that most computing professionals were male and most system trainers were female. Most females were employed in entry-level jobs, as were young inexperienced males. Females spent more time on entry-level tasks relating to programming and service support than males who spent more time on network architecture and project management.

With increased age and experience, functions such as marketing, project management and other management tasks assumed more importance. Whereas more experienced (>12 months in a job classification) males moved into management tasks, females continued the same task patterns as their younger, less experienced counterparts. These findings suggest major shortcomings in terms of productivity, career prospects and the commitment of industry to equal employment opportunities.

### 4.3. Industry's Commitment to IT

When devising curricula, curriculum developers need to know industry's immediate and long-term commitment to use IT as part of corporate strategies. Industry plans for future training needs are not as long term as those of educators, who normally work on a five or more year time span. When asking respondent companies to predict skill patterns in two or more years' time, they were very clear about what they needed now, less clear about two years on and even more unsure for the longer-term.

So the Delphi phase of the study was planned to articulate industry's views on future developments in IT and future skills required for its workforce. Industry experts identified IT developments in their own area of expertise and in the fifteen task groups used in the study. For example, a specific development in the telecommunications and networks technology indicated that experts saw modems as being fully exploited in industry now. ISDN was seen by most experts to be in the early research phase of the development life cycle while others believed that it was already exploited by industry.

Industry experts then predicted how technological advances over the next ten years might affect the nature of work in the fifteen task groups. It was assumed that all current work would be affected to some degree. The question was about the extent of the likely commitment by industry to incorporate technological changes, and how this would be done. A matrix was formed from the experts' predictions, showing the development stage of each technology and its impact on all task groups. The results enabled a consensus to be formed about the effect of IT developments over the next ten years.

Results showed that, for example, analyst-programmer functions would change significantly with developments in languages, knowledge based systems and software development tools impacting project leadership and programming particularly. Technical and support staff would be strongly affected by changes to design, systems architecture, telecommunications and networks and network architecture management, as computers and networks integrated business functions.

Finally, current tasks being done by the task groups were used to identify tasks that future computer people would need to perform and whether they would become more (or less) important or stay in equilibrium over the next ten years. Additional tasks were included where experts believed that technological advances and their impact would introduce new functions.

For example, technological developments were expected to have a relatively low impact on project management. However, the introduction of project management software would lead to a greater emphasis on new tasks, such as business awareness and cost monitoring, risk management, forecasting and project benefits, and could lead to changes in the levels of the organisation at which this task was done. Some tasks, such as developing standards and writing and editing user documentation, would decrease, although this was by no means a unanimous view. Acceptance testing tasks of writing a testing plan and running test routines were expected to disappear altogether.

New courses must take account of technological advances, and of how they are likely to change the context of computing work. Some of the predictions are already realities. Others may not come to fruition until later in the 1990s, if at all. In addition, the current economic recession may have a dramatic influence on the future structure of the computing workforce.

## 5. CONCLUSION

The conclusion of the study addressed training needs and demonstrated how relevant IT curricula may be developed. By defining the skills and knowledge required for particular tasks, the results of the study can be separated into series of study units for specific audience groups. Suggested delivery, techniques, context and issues are addressed. Curriculum developers can work out anticipated demands for specific knowledge and skills in the future, and design curricula that more closely fit industry's future needs.

The DEET education and training needs study is a substantial step toward providing a national long-term, strategic approach to IT education and training and provides a solid base on which to develop new curricula. The results can be critically evaluated, the methodology refined and the study replicated at any future time, accommodating further developments in the computing industry as they become known. Further work is needed to commit industry and education to work together and to develop more appropriate curricula encompassing the knowledge and skills that will lead to a productive and sustainable 21st century.

## 6. ACKNOWLEDGEMENT

I acknowledge that the major source of information on which this paper is based is the national study undertaken by the Economic and Policy Analysis Division of the Department of Employment, Education and Training.

## 7. REFERENCES

1 J. Hammond, Education and Training Needs for Computing Professionals, Education & Computing, North-Holland, Vol. 6 Nos. 1,2, 1990, pp73-80

2 DEET, Education and Training Needs of Computing Professionals and Paraprofessionals in Australia, Australian Government Publishing Service, Canberra, 1990

3 ibid, p. 15

Education and Society / R. Aiken (Editor)
Information Processing 92, Volume II
Elsevier Science Publishers B.V. (North-Holland)


# Strategies for Research - integrating outcomes into practice

Professor Robert Lewis

Chairman IFIP WG3.3 and Coordinator of Research, Neurope Lab, Centre Universitaire et de Recherche d'Archamps, Le Forum, 74166 Archamps, France.

**Abstract**

Those engaged in research have a strong interest in ensuring that their findings become well known. The way in which research outcomes are diffused will depend upon the audience which the researcher views as most important. Not only is there a desire to see that the outcomes are known, but also that they are used. The uses will vary according to the nature of the research being undertaken, perhaps by other researchers but perhaps exploited in industry or in society. The effectiveness of this diffusion process is not purely a matter of good publication practice.

Other factors include the original formulation of the research task and the execution of the research itself. Ahead of such concerns, though probably influenced by them, are questions concerning the strategy which helps to formulate the research agenda and the execution of the research itself.

These issues are discussed in the context of research into the uses of information and communication technologies to support learning and knowledge transfer.

Keyword Codes: K.3.0; K.3.1
Keywords: Computer Uses in Education; Research; Application

## 1. RESEARCH - WHAT AND WHY?

The overall theme of this Congress is labelled "From Research to Practice". As this paper is located in the Informatics and Education Stream it takes as its focus research on the role of information and communications technologies (ICT) in support of learning.

It is first necessary to establish a shared meaning by exploring "what is meant by research?". There are a number of ways of approaching this question depending on the way in which an individual is affected by research activities and outcomes.

### 1.1 The nature of research

A perspective on what counts as research is provided in the book arising from a colloquium organised by the European Science Foundation in 1983 (Hägerstrand, 1985). Having warned the reader that "a scientist working in an established discipline does not face a virgin natural world" and that "a feasible research project can only be achieved in relation to a specific scientific problem within the bounds of a specific scientific speciality", Professor Ziman claims that "a really important discovery is felt over substantial parts of one or more scientific disciplines". He suggests that "the influence of a discovery transcends the conventional boundaries of specialities and disciplines", "that the average 'half-life' of a primary paper in physics is about five years" but gives social scientists hope that "humanistic scholarship may change much more slowly, retaining its basic problem areas and frames for much longer than in the natural sciences" (pp. 8-11). Human behaviour manifests less rapid observable change than many phenomena in most of the natural, even environmental, sciences.

There is another related dimension to what is termed research which fundamentally concerns the audience for research outcomes. A basic distinction may be drawn between personal research and academic research, the latter being the theme of Ziman's remarks. The former is rarely published and may remain the intellectual property of the individual as part of their personal development; maybe this is what is usually called learning. What may distinguish learning from research is that new ideas in the latter are subject to scrutiny and the goal of sharing as well as appropriating meaning is a strong motivating force.

It is impossible to speak of the nature of research without considering the breadth of the field of research and the potential impact of the outcomes. The notion of the 'half-life' of an original paper can be extended to areas or fields of research. Ziman continues his analysis to speak of a 'subfield' having a lifetime of 10 years and broader fields as decaying or being taken over after 20 years. The point is that within the science community there are fashions (not used in a derogatory sense) which change. Those engaged in research need to be aware that, eventually, pursuing a rather narrow field may provide them with neither public acknowledgement nor personal fulfilment.

In terms of audience a useful view is provided by Weinberg's three-level scheme of classification of the effects of research (see Gyllenberg, 1985). Research may have:

- internal impact within its own discipline;
- external interdisciplinary impact on other disciplines;
- impact (either cultural or applied) on society.

The latter level leads to further thought about the 'audience' for research and how agenda for research are set.

**1.2 Agenda setting**

There are key questions which should be considered when formulating a research agenda. Whose research agenda? This may be a matter of who is paying? who are the stakeholders?

The stakeholders will each have their own needs or preoccupations. Maybe it is their position in the academic community; maybe their political authority; the productivity of their enterprise; their professional integrity as practitioners; and so on.

The previous section reflected an academic view. Policy makers may (implicitly) emphasise timescale when they speak of 'strategic' research. One example of this occurs in a UK Government paper (HMSO, 1986) when a strategic research area is defined in terms of social, economic and scientific timeliness as being "an area which promises significant advances in the medium term and will generate new knowledge . . . which must offer clear opportunities for economic exploitation." Very recently such a position was restated when Newby (1992) introduced the Corporate Plan (1992-97) of the Economic and Social Research Council (ESRC) in the UK and was already a feature of an ESRC research programme when justifying, as one of its continuing goals, the establishment of a 'map' of UK expertise:

> *" . . (the map) allows the Programme to match experience and expertise with the stated needs of policy makers and others in search of research partners (eg. European initiatives). Thus the opportunities for UK researchers to resource fundamental and strategic research are increased."* (Lewis, 1989, p. 10)

A critical role in defining the agenda for research is held by those whose professional work could be influenced by the outcomes of research. Such stakeholders are the practitioners who carry the professional responsibility of advancing their field by the adoption or adaptation of the outcomes of research and the products of development.

Once research moves beyond the quest for basic knowledge, that is it moves towards the applicable, even the medium term strategic, its value lies in the exploitation of its outcomes. It will usually be the case that such outcomes bring about pressure for change; but there is a natural human reaction to oppose change as the *status quo* is usually less threatening than the unknown.

If this premiss is accepted, the fear of the unknown needs to be minimised and one way to achieve this is to ensure that those implicated are a part of the rationale for undertaking the research, that is for defining the research agenda. In this way the outcomes are likely to address problems or issues which practitioners regard as important and can associate with readily.

## 2. PRACTICE

The 'practice' which is the underlying domain of this paper is learning and, in particular, the support that ICT may be able to bring to the learning process. It is necessary to review this practice before going further.

Most of what we believe about learning is derived from research which is not related to technology. There has been a recent emphasis on situated learning, on cognitive apprenticeship, scaffolding for learning, theories of language and thought, and the social and cultural dimensions of learning. Research in these areas has little or nothing to do with technology supported learning *per se*. It is important to remember that research and innovative teaching using technology has to carry with it the range of current thinking which stems from developmental psychology. To this must be added theories from the cognitive sciences with notions of learner models and formalisms for knowledge representation and, if we dare, concepts from the neurosciences.

So the unifying task is the formidable one of bringing together these fields of research in a constructive form, the more complex because the various schools of thought in academic circles tend to vary and be deeply entrenched.

One unique feature of IT is that it is considered as more than a passive learning resource. It should be pro-active in stimulating learning, providing feedback which may be to some extent adaptive, even attempting to diagnose misconceptions. The challenge for designers of software environments is to select a role for the technology which best meets their perception of learning needs. The technology can thus be viewed as a near-human partner in providing opportunities for learning.

The literature contains references to the technology 'behaving' in human ways. So in connection with the teacher/mentor role, there is mention of the surrogate teacher, the teacher, learner and computer as a trio, and the computer as having a peer role when reference is made to learner-learner interaction stimulated by the computer. One of the most active areas of research is into human-computer interaction, a particular interest being the case when the human is a learner. All these terms are ones which are unique to learning resources involving the use of computers and communications technologies.

Current educational theory and practice contains one favoured way of stimulating children's learning which is to engage them in problem solving and through that activity to develop understanding. For the children, this is research; the fact that some adult might know the answer is not relevant to their cognitive or manipulative tasks. Of course, children assume that adults (often the teacher) know 'the answer'; this may or may not be the case. In any event the children gain expertise by doing research and the special value of this expertise is often stressed because children develop a sense of owning the knowledge or skill.

Project-based or discovery learning methods blur the distinction between learning and research and in this sense, with children and adults alike, one person's research is another's learning. Perhaps a distinction which holds is that in research there exists a prime objective of sharing outcomes, making them common property; this is not true of learning. However, the cognitive processes remain similar, maybe even the same. The importance of such concerns become clear if learning is viewed as being a continuing process throughout life. Learning in schools is relatively modern and contributes only a small part to human learning. But, it remains a crucial element in providing the foundation for learning throughout life in an information rich world.

So, in considering what is meant by practice in the domain underlying this paper, it is necessary to take a broad view of learning as the role of ICT in the process goes far beyond traditional learning in institutions and may in fact have a far more important role in stimulating the exchange of knowledge in a much more general sense.

## 3. INTEGRATING RESEARCH AND PRACTICE

As discussed above, research outcomes potentially create pressure for change. Traditionally, the stages in research and development work have been roughly:

- identify a topic;
- carry out the work;
- 'sell' the outcome to the users.

These three stages should be compared with the commercial development of a product:

- undertake market research to see what customers want;
- develop a prototype product and obtain feedback from the market;
- adapt, produce and market the product.

The contrast is that at all stages of a commercial development the potential users of the product are engaged throughout the process. Of course, it doesn't always work according to such a theory but the exploitation of a product stands a reasonable chance of success if this process has been followed.

Can this paradigm be applied to research? If it is applied, can we expect research outcomes to have more influence of society? If outcomes have more influence, can we then expect society to be more supportive of the research we undertake? What implications does the paradigm have for the ways in which research is formulated, executed and exploited?

The starting point must be to engage practitioners in the evolution of a shared meaning and understanding of the field of research which is of mutual concern. This is essential if we are to communicate. The second stage must be to examine the perceived needs of practitioners and to join in debate about what are the barriers to progress which are not invincible. A major problem of research, as all new post-graduate students discover, is to define a well-defined, tractable problem which they have a chance of solving, or at least making progress towards a solution.

In 1980, I argued* that we needed time to gain "some years of experience of the use of CAL materials in regular courses (before it is) possible to formulate the questions which research can begin to answer...... In such experimental work it should be accepted that whilst the direct products of such innovation may be of value in the short-tern, the real gain will be in enhancing our understanding of the various mechanisms for learning involved."

---

* 'A pragmatic approach to advances in CAL' - invited paper at the Third Canadian Symposium on Instructional Technology, Vancouver, February 1980.

However, there is a stage, now reached, when substantive research is needed:

> *"The uncertain pragmatics of early work on classroom technologies must now give way to more clearly defined studies. Cognitive science, which promises to provide the basic concepts for work on teaching and learning, is now achieving some maturity. Nevertheless, present work remains somewhat scattered. Whilst diversity of approach is undoubtedly important when new problems are to be solved, the failure to invest in broadly managed programmes across this multidisciplinary field inhibits the development of 'critical mass' and the emergence of directions for change.*
>
> *The potential of this work will fail to be realised unless the most exciting lines of research are communicated in a way which makes them accessible to practitioners for wider trial and evaluation. In order to achieve this we need to bond some of the best research in cognitive science to that on classroom learning to the benefit of both areas of study."*
>
> (Lewis, 1989, p. 3)

As proposed above, defining a research agenda in any new field is a complex task and may require some years of pragmatism in order to establish what are the researchable issues and what priority should be placed upon them. This approach was taken in the field of IT uses to support learning as practitioners (teachers in this case) have been involved in creating those pragmatic experiences and then in contributing to the agenda setting. The more that this can be done, the better chance there is for the outcomes of research to be usable.

But the engagement of practitioners does not have to stop at the agenda setting stage. Experience of 'action research' over the last ten years has indicated that teachers make excellent co-researchers, bringing to the research activity a sensitivity of classrooms and of children's development. What is more, such practitioners are also able to communicate the outcomes of research to peers in ways which help the community at large feel a sense of ownership of the outcomes. Research outcomes will then not be imposed by clever, out-of-touch outsiders but negotiable with members of their own close community.

This scenario of an integrated 'research and practice' community has been achieved in a number of specific situations. Schwartz and colleagues (Educational Technology Center, 1988) report of work in Massachusetts and there are many examples of action research by teachers including that reported in the UK by (Eraut and Hoyles, 1989) and Portugal (Dias de Figueiredo, 1989). But such experiences are hard to institutionalise and generalise. How much can ICT itself assist in creating scenarios of this kind within the existing structures of research and practice?

## 5. LEARNING COMMUNITIES

Taking a new look at organisations and how knowledge within them can be exploited may offer some indication of ways which may be explored in creating learning communities. This is the approach being taken at Neurope Lab.

Neurope Lab is a non-profit international research and development centre focussed on the development of tools, technology and services to accelerate the process of learning and to support the management of knowledge as a fundamental corporate and community asset. It is a part of the Centre Universitaire et de Recherche d'Archamps (the French Geneva Campus) situated on the International Business Park at Archamps close to Geneva.

Neurope Lab is concerned with the formalisation and organisation of knowledge, the integration of technologies and methods to support an open learning network and the impact on society of the transition to the knowledge age.

Neurope Lab operates research projects and activities along four tightly coupled lines of enquiry:

- Open Learning, and the development of advanced approaches to knowledge transfer;
- Technologies of intelligence, and the development of new visual interfaces and applications of visualisation and simulation. Groupware, collaborative work technology, computer-mediated conferencing;
- Knowledge engineering applied to management, and the understanding, capture, retention and transfer of knowledge in the context of modern management;
- Economy of knowledge, and the valuation, protection and management of knowledge as a corporate asset.

In each field, the emphasis is on professionally run, practical research and the early development of technology-based tools and products to support the learning organisations.

A major project at Neurope Lab is supported within the European DELTA Programme*. The objective of the 'Just-in-Time Open Learning' (JITOL) Project is to develop and evaluate a learning environment for the professional development of individuals. The environment is based upon information-technology consisting of a telematic network linking and making accessible computer resources including data and knowledge bases, and using conferencing and communications software to facilitate access to human tutors and co-learners.

The underlying rationale has two aspects. Firstly, learning is basically a dynamic and continuous process. Therefore, structured courses at fixed times do not correspond to the nature of learning needs. A continuously evolving, interactive open learning environment is more appropriate.

Secondly, today's state of knowledge is becoming increasingly complex, quantitatively difficult to comprehend and constantly changing. Therefore, it is more and more a challenge to select appropriate information for individuals to enhance their knowledge or to solve specific problems. In consequence, *only knowledge bases which progressively integrate learners' requirements* stand a chance of meeting real needs. This approach is termed 'just-in-time knowledge' to refer to the dynamic aspect of learning and to the appropriateness of knowledge provided to assist in solving actual problems.

There are two specific foci within the JITOL environment:

**a. the computer mediated human-human interaction process (HHIP):**

In professional development contexts, the stimulus for a new learner action will often be a problem that arises in the process of the learner's work. A mentor or tutor and the learner will then engage in an iterative refinement (the human-human interaction process, HHIP) of their joint understanding of the learner's problem. Having established sufficient understanding of the learner's problem/question, the mentor may assemble a package of knowledge resources which the learner will study and then engage in further rounds of interaction with the mentor.

**b. the progressive construction of appropriate and evolving knowledge bases (EKB):**

The idea behind the Evolving Knowledge Bases (EKB) is that representations of the interactions between participants in the system should be stored and thereby become additional knowledge resources for subsequent use. Since the interactions will mostly emerge from problems that arise in the course of learners' professional work, indexing of these knowledge bases can be problem-oriented. In this way, learners will benefit both from actual interactions on the network and from subsequent up-dating and customising of resources.

---

* The DELTA programme is one of a number of projects within the Directorate XIII/F of the Commission of the European Communities. It is part of a four year programme of Research and Development in Advanced Communications-technologies in Europe (RACE) and Telematics Systems in Areas of General Interest. Its focus is Flexible and Distance Learning and this phase of work was preceded by the DELTA Exploratory Action (1988-90).

Experimentation with, and evaluation of the JITOL environment will be achieved through pilot investigations which are currently being put in place to engage professionals in banking, field maintenance, medical and learning technology domains.

In the context of the problem posed in this paper, the question is the extent to which an integrated research and practice community can be established to provide innovative solutions to the real problems of knowledge development and exchange.

## ELECTRONIC NETWORKS

The general case for electronic communication between academics is forcefully made in a paper to the Senate Committee on Commerce, Science and Transportation.

> *"There is a broad consensus among government, education and industry leaders that creation of a high-speed national research and educational computer network is a critical national priority. The benefits of such a network will be realised in greater research productivity and improved access to specialised knowledge databases and experimental facilities, such as supercomputers, accelerators and telescopes. The network will accelerate the transfer of research results to the private sector and substantially benefit our international economic competitiveness. . . . .*
> *Networking is making a major impact on the lives and productivity of scholars. First, it has reduced the isolation of scholars at small and remote institutions by enabling them to collaborate with colleagues and to have access to specialised research resources such as supercomputers, accelerators and telescopes, as well as information resources such as national bibliographic databases. Second, it has assisted in bringing these scholars more fully into research activities in their disciplines, which will not only enhance the rate of research progress in many fields but also help to keep instructional programs at small institutions current and help them recruit able faculty. an important role of government support for networking is to ensure the broadest possible connectivity and access to scholars at small and remote institutions. Without government support these institutions will be left out."*

(King, 1988)

Whilst some of this enthusiasm may be justified, there are some cautionary notes from experiences of such approaches in the past.

> *"The history of experience with telecommunications and computer-based information systems contains many instances of expensive technological failures that are at least partly attributable to designs that do not mesh well with the social and behavioral systems in which they are to be used. . . . .*
> *. . . . (there is a) long history of attempts to use telematics to improve communication among scientists and engineers. The goal of these attempts has been to capture the research literature of a discipline in computerized databases and to increase the scope of coverage, the number of researchers with access, the rapidity and accuracy of retrieval, and the ease of using retrieval systems. This goal continues to dominate thinking about the role of information technology in scientific communication. . . . .*
> *But studies of the dissemination of scientific information and patterns of interaction among scientists . . . . suggest that these efforts may to too limited. These studies have shown that scientists rely heavily on informal communication within a network of scholars working on related topics to find out about new research. Through their informal networks, researchers in some disciplines know about 60% of the literature relevant to their speciality before it appears in published form.*

(Galegher and Kraut, 1990)

Galegher and Kraut also quote Crane (1970) who suggests that if IT is to support links between scientists, it must be designed to support rich communication between individuals, rather than to provide an electronic warehouse for scientific research. It should not be forgotten, however, that the warehouse may still be useful for new and young researchers in the field, and for practitioners not a part of the informal academic networks.

The encouraging part of all this is that the methodologies that we are exploring at Neurope Lab, with their emphasis on human-human interaction, are coherent with the views expressed above.

## 6. NETWORKS FOR THE (NEAR) FUTURE

One vision for the near future is the creation of virtual, enlarged, interactive, sharing communities to support the integration of research and practice in Europe. The aim will be to set up in each EC country, and in others in a wider Europe, a node in an electronic network using existing communications infrastructures such as those currently provided by INTERNET. The national node or nodes would themselves be part of a regional networks. Researchers and practitioners in any organisation would have access to the network providing pathways to services initially seen as including:

- electronic conferencing and mail;
- a distributed database of "research people profiles";
- evolving knowledge bases reflecting the just-in-time issues of researchers and practitioners;
- gateways to relevant, existing databases in Europe and elsewhere;
- as found necessary, specialised databases of research reports, project outlines, etc. on themes not included elsewhere.

In the field of ICT to support learning, networking of researchers and practitioners is particularly important because:

- the field is multidisciplinary in that its community comprises those from various traditional disciplines: computer science, psychology, education, linguistics and from newer disciplines such as cognitive and neuroscience.
- the exploitation of research outcomes may suggest shifts in social and behavioural practice which are resistant to change; hence close collaboration is essential between research and practice if research outcomes are to become owned by those who are in a position to exploit them;
- those active in the field exist in very few, newly formed groups but most are widely dispersed and often isolated.

These features of constituency and distribution characterise many new fields of study and exploitation, in particular those involving new technologies where the rate of growth and innovation is large.

Critical dimensions are:

- the added value of electronic networks to research;
- the orientation of research and exploitation of research findings.

An important baseline is that networks already exist at a technological level and these are used by a proportion of the target community. Also, that human networks exist through professional associations, special interest groups and a whole range of well established forms of human interaction. Both forms of existing networks are highly valued and the aim is to capitalise on the strengths of each. How can human interaction, exchange of expertise, be assisted by the existing (and the exploitation of latent) communications and information handling technologies?

The network must take account of the infra-structures that already exist, and the institutional and personal commitment (ownership) that is a natural organisational and human characteristic. The effective exchange of researchers, the transferability of research training and substantive research experience, the recognised credits accumulated by such experience are an important part of the stimulation and development of a truly pan-European integrated research community.

The network must be seen as a complement to human-human interaction events, conferences, workshops, seminars etc. such as those of organisations such as EARLI, OECD, ESF, Council of Europe, IFIP, etc. in the ICT field.

Any vision for the future must be human-needs rather than technology-driven. There is no doubt that the informal networks to which Crane (*op cit*) refers have been extremely effective. Are they adequate for the future? But do they support only an elitist view of knowledge transfer? Can information and communication technologies open doors to knowledge for many more members of our community of researchers and professional practitioners?

## REFERENCES

Crane, D. (1970) The nature of scientific communication and influence. *International Sociology of Science Journal*, **22**, 38-41.

Dias de Figueiredo, A. (1989) Introducing informatics into education at the national level: objectives, opportunity, strategies. In *Education and Informatics*. UNESCO, Paris.

Educational Technology Center (1988) *Making Sense of the Future*. Harvard Graduate School of Education, Cambridge MA. Reprinted (1990) in the *Journal of Computer Assisted Learning*, **6**, 1, 14-33.

Eraut, M. and Hoyles, C. (1989) Groupwork with Computers. *Journal of Computer Assisted Learning*, **5**, 1, 12-24.

Galegher, J. and Kraut, R.E. (1990) Technology for Intellectual Teamwork: Perspectives on Research and Design. In *Intellectual Teamwork: social and technological foundations of cooperative work* (eds. J. Galegher, R.E. Kraut and C. Egido) pps. 1-20. Lawrence Erblaum, Hillsdale, New Jersey.

Gyllenberg, H. G. (1985) Progress and expectations in biology. In *The identification of progress in learning* (ed. T. Hägerstrand) p. 43. Cambridge University Press, Cambridge.

Hägerstrand, T. (ed) (1985) *The identification of progress in learning*. Cambridge University Press, Cambridge.

HMSO (1986) *Exploitable Areas of Science*. Her Majesty's Stationery Office, London.

King, K.N. (1988) *Statement of Remarks to the Science, Technology and Space Subcommittee of the Senate Committee on Commerce, Science and Transportation*. (mimeo) August 11, 1988.

Lewis, R. (1989) Information Technology in Education Research Programme 1988-93. *Journal of Computer Assisted Learning*, **5**, 1, 2-11.

Newby, H. (1992) *Social Sciences in the 1990's*. Economic and Social Research Council, Swindon.

UNESCO (1989) *Education and Informatics*. Proceedings of an International Congress, April 1989. UNESCO, Paris.

Ziman, J.M. (1985) Pushing back the frontiers - or redrawing maps! In *The identification of progress in learning* (ed. T. Hägerstrand) p. 11. Cambridge University Press, Cambridge.

Education and Society / R. Aiken (Editor)
Information Processing 92, Volume II
Elsevier Science Publishers B.V. (North-Holland)



# VISUAL OPERATIONAL THINKING AND COMMUNICATIVE COMPETENCE
## - a prerequisite for bringing multimedia network systems and learners into action

Lone Dirckinck-Holmfeld[a] and Janni Nielsen[b]

[a] Department of Communication, Aalborg University, P.O.Box 159, 9100 Aalborg, Denmark

[b] Department of Informatics and Management Accounting, Copenhagen Business School, Howitzvej 60, 2000 Copenhagen F, Denmark

**Abstract**

The authors take their starting point from two future and integrated trends in the development of educational technologies: the growth of dynamic graphics as well as the increasing use of computer mediated communications. On the basis of the results from two empirical research projects they argue that these new technologies will demand new qualifications of the users: that of visual operational thinking and that of (online) communicative competence. Discussing the two theoretical concepts, the authors point out new aspects in human-computer-interaction which have to be reflected in the support of the learners.

Keyword Codes: H.5.2.; I.2.6.; K.3.1.
Keywords: User Interfaces; Learning; Computer Uses in Education.

## 1. INTRODUCTION

A clear tendency in the development of information- and communications systems of the future is multimedia, with a growing use of icons, dynamic graphics and video. Whether one speaks of advanced systems for office work, monitoring or educational use, increasing amounts of information will be in the form of visual dynamic images which have to be read and understood. This means that alongside and interacting with a language culture there will be an image culture, demanding new cognitive qualifications of the learners. At the same time computer-mediated communication will grow as a consequence of the demand for more flexible ways of organizing communication and learning. The consequence is a demand for (online) communicative competence.

## 2. EMPIRICAL RESEARCH

In the following we shall introduce examples from two research projects within education which will illustrate the new required qualifications in human-computer-interaction with respect to visual dynamic graphics and computer mediated communications.

### 2.1. Use of text and dynamic graphics.

Part of the research project was an empirical investigation of the influence of image representation and written information on cognitive processes. To enhance this goal a simple software program in which text/dynamic graphics were integrated, was chosen, allowing for both a symbolic and/or dynamic graphical approach to problem solving.

The research is based on a qualitative investigation of 36 novice users - age 15-60 - who were videotaped[1] during their work with the computers. The empirical data were collected in two steps. First a group of school children who worked with the Danish edition of LOGO[2] in their math classes, was investigated. The second step was an investigation of a group of adults who participated in a computer course. The participant were university students, middle level managers in private companies, office workers, school teachers etc.

The novices were introduced to the computers given 6-10 hours of hands-on-experience, as well as instructions and worked through different examples together with an instructor. Following this the participants were given different problems to solve[3] and during this they were videotaped. They worked in pairs, and the following sources of information were available to them: Verbal explicit help and instructions, instruction on black-board, written explanations in the form of a manual, a book with exercises including explanations and illustrations, a list of system commands and finally the information on the screen, being both text and graphics.

### 2.1.1. Visual Operational Thinking

The analysis shows, that irrespective of age, there was a clear preference for graphics, only very few were able to handle the programming approach[4]. Nevertheless they succeeded reasonably well in solving problems, not always the problems posed, but they wrote functional programs. However, this happened only if they allowed their visual perception to rule (Nielsen 1987). Initially this was no problem, because they were clearly fascinated by the dynamic images. They all possessed - one may say, the very special ability of allowing themselves to be "seduced by the graphics" (Nielsen & Roepstorff 1985).

The dynamic graphics functioned as an enchantment, but to some of the participants it also worked as a hindrance. This happened when they got "caught" by the graphics, when the visual image, that which first meets the eyes, ruled. The graphic forms and in some cases also the dynamic movements captured their attention to the extent that they never sought beyond the dynamic image, hence it was not made the object of an analysis. The immediate visual sight was sufficient for them. As a consequence the dynamic graphics led to a fixation (Nielsen 1988).

To others the dynamic graphics enhanced learning and understanding. When successful, the users would move beyond the immediately perceivable and try to see the embedded information in the graphics. They would stare at the screen, their eyes glued to the cursor, heads nodding, following its moves. They would venture interpretations and comment on the stepwise movements. "Yes, that‘s it, we are turning to the right" (Nielsen 1987), and on the basis of the seen information make decisions about the next steps. They would solve the problems by reading and debugging the dynamic graphics - *not* the programs. In these cases we found that the dynamic graphics enhanced learning, hence understanding.

However, whether they succeeded or not, the dynamic graphics were the most important source of information. It was primarily the dynamic graphics - not the program and the a priori defined logic, nor other kinds of information and explanations - which they would rely on, respectively read and debug[5]. Yet the adults would state during an interview prior to the work with computers, that they primarily relied on the written instructions. And again, after the work with the computers were completed, they stated that the written instructions - exercise book or manual - were the main information sources. When confronted with the videotapes, they expressed surprise, even chock when realizing that they primarily relied on the dynamic graphics and the illustrations.

The analysis shows that it is not sufficient merely to see the graphics. One also has to be able to operationalize the visual knowledge gained. If one cannot see the embedded information in the graphics, one cannot make inferences. The inferences are based on an ability to read the dynamic graphics and imagine the outcome. We will suggest that the cognitive qualification, and the process underlying this ability, is that of *visual operational thinking*.

### 2.2. Computer-Mediated Communication in Distance Learning

The aim of this research was to investigate the use of computer conferencing as a communicative and pedagogical tool for enhancing cooperative and social learning in distance education. The research took its starting point from a field experiment at Jutland Open University 1987-89 (Lorentsen 1988). The experiment was small scaled, based on 48 students and 3 teachers using computer conferencing (PortaCOM) from their home in an one-year open university course (humanistic science). The students were partly taught through the conference system and partly on five residential weekend seminars. The pedagogical approach was project work. This means that the students acquired knowledge and understanding in the subject area by writing a project in cooperation with other students. The students were organized in groups. The purpose of introducing computer conferencing was exactly to enhance the students possibilities of communicating.[6]

Most of the students were edp novices. But they were familiar with and liked written communication. 75% of the students were teachers, nurses, librarians and academics.

On the bases of the field experiment we identified four interrelated levels in the users problems regarding computer conferencing (Dirckinck-Holmfeld 1990). Firstly, there were problems with regards to the communicative infrastructure, i.e. unstable telephone links which caused problems with data transmission. Secondly, the users had problems in handling the computers. Networking systems are very complex systems with shortcomings and many possibilities for mistakes. Thus it may be very difficult for the users (especially novices) to create a mental model and a semantic for the network system. Furthermore, the syntax caused problems, partly because it was not logic and consistent according to the task domain, and partly because the menus were not clearly designed. Thirdly, and most surprisingly, we noted some new types of problems which we define as meta-communicative problems, that is problems which occur because the user has no knowledge of how to communicate in this new media.

Computer-conferencing is a new "language game", a so called *written speech*.(Eklundh 1986, Dirckinck-Holmfeld 1990). It is a way of communicating which nobody has learned formally or informally. That is, it is not a competence embedded in our lifeworld/culture. We identified - among the users - great uncertainty with respect to the way of communicating. Examples of problems were: Turntaking, that is how to structure and manage the communication-act without the usual (and subconscious) tools which are used e.g. in face-to-face communication. Problems with how to avoid "overload" of irrelevant information and "underload" of relevant information, and difficulties with how to write a text in order that the message is carried clearly through.

Finally, we also identified problems with regard to communicating meaningfully and to carry out an academic discourse.

On the basis of the field experiment it became clear to us that to gain from computer based communication and to enhance cooperative learning, is not merely a question of implementation of a communication technology. It is - more precisely - a question of developing new qualifications in the learning organization. The central competence which is needed in relation to computer conferencing is (online) *communicative competence*.

#### 2.2.1 Online Communicative Competence

Communicative competence in computer conferencing is an interrelated and three-sided competence. It requires an elementary understanding of the semantics of the computer and the network, just as the user must be able to operate the computer on an elementary level. It embodies a meta-communicative competence, that is a consciousness of communication. This meta-competence is strongly integrated with a competence in operating the computer. The users have to be conscious of interpersonal communication, but at the same time they must be able to handle the communicative act. Finally, and strongly integrated with the meta-communicative competence it embodies an ability to and a competence in communicating meaningfully with regards to an academic discourse.[7]

Project pedagogy (Dirckinck-Holmfeld 1991) is based on the idea that the academic discourse - the communicative act - can be used as a means to help students to acquire knowledge, e.i. help the students to deepen and make probable that their argumentation is logic and true. The academic discourse also help make the knowledge constructing process cooperative, so that the discourse partly leads to a subject-oriented explication and partly to a creative, associative and mutually fruitful process.

The media through which the communication takes place is the computer conferencing. The function of this channel is to connect and regulate the communication and the communicators have to act according to the rules of the channel. These rules are to create, to maintain, to control and to break the connection between the communicators. Furthermore the channel determines the expression codes which the communicators must control - here the written speech act. As more multimedia are disseminated the greater the demands will be for the communicators to control the different codes: writing, speech, sound, graphics, pictures etc.

It is the ability to communicate meaningfully which is the essence in cooperative and communicative learning supported by computer conferencing. Yet, if the communicators are to succeed, they must be able to handle all three levels of competence.

## 3. CONTRIBUTIONS TO A THEORETICAL FRAMEWORK FOR LEARNING

M. Polanyi (1968) has given exceptional and profound contributions to the discussion on the nature of scientific knowledge. Making a distinction between logical knowledge and psychological knowledge (according to the author the latter being the ground upon which scientific knowledge rests) he discusses "the indeterminacy in scientific knowledge"(ibid p. 27). He argues that fundamentally knowledge rests upon an indeterminacy in content, in the coherence we see which will always be vaguely defined, as well as in the data upon which we base our results.

Polanyi suggests that "explanations must be understood as a particular form of insight"(p.37). This implies that there are other kinds of insights, other kind of understanding and other kinds of knowledge. These other kinds are of special interest to Polanyi, and he introduces these non-explicit or indefinable insights through examples of indeterminacy in knowledge where he shows that "we know far more than we can tell" (p.30).

The development of tacit knowledge and the tacit inference is intertwined with our focal awareness and subsidiary awareness. Polanyi explains these two concepts through a number of examples. When reading a text, the focal awareness is not oriented towards each single letter, nor towards each single word or the sequence of the words in a sentence. All of these function as subsidiaries for the focal awareness which is oriented towards what the reading is all about: the meaning of the text. The relationship between the letters, the words, the sentences is created via the tacit inference, via the cognitive ability of gaining insight. It is the same kind of tacit inference which takes place when one is looking through a stereoscope. Only looking with one eye, one sees one image. Looking with the other eye, one sees another image. Looking with both eyes, an image which - one may say - is not there is created. The eyes see a relation created by the tacit inference from the two images and born as a third image. Thus one see more than what is visible.

Whether trying to understand a written piece of communication or dynamic graphics unfolding on the screen, the underlying process is that of perception, of trying to gestalt, to make sense of what is seen.

Turning to the dynamic graphics, it should be no surprise then, that the most important source of information was the dynamic graphics. We have described how the learners were seduced by the graphics, to the extent that this was their primary source of information, thus visual perception ruled. To some of the users this led to a fixation whereas others attempted to see the embedded information by reading and debugging the dynamic graphics. The user who, with success, relied on graphics did so because they allowed their visual perception to rule, following the dynamic graphics so carefully - that they were "down there in the screen", moving around with the cursor. "Pouring one‘s body into it" is how Polanyi describes the process (ibid p. 33) and he argues that through this ability to project our senses out into an external space, essential knowledge is gained which could not be acquired by an act of detached intellectual interpretation. In this act of indwelling, the user does not focus on each particular step of the cursor, but these movements rather function as subsidiaries guiding the awareness away from each step and towards an integration of all the particular movements into an image - a coherent gestalt. It is a perceptual integration established through an inference.

Of course the users, when looking at the screen, are aware of each step of the cursor. The fact that their eyes are following the cursor around and their heads are nodding tells us that. However, this is not the focus of their attention, or rather they are aware of the particular steps in some unfocal way. The steps are perceived in relations to the whole, and the users make sense of what they see by establishing a coherence between the steps. Part of what they see is incoherent, but they gestalt an indeterminable coherence, thus seeing (imagining) a joint image.

This inference is based on the graphics which lead to understanding, it is not the result of detached contemplation. On the contrary, this is a spontaneous event, it happens suddenly and is never explicitly verbalized. Polanyi speaks of it as a tacit inference and sees it as a result of intuitive processes, of knowing more, or maybe seeing more than there is.

However, to some of the users the seduction would turn into an imprisonment. This could be a result of an expected graphical outcome not showing up on the screen. One could almost say that a breakdown in the "communication" occurred. They did not seem to have fully grasped the wholeness, or the interrelatedness of the graphics. As a result the process would often be trial and error and eventually haphazard changes. Most often they would get lost in the attempts to change the program in order to obtain a wanted result. As a consequence, they lost the overall view and sometimes experienced the frantic changes as if they were moving in a "maze". Others were so fascinated by the dynamic graphics, that even when the cursor‘s only moves were to circle around itself, they would laugh with expectant smiles on their faces, and their eyes glued to the screen, and execute the movements again (Nielsen 1986). Or they would be so fascinated by the graphical shapes, that they would perceive the form, not matter what, as the meaning of the activity. As a result no analysis would be attempted, not much understanding would be acquired. The users awareness became "frozen" in the graphical result on the screen. Attempts of indwelling were few, because the immediate fascination was so strong. However, it seems reasonable to speak of contemplation, though we cannot speak of a detached attitude. The contemplation would have, as starting point, the result on the screen, that is their focal awareness would be fixed on each particular step, or on the cursor, thus they could not perceive any coherence.

As to computer conferencing, the identified problems were on different levels. The focal awareness should have been on communicating meaningfully. However, either caused by problems with grasping the semantic and the syntax of the computer, or because of meta-communicative problems, the focal awareness was far too often on the technology or meta-communicative matters rather on the meaningfulness of the communication. Besides we noted that it was not a transfer of the focal awareness to the subsidiaries - which would then be the focus of the students attention - which lead to familiarity with the system, but rather arbitrary and sometimes frantically attempts (trial and error) to handle the technical problems. The shift in focal awareness from meaning- and knowledge production to the lower levels (the subsidiaries) resulted in the awareness being removed from the learning matters.

One may ask whether it is possible to talk about computer conferencing as embodying elements of tacit knowledge and requiring tacit inferences, when a prerequisite in computer conferencing where language is the game, is detached contemplation. Nevertheless, we shall argue that the written speech, whether being actively produced or perceptually received, requires tacit qualification in order to become meaningful. However, the learners need to go through a learning process in which they are made aware of, and has the possibility of acquiring the computer semantic/syntax and the written speech act. Only when these levels have been acquired and have become part of the learners knowledge one can say that these function as subsidiaries for the communicative act so that meaning among the participants can be produced as tacit inference.

## 4. DISCUSSION

We have pointed out new trends in the development of computers, that of dynamic graphics (multimedia) and that of computer conferencing (networking). On the basis of two empirically founded research projects we have argued that in order to obtain the best utilization of these technical possibilities, the development of visual operational thinking and online communicative competence are requirements. Furthermore it may be argued that visual operational thinking and language (as communication) are two different ways of acquiring knowledge, of becoming cognizant. Dynamic graphics may concretize and visualize processes which may be said to correspond to the subconsciousness of human cognition, whereas written communication is explicit and therefore may be said to correspond more to conscious processes. Thinking is traditionally thought of as being connected with the latter.

We will suggest, however, that thinking is neither language, nor pictures nor logic - all these "merely" function as subsidiaries for thinking. Thinking we understand as *condensation of meaning, insights which initially neither exist in language nor in pictures*. New insights and understandings may be perceived as "flashes", where one sees (mind‘s eye) something which one has never understood before (Polanyi 1968). A state, or experience like that is indeterminable, irreversible and tacit. In many working conditions, or situated actions, this kind of tacit knowing may be superior, e.g. in autonomous work processes where the user has to react to complex information (control room work or case work). In other connections such as in academic learning, tacit knowing is not sufficient in itself. Here the interest is to penetrate as deeply as possible into the understanding based on the tacit inference, in order to acquire a conscious and articulated understanding of the integration into coherent gestalts.

In this process of putting words to it, different tools may be used, e.g. the dynamic graphical codes or the linguistic codes. Just as different technics may be used, e.g. communication with others (in direct conversation), through own reflection or mediated through a media. In designing computers it is the conversational linguistic model (Norman 1986) which has been predominant. However, on the basis of the above, it is obvious that this is not necessarily the most suitable form of representation. Because it insists on actions being explicitly stated, which is not always possible - as they may be based in tacit knowledge, or because the wording of the action is not and never was necessary in order to enable it to be carried out. In relation to this the empirical analyses of the dynamic graphics point towards several conditions which may be relevant in design aiming at the learner: Graphics embody an element of seduction which enhances the users access to indwelling. Graphics also offer a way to concretize and enhance an overall and comprehensive view, without demanding explicit (and detached contemplative) cognitive activities of the users. However, the seduction is dangerous if it lures the users into focusing their awareness on the subsidiaries, instead of the meaning of the activity. But it is a force if it stimulates exploration. The implication for design is that the dynamic graphics have to be developed with due consideration to the specific meaning of the activity.

The empirical analyses of computer conferencing point towards another relevant aspect of design, namely the question of attention and whether this is focused on the task given (here communication) or if it is focused on the technic, e.g. that of sending messages. In the example with computer conferencing one cannot speak of the technical facilities functioning as subsidiaries in relation to the communication, but about two parallel processes which competed for the learners attention: the technical facilities of the system (which took up most of the users awareness) and the communicative ones (which got the least attention). When designing conference systems, in order that these may function as subsidiaries to communicative processes, it is obvious that the insights gained about the dynamic graphics could be used to develop systems which offer better conditions for the learner to indwell in the situation.

## 5. NOTES

1. The advantage of this method is obvious. The working process is captured, in detail, on the screen. The total process is visible, and "eternal" documentation. Others may work with you on the interpretations. And the participants themselves - as in this case - can participate in the analysis. Especially when breakdowns happen (Winograd & Flores 1987), this latter has proved extremely useful.
2. The LOGO program, developed at M.I.T. was very easy to handle. The philosophy behind the design was that a child should be able to use it without too much practice. Exactly because it has been designed in order to promote easy access for children it is, in terms of software development, a very advanced tool.
3. E.g. an illustration showing a triangle which was turning and at the same time growing, was given. The instructions would then be to try to write a program which would execute a similar figure.
4. The tapes showed that only one person - a yong man at the age of 15 - after approximately 1 year of working with computers, really reached a master level. He was brilliant - to the extend that he could make a change in a subroutine, mentally integrate it in a superroutine, and predict the outcome.
5. This was even true 1 year later, after approximately 50-60 hours of programming experience (Nielsen 1989).
6. In September 1991 two more courses were started at Aalborg University, building on the computer supportedproject work concept developed in the experiment. Computer supported distance learning is a main strategy for distance education at Aalborg University.
7. A model for an academic discourse may be found in Habermas theory of discourse (1979).

## 6. REFERENCES


Dirckinck-Holmfeld,L (1990) Kommunikation på kryds og på tværs, PICNIC-NYT nr. 9, Aalborg Universitets center.

Dirckinck-Holmfeld,L (1991) Making Project Pedagogy Function in Distance Learning through Use of Computer Conferencing, Lorentsen,A & Kolmos,A (eds.): Quality by Theory and Practice of Higher Education, TNP-Series No. 6, Aalborg University, p. 127-133.

Eklundh,K.S (1986) Dialogue Processes in Computer-Mediated Communication - A study of letters in the COM system, Linköping Studies in Arts and Science no. 6, Liber Förlag, Malmø.

Habermas,J (1979) Communication and the evolution of Society, Heinemann, London. (org. 1976).

Lorentsen,A (1988) Presentation and Analysis of 'Project Computer-Aided Distance Teaching'- A Research Project at Jutland Open University, PICNIC-NEWS 4E, Aalborg University.

Nielsen,J (1986) Not the computer but human interaction is the basis for cognitive development. Education and Computing, vol 2, no. 1,2, North Holland, p. 53-63.

Nielsen,J (1987) Datamater og erkendelsesprocesser. Danmarks Lærerhoejskole, PPP no.42.

Nielsen,J (1988) The Role of Dynamic Graphics when Learning Programming - implications for cognition. Lovis F. & E.D.Tagg (eds.) Computers in Education, North Holland, p. 337-343.

Nielsen,J (1989) 1 år efter. Unpublished empirical data.

Nielsen,J (1990) The Role of Text and Dynamic Graphics in Knowledge Acquisition. McDougall A. & C. Dowling (eds.) Computers in Education, North Holland, p.155-163.

Nielsen,J & Roepstorff,L (1985) Girls and Computers, a world of difference. rev. edition of Contribution of Third GASAT Conference, Univ.of London, vol I, p. 64-80.

Norman,D.A et.al. (1986) Direct Manipulation Interfaces, Draper & Norman (eds.) User centered system design, Lawrence Erlbaum associates, Publishers, London.

Polanyi,M (1968) Logic and Psychology. American Psychologist, 23, p. 27-43.

Winograd,T & Flores,F (1988) Understanding computers and cognition, Ablex Publishing Corporation, Norwood, New Jersey.

Education and Society / R. Aiken (Editor)
Information Processing 92, Volume II
Elsevier Science Publishers B.V. (North-Holland)


# Enhancing the scientist in the pupil: a computer environment supporting mathematical discoveries in the classroom

Evgenia Sendova

Institute of Mathematics, Bulgarian Academy of Sciences, P.O.Box 373, 1090 Sofia, Bulgaria
e-mail: banmat@bgearn.bitnet; fax: +359 2 752078

**Abstract**

The paper deals with research on creating a classroom culture in which students *do* mathematics naturally. The experience with Plane Geometry System - a computer environment supporting the growth and development of mathematical ideas in the classroom, has been described. A teaching style determining new roles for teachers and students alike has been suggested on the basis of an educational experiment in some Bulgarian schools.

Keyword Codes: D.2.6; K.3.1; K.3.2
Keywords: Programming Environments; Computer Uses in Education; Computer and Information Science Education

## 1. "WHAT IS MATHEMATICS ALL ABOUT?"

According to some researchers [1-3] the majority of junior high and secondary school students believe that:

- mathematics is mastering formal procedures;
- mathematics is completely divorced from real life, discovery, and from problem solving;
- all problems can be solved in 10 minutes;
- mathematics is merely a collection of already solved problems;
- teachers in mathematics know at least one (good) solution to any given problem;
- only geniuses are capable of discovering mathematics.

No wonder that such beliefs have a very strong negative effect on students' mathematical behaviour. Even if those beliefs are just plain wrong as far as the *real* mathematics is concerned, they are part of what Silver labels as *the hidden mathematics curriculum* [3]. Actually, most mathematical lessons are devoted to training pupils

- to complete *well posed problems* whose *solution is known* ;
- to memorize what is offered to them without attempting to make sense of it;
- to be passive consumers of mathematical thinking presented in a neat and clean form.

As a consequence the real flavour of mathematics - the false starts, the recoveries from them, the insights and discoveries remain entirely hidden from pupils. The latter are hardly ever given the chance to discover or invent by themselves.

To create a *microworld* supporting pupils to appreciate mathematics through exploration in the classroom was a challenge taken by a group of researchers under the guidance of Bojidar Sendov from the Educational Computer Systems Laboratory at the University of Sofia. Since 1986 they have been developing and experimenting with the *Plane Geometry System* (PGS) - educational software which is a kind of *mathematical laboratory* [4].

## 2. "YOU DO - YOU UNDERSTAND, YOU EXPLORE - YOU INVENT!"

That is the basic educational principle implied in PGS. The system enables pupils to create geometric objects, to experiment and play with them, to investigate their properties, to formulate and verify conjectures, i.e. to *discover mathematics*. The coordinate plane is the *room* where the laboratory is located and the computer screen is the *window* through which experiments are watched. The PGS language is a Logo extension enriched by tools for working directly with geometric objects: points, segments, lines, circles, vectors and sets of such objects. Each object is characterized by a name, a value, an image and its relationships to other objects [5].

Let us consider an example of exploring a situation formulated as follows:

*Triangle ABC is inscribed in circle K. Vertices A and B are fixed and vertex C is moving around circle K. What is the behaviour of the medicenter, the orthocenter and the incenter of triangle ABC?*

To solve this problem pupils make the initial construction by defining C as a *point on* circle K, which depends on parameter t - the angle that OC forms with the X-axis. Introducing a parameter makes the construction convenient for experiments and pupils are aware of this (Figure 1.).

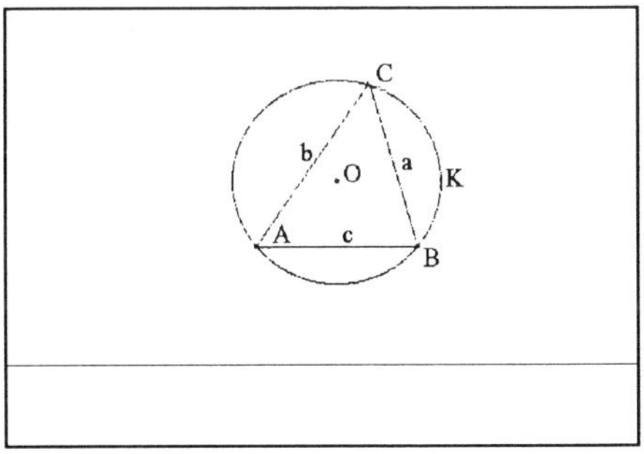


Figure 1.

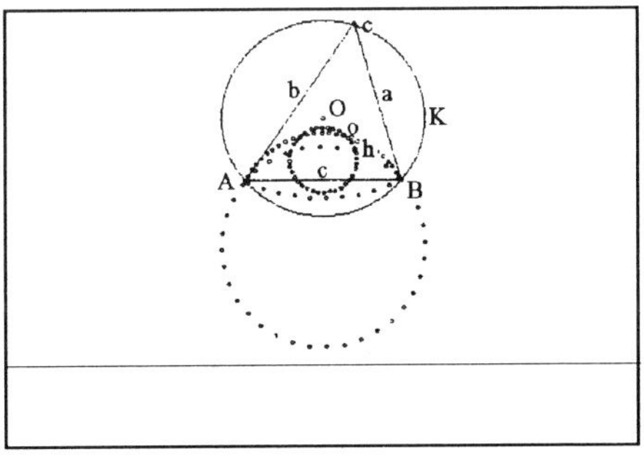


Figure 2.

Then they create procedures for constructing the special points, thus making their geometric definitions *workable*:

```
TO MEDIAN :P :S
    OUTPUT SEGMENT :P POINTON :S 0.5
END
```

```
TO MEDICENTER :A :B :C
    OUTPUT ISEC MEDIAN :A SEGMENT :B :C MEDIAN :B SEGMENT :A :C
END

TO ANGLE_BISECTOR :A :B :C
    OUTPUT LINE :B ((HEADING LINE :B :A) + HEADING LINE :B :C)/2
END

TO INCENTER :A :B :C
    OUTPUT ISEC ANGLE_BISECTOR :A :B :C ANGLE_BISECTOR :B :C :A
END

TO ALTITUDE :A :L
    LOCAL "C
    MAKE "C ISEC :L LINE :A 90 + HEADING :L
    OUTPUT SEGMENT :A :C
END

TO ORTHOCENTER :A :B :C
    OUTPUT ISEC ALTITUDE :A LINE :B :C ALTITUDE :B LINE :A :C
END
```

Thus pupils manifest that they do know the relevant geometric notions and can use them.

Next they can study the behaviour (the history) of C by saving its consecutive positions in the form of a set (Figure 2.).

Now it is not difficult for pupils to predict that the locus of the orthocenter like the locus of the medicenter is a circle. As for the locus of the incenter it seems to consist of two arcs. All these statements will be the pupils' own discoveries (not part of a problem's formulation which normally would be given in the *Prove-that* form).

Then comes the moment of verification, or the so called *experimental proof*. Pupils draw a circle through three points chosen from the corresponding *history* set and check if the remaining elements belong to that circle. Further on they try to invent more properties of the construction (e.g. they may predict that both the centres of the circles comprising the arcs are points on the original circle K).

To find interesting properties and to pose good problems is part of the mathematical adventures but the fun of discovering will be greater still if pupils feel that *the way has not been fully travelled before* [6]. This puts teachers in mathematics in a completely new situations - to teach with technology by using guided exploration which is exciting, challenging and sometimes...disturbing. A real story that happened in RCEI Vladimir Bashev School, Sofia, is a good illustration of this (RCEI stands for Research Centre for Educational Informatics):

## 3. MAY AN ERROR BE A SOURCE OF PROBLEMS?

A future teacher in mathematics was supposed to teach a geometry lesson (to 7th graders) to be evaluated by a special jury. The supervisor, Mrs Steliana Atanasova, has been involved in research on experimenting with a new style of teaching mathematics with PGS [7]. What follows is based on her report in a Bulgarian journal for mathematics and informatics teachers. She had recommended to the *teacher-might-be* a problem whose construction with PGS is easy but whose proof is a challenge for 7th graders. This is how the novice teacher formulated the problem:

*There is a triangle ABC and point M on BC. A line parallel to AB is drawn through M. Two lines are drawn through N and C so that they are perpendicular to AM and meet AB at points R and S, respectively. Compare the segments on AB. Are there equal ones?*

Although the problem was not formulated in the *prove-that* style, it was not as general as the guide teacher would have put it, e.g. *Find some interesting properties of the construction* or *Formulate as many conjectures as you can about the relationships among the segments, angles, quadrilaterals.* Such formulations, however, would be too great a jump for a novice.

Finally the construction appeared on the screen of each computer (Figure 3.).

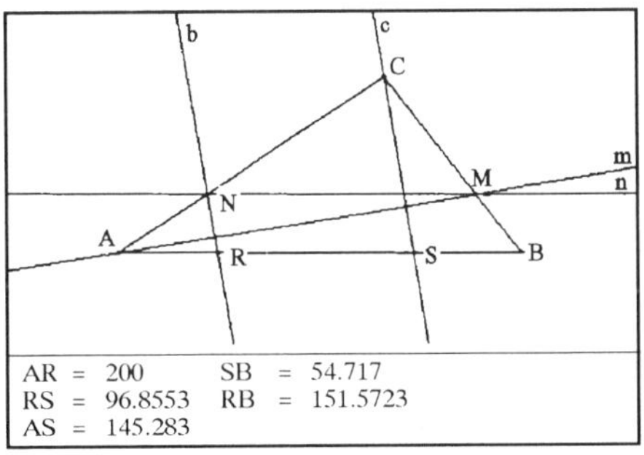


Figure 3.

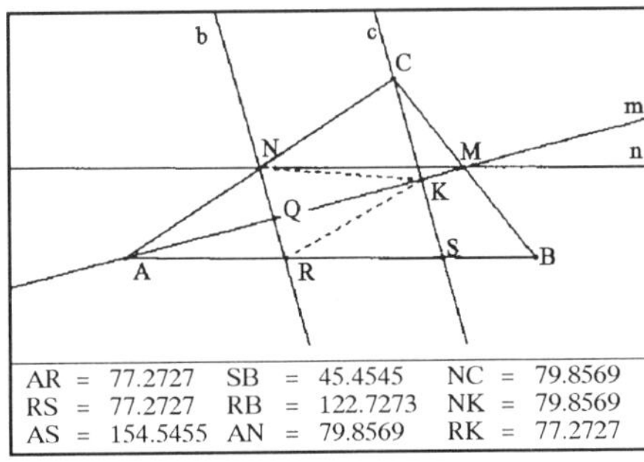


Figure 4.

Alas, no comments...(to the great surprise of the supervisor). The jury was satisfied though and left in a hurry for another lesson. All of a sudden everybody was shouting: *No equal segments! Why?* Obviously the silence before was only an expression of their solidarity with the novice teacher. Then, the expert teacher realized that she had forgotten the original formulation of the problem. The only thing she remembered was the result: *two equal segments are to be obtained on AB*. But under what conditions? - That was the question... After admitting her error

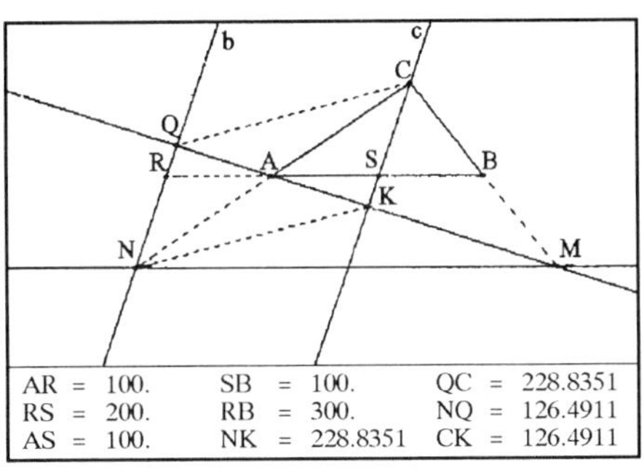


Figure 5.

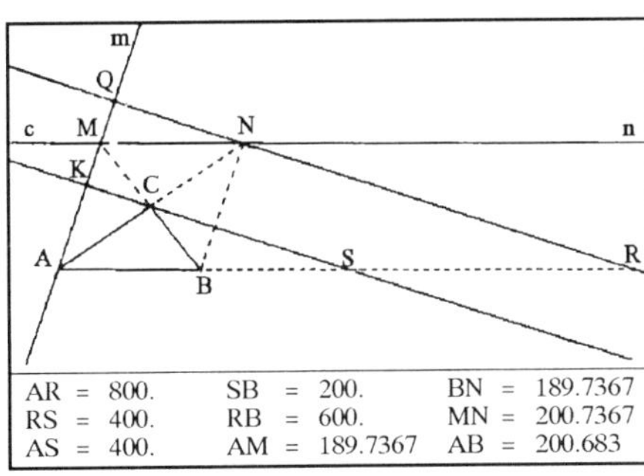


Figure 6.

she *threw down the gauntlet* to her pupils - *Find the initial conditions yielding equal segments.* Pupils decided to apply the *what-if* strategy by choosing some special position of M. *What if we make it the midpoint of BC*? - asked a girl. It worked! (Figure 4.)

But was this the only appropriate position? Some tried with moving M on the extension of BC with the ratio BM/BC being equal to -1 (Figure 5.) and equal to 2 (Figure 6.).

In these two cases they obtained equal segments as well. Everybody was absorbed in making measurements and forming conjectures in their notebooks. Some pupils noticed equal triangles, others found parallelograms, even a deltoidum (quadrilateral ARKN in Figure 4). Interesting relationships, (e.g. between the median and the hypotenuse of a right triangle) were stated. Everybody invented something of his own thus being motivated to attack the proof. The most impressive invention seemed to be that of two boys (Stefan and Zhivko) who investigated the relation of the ratios BM/BC and AR/AS (Figure 7.).

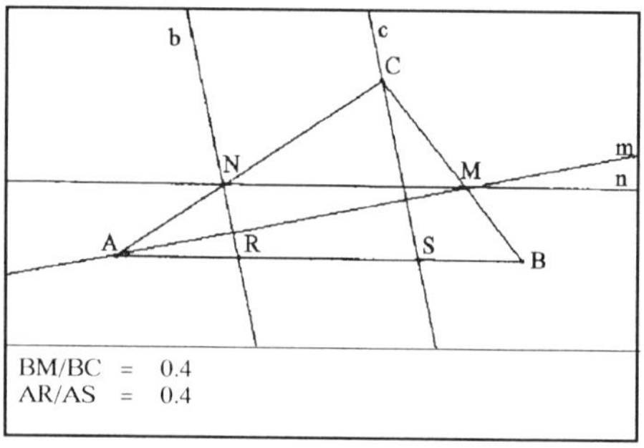


Figure 7.

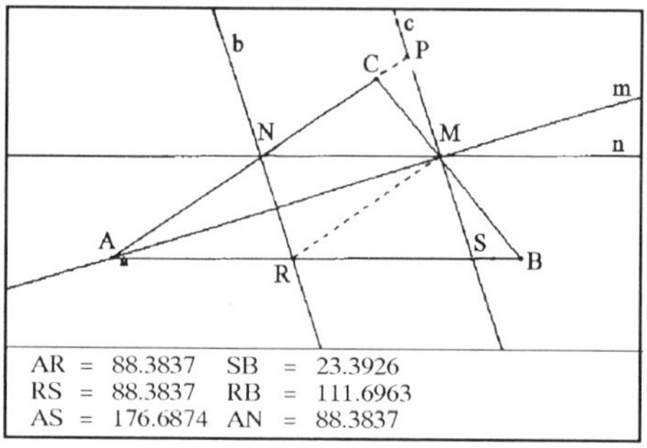


Figure 8.

Psychologists claim that *a problem is not a problem for you until you accept it and interpret it as your own.* In the traditional classroom, however, problems are rarely *your own*. In our case the statements made were no longer theorems of famous mathematicians, which pupils were supposed to know and to reproduce the proof of. These statements were *theorems* of Stefan, Zhivko, Daniela. That is why pupils felt fully motivated to prove them. Even if they happened to *reinvent the wheel*, the process of creative endeavour was something worth experiencing.

The measurements made with PGS are a good ground for the proof. In addition, pupils are used to construct auxiliary elements that might help. Of course it is not always possible to prove their conjectures on the basis of what they already know. But despite this, the geometric properties they have discovered will be valuable for their further mathematics lessons.

Let us come back to our story. A teacher's hint helped pupils to prove that N is the midpoint of AC and similarly, R is the midpoint of AS. Thus they invented and proved a theorem supposed to be considered at 8th grade.

Many interesting problems were generated but pupils were still eager to find the original formulation. The period was over, however, so they made sure they saved their achievements on a disk (as a PGS program). This would allow them to further their investigations.

## 4. TO DISCOVER THE PROBLEM - THAT IS THE PROBLEM

The next classes started with exploring a new idea - the position of line c was changed so as to pass through point M, not through C. This still did not give an interesting result. *What would happen if we change the function of m?* - they reflected. *Last time we started with a median. Let it be an altitude this time...* Nothing new. And finally - the insight: m becomes an angle bisector of A. Only then did the long expected equal segments - AR and RS, appear! (Figure 8.)

The children felt happy. Once again they had created a real problem - not one from the guide teacher, neither one from the novice teacher, but one of their own:

*Triangle ABC is given. The angle bisector of vertex A meets BC at point M. A line parallel to AB is drawn through M so that it meets AC at N. MS and NR are perpendicular to AM where R and S are on AB. Prove that AR = RS.*

Note the *prove-that* part in their statement.

The proof was facilitated by some measurements again. Pupils had checked experimentally that ARMN is a rhombus and RSMN - a parallelogram. They proved that M is the midpoint of SP and therefore AM is an angle bisector and a median for ASP, which implied that ASP is an isosceles triangle. Then a new question was put by the guide teacher: *When will NRMC become a parallelogram rather than a trapezium?* After some reasoning they reached the answer: *When P and C coincide, i.e. when the original triangle is isosceles!*

The *teacher-might-be* received a unique lesson - *to err is not only human, it is even teacher-like* since the only way to omit errors is to avoid new things. And the reward is great - now pupils can feel that the real spirit of mathematics *is searching for an adventure without knowing in advance what adventure they are likely to have* [6]. The role of the teacher in this adventure is that of a partner or navigator so unlike of the role of *a purveyor of information "Here's what is known, and here's how it's used..."*[8].

## 5. CONCLUSIONS

Our several year experience with integrating the Plane Geometry System into the teaching and learning of mathematics has shown that the new teaching style has readily been adopted since it responds to the natural wish of pupils *to learn rather than to be taught* [7]. They become used to exploring a given mathematical situation (by varying its key aspects) and to extracting the maximum from it. They create and discuss mathematics much as professional mathematicians do. Having experienced mathematics in that way, pupils will hopefully develop a view of mathematics as *vibrant, challenging, creative and constructive.*

Teachers, on the other hand, have gained a new image in students eyes - they are no longer people who know at least one true solution for each problem; they are able to take risks by saying: *I am not sure. Let us try and see what will happen...* Thus they break the myth that school mathematics is a collection of already solved problems. Furthermore, teachers are not only a *reality-check* for researchers - they become contributing partners in the research process.

As for researchers, they feel optimistic in their attempt to create a microcosm of mathematical culture - an environment that supports the growth and development of mathematical ideas thus enhancing the scientist in the pupil.

## 6. REFERENCES

1 T.P. Carpenter, M.M. Lindquist, W. Matthews and E.A. Silver, (1983). Results of the Third NAEP Mathematics Assessment; Secondary School, Mathematics Teacher, 76, 652-659.

2 A.H. Schoenfeld, What's All the Fuss About Metacognition, in A.H. Schoenfeld (ed.) Cognitive Science and Mathematics Education, 1987, Hillsdale, New Jersey (pp 189-215).

3 E.A. Silver, Foundations of Cognitive Theory and Research for Mathematics Problem-Solving Instruction, in A.H. Schoenfeld (ed.) Cognitive Science and Mathematics Education, 1987, Hillsdale, New Jersey (pp 33-60).

4 B. Sendov and D. Dicheva, Mathematics Laboratory in Logo Style, in F. Lovis and E.D. Tagg (eds.), Computers in Education, Proc. of the IFIP TC3 First European Conference on Computers in Education (ECCE'88), Lausanne, Switzerland, 24-29 July, 1988.

5 R. Filimonov and B. Sendov, Drawing Logo Closer to the Curriculum, in G. Schuyten and M. Valcke (eds.), Proceedings of the Second European Logo Conference 1989 (Eurologo'89), Gent, Belgium, 30 August - 1 September.

6 E.P. Goldenberg, On Problem Posing and Mathematical Behaviour: Notes on Pedagogy (a paper to be submit to MT)

7 M. Kolcheva and E. Sendova, Reinventing the Elements, a paper delivered at Colloque Logo et Apprentissage, Universite de Fribourg, Suisse, 3-6 October, 1990.

8 A. Henderson, From the Teacher's Side of the Desk, in A.H. Schoenfeld (ed.) Cognitive Science and Mathematics Education, 1987, Hillsdale, New Jersey (pp 149-165).

Education and Society / R. Aiken (Editor)
Information Processing 92, Volume II
Elsevier Science Publishers B.V. (North-Holland) 


# Should Smalltalk be Used in Educational Research?

A.C. Jones[a]

[a]Department of Computing Mathematics, University of Wales College of Cardiff, PO Box 916, Cardiff CF2 4YN, United Kingdom

**Abstract**

We describe the experience of implementing NOLOG—an ICAL system for children implemented in Smalltalk—and argue that Smalltalk is a powerful tool, well suited in many ways to implementing ICAL systems and educational software in general, but that currently Smalltalk has certain serious deficiencies. We highlight deficiencies in the *class library* and deficiencies in the *programming environment*. Our criticism of the *class library* is that it is too closely tied to what is used for implementation of the Smalltalk programming environment, leading to classes which are inflexible, and to a lack of example classes. We criticise the *programming environment* in that it does not adequately support class library navigation, the interactive creation of complex objects, or the debugging process. These deficiencies make Smalltalk difficult to learn and can hinder even an experienced Smalltalk programmer. We outline how Smalltalk could be improved in order to overcome these difficulties.

Keyword Codes: D.1.5; D.2.6; K.3.0
Keywords: Object-oriented Programming; Programming Environments; Computers and Education, General

## 1. INTRODUCTION

> '...the educational case for Smalltalk remains not proven. However the expressive power and aid to visualisation offered by Smalltalk makes it the existing programming system with the greatest educational *potential*. Before the potential can be achieved ways of making Smalltalk accessible to learners and teachers will have to be found' [1]
>
> '... Smalltalk-80 [is] an emerging language for expert systems and AI work' [2]

The NOLOG system has been implemented in Smalltalk (specifically, Smalltalk-80 version T2.1.2a running on a Tektronix 4404 workstation) in order to investigate the educational potential of Smalltalk, and also the suitability of Smalltalk for expert systems and AI work. The design of NOLOG necessitates the use of a variety of programming techniques including the implementation of a simple simulation, implementing a user interface (which departs from that directly supported by Smalltalk), knowledge-based programming, building an interpreter and implementing a constraint evaluator. We only consider the first three tasks in this paper.

We now proceed as follows. Commencing with a brief introduction to Smalltalk, we then cite relevant examples of existing applications implemented in Smalltalk. This is followed by a brief introduction to those aspects of the design of NOLOG which need to be understood in order to appreciate the subsequent discussion of the implementation of NOLOG, in which we aim to highlight strengths and weaknesses of the underlying Smalltalk system. We then outline how Smalltalk could be improved in the light of those weaknesses we identify, and finally we consider the anticipated effects of our proposals. We believe that Smalltalk is a very powerful system, but that improvements such as we propose are needed to increase the acceptability of Smalltalk, particularly to learners of the language.

## 2. SMALLTALK

Smalltalk is distinctive in combining an *object-oriented language* and an *interactive programming environment* [3-5]. Here, we outline the meaning of these two terms.

The Smalltalk language is *object-oriented* in that the programmer thinks in terms of *objects* which send *messages* to each other. Each object may possess *instance variables* (similar to record fields) and always belongs to a *class*. An object's class determines its structure and determines which *method* it will execute in response to a given message. Examples of classes are **SmallInteger** and **Compiler**; examples of messages are **printString** (obtain a textual description of an object) and **add:** (add an object to a collection). Classes are arranged in a *hierarchy;* a class *inherits* structure and behaviour from its *superclass.* For example, **SmallInteger** has a superclass **Integer**, which defines functionality common to integers. These classes implement the Smalltalk *programming environment,* but may also be used as ready-made components for one's own applications. Alternatively, it is possible to inherit from an existing class by creating a new *subclass* having behaviour similar to its *superclass,* but tailored to the programmer's specific needs. This facilitates code reuse; moreover separating responsibility among objects appears to benefit the structuring of large systems [6].

The *programming environment* includes *browsers* (supporting the interactive creation and modification of classes and methods); *workspaces* (windows in which Smalltalk code may be typed for immediate evaluation); *object inspectors* (allowing an object's instance variables to be inspected and modified) and a *debugger* (permitting Smalltalk code execution to be traced).

Object-oriented programming and interactive programming environments are not unique to Smalltalk, but Smalltalk is now a mature system (the Tektronix 4404 system was produced in 1985) which is readily available on relatively common computers such as the IBM PC and the Apple Macintosh. Smalltalk has developed somewhat over the years [7], but the changes have generally been changes of minor detail; in this paper our contention is that some rather more dramatic changes need to be made in order to increase the acceptability of Smalltalk.

## 3. RELEVANT SMALLTALK APPLICATIONS

Smalltalk was originally conceived as a programming language for both adults and children, but it is acknowledged that Smalltalk-80 itself (on which all present Smalltalk implementations are based) is no longer a language suitable for children [8]. There are also few educational applications *implemented* in Smalltalk, but notable examples include a 'dance kit' [9] (the child assembles a series of instructions for a 'dancer'); TRIP [10], a graphical system for time-rate-distance problems; Rehearsal World [11], a system for creating educational applications; and Playground [12], an object-oriented programming system for children.

A number of knowledge-based systems implemented in Smalltalk exist (e.g. Humble (see [13]) and Opus [14]). These generally implement existing knowledge-based techniques, but take advantage of Smalltalk's object-oriented programming paradigm in order to structure the implementation of the system.

Despite the success of systems such as the above, why is not Smalltalk more widely used? This is the question which we wish to address, but first we shall describe the NOLOG system.

## 4. THE NOLOG SYSTEM

NOLOG (Number LOGO) is a microworld inspired by LOGO [15], but intended for number-theoretical problems. As illustrated in Figure 1, there is a grid of numbered *islands* to which *planes* (aeroplanes) fly, controlled by a child's *flight plan* (i.e. a program). Visited islands are shaded black; the islands to be visited are specified in terms of relative motion along a number line or by *constraints* [16].

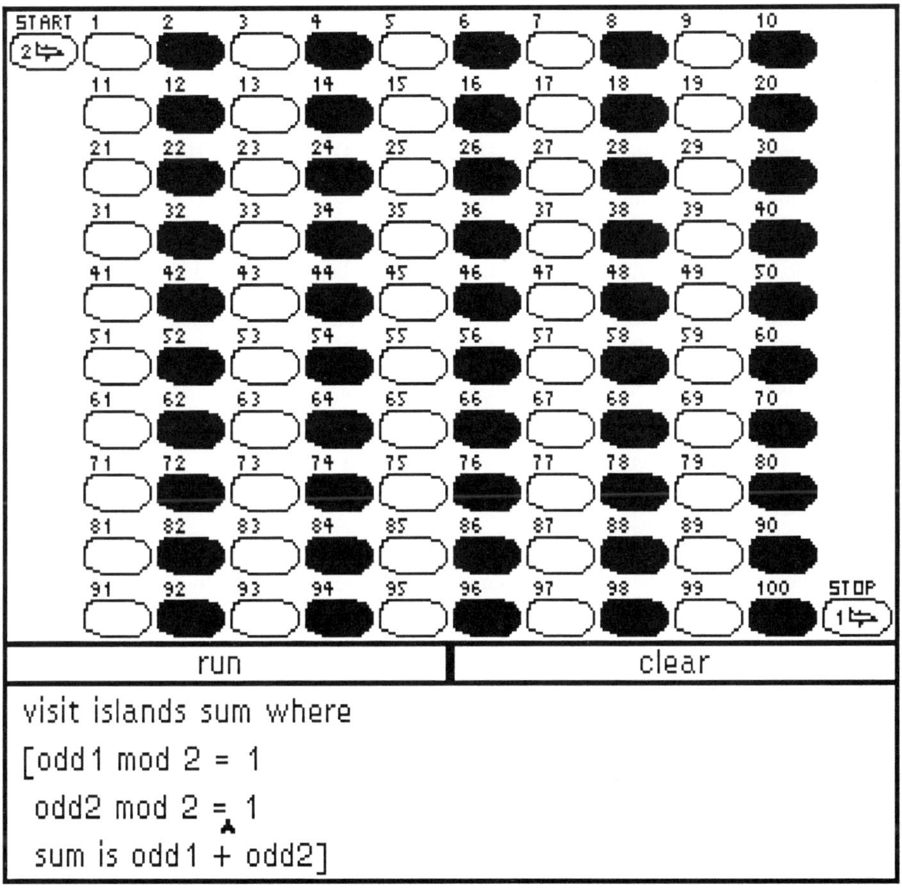


**Figure 1**. Part of the NOLOG system window.

NOLOG is supported by NUDGER [17]—an intelligent subsystem which provides programming assistance. NUDGER works with programs that are syntactically correct, but create unexpected results. Typically NUDGER highlights part of a child's flight plan and displays the corresponding programming assistance text in a *voice bubble* nearby.

## 5. IMPLEMENTATION OF NOLOG

NOLOG is a large system, but we highlight three aspects of the NOLOG implementation from which we can illustrate strengths and weaknesses of Smalltalk: the underlying plane-and-island system, the user interface and knowledge representation. Subsequently we discuss a general problem encountered when implementing NOLOG: that of searching for code.

### 5.1. The plane-and-island system

Smalltalk allows the separation of the user interface from the application using the *model-view-controller* (MVC) paradigm (Krasner & Pope [18] give a clear account of this paradigm). We shall return to this in section 5.2, but for now we note that in consequence we can implement the plane-and-island system and the user interface of NOLOG separately.

The two essential kinds of object in the plane-and-island system are **Plane** and **Island**. A **Plane** responds to messages such as **fly: aDistance**, **takeOff** and **land**. These are commands to fly a specified distance, to take off from and to land on the current island respectively. A **Plane** also maintains a reference to its current island and a *flight recorder* (a record of those islands visited). An **Island** responds to messages such as **movers** (the planes currently occupying the island) and **visit** (to visit the island). A **PlaneComponents** provides structured access to the different objects comprising the plane-and-island system and also maintains data from which the position of each plane and island on the screen may be calculated. When a plane or island changes state, it informs the **PlaneComponents**, since the latter is used by the user interface as a *model*. That is, when it changes, this change is reflected on the screen.

Smalltalk thus proves itself to be valuable for a straightforward means of simulation: the various items in the simulation can be implemented by Smalltalk objects. Moreover, we have noted the separation of the user interface from the plane-and-island system; similarly the interpreter controls the plane-and-island system by sending messages to it (in general, sending messages to the currently active plane), but is implemented separately.

### 5.2. The user interface

Smalltalk provides numerous classes for the implementation of the user interface. There is some variation between different versions of Smalltalk in the precise classes which are provided, but essentially they follow the same MVC paradigm, which divides an application into three parts: the *model* (containing the data for the application), the *view* (a window displaying the state of the model) and the *controller* (which co-ordinates user input for a given view). A given model may have more than one corresponding view-controller pair, viewing different aspects of the model. In this section we discuss the implementation of parts of the NOLOG user interface; we then consider the debugging of interactive applications.

In an early prototype of NOLOG, standard Smalltalk classes were used wherever possible, including list menus and text windows. Tests with children indicated that some features of the Smalltalk user interface caused them problems, including the complicated scroll bar mechanism and the distinction made between the three mouse buttons. Our implementation of the user interface elements required to overcome this problem utilises inheritance: our text editor consists of a **LogoCodeView** and a **LogoCodeController** (subclasses of **TextView** and **TextController** respectively), and our list view consists of a **SimpleListView** and a **SimpleSelectionInListController** (subclasses of **SelectionInListView** and **SelectionInListController** respectively). Three problems arise in implementing these classes:

1. We are inheriting from classes whose implementation is fairly complicated and thus requires significant effort to understand;
2. Little indication of how such inheritance should be approached is given in the Smalltalk programming environment, perhaps because the main purpose of the classes provided appears to be the implementation of the programming environment itself; and
3. Much of the coding for these new classes is duplicated.

The basic problem is that these classes are too large: the scroll bar implementation is an integral part of these controller classes (it is inherited from **ScrollController**), as is the interpretation of user input gestures. In section 6.1 we shall outline a solution to this problem.

Debugging an *interactive* system using the (otherwise powerful) debugger uncovers a serious limitation: interactive systems inspect the keyboard and mouse state, but when single-stepping through an application, the mouse pointer is generally over the debugger window rather than the window whose operation is being debugged. Moreover, certain essential state information, such as the active window and process, will refer to the debugger rather than what is being debugged, leading ultimately to a crash.

### 5.3. Knowledge representation

To represent programming knowledge, we follow Johnson [19] in using *plans* for correct and incorrect programs and parts of programs. Our plans are essentially structured objects, containing patterns to match against the parsed program; we also use Smalltalk *blocks:* these are pieces of Smalltalk code which may be evaluated at any time. For example, we employ blocks to implement *pre-conditions* which must hold before a plan is tried.

We maintain a **PlanConstructor** for each plan, which contains a method to create the **Plan** when required. Two reasons for this are that a new instantiation of a plan may thereby be created without having to implement a specialised copying method, and that the Smalltalk programming environment does not readily support the creation of complex objects such as a **Plan**. These **PlanConstructors** are organised into a number of **PlanCollections**. It is necessary to implement our own browser to maintain even this relatively simple arrangement: the Smalltalk object inspectors are unsuitable since they are based upon editing an object's *structure,* which may lead to inconsistencies. For example, a **PlanConstructor** contains an instance variable referring back to its **PlanCollection**: using the object inspectors to add a new **PlanConstructor** to a **PlanCollection** and using the object inspectors to set the back-pointer to the **PlanCollection** must be done as two separate operations.

In implementing this part of the system, it would have been useful if some knowledge-based examples had been provided in the Smalltalk class library as a source of ideas.

### 5.4. Searching for code

The provision of classes which can be reused directly (e.g. the user interface classes) makes prototyping easy, but *finding* such classes in the programming environment is not a particularly easy task. The browsing tools provide structural access to classes and methods, and they support *exploratory programming* [20]. However, the organisation is not *prescriptive*. That is, the tools support investigation of the *structure* of the class library, but provide no *guidance* as to what parts of the class library to explore, or how to build a particular kind of application (e.g. how to use the MVC system). A programmer may also wish to know how to inherit from existing classes. But generally there is no information given in the system as to how one might achieve this for a given class: thus the programmer needs to read the source code in order to understand the implementation of a class. There are a number of books now available which would have helped in the understanding of the class library (notably [21-22]), but to have to revert to books in order to discover how to use the Smalltalk class library means that the programming environment has failed.

## 6. PROPOSALS FOR IMPROVEMENT OF SMALLTALK

We now propose improvements to the Smalltalk class library and programming environment. These are closely interrelated: an improved programming environment should facilitate more effective use of the class library. The help given by the programming environment is particularly important because of the diffuse nature of the class library [23].

### 6.1. The class library

It is well-known that designing a class library for reuse is an important issue and that this can be facilitated by *pluggability* (designing classes to have the same interface so that they can be interchanged) [24]. Nevertheless, although Smalltalk has been available for so long, the reusability of the class library has yet to be significantly improved.

In particular, the user interface classes are difficult to use because of their size. We propose that the scrolling behaviour be delegated to a separate object from the controller (this is already done in some versions of Smalltalk) but that the controller itself be separated into a *front end* and a *back end.* The front end should interpret events such as depression of a mouse button and relay the appropriate message to the back end. As an example, we have implemented a prototype dividing a **TextController** into a **TextConFront** and a

**TextConBack**. When the left mouse button is depressed, the **TextConFront** sends the message **startSelectionAt:** to the **TextConBack**, indicating that text is being highlighted. While the left mouse button is held down the message **extendSelectionTo:** is sent. If the middle mouse button is depressed, the message **startUpYellowMenuAt:** is sent (a pop-up menu appears on the screen). Similar coding supports other input events. We may obtain behaviour other than the default Smalltalk behaviour by substituting a different front end: for example, a **NOLOGFront** sends the same messages whichever mouse button is depressed.

We also mentioned the desirability of the classes supplied being less closely tied to the implementation of the Smalltalk programming environment. Purchasing additional class libraries to augment the standard library can lead to difficulties with clashes of libraries from different suppliers [25]. It therefore seems vital for these libraries to be supplied as standard.

### 6.2. The programming environment

The programming environment could be significantly improved. Although code reading is a typical means of developing Smalltalk applications [26] this is inevitably difficult for the novice programmer, and inconvenient for the experienced programmer. What is needed is a system which allows the programmer to select a topic in the browser such as 'creating a user interface' and investigate the class structure in a more organised manner.

Moreover, we propose that an object inspector should be implemented allowing access to objects via *messages* rather than allowing direct access to instance variables. For example, the messages to be used in updating a **PlanCollection** would include **addPlan:** and **removePlan:**. The corresponding methods would ensure that the reference from the **PlanConstructor** back to the **PlanCollection** was set correctly. This inspection facility could be integrated with the other exploration tools in order to improve the ease with which one may move from inspecting a class to inspecting instances of a class and vice-versa.

The debugging difficulty mentioned in section 5.2 stems partially from the fact that the debugger is a part of the Smalltalk system which is currently executing. One possibility would be to implement a debugger which runs entirely separately from the Smalltalk system, but we propose that advantage could instead be taken of the fact that window management, event management and process scheduling are each almost entirely implemented in Smalltalk. The methods which check for the currently active process and window would be amended to check whether the code was being executed from the debugger, and if so, to return the process and window being debugged. Similarly, while the debugger is executing code, one of the primitive event management objects (an **InputSensor**) could be replaced by a **DummySensor** designed to access a control panel simulating the keyboard queue and mouse state.

## 7. ANTICIPATED EFFECTS OF OUR PROPOSALS

Of necessity we have outlined our proposals very briefly. Clearly we need to implement our proposals in full, and systematically test our implementation. Working through the entire class library searching for ways of improving it would be a major undertaking; implementation of our proposed changes to the programming environment would be a smaller undertaking. Nevertheless we predict that an improved class library and programming environment would increase productivity. In particular, an improved programming environment intended to facilitate navigation should be especially valuable to the novice Smalltalk programmer, for whom almost the entire class library is unexplored territory.

We have seen that Smalltalk is a powerful tool for implementing interactive applications such as are required in educational contexts, but that Smalltalk is currently difficult to use. Our proposals are intended to rectify this.

**Acknowledgement**

Implementation of NOLOG commenced while the author was in receipt of a UK Science and Engineering Research Council studentship.

## 8. REFERENCES

1 T. O'Shea & J. Self, *Learning and Teaching with Computers: Artificial Intelligence in Education,* Harvester, Brighton, UK (1983) 209.

2 J.H. Alexander & M.J. Freiling, *Smalltalk-80 Aids Troubleshooting System Development,* Systems & Software (April 1985) 111-118.

3 A. Goldberg & D. Robson, *Smalltalk-80: The Language and its Implementation,* Addison-Wesley, Reading, Ma. (1983).

4 A. Goldberg, *Smalltalk-80: The Interactive Programming Environment,* Addison-Wesley, Reading, Ma. (1984).

5 A. Goldberg, The Influence of an Object-Oriented Language on the Programming Environment. In: D.R. Barstow et al. (eds.), *Interactive Programming Environments,* McGraw-Hill, NY (1984) 141-174.

6 G. Booch, *Object-Oriented Design, With Applications,* Benjamin-Cummings, Wokingham, UK (1991).

7 L.P. Deutsch, *The Past, Present and Future of Smalltalk,* Proc. ECOOP 89, Cambridge University Press (1989) 73-87.

8 A. Goldberg & J. Ross, *Is the Smalltalk-80 System for Children?,* Byte (Aug. 1981) 348-368.

9 A. Goldberg & J. Ross, *Is the Smalltalk-80 System for Children?,* Byte (Aug. 1981) 348-368.

10 L. Gould & W. Finzer, *A study of TRIP: a Computer System for Animating Time-Rate-Distance Problems,* Int. J. Man-Machine Studies 17 (1982) 109-126.

11 W. Finzer & L. Gould, *Programming By Rehearsal,* Byte (June 1984) 187-210.

12 J. Fenton & K. Beck, *Playground: An Object-Oriented Simulation System with Agent Rules for Children of All Ages,* Proc. OOPSLA 89 (ACM SIGPLAN Notices 24(10), 1989), 123-137.

13 E.R. Tello, *Object-Oriented Programming for Artificial Intelligence,* Addison-Wesley, Reading, Ma. (1989).

14 J. Laursen & R. Atkinson, *Opus: A Smalltalk Production System,* Proc. OOPSLA 87 (ACM SIGPLAN Notices 22(12), 1987) 377-387.

15 S. Papert, *Mindstorms: Children, Computers, and Powerful Ideas,* Harvester, Brighton, UK (1980).

16 A.C. Jones & M.P. Thorne, *Intelligent Computer Aided Mathematical Problem Solving in a Modified Logo Environment,* Proc. ECCE 88, North-Holland, Amsterdam (1988) 207-211.

17 A.C. Jones & M.P. Thorne, *An Application of NUDGES to Intelligent Tutoring,* Proc. 6th ICTE, CEP Consultants (1989) 120-123.

18 G.E. Krasner & S.T. Pope, *A Cookbook for Using the Model-View-Controller User Interface Paradigm in Smalltalk-80,* J. Object-Oriented Programming 1(3) (1988) 26-49.

19 W.L. Johnson, *Intention-Based Diagnosis of Novice Programming Errors,* Pitman, London (1986).

20 J. Diedrich & J. Milton, *Experimental Prototyping in Smalltalk,* IEEE Software (May 1987) 50-64.

21 W. LaLonde & J. Pugh, *Inside Smalltalk Vol. 1,* Prentice-Hall, London, 1990.

22 W. LaLonde & J. Pugh, *Inside Smalltalk Vol. 2,* Prentice-Hall, London, 1991.

23 J. Nielsen & J.T. Richards, *The Experience of Learning and Using Smalltalk,* IEEE Software (May 1989) 73-77.

24 R.E. Johnson & B. Foote, *Designing Reusable Classes,* J. Object-Oriented Programming 1(2) (1988) 22-35.

25 L. Berlin, *When Objects Collide: Experiences with Reusing Multiple Class Hierarchies,* Proc. OOPSLA/ECOOP 90 (ACM SIGPLAN Notices 25(10), 1990) 181-193.

26 D.W. Sandberg, *Smalltalk and Exploratory Programming,* ACM SIGPLAN Notices 23(10) (1988) 85-92.

Education and Society / R. Aiken (Editor)
Information Processing 92, Volume II
Elsevier Science Publishers B.V. (North-Holland)


# CO-EXPLAINER: A MACHINE-LEARNING COMPANION

N. Hoskin and R. M. Aiken

CIS Dept., 038-024, Temple University, Philadelphia, PA, 19121, USA

**Abstract**

The Co-Explainer model for an interactive intelligent learning system is developed. This model features a collaborative computer learning partner that participates in joint problem-solving with the student user. Interaction with the co-explainer module serves to make explicit the student's own explanations for each problem-solving step. This model is related to its place among other such teaching/learning systems. Work in the fields of human learning and machine learning is described which serves to, respectively, justify the development of the model and its potential for current implementation.

Keyword Codes: I.2.1; I.2.6; I.2.8
Keywords: Applications and Expert Systems; Learning; Problem Solving, Control Methods, and Search

## 1. INTRODUCTION

The intelligent tutoring systems (ITS) field is concerned with the development of computerized systems which can provide a learning experience equivalent to that of a human tutor in a one-on-one teaching session. The basic ITS has been widely envisioned as containing the subject knowledge of a domain expert, the pedagogical (instructional planning) and discourse planning knowledge of an experienced human tutor, and an adaptive internal model of the student's current domain-knowledge state [1]. In behavioral terms, the ITS tutor component has been most commonly conceptualized as an omniscient teacher whose role is to immediately recognize and correct any student error.

ITS researchers are in the process of developing new paradigms that diverge from that of the fundamental ITS model. These new models attempt to incorporate the latest knowledge available from such areas as educational psychology, human learning theory and cognitive psychology into systems that will provide students with adaptive, flexible computerized learning systems. Such systems will often rely on the latest developments in AI architectures and machine learning to provide versatility and sensitivity to humans.

This paper presents a potential new paradigm for such a learning system, the Co-Explainer (Co-Ex) Model. Section 2 describes the ITS models that have contributed to the Co-Ex model. The following section provides a description of the Co-Ex model, the general principles upon which it is based and the issues which it is expected to address. Section 4 describes how some current conceptualizations of human learning relate to the Co-Ex model. Section 5 describes the role of machine learning in the Co-Ex model more fully. It also presents some important studies of machine learning that relate to the development of the model prototype. The summary restates the main features of the model, answers a possible objection to the development of systems based on the model and considers some possible implementation domains for the co- exploration model.

## 2. THE COMPANION AND COLLABORATOR MODELS

At least two ITS research groups have been concerned with deficiencies in the traditional ITS model and have proposed independent yet isomorphic solutions to these perceived weaknesses. One group, Chan and Baskin [2], has developed the Learning Companion System (LCS) model and the other, Cumming and Self [3], the concept of a computer-based collaborative learning partner (the collaborative learning model).

The LCS evolved out of the recognition of the useful effect of social interaction upon cognitive development, and the inhibiting effect on such interaction of the vastly different knowledge levels in the usual tutor-student interaction. Vygotsky's theory of the zone of proximal development recognizes the distance between the problem-solving abilities of a student working alone and that student under adult guidance or peer collaboration [4]. Vygotsky postulates that in peer interaction, if the peer's input is credible, the problem solver is motivated to modify any claims that are not supportable. The consequence is a collaborative solution that is superior to what either individual could manage alone.

Among the recent research which supports the such theories is that done on the practice of reciprocal peer-tutoring (Brown and Palincsar [5]), a procedure that requires students to alternately assume both the tutor and student role as they assist each other. This work shows that explanatory processes, as part of the reciprocal teaching activity, motivate learners and encourage the search for deeper levels of understanding and subject mastery. Brown and Palincsar characterize these explanatory- based interactive learning activities as inducing the learners to explain and represent knowledge in multiple ways and therefore, in the process, to comprehend it more fully themselves..

The LCS envisioned by Chan and Baskin would contain all of the four components of the traditional ITS, but would include in addition a 'companion' module. This fifth module approximates the presence of a learning peer for the human student, while the other components continue to act in the role of teacher. In a sense, the ITS has a multiple personality, without exhibiting the problematic behavior of humans with such a disorder. The 'teacher' personality generates problems, demonstrates examples, explains learning activities, and intervenes to break learning impasses when both partners are unable to make progress. The teacher's main role is seen as the management of educational goals through the monitoring of the student's learning stages, with rare remedial interventions.

Self argues that current ITS's are often incapable of ascertaining the true state of a student's knowledge, and even when they correctly identify student misconceptions, are often lacking in the pedagogical expertise to properly address them. Indeed, it may be arrogant and counterproductive to label student beliefs as 'bugs'. Instead, the ITS should act as an empathetic and fallible 'collaborator', participating in learning with the student through its offering of advice and suggestions on the domain material and learning process.

Gilmore and Self propose an alternative role for both machine learning and student modeling -- the generation of a peer learning collaborator [6]. For such a role, the machine learning techniques need only have psychological credibility (the student must consider the model's learning performance to be possible for her to emulate), not psychological fidelity. The model developed by Cumming and Self represents an attempt to re-define the utilization of intelligence in educational systems, and has also been called the Collaborator model.

## 3. THE CO-EXPLAINER MODEL

In the Co-Explainer model, the learning system's intelligent component (the co-explainer) is a collaborative module. It and the student would act together to co-operatively solve problems posed to them by another system component, the teacher module. The student and system would move jointly through a series of increasingly complex and diverse problems. The purpose of the teacher module is simply to present problems and intervene with correct solution steps in the event that the student and co-explainer reach an impasse.

The use of an increasingly-complex problem set serves two purposes. The first is to maintain the interest of the student, through continuing to constantly challenge and stimulate her. The second is to not allow the co- explainer module to become so competent with the concepts and procedures currently under study as to dominate the interaction with the student. This would ensure that the behavior of the co-explainer module remains constant throughout its sessions with the student -- the student would always be able to conceptualize the co-explainer as a fallible partner, generally reliable for some cogent advice and explanation, but never available as a crutch. While the same behavior could be accomplished in other manners (such as explicitly incorporating into the co- explainer module rules that constrain its provision of suggestions or answers), the suggested mechanism would seem to be a more natural one.

The co-explainer module would not incorporate large amounts of pre-compiled knowledge . Instead, the student and co-explainer would begin on an equal footing; the co-explainer building its own internal model of the domain in parallel with the student. The co-explainer is envisioned as begining a problem-solving session with a case-based component containing the same set of worked example problems as the student has been exposed to in class lessons. The problem-oriented nature of their interaction would serve the purpose of explicitly establishing the goals of their interaction. Much work in AI and cognitive science points to the obligatorily goal-oriented and situated nature of the cognitive activities of any intelligent agent. By placing the student and co-explorer module firmly in a problem-oriented environment, the context of their behaviors is firmly established.

The Co-Ex model owes much to the Cumming and Self concept of a collaborative educational system. As with their model, the Co-Ex model sees the purpose of the learning system as offering advice instead of instruction, and acting in a fashion that is intended as much to increase the metacognitive skills of the student as to increase her factual or procedural knowledge base. Both models see the envisioned collaborative interaction as ceding to the learner a large measure of both the global and local control of the learning experience. Another central concept to both models is the separation of task and discussion levels within a collaborative system [7]. As with the constructionist approach of Papert, each model sees the learner as not only performing a task (the task level), but reflecting upon the task and the learning experience (the discussion level), with this reflection being vital to the development of metacognitive abilities. The elicitation of, and full participation of the learning system in this discussion level, as a natural component of the student-system interaction, is thus critical to the fulfillment of the goals envisioned for the co-explainer system.

The use of recent paradigms in machine learning is vital to the realization of the Co-Ex model. Because of the rapidly advancing nature of the machine learning field, it is difficult to say which of such machine learning models would be usefully incorporated into such a prototype. However, the role of machine learning within a Co-Explainer model prototype can be developed through the discussion of three major points:

(1) the co-explainer module should incorporate human-like learning capabilities;

(2) the co-explainer module should incorporate multiple types of machine learning and hence reasoning capabilities; and,

(3) the emphasis of the machine learning techniques incorporated within the co-explainer module should be on their explanator capabilities.

As previously stated, the co-explainer module is seen as beginning any interaction with a student with an approximation of the domain knowledge of the student. The difference between the co-explainer and student lies in the incorporation into the module of machine learning capabilities that are designed to enable the module to become an 'expert' in the domain. The high-level purpose of the interaction between the student and system can thus be seen as the induction of homomorphic learning procedures in the student. This should occur through the ability of the system to explain both its view of the domain and its own ability to reason within it (operating on both the task and discussion levels).

The co-explainer module is not expected to have machine learning capabilities that are identical to those in the student, but capabilities that mirror those which can be elicited in the student. The machine learning ability of the system should be psychologically feasible, not necessarily psychologically valid. This is not to say that they cannot be psychologically valid, since many of the researchers in the machine learning community base their models on human learning data, viewing psychological validity as an important goal of their work.

The second point above is that the co-explainer module should include multiple machine learning techniques and models. This follows logically from the many analyses of human intelligence which show that human performance is dependent upon the functioning of multiple reasoning methodologies [8]. Any learning system designed to elicit effective domain performance in humans should, therefore, model the multiplicity of these mechanisms. The machine learning field has focused on many of the learning behaviors exhibited by humans - similarity-based generalization and discrimination, case-based learning, analogical learning, and explanation-based learning to note several major approaches. Operational machine learning models are available in each of these areas and should be appropriately incorporated into the co- explainer module.

The presence of multiple reasoning methodologies in the co-explainer would also serve the purpose of providing the system with multiple representations of the domain. Cumming and Self have stressed the need for the collaborative system to be able to reason from multiple viewpoints. In addition to the ability to introduce the student to such viewpoints, the presence of a variety of reasoning methods should enable the system to avoid or sidestep learning impasses. The system as well as the user needs to have the ability to back away from such a blockage and attempt a reformulation of the problem. Such a system should be able to offer multiple paths forward from any point in the solution space, as well as multiple ways of explaining the path that was taken to any such point.

The third point, concerning an emphasis on the explanatory power of the co-explainer module (and hence the models name), follows from a major goal of the system being the elicitation of metacognitive skills in the student. The ability of the system to explain its reasoning processes is essential to its ability to function on the metalevel of discussion. This facility would allow the module to function as a "glass box" model which the student can emulate. The system should be capable of requesting an explanation of any student action or statement for which it cannot find a justification in its own domain model. This will serve the function of requiring the student to make explicit the state of her domain knowledge. This behavior of the system should approximate the mutual questioning and explanatory interactions that occur with human peers. It is thus expected that these capabilities of the co-explainer module should produce the learning benefits seen in such human-to-human interactions as collaborative learning and reciprocal peer tutoring.

## 4. HUMAN LEARNING STUDIES

On-going work in the field of human learning research is spread over such areas as education studies, educational psychology, cognitive psychology and cognitive science. This section will focus upon the recent research efforts whose results served to inspire the Co-Ex Model, specifically in the areas of explanation-based and case-based reasoning in humans.

A research program by Chi and colleagues has demonstrated the central role that self-generated explanations play in the comprehension and performance of students studying physics [9, 10]. Example problems form an important component of any physics text and often provide the only place where many concepts and procedures are presented. The results of their protocol studies show that good students tend to study example-exercises in a text by explaining and providing justifications for each solution step. This generation of explanations serves to create inference rules that form internal functional and causal models for the systems under study.

Poorly-performing students do not exhibit the ability to monitor their comprehension failures and successes as good students do, and this may account for their significant lack of self-explanatory behaviors. This supports the emphasis in the Co-Ex model of the co-explainer module's ability to both generate and elicit explanations. The questioning of the student on domain knowledge by the system should force students to confront the state of their knowledge, while the provision of the system's own explanations helps students to develop and deepen their own models of the domain.

There is an accumulation of evidence that textbook-derived or classroom-derived worked examples provide the prime knowledge resource of students in their subsequent problem-solving behavior. Sweller and Cooper have shown that worked examples can lead to a decrease in both solution times and errors in later problem-solving sessions [11]. This research supports the role of the co-explainer in helping the student to recall and explain previous problem solutions, and its acting to lessen the cognitive load of the user.

A number of research groups have focused on the differences in the cognitive structures and procedures between novices and experts or between good and poor problem solvers [12, 13]. The usual interpretation of the results of such studies focuses upon the ability of good problem solvers/domain experts to utilize the deep structure of a problem or concept to organize their knowledge and their categorization procedures. Poor problem solvers/novices rely predominantly on surface features of the problems to retrieve possible solutions, and so often make incorrect choices. Viewing such studies from the context of case-based reasoning, it could be said that good problem solvers/experts use the deep structure (the functional and causal attributes) of a case to index and access it.

A study of the use of transfer problems (problems that are structurally, but not conceptually unfamiliar to the solver) by Robertson has analyzed its results from the viewpoint of differences in indexing [14]. The role of problem indexing has also been stressed in a study of the transfer of problem-solving ability between presentations of insight problems (problems requiring a reorganization of the user's initial conceptualization of the problem in order to solve it, usually resulting in an aha! reaction). Some forms of human problem solving thus seem to occur not through the application of a sequence of separately-retrieved procedures but via the recovery of a particular complete problem-solving episode (case) from memory. The procedures associated with this retrieved case are then applied to the new problem, perhaps with appropriate adjustment. This provides evidence that case-based reasoning as realized in computer systems has psychological feasibility, if not validity.

## 5. MACHINE LEARNING AND THE CO-EXPLANATION MODEL

There is a growing body of research into what can be termed psychologically plausible machine learning techniques. These are approaches to machine learning research that take as their starting points data observed from human learning experimentation, and aspire to incorporate similar behaviors into a computational system. A (perhaps not exhaustive) list of such machine learning paradigms would include explanation-based learning, case-based reasoning, and analogical reasoning. It is with these psychologically plausible machine learning mechanisms that any current attempt to realize the Co-Ex model will best concern itself. These learning behaviors are those which the co- explainer module should exhibit to the student in order to stimulate the student's own metacognitive abilities. The co-explainer should be able to hold a dialogue with the student on its own cognitive abilities in order to elicit similar abilities in the student. This area was addressed previously (Section 4) in relation to the task and discussion levels of dialogue between the student and co-explorer module.

This point also relates to the necessarily 'glass-box' nature of the co-explainer module. The reasoning performed by the system in an explanation-based, case-based or analogical manner will be easily recognizable by the student. This would not be so for such mechanisms as conceptual clustering or the operation of the ID3 induction algorithm. A co-explainer module which exhibited the same behavior as a student through the use of such non-psychologically-feasible mechanisms could not be said to be plausibly modeling the student, which is a goal of the Co- Ex model. While important for other uses, these types of machine language approaches are too opaque for their incorporation into a co-explainer module.

The following subsections describe two areas of machine learning where the existing models are psychologically plausible and offer themselves as promising components of a co-explorer module.

I. Explanation-Based Reasoning

Explanation-based reasoning (EBR) is a type of machine learning whose models rely on the generation of explanatory hypothesis to improve their performance. Currently-existing computational models of abduction fall into two broad categories: explanation-based learning (EBL) [15] and explanation completion (EC) [16]. EBL is a large class of machine learning algorithms that work as follows. The machine has a domain theory that is sufficient to solve a wide class of problems. However, the theory is expressed in a way that makes solution of most problems computationally infeasible. EBL increases the performance of the system as measured by the number of problems it can feasibly solve, but EBL does not change the set of problems that it can solve in principle.

Explanation completion is a class of learning algorithms that increase the set of problems that are solvable in principle. It does this by attempting to complete a partial explanation, and then testing the resulting piece of knowledge for its plausibility. Plausibility can be determined by a variety of means, ranging from syntactic measurements to a determination of consistency in known explanation patterns.

II. Case-Based Reasoning

Case-based reasoning (CBR) is the process of using the results of past problem-solving episodes (cases) to analyse or solve a new problem, explaining why the past analysis or solution is, or is not, similar and therefore whether it can justifiably be followed, and/or adapted to the new situation. When presented with a problem, a CBR system typically first analyzes it in order to develop a set of index parameters with which to search its case base. It then retrieves the closest-matching case, and attempts to map its features to the new problem. The result of such a mapping is then adapted to the solution of the new problem. Case-based learning consists of adding the new problem solution, properly indexed to the case base of the system so that it can aid future problem-solving episodes. There is considerable evidence that CBR methods are implicitly used in human reasoning and play an important role in the progress from novice to expert status in a domain [17].

CBR systems have intimate connections with explanation-based and analogical reasoning systems. Typically a CBR system may use EBR in order to analyze and index new cases [18], while using analogical reasoning methods to perform the mapping of old to new cases. Thus there is often not a clear distinction between systems that are termed declared as using'case-based', 'explanation-based' or 'analogical' reasoning.

## 6. CONCLUSIONS

Two considerations should help determine possible implementation domains for the first co- explanation model system: (1) sufficient studies of human novices and experts existing to provide the foundation for a principled development of a such a model system; and, (2) existing ITS or expert systems that serve to provide a basis for co-explorer model system development. A promising domain is computer program design. Multiple studies of expert and novice performance have been performed, and plausible cognitive and computational models exist for skill acquisition. Bonar's plan-based tutoring system BRIDGE offers an example of an icon-based system which could be used as a basis for a program design co-explainer prototype [19].

To summarize, a Co-explainer model for an interactive intelligent learning system has been developed and related to its place among the companion and collaborator learning system models. Work in the fields of human learning and machine learning has been described which serves to, respectively, justify the development of the model and its potential for current implementation

Work toward development of a co-explorer learning system would contribute to both the ITS and AI fields. It would also represent a contribution to the research being performed on intelligent assistant programs and learning apprenticeship systems. The development of human- computer collaborative systems is an idea which has occurred to researchers in a variety of fields. It would seem that systems such as the co-explorer represent an idea whose time is here.

## 7. REFERENCES

1. E. Wenger, Artificial Intelligence and Tutoring Systems: Computational and Cognitive Approaches to the Communication of Knowledge. Morgan Kaufmann Publishers, Los Altos, California, 1987
2. T.-K. Chan and A.B. Baskin, "Learning Companion Systems." in Frasson, C. and Gauthier, G. (Eds) Intelligent Tutoring Systems: At the Crossroads of Artificial

Intelligence and Education. Ablex Publishing, Norwood, New Jersey, 1990.

3. G. Cumming and J. Self, "Collaborative Intelligent Educational Systems." in Bierman, D., Breuker, J. and Sandberg, J. (Eds) Arificial Intelligence and Education: Synthesis and Reflectio IOS, Amsterdam, The Netherlands, 1989.
4. L. Vygotsky, Mind in Society (Cole M., John-Steiner V., Scribner S., and Souberman E., Trans.) Harvard University Press, Cambridge, MA, 1978.
5. A.L. Brown. and A.S> Palincsar, "Guided, Cooperative Learning and Individual Knowledge Acquisition." in Resnick, L.B. (Ed) Knowing, Learning, and Instruction: Essays in Honor of Robert Glaser. Lawrence Erlbaum, New Jersey, 1989.
6. G. Gilmore and J. Self, "The Application of Machine Learning to Intelligent Tutoring Systems in Self, J. (Ed) AI and Human Learning: Intelligent Computer Aided Instruction. Chapman and Hall, London, 1988.
7. G. Cumming and J. Self, "Intelligent Educational Systems: Identifying and Decoupling the Conversational Levels." Instructional Science, 19, 11-27, 1990.
8. R.J. Sternberg, Beyond IQ: A Triarchic Theory of Human Intelligence. Cambridge University Press, Cambridge, U.K., 1985.
9. M.T.H. Chi, and M. Bassok, "Learning from Examples Via Self-Explanations." in Resnick, L.B. (Ed.) Knowing, Learning and Instruction: Essays in Honor of Robert Glaser. Lawrence Erlbaum Assoc., Inc., Hillsdale, New Jersey, 1989.
10. M.T.H. Chi, M.W. Lewis, P. Reimann and R. Glaser "Self-Explanations: How Students Study and Use Examples in Learning to Solve Problems." Cognitive Science, 13, 145-182, 1989.
11. J. Sweller and G.A. Cooper, "The Use of Worked Examples as a Substitute for Problem Solvin in Learning Algebra" Cogn. and Instruction, 2, 59-89, 1985.
12. T. de Jong and M.G.M. Ferguson-Hessler, M.G.M. "Cognitive Structures of Good and Poor Novice Problem Solvers in Physics." Journal of Educational Psychology, 78(4), 279-288, 1986
13. P.T. Hardiman , R. Dufresne and J.P. Mestre "The Relation Between Problem Categorization and Problem Solving Among Experts and Novices." Mem and Cogni, 17(5), 627-638, 1989.
14. W.C. Robertson, "Detection of Cognitive Structure with Protocol Data: Predicting Performanc on Physics Transfer Problems." Cognitive Science, 14, 253-280,1990.
15. G. de Jong and R. Mooney, "Explanation-Based Learning: An Alternative View." Machine Learning, 1(2), 145-176, 1986.
16. K. VanLehn, W. Ball and B. Kowalski "Explanation-Based Learning of Correctness: Towards Model of the Self-Explanation Effect." Proceedings of the Cognitive Science Society, Lawrenc Erlbaum, Hillsdale, NJ, 1990.
17. J.L. Kolodner, J.L. "Towards an Understanding of the Role of Experience in the Evolution fro Novice to Expert." Int. J. Man-Machine Studies, 19, 497-518, 1983.
18. R.C. Schank and D.B. Leake, "Creativity and Learning in a Case-Based Explainer", Art. Intel 40,353-385, 1989.
19. J.G. Bonar, R. Cunningham, P. Beatty, J. Corbett and W. Weil "BRIDGE: Intelligent Tutorin with Intermediate Representations." ONR Technical Report LSP-5, 1988.

Education and Society / R. Aiken (Editor)
Information Processing 92, Volume II
Elsevier Science Publishers B.V. (North-Holland)



# Courseware to help readers trace the ties in text as an aid to comprehension

J. Anderson

School of Education, Flinders University of South Australia, GPO Box 2100 Adelaide, South Australia 5001, Australia.

**Abstract**

Researchers in different parts of the world have been mapping the cue systems that readers utilise to derive meaning from text. Goodman and Smith, for example, in the United States describe the graphophonic, syntactic and semantic cues available to readers; Halliday and Hasan in Australia and Chapman in Britain propose a further layer termed cohesive ties as the fundamental building blocks of text. Building on these insights, our work at Flinders University has been directed to developing computer software where students may trace ties in text and, as they perceive and make connections, are aided in comprehending a writer's meaning. This paper describes a program called *Tie Tracer* and its forerunner *GapMaker...GapTaker* and the developmental work as we have moved from research to practice. The resulting courseware – computer programs and teaching materials – has been trialled with many groups including young children, adults with learning difficulties, and learners for whom English is not the mother tongue.

Keyword Codes: K.3.1; K.3.2; J.4
Keywords: Computers and Education, Computer Uses in Education; Computer and Information Science Education; Computer Applications, Social and Behavioral Sciences

## 1. THEORETICAL BASIS FOR COURSEWARE DEVELOPMENT

The theoretical basis for the courseware development described in this paper stems from two separate lines of research endeavour. One line comes principally from Goodman and Smith in the United States of America whose work is well known to reading researchers and practioners alike. The second line stems from linguistic analyses conducted in Australia and Britain into the mechanisms that bind text, and associated psycholinguistic studies relating students' perceptions of these same mechanisms to comprehension.

This paper presents first a brief outline of the theoretical underpinnings for the literacy courseware being designed and developed at Flinders University of South Australia. There follows a description of the developmental work of two computer programs, *GapMaker...GapTaker* and *Tie Tracer*, as the work has moved from theory and research to practice, in classroom trials with children and adults, with native English speakers and with learners for whom English is not the mother tongue.

## 2. CUE SYSTEMS AND COHESION

A selection of Goodman's writings, such his classic papers *Reading: a psycholinguistic guessing game* and *Miscues: windows on the reading process*, is collected in Goodman (1982). At the risk of oversimplifying, Goodman postulates that readers utilise three overlapping cuing systems as they attempt to make meaning of written text. First, there are graphophonic cues. These are the sound relationships between the written form of words and their meanings. Second, there are syntactic cues, the cues realised through the grammar of language. And third, there are semantic cues, cues realised through the meanings of words. Reading is a psycholinguistic game as readers utilise these cue systems to make predictions. As text becomes more difficult, or with less fluent readers, recourse needs to be made to all three sets of cues, especially graphophonic cues leading to sounding out of individual words. This use of what Smith (1978) calls *visual information* slows reading down causing bottlenecks to comprehension.

Quite separately from Goodman, two linguists now resident in Australia – Halliday and Hasan – postulate another major source of linguistic information which they term cohesion. Cohesive ties, according to Halliday and Hasan (1976), are the links within text that make a text a text, in contrast to a set of unrelated sentences. Other writers have described cohesive ties as *a kind of linguistic mortar* (Tierney and Mosenthal 1980). In Britain, Chapman tested the educational validity of these linguistic theories in a large-scale longitudinal project designed to gauge the extent to which students' perception of textual ties was related to more traditional measures of reading comprehension (Chapman 1983). The importance of the concept of cohesion to reading teachers is slowly being recognised (see, for example, Irwin 1986).

Some examples might clarify these concepts of cue systems and cohesive ties. Consider the sentence:

```
The wind xxxxx in the trees.
```

And suppose that for some reason the third word is misprinted or smudged to make it illegible. To reconstruct the sentence, a reader might make use of syntactic cues, that English grammar requires some verb to complete the meaning (e.g. *spoke*, *knocks*, *blows*, *howled*) though the tense of the verb is not indicated. The reader might also utilise semantic cues to complete the meaning since certain words are more likely than others. Thus *blows* or *howled*, even in the very limited context, are more probable than *ran* or *climbs*. Suppose, further, the reader could just make out the outline of the blurred letters but did not *know* the word. Such a reader might then sound it out – for example, b-l-o-w-s – and attempt to use sound relationship or graphophonic cues.

Cohesive ties, by contrast with syntactic, semantic and graphophonic cues, extend beyond the sentence and serve to bind sentences together. A native speaker of English, if confronted with the following jumbled sentences, would generally have little difficulty in rearranging them to make a meaningful text:

- It was small and black.
- A cat came to my house.
- Now I have it for a pet.

What allows a meaningful arrangement of these sentences into a single text are cohesive ties (here the anaphoric *it* referring back to *cat* and the conjunction *Now* linking the third sentence with all that has gone before).

## 3. A PROGRAM TO PROVIDE A WINDOW ON THE READING PROCESS

It was these two lines of research, one concerned with the cue systems of language and the other relating to the cohesive properties of language, that provided the springboard for the design and development of courseware at Flinders University as part of a larger research program into student learning through computer-mediated text. Described first is a computer program that allows one to observe (although only to a limited extent) what happens when a subject reads text, reading normally being a silent and invisible process. Next, an overview of a second computer program is given where subjects are aided in tracing the threads that tie text together.

*GapMaker...GapTaker* is a dual purpose program in that it is both a reading and a writing tool. One part of the program (*GapMaker*) allows users to construct meaningful cloze activities, that is passages of text in which certain parts are deleted, while in the second part of the program (*GapTaker*) subjects attempt to reconstruct the deleted parts and restore the text to a meaningful whole. The underlying theory posits that at each deletion or choice point, the degree to which readers' replacements of text match the choices made by the writer when composing the text is a measure of the comprehension of the passage.

The *GapMaker* component of the computer program is quite flexible. The built-in word processor allows all kinds of texts to be entered and in this sense the program is content-free. If teachers were using the program with young pupils for instance, they might employ appropriate narrative or fictional texts, whereas secondary teachers might choose passages from textbooks – science, history or geography – whatever the teaching purpose determines. Traditional cloze procedure involves the deletion of words on a regular pattern through texts, often every fifth word. *GapMaker* allows the user to adopt *any* regular deletion pattern of words. As well, the program permits the deletion of particular words or even parts of words, such as verb endings for example. Another feature is that the user may specify the starting point for deletion commencing, for instance, at the beginning of the second or third sentence in order to allow a lead-in to the passage. In other words, the user has full control of what parts of a text are deleted – regular or irregular word deletion, words or parts of words, and parts of text to keep intact.

Other computer programs like, for example, *Clozemaster* and *Gapkit* (available for Apple and BBC microcomputers) can also generate cloze reading activities but *GapMaker...GapTaker* goes further for in the *GapTaker* part of the program, subjects reconstruct texts at the keyboard, attempting to fill gaps and make texts whole again. The computer program accepts all readers' responses, the text adjusting according as responses are longer or shorter than the original. On completion, students may match their responses with those in the original text and obtain feedback on their performance.

Another function available in *GapMaker...GapTaker* is the deletion of all words in a text which readers attempt to replace by making certain hypotheses and confirming or rejecting these as the text slowly emerges. This reading activity was first devised in a program called *Developing Tray* and later in *Word Search* (programs for the BBC) and described by Govier (1983) as "a significant new teaching tool". The original program was called *Developing Tray* because text is initially hidden, rather like an undeveloped photo, the task for students being to make the text progressively appear in the same way that a photo gradually becomes visible in a developing tray.

Many trials have been conducted of *GapMaker...GapTaker* with students at different levels of schooling, with subjects of differing language ability, and with subjects for whom English is not the mother tongue. While space precludes a full description of these trials, it should be noted that results with computer-mediated texts mirror quite closely those with *book texts*. That is, performance at the computer with text reconstruction correlates well with standard measures of reading comprehension whether these latter are administered in pencil-and-paper format or on computer. The program thus provides a window on the reading process by creating choice points in text and allowing teachers, and researchers, to observe students' responses at these choice points. The use of computers additionally allows researchers to record students' different attempts at replacement, the order in which replacements are made, and even the time spent in completing each replacement. The program may be said therefore to simulate both an eye camera and mark sensing equipment, in so far as it records students' processing of text as well as the product or comprehension of text.

From an instructional point of view, *GapMaker...GapTaker* has proved highly motivating as a class activity even after the novelty of working with computers (the Hawthorn effect) is taken into account. Following the trials, teachers reported that they found it useful for students to enter their own stories into the program and from these for students themselves to create reading puzzles for other students to solve. In this way the program serves as both a writing and a reading and reasoning tool.

## 4. A PROGRAM TO TRACE TEXT CONTINUITY AND CONTENT

Another computer program developed at Flinders University as part of the research project reported here on computer-mediated text and comprehension is *Tie Tracer*, a program utilising the colour capabilities of computers. Examples from the accompanying program documentation describe the key functions of *Tie Tracer*.

### 4.1. Tracing continuity in text

One of the major categories of textual cohesion allows readers to trace the key actors in narrative and so maintain the threads of a story. Consider the nursery rhyme, Dr Foster, shown below with four deletions:

```
Dr Foster went to Gloucester in a shower of rain. ..
stepped in a puddle right up to ... middle. And .. never
went ..... again.
```

The rhyme is shown in *Tie Tracer* with blanks colour-coded, one chain perhaps green and the other red. In each case, the colour provides a clue to the missing words by highlighting the referent items (*Dr Foster* and *Gloucester* respectively). Although a very short text, the colour coding can help readers keep track of events (that is, comprehend) by seeing the main actor, Dr Foster (through the chain *Dr Foster ... he ... his ... he*), and places (through the chain *Gloucester ... there*).

As a further example, consider the two key groups of actors in the following passage. In printed form, as here, these two groups are indicated in italics and bold respectively:

*The two children* had an idea who **the culprit** was. *Mary and Joan* had seen **him** near *their* letter box. The next day *they* decided to challenge **the young boy.**

As a measure of students' perception of the continuity in this text, ends of cohesive ties may be deleted (e.g. **him** in the second sentence and *they* in the third) and students then asked to restore the missing text. What *Tie Tracer* uniquely does is separately colour-code the two groups of actors, in place of the italics and bold, so that readers are helped in keeping track of the two threads running through this text. In addition, the program can colour-code the referent items, namely *the two children* and **the culprit**, to facilitate tracing the connections for comprehension. The user has full control over which words are deleted in stories and the choice, too, of colours, and whether the referent item is colour-coded or not. In other words, *Tie Tracer* may be used to produce conventional cloze texts, or the colour facility may be employed as an aid in tracing continuity ties in text.

### 4.2. Tracing text content

A second major category of textual cohesion serves to determine the content of text. This is achieved principally through repetition and association of the meanings of lexical items. To illustrate just how important these ties are to comprehension, the following short excerpt has most lexical items deleted:

```
One of my ........ ....... is ........ I find it
........to ......or ..... To ..... is really quite a
....... .........
```

As this excerpt demonstrates, there is little meaning when key lexical items are hidden. Here is the text with lexical items restored:

```
One of my favourite hobbies is painting. I find it relaxing
to sketch or draw. To paint is really quite a restful
activity.
```

Several threads run through this text: one thread is conveyed by the words *painting ... sketch ... draw.... paint*; another thread by the words *favourite ... relaxing ... restful*; and a third thread by the words *hobbies ... activity*. (Yet another thread is the continuity component conveyed by *my ... I*, already described.) It is the threads conveyed through the vocabulary that determine in large measure the content of this particular text, namely that it is about a pleasurable past-time or hobby.

As in the previous examples, some of these elements may be deleted for students to restore, and the degree to which the text is made whole again is a measure of students' comprehension of content. Again, the use of different colours for each separate thread (up to six are available) is something the computer can effectively show but which is less easy to simulate in a printed description, as here.

### 4.3. Sorting the parts

There are other components of *Tie Tracer* which combine tracing of text content and text continuity. In Sentence Sort, for instance, students are presented with sentences (or even parts of sentences) in jumbled order to rearrange so that they *make sense*. Students are successful to the extent that they are able to perceive the threads or cohesive ties in text.

The computer shuffles the parts very thoroughly in Sentence Sort. However, if teachers wish, they can control the shuffling, which they may want to do, for instance, to make the task easier for some students. Thus, for example, just the first two sentences of a story could be reversed, the remaining sentences being in the original order. An option within *Tie Tracer* allows this. With pencil and paper, an activity such as Sentence Sort would require individual sentences to be cut up and rearranged. What the computer does is shuffle the parts, administer these to students to sort, and then compare students' rearrangements with the original ordering. A text editor allows teachers or students to enter groups of sentences that form whole texts for subsequent sorting.

### 4.4. Trialling Tie Tracer in classrooms

As with *GapMaker...GapTaker*, *Tie Tracer* has been extensively trialled with students and their teachers and these trials evidenced even further uses of the program. Teachers reported, as before, that it was useful for students to enter their own texts and create reading puzzles for other students. In particular, younger students enjoy entering jokes and riddles and these, with their punch lines and answers, lend themselves especially to sentence sorting.

When students enter their own stories, they usually want to indicate the author (e.g. By Samantha Jones). This practice highlighted a *bug* in one of the early versions of the program because, unless a full stop is entered after the name (the method by which the program identifies components for shuffling), the author caption is omitted. In one school where *Tie Tracer* was being tested and where this problem was first detected, one Year 3 student aged just 10 suggested that the program could even be used to shuffle items such as students' names with the task for students then to rearrange these alphabetically. The boy went on to suggest that this would only work if full stops were entered after each name.

This insight from the 10-year-old pupil led to a new teaching activity, for the same idea may be used to order words into phrases or sentences, provided full stops are entered after the parts for sorting. For example, the following short story contains just six words:

```
my. little. cat. is. called. Spot.
```

If a full stop is placed after each word when the story is entered, as shown, Sentence Sort may be used to shuffle the parts, with students now sorting the words so that they make sense. Such an activity may be appropriate for some children before attempting to sort longer units. The same idea may be used to sort phrases and clauses or, as the Year 3 student first suggested, to sort items alphabetically.

## 5. CONCLUSION

The two computer programs described briefly here, *Tie Tracer* and its predecessor *GapMaker...GapTaker*, were developed to meet the reading needs of students and teachers. Their development was part of a larger research project investigating the use of computers in language. The major purposes of the research were to provide a window on the reading process and to gauge the degree to which students' perception of cohesive ties, the mechanisms which bind text, is an aid to comprehension.

Although it is stated that the two programs provide a window on the reading process, clearly the deletion of parts of texts and the subsequent attempts to make the texts whole again disrupt normal reading. It is because reading comprehension is a largely hidden process that some kind of interruption – in this research by creating choice points similar to those encountered by writers when writing – is inevitable if the process is to be examined by researchers.

Both computer programs presented in this paper are firmly grounded in theory. As well, each is content free, by which is meant that the programs may be used with any text of the user's choice. Thus the programs may be applied across different grade levels or with students of differing abilities. In the course of trialling the programs in classrooms, new types of teaching activities were suggested . There are no doubt yet other ways to use *Tie Tracer* and *GapMaker...GapTaker* to promote language learning, ways waiting to be discovered by imaginative teachers and their students.

## 6. REFERENCES

L.J. Chapman, Reading Development and Cohesion, Heinemann, London, 1983.

K.S. Goodman, Language and Literacy: The Selected Writings of Kenneth S. Goodman (Vol. 1), Routledge and Kegan Paul, Boston, 1982.

H. Govier, Primary language development, Acorn User, 10 (1983), 45-51.

M.A.K. Halliday and R. Hasan, Cohesion in English, Longman, London, 1976.

J.W. Irwin (ed.), Understanding and Teaching Cohesion Comprehension, International Reading Association, Delaware, 1986.

F. Smith, Understanding Reading: A Psycholinguistic Analysis of Reading and Learning to Read (2nd ed.), Holt, Rinehart and Winston, New York, 1978.

R.J. Tierney and J. Mosenthal, Discourse Comprehension and Production: Analysing Text Structure and Cohesion (Technical Report No. 152), Center for the Study of Reading, University of Illinois, Urbana, 1980.

### Courseware

GapMaker...GapTaker, Prologic, Melbourne (for IBM and Apple computers).

Tie Tracer, Jacaranda Software, Brisbane (for Apple and BBC computers).

Education and Society / R. Aiken (Editor)
Information Processing 92, Volume II
Elsevier Science Publishers B.V. (North-Holland)
1992 IFIP.

# New intellectualized software for statistical informatics education and research

Igor N. Sinitsyn

Institute of Informatics Problems, Russian Academy of Sciences
117900, 30/6, str. Vavilova, Moscow, Russia

Abstract

Stochastic systems (StS) serve as a suitable mathematical model for a lot of real-life phenomena in statistical informatics. The main results of Stochastic Systems Research Program in the field of StS software tools for model validation and analysis and its education and research applications are given.

Keyword Codes: K.8.1; I.6.4; D.2.2
Keywords: Personal computing, Application Packages; Model Validation and Analysis; Tools and Techniques

## 1. INTRODUCTION

Any application of mathematical and informatical methods implies the design and validation of a suitable mathematical model for the system or process under study, the necessary theoretical evaluations (sometimes very complex and sophisticated), based on this model, the problem algorithmization and at last producing the respective software. But almost all the specialists working in various fields of human activity have neither the necessary mathematical nor informatical knowledge. What then must these specialists do? Postpone all their daily work and study mathematics? We say no. People must not go to mathematics but mathematics must come to people. The mathematicians and scientists in informatics must create such informational technology, tools and software for personal computing which give the possibility to solve various mathematical problems without any special knowledge of mathematics and informatics.

Aiming at this goal, the Stochastic Systems Research Program was started in 1984 in the Institute of Informatic Problems of the Russian Academy of Science [1, 2] . The choice of a stochastic system (StS) for study was motivated by the fact that it serves as a suitable model for a lot of real-life phenomena.

The first stage of the Program covers the problems of the statistical analysis of StS described by differential,integro-differential, difference, mixed differential and difference equations. The resulting methods, algorithms and software are designed for studying such systems whose mathematical model in the form of some of the above mentioned equations is completely known.

The second stage of the Program covers the problems of real-time estimation of the state and unknown parameters in a partially observed StS of one of the above mentioned classes. The resulting methods, algorithms and software are designed for computer aided design of filters and identificators realizing the estimation processes. This part of the Program yields the tools for solving that part of the general identification problem which concerns the estimation of unknown parameters.

The third and the last stage of the Program covers the problems of automatic design of mathematical models from experimental and off line statistical data. At this stage the theory of model fitting is reviewed and developed including mathematical tools for the choice of an adequate model consistent with the available data and their uncertainly, estimation of its parameters, testing hypotheses and validation of the model chosen. Then the intelligent software and appropriate computer implementation are elaborated to provide users with the tools for fully automatic design of mathematical models with possible user's guidance (depending on his desire and competence). Once the model is built, it may be used for studying the system functioning, to predict its behavior under various kind decisions and thus supporting the decision making processes. This part of the Program solves the most important and most difficult identification problem, i.e. the establishing of the adequate set of equations describing the system or process to be studied.

Main results of Stochastic Systems Research Program are realized in educational and research practice in the form of intellectualized PC-based tutoring software "MOMENT", "NALib", "StS-ANALYSIS", "StS-MODEL" and "StS-FILTER" [1-4].

## 2. MATHEMATICAL BACKGROUND

The great importance for practice has the problem of building mathematical models of real systems on experimental data. One of the approaches to building models of studied system is the preliminary study of general regularities of the system behaviour and the spelling of the supposed equation of its model with the unknown parameters what is necessary to estimate by the results of the observations (the identification of parameters). Modern mathematical background of StS software based on the applied StS theory is given in [3].

## 3. DESIGN PRINCIPLES OF INTELLECTUATIZED SOFTWARE FOR STOCHASTIC SYSTEMS EDUCATION AND RESEARCH

The StS software requirements imply the following design principles: 1) realization on universal non-expensive computers functioning in the interactive regime (first of all on personal computers); 2) orientation to mass users being non specialists in computing and StS theory; 3) automatization of all stages of StS education and research.

One of the most important requirements to modern StS software products is the application of well developed interactive man-machine interface. This is explained by the fact that a StS research is a specific intellectual work where intuition and experience of the researcher are of great importance. Besides this, the convenient dialogue interface provides such a high level of comfortness for a user which permits to speak about StS software as an everyday instrument for the researchers.

The StS software must represent a closed system from the connection of software modules and components point of view. Meanwhile this software should be open for the information interchange on the file data level with other software products. The special converting modules in StS software assigned for the data transformation into the widely spread unified formats allow to use some well known specialized software products for the nonstandard data processing. Such an approach allows to: a) restrict oneself by only minimal set of necessary standard service functions, and thus to make the StS software application easier; b) better include the StS software into the modern program medium and raise the adaptive properties to quickly increasing service functions requirements; c) simplify the integration of the StS software with other software products in the composition of complex software and hardware systems.

The characteristic disadvantage of most of all scientifical software is that the user must know special languages for the mathematical model description (high level non-procedure languages, as a rule). That is why the necessity of the software design for inputting and natural visualization of the model arises. Only quite natural description of a mathematical model will permit the user to interact effeciently with a computer.

Special full screen word processor for the corresponding stochastic equations, initial conditions and parameters inputting, modification and mapping in the natural form be an important component of StS software. The naturality is achieved by the usage of the non-standard software signgeneratior with the original set of signs and symbols. The symbol size and relative position must correspond with the proportions of the natural mathematical expressions. Other important component is the translator of the natural text mathematical model description into the internal representation in PC for the quick inter activeness. While translating the lexical, syntaxical and partially semantical correctness of the model should be checked out.

The StS software after sufficient experience of application should provide the possibility to create the blank of stochastical models and support the process of administration of new models.

In general for a mass researcher it is expedient to have StS software in the form of the integrated applied package compounding different functional blocks.

## 4. INTELLECTUALIZED PACKAGE FOR STOCHASTIC PROCESSES ANALYSIS AND MODELING, COMPUTER AIDED FILTER AND IDENTIFICATOR DESIGN "StS-FILTER"

Intellectualized package "StS-filter" for IBM PC/AT, PS/2 compatible computers realizes the methods of statistical analysis, modeling, Kalman and Pugachev filtering and identification processes and parameters. It allows to perform statistical PC-based research and design for high dimension linear and non-linear StS(modeling, accuracy and sensivity analysis, parameter identification and optimization, computer aided optimal filters and identificators design).

The package represents the integrated environment including modules:

1. Original mathematical word processor allowing: input; edit models and text comments on them; perform syntax and semantix analysis.

2. Compiler.

3. Mathematical module realizing: installation of initial data; calculation of model probabilistic characteristics; calculation of filters and identificators coefficients; modeling; calculation of mean square errors; saving the results of calculation on disk.

4. Graphical visualization module providing: simultaneous overview of several characteristics while computer experiment; output of several graphs for required characteristics; scaling and microscope regime; hard copy reception of any graphs; output for results table on printer.

Modules control, selection, copying and deleting of models performs using the hierarchical menu systems. "StS-FILTER" is functioning under control of operational systems MS-DOS (versions 3.00 and higher), realized on C language.

## 5. APPLICATION OF INTELLECTUALIZED StS SOFTWARE

The designed StS software is used in the spheres of education, science and technics where stochastic differential or difference equations serve as an adequate models. They are studied in the following courses: Probability theory and mathematical statistics, Random processes, Mathematical modeling, Statistical control theory, Statistical informatics, Mechanics, Flight dynamics, etc. in the Russian Universities and Colledges.

Forms and methods of education are usually based on speciality and mathematical level of students. The application of the described StS software by the students of mathematical and some applied specialities may be organized for the 4-5 year students of Russian Universities and Colledges and for last terms of Bachelor degree course in the Western Universities in the form of options or studying additional chapters of standard courses. In this case the methodical material usually correspond to the description of StS software It's no use to give technically minded students a strict mathematical background of models. It's better to fix their attention to a short theoretical introduction giving a good variety of different examples. For students of biological, chemical, economical faculties it's possible to prepare short course on analysis, modeling and building of stochastic models in certain area and with certain examples but after an minimal introduction course of mathematics. This variety of approaches is possible due to a high grade of software intellectualization (there is no need for a special preparation in the StS theory and programming).

Following [4-5] some classical stochastic problems in informatics (estimation, calibration of computer systems analytical models, software performance evaluation), signal processing (analysis and modeling, Kalman and Pugachev filtering and extrapolation) and mechanics and biology modeling (models of neutral stable ship, rigid body and physical pendulum in a random environment, stochastic population dynamics, stochastic biochemical reactions) are outlined.

StS software may be also considered as basic functional, problem and subject-oriented tools for new informatical research and education StS technologies.

## 6. REFERENCES

1 V.S. Pugachev, Stochastic Systems Research in the USSR Academy of Sciences, IIASA, Laxenburg, Austria, 1989.

2 V.S. Pugachev, Tutorial. Lectures on Applied Methods for Analysis and Filtering in Stochastic Differential Systems, IIASA, Luxenbourg, Austria, 1991.

3 V.S. Pugachev and I.N. Sinitsyn, Stochastic Differential Systems. Analysis and Filtering, Chichester. John Wiley, 1987.

4 I.N. Sinitsyn, V.I. Shin, N.K. Moshchuk et al, PC-based intellectual tutoring software for analyzing and modeling processes in dynamic systems with random disturbances. Proceeding of Soviet-British Modeling Colloquium, Moscow, 19-23 Nov. 1990.

5 I.N. Sinitsyn, Statistical problems of informatics and computer aided scientific engineering (survey), Preprints of 8 International Symposium "Information Modular Computer Systems and Networks", Russia, Dubna, 8-12 Sept. 1991.

Education and Society / R. Aiken (Editor)
Information Processing 92, Volume II
Elsevier Science Publishers B.V. (North-Holland)
1992 IFIP.



# Knowledge Based Systems in Education: An Instructional Method that Places the Responsibility for Learning on the Students

Bent B. Andresen

Royal Danish School of Educational Studies
Emdrupvej 115B, DK-2400 Copenhagen NV, Denmark
Fax:+45 39 66 00 83

**Abstract**

This paper deals with applications of knowledge based learning environments.

It considers in particular the use of critiquing systems. Critiquing systems are second generation expert systems tailored to evaluate the students' problem solving. Instead of telling the students what to do (like main stream expert systems), critiquing systems use the students' problem solving approaches as a starting point. This mode of critiquing focuses the analysis of the system around the students' thinking in a natural and direct way. It provides an instructional method that places the responsibility for learning on the students.

The paper presents research evidence indicating that the critiquing approach can foster independent problem solving and encourage students to become self-directed, autonomous learners.

Keyword Codes: I.2.1; I.2.8; J.3
Keywords: Applications of Expert Systems; Problem Solving, Control Methods, and Search; Life and Medical Science

## 1. WHO SOLVES THE PROBLEM?

This section explores the premise that critiquing systems can facilitate independent problem solving and encourage students to become self-directed, autonomous learners. The systems are not replacements for human teachers. They support students who have already been taught a subject matter by a teacher. They are means for the students for self-monitoring of their learning after the lessons with the teacher.

### 1.1 The Teaching and Learning of Ideas and Concepts

The section considers two scenarios in which this takes place. The first one deals with the teaching of *ideas and concepts*. The process often goes on like this: at first, the teacher presents new ideas and concepts. Then, the students and the teacher discuss these, and contrast them with alternative ideas and concepts. Finally, the students apply them in various ways. The purpose of this is to give the students opportunities to understand the new ideas and concepts. This can not be done by heart.

We have various approaches to ease understanding [1]. One often used strategy is to teach new ideas and concepts in more than one way. Another basic strategy is to apply the concepts and ideas considered in different contexts. The goal is to put them to practical use in a setting where close, individual attention can be paid to each step.

At this stage the students benefit from feedback. The feedback make them sure that progress is being made in the desired direction. Students' prior understanding usually varies so some of them misunderstand or forget previous presentations. Many students have misconceptions even after taking a course because they have not had the opportunities to test and witness the evidence that would change their minds. To clear up misconceptions, students need to be given the chance to predict the results they anticipate in an experiment or investigation. Someone can then explain why the original hypothesis was faulty. In this way experiments help students use the scientific method to distinguish facts from opinions and misconceptions [2].

The feedback is supplied in various ways [1]. The students can receive feedback from question and answer sessions with the teacher, through peer-group discussions, and by use of more or less standardized test procedures.

The students can also receive feedback by a critiquing system. Critiquing systems are second generation expert systems tailored to support students when they need feedback to be able to evaluate and refine their problem solving by showing mistakes, offering suggestions, alternatives, improvements, etc.

Knowledge based systems usually contain an explanation capability. This capability allows the advice of the system to be adapted to the particular questions and concerns of the students, using the recommendations of the system as a starting point. There is, however, a much more direct way to adapt the analysis of the computer to the student's thinking. It is to use a different approach to advice-giving: the critiquing approach. Here, instead of initially telling the students what to do, the system asks what approach they are contemplating and then criticizes that plan. This mode of advice immediately focuses the analysis of the system around the particular concerns of the students [3].

The students have a much more active role in comparison with the use of a main stream expert system. They must provide a plan of their own before they can get advice. The advice supplied by the system is a critique of the students' suggestions and hypotheses. The advice can take the form of suggestions of corrections, extensions, critique of the students' perspective etc. This feedback, when appropriate, confirms the students' expectancy, directs attention to relevant factors, etc.

Often the feedback from critiquing systems is accompanied by verbal advice from the teacher. The relationship between the two kinds of feedback requires research. Apparently, the two kinds of feedback are supplementary. Teachers almost never offer detailed analysis and explicit diagnosis of students' (mis)understandings [4] as critiquing systems and other intelligent systems do.

### 1.2 The Teaching and Learning of Skills

The second scenario deals with the teaching and learning of *skills*. The process is somewhat different from the acquisition of concepts and ideas. Students do not learn skills by watching the teacher or others doing what has to be learned. Therefore, the teaching of skills consists of two parts. The first part is instruction and demonstration. The second part is practice [1]. The students must have opportunities to practise any new skill to acquire it. During the practise the students need feedback.

There are many ways in which one can monitor the students' steps and give appropriate feedback. Feedback can be given, among others, through supervision and through self-checking of skills by use of more or less standardized test procedures.

If students' performance is sufficiently well codified, it can also be tirelessly monitored through critiquing systems. Critiquing systems can provide a non-threatening means to generate feedback. They can help students focus on details performed successfully as well as negative details. Other sources of feedback might tend to concentrate on failures of problem solving activities.

## 2. RESEARCH ABOUT THE USE OF CRITIQUING SYSTEMS

This section presents findings from a research project called *The Critiquing Project*. The research explores the pedagogical potentials of critiquing systems. A prototype critiquing system, VANDVID, has been build to be used in environmental education. Details of the function of the system can be found in [5].

VANDVID embodies the expertise needed to point out areas with on going pollution in streams and rivers. The use of it helps students in judging about the quality of the water and about sources of pollution. The problem is to judge whether, and eventually where, the stream or river investigated is polluted. The procedure is the following. First, students go to the stream or river considered and collect data about the quality of the water. This is done at several places. Second, the students analyze these data. Third, they judge about the quality of the water and eventually sources of pollution. Fourth, they use the critiquing system to evaluate their hypotheses about the pollution.

In the years 1989-91 several hundred students in Danish primary and lower secondary schools have used VANDVID. Afterwards, their teachers were interviewed by the author.

## 2.1 Teachers evaluation

The teachers were asked to evaluate the classroom activities with the critiquing system. The focal point was the students' enthusiasm for learning. It is well known that passive learners usually do not learn much and hostile students rarely learn anything worthwhile. How much time students are actively engaged in learning contributes strongly to their achievement [6].

Is the critiquing approach one of the sorts of actions that teachers can take to increase this time? Does the process of learning associated with the use of the critiquing system foster actively engaged students and cooperative work in the classroom, i.e. students tutoring other students? Without expectations, the teachers' answers to these research questions were *yes, it does.*

The use of VANDVID introduces an unprecedented level of autonomy into environmental education. And the feedback of the system motivates students to become self-directed learners inside as well as outside the structured classroom environment.

The teachers emphasize that students learn procedural skills. According to previous research [7], procedural skills are essential in self-directed learning. The study shows that the students acquire abilities to analyze, plan, synthesize, and evaluate. They learn to organize their approach to a problem in a systematic way, to handle important variables involved in the solution and to recognize interrelationships among them.

Previous research shows that another important skill of self-directed learning is the ability to gather information [7]. The study shows that the students learn to retrieve topic knowledge they might lack from sources outside the classroom; and they learn to apply the topic knowledge to the problem-solving task.

The students also learn self-monitoring skills. They learn how to evaluate their progress. The use of the critiquing system is an iterating process. After the first trip to the stream or river considered, the students analyze the data and plan the next step. They plan new measurements to investigate suspected areas of the stream/river in greater detail. This bracketing method can be used as many times as needed. Each time the students go to the stream or river and investigate new places, the average distance between the places decreases. After two or three steps, the students usually have discovered the source of pollution. Between each step, the students benefit from the feedback from VANDVID. They use the feedback to confirm their expectations, so they can be sure to trace in the right directions.

Finally, the study shows that the students develop communications skills. They learn how to communicate their findings to others. The communication process is not the usual 'as if' communication but real communication to a real audience about real world research questions based on personal experiences and observations. One group of students, for example, produced several articles about their findings to a Danish newspaper to tell other students and adults about their research and findings and opinions.

## 3. A THEORY OF SELF-DIRECTED LEARNING

Theories of self-directed learning usually emphasise the need for structure if a self-directed learning group is to succeed in their efforts. In the classroom, the teacher first provides this structure. Later, the students provide some of it. Five elements of it are essential according to previous research [8]:

- clearly defined goals;
- availability of resources;
- well-defined roles of both students and teachers;
- motivation and preparation to meet the demands of the learning situation;
- means for monitoring and altering the course as it proceeds.

The study reported in this paper confirms this list. It also shows that another element should be added:

- the students' ability to formulate and evaluate hypotheses.

The learning process requires hypotheses about what is going on in the domain considered. The students formulate a position on the quality of water, the amount and sources of pollution, etc., and receive feedback supplied by other students or the teacher. Last, but not least, they receive feedback from the critiquing system. Thus, the ability to formulate guiding hypotheses for ones own work is an important, sixth element in self-directed learning.

## 4. CONCLUSION

This paper considers self-directed learning associated with the use of critiquing systems. Critiquing systems are expert systems that embody knowledge about a subject matter and about a way to evaluate the students' problem solving. They augment and do not replace previous channels to expertise. The teacher's knowledge and skills are still available.

Critiquing systems supply feedback to confirm the students' expectancy, direct attention to relevant factors, and stimulate recall of ideas, concepts and skills. They assemble the feedback dynamically and tailor it to the particular data and hypothesis of the students. The aim is to elicit the introspective participation of the students showing their mistakes and offering suggestions and improvements.

Feedback generated by a critiquing system is timely. Students use the system at a time where corrective feedback is most valuable.

The paper reports on research evidence showing that a critiquing system provide a non-threatening means to generate feedback and help students focus on details performed successfully as well as negative details. Other sources of feedback might tend to concentrate on failures of problem solving activities.

The critiquing can be repeated several times. The students take the critique into consideration, generate new hypotheses until finally, they end the session and take the proper action.

During this process, the students gain topic knowledge and develop procedural skills, self-monitoring skills, and communication skills. They learn by doing.

The important point is that the use of critiquing systems provides an instructional method that places the responsibility for learning on the student.

## 5. REFERENCES


1 Sparkes, J. (1984): *Pedagogic Differences Between Media.* In: A.W. Bates (ed.): *The Role of Technology in Distance Education*, Beckenham.

2 *What Works - Research about Teaching and Learning* (1986), U.S. Department of Education, Washington DC, p. 23.

3 Miller, P.L. (1984): *A Critiquing Approach to Expert Computer Advice: ATTENDING*, London.

4 Cox, R, & Cumming, G. (1990): *The Role of Exploration-based Learning in the Development of Expertise.* In McDougall & Dowling (eds.): *Computers in Education, Proceedings of the Fifth World Conference on Computers in Education, Sydney, July 9-13*, pp. 359-364.

5 Andresen, B.B. (1990): *Applying Second Generation Expert Systems in Education. The Critiquing Approach.* In McDougall & Dowling (eds.): *Computers in Education, Proceedings of the Fifth World Conference on Computers in Education, Sydney, July 9-13*, pp. 1051-1054.

6 *What Works - Research about Teaching and Learning* (1986), U.S. Department of Education, Washington DC, p. 34.

7 Lieberman, D.A. & Linn, M.C. (1991): *Learning to Learn Revisited: Computers and the Development of Self-Directed Learning Skills*, Journal. of Research on Computing in Education, Vol 23, No. 3, pp. 373-395.

8 Husen, T. & Postlethwaite, T.N. (1975): *The Int. Encyclopedia of Education*, Oxford, p. 4518

Education and Society / R. Aiken (Editor)
Information Processing 92, Volume II
Elsevier Science Publishers B.V. (North-Holland)



# Knowledge-based simulation in memory re-education

Mohand-Saïd HACID, Christine BONNET and Jacques KOULOUMDJIAN

Insa de Lyon, Dépt. Informatique, 69621 Villeurbanne, France

**Abstract**

The use of Artificial Intelligence (AI) do open new possibilities for building systems so powerful that complex problems can be solved with little effort from the user. In tutorial applications, intelligence is asked to the system to customize adaptative strategies and to plan [1]. This paper presents a Knowledge-based simulation system, REMISSION (Rééducation Ecologique de la Mémolre par un Système de SimulatlON) for memory re-education. Among the possible ways of implementing knowledge-based simulation system, it exists those based on the cooperation of expert system and simulation tools [2]. REMISION is based on the cooperation of an expert system builder (Nexpert Object [3]) and a graphical software with extended capabilities (DataViews [4]). The resulting architecture of the REMISSION system combines techniques of AI, Animation, and explanation. A versatile graphics language for knowledge base and animation description, LASER, surrounds the kernel of the system.

Keyword codes: I.2.0; I.6.7; K.3.1
Keywords: Artificial Intelligence, general; Simulation Support Systems; Computer Uses in Education

## 1. INTRODUCTION

The Rhône-Alpes region research project for designing and developing Artificial Intelligence tools in medecine was started in 1989 and represents a broad research initiative to investigate the process of re-education. As part of this research program, we have created the REMISSION (Rééducation Ecologique de la Mémolre par un Système de SimulatlON) system.

REMISSION is an object and rule oriented simulation and animation environment that allows neuropsychologists to construct simulations by endowing graphical objects with conceptual components describing their behavior in response to the external actions.

The task of the re-educational design extends from analysis of the domain knowledge to be transmitted, to the development and delivery of the re-educational materials. During analysis, the designer (neuropsylogist) determines re-educational goals, collects and analyzes knowledge to be transmitted, and then structures this knowledge to achieve the re-educational goals. Decisions are made about the material to include. Finally, a set of deliverable materials-presentations, instructions, exercises, interferences, helps, etc. is created and organized into a scenario sequence to achieve the re-educational goals. Viewed from a design perspective, the re-educational design process is a serie of analysis and synthesis steps that transforms a large amount of knowledge (about patients, tasks, etc.) from its original form to a form that can be used for re-education.

## 2. MEMORY RE-EDUCATION IN THE REMISSION SYSTEM

This section globally describes the re-educational process and environment of the REMISSION system. The technical aspects of the system are described in the next section.

The REMISSION system is an intelligent rehabilitation system used for people suffering memory problems. It is aimed at simulating everyday "ecological" situations by means of graphical scenes: patients are asked to accomplish more or less complex tasks on the displayed objects.

### 2.1. Source elements: scenarii and exercises

The system asks the patient, each session, to work on scenarii. A scenario is composed of a sample of variable level exercises which are linked by the context (set of scenes about the same place, for instance, the garage, the kitchen, the garden) in which the patient will act. The neuropsychologists and therapists determined for each scenario and exercise, a maximum duration (about 30 minutes per scenario, 5 minutes per exercise) in order to keep the patient concentrated and attentive during a session. For the same reason, two contexts at most (two scenarii) are presented to a patient in a single session.

The exercises fall into two categories:

•training exercises: the patient learns the re-educational environment by manipulating the elements of the graphical scenes. For instance, we can teach the patient the location of the objects in a room, the cupboards' contents, the plan of an apartment and so on. One example of this type of exercise is programmed into the system (Figure 1). A cupboard opens, leaving the patient time to visualize the objects in it (bowl, pan, fork and spoon) and then closes after a given time which is proportional to the number of items to be memorized. The patient must then recognize the objects in the cupboard by pointing out the reproductions of the objects which appear at the bottom of the screen. If the patient succeeds, a fuller cupboard opens and so on until either the patient reaches the maximum level (the last cupboard) or the patient fails.

•re-educational exercises: the patient learns to do various tasks by using what he has previously learned. For instance, we can ask him to set the table, to tidy away plates and dishes and so on. These exercises involve manipulating objects and/or walking and/or recognition of objects.

At the beginning of each exercise, an instruction showing the patient the task(s) he has to do, is diplayed on the screen and fades away after five seconds (necessary and sufficient time to memorize the instruction). The patient then has a time t (t is specific to an exercise) to realize the tasks. If the patient ends before time t, he can stop the exercise by himself, if not the system interrupts the patient.

Figure 1: An Example of an exercise's scene

When a patient begins a new scenario, he has to start with one or several training exercises. A scenario includes exercises whose chain is predefined and/or exercises which can be independently developed. Each exercise is conceived to especially engage a particular type of memory. The graphical scenes constitute the working environment of the patient and their only interface with the system. In each exercise, the patient works on a particular scene.

Thanks to its flexibility, the system supplies the neuropsychologists with access and control. They can give a personal touch to the extant, define new scenarii, exercises and so on thanks to LASER langage (Langage de Spécification de l'Environnement de Rééducation) which we developed [5].

### 2.2. The system's adaptation: individually taking the patients into account

The system has knowledge on each patient which are saved in the patient's profile (the civil status of the patient, his clinical diagnosis, his medical history, the prescribed drugs and specific information about his memory problems). A report of the re-educational session being followed by the patient is saved in the patient's history (undertaken scenarii, developed exercises in each scenario and so on). The re-educational strategy is adaptive. The exercises are selected for a patient according to a set C of criteria: C= { memory involved in the exercise, exercise's level, patient's progress, history and affinities }.

Within an exercise, either more or less complex unexepected events (interferences) take place, or, on the contrary, help can be triggered by the system according to a set of constraints, which take into account the patient's progress. The system decides on the usefulness of an interference/help. The interferences must be simple to resolve and often involves prior training. Several interferences with a maximum of three, can occur during the same exercise. The interferences are more or less difficult according to their level and the closeness of their trigger actions with regard to the task being done by the patient.

### 2.3. Evaluations and corrections

In re-educational or training mode, the patient's actions are automatically valued and the impact of the possible interferences is measured. This evaluation allows to correct the patient's mistakes. The correction, generally ensured in all tutoring systems allows the patient to improve and reinforce his training, especially through repetition (see [6-8]). One or more system's solution(s) correspond to each exercise (several if a task can be solved in different manners). The re-educational exercises' solutions are modelled in the form of task trees. The trees are built during the construction of the solutions which process was defined by the designers via a Solutions Generator. This generator has two working modes according to the kind of exercise: training (Figure 2)/ re-educational (Figure 3).

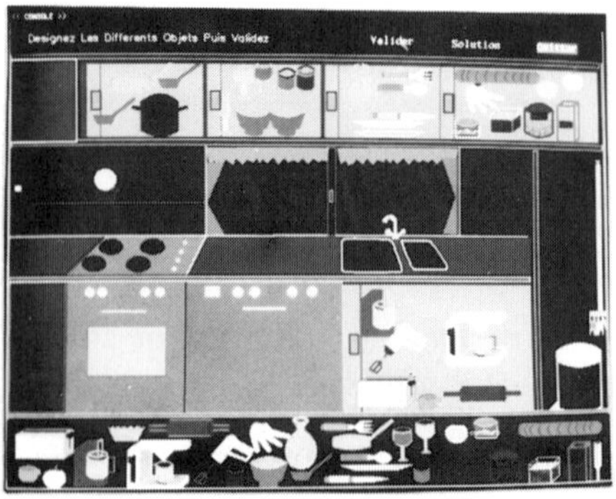

Figure 2: An example of training exercise's solution generation

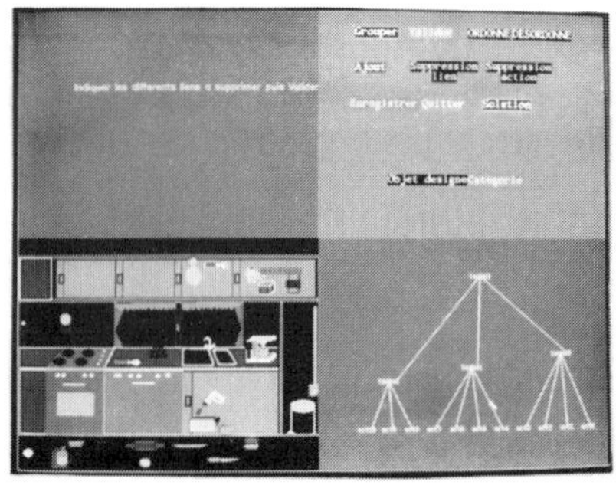

Figure 3: An example of re-educational exercise's solution generation

In training mode, the evaluation is executed in real time so that the correction is given instantaneously. When the patient makes a mistake, a signal (twinkling) is emitted showing the location of the mistake (involved object). According to the exercise, the patient may be able to correct himself. Each correct manipulation is shown by another signal which encourages the patient (sonorous beep followed by the deletion of the graphical object). At the end of an exercise, a final correction is shown: all the objects forgotten by the patient during the recognition twinkle.

In re-educational mode, the evaluation is carried out at the end of the exercise. It takes into account all the patient's actions including his incorrect manipulations (pointing out the wrong object). A module called "The evaluator" evaluates the patient's solution by putting his various actions into sets : correct actions, non optimal actions, incorrect actions (not necessary), incorrect manipulations (click into space), forbidden actions, unidentified system actions (not carried out by the patient).

The graphical animation of the scene, and the explanation generation adapted to the development of an exercise by a patient, are produced in real time and should not be penalized by a prohibitive research time. Therefore, the results have been modelled into dynamic list structures, because the size of the solution is unknown at the beginning of an exercise. Several system solutions can be defined for one exercise. The Evaluator chooses a solution corresponding to the smallest number of patient's errors and provides the corresponding results. The patient's solution is successively evaluated with regard to the various system solutions. Results are compared two by two (old, new one). The evaluation is accomplished in two steps:

1- Screening, by pattern-matching, of the patient's solution in order to exclude the forbidden actions.
2- The nodes of the tree are processed by an exhaustive depth first search forward in the system solution tree.
The various sets of actions are then constructed, the dynamic list structures are updated, and the results are generated.

A personalized correction is then presented to the patient in the form of an animation (The correction is performed by "The Corrector"). The patient sees step by step his correct, his forgotten actions and optimal ways to do actions (Figure 4). At the end of the correction, forbidden actions are shown in textual form with a twinkling of the affected graphical objects. Before each action simulation, a message is displayed to the patient which explains the action he is going to visualize. The Corrector loads the Evaluator's results (dynamic list structures) and processes them by following the correct chronology of the exercise's actions. Various message skeletons were created to correspond to the explanations: correct moving actions and/or handling actions, non optimal actions, forgotten moving actions and/or handling actions.

Another more detailed correction (Figure 5) is provided for the neuropsychologists and therapists so that they can follow up on the patient's development of exercise (The detailed correction is performed by "The Explanations Generator"). In particular, the neuropsychologists need to know the number of wrong manipulations carried out by the patients as well as whether or not he respected the order of the given 'ordered' task.

In order to decide if an interference/help should be triggered, an evaluation is performed at given times, in real time, to give a partial diagnosis. This diagnosis represents the patient's progress during an exercise.

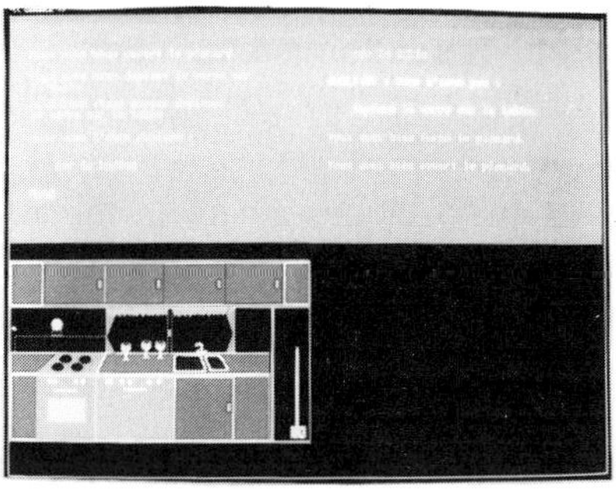

Figure 4: A correction for a patient

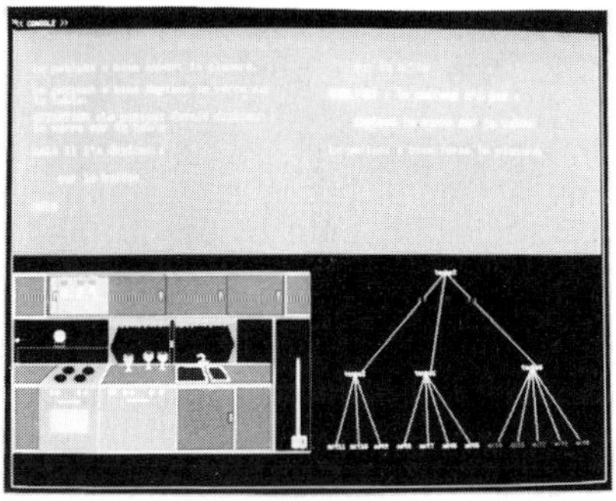

Figure5: Explanations for the neuropsychologists

## 3. ARCHITECTURE AND GENERAL WORKING OF THE REMISSION SYSTEM

The system is based on a modular architecture [9] (Figure 6). This modularity (decomposition by functions) responds to the needs imposed by a real time processing: the response time must be as short as possible.

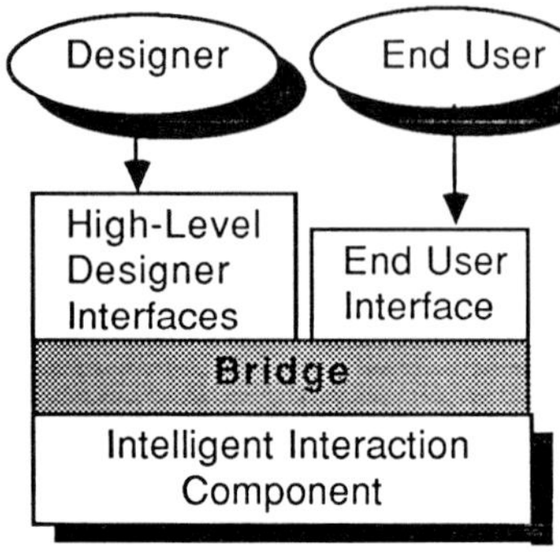


Figure 6: simplified architecture of REMISSION

In this architecture, we distinguish four main components:

**3.1. The graphical component: end-user interface**
It interfaces directly with the patient. During an exercise, the component waits for the patient's response. It graphically manages actions which result from the response (i.e switch on a hotplate, open the door of a cupboard, and so on).
The graphical component manages all the graphical objects associated with a scene. The ending of a re-educational exercise can be induced either by the patient: he considers the exercise as finished, or by the graphical component: if the time elapsed has reached the allowable limit.

**3.2. The decisional component: intelligent interaction component**
It provides a re-education adapted to each patient's memory level. It logically interprets the patient's handling of objects in the graphical scenes and evaluates these manipulations in real time or in delayed time. It is made up of several packages. Some of which take part in the training mode, others in the re-educational mode.

**3.3. The acquisition component: high-level designer interfaces**
It consists of four user-interfaces:
•one supplied by DV: DV-Draw graphical editor [4],
•one which allows the generation of the system's solutions: the Solutions Generator.
•one which allows the acquisition of the LASER language elements. After the data is acquired via this user-interface, the compiler generates two bases: "re-educational elements", "elements of the simulation environment".
•one for the observer (designers) in order to acquire information about patients (patient's profile). This interface was developed with ORACLE DBMS tools.

### 3.4. The communication interface (Bridge)

It allows the bi-directional communication between the graphical and the decisional components. It performs this function by transforming information provided by the graphical component into a form processible by the decisional component.

## 4. CONCLUSION

This paper has shown the usefulness of combining Artificial Intelligence and simulation techniques, and described the REMISSION's architecture which implement it.

Our experience with the system has been positive, and we feel that it advances the state of the art in knowledge based simulation . This is a field where research is concentrating on making the specification of simulation environment easier. The system described here provides us with a platform on wich to perform this research, and upon which we can build to achieve higher goals. Our belief is that the most powerful and expressive feature that must be incorporated in a knowledge based simulation is object and rule orientation. Further developments of the research are devoted to the investigation of multi-media aspects.

## 5. REFERENCES

[1]: Peachey D.R. & McCalla G.I. "Using planning techniques in intelligent tutoring systems", Int. J. Man-Machine Studies, 1986, N° 24, pp. 77-98.

[2]: O'KEEFE, R.M. "Simulation and expert systems - A taxonomy and some examples", SIMULATION, January 1986, Vol. 46, n° 1, p. 10-16.

[3]: NEURON DATA INC. "NEXPERT OBJECT FUNDAMENTALS", Palo Alto, California : Neuron Data Inc., 1989. 596 p.

[4]: V.I. CORPORATION "DV-Draw and DV-Tools : User's Guide". Amherst Research Park, Massachusetts : V.I. Corporation, October 1989, 480 p.

[5]: BONNET, C. "Simulation dans un Contexte Rééducationnel : Acquisition des Eléments de l'Environnement de Simulation et Analyse des Interactions de l'Utilisateur". Doctorat thesis : INSA de LYON, Laboratoire LISI, 1991, 156p.

[6]: DION, P. & LELOUCHE, R. "Architecture of an intelligent system to teach introductory programming", Intelligent Tutoring System Conference,Montréal (Canada), June 1-3, 1988, p. 387-394.

[7]: RICKEL, J. "An Intelligent Tutoring Framework for Task-oriented Domains", Intelligent Tutoring System Conference, Montréal (CA), June 1-3, 1988, p. 109-115.

[8]: WENGER, E. "Artificial Intelligence and Tutoring Systems Computational and Cognitive Approaches to the communication of knowledge", Los Altos (CA) : Morgan Kaufmann Publishers, 1987. 486p.

[9]: HACID, M.S. "Integration des Techniques d'Intelligence Artificielle dans un Environnement de Simulation : Application à la Rééducation de la Mémoire". Doctorat thesis: INSA de LYON, Laboratoire LISI, 1991, 123p.

Education and Society / R. Aiken (Editor)
Information Processing 92, Volume II
Elsevier Science Publishers B.V. (North-Holland)


# A CENTURY AFTER LADY LOVELACE' TRAGEDY

drs. A.M. Bruin

director of The Foundation of Women and Computer Science.
WG-PLEIN 220 1054 SE Amsterdam, The Netherlands

## 1. ABSTRACT

Did you know that a century ago the daughter of Lord Byron, Lady Lovelace, was the first to be involved in computer programming? At the birth of Computer Science men and women were present. The tragic part of this story is that no one knows a woman was involved. Hardly any history book mentions this fact.
Now a century after Lady Lovelace another tragedy, even on a larger scale, is at stage. Women working in computer science are really invisible now, because they form an extreme minority. Mostly men are working in the professional and training field of Information Technology. This development did not take place a hundred but only ten years ago in a society in which each right-thinking person acknowledges the importance of emancipation.
It is interesting to overview the political measures taken at the introduction of computer use in the Dutch educational system. Was there any attention payed to the gender issue?
Action now requires knowledge of the underlying principles of the lack of interest by girls. Recently two studies -in primary and in secondary education- are performed to investigate the possibilities and effects of computer use in education. The results clearly show the difference in interest between boys and girls. Given these results a few recommendations can be made for education. For instance recognizing the differences in learning styles. But also the image of computer science.

## 2. SCIENCE AND GENDER; AN OLD HISTORY

In the Netherlands only 10% of careers in computer science are filled by women. This fact tallies with the situation in most other European countries.
From the point of view of society it is, to say the least, surprising that a field which is only ten years old should be occupied in such a traditional way as regards man-woman relationships.
In other words, in those ten years computer science has developed into a technical subject which is no appeal to girls.

That math or physics real boy's subjects are, is deemed to be explicable from a historical perspective. They used only to be male scientists. But that a field like computer science in which there were more than enough chances for a sexually neutral occupation has gone the same way is, to put it mildly, surprising.
In a society in which each thinking person acknowledges the importance of

emancipation, it is apparently still possible that a new professional and training field should be filled exclusively by males.

Of course, girls nowadays receive the same training opportunities as boys. However, they use them differently. Durndell (UK, 1990) interviewed 210 first year economics and science students who were capable but did not want to study computer science. Women students indicated more frequently than men that they are more interested in people than things. Often too, girls have the impression that computer science involves little contact with people. Computer science was associated with the idea of spending the whole day behind a terminal. In itself, working in a male environment was not an important reason for choosing against a study in computer science.

## 3. EDUCATION AND INFORATION; AN OVERVIEW

What direct measures has the Dutch Ministry for Education found to make sure that by the introduction of computers throughout education - from nursery school to high education - the differences between boys and girls is taken into account?
After all, the basic assumption by the large scale introduction of computers into education, was that pupils should develop into full participance in our computer society. In the early eighties a policy for technology came high on the list of priorities. Education seemed to be an important factor in stimulating the use of new technologies in all parts of society. University and vocational training were first. These had the highest priority as they link with the professional market. To realise linkage between education and the employment market two billion guilders were invested. In 1984 a new large-scale plan was introduced in which it was also the turn of the other forms of education. 1,7 Billion guilders was invested. This project ended in 1988 and was followed by yet another. This project was to be under the motto of the propagation of the use of computers in education. It will continue until the end of this year and has cost about 300 million guilders.
Has this been the last effort of the Dutch government to introduce new technologies to the educational system? No, also for the coming four years 400 million guilders has been set aside to enable schools to give lessons in an adequate way.
Meanwhile, the universities have apparatus, all of the 1700 secondary schools have a computer room anyway and at the moment all the (9400) primary schools are receiving computers at a ratio of one to every sixty pupils.
The last ten years about 4,5 billion guilders has been invested in the introduction of new technology to education with the aim of producing people for full participance in our computer society.
A large expenditure for such a small country as the Netherlands with a population of only 14 millions.

### The Foundation of Women and Informatics.

Ten years ago there was little concern about the risk that computer science in schools would be a province of male teachers and students. The risk was located in 1984 by the Women in Computer Science Foundation. This then led to for example the measure that one in three of the secondary school teachers given extra training should be a woman. There have been no further special government measures to involve female teachers or pupils in new technology. Since 1984 the Women in Computer Science Foundation has received a subsidy from the government. All together 0,03 percent has been invested in attracting more women and girls to computer science.

**Information technology and female teachers.**

What about the participation of women in education? In secondary education 33% of the computer science teachers should in principal be women. This was namely one of the conditions in providing computers. Of course all 1700 schools agreed to this. A simple calculation indicates that 33,3% of computer science teachers in secondary education should be women. Now, three years after the last training round, the percentage of women computer science teachers appears to be 15%. The tendency is that it is going to sink to 10%, which is also the norm for other sectors where no special measures have been taken. It is not known what has happened to the women computer science teachers.

In the introduction of computers to primary education there is the same situation at the moment. In primary education 80% of the teachers are women. One teacher per school is trained to enable them to give support and advice to their colleagues. Only 25% of these teachers are women. Here too there is a clear case of an imbalance in participation. Real measures are not taken. Though more attention is being given to more information. Image making in the media show that working with computers is for men. Through socialisation the image is communicated to children. This expresses itself in the professional preference of school children (9 to 12 years). For boys working with computers is third choice after policemen and pilot. For girls working with computers is not in the top-9 list. The first three choices of girls are: nurse, primary teacher and carer (Klopper and Schleyper, 1989).

**A conclusion.**

The conclusion which can be drawn is that in education as well as elsewhere no real attention is paid to emancipation at the introduction of new technologies. In this way the field has been developed in a one sided manner and so has become even less attractive to women and girls.

The introduction of new technologies can not be wiped out an done again. That's the way it is. It is however useful to investigate what consequences this has for computer science education, so subsequently, some remedy can be attempted.

## 4. IN SEARCH OF THE REMEDY.

Results of recent studies.

To investigate the possibilities and effects of new media in education the project 'test school new media' was carried out from 1988 to 1990. In secondary education the possibilities of advanced data machines for the subject geography, for example video-discs, CD-ROM and video-tex were investigated. The basis of the lessons was a model for the processing of information. This model was a modified version of the 'crackermodel' of Diane Freeman. The simplified version for the geography lessons is:
step 1: question
step 2: sources
step 3: processing
step 4: reproduction
step 5: answer.
The central question of this study was to what extend pupils learn significantly more

about the processing of information with the help of new media.
In any case, in 20% of the lessons of second and third years use was made of new media such as video-discs, CD-ROM and video-tex. It is important to note that these are not primitive forms of computer use but advanced adaptations in which the machine-concept is largely suppressed.

**Before.**
More than half of the pupils liked working with computers in geography lessons. The difference between boys and girls is conspicuous. Almost three-quarters of the boys were enthusiastic about the new media at the beginning of the project compared to more than a third of the girls.
Boys were also more positive in advance about the educational value of new media for geography.
The last question before starting the project was if the pupils prefer to work alone or in pairs behind the computer. The majority of the girls, more than 60%, stated prior to the project that they wanted to work with the computer in pairs. Only a quarter of the boys wanted this.

**After.**
During the course of the project the difference between boys and girls became even wider. More than 80% of the girls expressed preference for working in pairs and the boys had no clear preference.
Boys and girls valued working with new media differently. Only one in six girls said they really liked it while two-thirds were desinterested. In contrast, two-third of the boys liked working with new media.

**Comparisons.**
If we compare the average scores for the before questions with those for the after questions, we see that the boys' enthusiasm remained constant throughout the project while the girls' opinion, which was already more reserved, became even more negative.
In addition, after two years the girls are considerably more pessimistic than the boys about educational returns. While 40% of the boys say they have profited from the use of new media, this supplies for only 10% of the girls. A third of the girls even think they learned less than from ordinary lessons. Only one in seven boys feels the same way.

**Conclusions.**
Girls learn computer science technique considerably less well. There is a significant correlation between the answers to the question if they liked working with new media and the answers to the question if geography could be learned better in this way. The more they enjoyed it the better the learning results they expected.

The entire research shows that the learning results of the experiment group are no better than those of the control group. The other hypothesis, that pupils learn how to cope with computer science better if they use new media, is being restrictively confirmed.
However, for second and third years there are significant differences between boys and girls. From the differentations test between the before and after test, it appears that girls achieve considerably less than boys. In other words, girls learn computer science skills

with the help of the computer significantly less well than boys.

**Same results with younger children.**
These are data which have been collected from secondary school pupils (13 and 14 years). A reaction to this can be that socialisation has already have such a strong influence on the way girls think, that computer science and the use of computers has been pushed into the science corner. Another recent research conflicts with this explanation. Among primary school pupils in the ages 9, 10 and 11 years research has also been done into the development of the attitude towards computers to repeated use of them. This research conducted in 500 primary schools reveals that boys develope a more positive attitude than girls. They have a higher estimate of their abilities. Also they acquire more self- confidence. Further, their interest and pleasure increases. None of this applies to girls. Their attitude remains the same. The opposite is sooner true: fear of computers increases and the more experience they have of working with computers at school the more difficult they find it. Needless to say boys and girls received the same lessons.

## 5. BUT GIRLS LEARN DIFFERENTLY.

**Context-bound learning.**
This last fact agrees with the experiences of Rose Flower, math teacher of the year in England, who indicates that girls have less self-confidence in math lessons than boys. She suggests that learning math is not an individual process but must be seen in the context of the group. Self-respect and feeling appreciated by others is essential in the learning process. The exchange of ideas is as important as working by oneself.

**Quality versus quantity.**
Girls are just as capable of learning with the aid of computers. But girls learn differently. They attache great importance to the social context in which they learn. Learning with and about the computer by placing it in the social context, the imbalanced development of attitude could be neutralised. This demands a specific approach. Usually on the assumption that girls are behind. The research results disapprove this: girls fall behind on the basis of the context in which the use of computers occurs.

**More interest in people then in machines.**
In itself, there is nothing wrong with girls having more interest in people than in machines. It becomes worrying if a decisive negative position in the employment market goes with it. Attempting to bring girls from behind does not work because they are not behind. It is another way of learning in which the human interaction scores higher than interest in machines.

## 6. HOW TO HANDLE THE DIFFERENCES IN THE CLASSROOM.

**First action; awareness.**
At the moment all of the 9400 primary schools in the Netherlands receive computers from the government. A good opportunity to do something about the girl/boy problem.

However, it is important to take a step back and to create conciousness of the phenomenon among teachers. In May a disc will be distributed to all the primary schools containing the computer attitude test "compass".
With this the teacher can measure the average computer attitude of each group and the difference between boys and girls. After six weeks the test will be taken for a second time. The difference in attitude development between boys and girls will be statistically demonstrated to a significant level by this means. With this approach you bring the phenomenon into the class. The test shows that it simply happens while you are standing there. Behind the testscore suggestions are given for doing something about the difference.
An obvious suggestion is to always have several pupils behind the computer and to allow them to talk. We also know that girls find war games less exciting. Other suggestions are connected with the difference in learning styles. In the girls' styles the importance of the social learning context clearly arises.

**Adjusting to learning differences.**
**1.** Do not simplify a problem, but look at it from all angles. Do not reduce a social problem to a technical problem.
Girls' thinking is divergent rather than convergent; several simultaneous solutions are possible. It is obvious that convergent thinking should be related to math, and so to a part of computer science. In making structure diagrams hypothetical-deductive thinking is important. Convergent thinkers excel in this. However, to collect data necessary for the solution of a problem, divergent thinking is better. That this difference in ways of learning should be the reason for the difference in performance in computer science and other scientific subjects is, therefore, unfounded.
**2.** Wanting to give new information an appropriate place in the familiar.
Girls ask 'why' more often as they wish to relate the new to the familiar. When girls do not receive an opportunity to make this relationship, they do not understand. In computer science logical abstract thinking dominates: just accept what you are told. Boys easily accept these rules and do not ask themselves if they are stupid if they do not understand them.
**3.** Solving by organising and reorganising.
Girls deal with a problem by organising and reorganising it, boys tend to make a plan and carry it out. From English research it emerges that girls in programming education learn by organising and reorganising the elements together with the computer while boys program in a more systematic and step-by-step way. The results of both groups are good. But the learning of girls was called not-systematic and not-planned. They give it up and have to adopt another style which they are not at home with.

## 7. THE SOLUTION; COMPUTER SCIENCE MUST CHANGE.

A broad problem orientated and insight stimulating approach to computer science education is more stimulating to girls and women. There must be more attention paid to the reasons for automatic systems, the principles behind computer adaptations and the social effects of professions and work.
This means that computer science must change. Social, organisation and social aspects are also of the greatest importance in this subject. That there is no place for people if you choose this profession is a widely spread conception. A real computer scientist sits the whole day in a temperature controlled space where people are only admitted if they

can show a pass. As long as computer science has this image the field is uninteresting to girls. But to who than? Working in computer science is not bound to cellars full of apparatus. People play an important role in dealing with information, According to the prospectus of the universities communicative skills are obligatory for studying computer science. Also in the employment advertisement people who can work in a team and can organise are expressly demanded. If these skills are of crucial importance in the exercise of the profession, it is not bad to begin with education and to strip the subject of computer science of its laboratory image.

## LITERATURE

Aanholt, Th.C.C.M. van ; Smeets, E.F.L.
1991 Eindrapportage proefschool nieuwe media. Instituut voor toegepaste wetenschappen.

Beusekamp, M.F. (et al.)
1991 Vergroting instroom van vrouwelijke studenten informatica : Eindrapportage, Memoranda Informatica 91-59, Enschede, Universiteit Twente.

Bruin, Magda ; Burg, Arda van ; Hezewijk, Irma van
1991 Vrouwen achter de schermen : hoe vrouwen te betrekken bij PRINT, Amsterdam, APS.

Dam, G. ten ; Urlings, M. ; Volman, M.
1991 Sekseverschillen in het onderwijs : curriculum, didactiek en organisatie, Groningen, Wolters-Noordhoff

Dorp, Saskia van ; Joukes, Gertje
1991 Meisjes in het informatica-onderwijs : boekrecensie. In: TVI jrg. 5, nr. 19, p. 19-20.

Greenbaum, Joan
1991 Participerend ontwerpen; naar een andere benadering van van systeemontwikkeling. Congreslezing 10 jaar Vrouwen en Informatica. Amsterdam : in congresverslag Vrouwen en Informatica.

Joukes, Gertje
1992 Het tijdperk na PRINT : informatica-onderwijsbeleid na 1992. In. TVI, jrg. 6, nr. 21, p. 10-13.

Klopper, D.L. ; Schleyper, Y.G.M.
1990 Zij wel, ik ook: een onderzoek naar meisjes en computers. Technika 10, Utrecht.

Martin, Dianne
1991 Op naar sekseneutrale kaders van informatica-onderwijs. Congreslezing 10 jaar Vrouwen en Informatica. Amsterdam: in congresverslag Vrouwen en Informatica.

Rikhof-van Eijck, Marlies
1991 Informatica-didactiek, ook voor meisjes. In: Informatiekunde en informatica in LBO/IBO, conferentieverslag, Enschede, VALO.

Schelhöwe, Heidi
1991 Fundamenten van informatica vanuit feministisch perspectief. Congreslezing 10 jaar Vrouwen en Informatica. Amsterdam: in congresbundel Vrouwen en Informatica.

Vlas, W.D.J. ; Feteris, A.
1991 Meisjes en informatica: de laatste barrières, Enschede, Universiteit Twente.

Waal, Mieke de
1989 Meisjes: een wereld apart: een etnografie van meisjes op de middelbare school. Amsterdam, Boom Meppel.

Education and Society / R. Aiken (Editor)
Information Processing 92, Volume II
Elsevier Science Publishers B.V. (North-Holland)




# Cross-cultural gender differences in student self-efficacy: the impact of culture

Vasilios Makrakis*

Department of Teacher Education, University of Crete, 74 100 Rethymnon, Crete, Greece

**Abstract**

Educators and policy makers are increasingly being confronted with the question of gender equality in educational computing. This study investigates the impact of culture on the "We can, but I can't" phenomenon, a tendency for females to be unsure of their own individual ability to use computers, but to feel that women as a group in general are as able as men in computers. The study was administered among a sample of 773 Swedish and Japanese ninth-grade pupils. Results from two-way analyses of variance and multiple regression analyses indicate that this phenomenon is largely a reflection of socio-cultural differences and perceptions concerning gender equality in computers as well as gender equality in student aptitude in major school subjects.

Keyword Codes: K.3.0; K.4.2
Keywords: Computer Attitudes, General; Social Issues

## 1. INTRODUCTION

The increasing use of computers has urged school authorities to adopt computers either as an instructional and learning instrument or as an object of instruction. A strong background in computers seems therefore to be critical for many career and job opportunities in today's increasingly computerized world. However, several studies show that women's participation in computer-related studies or programs is decreasing, at least in Europe [1-3]. This trend may be related to the phenomenon "We can, but I can't": a tendency for females to be unsure of their own individual ability to use computers, but to feel that women as a group are as able as men in computers [4-5].

---

* The research on which this paper is based was carried out while the author was a Japan Foundation research fellow affiliated with the National Institute of Educational Research of Japan (1989-90) and an assistant professor at the Institute of International Education, University of Stockholm (1988-89). The financial support received by the Japan Foundation and the Stockholm School Administration is highly acknowledged.

Considering that pupils' perceptions of their computer capabilities (self-efficacy) are likely to influence both behavioural and achievement outcomes [6], the factors which predict pupil self-efficacy in computers deserves close investigation. Bandura has proposed that pupil perceptions of self-efficacy regarding a task can influence the choice to engage in that task, the effort that will be expended in performing it, and the persistence that will be shown in accomplishing it [7]. Computer self-efficacy can be defined as a general self-esteem or personal confidence in the ability to learn computers and to perform well on computer-related tasks.

A number of studies suggest that prior computer experience constitutes a significant predictor of computer self-efficacy [8-9]. Similarly, perceptions of usefulness of computing skills for one's future career and interest in knowing more about computers have also received considerable attention for their role in explaining gender-related differences in computer self-efficacy [9]. Perceptions of computer self-efficacy may be affected by another factor, possession of a personal computer. Parental and teacher encouragement for the involvement of pupils in computer-related activities also seem to be important factors for computer self-efficacy [6,8,10], despite some controversial results [11-13]. Gender equality in computer competence (we equally can) may be influenced by females' perceptions of gender equality in computers and/or in the perceived gender equality in pupil aptitude in major school subjects.

The study reported here was designed to investigate gender differences among Japanese and Swedish ninth-grade puplis in their perceptions of self-efficacy and gender equality in computer competence and the factors which could affect these perceptions. The central thesis in this study is that the "We can, but I can't" paradox is a social construct, highly driven by the culture of a particular social group.

## 2. THE METHOD OF THE STUDY

This study is primarily concerned with the impact of two factors (country and gender) on students' self-efficacy as measured by a five point Likert-type scale. The literature review identified several factors related to self-efficacy in computers. The data were collected from a questionnaire administered to 773 Japanese and Swedish pupils (470 in Japan and 303 in Sweden). The samples consisted of an entire ninth-grade class in each of the 13 Japanese and 16 Swedish schools selected from the metropolitan areas of Tokyo and Stockholm. The Japanese schools were selected from those lower secondary schools identified as computer-using schools in the area of Tokyo by a national computer study. The Swedish schools were randomly selected from all lower secondary schools in the area of Stockholm. An analysis of variance (ANOVA) was used for testing the effects of country and gender on the two dimensions: "We can" and "I can't" and t-tests were used to compare the means of the two socio-cultural groups. Also, stepwise multiple regressions were performed to indicate which attitudes are significant predictors of the dependent variables: computer self-efficacy and gender equality in computer competence. The reliability of the instrument for this study was assessed with correlations between items and subscale scores. Correlations between items that formed a subscale were positive and exceeded .60 for all items. Item/total correlations were positive and exceeded .75 for all items. These correlations indicated that all items discriminated well between subjects and were satisfactory for retention in the scales for final analysis.

## 3. RESULTS OF THE STUDY

Table 1 shows the results of two ANOVA procedures, each of which relates to pupils' self-efficacy and gender equality in computer competence. The results of the first ANOVA reveals a non-significant interaction effect between country and gender. This means that the effect of the pupil's gender on computer self-efficacy, if any, seems to be the same among the Japanese pupils investigated as among the Swedish pupils.

**Table 1**
**Analysis of variance (ANOVA) procedures**

| | F | | |
|---|---|---|---|
| Dependent Variable | Country | Sex | Interaction |
| I feel confident with my ability to learn about computers. | 309.67 (0.0001) | .627 ns | .237 ns |
| Girls can do just well as boys in learning about computers. | 3.88 (0.049) | 15.70 (0.0001) | 4.94 (.016) |

Inspection of individual means for these two variables using t-tests statistics shows that the Swedish pupils have a considerably higher self-efficacy score in computers than the Japanese pupils, $t(522) = -16.85$, $p < 0.0001$. However, both boys and girls in each individual country had almost the same computer self-efficacy score (see Table 2).

Similarly, no statistically significant interaction between gender and country was found concerning computer self-efficacy. The reverse was, however, true for the pupils' perceptions on gender equality in computer competence. The effect of gender, therefore, on the "we equally can" dimension of the "We can, but I can't" paradox is not the same among those Japanese and Swedish pupils investigated.

Significant main effects are also found for both gender and country. This implies that Japanese pupils do not have the same average perceptions compared to the Swedish pupils investigated with respect to the above statement and girls do not have the same average score in this variable as boys. Indeed, girls whether in Japan or Sweden were more convinced than boys regarding perceptions of gender equality in computer competence. This is more pronounced among the Swedish pupils rather than the Japanese pupils (see Table 2).

Table 2
**Descriptive statistics and t's for sex-related differences on all measures for Japanese and Swedish pupils**

| Variable | | Possible max/min scores | Girls M | Girls SD | Boys M | Boys SD | t | p | df |
|---|---|---|---|---|---|---|---|---|---|
| | J | 5-1 | 3.09 | .620 | 3.10 | .879 | -.28 | ns | 458 |
| Efficacy | S | | 4.17 | 1.02 | 4.26 | .902 | -.72 | ns | 290 |
| | J | " | 3.71 | .825 | 3.58 | .938 | 1.61 | ns | 463 |
| Equality | S | | 4.03 | 1.13 | 3.56 | 1.21 | 3.40 | .001 | 292 |
| | J | 4-0 | 1.04 | .906 | 1.45 | 1.16 | -4.27 | .001 | 464 |
| Experience | S | | 4.00 | - | 4.00 | - | - | - | - |
| | J | 4-1 | 1.13 | .456 | 1.36 | .702 | -4.22 | .001 | 434 |
| Teac. Enc. | S | | 1.41 | .666 | 1.58 | .784 | -1.99 | .047 | 297 |
| | J | " | 1.30 | .665 | 1.28 | .625 | .25 | ns | 404 |
| Parent Enc | S | | 1.71 | .859 | 1.85 | .866 | -1.40 | ns | 296 |
| | J | " | 1.11 | .468 | 1.22 | .582 | -2.12 | .035 | 401 |
| Peer Enc. | S | | 1.23 | .533 | 1.54 | .745 | -4.12 | .001 | 283 |
| | J | 1-2 | 1.57 | .495 | 1.37 | .485 | 4.43 | .001 | 465 |
| Comp Owner | S | | 1.43 | .497 | 1.66 | .473 | -4.24 | .001 | 301 |
| | J | 5-1 | 3.57 | .630 | 3.72 | .700 | -2.48 | .014 | 463 |
| Usefulness | S | | 3.20 | .856 | 3.71 | .823 | -5.03 | .001 | 276 |
| | J | " | 3.27 | .714 | 3.39 | .858 | -1.58 | ns | 459 |
| Interest | S | | 2.74 | 1.05 | 3.33 | 1.16 | -4.57 | .001 | 290 |

Swedish pupils, in general, were also found to be a little more positive with respect to the "we equally can" dimension than Japanese pupils, but the difference was at the edge level of $p<0.05$. A paired samples t-test between computer self-efficacy and gender equality in computer competence showed statistically significant differences in both countries, but in a different direction. While among Japanese the "We can, but I can't" paradox was clearly identified for both genders, $t(463)=-10.85$, $p<0.0001$, the computer self-efficacy score for Swedish pupils was significantly higher than that of the gender equality in computer competence score, $t(286)= 5.97$, $p<0.0001$. A similar trend was evidenced for males, $t(258)=-6.64$, $p<0.0001$. Swedish girls, however, revealed a similar score in their computer efficacy both as individuals and as a gender group, but boys felt a much higher self-efficacy as individuals rather than as a gender group, $t(150)=6.78$, $p<0.0001$.

The stepwise multiple regression results are presented in Table 3. As it can be seen from this Table, the overall student computer self-efficacy model accounted for 42.1 per cent of the computer self-efficacy variability. The country variable was found to be the strongest factor which alone accounted for 29.4 per cent of the variance, followed by computer usefulness, adding another 10.6 per cent of the total variance explained. The increase provided by the intrinsic motivation towards computers (computer interest) was very small ($R^2ch=.020$).

With respect to the "We equally can" dimension of the investigated paradox, the regression analysis shows that this aspect is highly influenced by pupils' perceptions concerning gender equality in major school subjects as well as gender equality in computers. This composite variable by itself accounted for 57.8 per cent of the explained variance and exerted a considerably high influence (Beta = 0.75, at $p<0.0001$).

Table 3
**Stepwise Multiple Regression Models**

| Regressors | $R^2$ | $R^2$ch | Fch | p | Beta | p |
|---|---|---|---|---|---|---|
| | I feel confident with my ability to learn about computers | | | | | |
| Country | .294 | .294 | 270.93 | .0001 | .59 | .0001 |
| Comp. usefulness | .400 | .106 | 115.64 | .0001 | .21 | .0001 |
| Comp. interest | .421 | .020 | 22.63 | .0001 | .18 | .0001 |
| | Girls can do just well as boys in learning about computers | | | | | |
| GenEqCompApScS* | .578 | .578 | 889.92 | .0001 | .75 | .0001 |
| Country | .590 | .011 | 18.57 | .0001 | .13 | .0001 |
| Comp. usefulness | .601 | .011 | 18.47 | .0001 | .12 | .0001 |

* Gender equality in computers and gender equality in pupil aptitude in school subjects

Concerning the mean scores of the variables included in this study, t-test statistics presented in Table 2 show that boys outscored girls in computer experience acquired at school ($p<0.001$). This finding refers to the Japanese pupils rather than to the Swedish pupils who all receive the same amount of computer literacy instruction, normally ranged from 70 to 80 hours during the last three grades of the compulsory school. Interestingly, the intrinsic motivation towards computers- described as interest and enjoyment in the study of computers was found to be similar among the Japanese pupils, but as expected boys outscored girls among the Swedish pupils ($p<0.001$). Similarly, Japanese and Swedish boys outscored girls with respect to the usefulness of computers in future career ($p<0.01$ and $p<0.001$, respectively). Despite the fact that teacher encouragement in getting students involved in learning more about computers was very small, it was significantly directed more to boys rather than to girls, especially among the Japanese female pupils.

A similar trend was also identified regarding peer encouragement, especially among the Swedish pupils investigated. However, parental encouragement was almost equally distributed to both genders, regardless of country. Interestingly, the Swedish parents were found to exert significantly a higher rate of encouragement rather than the Japanese parents ($p<0.001$).

## 4. CONCLUSION

The first striking point revealed in this study concerns the lack of gender differences in computer self-efficacy scores. Although boys were found to be a fraction ahead of the girls, the difference was not statistically significant in none of the countries investigated. This is not, however, in the line of previous research, which identifies girls as less competent in dealing with computers than boys [8]. The second striking point is that the "We can, but I can't" paradox appeared clearly only among the Japanese pupils investigated. It was clearly shown that, the only computer-related item to which Japanese females responded with more positive conviction was "Females can do just as well as boys in learning more about computers". However, as soon as females were asked to assess their own self-efficacy, they shifted in their judgments, reporting less conviction to their self-efficacy in computers as individuals.

One set of factors underlying the appearance of this paradox in the case of Japan, but not in Sweden is, of course, cultural and attitudinal and the role played by the institutional structures of society, such as the family and the school. A possible explanatory factor may derive from the fact that the group is most fundamental to all aspects of the Japanese social fabric and Japanese feel more confident and secure as a group members rather than as individuals. As it has been consistently reported, Japanese are not so much concerned with the realization of self or individuality as with group identity [14]. The "we equally can" dimension of the investigated paradox is also considerably reinforced by the high score of pupils' perceptions concerning gender equality in computers and gender equality in pupil aptitude in school subjects.

## 5. REFERENCES


1 A. Durndell, The Persistence of the gender gap in computing. Computers and Education. Vol.16, No.4, 283-287 (1991).

2 G. Lovegrove, Experiences in running workshops for schoolgirls. Proceedings of the EURIT '90 Conference on Technology and Education, April 23-27, Herning, Denmark (1990).

3 G. Siann et al., Stereotyping in relation to the gender gap in participation in computing. Educational Research. Vol.30, No.2, 90-103 (1988).

4 G. Siann et al., The Effect of computer use on gender differences in attitudes to computers. Computers and Education. Vol.14, No.2, 183-191 (1990).

5 B.A. Collis and R.L. Williams, Cross-Cultural comparison of gender differences in adolescents‘ attitudes toward computers and selected school subjects. Journal of Educational Research, Vol.81, No.1, 17-27 (1987).

6 R.D. Hess and I.T. Miura, Gender differences in enrollment in computer camps and classes. Sex Roles, Vol.13, 193-203 (1985).

7 A. Bandura, Self-efficacy mechanism in human agency. American Psychologist, Vol.37, 122-147 (1982).

8 I.T. Miura, Computer self efficacy: a factor in understanding gender differences in computer course enrolment. Paper presented at the Annual Meeting of the American Educational Research Association, San Fransisco (1986).

9 I.T. Miura, The relationship of computer self-efficacy expectations to computer interest and course enrollment in college. Sex Roles, Vol.16, Nos. 5/6, 303-311 (1987).

10 I.T. Miura and R.D. Hess, Sex differences in computer access, interest and usage. ERIC, Washington (1983).

11 M. Chen, Gender and computers: the beneficial effects of experience on attitudes. Paper presented at the Annual Meeting of the American Educational Research Association, San Fransisco (1986).

12 S.K. Kwan et al., Gender differences and computing: students' assessment of social influences. Education and Computing Vol.1, No.3,187-194 (1985).

13 J. Moore and L. Steele, Sex and the choice of computer studies. Computers and Education, Vol.49, 2-3 (1985).

14 N.K. Shimahara, Adaptation and Education in Japan. Praeger, New York (1987).

Education and Society / R. Aiken (Editor)
Information Processing 92, Volume II
Elsevier Science Publishers B.V. (North-Holland)



# Addressing the Gender Gap in Informatics Education

C. D. Martin
Department of Electrical Engineering and Computer Science, The George Washington University, Washington, D.C. 20052, USA

Keyword Codes: K.3.1, K.3.2, K.4.1, K.4.2
Keywords: Computer Uses in Education, Computer and Information Science Education, Public Policy Issues, Social Issues

**Abstract**

The problem of the significant decline in young women studying informatics and subsequently pursuing careers in the informatics profession is addressed. The hypothesis is made that part of this decline can be attributed to the male-oriented paradigm pervasive throughout the study and practice of informatics. Results from a gender and informatics workshop held in the United States in 1990 and related research findings are presented as well as specific recommendations for addressing the problem.

## 1. INTRODUCTION

The work force in the year 2000 will require many more engineers and computer scientists. New jobs which require a highly trained, technically competent work force are being created at the same time that the engineering and informatics work force is aging. At the same time that the need for technically trained professionals is increasing, there is a diminishing interest in informatics and engineering among the traditional talent pool of white males. As a result, there has been a significant decline of students enrolling in informatics programs over the past three years. This decline warrants the serious concern of both informatics professionals and educators since it will eventually have an adverse impact on the profession and on the world economy.. The most significant portion of the decline can be attributed to young women. This is particularly startling because informatics is a relatively new field that has been open to women since its beginning approximately twenty-five years ago. When the flood of informatics undergraduate students hit the universities from 1978 - 1985, almost half of them were women. Now interest in informatics on the part of young women has significantly declined (Levenson, 1990).

Numerous studies have demonstrated that preadolescent girls show superior aptitude for mathematical concepts and operations when compared to their male counterparts. Some researchers have found, however, that during early adolescence an explicit disinterest in math and science is developed in young women because of social pressures (AAUW, 1991). The result is a stagnation of inherent ability and the retarded development of subsequent skills necessary to undertake college studies involving math or science, such as informatics. The fact that social attitudes become fixed during the early teenage years clearly suggests that efforts to influence young women's attitudes about future careers, personal abilities, and professional role models should occur during the early teen years. Attitude changes are required at this time to ensure that a curricular track is chosen which provides an adequate academic background for careers in informatics.

### 1.1 The Power of Paradigms

One premise is that the decline in young women selecting educational curricula that lead to careers in informatics can be attributed to the existing educational paradigm that separates studies of science, math and informatics from studies of the humanities starting in the secondary schools. Several studies have suggested that the way informatics material in particular is taught at the elementary and secondary levels is gender-biased toward males. If a new gender-free paradigm can be created that presents an integrated approach to these disciplines, more young women would continue to be interested in them as future career options. This paradigm should include greater attention to values, human issues and social impact as well as to the mathematical and theoretical foundations of informatics.

Eric Roberts (1989) found the unique aspect of informatics as a discipline to be the encouragement of highly focused, almost obsessive behavior as a road to success. Males have been given license by society to be obsessive, whereas women are expected to be more "balanced." This view echoes Sherry Turkle's comments in her book *The Second Self* (1984), where she examines the social and psychological aspects of the computer revolution and presents descriptions of computer hackers at MIT as the ultimate "nerds," antisocial and obsessive to the extreme in their behavior. Such a paradigm for computing is decidedly unappealing to women who are nurtured to value interpersonal relations.

In their well-known study "Poolhalls, Chips and Wargames (1985)," Kiesler, Sproull and Eccles of Carnegie Mellon University examined why computers seemed to be more attractive to boys than girls. They offered a cultural framework for explaining the apparent gender differences and suggested that the world of computing was more consistent with male adolescent culture than with feminine values and goals. Computing itself was neither inherently difficult nor uninteresting to girls, but computer games, educational software and curriculum were designed using a male paradigm.

In looking at the undergraduate and graduate informatics curriculum, again the paradigm issue enters in. The typical student that most professors have in mind when they design their courses, problems, and lectures is the white male. A 1987 Burton study found that most female undergraduate and graduate students in informatics experience a lack of role models, feeling of isolation and a reduced social support structure when compared to their male counterparts. So-called "killer" courses taught in the freshman year - courses designed to cull rather than cultivate students for the discipline - have impacted both female and minority students more adversely than white male students. Women are attracted to and learn better in a cooperative rather than a competitive environment. The typical informatics curriculum taught by predominantly male professors, many of whom are foreign and come from cultures that do not regard females as serious students, all contribute to what Sheila Widnall (1988) describes as the "chilly classroom" for female students.

A Cooper Union study (1989) surveyed female science, engineering, and computer students and professionals and found that the chilly classroom carries forward into a chilly work environment as well. Researchers found that 70% of the women felt they had to work harder than their male counterparts, 50% felt that they viewed ethical issues differently than their male counterparts, 39% felt that they would be penalized if they took maternity leave, 30% felt that the wives of their male colleagues felt threatened by them, 58% felt that harassment of some sort was prevalent in the workplace, and 78% felt they received comparable pay when they started, but were not promoted as rapidly. Another study supported the last belief. It found that most women begin with comparable wages, but within 10 years, they earn 25% less than males.

## 2. A RESEARCH WORKSHOP ON THE GENDER GAP IN INFORMATICS

An all day preconference research workshop entitled "In Search of Gender-Free Paradigms for Computer Science Education" was held on June 24, 1990, at the National Educational Computing Conference (NECC/90) in Nashville, Tennessee. The workshop was jointly sponsored by NECC, the Education Division of IBM and the ACM Subcommittee on Precollege Education. The premise of the call for papers was that the decline in the number of young women selecting computer science majors was attributable to the existence of a male-oriented paradigm in computer science. The workshop brought together researchers who had been conducting gender-related research in computer science education to examine all of the issues and to make recommendations to solve the problem.

The workshop format included nine research presentations given by Danielle R. Bernstein from Kean College of New Jersey; Valerie Clarke from Deakin University, Australia; Carol Edwards of the Southern Coalition for Educational Equity; Henry Etzkowitz from SUNY and Columbia University, New York; Cindy Meyer Hanchey from Oklahoma Baptist University; Charles Huff from St. Olaf College, Minnesota; Robin Kay from the University of Toronto, Canada; Lesley Klein, Pace University, New York; and Elizabeth Wolf representing the Women of the ACM (WACM) Subcommittee. The result of the workshop is a monograph (Martin and Murchie-Beyma, 1992) containing all of the papers and recommendations presented by the participants as well as several other papers germaine to the topic. This paper summarizes the findings from the workshop and presents a set of recommendations for the solving the gender gap in informatics

## 2.1 The Research Findings

Kay (1992) suggested shifting from a construct methaphor which masks process, emphasizes generalization, and produces arbitrary interpretation of results to a process methaphor that would encompass dynamic and complex interactions, social construction and context. The goal would be to provide a coherent model to explain the complex interaction of many factors, It would allow researchers to move from merely identifying gender differences to understanding them.

Huff, Fleming and Cooper(1992) described a research program that has investigated the social psychology of human computer interaction. In a number of carefully constructed experiments, they have confirmed that males and females approach the task of computing in recognizably different ways and that the design of the software itself carries with it a gender-loaded paradigm that can produce differential stress to users depending upon gender.

Aman(1992) looked at two broadly gender appropriate computer applications, problem-solving and written composition, as well as overall attitude indicators. The study was conducted at two gender-segregated high schools, one male and one female. It found that gender was a significant predictor of computer attitude and that females held persistently more positive computer attitudes than males. On the other hand, females showed less confidence in their abilities on the computer. Additionally, males overwhelmingly spent substantial amounts of time each week on the computer when compared to females.

Klein (1992) synthesized past studies to trace the behavior of female students in mathematics and attitudes toward informatics from elementary mathematics through college mathematics. Results of previous studies concluded that girls excel in such areas as computation skills and symbolic relationships while boys dominate in spatial relations and problem solving. While women generally did not agree that mathematics was a "male domain," they reported more math anxiety. Males, on the other hand had more confidence in their ability to learn math, and stated a significantly greater intention to take math courses in the future than women. Men perceived women to be not as able to handle computers. Several studies suggested that masculine software design has precluded girls from developing a sense of "ownership" toward computers, beginning with video arcade games where girls are usually the spectators. The Klein study concludes with recommendations to clarify and formalize informatics curriculum at the precollege level and make an introduction to informatics mandatory for all high school students, incorporate computer usage across the curriculum to provide a variety of computer experience for all students, decrease competitiveness in the design of education software and incorporate cooperative group projects in the classroom as often as individual projects.

Edwards(1992) reported that young women of color experience all of the gender problems found in previous studies to a greater degree. They face tremendous cultural and educational barriers that prevent most of them from venturing into majors and therefore careers in math, science, engineering and informatics. They experience the educational barriers of a frequent lack of resources in predominantly minority schools, lower teacher expectations, more substitute teachers, less experienced teachers, and the frequent relegation to lower educational tracks, even through tracking has been found to benefit only the top 1% of students. The cultural barriers include the lack of role models, the lack of encouragement by parents and teachers, the responsibility for the care of siblings, and an anti-intellectual culture which measures self-esteem in non-academic ways. Sadly, the effects of disadvantage are cumulative; that is, the combination of being poor and minority and female lowers perceptions and aptitudes towards math and computers proportionally to the level of disadvantage.

Clarke(1992) described research conducted over the past five years that examined gender-based factors related to primary, secondary and university students. She identified 13 barriers inhibiting the participation of girls in computing and suggests practical strategies for overcoming them. At all levels she found gender stereotyping and expectations to be a major cause of the differences found. She also found gender stereotyping to be situational as illustrated by one study in which a coeducational primary school was compared to an all-girl primary school. In her research Clarke has noted the presence of sex bias in parental and teacher behavior reflected by greater home ownership of computers by families with boys and encouragement to enroll in summer camps and courses for boys.

At the secondary and university levels, the major factors reflecting gender differences were previous computer experience, type of computer experience (ie, word processing versus programming), differences in mathematics experience related to high school math courses taken, male-oriented software design, the different social needs of girls and boys, and the perception of computing as a male activity. The dearth of female role models and lack of encouragement by high school counselors to steer girls toward informatics were also seen as factors affecting female enrollment in college informatics.

Bernstein (1992) stated that her research has shown that the feeling of self-efficacy is a major predictor of success in informatics. Self-efficacy with computers can be defined as the feeling that one is in control of the machine and can make a difference in the operation of the machine. As a group women rate themselves lower than men for perceived self-efficacy on computers. The factor most influencing feelings of self-efficacy is previous experience with computers. Research has shown that from the first encounter men approach the computer as a passion or a preoccupation, whereas women view the computer as a tool to complete a specific task.

Bernstein suggested that a new curriculum paradigm for informatics courses, especially the introductory course, is needed to increase confidence and the sense of being in control. This new approach would be based upon the use of applications packages such as spreadsheets and databases to introduce the fundamental concepts of informatics, rather than programming. Such a course would tend to be an equalizer, empowering those who had not had high school programming as well as those who had. Women would see the usefulness of computers immediately and might thereby have incentive to continue studying about computers.

Female faculty and graduate students in four academic departments (chemistry, physics, informatics and electrical engineering) at two research universities were surveyed by Etzkowitz et al. (1992). They found that all the traditional norms of the academic system work to exclude women or hold them back on the promotion ladder. Women who attempt to define an alternative scientific role, balancing research with other roles and limiting time at the work site, encounter structural obstacles such as severe limitations on arranging parttime appointments during pregnancy or childrearing years. Men in some areas of research such as theory are resistant to participation by women. Female graduate students with children often have difficulties finding thesis advisors who understand their family responsibilities.

Etzkowitz et al. concluded that the development of a critical mass of of women faculty and graduate students within a department would result in a reduction of structural barriers, positively affect the culture of a department, and either restrict the expression of or change negative male attitudes, thereby increasing the success rate of women faculty and graduate students in achieving tenure, promotions and degrees. To accomplish this, they proposed the involvement of students and faculty in the faculty recruiting process, a change in the tenure structure to allow a more flexible timeclock, and the removal of the geographic constraints encountered by female graduate students who may not be in a position to move to another location after graduation but are prevented from being hired by their department

The preliminary report of the ACM Subcommittee on the Status of Women in Computer Science (Pearl, et al, 1991) was presented at the workshop. It detailed the discouraging statistics from the informatics pipeline over the past decade that reveal the declining participation of women at all levels in the field. Approximately 36% of all B.S. degrees, 30% of all M.S. degrees, 11% of all Ph.D.'s, and only 6.5% of all informatics faculty appointments are earned by women. The numbers are more encouraging in industry where 30% of all employed computer scientists are women. However, even in industry where women find a more flexible environment better suited to their special needs, they still encounter the glass ceiling and the "mommy track" mentality blocking career advancement. This preliminary report called for a systematic study of the structural changes needed in both academia and industry to reopen the pipeline for women.

## 2.2 Recommendations from the Gender Workshop

After the paper presentations, the workshop participants formed three subgroups to discuss the issues of *exposure*, *attraction* and *retention* of young women to informatics. Each group was asked to identify major problems and obstacles that hindered women in each topic area and to recommend both visionary and practical solutions to the problems.

2.2.1. *Exposure:* Regarding early exposure to computers and computing, the first subgroup identified gender stereotyping, low expectations, limited access to computers, bias in counseling by teachers and parents, male-oriented software, and the lack of role models in the media and in daily life as the major obstacles to providing early, positive exposure to computers for girls. The group recommended that to counteract these obstacles there should be an immediate national effort at the middle school level to develop programs to appeal to girls since that is the age when most girls lose interest in math, science and computers. They saw the need to improve curriculum, educational software and teacher training to address this concern. The focus on computers at this level should not be on programming, but on the relevance of the computer to social needs through the use of applications software in cooperative learning environments. Computers should be used throughout the curriculum with equitable access for all children.

2.2.2 *Attraction:* Similar themes were discussed by the second group who looked at why girls are not attracted to computers and informatics. They identified computer games and software, lower home ownership of computers, parent /teacher expectations and advising, and the early emphasis on programming as the major culprits in turning off girls to computers. They suggested a national parent education program through the media and parent teacher organizations, inservice training for teachers and guidance counselors, the allocation of more resources to provide more computers in schools, and a more tools-oriented approach to computer studies in both high school and college. They also suggested an active role by industry to provide role models in the schools, to develop gender neutral software, and to provide funding for special projects related to attracting young women to informatics.

2.3.3 *Retention:* The third group looked at the retention issue since the data have shown that simply attracting women to informatics is not enough. There is a significantly higher dropout rate among female informatics students than among their male counterparts. Recommendations from the third group were targeted for high school, college and graduate informatics programs. They recommended structured labs using group projects based upon cooperative learning models, formal peer, faculty, and alumni mentoring programs for women and minority students, pairing of college students with high school students and pairing of graduate students with college students to provide positive peer role models, guest lecture programs fed by government and industry to provide role models, a computer for every student in their dorm room, more financial aid in the form of grants rather than loans, and programming courses which emphasize computer applications and which focus on reading good programs before writing them.

The final recommendation of this group was related to the reward structure for faculty members. Recognizing that the programs they recommended take a tremendous amount of time to develop and administer, they proposed that the criteria for tenure and promotion should include developing new teaching strategies, developing innovative curriculum, mentoring, and administering programs to meet the needs of special categories of students as well as the traditional research and publishing.

## 3. CONCLUSIONS

A gender-free paradigm for computing probably does not exist. What is needed instead is the pluralistic approach called for by Turkle and Papert (1991). Both the popular and technical culture have presented computation as the ultimate embodiment of the abstract and formal, ignoring the concrete and personal aspects of computation. In their in-depth examination of successful programmers at many different levels over two decades, they found a "diversity of approaches to programming that suggests that equal access to even the most basic elements of computation requires accepting the validity of multiple ways of knowing and thinking." Despite the dominant ideology of the computer culture which privileges the structured, hierarchical, "black box" style, they cite evidence that the main difference between the formal and concrete approaches to programming is not in the quality of the final product, but in the process of creating the product.

The trend of the declining number of students choosing to study math, science, and informatics can be reversed by tapping into the reservoir of female members of our society (Berryman, 1985; Betz, 1990). This workshop provided a forum for identifying both problems and solutions that address the gender gap in informatics. The lack of women in the informatics professional fields is a major social issue that needs to be addressed by businesses, educational institutions and governments. Simply opening doors to once restricted career fields has not proven to be enough (Tobias, 1990; Widnall, 1988). The challenge is to identify programs that work in attracting this population to informatics and to cultivate sustaining support systems for them once they take the plunge into the previously male domain of informatics.

## 4. REFERENCES


Aman, J.R. (1992) Gender and attitude toward computers.*

American Association of University Women (AAUW). *Shortchanging girls, Shortchanging America.* Washington , D.C. January, 1991.

Berryman, S. Minorities and women in mathematics and science: Who chooses these fields and why? Paper presented at the annual meeting of the American Association for the Advancement of Science(AAAS), Los Angeles, May, 1985.

Bernstein, D.R. (1992). A new introduction to computer science.*

Betz, N.E. What stops women and minorities from choosing and completing majors in science and engineering? Science and Public Policy Seminars. Washington, D.C.: Federation of Behavioral, Psychological and Cognitive Sciences, June, 1990.

Burton, M.D. (1987). Gender differences in professional socialization: A study of women and men becoming computer scientists. Technical Report, Pittsburgh: Cagnegie Mellon University.

Clark, V.(1992). Strategies for involving girls in computer science.*

Cooper Union 1989 national survey of undergraduate women engineering students. (1989). The Cooper Union for the Advancement of Science and Art, New York, NY.

Cooper Union 1989 national survey of women engineers. (1989). The Cooper Union for the Advancement of Science and Art, New York, NY.

Edwards, C. (1992). Implications of the computer culture for women of color.*
Etzkowitz, H., Kemelgor, C., Neuschatz, M. and Uzzi, B. (1992). Restructuring departments for equality.*
Hanchey, C. M. (1992). Gender Equity Resource List.*
Huff, C. W., Fleming, J.H. and Cooper, J. (1992) Gender differences in human computer interaction.*
Kay, R. (1992) Understanding gender biases in computer-related Behaviour: Are we using the wrong metaphor?*
Kiesler, S., Sproull, L., & Eccles, J.S. (1985). Poolhalls, chips and wargames: Women in the culture of computing. *Psychology of Women Quarterly,* 9, 451-462.
Klein, L. S. (1992). Female students' underachievement in computer science and mathematics: Reasons and recommendations.*
Levenson, N.(1990). Educational pipeline issues for women. *Computing Research News*, 11-13, October, 1990.
Pearl, A. Pollack, M. Riskin, E. Thomas, R. Wolf, E. Wu, A. (1990) Becoming a computer scientist: A report by the ACM committee on the status of women in computing science. *Communications of the ACM,* November, 1990.
Turkle, S. (1984). *The second self: Computers and the human spirit.* New York: Simon and Schuster.
Turkle, S. and Papert, S. (1990). Epistomological pluralism: Styles and voices within the computer culture. *Signs Magazine*, University of Chicago Press, November, 1990)
Roberts, E. (1989) Women and computer science. *Tough Questions*, Student Pugwash Magazine, Fall issue,4-5.
Tobias, S. (1990). *They're not dumb, they're different: Stalking the second tier.* Tuscon, AZ: Research Corporation
Widnall, S.E. (1988). Voices from the pipeline. *Science*, 214, 1740-1745.

*found in Martin, C. D. and Murchie-Beyma, E. (editors) (1992) *In Search of Gender-Free Paradigms for Computer Science Education.* The NECC Monograph Series, International Society for Technology in Education (ISTE),1787 Agate Street, Eugene, OR, 97403, USA.

Education and Society / R. Aiken (Editor)
Information Processing 92, Volume II
Elsevier Science Publishers B.V. (North-Holland)


# Structured Hypertext Applied to Software Measurement

D. Meyerhoff and M. Müllerburg

GMD, Schloss Birlinghoven, Postbox 1316, D–5205 Sankt Augustin, Germany

**Abstract**

In this article the concept of Set Structured Hypertext is introduced as a possible solution of the navigation problem in plain hypertext. A standard answer to the navigation problem is to impose a classical document structure. This fall back to the structuring means of chapters, sections, and subsections suggests a linear sequence of browsing through the hypertext and pushes it thereby back into one row with papers and text books. The main idea of Set Structured Hypertext is to use the content itself for structuring the electronic document. This usage of the potential power of the hypertext concept makes locating information much easier.
A system implementing this concept was developed in order to make conceptual knowledge about the domain of software measurement available for software engineers in their daily working environment.

Keyword Codes: D.2.8 D.2.2 H.5.0 K.3.2
Keywords: Hypertext, Software Measurement, Instructional Environment

## 1. Introduction

Today hypertext is a very popular idea for making information available. There are many hypertext systems and a lot of enhancements and extensions of the original hypertext concept [2] have been developed. In this paper we focus on the location question, i.e. on how to find information in a hypertext and how to organize a hypertext in order to enhance locatability of information. This is just another aspect of the often addressed navigational problem (see also [3]).

Plain hypertext makes it very difficult for the authors as well as the readers to generate a mental model of the document and of its content. The problem is caused by a lack of structuring mechanisms. This lack is often circumvented by supplying graphic browsers to traverse the hypertext, supplying overview cards for a group of cards (sometimes called browsers, too, see [7], p. 837), providing query facilities (see [3]), or by imposing a hierarchy onto such a hypertext. As documented in the literature (see e.g. [3], p. 35] a hierarchic organisation of hypertexts is especially adequate w.r.t. the understandability of the document and orientation of the users.

In several hypertext systems such hierarchies are supported, however these are mostly document hierarchies. As an example the top node of a hierarchic hypertext could represent the document as a whole, while its children would refer to an introduction, several chapters and a summary. This kind of hierarchy does not refer to the content of the hypertext and therefore is not a means for enhancing the users perception of the content structure, i.e. the categorization and relationships of the concepts of the domain. Another drawback is that this kind of document structure is always tuned to the requirements of a specific target group. Readers with different background have to reorganize such a hypertext by using its associative links rather than its organizing links, just like they would restructure a book by making use of the subject index.

For avoiding such problems we here suggest to structure the information based on the structure of the content itself. We therefore introduce the concept of *Set Structured Hypertext*, which on the one hand supports the reader in the process of locating the desired information within the hypertext, and, on the other hand, supports the author of a hypertext in his or her design decisions, giving criteria how to organize the document and where to add new information.

In Section 2. we discuss problems of hypertext with respect to the development of a hypertext document for the domain of software (engineering) measurement, motivating the development of Set Structured Hypertext (SSH). Section 3. introduces the concept of SSH and demonstrates its application for the domain of software measurement. Section 4. presents a prototype system for SSH and discusses its usage for accessing information about software measurement. The results are summarized in Section 5.

## 2. Hypertext for Software Measurement

Wanting to make knowledge about measurement in software quality assurance available at the software engineer's computer we investigated the possible application of the hypertext concept. Before we discuss some problems we encountered we briefly introduce the topic of software measurement.

### Software Measurement

Software measurement (for an introduction see [5]) is a subdiscipline of software engineering. The entities we might be interested in measuring include the process of software development, the programs resulting from this process and all the other documents that are usually developed during this process as well as the resources needed for the process. A measure can be regarded as a mapping of an entity onto a number. As an example the measure *number of lines of code* maps a program onto a number, which is the number of text lines in a textual representation of a program.

Because software measurement is not a trivial task there are a lot of tools (software tools) available that support the personnel doing the measurement in determinig the values, e.g. tools that count, among other things, the *number of lines of code* of a program.

Software measurement is not an end in itself but rather is applied in order to get control of the relevant factors involved in software development, e.g. control over resources of the software development process or quality of the resulting progams and documents. In our application we are mainly interested in measures that are applied to the outputs of a software development process, i.e. programs and documents. Naturally these measures are used in software quality assurance, another subdiscipline of software engineering which is interested in the quality, for example reliability or maintainability, of software.

### Problems with Hypertext

The system we intended to develop was to aid a software engineer in applying software measurement by aiding the selection of appropriate measures, tools etc. for a specific software project. The advantage of using an electronic media here was the ease of modification with respect to newest results in this fast developing area and the possibility to adapt the content of the document to the specific needs of companies using it.

Developing a hypertext for software measurement, the author is confronted with the question of how to organize the information. Adding, for instance, information about a new measure to the already existing information the author has to decide whether to add it to an existing node (and to which one). If the measure can be used to assess maintainability and reliability of a program, do we add the information to the node dealing with maintainability and reliability or to the one dealing with program, or, is the information worth an individual node (and to which nodes is this going to be linked)? Related problems come up when accessing the hypertext. Halasz says ([7], p. 842) "often these users can describe exactly what information they are looking for, but simply they cannot find it in the network."

According to good design principles [1] we started the development of the hypertext with thorough planning and analysing, which led to a grouping of the concepts to be dealt with into six categories. Although we anticipated the need for continuous maintainance these six categories seemed to be stable, so that extension of the hypertext would probably lead to new members of categories and even new categories but not to the change of these categories themselves.

Having developed these categories we found that the users of a hypertext on software measurement would benefit more from these categories themselves than from some arbitrarily chosen document structure. Therefore we made this categorization the organizing structure of the hypertext, leading to the concept of Set Structured Hypertext.

## 3. Set Structured Hypertext

In this section we present the concept of Set Structured Hypertext (SSH) and demonstrate its usage for the example domain of software measurement.

A Set Structured Hypertext organizes the content of an electronic document by grouping the nodes to socalled *node sets* and accordingly the links to *link sets* or link types. Since a node in Set Structured Hypertext represents a concept (and information about it) a node set refers to a respective set of concepts that share some vital commonalities which can be captured by a broader term. This term is then the name of the node set.

Having grouped the nodes to node sets it should be possible to identify binary relations between some of these node sets. These relations are also mirrored on the level of the elements as relations between elements of these sets (and therefore are related to the hygraph formalism [8] in this aspect). For example in our domain there is a relationship between the node sets *measures* and *tools*, so that for every node of node set *measures* there may be some related nodes in node set *tools* and vice versa, which means that those tools can be used to compute the measure.

We can also define consistency of the resulting hypertext: For every node there is a node set that it belongs to, and for every relation between two nodes there is a relationship between their respective node sets.

This content based structuring of Set Structured Hypertext results in a clear understanding where some information should be located in the document, i.e. where an author should put it and where a reader should look for it. Content based hypertext structuring mechanisms have also been proposed by [6]. The usefulness of structures derived from the application domain is also subject of research in the area of computer aided instruction (see e.g. [4]). A more formal description of the concept of Set Structured Hypertext is given in [10].

### Applying the Concept to Software Measurement

Our example application for SSH is software measurement. For this domain a grouping of the concepts into six sets (at the moment) seemed appropriate. The resulting node sets are the following: *Measures* are mathematical functions that map entities (e.g. programs) onto numbers, and *Tools* help to apply these measures, e.g. they compute the actual measurement value. *Entities* are what we are actually interested in with respect to measurement, assessment and prediction, such as programs and documents. *Quality Attributes* of entities are those attributes or characteristics that we want to assess or predict. *Quantitative Attributes* of entities are those attributes that we may be able to measure based solemly on the entity itself, and *models* are abstract representations of entities and are used as a basis for defining measures.

The relations identified between these sets are visualized in Figure 1: *Models* can be derived from *Entities*, *Measures* are defined on *Models*, *Tools* may implement *Measures*, *Entities* have *Qualitative Attributes*, *Entities* have *Quantitative Attributes*, *Qualitative Attributes* have to be defined in terms of *Quantitative Attributes*, and *Quantitative Attributes* can be measured (relation to *Measures*).

The questions about where and how to add information to the hypertext can now be answered on the basis of such a structure. Adding information about a measure for instance is done by creating a new node in the set *Measures* and relating this node to other nodes appropriately. Linking is done with respect to the identified relations, so a measure is typically related to some tools (that implement the measure), to a model (that the measure is based on), and to quantitative attributes (that are measured).

## 4. The Prototype

We here describe the implemented prototype system for SSH and how we used it for the domain of software measurement.

The main components of the prototype system are a data structure representing the hypertext, an editor, a network browser and a dictionary. The dictionary provides alphabetical access to the named nodes of the document whereas the network browser provides

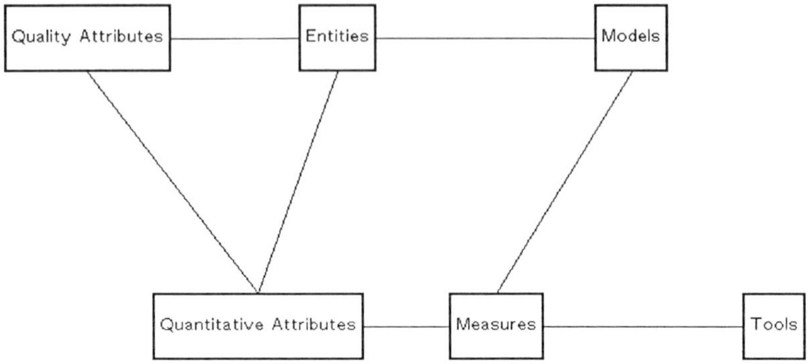


Figure 1: Node Sets and Link Sets

access via the structure. The editor is used for defining and updating the document. We here concentrate on the network browser, for a description of the other tools see [9].

The network browser provides a graphical presentation of the hypertext as a network and functionality to access the items of and browse through the document. The start up situation, the socalled high level view, is a view of the network defined by the node sets and the link sets between them, similar to that of Figure 1. The user here can access either the text attached to each of these items or the elements of any node set he or she is interested in.

Selecting an element of a node set and wanting more detailed information, its text can be accessed. In addition, the user can get a graphic presentation of the socalled context of the node, i.e. the node itself, its links and the linked nodes are displayed, accompanied by some information about which node set each of the nodes belongs to. This visualization, called a low level view, allows a repeated application of the context and delete-from-display functionality, so that the user can get the nodes and links onto the display that suit his special interests.

## Using the Prototype for Software Measurement

Using the network browser for accessing information in the SSH document on software measurement, the reader may start by accessing for example the elements of the node set *measures*. When the reader is interested in the context of the element named *Cyclomatic Complexity*, the resulting network will show all the tools that support this measure, it will show the models that the measure is defined on, and finally it will show the quantitative attributes that the measure can be used for. These are the only (direct) links allowed for measures, i.e. defined by the node and link sets.

The really interesting part of navigating in such a network begins, when the different features are used in combination. For example, looking at the explanation of a measure, we may find it interesting and wonder what tool there is to support this measure, or what sort of software object it can be applied to. In this case we would use several context commands, one after the other, in order to find the concepts and the relationships we want to focus on. Figure 2 shows an example network that has been created by accessing the context of the measure *Cyclomatic Complexity* and applying an additional context to the model *Flow Graph*. The default layout shown on the screendump of Figure 2 places elements belonging to the same set into a single column which is annotated with the name of that set. Because each of the sets has a standard position on the screen it is easy for the user to remember where to expect which kind of information.

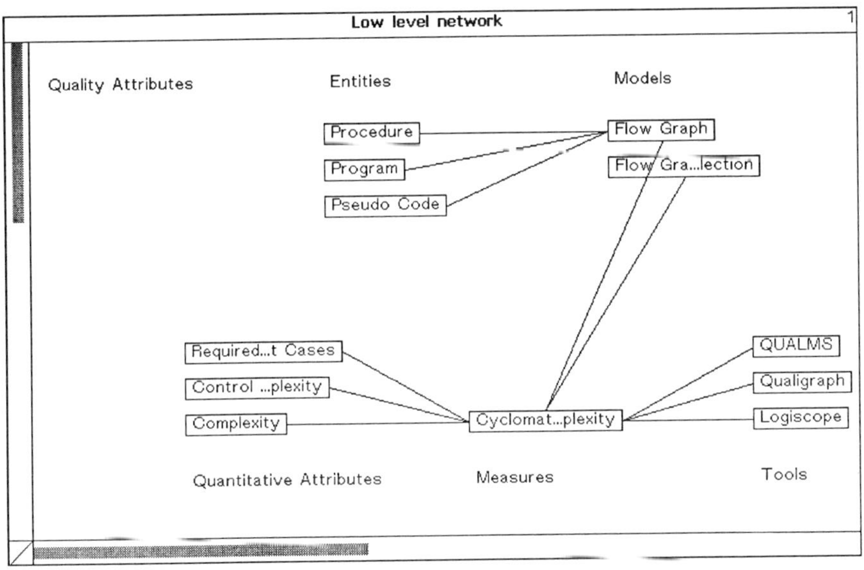


Figure 2: The Context of a Software Measure

Obviously this dynamically computed browser view is more flexible than the static browser cards that are for example used in NoteCards (see [7]). The number of associated texts visible at the same time is also not restricted and the browser can show several contexts at a time. Therefore the notion of the position of the user is no more relevant. This leads to a more free form of working with the hypertext.

## 5. Conclusion and Outlook

In this paper the problem of locating information in a hypertext (navigation problem) was discussed using examples from the domain of software measurement. It was shown that a hierarchic organization of a hypertext based on content relationships allows to maintain the powerful means of a strong interconnectedness while also enhancing the orientation of users. It seems that this approach is useful for domains where very many concepts are to be handled and where a categorization of these concepts into larger groups is possible and helpful.

The prototype was implemented in Smalltalk80 (Version 2.5) and runs on Apple MacIntosh II computers and Sun workstations. The usage of this prototype for the domain of software measurement proved the usefulness of the concept of SSH for a real life application.

Our current work focusses on providing guided tours through the hypertext, allowing more efficient learning for beginners. In addition, we think about implementing additional structuring mechanisms, in particular different link types for links within node sets for describing subpart and subtype relations. The usefulness of recursive refinement of sets in subsets is considered, too.

**Acknowledgments**
This work was carried out in the METKIT Project which is partly sponsored by the CEC under the ESPRIT-II Programme (P-2384). The authors want to thank Uwe Dumslaff and Susanne Flacke for many fruitful discussions which substantially contributed to the results described in this paper and Professor Gunzenhäuser for carefully reviewing it.

## References

[1] P. J. Brown. Assessing the quality of hypertext documents. In N. Streitz, A. Rizk, and J.André, editors, *Hypertext: Concepts, systems, and applications*, pages 1–12, Cambridge, November 1990. Cambridge University Press.

[2] V. Bush. As we may think. *Atlantic Monthly*, 176:101–108, 1945.

[3] J. Conklin. Hypertext: An introduction and survey. *IEEE Computer*, 20(9):17–41, 1987.

[4] U. Dumslaff and D. Meyerhoff. A tutoring system architecture to support the design process. In H.J. Bullinger, editor, *Proceedings of the 4th International Conference on Human–Computer Interaction, Stuttgart 1991*, Elsevier 1991.

[5] N. Fenton. *Software Metrics: A rigorous approach.* Chapman & Hall, London, 1991.

[6] P. K. Garg. Abstraction mechanisms in hypertext. *Communications of the ACM*, 31:862–870, 1988.

[7] F. G. Halasz. Reflections on notecards: Seven issues for the next generation of hypermedia systems. *Communications of the ACM*, 31:836–852, 1988.

[8] D. Harel. On visual formalisms. *Communications of the ACM*, 31:514–530, 1988.

[9] M. Müllerburg, D. Meyerhoff, S. Flacke. Knowledge about Software Measurement on the Computer: The METKIT CAI System. In *Proceedings of the 3rd European Conference on Software Quality.* European Organization for Quality, 1992.

[10] M. Müllerburg, D. Meyerhoff, S. Flacke. *Report of Work Package 10: Computer Aided Instruction of Measurement in Software Quality Assurance.* Technical Report, GMD, St. Augustin, Germany, 1992.

Education and Society / R. Aiken (Editor)
Information Processing 92, Volume II
Elsevier Science Publishers B.V. (North-Holland)



# The Irvine-Geneva Course Development System

Alfred Bork, Bertrand Ibrahim, Bernard Levrat, Alastair Milne, and Rika Yoshii

Educational Technology Center, Department of Information and Computer Science, University of California, Irvine, California 92717, U.S.A.

Centre Universitaire d'Informatique, Université de Genève, CH-1211 Genève 4, Suisse

**ABSTRACT**

This paper outlines a system for the production of significant amounts of high quality highly interactive technology-based learning material. This system has been under development for over twenty-three years, first at the University of California, Irvine, and in the last ten years, jointly with the University of Geneva. The approach emphasizes a systems point of view; that is, we delineate the various tasks, seek the best possible people for each task, and develop suitable interfaces between the different types of people involved. The approach recently has been used extensively for multimedia material. The system is applicable to widely differing styles. Major changes have occurred recently.

Keyword Codes: K.3.1, D.1.2, D.2.2
Keywords: Computer Uses in Education, Automatic Programming, Tools and Techniques

## 1. INTRODUCTION

In textbook publishing, and the making of educational films, we see mature production systems for creating sizable amounts of commercially viable curriculum material. The models in these activities are similar, although there are many variations.

If one examines however the production of technology-based learning material, such as that involving the computer, the videodisc, the CD-ROM drive, and other auxiliary devices, one sees a variety of methods and strategies in use. Furthermore one sees little full-scale high quality material, in spite of a long period of development. We regard the period so far as experimental. The issue was learning how to use the technology, and learning how to modify older production systems, such as those for textbooks, for the new medium.

Many developments are not adequate to a full production strategy. Although we will not argue the case, since we discuss a system we believe will be successful, the use of authoring languages and authoring systems is an unfortunate direction.

The development of the production system discussed in this paper was started over twenty-three years ago at the University of California, Irvine. About ten years ago we were joined by colleagues at the University of Geneva, and since then the two groups have been closely affiliated. Many aspects of the system, such as pedagogical design, have changed little over time, even as new media and new computer capabilities were added. Other aspects, such as the technical implementation, have changed; they are still under evolution. The system has produced commercially viable material in varying subject areas, and continues to be used in a wide range of current projects.

## 2. PRODUCTION SYSTEMS

The production system discussed in this paper has clearly defined goals.

- The learning materials should be of the highest quality.
- The learning materials should work for a wide variety of students, aiming for mastery for all. Learning should be interactive.
- The learning materials must be motivational, so students will stay at difficult tasks.
- Material must be produced within the times initially specified.
- Material must be produced within the costs initially specified.
- Units should be adaptable to changing pedagogy and technology.
- Pedagogical design should not be influenced by implementation considerations.

We divide the discussion into several headings. First we discuss the four major aspects of the production system; management, pedagogical design, technical implementation, and formative evaluation and improvement. In some sections we distinguish between past and current situations, and we will consider some future possibilities. Then we will consider maintenance and time and money, critical if a course development system is to prove effective.

## 3. MANAGEMENT

The production of sizable amounts of high quality material, regardless of media, is complex, involving many people with different qualifications. Hence a very important consideration is project management. Many projects involving technology have failed because of the lack of any careful management system.

There is much to be learned from industry concerning management. The use of the standard project management techniques, many now available on computers, is essential for large projects. The computer is used in several of the developmental stages, easing the management tasks to some extent, as full use of the computer capability is considered.

## 4. PEDAGOGICAL DESIGN

The most important component in development is pedagogical design, the decisions that determine how the material is to react with each individual learner. If the material is weak pedagogically, then fancy programming or evaluation will not make it work better. Hence this is the most critical stage in production.

### 4.1. Emphasis on very good teachers

The key individuals in pedagogical design are excellent teachers.

- The teachers must like students, and must spend much time talking individually with students in the area to be developed.
- The teachers should be primarily interested in active learning, not passive learning.
- Teachers should realize that each student has individual needs. The teachers should be concerned with providing the best learning experience for each student.
- Teachers should be willing to work with groups of several other teachers in the design of the material. Compromise is essential.

We cannot stress too highly the role of these very good teachers. They are critical in the product. We call our production system a teacher-based system, to emphasize the importance of good teachers. This is opposed to systems that are theory-based, technology-based, or tool-based. Not enough is known about the learning process either from a behavioral or cognitive point of view to base a production system on learning theory, although there are such systems. The critical things to capture in production are the insights of very good teachers. We want teachers who understand the students' problems, and know how to recognize those problems, and who know how to help students with the problems that occur. Nor should technology take precedence over pedagogy.

We emphasize that the teachers must be familiar with the subject area, and see students daily in classes, in just the area we are working in. Thus if we are developing material in middle school science we expect that most of the good teachers involved in the design process will be middle school science teachers.

In addition to the good teachers, other types of individuals may be present. First there may be researchers in the learning areas involved. In some areas, such as science education, there is considerable research. In some areas there is little available. If something is known about how people learn in a particular area we want to make use of that, to the maximum extent possible. We also like to have people familiar with highly interactive learning material.

We do not involve programmers at this stage. We want the designers to feel free to make any choices they think pedagogically best, and we do not want to restrict them in these choices. Furthermore, we do not typically have screen designers involved. They will appear later in the production process.

### 4.2. Overall design

It is convenient to divide the process of pedagogical design in at least two stages. If several media are used then more than these two stages may be involved. The general point of view is top-down.

Overall design starts with the broadest considerations of the units to be developed, including the general principles of this material. It does not get down to minute details of how individual modules behave when used by students; such details occur in detail design.

Overall design sessions produce an outline of the material to be produced and module descriptions, so that those who work on the detail design of each module will have guidance as to how to proceed, and will see how their module fits into the overall production program.

Designers in both overall design and detail design work in groups, generally with larger groups in the overall design activities. Overall design begins with the project proposal, a document already approved, that gives guidance to the project.

The first new activity in overall design is likely to be brainstorming, in the formal sense of the term. Since developers will probably not be familiar with brainstorming it is necessary to give them a brief description of the process including strong emphasis that in the first stages of brainstorming there is no criticism or discussion of the ideas presented. Developers are urged not to worry about the details of what they are proposing or whether they have already been suggested, but to generate many ideas quickly. A person experienced at brainstorming should run the session.

Brainstorming produces a variety of ideas that can be classified. Some represent pedagogical techniques. Others refer to subject areas to be covered. Some may be general philosophical principles. No attempt is made to separate these initially, but at a later stage one can begin to break them into categories, and use them as guidance for the more formal development of outline and module descriptions.

We have found it useful for overall designers to state what they regard as the major learning difficulties with each unit. These are not restrictive on the detail designers who follow, but give clues to them.

### 4.3. Detail design

Detail design starts with the outlines and module descriptions from overall design and produces documents, scripts, with all the information on how the material is to work with students. Details about screen design and user interface will usually not be present at this stage.

We have groups of about four teachers working together. A typical session is one week, full time. Design sessions that occupy only a part of the individual's time, such as two hours a day, are inefficient, because teachers do not remember all the minute details of the discussions that have ensued. Several groups will work together in a sizable project, meeting early in the morning and at meals, but maintaining their groups during the week or two in which they are working.

Many of our designers have never been involved in design of extensive curriculum material, and most are not familiar with interactive techniques, so the first morning is an introductory session. We do not expect designers to know anything about computers. The introduction must include information about group dynamics. Teachers are usually not familiar with working in small groups, although this activity is well known within industry. So they must be prepared for the often almost violent disagreements likely to occur in these groups and for the necessity of quickly reaching consensus.

Teachers learn about the script strategies for recording detail design decisions in the early hours of working on the design, although they have seen scripts in advance. The script has varied little in style in the twenty four years we have been using this process.

Scripts give all the details of what is to happen. They are a semi-formal visual programming language, oriented to the needs of learning. They show the text, the media to appear, the information for programmers, comments to help later designers, the tests to be performed on student performance or on user input, and the paths followed as the results of these tests. Examples of scripts are contained in our literature. The natural language components of the script formalism make it easy for newcomers to quickly gain speed in developing scripts.

## 5. DESIGN INVOLVING MANY MEDIA

If media such as video, still pictures, and sound are to be in the final product, then these too must be designed. This may necessitate additional design sessions and production sessions. Since specialized talents are needed for these media it is likely that separate groups will be involved in their design and production.

We find it useful to have the media partially available before the final detail design session. It is difficult to design highly interactive material involving video unless the video is fully known to the designers, available at the design sessions. They need to examine it over and over to see just which portions can be used for what purposes. We will not discuss the questions of how media are selected and developed, but we have additional tentative information on these issues for those interested.

## 6. TECHNICAL IMPLEMENTATION

As already mentioned technical implementation may include the various media to be developed. Two different processes involving different people, are needed for technical implementation. One concerns getting the material running on the computer, with the media integrated. The second task is the issue of screen design and user interface.

With regard to programming we discuss two possibilities. One represents our older strategy, involving direct programming of the modules. The second involves an automatic programming environment, now in working form through recent efforts at the University of Geneva.

### 6.1. Production of computer programs

The material must eventually run in a computer environment. How do we proceed from the script to the running program?

#### 6.1.1. Older strategies

In our older strategies for the development of technology-based learning material, the stage of implementation involving programming often involved undergraduate student programmers. The programming was done directly by programmers.

- Language and Style

  We typically have used a higher level language, TurboPascal in recent efforts. But occasionally we have been forced to use other languages too.

  Since the material will need to be frequently revised, particularly in the early stages and through formative evaluation, it is important to work in a structured language allowing easy revision. It is also very important to follow the structures of good modern software engineering. Programs must be carefully reviewed to see that these standards are met.

- Tools

  We have found it important to develop tools to assist programming activities. Most high level programming languages do not allow effective control of the screen. This is somewhat aided by modern windowing environments, but they do not provide the best capabilities. We have for over ten years had our own windowing environment, particularly oriented to the screens we wish to present in technology-based learning material.

We also have tools to separate everything dependent on natural language from the rest of the material so it would be relatively easy to move materials to different languages, important for future international development projects.

### 6.1.2. Newly Developed Computer Supported Course Development

Newer work in this area is based on direct entry of the script, as soon as possible, into the computer. Then, from the internal representation of the script, the script can be modified, or the program can be directly written by the computer itself (automatic programming).

A full course development environment has been built, using the script as a semi-format visual specification for modules. This environment supports script entry, script update, version control, (partial) automatic program generation, computer supported editing of the hand-programmed parts, and computer supported translations of the computer dialogs.

We do not expect to write the full program automatically, but we estimate that we should write more than 80% in this fashion. Our current developments, programmed in Ada at the University of Geneva on Suns under X-11, do not yet attain this figure. But they are operational, and we have used them in several recent projects.

We estimate that the overall savings in cost will be about 30%, and the overall savings in time will be about 45%, when these facilities are complete. These figures are for the entire development process. Additional funding will be needed. Information about the automatic programming environment is available from the authors and in recent papers.

### 6.2. Screen design and user interface

The specialists in screen design for the use in projects involving technology-based learning material should be graphic artists, with some background in learning issues.

Generally we want the screen to have only the relevant information on it at any given time, as we want to focus students' attention on what is important at the moment, not on older material now only garbage from the standpoint of learning. Blank space is one of the most valuable commodities here. Unlike blank space in books, blank space is free on the screen.

## 7. FORMATIVE EVALUATION AND IMPROVEMENT

An important component of the production process is the use of the materials by students. Particularly with computers, very useful information can be gathered about how the materials work with the target audience, and the materials can be improved based on this evaluation before they are released. It should be understood that this is a much more extensive process than beta testing of computer software. Professional evaluators should structure this process.

We recommend two rounds of formative evaluation and improvement. That is, after the materials have been improved, they can be tested once again and improved a second time.

In addition to the usual purposes of formative evaluation, computers allow the possibility of determining whether the material is motivationally captivating for the users. It can be used in environments in which the student is under no pressure to continue to run the material, such as public library environments, where no exam is expected by the students. Then one can record where students frequently leave the program, indicating sections that do not hold the attention of the student. Then these sections can be reworked. Our previous experience with this type of formative evaluation indicates that a primary cause of students losing interest is a lack of interaction in passive material, with large amounts of reading or viewing video. Often it is possible to make dramatic improvements in motivation at such locations.

## 8. SUMMATIVE EVALUATION

Summative evaluation compares the technology-based learning material with other material, possibly using other media, from the standpoint of learning. Summative evaluation is an expensive activity, and so has seldom been done at a reasonable scale. But it is important in understanding in how effective technology-based learning material is, as compared with other methods of student learning. We need to have far more detailed summative evaluations, as we begin to develop sizable amounts of technology-based learning units. It is only through this process that we can begin to get the detailed information we need for improving our learning systems.

Summative evaluation is typically not part of the development process. The original design group should not be involved in summative evaluation.

## 9. MAINTENANCE

After the material is available, there will still be a need for maintenance activity, as with all software and all curriculum material. Hence there must be a mechanism devised to consider this problem, and to react to the needs of improving the material as problems are found. Maintenance will be very much eased if the program is well-structured and well-commented.

Maintenance is now computer supported. When the specification (the script) is changed, the system indicates to the programmer the parts of the program that need to be updated. During this process, the programmer can see, at any moment, the part of the specification that corresponds to the relevant part of the program. Similarly, the system can show a translator changes in text since the last translation, so that the different translations can be brought up to date quickly, without having to compare the different language versions manually.

## 10. TIME AND MONEY

Our experience indicates that it costs, in a sizable project with a production system already in place, about $30,000 to produce an hour of material, or about $2,000,000 to produce a full year-long course. These figures are similar to those in developments of courses at the Open University in the United Kingdom. They do not include the production of video, as these costs are dependent on the quality of the video.

These costs are roughly in four equal parts, reflecting the four stages of the development process indicated in this paper, management, pedagogical design, technical implementation, and formative evaluation and improvement.

Development of a course will typically be a three year period, with the last year devoted to formative evaluation and improvement. Again this is similar to the Open University.

## REFERENCES

*Getting to Yes*, Roger Fisher and William Ury, Bruce Patton, ed., Penguin Books, New York, NY, 1983.

Production Systems for Computer-Based Learning, Alfred Bork, *Instructional Software: Principles and Perspectives for Design and Use*, D. F. Walker and R. D. Hess, eds., Wadsworth Publishing Company, Belmont, California, 1984.

Production of Technology-based Learning Material Tools vs. Authoring Systems, Alfred Bork, *Instruction Delivery Systems*, Vol. 3, No. 2, March/April Belmont, California, 1984.

Pedagogical Development of Computer-Based Learning Material, Alfred Bork, *Designing Computer-Based Learning Materials*, NATO ASI Series, Series F: Computer and Systems Sciences, Vol. 23, Springer Verlag, Berlin, Germany, 1986.

How to Develop Quality Courseware: Results of a Survey, Urs Karrer, *Journal of Educational Technology Systems*, Vol 16(4), 1987-88.

*Software Engineering Techniques for CAL*, Bertrand Ibrahim, *Education & Computing*, Vol. 5, pp. 215-222, 1989.

Courseware CAD, Bertrand Ibrahim et al., *WCCE/90, Conference Proceedings*, North-Holland, 1990.

Practical Techniques Useful in Authoring Technology-Based Learning Material, Alfred Bork, Nancy Pomicter, *Journal of Computer-Based Instruction*, Vol. 17, 53-69, Spring 1990.

Interpretation des Intentions des Concepteurs de didacticiels, Alain Aubord et al., *13emes Journees Francophones sur l'Informatique*, pp. 181-195, Geneva, January 9-10, 1991.

Education and Society / R. Aiken (Editor)
Information Processing 92, Volume II
Elsevier Science Publishers B.V. (North-Holland)


# A COMPLETE COMPUTERIZED INSTRUCTIONAL SYSTEM AND ITS AUTHORING FACILITY

Luis Osin
Centre for Educational Technology
Ramat Aviv, Israel

## ABSTRACT

A **complete** computerized instructional system is much more than just a collection of isolated personal computers. A system composed of an instructional facility, an administration facility, an instructional library and an authoring facility is described. Within such a system students may work in **monitored** mode, where an internal student model is updated according to the student performance, or in **free** mode, where the system resources are freely available to the student. The efficient development of courseware for such an instructional system required the design and implementation of a state-of-the-art authoring facility, whose conception and major features are described. This complete instructional system is implemented with off-the-shelf components, within the IBM-Microsoft families.

## A COMPLETE COMPUTERIZED INSTRUCTIONAL SYSTEM

The adjective "complete" is used here to denote that the instructional system we have in mind includes much more than a set of unrelated personal computers which serve as a delivery system. Quoting from Venezky and Osin (1991): "the complete instructional system presented in figure 1, includes four main subsystems:

The **Instructional Facility** epitomizes the whole purpose of the system - the provision of instruction, the on-line facilitation of student learning. In practical terms, the core of the instructional facility consists of those programs that interact with the student at her terminal.

The **Administration Facility** is the repository of student, course, and statistical records that are necessary for the delivery of instruction and for the evaluation and improvement of instructional materials.

The **Library** includes all the computerized instructional materials in any possible form, including courseware, tools, games, simulations, and other instructional programs that will be presented to the student or used by him.

The **Authoring Facility** serves primarily to create, update, and improve the library."

Classical implementations of complete instructional systems, like the PLATO system, had a powerful central computer, serving a large number of special purpose instructional terminals (Bitzer & Skaperdas, 1970). Unfortunately, very few schools could afford a PLATO system. What schools could indeed buy, when they appeared in the market, were isolated personal computers, but very rarely were they integrated in a system like the one we described.

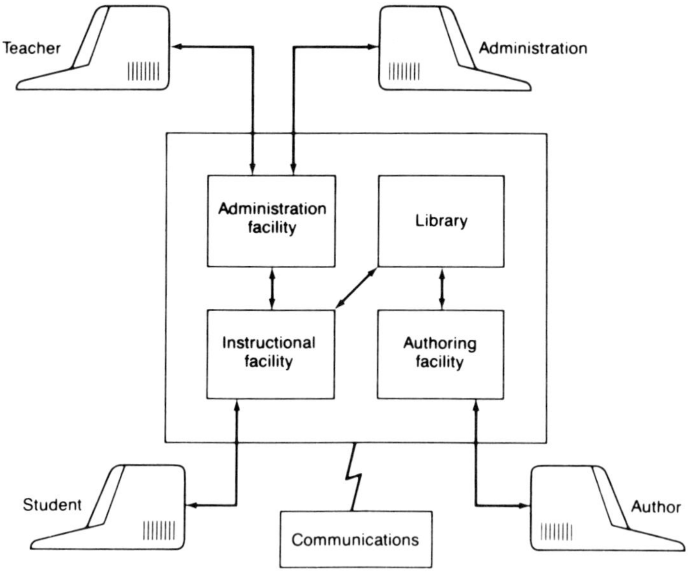


Figure 1. A Complete CAI System

Today, it is possible to implement a complete instructional system with off-the-shelf components, using personal computers as student stations, and linking them via a reliable network to a reasonably powerful computer, which acts as the net server. The server controls a large disk, containing the library and the administration files, and transfers the instructional programs to each personal computer, according to each learner's requests or requirements.

The advantages of such a system, from a school standpoint, are obvious: gone is the tedious and time consuming process of dealing with diskettes, and the teacher can receive a full report of all the activities performed by her class' students, evaluated or graded when possible. The same applies for group training in large organizations.

Let us analyze now how the instructional dialog takes place, by zooming into the instructional facility and its links with the other modules (see figure 2).

A session starts with the student's identification, which results in her instructional profile being downloaded from her student record stored in the Administration Facility, into the on-line student model, which will be the actual partner in the instructional dialog conducted with the pedagogical model stored in the system. The (real) student may switch between two modes of interaction: **monitored** or **free**. In free mode, the student makes use of the system resources (lower loop), and the pedagogical model is not active. In monitored mode, each student activity results in an updating of the student model, which is analyzed by the pedagogical model in order to provide support and guidance (upper loop). At the end of each session, the updated student model is stored in the corresponding file record, while usage statistics related to the instructional programs that were activated are stored for future evaluation, whose objective is courseware improvement.

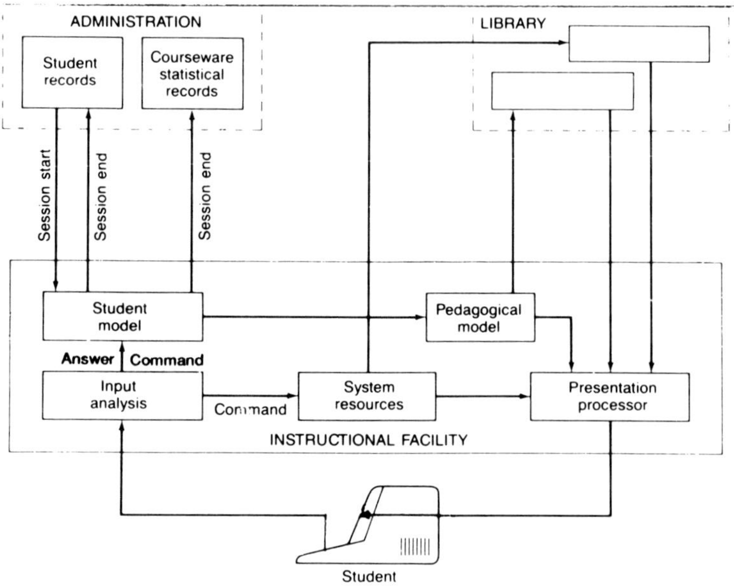


Figure 2. The Instructional Facility

## THE REQUIREMENTS OF AN AUTHORING SYSTEM

Monitored instructional programs are usually built as a set of interaction units, "visited" by the student in an order which is dependent on the student's performance in the program. The number of instructional units may be very large, in the order of thousands, when the program covers a complete curriculum, or relatively small, in the order of units or tens, when dealing with a lesson that covers a specific topic.

Both in the first case ("courseware") or in the second ("lessonware"), running an instructional program in a complete facility requires attention to the following functions:

1. Student-computer dialog in each unit
2. Student "navigation" among the interaction units
3. Data collection and file administration
4. Student utilization of system resources

The **authoring languages** which appeared in the 60's provided easy tools to the authors for the definition of textual dialogs, and included **jump** or **goto** commands from unit to unit to define the student path. These languages are obsolete for several reasons. Most prominent:

a. When dealing with courseware which may include hundreds or thousands of interaction units, the embedding of the branching commands within each unit is not only a very hard task of decision making during the development process, but poses an impossible task for an efficient process of upgrading and debugging. The goto's and jump's make sense for lessonware only.
b. Present technology emphasizes graphic presentation, and is more likely to have the student reacting by pointing to an object on the screen than by writing a name.
c. Current windowing techniques were non-existent at that time.
d. Multimedia presentations are just in the beginning stages.

Some five years ago, the Centre for Educational Technology (CET) decided to develop its own authoring system, taking advantage of the state of the art technology. An **authoring system**, as opposed to an **authoring language**, not only provides the author with the tools to take care of the first function (dialog), previously mentioned, but deals also with the three other functions in a form which is transparent to the author.

Since 1977 CET pioneered the introduction of Integrated Instructional Systems into the Israeli educational environment, and is today the largest organization in Israel devoted to the task of improving education through the appropriate use of technology (with 440 systems installed, serving 120,000 pupils on 12,000 terminals). The Centre, with a staff of 270 people, provides schools with hardware, software, courseware and other instructional computer programs, pedagogical training in the integration of those programs within class activities and, of course, maintenance and system upgrading.

The new authoring system was designed based on the experience developed at CET, making use of sound software engineering techniques, and incorporating standards that, hopefully, would be prevalent in the computing environment. From the author's standpoint, the great advantages would be: modularity, ease of development, modifications and debugging, hardware independence (within a given family), and the possibility of concentrating on the educational aspects, while the ancillary aspects are transparent.

## ARCHITECTURE OF A COMPLETE INSTRUCTIONAL SYSTEM

The architecture selected by CET for a school (or training) system consists of a number of personal computers, acting as student (or trainee) stations, and linked by a network to a central computer, the net server, which controls a large magnetic disk, repository of the library and administration files. Having the computational resources distributed at two levels is the logical solution when there are, on the one hand, central functions like library management and administration facility management and, on the other hand, individual functions like maintaining an instructional dialog with each student or transmitting his requests.

Instructional programs are usually downloaded from the library to the student's personal computer which handles the corresponding interaction. If the student is in free mode, the system resources are at her disposal. If the student is in monitored mode then, when the active unit of interaction is finished, the performance parameters are used to update the student model, and the pedagogical model decides which is the next unit to present. In most cases, the interaction is handled entirely at the student station level. In other cases, more demanding in terms of computing resources, the program handling the interaction at the student's personal computer requests services from the central computer. To give just two examples: 1. A student may be reading a story in "The Computerized Reader" (in Hebrew) and finds a concatenated word (a string of letters) whose structure escapes him (there are 100,000,000 valid strings in the Hebrew language). Then he asks for help from the Hebrew Morphological Analyzer, resident in the central computer, which receives the string pointed at by the student, and returns its structure. 2. A student solving an equation at her terminal writes, using a mathematical editor, a (hopefully) equivalent equation. The system sends this equation to the central computer, where a resident symbolic algebra manipulator determines whether the equation written by the student is correct (this instructional program is under development).

In terms of hardware-software, CET decided on the IBM-Microsoft family, hoping that their market dominance would help in determining de-facto standards and an abundance of software and peripherals - thus improving quality and reducing prices. As a result, we are using MS/DOS as operating system at the student stations, Microsoft Windows for the user interface, LAN Manager as network software, OS/2 as operating system at the server, and SQL Server for the relational database management system, where all the information is stored, be it courseware, student or school related. At the time of writing, the student stations are IBM (or compatible) AT 286 PC's or 386 SX's, with VGA graphic cards, and the server has an Intel 386 or 486 processor, with 400 MB of hard disk memory.

It is worth mentioning that the use of Windows reduces the dependency on graphic cards, and that the use of SQL allows for ease of transportability among different systems.

## THE DESIGN OF THE AUTHORING SYSTEM

The great advantage of designing one's own authoring system is that it is possible to tailor it to the exact needs of the organization that is going to use it. The great disadvantage is the high cost of developing such an authoring system. In 1986, CET looked at the commercially available authoring systems and couldn't find any one answering all of its requirements. The decision was taken to develop such a system in-house, based on the assumption that the high volume of courseware development at CET justified the investment.

What characterizes CET's authoring system?

1. The separation between the design of the interaction units for a certain courseware, and the writing of the program that controls student navigation among these units. This program is called a **strategy**. Having the strategy separated from the specific interaction units has major advantages:

a. Each interaction unit may be developed, tested and debugged independently. The possibilities of making mistakes in a program, and the difficulty of finding and correcting those mistakes, grow (if not exponentially, then probably quadratically) with program size. Working in relatively small units of interaction increases the reliability of the units and reduces drastically the debugging cost.

b. The same strategy may be used for different pieces of courseware, thus reducing development costs. For instance, strategies for tutorial mixed-initiative interaction, for testing and practice, and for test-and-question banks, are available to every author. If none of the available strategies matches the author requirements, then a new strategy is written, and added to the collection of available strategies.

c. The same units may be used under different strategies. For instance, the exercises prepared for a testing and practice courseware may be used, without any change, in a test-and- question bank. Thus, an author that prepares testing and practice courseware gets for free a test-and-question bank. By the same token, explanation or definition units that are developed for a tutorial course, may be used as entries for an information-retrieval system.

d. The author is free from the burden of having to consider all the branching possibilities for each interaction unit.

2. Within each interaction unit, there is a further separation between the logic of the interaction and the items or objects of the interaction. The logic of the interaction is defined in a **script**, written in an authoring language called **PAL** (the acronym of: Professional Authoring Language). The script refers to every **item** (text, graphics, animation sequence, audio segment, etc.) by name. Items are generated, independently of each script, by using the appropriate editors. The advantages of this approach are:

a. The same script may be utilized with different items, thus providing interactions that may be totally different from the student's standpoint, without any additional cost in script-writing.

b. The same items may be used in different scripts, with great savings in graphics, animation or audio development costs.

3. As a result of 1. and 2., it is possible to work with specialists, and develop the materials for a large number of interaction units of the same or different courses in parallel. Subject matter experts work with instructional designers in the definition or selection of a given strategy, and then design the units whose execution will be assigned to graphic artists and programmers. Nothing excludes the possibility of one person being able to fulfill all the tasks at the desirable level of competency, but for the moment we have not found such a case at CET.

4. The authoring system is written as a set of Microsoft Windows applications, and its capabilities increase with the evolution of its host. As more and more tools are written for Microsoft Windows, those of interest are incorporated into the system.

5. PAL is a full fledged authoring language, including the usual statements of a general purpose programming language, with the addition of commands and features which are specially tailored for instructional dialogs. PAL is fully described in its reference manual (CET, 1991), but this manual contains 340 pages, so that we will present, in the next and final section, its highlights only.

## PAL: PROFESSIONAL AUTHORING LANGUAGE

A block diagram, showing the structure and the execution process of courseware written in PAL, is presented in figure 3. The strategy selects an interaction unit, among those available in the library, based on the student's performance (including long-term student history and performance in the course being presented). The student "dialog" with the selected interaction results in the updating of the student record, on the basis of which a new interaction unit is selected, and so on and so forth, until the course is finished.

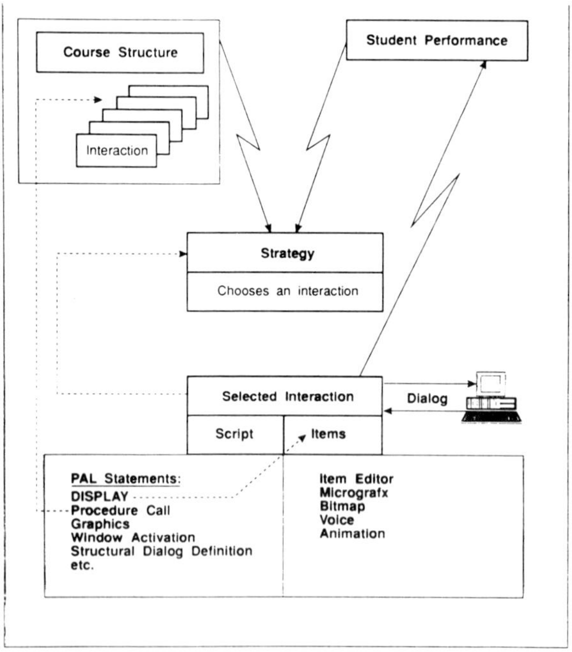


Figure 3 : PAL's courseware structure and execution

PAL offers authors the opportunity to integrate two levels of student-computer dialog: a sequential logic in the foreground, with presentation of information and expected student answers, in parallel with an event-driven logic in the background, where the student may branch out of the sequential dialog and make use of the computer resources placed at his disposal. Every author may, according to personal style, emphasize foreground or background activities.

The sequential logic is organized in terms of a collection of pre-programmed patterns, with a set of default options for the interaction, where the author's task is to define the items to be presented to the student. The author may change the default options according to her needs or taste, and may define new patterns, using PAL's programming capabilities. New patterns may be structured as procedures, to be called when needed.

The event-driven logic is interrupt-based, and it is activated according to student requests (e.g., a dictionary search), or to constraints determined within the sequential logic (e.g. a time limit for an exercise). Besides the system-defined events, the author may define an event block by establishing which is the **event** (i.e., an action, condition or situation), and the **event-body** (i.e., the sequence of statements to be executed when an event occurs).

The disjunction between the sequential and the event-driven logic allow for a very clean design, and the author may concentrate, in each stage, on the aspects relevant to the level being considered.

As a final consideration, Microsoft Windows standards and style have been adhered to in the development of the authoring system. The entry to the system is through the **interaction builder**, which presents a menu with the following options:

**Edit Script** enters the Microsoft WRITE editor.
**View** loads a script from the course database and presents it on the screen.
**Rename** renames a script.
**Remove** removes a script, and the items that belong to it only, from the course database.
**Compile** activates the PAL compiler.
**Edit Item** enters the item editor used to create/edit items.
**Run** activates the PAL interpreter to run a script.
**Misc** accesses miscellaneous options for handling the course database.

If possible, the lecture will be accompanied by a live demonstration of the authoring system here described.

REFERENCES

Bitzer, D. and Skaperdas, D. (1970) **The Economics of a Large-scale Computer-Based Education System: PLATO IV** . In: Holtzman, W.H. (Ed.) **Computer-Assisted Instruction, Testing and Guidance.** New York: Harper and Row.

CET (1991) **PAL Reference Manual.** Tel Aviv: Centre for Educational Technology.

Venezky, R.L. and Osin, L. (1991) **The Intelligent Design of Computer-Assisted Instruction.** New York: Longman.

# STREAM 5: THE VULNERABILITY OF THE INFORMATION SOCIETY: SOCIAL, LEGAL, AND SECURITY ASPECTS

## Klaus Brunnstein Chair

Klaus Brunnstein, *Chair*
University of Hamburg
Germany

William J. Caelli
Queensland University of Technology
Brisbane, Australia

Fernando Saez-Vacas
Technical University of Madrid
Spain

Robert R. Moeller
Sears, Roebuck & Company
Chicago, IL USA

Jose Pino
University of Santiago de Chile
Santiago de Chile

Education and Society / R. Aiken (Editor)
Information Processing 92, Volume II
Elsevier Science Publishers B.V. (North-Holland)




# Innovation as a Critical Success Factor for the Development of an Information Technology Industry in Chile

Ricardo A. Baeza-Yates[a], David A. Fuller[b] and José A. Pino[a]

[a]Depto. de Ciencias de la Computación, Universidad de Chile, Casilla 2777, Santiago, Chile. E-mail: {rbaeza,jpino}@dcc.uchile.cl. [1]

[b]Depto. Ciencia de la Computación, Pontificia Universidad Católica de Chile, Casilla 306, Santiago 22, Chile. E-mail: dfuller@lascar.puc.cl.

**Abstract**

Chile presents an interesting case of development of information processing and technology. Its open-market policies, good education level and early adoption of computer technology have allowed its exports to become competitive on an international basis. The Chilean software industry is attempting to grow to become an international player. It is argued that several factors must be present to reach this objective and that these elements must have innovation as a common floor. An assessment of the feasibility of these ideas in Chile and other developing countries is made.

Keyword Codes: K.4, K.1, K.5
Keywords: Computers and Society; Computer Industry; Legal Aspects of Computing

## 1 Introduction

Chile, a Latin-America country with a population of 13 million, used to be a one product producer: copper. Its entire economy was based on the international price of this mineral and this implied enormous problems to the stability of the economy.

Chile was the first to implant the open market economy model in the region, and currently enjoys one of the healthiest and most stable economies in Latin America. Its exports have diversified both in products and markets. The country has been successful exporting raw materials with little added value, but in order to sustain and increase its GNP growth in the future, it will have to develop industries with high value added products. In that sense, the development of an IT industry could appear as a good opportunity, since software products are essentially "pure added value". There are other advantages of this industry as well: it is non-polluting, it requires less initial investment than other industries, and it provides relatively high income to entrepreneurs and employees.

Chile has recently demonstrated a capacity for producing and exporting IT products to the international community [1] and has been proposed as the country which could lead the way to other Latin-American nations in developing IT industries [2, 4]. In this paper, we expect to give evidence to show that innovation has been the critical factor that has made the Chilean IT Industry to develop. For that, we describe the main innovative

[1]This work was partly supported by grant No. I-3084-9222 from DTI (Universidad de Chile).

factors introduced in the past by the agents involved in the process: Government, users, producers and universities.

# 2 Background

## 2.1 IT Development

The country has had a relatively long history in terms of developing and introducing IT. It starts in the late 50's with an incipient technology transfer process done in a few universities, on areas such as analog and digital systems. In the second part of the 60's, some universities and industries bought third generation computers. They rented time slots to companies to process a few administrative applications. At that time, companies producing "tailor-made" software appeared. By the end of the 70's, many companies had automatized their administrative processes. Also, people incrementally were exposed to the benefits of the IT. Moreover, most public services were being computerized.

In the 80's, the Chilean IT industry grew steadily. Since the demand on IT systems increased, and since qualified people in information technologies already existed in Chile, this decade is characterized by the appearance of many specialized IT companies, some of them offering locally-produced quality products. Large contracts for customized software also appeared during this time, as a consequence of the technological transformation of the national industry.

Nowadays, Government is a large consumer of IT products. During the last ten years, the country has had to reduce the size of the Government machinery to one third of its original one. This could not have been done without the introduction of IT systems.

Also during this decade, the software industry started to export locally produced IT systems. Software companies have grown from 40 in 1980 to 256 in 1991 [1]. The software industry is organized through the Chilean Software Association (ACS) since 1985. Exports have risen from US$ 1.4 million in 1989 to an estimated US$ 10 million in 1991.

## 2.2 Education

We consider education as one of the most critical factors of success in the development of an IT industry. In this area, Chile has been investing to create opportunities of education at all levels: it enjoys a well established tradition in education, supported by good international school teaching standards and some of the best universities in the region. Thus, Chile has one of the highest literacy rates in Latin-America, and Chilean universities have become a pole of attraction to students who want to do graduate studies in the region.

Education in IT is provided at various levels and places, being heavily demanded. The professional level is taught at universities, with a duration of 5 years or more. There are currently traditional and private universities in Chile. The former have a long tradition in education and research. The latter correspond to universities with less than 10 years of life, managed as a business. The strongest Engineering Faculties belong to the traditional Universidad de Chile and Pontificia Universidad Catolica de Chile. Both have been investing in sending their academic staff to do graduate studies abroad during the last decade. In general almost all universities in Chile are currently teaching Engineering degrees in computer science and other IT related subjects.

Graduate courses in IT are taught by a few universities, conferring Master's degrees with a typical duration of 2 years. Also, continuing education and short courses are offered by universities and private centers.

### 2.3 Research

Research in information technologies is being done at a few traditional universities, encouraged by research grants such as Science and Technology Fund (FONDECYT), Andes Foundation, and a few international sponsors. The results: internationally competitive research in areas such as algorithm design and complexity, software engineering, expert systems, performance evaluation, information systems, text retrieval, optimization and automatic control.

In 1984, the academic community founded the Chilean Computer Science Society (SCCC), whose main achievement has been an annual international conference [3]. Another scientific conference, the Latin-American Conference on Informatics was started in Chile in 1974, and was held there until 1979. From 1980 onwards, the conference has been organized by most of the Southamerican countries. Also, Chile was one of the first countries in the region to introduce the Unix operating system in 1984 and to be connected to international academic computer networks in 1986. A national academic network covers several universities throughout the country.

## 3 Current Status

### 3.1 Level of IT utilization of the country

Users are informed of the power of IT systems, and hence, they play an active role demanding such systems. In fact, there are many organizations which have developed or bought complex systems. For example, banks have heavily invested during the last five years in developing IT systems. They have their branches on-line throughout the country, they are connected on-line to banks abroad providing services such as SWIFT operations, automated cash dispensers along the country, and some offer the possibility of using a microcomputer at home to connect to the bank's computer. The stock market and the electronic stock market in Santiago also provide users connectability to their computers.

In the productive sector, mining industry is the largest IT consumer. They use from small systems with spreadsheets and word processors, to large management information systems, expert systems, collaborative systems, planning systems, etc.

Almost all Ministries have some kind of IT systems available to their use, providing speed ups and cost reductions in the decision making process. Most of these systems will be connected through an inter-ministry network, which will enable the Ministries to obtain the required information faster and cheaper. Another example is the quality of telecommunications: it is possible to rent satellite data links to anywhere in the world, there are fibber optic link services in Santiago, cellular telephones, etc.

### 3.2 Government

Since 1990 Chile has been in democracy allowing Chilean organizations to open to the world and benefit from an enriched relationship with foreign governments, companies and universities.

During 1991, the Science and Technology Council (CONICYT) opened special funds, FONDEF and FONTEC, oriented to large applied research projects with transfer of technology. IT was one of the priority sectors considered in this initiative. Also in 1991, the Ministry of Economics created an intersector committee for the software industry

(CIDS), with the participation of the IT industry through the ACS, the universities, and the SCCC. This committee will discuss and coordinate actions to expand the software industry.

Software exporters can benefit from loans and a few tax breaks open to any exporting company, but Government has not yet shown a special treatment to IT exporters, with policies and incentives specifically applied to this industry to motivate investment in this area.

## 3.3 IT Industry

The Chilean Software Association (ACS) has effectively promoted the IT industry through several pioneering efforts. First, with the help of ProChile, a Government organization to promote exports, five local software companies were present in 1990 at Cebit, the largest software trade show in the world. This participation was repeated in 1991 and 1992, when also Mexico (1991), Brazil (1992), and Uruguay (1992) were sharing representation from Latin-America. Second, the ACS organized in 1990 and 1991 the Iberoamerican Meeting of Software Exporters with the participation of several Latin-American countries and Spain [3, 4].

Annually, Chile hosts a trade show on IT, called SOFTEL, which has become one of the most important event of its kind in the region [3]. Finally, Fundación Chile, a private organization with experience in boosting exports in other areas, has started an IT group whose main goal is the transfer of state-of-the-art technology to industry.

An interesting issue which is being noticed recently, is that local IT companies are exploring horizontal markets in Chile and the U.S. such as microcomputer anti-virus, text retrieval systems, fourth generation software, etc. Products for these markets usually need higher initial investment, with longer return periods, and larger risks than products for vertical markets. This seems to be a sign of maturity and credibility of the current IT local industry.

## 3.4 Education

Despite the growth of demand for education in IT related matters already mentioned in section 2.3, the universities and other educational institutions have structured a reasonable scheme of degrees and professional titles offered throughout the country. Thus, a reduced number of standardized degrees and titles offer employers a clear guideline on the type of graduates they hire. It is also advantageous to high school students who can easily know in advance the effort required to graduate and the professional market they intend to enter. Specifically, all "licensed" degrees are conferred by universities after 8 semesters of regular study, and "engineering" professional titles are awarded by Engineering Faculties after 3 or 4 further semesters of regular study. This degree standardization is unusual in many countries of the Region.

## 3.5 Research

One of our working hypothesis is that research in IT is an important factor for success in developing an IT industry. The first three columns of Table 1 show the number of papers in IT related subjects published in international journals by authors from Latin-America, extracted from [5].

Table 1: Number of papers in IT subjects from Latin-America.

| Country | Year 1988 | 1989 | 1990 | papers/Inh (89) ($\times 10^{-6}$) | papers/GNP (88) ($\times 10^{-9}$ US$) |
|---|---|---|---|---|---|
| Argentina | 94 | 100 | 89 | 3.04 | 1.33 |
| Brazil | 244 | 257 | 285 | 1.74 | 0.75 |
| Chile | 71 | 63 | 69 | 4.85 | 3.22 |
| Colombia | 1 | 7 | 3 | 0.22 | 0.03 |
| Costa Rica | 6 | 3 | 2 | 1.00 | 1.28 |
| Cuba | 5 | 18 | 4 | 1.71 | 0.19 |
| Guatemala | 2 | 3 | 0 | 0.34 | 0.25 |
| Mexico | 130 | 134 | 111 | 1.58 | 0.74 |
| Panama | 1 | 2 | 0 | 0.83 | 0.18 |
| Uruguay | 3 | 3 | 3 | 0.97 | 0.45 |
| Venezuela | 33 | 50 | 48 | 2.60 | 0.52 |
| Other countries | 0 | 2 | 1 | 0.00 | 0.00 |
| TOTAL | 590 | 642 | 615 | 1.59 | 0.75 |

The last two columns of Table 1 show for each Latin-American country, the number of papers per million of inhabitants during 1989, and the number of papers per billion of US$ of GNP during 1988. We consider that these values show the state of maturity of Chilean IT research. The implication of research being a driving force for the creation of new products and services in the IT industry is clear. However, the Chilean research has not had a close relationship to industry and its theoretical developments may have not being exploited by the software producers (with some exceptions).

Lately, the Chilean academic community has been involved in key positions of the Latin-American CS organization (CLEI) and in the program committees of regional and international conferences. During 1991, the SCCC has become a sister society of ACM and CS/IEEE. At the same time the International Conference of the SCCC has become the top quality conference in the region. Recently, Chile entered to Internet, an advanced international computer network. A national academic network of the same type is also under way.

As examples of active innovative applied research projects, we can mention the introduction to industry of knowledge based systems forcing the technology transfer process; the successful development of complex planning systems in a local university for a European Chemical company; a text retrieval software for Windows based on state-of-the-art technology through the collaboration of a local software house with a local university [4]; a joint initiative between university and industry on developing complex collaborative systems based on state-of-the-art technology; and the a research and development project to build a complex merge of software, hardware and communication systems to link basic schools in southern Chile, a less developed region of the country (funded by the Ministry of Education and the World Bank).

# 4 A Strategy for the Future

An IT export industry can only grow and become an important player in the Chilean economy if a conjunction of factors is present. These critical factors are analyzed below.

## 4.1 Enhancement of the industry marketing activity

Currently, there are some local IT companies exporting to U.S.A. which are doing their own publishing, that is, they have established offices abroad, done marketing, provided maintenance and training, etc. Obviously, this is too expensive to be done by individual companies. Lower cost alternatives exist and these should be explored. It is necessary to have local publishers with the responsibility of selling locally developed software systems in the world market. These publishers could operate via the following mechanisms: association with foreign distributors, either multinational companies or small local companies; selling the rights of locally produced IT products to established foreign distributors; exchange of distribution rights with foreign producers; etc. Another solution could be a common publisher fostered by the ACS and/or the Government.

In addition, IT exporters should exploit market niches where Chile has comparative advantages. For instance, the Spanish language is spoken by more than 400 million people in the world; any product exploiting particularities of this language could be advantageous in this market. Another example comes from Chile's past experience with high inflation rates: most information systems have automatic indexing features not available in countries with traditionally low inflation rates but having now double-digit figures. Know-how in IT systems for exploitation of natural resources (mining, forestry) could be applied as well.

Consultancy services can also be exported and they should be promoted by professional societies. Especially interesting markets are the other Latin-American countries which are following a similar open-market policy [2] . An important asset to Chilean consultants compared to out-of-region competitors is the knowledge of the local procedures, traditions and a common language.

## 4.2 Government involvement

Government should support the IT industry with special policies to finance research in IT to create a mature scientific and technological ability in the country, passing tighter copyright laws, supporting the creation of new IT enterprises, creating export channels for locally produced products, supporting graduate and undergraduate students in IT, supporting IT events, etc.

We would like to see the Government as a more active agent to develop this new IT market than its current record. Otherwise, Chile runs the risk of not being able to grow at the necessary rate, and therefore, never be able to have a successful IT industry. We think that IT products cannot be treated as yet another product to be developed in the country. The reasons are: first, an IT product requires "brain ware", a scarce human resource which has to be cultivated locally. Second, software can trivially be reproduced by users, and hence, it needs special legal protection. Third, it is quite easy to smuggle software to or from the country (some companies might be paying custom taxes for the used and produced products, and some others might not). Finally, this product requires special maintenance and continuous updates.

A possible action the Government may take is to provide financial partnerships to selected high-technology projects. Other actions involve tax exemptions to specific goals. For instance, it could offer tax incentives to companies wishing to establish themselves in geographical areas with high unemployment or which the Government wants to foster economic development. Another objective could be the attraction of foreign capital. Off-shore programming in Chile could be an activity that the Government could emphasize through tax incentives and promotion abroad through ProChile.

## 4.3 User issues

IT users, including companies which develop software for their particular needs, should also take initiatives to make the best use of the broad offer of the IT market.

A first aspect is to change the way that IT products are traditionally purchased by many companies. The purchasing process should start by choosing application software first and then worry about basic software and hardware platforms.

A second aspect related to the above, is the certification of the software quality. Certification helps the user by simplifying the purchasing decision. On the other hand, it improves and standardizes the quality of IT products, as well as the distribution channels. Certification should be done by an independent organization with the participation of IT industry, Government and users. Some initiatives have been proposed, but they have not yet been implemented.

## 4.4 Education

In this area, we think that a closer relationship between universities and producers has to be developed. For example, better acceptance for continuing education and advanced seminars is needed from the producers. Currently, it is very difficult to keep people at IT companies aware of state of the art technology. One way of improving this is by implementing residence periods for graduate students at producers' premises, as well as having people from IT companies coming to spend some time at university laboratories.

There is also a need to update the CS curriculum at the universities. It is necessary to include important aspects such as ethics, graphic design, notions of marketing, documentation writing, etc.

Finally, a voluntary accreditation procedure for the different education statements is needed. This mechanism would certify the level and quality of the IT programs, as well as enforcing a uniform quality for the degrees and titles granted by the various institutions.

## 4.5 Research

Since Chile is not known in the international community as a technology producer, university IT departments will need to be extremely active to show that the country has a scientific and technological capability. We estimate that by 1994, there will be approximately 70 academic staff with PhDs in IT related fields in the country.

This is not enough if they have to train undergraduate and graduate students in the latest IT developments, do state of the art research and do technology transfer and applied research. It is clear that the strongest CS departments should help the CS departments of other universities. There is a main action which must be taken: to launch a *Computer Science Development Program* (CSDP), which should define the way of making the CS departments of the two main traditional universities to grow and collaborate among themselves and industry. This plan should be financed by industry and Government. It is necessary to increase the academic staff members of both Departments, hiring interested people with PhDs abroad. Also, additional computer equipment, and a PhD program in CS is needed.

Also, there should be a *Development Program* for computer science departments of other universities. This starts by sending their academic staff to get PhD studies to the CSDP. This will be considerably less expensive than sending them abroad. Also, staff from other universities with acceptable research levels should have the opportunity to spend time as guest members, collaborating with people of the CSDP and industry.

Finally, universities should encourage the participation of industry in their research and development. Effective communication channels between industry and universities must be established to this end.

# 5 Conclusions

Chile has achieved success in an initial stage of using IT technology to make its exports competitive in the international market. It has also established a good small software industry. However, to succeed in developing its software industry to become a player of some international weight, Chilean society must agree on certain tasks to be coordinatedly undertaken by members of Government, industry and universities. This concerted effort should be sustained in time, independently of economic cycles, political parties in Government, etc. This effort must also take an innovative approach in the various tasks involved.

This open-market policy, which encourages international competitiveness, fits well and is consistent with the general economic policies of the country. Therefore, other developing countries without a similar foundation and perhaps without the other factors described in the paper - such as education level, IT use and research level - may have serious problems to follow the same approach. Nevertheless, some of the ideas presented in this paper may be applicable to other developing countries.

# References

[1] D. A. Fuller and J. A. Pino, A Strategy for the Successful Development of an Information Technology Industry in Chile, International Conference on Social Implications of Computers in Developing Countries, Nairobi, Kenya (IFIP WG 9.4), March 1992.

[2] S. E. Goodman, Computing in a Less-Developed Country, Communications of the ACM, Vol. 34, No. 12, pp.25-29, December 1991.

[3] L. Press, Personal Computing and the World Software Market, Communications of the ACM, Vol. 34, No. 2, pp.23-28, February 1991.

[4] L. Press, Computing in Chile: Leading the Way for Other South American LDCs?, Communications of the ACM, Vol. 34, No. 12, pp.27, December 1991.

[5] CompuMath Citation Index, Institute for Scientific Information, 3501 Market St., Philadelphia, PA 19104, ISSN 0730-6199.

Education and Society / R. Aiken (Editor)
Information Processing 92, Volume II
Elsevier Science Publishers B.V. (North-Holland)




# Informatics and Democracy

**Enrique Calderon A.** [a], **Elvia Martinez V.**[a] **and Daniel Cazes.** [b]

[a]**Fundacion Arturo Rosenblueth, Mexico**

[b]**National University of Mexico,Mexico**

### Abstract

Personal computers, telephone computer networks and communications technology are now important tools for democratic efforts in many countries. The document describes a project in progress in Mexico, with the participation of civil organizations, including political parties and a research institution. Some of the most important results, related to the last two federal elections, are reported, while a new nationwide effort is proposed for 1994.

Keyword Codes: K.4; K.4.2; K.8
Keywords: Computers and society; Social Issues; Personal Computing.

## 1. The Democratic Vocation of Informatics.

Having a principle associated to the production of the most dreadful weapons, including the nuclear kind, the computer began to be employed by civilians a few years later. During the sixties and seventies government institutions and big financial organizations, began to build successfully great information systems on their employees, their users, clients and creditors, improving in this way their capacity and the quality of their services, as well as incrementing the dimensions of their activities and businesses.

From another point of view, the computers were in hands of the powerful, providing them with information and power over the common citizens, whose financial, commercial and professional history was better known by the great corporations than by their owners. With this vision, widely known and propagated a bit more of a decade ago, the era of automatization necessarily came with the establishment of future regional dictatorships.

With the introduction to the market of personal computers, which come in a more powerful version each day, along with the evolution of telephone networks that allowed long distance communications for those computers, the previous vision began to disappear and started to be replaced by another one, in which common citizens, specially the youngest, were provided with an individual capacity to process information and to have it available, which before was only at the reach of corporations.

Personal computers made possible for professionals, students and small organizations to compete with equal conditions, against larger enterprises, a phenomenon that has induced a healthy proliferation of new and strong organizations in the most diverse fields of activities.

At the same time, the efficient production systems that generate thousands of identical copies of all kinds of things, are leaving the way to new forms of manufacturing, more evolved and capable of generating products and services tailored to the preferences, needs and possibilities of each person, in this way strengthening the presence of the individual. With this, populations, citizens, men and women have stopped being simple statistical figures to be considered as what they are: Persons!

Of course that this conception is today only valid in developed countries. In fact, through it, it is possible to evaluate, or could be evaluated, the level of development of each nation. How much each man, each woman, each citizen has his/her individual rights insured, how well he/she knows them, how much they can be claimed and be heard by the community, how much capacity he/she possesses to express his/her ideas and to be informed of what is happening around him/her, in his/her city and country. Only this can measure today the level of development and the will for progress of nations and their governments.

It is easy to observe that our development scheme turns out to be closely linked to the one of democracy, for which the technological tools of computation and telecommunications have turned out to have a greater value, as represented by the recent happenings in East Europe, where the population has been informed of real events, almost at the same time when they take place.

## 2. The Case of Mexico.

For the analysis and discussion of our project, it is necessary to describe the case of Mexico as it is today, its peculiarities and political contradictions. This is a nation with abundant natural resources, where today live a bit more of 80 million people, in a great diversity of environments differentiated by the climate and the cultural history. Mexico City highlights among these, one of the largest cities in the world, where more than a fifth of the national population is concentrated.

The wealth is presently in hands of about five hundred families, who have the control of the finances, industry, mass media and communications. Also, they are closely related to the group that has governed the country during the past decades.

Until a few years ago, the political control of the group in power was accomplished through corporative mechanisms that controlled the peasants and city workers, administrating prizes and punishments in a brutal and severe way. Above this fascist outlined system, was the governing group, headed by the President of the country, granting everyone an image of remarkable stability and democracy, while the opposition languished as a victim of inanition.

During the eighties, the economic crisis of Latin America was translated into great upset, as the contrast between the wealth of a few and the pauperism of the rest became obvious and the deterioration of education and public services was evident. As a political result, the opposition emerged with intensity and began to give trouble to the government. In some local elections for state governor, the Partido de Accion Nacional (National Action Party, moderate right) made electoral fraud accusations.

The process came to its climax with the presidential elections of 1988, when two opposition candidates contended with an unusual strength against the official candidate, who won the elections facing the general suspicion of a major fraud and without having the foundations to prove the opposite. A significative element were the computers, which remained silent for over a week, creating a total information emptiness and the conviction that the results were "being fixed". This conviction prevails to this day within wide sectors of the population. An important fact was the victory of the center left candidate Cuauhtemoc Cardenas in most of the cities in the country, including Mexico City, while voters for the official candidate were from rural areas with low resources and the most forgotten by the governing group, but also the most vulnerable to have electoral irregularities.

Facing the seriousness of these facts and some other which have been happening later on, in spite of the image improvement by the new government by means of populist measures (solidarity program), and the reactivation of the economy by selling state companies, several groups demand and work actively for the establishment of democracy, which has been called "a democracy without adjectives."

The present paper describes one of these efforts employing a computer network connected (until now) through telephone lines in Mexico City. The project of the Arturo Rosenblueth Foundation is in coordination with the Council for Democracy, and has the support of the two main opposition parties, the Partido de Accion Nacional (National Action Party) and the Partido de la Revolucion Democratica (Democratic Revolution Party).

## 3.The Fast Counting Project for the Federal District.

Having ahead the elections to renew Congress in August of 1991, the Arturo Rosenblueth Foundation and the Council for Democracy, started the organization of a citizen network, that would allow to know the election results for the Federal District (where an important section of Mexico City is located), a few hours after the process to elect the Federal Congress ended, in which one senator and 40 representatives were to be chosen.

The use of conventional sampling techniques allowed us to determine that the 40 samples required the observation and the gathering of the results of 2300 voting booths out of a total of 9780, establishing a network with three layers, by means of which the information could flow promptly.

The first layer was made up by 2300 informants that were to observe results at voting booths. The information was transmitted by phone to a node that had been assigned to each of them, which in turn was part of a set of 180 telephone centers, operated voluntarily by 300 people, who registered and concentrated the information by hand. Then it was transmitted, by means of telephone, to 20 computer centers distributed among the city and connected to a server with a 386 processor.

The operators of this equipment, the same as the ones at the telephone centers, were voluntary, from among the civil population, most of them students, professionals and housewives. To insure the success of the project, some load calculations and simulation processes were carried out, some redundance elements were also added. With this machinery, it was possible to have the information of 37 of the 40 districts, 11 hours after the voting sites were closed and seven days before the official results were known; the differences were less to one percent in most of the districts.

Nevertheless, the results were not propagated by the press with the relevance they deserved. Among political circles tis was considered a success, in spite of the fact that the results were not the expected or desired ones, as the official party won all of the districts.

For us, this meant an important experiment, with two things to conclude. First, that a similar counting at a national level for the '94 presidential elections is totally feasible, by means of making up a citizen network.

Secondly, it was clear that the mere counting of the votes at the end of the elections brought up some other diverse substantial aspects, that the governing group could use to modify the electoral processes to its convenience, before these even took place; as a result the citizen network would be alert to inform other things too.

### 3.1 The geography of the elections.

At the end of the 1988 presidential elections, Mexican society faced an emptiness of official information that lasted about ten days, and the only explanation for it was that "there had been a collapse in the computer system." When the government finally released the official results, a suspicion aroused that these had been altered to favor the government's candidate, who resisted to face the election returns. A political crisis of a great proportion was genreated.

With the purpose of analyzing the official information with the greatest impartiality possible, this was used to build a geographical data base, where information of the 1980 population and housing counting was added to the results of each electoral district, projected to 1988.

The most important results of the analysis performed during the following weeks allowed to generate a document, which was published later by one of the most important newspapers in the country. The most relevant facts were the following:

1 The vote of the urban population, from the areas having more substructure, the best earnings and more capability for surveyance, favored the opposition candidate of the moderate left (Cuauhtemoc Cardenas).

2 The vote of the rural areas and indian communities least observed favored the official candidate, in spite of the fact that in many of these areas the preference for Cardenas was open and widely known.

3 In the north region of the country most of the votes also favored the official candidate, in spite of the strength the candidate of the center right had.

4 The districts where the official candidate had greater percentages favoring him, the ballots turned out to be excessive, in spite of the low cultural level of the population.

Although the research paper left for the reader to draw his own conclusions, the figures proved clearly that the results were altered. It was impossible to estimate the dimension of the alteration. Therefore, the best of cases was to strengthen the uncertainty of who had really won.

Moreover, the research studies that were performed, offered from then on, the possibility to locate the points where the surveyance should be centered for the 1994 elections, with the aim of guarantying the respect for the citizen's vote.

**3.2 The national citizen network.**

Considering the experiences mentioned above, the Rosenblueth Foundation works in the development of a project to integrate a citizen information network, capable of contributing significantly to the advancement of democracy in Mexico.

With the establishment of this network, it is intended to provide the Mexican society with an instrument that would allow to:

1 Know in an immediate and reliable way the results of the elections, a few hours after election booths are closed, in order to conform a public opinion to make difficult the traditional alteration of the results.
2 To know in a faithful way the development of political campaigns and the cost of the political acts that take place all over the national territory (detecting and making difficult the illegal use of public resources, that are frequently used to favor official candidates).
3 To keep a permanent nationwide record of the space and time the media dedicates to the different political parties (to know and report any obvious preference and illegal support of the media toward official candidates).
4 To keep a record of violent happenings or abnormal actions taking place anywhere in the country, having the elections coming up, and that would indicate the possible preparation of electoral frauds.

The fundamental aspect of the project lies in the possibility of informing the whole society beforehand, providing a global image of what is happening, changing the present situation, where only the parties get to know what is going on, in a casuistical way and several weeks, or even months later.

### 3.3 Conformation of the Network.

Having present the information available and the experience gathered, the citizen network would count on nearly 4,000 located observation points, 60% of them at the major 50 cities of the country (2,400 points distributed in proportion to the number of inhabitants at each urban center). From the remaining 1,600 points, 600 would be placed in towns having 2,000 to 100,000 inhabitants and the last 1,000 in areas typically rural.

At each one of the 32 entities that conform the country would exist a statal coordination generally related to a local university, which would work as a node to concentrate information that would be fed by various gathering centers. These in turn would receive the information coming from the observation points, making up the four level structure shown in the figure.

National coordination (1)
Statal coordinations (32)
Gathering centers (300 approximately)
Observation points (4,000)

The conformation of the network, including the distribution and location of the gathering centers would be done taking into account the social-political information available and some logistic considerations.

### 3.4 The technological substructure.

The capacity and response speed of the network, which should cover a territory of 2'000,000 squared meters, is obviously one of the elements that will determine the success of the project, this is why it is necessary to have available enough technology in terms of computers and telecommunications.

For the computer aspect, it is intended that the 32 statal coordinations as well as the 300 data gathering centers have available computers provided with a rigid disk, a 286 processor and modems to make up a computer network (WAN), connecting its nodes through telephone, as well as to a local network with a server, installed at the national coordination.

All of the nodes of the computer network should be at urban centers, that would allow them to use the conventional telephone network, which would be useful for the communications at the urban areas and some rural settlements. For the other observation points it has been planned the use of radio transmitters with a range of 50 to 100 km. These would be received by receptors at determined gathering centers.

Additionally, cellular telephone units will be employed at some areas of the country that have this service available, as well as additional radio, telephone and computer equipment in order to obtain reasonable redundance levels.

The estimated amount for this technological substructure is one million dollars. Its financing would come from the civil population, complemented by international funds.

### 3.5 Security and Viability Aspects.

Although all of what is intended lies within the Mexican law, the development of the project implies risks that should be taken into account, considering the political interests it could affect, and the environments of political violence that still prevail in some regions of the country.

To confront this risk, the alternative to keep the project secret must be discarded, not only because of the high costs that an operation of this kind would represent, also because it would be opposite to the same philosophy of the citizen network, which should operate at everyone's sight. The other alternative, consists on the diffusion of its existence and having its objectives clear and transparent, not only to confront the Mexican society, but also to confront the international community as well, being this the only way to guarantee its existence. That is why its presentation at this International Congress becomes extrememly relevant for us. In this way, its preparation does not obey academic reasons, rather it responds to a practical need.

The development of the project publicly does not stops the use of security mechanisms to validate and filter the information received; in fact, the project includes the use of access and identification keys throughout the network, in order to guarantee the integrity of the information.

## 4. Conclusion

For all of us who work in the project, its development implies a trascendental gaol, not just because its technical, logistics and strategy achievments, but also for its real implications in the struggle held by Hispanic American countries to try to acheive broader and more just development states.

Education and Society / R. Aiken (Editor)
Information Processing 92, Volume II
Elsevier Science Publishers B.V. (North-Holland)


# Information Technology Usage and Industry in Developing Countries

Jose A. Pino

Depto. de Ciencias de la Computacion
Universidad de Chile
Casilla 2777, Santiago, Chile
E-mail: jpino@dcc.uchile.cl

Keyword codes: ***K.4, K.1***
Keywords: ***Computers and Society; Computer Industry***

**ABSTRACT**

It is frequently stated that the development of a computer industry - especially the software industry - is desirable and feasible for a developing nation. However, it is less commonly emphasized that the chances of success in this industry are highly correlated to the level of computer usage in the country.

A strong user community is an important asset for a computer industry. It provides a stimulus and initial market for new applications and developments. Even for a decidedly export-oriented industry, this is a necessary ingredient. It also provides nearby test sites and immediate feed-back from first users.

A highly developed user environment demands services and materials which are needed for a computer industry as well. Thus, it is important for a software industry to have available computer networks, new hardware, software tools, etc.

Two other factors are shared by users and industry: personnel and research. High information technology usage is only achieved by the work of well educated technicians, whose training perhaps does not differ much from that required by information technology goods and services production. Research is the basis for innovation, both in usage and industry.

Education and Society / R. Aiken (Editor)
Information Processing 92, Volume II
Elsevier Science Publishers B.V. (North-Holland)



# Informatics and Development

S.C. Bhatnagar

Indian Institute of Management, Ahmedabad-380 015, India

In identifying a role for informatics in development the broad spectrum of activities covered under development would have to be understood. Development can be created by accelerated economic activity through policy measures which will promote growth of industry and agriculture. Development also means creating equitable access to social services such as, health, education, drinking water, communication services and providing direct financial assistance to rural/urban poor. Whereas the role of informatics in the management of an enterprise to increase its productivity and competitiveness is well recognised, its role in improving delivery of social services and monitoring of poverty alleviation programmes is not well documented. In developing countries like China and India, governments have embarked on ambitious programmes of computerisation. China uses nearly 100 computers for monitoring the performance of its family planning programme at various levels. India has installed two micro computers in each of its 440 districts to plan and monitor rural development programmes.

The impact of such computerisation is yet to be assessed formally. Some advantages that have been reported are: more effective utilisation of funds through integrated planning focusing on the special needs of each region; tighter monitoring of programmes by allowing access to detailed data which is otherwise lost in aggregation at different levels. The quality of data is improved because computerisation has created a positive dependence of field level functionaries on computers. Computers reduce record keeping work, and help in planning of their own activities. Use of computers for handling correspondence, maintaining work lists and schedules increases personal productivity and releases time. Most important, a culture of open information has been created because information is now accessible to all the stakeholders.

For promoting successful use of informatics in development governments should play an enabling role by setting policies which result in easy access to computing equipment at reasonable prices. Creation of educational and maintenance infrastructure are also critical. Applications development is best done in a decentralised fashion. The field levels understand their critical area of concern and information needs much better than federal levels. They need technical support to handle unusual problems in application development. Extensive user training is necessary. Diffusion of use of IT can be accelerated through sharing of experiences of successes and failures. Developing countries share common problems and can learn from each others experience but must develop their own approach to use of IT. Hardware and generic software can be imported but application choice must be indigenous. International cooperation is needed for development of low cost communication technologies and more robust hardware.

Education and Society / R. Aiken (Editor)
Information Processing 92, Volume II
Elsevier Science Publishers B.V. (North-Holland)


# Systems development for development — is it possible, how, by whom?

M. Korpela[a]

[a]Computing Centre, University of Kuopio, PL 1627, SF-70211 Kuopio, Finland

**Abstract**

There is a strong general opinion that computer systems in developing countries should contribute in the national development and address the priority needs of the ordinary people. If double standards are to be avoided, the same criteria should be applied to computer systems everywhere. However, systems development in industrialized countries is not explicitly directed by priority needs, rather by payable demand. This contradiction should be addressed by the academia and the professional societies of the North.

Keyword Codes: K.4.2; H.1.0
Keywords: Social Issues; Information Systems Models and Principles, General

When you tell a layman, or a development agency officer for that matter, that you are developing computer systems for a developing country, the next question will be: "But ... are computers really appropriate to those countries? Can your systems benefit the ordinary people, or are they just for the elite?"

The question is paternalistic, but a good one. It just needs to be put in a more general way. There cannot be double standards, one for the rich and one for the poor countries. The real question every computer professional in any country needs to ask herself is: *Does my work address the priority needs of the ordinary people of the world?* Do my systems benefit the underprivileged, or the elite?

The criteria above should not only be used in evaluating computer projects in developing countries, but in the North as well. However, in the North we are told that profitability and market forces should decide — in plain language, the *payable* demand, not the needs; in plainer language still, those who have money and power.

In any country, the next question to ask is, how systems development *could* be directed by priority human needs. Many empirical, action oriented studies, notably in Scandinavia, point out that the key issue is whether the users and the "clients" (or beneficiaries, customers, patients; victims?) of computer systems are empowered to direct the development in cooperation with the computer experts.

But is it possible in real world that users and clients can take the helmet? This crucial issue should be discussed by the computer academia and practitioners.

Education and Society / R. Aiken (Editor)
Information Processing 92, Volume II
Elsevier Science Publishers B.V. (North-Holland)



# African Development Through Information Technology?

**Mayuri Odedra**
PC WORLD Africa, 16 Avon Court, 34 Keswick Road, London, SW15 2JU, United Kingdom

Few doubt the significance of information technology (IT) for economic and social development. IT is widely preached as having the power to narrow the gap between the developed and the developing countries (DCs). Yet, how many DCs, especially those in Africa, have succeeded in exploiting this developmental potential? Very few. There is extensive under-utilisation of equipment and failure of major computer based projects; signs which may indicate why IT has played little role in African development.

Much of the spread of computers that has taken place has not been need-based. Hard-selling from manufacturers and vendors, the urge to keep up with the latest technology, self-interest, and pressure from computer professionals have all contributed to the spread. African's have accepted the technology in a blind-folded manner. No policies or clear strategic buying plans exist which clearly identify the needs that are likely to bring overall benefit to the nation.

Although IT has had different implications on different countries, overall there have been many negative consequences inflicted by this technology. Scarce foreign currency has been spent on equipment which is under-utilised, the dependency on MNCs and expatriate personnel has been increased, and socio-cultural conflicts introduced. Moreover, what Africa has experienced so far is not IT transfer but "transplantation", the dumping of hardware without the necessary knowhow. The acute shortage of computer professionals and lack of computer awareness at the national level have also been a major hindrance. Computers are still largely used for routine data processing with very little decision-making based on computer output. There is still a lack of recognition of the importance of information as a resource. Little computer literacy and awareness exists at the national level which has not only allowed the "foreign forces" to take advantage of the situation but has led to an increase in dependency on the advanced nations.

However, even if they had achieved the benefits of IT, this would not necessarily have led to economic development nor would it have accelerated the process. This is because development is a very complicated and controversial issue. Africa is largely held back by economic and social structures, and value systems which have perpetuated underdevelopment. Technology alone is not able to change such structures. In fact, automation may be totally irrelevant to the development problems facing Africa.

Education and Society / R. Aiken (Editor)
Information Processing 92, Volume II
Elsevier Science Publishers B.V. (North-Holland)


# PARTICIPANT: PANEL ON INFORMATICS AND DEVELOPMENT

Sam Lanfranco[a]

[a]Distributed Knowledge Project, CERLAC & YCHS, York Lanes, York University, 4700 Keele Street, Toronto, CANADA M3J 1P3

Keyword Codes: K.3.1;K.4.1;K.4.2
Keywords: Computer Uses in Education; Public Policy Issues; Social Issues

## 1. Appropriate Technology

Informatics in development can be viewed from two perspectives. The economist sees informatics as a technology and input in production. The social scientist sees informatics as an input and output of social process. Computer mediated processes are increasingly appropriate for developing countries. They offer a discrete-jump to "better" technologies, are becoming easier to adapt, and are well suited to input endowments, relative prices and market conditions.

## 2. Reliance and Resilience

Successful development requires "groupings" which combine reliance on global linkages with resilience at the "group" level. The "Think Globally, Act Locally" environmental motto is echoed in the call for "Global Access, Local Process". Fights over the control of labour, land and capital will be replaced by struggles over access to and the use of information. Developing areas require strategies to build local informatic capabilities while joining forces to protect global information access. Latin America is active on the first front but not the second.

## 3. Building Skills, Knowledge and Wisdom

Information is both the input and the output in computer mediated process. This is important for developing areas. Informatic capacities and resource abundance are acquired, not endowed. Production process can be "decomposed" into informated steps. Skills, expertise and knowledge can be "composed" for use by individuals and groups. Computer augmented labour, computer assisted production and computer managed knowledge change how the citizen and expert participate in social process. This has important implications for what it means to educate the citizen and train the expert. It has profound implications for the location and use of wisdom is society and how wisdom is mobilized in social process. Latin American approaches to computer mediated education must address these issues.

Education and Society / R. Aiken (Editor)
Information Processing 92, Volume II
Elsevier Science Publishers B.V. (North-Holland)



# Computer-based information systems in their social context : Use of different perspectives

T.M. Waema and A.J. Rodrigues

Institute of Computer Science, University of Nairobi, P.O.Box 30197, Nairobi, Kenya

Abstract

In developing countries computer-based information systems (CBIS) initially tend, in general, to be literally "implanted" into complex social contexts in organizations. If effectively used, they acquire institutional character and become inextricably entwined with these contexts. For instance, they become inseparable from human judgments and actions and are often influenced by political power plays, structural constraints, and participants' perception of their situation. This has a number of implications for understanding CBIS in their social contexts.

Firstly, CBIS can be better understood if different perspectives are used to analyse their complexity in their social contexts. Each perspective represents only one way of "seeing" and "not seeing" since its use may exclude other views of the same phenomenon. Thus to understand more deeply CBIS and their relationship with the social context in which they are implemented, developed and used, it is necessary to integrate a number of perspectives.

Secondly, the technologies used to deliver the systems required should be maintainable and flexible so as to meet the challenges posed by changes in the social context. In our case study, the Public Universities Admission System's in-built technical flexibility enabled it to be easily modified to meet the changing demands imposed by both the Universities as well as the wider public. This demonstrates that an off-the-shelf package may be inappropriate except in standard areas and situations where source code is availed to meet desired modifications.

Thirdly, specialised skills need to be available, such as the analyst/programmer in the case study, so as to modify existing systems to meet the changing technical and socio-political needs of the client oranization and the wider context. The Public Universities Admission System had to be modified initially to cater for the change from a specialised to a broad based educational system while maintaining specialised Faculty interests. Subsequent pressure exerted by the public's perception of a "fair" admission criteria necessitated the adoption of broad based criteria with adverse foreseen consequences on the quality of the Basic Sciences intake, thus illustrating the "power play" factor. In this case study, the socio-political aspects were provided by the public supported by the media and interpreted by the Joint Admissions Board of the Public Universities with full cognizance of the consequence.

Keyword Codes: H.4.m; K.3.1; K.4.2
Keywords: Information Systems Applications, Miscellaneous; Computers and Education, Computer Uses in Education; Computers and Society, Social Issues

Education and Society / R. Aiken (Editor)
Information Processing 92, Volume II
Elsevier Science Publishers B.V. (North-Holland)


# RISK AND VULNERABILITY IN AN INFORMATION AND ARTIFICIAL SOCIETY

Jacques BERLEUR
On behalf of IFIP-WG9.2 *

Institut d'Informatique, Facultés Universitaires Notre-Dame de la Paix, Namur, Belgium

Keywords Codes: K.4.2; K.4.3; K.6.5
Keywords: Social Issues, Legitimacy; Organizational Impacts, Social Responsibility; Risk, Social Vulnerability

The concept of the vulnerability of an information society is frequently spoken about,[1] but what does it mean? Is there something that makes our age more vulnerable than any other? What is the role of technology in it? Can we measure vulnerability? Can we diminish it? Can we insure against it? What is to be protected: data, systems, knowledge, management, society or all of these?

We would like to emphasize here the social aspect of vulnerability: it is said that society is vulnerable and that technology is making it more vulnerable. It has often been said that technology contains dangers: the myth of Prometheus teaches us that technology must be submissive. What raises new questions today, when systems are felt to be less reliable, is our increasing dependence on information systems' producers and designers. The vulnerability of systems, from the point of view of hardware and software, seems also to initiate new fears and threats.[2]

Starting with an examination of social vulnerability as perceived in fiction and cartoons, the first part of this paper will report on existing surveys and specific examples at the levels of society, and public and private firms in order to give a first approximate overview of risk. But, as it will appear, the concepts are far from clear.

The second part will try to give a conceptual framework of reference in which we shall explicitly state our thesis: the concepts of risk and vulnerability cannot be understood unless several factors are examined together. The systems of knowledge, of power of action and the status of technology are interlinked in a symbolic structure which decide the social legitimacy of actors and the status of risk in a given society. The analysis of risk must at least include the status of the actors involved (including organizations and enterprises), the nature of action, the technology which is used, the effects which should result from this action and the visibility of those effects. Social vulnerability is defined in relation to what will be called the crisis of legitimacy.

The symbolic structure may also indicate the ways to effectively reduce or control vulnerability. We believe that every preventative or curative measure gets its interpretation from the fact that it has an impact on one or more of the distinctive features of the symbolic structure. The third part will enumerate the measures which are taken (or envisaged) today and will try to assess how they may relate to those features.

This paper is not a state of the art paper regarding risk and vulnerability;[3] it is rather a position paper providing the basis for a discussion of the most appropriate ways of preventing what is today perceived as a significant social threat: risk and vulnerability in a computerized society.

## 1. A Panorama of Present and Future Vulnerabilities

### *The Future Environment As Seen In Tales and Cartoons*

The vulnerability of society through excessive dependence on technology is a common theme in literature and folklore. Typically human beings or communities are depicted as overreaching themselves and suffering disastrous consequences as a result. Throughout human history there have been tales of artificial men (like the Golem of Prague) running amok, or of instruments (like the bewitched broom of the Sorcerer's Apprentice) failing to respond to their creator's commands. Perhaps the best known of these kinds of stories is Mary Shelley's "Frankenstein"; or, "The Modern Prometheus" written in the early 19th century.

In twentieth century literature whole societies, as well as individuals, are held to account for the Faustian bargain with technology. Eugene Zamiatin's "We", Aldous Huxley's "Brave New World", and other works of fiction are powerful cautionary tales, telling us that it is always dangerous - and often disastrous - to relinquish human choice to machines.

Two stories of special relevance in the age of information are "The Machine Stops" by E.M. Forster and "Ms Fnd in a Lbry" by Hal Draper.[4] In Forster's tale people live in an entirely artificial environment underground. They never experience the natural world directly, and communication with each other is mediated by the machine on which they depend for their very existence. Having lost the capacity to act independently of the machine, they are powerless to avert disaster when the machine malfunctions in unanticipated ways.

In his short story, Draper explores the idea of computer-mediated knowledge. Advances in information storage and retrieval technology have made it possible, in the fictional world of the story, to store vast amounts of information in ever smaller media. Direct knowledge of experience becomes ever more attenuated as people come to depend on indexes to written texts, then indexes of indexes, and ultimately on indexes of indexes of indexes n-times removed. Disaster strikes this fictional realm when some critical keys to a high level index are lost or destroyed. Lacking direct knowledge of the world, and bereft of their mediating information technology, people are unable to function in their accustomed roles.

Cartoonists very often reveal the living truth with accuracy and surely express some general feelings of the public who recognizes itself with humor ... and anxiety! "We sense the effects of information technology. I.T. follows us to work and from work - it is a prison, there are no pictures; the rooms in which we found ourselves today are the environments in which we will find ourselves tomorrow. They echo melancholy; they are cold. We feel a sense of loss for things we once possessed. The overt symbols of power are disappearing. We are far away from power, power is becoming invisible, it hides away in buildings, in corporate and administrative decision-making. The buildings, however, are enhanced by light and air, they are enrobed in a designer touch. The traditional responses to power become ludicrous - or worse, ... closing our eyes to these developments is as useless as closing our eyes against the testing of the first hydrogen bomb ..."[5]

### *Surveys on Vulnerability*

Few data are available which would permit measurement of the phenomenon of vulnerability at the organisational level. A 1982 study seems to show that the survivability of enterprises in the event of a computer emergency varied from 1-2 days (banks), 4-5 days (insurance and industry) to 6-7 days (trade) but the methodology of this study remains unclear and the detailed results are confidential. A more extensive survey was undertaken by the University of Texas, Arlington in 1987.[6] A questionnaire was sent to 1,444 USA enterprises and from the 160 answers it appears that most feel very dependent on their computers, not only financially but also in terms of their activities. The mean duration of emergencies extends from 2 to 4 days; the loss is equivalent to 15- 40% of their activity, without considering additional costs of 10-20%. Unfortunately, it seems that large businesses with significant experience of emergencies did not reply. An equivalent survey is presently being undertaken by the University of Hamburg, and will cover experiences in Germany, Austria and Switzerland and probably also Australia and Sweden.[7]

The present lack of statistical data leads us to look at some cases which are seen as typical of the phenomenon of "social vulnerability".

### *Wall Street 1987*

The vulnerability of the information and artificial society can be well illustrated by the Wall Street stock market collapse of October 19, 1987. Of course, it is said that the "immediate cause of the break was incidental. The market plunge was an accident waiting to happen."[8] But, "*modern technology* coupled with the greater presence of sophisticated institutional investors *undoubtedly contributed to the suddenness of the October drop.* Through modern telecommunications and information processing, investors can follow events as they unfold and react very promptly. What formerly took hours and days now can be done in seconds or minutes."[9] Indeed, as officially explained by A.Greenspan, Chairman of the Board of Governors of the Federal Reserve System, this crash pointed out "dramatically the many changes that have occurred in our market for equity products and the resulting *vulnerabilities* of the system. Some of those changes, such as the use of so called portfolio insurance strategies *based on the faulty premise* of a high degree of market liquidity, have at least to a degree be corrected by the October experience. Other changes such as the *heavier dependence of market participants on high speed computers and telecommunication devices* and the growing role of institutions ... are here to stay."[10]

Many of the new trading strategies (portfolio insurances, index arbitrage, ...) "were *based on mathematical models and executed by computers.*"[11]. Indeed, "advances in computer technology have facilitated the development of computerized procedures that process information for use by market participants, produce buy and sell orders, and send these orders to exchanges for execution. This technique, the program trading, permits large portfolios to be traded as though they were individual stocks."[12]

Now a coordinated intermarket circuit breaker has been established which is triggered by a determined decline of the Dow Index.[13] "The resulting trading halt is intended to give the market a breather to digest available information ... "[14]

We leave to the authors the appreciation of the real impact of those measures. We believe that they are more psychological than real.

### *Potential Problems in Hospitals*

Other case studies may illustrate our approach. The example of hospitals may be instructive, since health is always a sensitive question and consequently the maximum preventative measures seem to have been taken to protect systems.

Experts stress that when considering the potential harm of computorized integrated Hospitals Information Systems (HIS), one should first realize that the manual handling of data also implies risks: misinterpretation, errors of transcription, absence of data at the required location, unavailability of updated data, lack of consistency between different data (e.g. diagnosis and drugs), etc. Nevertheless, the specialized Working Group 4 of the International Medical Informatics Association (IMIA) recognizes that with HIS new risks have emerged regarding unauthorized access to medical data, the integrity of data and programs, and the availability of data.[15]

"In health care, absolute privacy is not possible; to be able to function, the members of the health care team need data on the health status of the patient. This principle of 'need to know' should be made explicit and implemented in software properly supported by organizational measures."[16] Although regulatory recommendations are stressed,[17] data protection legislation is not always forthcoming and, moreover, "awareness amongst the users is limited."[18]

As far as the integrity of data and programs is concerned, "whereas errors in the manual situation in general will affect only one patient, when using computers we may expect both incidental and systematic errors. The latter category, 'errors in knowledge', may affect large groups of patients. Examples which have occurred are:

- "an error in a radiotherapy system caused an extremely high radiation dose, killing a patient;
- an error in a dosage prescription program caused, under special circumstances, a patient to get the dosage prescribed for the previous patient. This led in one reported case to an emergency admission at the hospital, where fortunately the bleeding that occurred could be stopped;
- a modified textual interface led sometimes to the loss of the first character of each line on a histology report; in some cases this changed the meaning completely. Fortunately, no wrong clinical decision was made on this misleading information."[19]

The system becoming unavailable also involves potential harm, since it has to be backed up by manual procedures that, if invoked, will reduce the quality of care: only urgent testing will be done in the laboratory, no checks will be possible on the supply of drugs, etc. "It is surprising that this dependency of the hospital on the proper functioning of its information processing has not yet received attention till now. It is needed to pay more attention to this problem and come to some guidelines on the acceptable level of availability and the measures to be implemented."[20]

Risks are high in hospitals, according to the people in charge. "The primary problem ... in health information systems is the lack of awareness. ... Software errors may cause situations that are a direct threat to the health of the patient, e.g. in supporting the administration of drugs or in reporting the result of diagnostic tests. The quality control of software to be used for medical applications is absolutely inadequate. If we handled pharmaceuticals in the same way that we deal with software, we would be put in jail. ... Regulations for the certification of software are needed. With the maturation of HIS, a complete breakdown for a period of several days would lead to chaos. ... More attention is needed for back-up facilities and other measures that reduce the risks."[21]

Is it true that most of the preventative measures do not address the issues at stake? The measures most often mentioned are: privacy law, password control, dual operation, a separate energy supply, back-up testing, failure and disturbance registration and analysis, special control committees, etc. Are those measures sufficient? The activity of patients' organizations in some countries, such as the Netherlands, with a special desk at the entrance of the hospital, shows that most of the time the solution is unsatisfactory![22]

### *Electronic Data Interchange (EDI)*

Amongst telecommunication devices, one which promises to have an impact on economic life is Electronic Data Interchange. Phenomena such as globalization, concentration, delocalisation and task- externalisation have already been suggested. One may also surmise, at the micro-economic level, the modification of management and strategical choices, the financial consequences of undetected errors or of systems breakdowns, new fraud opportunities, the impact of standards choices on the processes of rationalization, etc. At the macro-economic level, inter-firm relations and the market structure will surely influence the aggregated effects on society.

EDI systems also introduce new legal problems. How do we process, for instance, documents that legally require a signature? Do we need new rules or laws to cover EDI in the private sector? Moreover, EDI creates new boundaries within private and public sectors so that the internationalisation of information flow is leading to the need for international laws and at the same time to the emergence of a dual legal system, one for computers and one for traditional systems. Will the law not be reduced to a pure "administrative skeleton"? Huge problems also reside today in defining and standardizing all the information which is needed to run such systems which, by definition, tend to be worldwide. Who is defining what, for whom and for what purpose?

### *A Concept To Be Elucidated*

Case studies could be multiplied. But would they deeply modify the first perception that we already have? What impression can be derived? We can probably say in the first approximation that we are facing a classic problem of the relation between computers, organizations and society: technology is sometimes seen as influencing society while, on the other hand, sociological approaches determine that technology has no autonomy and remains subject to societal or organizational determination. We are facing a dilemma which should be pointed out: on the one hand, computer science and data processing is partly responsible for the vulnerability of society, but on the other, society is fully in charge of the ways in which these new techniques develop.

As we have seen, the concept of vulnerability most often emerges from technology, even though - as it will appear later - this view is probably biased. The word "vulnerability" is practically understood as being equivalent to "technical fallibility". In the context of an information society, this fallibility can occur at several levels:

1) hardware: breakdowns, incidents, hitches, ...
2) software: bugs, viruses, inadequate and too simplistic expert systems, ...
3) organization and man. At this last level, two cases must be considered: errors and cheating. Firstly, errors can be due to users (when they perform data capture or handle a computer program) or to designers (when they carry out conception or realization or exploitation of programs). The organization may be responsible for the absence of access rules or for the simplicity of security measures. Computer scientists can also try to cheat (pirating and hacking, software theft, computer abuse, divulgence of secret data, creation of erroneous data - for example, fictitious voters -[23], modification or deletion of data - for example, fines in a police file).[24] But it can also be a means of pirating (for example, when money is embezzled with the help of a bank card). According to several studies computer cheating is responsible for major losses in banks and insurance companies[25] and in production systems, as has been the case in a large car company which lost the equivalent of one year's profit.

Technical fallibility implies less explicit control, a narrower dependence on technical systems (particularly on computer systems) and a transfer of responsibility to these systems. People feel that "the responsibility is in practice moved to the information system". "In a technological society, man is regarded as the weakest point. Although this assumption can be questioned, in reality information technology is used for controlling this weakest point."[26]

But what about "social vulnerability"? It is not unambiguously defined. Several levels appear: individual, organizational, political and economical.

The information society can be described as "artificial" because it uses the technique of representation and simulation and is based on theoretical models.[27] "The art of simulation consists in choosing the right specifications for the model..."[28], but perhaps the model cannot be applied, in an adequate and suitable way, to the concrete reality of the world.[29] We shall come back later to this link between representation, simulation, models and artificiality.

In this "artificial society", vulnerability is more or less linked with *risk*. This last notion is defined by classical authors and adopted by R. Laufer[30] as expressing "the gap between the anticipation of the consequences of a given action and its actual outcome." For Laufer[31], three types of risk can be defined, according to the way in which it is connected to human action:

1) *Speculative risk*, which is taken voluntarily and is directly linked to the goal of the economic actor (for example, the risk of the contractor); it can be generalized to the social actor (for example, the racing driver),
2) *Pure risk*, which is assumed voluntarily but is not considered by the economic and social actors as related to the aim of the action (for example: the risk of cutting oneself for a glassworker, or the risk of having bugs in a programme). These types can be distinguished as insurable and uninsurable risks.[32]
3) *Involuntary risk* which "could not even be anticipated when considering the normal 'pattern' of the action" (for example a factory affecting a local community by pollution).

Without going into detail, it would be interesting to compare these different types of risks with those events that the specialized insurance companies do not normally cover. We can mention: gradual degradation, corrosion, rust, dampness or dryness of the atmosphere, dishonest acts, loss of market, declared or undeclared war, insurrection, rebellion, revolution, nuclear radiation, programming errors or faulty machine instructions, interference by strikers or other persons, etc. Virus perils may sometimes be covered by an extension of an EDP All Risk Policy. Rare is the Systems Perils Policy which offers cover for full related "consequential loss". Lloyd's of London seems to be one of the few to insure against Computer Fraud.[33]

Let us conclude the first part. The concept of vulnerability still remains unclear:

- Vulnerability may be seen from the point of view of an increased dependence upon technical systems to which responsibility is transferred. It would then be seen as technical fallibility or the production of norms and the standardization of social behaviour resulting in a threat to social values (liberties, democracy, culture, ...)
- Vulnerability may be looked at according to various dimensions: individuals, organizations, economic mechanisms, political systems, ...
- We may question the role of the technological imperative in the analysis of vulnerability. Are we speaking in terms of technological determinism at the level of organizational and societal changes, which would be opposed to the results of many sociological and organizational studies?[34]

## 2. Risk, Vulnerability and Crisis of Legitimacy

Several attempts to classify the different kinds of risk and the appropriate means to control them have been described. Let us mention one which is inspired by the Swedish SÅRK Report:[35]

- *Acts of God*: earthquakes, tidal waves, landslides, lightning strikes, flood, fire, ...;
- *Acts of people*: criminal acts, misuse for political purposes, acts of war, ...;
- *Deficiencies of people*: human error, deficiency of education, dependency on key persons, strikes, ...;
- *Deficiencies of organizations*: lack of documentation or training, deficient quality of hardware or software, profit motivation, ...;
- *Dependency on others*: organizations, people, ...;
- *Complexity of systems*: volume of data, centralisation, integration, dependency, ...

This classification may help: one may consider the legal, organizational, social or technical measures which could prevent society from some specific risk: better training, reinforced control, etc. But it does not clarify its presuppositions and it is not sure that such measures will solve problems without creating others. One may also have noticed that the classification is such that it allows us to identify who is guilty!

But the question of risk and vulnerability must be taken in all its dimensions and seen and studied *within a global framework.* Let us state briefly what will appear in more detail later: to take risks under the law of free-market democracy is different from taking risks under anti-monopoly rules or when there is a crisis of belief in "progress". It is different again when consumers associations question the "invisible hand" of the "natural" market and speak instead of the "visible hand" of the "cultural" managers who manipulate their needs.[36]

The way to think about risk and technology differs according to the frame of reference, i.e. according to the way relationships are established or symbolized between the specific features which constitute society.[37] There is a need for some theoretical background which permits the control of anticipation, since as said earlier, risks are expressing "the gap between the anticipation of the consequences of a given action and its actual outcome". Furthermore, we cannot assert that there are "major risks" when there are no criteria to judge or in a situation of global anomie. Pragmatism is sometimes worse than doing nothing since it tackles the symptoms of vulnerability and not the causes. Are we sure that "risk management" or "management of uncertainty", for instance, will really reduce vulnerability?[38] If social vulnerability corresponds to a stage of degradation of social cohesion, or to a threat to a supposed cohesion which could result from an apparent stability of the social regulatory mechanisms, we must at least try to identify the different factors which ensure or symbolize the functioning of those mechanisms.

We suggest studying the question of risk and vulnerability in relation to the crisis of the system of legitimacy of action and power, where we shall try to explain the links between:

- the system of knowledge (its relevance, its organization, its methods, ...),
- the system of power (private and public) and organizations,
- the systems of action, and
- the status of technology.

Let us remember that according to Max Weber[39] there are three types of power and that these three types constitute a theory:

- charismatic power, related to a "sacred/profane" *Weltanschauung*, is able to install in the profane world the order and the harmony of the sacred sphere;
- traditional power, related to a "culture/nature" *Weltanschauung*, submits nature to the laws of culture, (e.g. to the wisdom of ancients);
- rational-legal power, related to a "nature/culture" *Weltanschauung*, understands culture according to the laws of nature.

One may be immediately convinced that the third type of power is the only one which could be legitimate today, since in our world the nature/culture *Weltanschauung* is predominant.[40] But we must proceed further and examine, for the rational-legal system of power, again three periods in which the status of risk could appear in different ways. These three periods correspond to three epistemological paradigms characterized as:

- determinism, within a Kantian epistemology (i.e. natural laws of economy and an atomistic market),

- positivism or pragmatism under the epistemology of A. Comte,
- system analysis, the reign of the artificial, a radical form of pragmatism which adopts H. Simon's science of systems.[41]

In order to explain the status of risk and the role of technology we must briefly indicate, for each period, the system of knowledge (rational-), the system of power (-legal), the legitimacy of the system of action and the related status of risk, and finally the status of technology. As far as the system of power is concerned, we shall concentrate on the so-called private sector without consideration of the public sector and the way it regulates or enforces the system of power.[42]

*During the first period* [1800 -> 1880-1900]:

- Knowledge is dominated by the epistemology of Emmanuel Kant (1724-1804): the model of science is Newtonian physics and is deterministic; consensus is obtained by the fact that every rational being is capable of discovering the laws of nature and has direct access to scientific truth; there is no place for opinion.
- Political economy is developed according to the model of Newtonian physics: atomistic free-market democracy is the rule and no firm has the power to upset the "natural equilibrium" (the "social optimum" of Walras and Pareto); this also defines the laws of society (rights of property); every individual by the same token complies with the laws of nature.
- The legitimacy of action relies upon the nature of its cause, since there are laws.
- In these conditions, risks are legitimate inasmuch as they result from the functioning of the laws of nature (be it an earthquake or the risk of the entrepreneur, also called *speculative risk*). This risk, however painful it is, has to be accepted. The only illegitimate risks are those which result from a disruption of the order of nature by some cultural being, which corresponds to "guilty behaviour": there is personal responsibility and it is associated with personal fault.
- Technology has no specific status, nature being completely separated from culture; there is no place for artifacts in science and the law of the market allows the entrepreneur to choose any technology he wants, provided he is subject to the legal system.

*During the second period* [1880-1900 -> 1945-1960]:

- Knowledge is under the positivist epistemology of Auguste Comte (1798-1857) and the models of science may be characterized as closed systems. Laws are still deterministic, but a consensus is now reached by the experts of each field of science; consequently, opinion plays a role inasmuch as one must distinguish between the knowledge of the expert and the knowledge of the one who knows that he does not know but that somebody knows. Let us add that Comtean epistemology strictly excludes multidisciplinarity.
- Political economy corresponds to the development of large enterprises which threaten the rule of atomistic free-market democracy; therefore, a new legal mechanism intervenes through anti-trust legislation which requires the size of firms to be measured and action taken according to whether they are still closed systems. Inside organizations, the principles of scientific management are typical of this period: they ensure the authority of managers.
- The legitimacy of action does not rely any more on the cause, but on the finality of power; the positivist knowledge of the experts establishes the principle of the "one best way" in order to control the means necessary for desired results, as well as to regulate the market. The consensus on the measure of action is reached through

an oriented (finality) hypostasis which, in the work of A. Comte, is God, or more precisely "God Progress".

- Unacceptable risks of two types appear. The first is due to firms becoming too large and is controlled, as has been explained, by anti-trust laws. The second is accidents inside firms. To deal with them the insurance system is created, based on the principle of responsibility without fault. A new notion appears, distinguished from speculative risk: *pure risk* which recognizes that there are risks to be borne although they do not pertain to the goal of action.[43] A racing driver takes a speculative risk whereas the loss of a finger at work is a pure risk. Companies only insure pure risk. As soon as the subject is considered to influence the occurrence of a given accident, when there is fault without responsibility, we have a "moral hazard", which is illegitimate and therefore uninsurable.
- Technology becomes predominant in itself and as an aid to management. It is linked by essence to God Progress: development of science and technology is equivalent to progress for the whole of humanity. Scientific management is also the rule. As long as both technology and scientific management remain positivist, i.e. limited to the closed systems where they have their role to play, vulnerability does not increase.

*The third period* [1945-1960 -> today] is dominated by the increasing confusion between nature and culture; it is the reign of the "artificial":

- Science becomes the science of the artificial, or the science of systems.[44] Rather than a science, it is an art: the art of representation and of specification of models. But as there are many different ways to specify models, the consensus is more and more becoming a "consensus of opinions". Scientific knowledge abandons its pretension to determinism, since positivism is less in favour![45] Increasing demand for interdisciplinarity is one symptom of the state of confusion of most paradigms.[46] As it emphasizes global and holistic approaches, it refers to culture, which means that it reverses the relationship nature/culture and favour the *Weltanschauung* culture/nature.
- The market mechanism breaks down since firms are becoming bigger and bigger and are no longer subject to the laws of nature, i.e. to the "invisible hand of the market", but more clearly to the "hands of the visible managers"![47] This situation of imperfect competition is considered as illegitimate, as shown in a large part of the literature about multinational firms.
- The legitimacy of action can only be obtained by direct approval of the pursued goals and of the methods which are used: public opinion again plays a determinant role and consensus is obtained most of the time by directly creating it. The legitimacy of action no longer relies on the cause or on the finality, but mainly on the method of action.
- The status of risk is also clear : the situation of imperfect competition creates permanent risk and uncertainty and becomes a source of social concern.[48] The breakdown of the principle of the risk of the entrepreneur is complete when it is managers who decide how to act while it is financial shareholders who take the so-called financial risks. Sometimes the situation of risk resembles that of a game, if not of gambling.
- Finally, technology plays a dominant role as it cannot be said that it is subject to the laws of nature, be they the laws of the market or the laws of science. The new paradigm speaks of "techno-sciences" (e.g. "bio-technology", computer science, ...).

This third period - the current period - is thus characterized by a crisis of law (laws of political economy as well as associated rules) and by a crisis of science with - from the point of view of epistemology - an increasing confusion between the subject of knowledge and its object. Artificial Intelligence is defined as the tool that allows us to symbolically reconstruct action and thought. Artificial Intelligence is the ultimate expression of confusion between the subject of knowledge (man) and its object (for instance the computer) to such a point that man is ready to give up his place to it.

All these phenomena can be taken as an expression of a crisis of the symbolic system which allows societies to describe and interpret their actions, related and associated risks, and finally the judgments by which their legitimacy was recognized.

*
* *

We suggest adopting this *frame of reference* to analyse the current status of risk. Of course, the three periods may overlap: an earthquake or any natural catastrophe is considered as an act of God so long as the predominant *Weltanschauung* has the sacred opposed to the profane. But when it includes the domination of nature then this interpretation becomes irrelevant, even though the event is still considered a major risk. A change in the system of legitimacy - i.e. a change in the rational or legal system - may create risks which are as serious as the previous ones.

Our thesis is that a risk is major as soon as the legitimacy of the action is questioned, or as soon as the legitimacy system cannot gain the support of an accepted "rational-legal system". Moreover, when we qualify risks as "speculative", "pure ", "acceptable" or "unacceptable", "legitimate" or "not legitimate", "voluntary" or "involuntary", we always refer to a well determined frame of reference where those terms have a specific meaning and determine some attitude: we have said, for instance, that in the third period speculative and pure risks cannot be properly distinguished.

When we speak of "social vulnerability", we imply that risks are not originated only in the organization of science (which is related to epistemology) or in the technology which can be derived from it (to be quite correct, technology is always a *socio*-scientific device), but also in the organization of society and particularly in the way the private and public actors behave on the market.

Risks do not arise from technology alone; they may be encouraged by the advanced status of technologies as they become embedded in an organizational environment which is not *a priori* legitimate.

It should be clear by now that the analysis of risk must at least include the status of the actors involved (including organizations and enterprises), the nature of the action, the technology which is used, the effects which are expected to result from the action and the visibility of those effects. There is vulnerability as soon as the legitimacy system is not obvious or not generally accepted. This means that disturbances in the symbolic systems of society are as responsible for vulnerability as the systems of knowledge and technology. Risks appear as unbearable as soon as they cannot be interpreted in a frame of reference. *Risks* - be they major or not -

are present as such when there is a threat on the constitutive features of the symbolic structure within which action keeps its legitimacy.

Briefly, there is vulnerability:

- when the symbolic structure does not function anymore,
- when responsibilities cannot be assigned (Who are the actors? Do they obey some recognized laws?, etc.),
- when the system of regulation of a specific society seriously lacks stability,
- when there is no consensus on what has to be done or on the nature of action,
- when technology introduces confusion in the knowledge system.

Vulnerability of society is not, by essence, the consequence of a given technology but increases insofar as technology plays a role in the construction (some people would prefer to say "deconstruction") of the symbolic structure which provides coherence in society. From this point of view new technologies, and especially the technologies of the artificial, have a mimetic role with respect to the crisis of legitimacy of action and power in our time. But there are also specific features in them which precipitate the deconstruction. Communication technologies, for instance, may increase the deregulation of an accepted hierarchical structure in an organization by favouring the lateral exchange of information and, as a consequence, favouring the role of opinion. It may be advantageous (see, for example, the role of ARPANET, set up by the Department of Defense but used during the Vietnam War against its own interests) or disadvantageous (e.g. promoting the destruction of an accepted decision making process).

## 3.What Ought People to Do to Try to Reduce Risks and Vulnerability?

As indicated, the third part will mainly consist of a catalogue of measures which are taken or envisaged today in order to either prevent risks, reduce them or to control and limit their effects. We shall leave until the conclusion the question of knowing whether these measures are successful in reducing the vulnerability of our societies.

One might expect that our aim is to find measures that are effective in protecting our societies. We must say however that we have been tempted to classify measures as "efficiency measures" and "effectiveness measures". The definition is not constant amongst the authors but most of the time "efficiency" expresses the notion of "doing the thing right" while "effectiveness" expresses the notion of "doing the right thing".[49] Management Control manuals say that efficiency stresses the inner relation between input and throughput (i.e. within the organization process) and that effectiveness is more linked to the output and to what is expected from the inner process. We surmise that the question of legitimacy is more linked to effectiveness, since it raises the question of whether the product is socially acceptable.

Thus, efficiency measures do not address the cause or origin of increased vulnerability, but only attempt to manage its effects and consequences. They aim to reinforce the reliability of technological development and its applications ("doing the thing right"), and at the management of a situation rather than at its radical cure. Effectiveness measures address the real causes of vulnerability and raise the question "why?". A medium or long term change is envisaged, attempting to restore the legitimacy of certain technological developments ("doing the right thing").

Computer scientists distinguish syntax and semantics. Risk and vulnerability belong to the semantic field and security measures, for instance, are purely syntactic. The analogy would be between efficiency and syntax and between effectiveness and semantics. Others might prefer to link efficiency with pragmatism and effectiveness with action at the symbolic level.

We shall not go further with these distinctions, leaving further discussion until the conclusion.

We prefer to concentrate our attention on the fact that some measures are more directly linked to the symbolic structure and its distinctive features - systems of knowledge, of power or of action, and the status of technology. One may think that they would be "more effective" in preventing and reducing risks and vulnerability since they play a more important role on the factors which provoke the crisis of legitimacy.

Let us now enumerate these measures as they are promoted in the literature or in practice.

### *Measures of security*

- Technological systems measures (*hardware* and *software*)
  - A first condition to be fulfilled is the technical reliability of the computing systems. "To rely on a given equipment, on the service's continuity, on a total reliability (!), a total protection (!): isn't it a necessary condition for the respect of liberties?"[50] "Two pitfalls must be avoided: to give to the computers the security of other computers or automated systems; to accompany the security of systems by an increasing control which would attend to the liberties (...)";[51]
  - To guarantee the reliability of programs and of processing.

- Organizational/management measures (*human*)
  - related to the design:
    - to increase measures which will reduce dependence upon designers,
    - to guarantee good documentation, sufficient training of users, ...
    - to set up a code of practice for designers.
  - related to the use:
    - access control, control of diffusion and of information use.

### *Legal measures*

- produce a clear definition of contracts taking into account the specificity of information systems,
- protect the right to information, and of civil liberties (rights of "filer"/rights of "filed"),
- build up automated legal systems,
- enhance insurance measures,
- define the fields and domains which are to be considered as computer crime and abuse; what are these specific crimes and abuses? What is the specific role of computers when these crimes and abuses are described? Consider:
  - the computer as the object of crime (sabotage, theft of machine-time or of software, data transformation or alteration),

- the computer as the tool where the act could have been performed by other means (money derouting),
- the computer as the occasion of the crime (anti-competition practices, for instance).

Two ways to tackle computer crime may be envisaged: either by extension of existing measures against other forms of crime, taking into account the specificity of computing, but within the framework of the general law; or introducing new laws which are appropriate to the specificity of computer crime. The first approach is centered on the *result* and is mainly linked to four domains: the false and the use of the false, fraud, the abuse of confidence, and espionage; the second is linked to *domains* which seem to be really *specific to computing*: fraudulent access, software modification and destruction, ...[52]

***Social Measures***

- provide information on existing possibilities, and on the risks to be taken into account,
- provide training that allows for the control of IT,
- educate usees, develop a "common language" among them, paying attention to psychological dimensions in the computing world, etc.
- encourage participation of the public in decisions (See, for instance, "Consensus Conferences"),
- develop ways to empower people to act and to participate in decision processes,
- organize groups with common interests, consumers association,
- appoint Data Ombudsmen,
- etc.

***Economic Measures***

- Some measures may be taken to regulate the market: most often they are legislative, but they may be organizational. For example, the creation of the I.M.F. to control international exchange rates or, in Europe, the "Monetary Snake"; a specific taxation system on firms may also reduce the amount of pollution. One may also think of measures which enforce freedom of information as in the Purchase Public Offer cases.
- Even if information should be made public, mechanisms like patents lead to privatisation, which means that by manipulating information one may influence the market. Some measures to reduce these influences are regulatory or legal proceedings and possibly more specific measures such as "contractual design mechanisms" which oblige the revelation of information.[53]
- What appears more clearly today is that it is necessary to restore moral norms, because dishonesty creates externalities and thus the greatest disturbances on the market. In terms of information, L. Walras wrote that information was "perfect ... until one actor is in the situation where he knows that I know something he does not". Regulation by moral norms or developing entrepreneurial ethics is increasingly studied by economists; it seems to be agreed that "less ethics" leads to "more State" and "more control and repression" and that capitalism through its "self-preoccupation doctrine"[54] - without sufficient consideration for alternatives

and for pain, grief and death (i.e. for moral norms) - is facing growing difficulties if not a major crisis.[55]

### *Other Measures*

- A method for anticipating the effects of technological development ('Early Warning') could be a tool for better grounded choices, for supporting political decision making, making it more aware of technological implications for the future of societies.
- A broader participation of the public in decisions and the reaching of consensus also presuppose democratic mechanisms of decision making related to technological choices.
- Questions can also be raised about the process of representation and modelling. Models are created today which have no other justification than their own functioning. They have their inner coherence, but they have no correspondence to external reality. It would be justified to set up some auditing procedures to ensure that systems are representing what they are supposed to represent.
- Other means of restoring the symbolic structure or to "manage the impossible":[56]
    - Produce laws preventing the abuse of technology,
    - Create commissions to report on abuses and their prevention,
    - Mr."Technological Danger" (see above "Early Warning"),
    - Establish Safety Norms,
    - Create Ethical Committees,
    - etc.

*
* *

Returning to our previous distinction, some authors have noticed that the difference between efficiency and effectiveness measures corresponds to the difference between a *rational* approach, based on objective data, and a *political* approach, giving weight to subjective data and factual experience.[57] This rational-political difference is probably close to our rational-legal system of power, showing that effectiveness measures, related to the legal subsystem, are more related to the system of legitimacy of action.

If, as we have supposed throughout our paper, vulnerability is defined in relation to the crisis of legitimacy, the proposed solutions must go beyond the management of the situation - the efficiency measures could only tackle the symptoms and remain pragmatic - and, considering the causes of the situation, favour the restoration of the legitimacy of specified technological and social choices.

But the history of systems of legitimacy shows that legitimacy is the result of a set of factors which cannot be fully controlled and do not only result from voluntary action. Actions which can help to "restore the symbolic structure" may only be guidelines, trying to *turn* the evolution of the legitimacy systems, without any determinism.

In a way, "efficiency" belongs to the level of pragmatic action, where "syntactic rules" do exist (e.g. "Go to the Ethics Commission"), while effectiveness or the symbolic structures belong to a "meta-rules level" which is not fully reachable. One is obliged, in action, to follow the rule "as if the situation was supposed to be such", since we recognise the paradigmatic confusion of our present time. We are faced with "the management of the possible and of the impossible".[58] Efficiency and effectiveness measures do not exclude themselves, but they do not function at the same level. What is to be avoided is their contradiction.

As we have said, the most important point is not to clarify the distinction between efficiency and effectiveness but to assess how a specific measure is interacting with one or several features of the symbolic structure. The measures of security must be evaluated in relation to the status of technology in a given period. Some of the organizational measures may have a very favourable impact as soon as they increase the consensus for a given paradigm or promote the legitimacy of the actors. Legal measures may remove suspicion over types of behaviour or increase social confidence towards given actors. Specific economic measures may restore the moral climate and then reduce the externalities and improve the functionality of an accepted "state of the art", etc. The efficient or effective aspect of a measure cannot be appreciated unless it is examined specifically.

In itself, the concept of vulnerability seems to suggest something irreversible and to contain risks which multiply out of proportion, without our being able to stop their effects. One may think that vulnerability is incurable. This is not the position of this paper!

## Conclusion

"Philosophers have only sought to interpret the world; the point however is to change it!" Does this mean that the time has come to look for an alternative to the dominance of technology and business? Some are advocating the necessity of restoring a culture - or a "counter-culture" to distinguish it from the present one - which would not be dominated by technology, but would involve a reversal of the *Weltanschauung* which supports the third type of power of Max Weber. None can however deny that culture may affect the social environment, lifestyle, etc., and that in the long run we could develop a socially accountable approach to computers which, in turn, implies cultural understanding.[59]

There is a danger that dominant culture incorporates change and that change simply means "putting green chambers into the Titanic". Is it not better to act as a Trojan Horse, instilling day after day a sense of the daily needs of people into systems which seem to ignore them except as consumers. The gap between "the market" and individuals requires to be bridged in order to make society *sustainable*. It involves reshaping "civil society", creating "intermediary bodies" in the lacuna between individuals and society.

The main concept to be promoted is *social responsibility*. For most people it means awareness and knowledge about security and vulnerability problems, for others a duty to inform. For computer scientists it means the breakdown of their isolation and their participation in social movements (they are rarely members of trade unions for instance). For managers it means to promote reactive, participatory and anticipatory control. Social responsibility urgently requires the development of specific rules of ethics and a greater awareness of the social consequences of present developments: computer use and abuse may lead to irreversible situations as has been the case in other scientific and managerial domains. Social responsibility is not a concept which is defined once for ever. It searches for its truth in everyday life without being assigned its meaning before each individual has found it. It is a kind of wisdom - with its rights and duties - that is waiting at the doorstep of our home when we start the day and that helps us to face fears and threats.[60]

---

* This "paper of positions", to be discussed, has been adopted by IFIP-WG9.2 as the result of a common study started in January 1989. The Working Group decided to have, in each of its meetings, a "Teach-In" to give it "food for thought". The theme of risk and vulnerability progressively emerged and was refined during further meetings. We are indebted to the members who contributed during the several "Teach- Ins" under the chairmanship of Dick SIZER (UK): Abbe MOWSHOWITZ (USA), Colin BEARDON (UK), Klaus BRUNNSTEIN (D), Herbert BURKERT (D), Julie CAMERON (AUS), Roger CLARKE (AUS), Gonzales d'ALCANTARA (B), Bart de GREEF (NL), Paula GOOSSENS (NL), Jan HOLVAST (NL), Heinz KLAMET (NL), Romain LAUFER (F), Peter NILSSON (Sw), Jean-Louis RIGAL (F), Wilhelm STEINMÜLLER (D), Felix VAN RIJN (NL), Diane WHITEHOUSE (UK), Joseph WEIZENBAUM (USA) and Louise YNGTRÖM (Sw). We are also grateful to those who joined us in a One-Day Seminar (January 1991) and expressed their views, helping the Working Group to take into account some practical experiences: A.R. BAKKER (NL), Jan FREESE (Sw) and Dan SIMPSON (UK). We are finally indebted to Marie d'UDEKEM-GEVERS, Benoît KUSTERS and Claire LOBET-MARIS (FUNDP-B) who prepared material for Parts 1 & 3.
Our acknowledgement finally goes to the Belgian Scientific Services for the Programme "Pôle d'attraction interuniversitaire, Convention n°32" which financially supports the FUNDP-Namur team.

1 See, for example, République Francaise, Sénat, Jacques THYRAUD, Rapport fait au nom de la commission des Lois constitutionnelles, de Législation, du Suffrage universel, du Règlement et d'Administration générale sur la proposition de loi adoptée par l'Assemblée nationale, relative à la *fraude informatique*, 1ère Session ordinaire 1987-88, Annexe au Procès-Verbal de la séance du 2.X.1987, p. 13.

2 A review of data available from the field of investigative journalism provided T. FORESTER and P. MORRISON with a general overview of technical vulnerability as it relates to information technology: *Computers Ethics: Cautionary Tales and Ethical Dilemmas in Computing,* Oxford: Basic Blackwell, 1990.

3 One could refer, f.i., to the Proceedings of the EUROPROSPECTIVE-1 Conference (CEC-FAST, CGP, CNRS and CPE), and particularly to Jean-Paul MOATTI, Des sociétés vulnérables, (Chapter 15 of *Le monde vu d'Europe*, sous la direction de Bernard CASSEN & Philippe de la SAUSSAY, Paris, Economica & CPE, 1989). Several papers have also circulated among the participants to Workshop 4, "Risk and Vulnerability In Industrial Societies".

4 FORSTER, E. M., The Machine Stops, in: E. M. FORSTER, *The Eternal Moment and Other Stories,* New York: Harcourt Brace Jovanovich, 1928.
DRAPER, Hal, Ms Fnd In A Lbry, in: A. MOWSHOWITZ, *Inside Information: Computers in Fiction,* Reading, MA: Addison-Wesley, 1977.

5 Herbert BURKERT, A Comic Book Approach, IFIP-WG9.2 Meeting, Namur, January 1990.

6 Steven R. CHRISTENSEN and Lawrence L. SCHKADE, Financial and Functional Impact of Computer Outages on Business, Texas University of Arlington, 1987 (Paper CRIS-87-01).

7 Vulnerability of Information Economy, Verletzlichkeit der Informations Wirtschaft, Eine Umfrage der Universität Hamburg unter Leitung von Prof. Kl. BRUNNSTEIN (Projektteam: Uwe ELLERMANN, Ronald GREINKE and Daniel LÖFFLER), Vorabversion, dezember 1990. The questionnaire is available on diskette. The survey should be completed by the end of 1992.

8 A. GREENSPAN, *Federal Reserve Bulletin*, April 1988, p. 221.

9 ibid. *We underline.*

10 *Federal Reserve Bulletin,* July 1988, p. 446. *We also underline.*

11 ibid., p. 447.

[12] cf. C. D. DAVIS and A. P. WHITE, *Federal Reserve Bulletin,* September 1987, p. 699.

[13] See *Les Echos,* Paris, 20 novembre 1991.

[14] A. GREENSPAN, *Federal Reserve Bulletin,* July 1988, p. 448.

[15] A. R. BAKKER, "Computers in Hospitals, Vulnerability Aspects", Lecture presented in the IFIP WG9.2 One-Day Seminar (January 11, 1991), *ad instar manuscr.* See also, same author, An Integrated Hospital Information System in the Netherlands, in: *Clinical Computing,* 1991, vol. 7, n.2, pp. 91- 97.

[16] ibid.

[17] See, for instance, The Recommendation R (81/1) "Regulations for Automated Medical Data Banks" adopted by the Committee of Ministers of the Council of Europe on January 23, 1981.

[18] A. R. BAKKER, "Computers in Hospitals, Vulnerability Aspects", doc.cit.

[19] ibid.

[20] ibid.

[21] ibid.

[22] Paula GOOSSENS, Comments on "Vulnerability in Hospitals", IFIP-WG9.2 Meeting, Brighton, 1991.

[23] As has been the case in the USA.

[24] According to cases registered in Dallas.

[25] See *Computer World* 1984, n°45 and 52.

[26] Jan HOLVAST, Vulnerability of Information Society: The Conflicting Demands of Security and Privacy, in: *Proceedings Conference SOST'89,* Terrigal, Australia, 3-5 May 1989, Australian Computer Society, Sydney. Republished in: Roger CLARKE & Julie CAMERON eds, *Managing Information Technology's Organizational Impact,* Elsevier/North-Holland, 1991, pp. 411-424.

[27] Pierre LEVY, "Temps réel et simulation", in: *Culture Technique,* n°.21, juillet 1990.

[28] cf. Romain LAUFER, Organization and Legitimacy: The Case of the History of Insurance Companies in France, *ad instar manuscr.*, 1991, p. 8.

[29] Francis PAVE, 1989, *L'illusion informaticienne,* Editions l'Harmattan, Paris, 1989, p.14. See particularly chapter 6: L'hyperfonctionnalisme cybernétique et ses insuffisances.

[30] Romain LAUFER, Organization and Legitimacy: The Case of the History of Insurance Companies in France, doc. cit., p. 10.

[31] Romain LAUFER, Towards a typology of "major risks", doc. presented at IFIP-WG 9.2 Meeting, Brighton 1991.

[32] See *The Geneva Papers on Risks and Insurance,* and especially the issues on "Natural Disaster and Insurance" (vol. 9, 1984, n° 30, 31 & 32) and on "Limits of Insurability and Risks" (vol. 11, 1986, n° 39), Assurances de Genève.

[33] Yasar TÜMBAS, Computer Related Risks and Insurance, Paper prepared for the IFIP-WG9.2 One-Day Seminar, Namur, January 1991, on behalf of the CIGNA Insurance Company of Europe.

[34] "Vers une société vulnérable?", Editorial, in: *Journal de Réflexion sur l'Informatique,* numero spécial, Namur, Institut d'Informatique, n° 6, juillet 1987. See also: Colette HOFFSAES, L'informatique dans l'organisation: changement ou stabilité?, in: *Sociologie du Travail,* n° 3, juillet-août 1978, pp. 280-301.

[35] Swedish SÅRK Report, *The Vulnerability of Computerized Society. Considerations and Proposals.* Stockholm 1979, Liberförlag. Presentation by Jan HOLVAST, IFIP-WG9.2 Meeting, 1989. See also, Jan HOLVAST, Vulnerability of Information Society: The Conflicting Demands of Security and Privacy, art.cit.

[36] Romain LAUFER, The Question of the Legitimacy of the Computer: An Epistemological Point of View, in: *The Information Society: Evolving Landscapes. Report from Namur,* J. BERLEUR, A. CLEMENT, T.R.H. SIZER & D. WHITEHOUSE, eds. An IFIP-WG9.2. Reader on Social Accountability of Computing and Telecommunication, Springer Verlag New York - Captus University Publications, 1990.

37 Romain LAUFER & Catherine PARADEISE, *Marketing Democracy: Public Opinion and Media Formation in Democratic Societies,* Transaction Books, New Brunswick, 1990 (English translation of *Le Prince Bureaucrate, Machiavel au pays du marketing,* Paris, Flammarion, 1982).

38 R. BASKERVILLE, Risk Analysis: An Interpretive Feasibility Tool in Justifying Systems Security, in: *European Journal of Information Systems,* 1991, vol 1. n 2, pp. 121-130. See also, same author: *Designing Information Systems Security.* Chichester: Wiley, 1988.

39 Max WEBER, *Economy and Reality,* New York, Bedminster Press, 1968.

40 Let us remember that Max WEBER was explaining different existing types of power in a given society.

41 Emmanuel KANT, *Critique de la raison pure,* Transl. of A. Tremesaygues and B. Pacaud, New edition, Paris, Presses Universitaires de France, 1944.
Auguste COMTE, *Cours de philosophie positive,* 1830-1842, 6 t., Paris, réed. Hermann 2 vol., 1975.
Herbert A. SIMON, *The Science of the Artificial,* MIT Press, Cambridge Mass., 1971.
A more extensive description of our theoretical background may be found in: Romain LAUFER & Catherine PARADEISE, From Natural Science to Cybernetic Science and to Artificial Intelligence (pp. 170-189 of Chap. 8, Pragmatism: The Formation of the Cybernetic Ideology, in: *Marketing Democracy: Public Opinion and Media Formation in Democratic Societies,* op.cit.)
See also, Romain LAUFER, The Question of the Legitimacy of the Computer: An Epistemological Point of View, in: *The Information Society: Evolving Landscapes. Report from Namur,* J. BERLEUR & al., op. cit., pp. 31-61.
Or, same author, Cybernetics, Legitimacy and Society, in: *Can Information Technology Result in Benevolent Bureaucracies?* , T.R.H. SIZER, L. YNGSTRÖM, J. BERLEUR & R. LAUFER eds., North-Holland, 1985, Proceedings of the IFIP-WG9.2 Namur Working Conference, January 3-6, 1985, pp. 29-41.
See also, Jürgen HABERMAS, *Raison et légitimité: Problèmes de légitimation dans le capitalisme avancé,* Paris, Payot, 1980. (*The Crisis of Legitimacy,* Boston: Beacon, 1973)

42 It can be shown that the crisis of the public sector coincides with the crisis of the Administrative Law Criterion and is at the basis of the distinction between what are referred to above as "the three periods".

43 The distinction between speculative and pure risk may be considered as closed with respect to the difference between banks and insurances.

44 The famous book of Herbert A. SIMON, *The Science of the Artificial,* op.cit., was translated into French as *La Science des systèmes.* More recently Simon extended the notion to a new field; see: Simon, H. A., Cognitive Science: the Newest Science of the Artificial, in: *Cognitive Science*, 1980, vol. 4, pp. 33-46

45 Let us recall the famous *Zero Growth* of the Club of Rome and the predictive value of Forrester's models!

46 One could also interpret this evolution by saying that leaving the deterministic and positivistic attitudes of the two previous periods based on pure linear causality, systems analysis tries to develop a kind of "circular causality" where complexity and uncertainty may be taken into account. The result is that interests are more focussed on the state and functioning of the system (see the importance of concepts like regulation, equilibrium, etc.). It may explain the predominance of modelling.

47 Alfred D. CHANDLER, *The Visible Hand,* The Belknap Press, Cambridge (Mass.), 1977.

48 Franck H. KNIGHT, *Risk Uncertainty Profit,* University of Chicago Press, 1971. See also, Jos LEYTEN, Paul KALFF and Thea WEYERS, *Kunsmatige Intelligentie: Vragen over Maatschappelijke Kansen, Risico's en Problemen* (Artificial Intelligence: Questions on Social Chance, Risks and Problems), STB-TNO Report to the Nederlands Organisatie voor Technologisch Aspectenonderzoek (NOTA), Apeldoorn, November 1987.

49 Benoît KUSTERS, L'évaluation des sytèmes informatiques en entreprise: quelques repères, in: *Journal de Réflexion sur l'Informatique,* n° 19, Namur mai 1991, pp. 4-12.

50 Daniel NAULLEAU, "Vulnérabilité et libertés", in: *Journal de Réflexion sur l'Informatique,* n° 17, Namur, juillet 1990, p.14.

51 ibid. p.12.

52 République Francaise, Sénat, Jacques THYRAUD, Rapport fait au nom de la commission des Lois constitutionnelles, de Législation, du Suffrage universel, du Règlement et d'Administration générale sur la proposition de loi adoptée par l'Assemblée nationale, relative à la *fraude informatique*, 1ère Session ordinaire 1987-88, Annexe au Procès-Verbal de la séance du 2.X.1987, doc. cit.

53 This is linked to the "theory of contracts with imperfect information".

54 L. BERKOWITZ, The Self, Selfishness, and Altruism, in: J. MACAULAY and L. BERKOWITZ eds., *Altruism and Helping Behavior,* New York, San Francisco and London: Academic Press, 1970, pp. 143-151.

55 "Capitalist development being based upon a high degree of division of labour and upon continuous processes of competitive innovation that call for ever avid consumers tends to cause a gradual erosion of the moral norms on which the effective functioning of the market rests." In: Jean-Philippe PLATTEAU, The Free Market is not Readily Transferable: Reflections on the Links Between Market, Social Relations and Moral Norms, Paper presented to the Silver Jubilee Conference at the University of Sussex, 1991. Namur, *Cahiers de la Faculté des Sciences Economiques et Sociales,* november 1991, p. 53. See also, A. ETZIONI, *The Moral Dimension - Towards a New Economics,* New York and London: The Free Press, 1988.

56 Romain LAUFER, The Question of the Legitimacy of the Computer: An Epistemological Point of View, in: *The Information Society: Evolving Landscapes. Report from Namur,* J. BERLEUR & al. eds, op. cit., p.59.

57 R. HIRSCHHEIM and S. SMITHSON, A critical Analysis of Information Systems Evaluation, in: *Proceedings of the IFIP-WG8.2 Working Conference,* 27-29 august 1989, North-Holland Publ.

58 ibid.

59 Jean-Louis le MOIGNE, "La science informatique va-t-elle construire sa propre épistémologie?", in: *Culture Technique,* n° 21, juillet 1990.

60 "Wisdom is glorious, and never fadeth away, and is easily seen by them that love her, and is found by them that seek her. She preventeth them that covet her, so that she first sheweth herself unto them. He that awaketh early to seek her, shall not labour: for he shall find her sitting at his door. To think therefore upon her, is perfect understanding: and he that watched for her, shall quickly be secure. For she goeth about seeking such as are worhty of her, and she sheweth herself to them cheerfully in the ways, and meeteth them with all providence." (Book of Wisdom, chapter 6, vv. 13-17, *The Holy Bible*, First published with the approbation of The Most Reverend Dr. Crolly, A new Edition with the approbation of the Cardinal Archbishop of Westminster, London: Burns and Oates Ltd, p. 543.

Education and Society / R. Aiken (Editor)
Information Processing 92, Volume II
Elsevier Science Publishers B.V. (North-Holland)


# Addressing Vulnerability and Privacy Problems generated by the Use of IT-Security Mechanisms

**Simone Fischer-Hübner[a], Louise Yngström[b] and Jan Holvast[c]**

[a] Faculty for Informatics, University of Hamburg, Vogt-Kölln-Straße 30, 2000 Hamburg 54, Germany

[b] Department of Computer and System Sciences, University of Stockholm and Royal Institute of Technology, Electrum 230, 16440 Kista, Sweden

[c] Jan Holvast, Stichting Waakzaamheid Persoonregistratie, Geldersekade 101, Postbus 711, 1000 AS Amsterdam, The Netherlands

**Abstract**

As systems become more and more complex, the system's vulnerability to all kinds of threats increases at the same time. Security mechanisms are often used to deal with the problem of vulnerability. Unfortunately, IT-security structures are often based on some misconceptions that are generally made. Besides, there is a conflict that security mechanisms on one hand can be used for fighting vulnerability and protecting personal data from misusage, but on the other hand mean an additional level of control and therefore endangers privacy. In this paper, these problems are discussed and an alternative holistic approach - technology, management and social structures together - to solutions that cope with vulnerability and that consider privacy interests at the same time, is presented.

## 1. INTRODUCTION

Recently a growing number of security violations, such as external system breakins by hackers and especially computer anomalies, such as viruses, worms or trojans, have been reported and have demonstrated the vulnerability of today's systems. With the trend of growing system complexity, systems are at the same time becoming much more vulnerable to all kinds of threats. Many economic and public organisations rely on the availability and the correct functioning of information systems as well as on data integrity and data secrecy. Threats to privacy through the misuse of personal data is also an aspect of vulnerability. Security mechanisms can help to protect against such kinds of threats.

Security mechanisms are only a part of the total measure that need to be taken when vulnerability is raising, as vulnerability is only for a part a technical problem. It is necessary to bear in mind that there ought to be many more disciplines but computer science involved in such a discussion [NCR 91,p.17].

The emphasis on technical security measures is caused by a number of usual misunderstandings and has the consequence that fighting vulnerability can lead to building fortresses in which freedom of people in general and privacy in special is disaproportiante invaded. On one side technical security mechanisms can help to protect from illegal disclosure or usage of personal data stored in a system and to guarantee privacy interests. But on the other side they also mean an additional level of control and thus a threat to privacy. We therefore need a combination of measures that respect privacy.

## 2. VULNERABILITY

The main conclusion of the report of the Swedish Sarbarhetskommitten [SARK 79] that 'vulnerability is unacceptably high in todays computerizd society' is affirmed by several studies in other countries (see [TDR 81] [GAO 82] [European Commission 84], [Coopers/Lybrand 88]). All these studies relate the problem of vulnerability to technical development in general and make clear that it is the result of increasing complexity of organization and technical systems. A system is defined as complex, when it is coupled to other systems or the volume of the system is extensive. Information technology is increasing vulnerability while it offers possibilities for collecting and storing more information, exchange of information and is responsible for a growing dependency on networks.

> *"Therefore, vulnerability can be defined as the state of a system in which complexity, in the sense of dependency, volume of data, centralisation, integration and interdependency, is so high that a small cause during a short time can have an enormous effect on the total environment of the system and on the system itself."* [Holvast 91]

Vulnerability is influenced by a lot of external and internal factors. The external factors are related to causes and attacks from outside the system: Acts of God (catastrophies, earthquakes), acts of people (criminal acts, hacking) and dependency of others (dependency on foreign sources, electricity, suppliers). The internal factors are organizational factors, such as lack of system documentation and system errors.

## 3. FIGHTING VULNERABILITY

Countermeasures in general are oriented towards the factors influencing vulnerability and not on vulnerability itself. That means that in general security mechanisms for fighting threats to a system's *confidentiality, integrity* and *availability* are used. Security criteria such as the American TCSEC [DoD 85] and also the European ITSEC [ITSEC 91] define different security classes for security means that could be taken for special applications. They are concentrated on dealing with confidentiality and neglect aspects of integrity or availability, although the last two aspects seem to be not less important for fighting vulnerability in commercial applications (see [Brunnstein/Fischer-Hübner 90]). So most security mechanisms in use are mechanisms to control the legality of the system usage to guarantee confidentialy. Mainly the following mechanisms are used:
**Identification and authentication mechanisms** are used to control the legitimate system usage and to identify a user so that her/his further actions will be controlable. **Discretionary and mandatory access controls** are used to control the accesses of subjects to objects in a system and often enforce formal security models such as the Bell LaPadula model [Bell LaPadula 76]. **Auditing and Monitoring** of unusual activities shall help to enforce user accountability. These measures shall detect and deter penetration of a system and reveal behaviour that identifies misuses.

For enforcing integrity the same or similar mechanisms are used. Integrity models such as the Biba-model [Biba 77] or Clark Wilson- model [Clark/Wilson 87] are not widely in usage and require also access control mechanisms for enforcement. Availability has not either traditionally been a topic of security research either and for its enforcement quite other techniques are used, such as for enforcing fault tolerance of a system, or organisational means, such as contingency planning.

Besides these mechanisms that are based on formal methods, new **heuristic methods for intrusion detection** has been developed during the last years. Real Time Intrusion Detection Expert Systems, that are based on Dorothy Denning's Intrusion Detection Model [Denning 86], can help to detect intrusions in real time. As these systems are based on the hypothesis that intrusions can be detected by statistical abnormal behavior and as this statistical method is independent of any particular system vulnerability, they are capable to detect new kinds of attack-strategies and generally undecideable security threats (e.g. viruses) that cannot be prevented by other security mechanisms. Besides, they also use so called a priori-rules that encode information about known vulnerabilities hacker-strategies.

## 4. UNRAVELLING SOME FREQUENT MISCONCEPTIONS

Vulnerability is a consequence of increasing complexity in organisational and technical systems - alone and in interaction with each other. In order to control organisations and their interacting IT systems sufficiently well and in real time some usual misconceptions will be enhanced.

**Misconception 1: Data and information is the same concept :**
Data is a message about an event at a certain time and date - a report to an automatic or a human decision maker. When used, data must fit into some sort of pattern or form. Many examples of file-merging show that automatic decisions were wrong because data itself was not the correct message about the event, even though data was presented in the correct format - and humans as decision makers would not have made the same mistakes [Nilsson 90]. This attribute is often referred to as quality of information/data and is touched upon in the definition of integrity as offered in the IDA-report: "Integrity denotes the goal of ensuring that data continues to be a proper physical and semantic representation of information, and that information processing resourses continue to perform correct processing operations" [IDA 90, p. 4]. The recieving process, human or automatic, must be facilitated with "enough" antecedents on (the context of) the information in order to judge if it is useful for decision making.

Few IT-security models of today offer the possibility for the recieving process to do this judgement - neither TCSEC nor ITSEC explicitly addresses this demand. Until measures of level of integrity or quality can be stated for IT systems, data from computers can be looked upon as rumors from an automat.

**Misconception 2: Humans as users of IT systems can, in broad, be treated in the same way :**
Humans perform different roles vis-a-vis IT-systems; as users: either employees of or customers to an organisation which uses IT-systems and as usees: a person which the IT-system produces and processes data about. Most studies on computer mis-uses or computer related crimes underlines this by agreeing to that at least 80% of inappropriate manipulations in computer systems are done by employees. On the other hand, most studies on participatory system design show positive effects for safe and secure EDP-processing as a result of user involvements. Human factors as inappropriate training, unlogical system design, insufficient work environment etc are all negative factors but non-intentional threats to IT-systems.

Thus: in order to deal with intentional threats, security systems must hinder the user as much as possible, and in order to deal with unintentional threats, security systems must aid the user as much as possible. In trying to cope with this contradiction, using the power of states and enterprises, privacy of individuals is violated. Data on users are treated as data on usees, a human who is personally affected by data collected, processed, stored and disseminated about her but who has no control of the processes. These matters are proposed to be dealt with within legal frameworks, but it is highly questionable whether this works.

**Misconception 3: Correct input generates correct output :**
Studies on how to minimise errors entering EDP systems show that 50% of all errors are inherited from other systems and thus cannot be corrected in receiving systems. Additionally, many input errors are due to human factors [Bailey 83]. And even if above stated could be waved away with references to human misunderstandings, the mere construction of a computer makes it impossible, since the von Neuman architecture can't solve complex problems in a completely controlled and at every time in excactly the same way. Viruses on von Neumann machines are examples for integrity threats that are generally not detectable. von Neumann discussed complexity vs. controllability and suggested using the concept of voting for solving this problem [von Neuman 56].

Since nothing a priori could be supposed about the correctness of input, throughput or output, a continious use of different inbuilt checks is needed in IT security systems. Some of these checks need to act intelligently to some extent, that is the security functions themselves must be able to modify their behaviour when circumstances call for it, as expressed more generally by Beer and more specifically in Denning's Intrusion Detection Model [Denning 86].

**Misconception 4: Security techniques raises the level of security - or it will be OK when we use crypto :**
Implemented security mechanisms need to be controlled - or "any system left uncontrolled, will go out

of control - and by means of going out of control, can it be brought back into control" [Schoederbek et al 90]. Control of security systems has to be seperately performed by EDP-auditing, since partly or falsely implemented security rather give a false picture of security.

**Misconception 5: IT security is primarily a concern for the administration of a company :**
It is true that security needs to be managed and administrated, but security itself -in its accepted definition of confidentiality, integrity and availability- is needed in production as well as in the administration. Most goods today are produced by IT systems - and many products contain IT elements. This implies that standards for specification of security enforcing mechanisms in IT-systems and -products are needed. The currently available structures TCSEC and ITSEC will together with forthcoming new structures affect every part of the IT and IT security business in the future - administration as well as development and production. To cope with this, security has to be handled by an holistic approach -technology, management and social structures together,that in turn has to involve many different groups of specialists. This is called for in the Computers at Risk-report [NRC 91].

## 5. VULNERABILITY AND PRIVACY

More than a century ago the privacy discussion started in the United States with the publication of the article 'The Right to Privacy' by Samuel D. Warren and Louis D. Brandeis. The reason for this publication was the development of new forms of technologies that was coupled with other developments. Photography in combination with the press, was in the view of the authors an attack on personal privacy in the sense of the right to be let alone. After this first discussion numerous articles on this subject appeared, all of them more or less in response to other develpoments of information technology: eavesdropping, hidden cameras, lie-detectors, computer, telecommunications networking , a.s.o. As a consequence the concept of privacy was broaded up and now generally is seen as - within limited boudaries - a person's seldetermination on her/his body, space, data, also defined as the bodily, spacely and informational dimension of privacy.

Informational self-determination was defined by the German Federal Constitutional Court in the so called 'Census Decree' in 1983 as the freedom of an individual to determine in principle on herself/himself on the disclosure and use of her/his personal information. In order to ensure informational self-determination, protection from illegal dissemination or misuse of data, from illegal collecting and storing of data and also from data-manipulation and use of incorrect data (to prevent infamation) have to be guaranteed.

Fighting vulnerability also means protection against illegal disclosure of personal information. Therefore privacy laws try to guarantee the right of privacy by enforcing technical safeguards. The Proposal of the European Commission [European Commission 90] specifies in Article 18 the requirement of appropriate technical and administrative measures, that protect personal data from accidental or illegal destruction, modification or loss and from illegal access. The German privacy protection law (BDSG: Bundesdatenschutzgesetz) also specifies in § 9 BDSG a general requirement of appropriate technical and administrive controls and lists in its enclosure specific technical safeguards that have to be taken. Also the Swedish and the Dutch laws include such requirements.

But using security mechanisms as the only solution for the vulnerability problem means in an information society more use of information technology. This technology is a control technology on system and people and is dimishing personal freedom or personal privacy. This leads to a conflict between the use of security mechanisms to guarantee privacy and the use of the control capability of security mechanisms that endangers privacy. By the development of nowadays information technology the bodily, spacely and informational dimensions of privacy are under attack, although the emphasis is on the informational dimension. When we are looking at the control mechanisms in use for fighting vulnerability, it is clear that the amount of control functions are increasing. The following examples demonstrate how security mechanisms endanger the privacy of the system's users, about whom personal data are collected and who therefore at the same time can be regarded as usees, and of other usees, that are not actively involved:

**Authentication mechanisms:**
The authentication process of a user and especially continuous authentication, such as through keystroke dynamics, produce information about the user's presence. Furthermore, if mechanisms, such as smartcards, are used as a ticket for an employee to enter certain security relevant areas, information about the employee's movements and relations to other employees can be collected.

**Discretionary and mandatory access controls:**
Discretionary access control mechanisms, as access control lists, require the storage and usage of information about the user's access rights. Mandatory secrecy and integrity access controls use security and integrity levels, that are attached to users and to objects. These access control information reveal personal information about the user's status. Furthermore, in order to attach a security or an integrity-level to an user, her/his trustworthiness has to be checked e.g. by observations. That means an additional limitation to the user's privacy sphere.

**Monitoring, Auditing and Intrusion Detection:**
Audit trails reveal information about the activities and behavior of the users. Furthermore, if activities of users with respect to other people (usees) are audited, the audit trails can also contain critical information about usees. For example, the german police is recently allowed to have online access to the German central traffic information system (ZEVIS). Some of these online accesses are audited in order to check their legality. These audit data do not only contain information about the request-activities of the policemen, they also reveal sensitive information about the car drivers that are observed by the police.

Monitoring of unusual and security relevant activities on a system through system status information also means a continous control of an user's actions.

Intrusion Detection Expert Systems that are based on Dorothy Denning's Intrusion Detection Model in order to detect statistical abnormal behavior produce and use statistical profiles, that store statistics about the behavior of subjects (e.g. users) with respect to objects. These statistics can be directly misused for employee performance control without any further analyzation [Denning et al. 87] [Fischer-Hübner/Brunnstein 89]. Recent studies shows that the knowledge of the existence of a computerized performance monitoring system may result in decrease of productivity, increase of stress and lower level of job-satisfaction [Irving et al. 86].

The need for this control for fighting vulnerability is seen so vital that a discussion about the dangers to privacy is scarely tolerated. However, use of one-sides technical mechanisms, based on misunderstandings, has the potential danger that we are leaping in a control society in which the defense of a in itself vulnerable information technology is taken for an excuse for extensive use of more information technology for control purposes. We have to look for alternative solutions for dealing with vulnerability, unless in fighting vulnerability we shall not create an even greater vulnerability caused by that chaos created by humans who will -in every way possible- strike back at the vulnerable systems.

## 6. TOWARDS IMPROVED SOLUTIONS: AN HOLISTIC APPROACH

To cope with this, vulnerability has to be handled by an holistic approach -technology, management and social structures together-, which in turn has to involve many different groups of specialists. For this approach we will esspecially point at the following solutions:

### a.) Educational Mechanisms

An holistic approach has succesfully been used in an one year academic programme in Security Informatics at the department of Computer Science and System Science at the University of Stockholm and the Royal Institute of Technology in Sweden. The programme is based on General Systems Theory GST and Cybernetics. The target group of the programme are IT-security managers, risks managers and EDP auditors [Yngström 83, 89]. A study in 1991 shows that previous students, now security professionals, consider GST and Cybernetics as an important and efficient base for assesment and understanding of security-relevant problems, work efficiency and effectiveness and continious learning within the field of security and IT-Security [Yngström 91]. Based on GST and Cybernetics it is possible to give this course even a more general base to offer the best countermeasures to vulnerability: information and understanding and -hopefully- wisdom to planners and practitioners of IT-security as well as to users and usees.

**b.) Legal Mechanisms**

Furthermore, special legal attention is needed [Fischer-Hübner/Brunnstein 89]:

**Restrictions for security purposes only:**

A basic principle of privacy is that it has to be prevented, that information of an individual obtained for one purpose has to be prevented from being used or made available for other purposes without the consent of the individual. This principle is guiding thr Swedish Data Protection Law since 1973 and was also formulated in the German census decree. The German privacy protection law in § 14 IV BDSG therefore restricts the use of personal data collected for privacy protection controls, back-up or operation maintainance only to those purposes.

**The right to be informed:**

Furthermore, according to another basic principle, also formulated in the German census decree, everybody, about whom personal data are stored has the right to be informed about the data that are stored, and about how these data are processed, as well as the right to have wrong data corrected and data, that are illegally stored, deleted. An user, whose activities are audited for security purposes shall at least have the right to control the collection of audit data referring to her/him and the information produced by them, unless this control has an influence on the security process. We take the postion that at least the kind of events being audited should be known.

For intrusion detection expert systems the question is raised, whether rules, that produce personal information out of audit data should be known by the users. Otherwise, they would not have the chance to control the correctnes of the produced personal data. On the other hand, if so called a priori-rules, that encode information about system-vulnerabilities and hacker-strategies, are known by the users, they wont be capable of protecting against such kinds of attacks any longer. Furthermore, these rules can also contain sensitive information about the system's vulnerabilities, e.g. about bugs or virus replication techniques - if rules for dynamic virus detection are used -, that should be kept secret, as otherwise it could be misused. Consequently users should just have the right to be informed about the kind of rules being used.

**Participation of the work council:**

According to the German "Betriebsverfassungsgesetz" the work council of a company ("Betriebsrat") must participate in the decision to introduce any system, that can be misused for monitoring performance. Arrangements, that were met without the participation of the work council are regarded as invalid. Therefore, security mechanism, that can be misused, must therefore be accepted by the work council.

**c.) Humane use of information technology**

Besides the legislative means to control the collection and use of personal data used by security mechanisms, legislative regulations for technical protection of that data are also needed [Fischer-Hübner/Brunnstein 89].

**Protection from illegal and unnecessary accesses:**

Security-relevant data, such as data in password-files and access right-databases, used for authentication and access control, have to be protected from illegal and unnecessary accesses. Access control information should be read only by the access control mechanism, and be altered only by the user, to that the information refer, or by a security administrator. Audit trail information should just be read by an auditor for security relevant analyzations only. For intrusion detection systems, further control mechanisms are needed, that restrict accesses to the profiles in the knowledge base. The auditor shall just have write-access to the knowledge base to influence the intrusion detection process by defining the statistical profiles. He/she should just have 'read-access to the knowledge base in cooperation with the work council. Only alarm messages should be accessible directly.

**Reaching anonymity inside a system through the use of aliases:**
Another approach to protect personal access control information or personal information in audit trails or intrusion detection profiles could be the use of aliases instead of real subject-names.

Formal anonymity inside a system could be reached by replacing the subject identifiers in the access control database (e.g. in access control lists or in process security level tables) by aliases. The replacement-function could be implemented by an encryption procedure. By implementing a mechanism for encrypting the subject- and object- patterns of the profiles, formal anonymity of the profiles of an intrusion detection system can be reached [Fischer-Hübner/Brunnstein 89]. Proper key management has to guarantee that the key is kept secret and can just be derived by an auditor in cooperation with the work council in case of an security alarm, that has to be analyzed in more detail (e.g. in order to unmask an intruder). The question, whether the access control lists or profiles still describe personal data, depends on the question, whether a reidentification of subject- and object-identifers and patterns is comparatively easy. This question in turn depends first of all on whether the encryption key can be considered as secret and on the additional knowledge, that could be known and used by an potential attacker for reidentification. In any case, the problem of reidentification has to be carefully analyzed from case to case.

**d.) Development and usage of mechanisms other than checking of access rights:**
Besides security mechanisms based on the checking of access rights, we need mechanisms to enforce the two neglected aspects of security: integrity and availability. These mechanisms should be designed, in a way that they do not excert control of users or usees. Especially for fighting integrity threats other kinds of models and mechanisms , that consider, amongst others, the semantics of stored data should be developed.

## 7. CONCLUSIONS

More than in the past vulnerability itself as a consequence of complex structures must be studied and not only the details influencing vulnerability. Only then it will be possible to grasp vulnerability in an holistic oriented way without violating privacy in an unacceptable way.

## 8. REFERENCES

**[Bailey 83]** R.W. Bailey, "Human Error in Computer Systems", Prentice Hall, 1983

**[Bell Lapadula 76]** D.E.Bell, L.J.LaPadula, "Secure Computer System: Unified Exposition and Multics Interpretation", Mitre Corporation, Bedford, Mass., January 1976

**[Biba 77]** K.J.Biba, "Integrity Considerations for Secure Computer Systems", USAF Electronic Systems Division, Bedford, Mass., April 1977

**[Brunnstein/Fischer-Hübner 90]** K. Brunnstein, S. Fischer-Hübner, "Risk Analysis of 'Trusted Computer Systems'", IFIP/Sec'90 Conference-Proceedings, Helsinki, May 1990.

**[Clark/Wilson 87]** D.D.Clark, D.R.Wilson, "A Comparison of Commercial and Military Computer Security Policies", Proceedings of the IEEE Symposium on Security and Privacy, 1987

**[Coopers/Lybrand 88]** "A consolidated report of case findings", Rep. No.2, Coopers&Lybrand, 1988.

**[DoD 85]** Department of Defense, Trusted Computer System, Evaluation Criteria, Washington, 1985.

**[European Commission 84]** Commission of the European Communities, Information Task Group, "The Vulnerability of the Information Consious Society, European Situation.", 1984.

**[European Commission 90]** Commission of the European Communities, Proposal for a standardization of the privacy laws of the member states, 1990.

**[Denning 86]** D. Denning, "An Intrusion Detection Model", Proceedings of the 1986 Symposium on Security and Privacy, IEEE Computer Society 1986.

**[Denning et al. 87]** D.Denning, P.Neumann, D.Parker, "Social Aspects of Computer Security", Proceedings, 10th National Computer Security Conference, Baltimore, 1987.

**[Fischer-Hübner/Brunnstein 89]** S.Fischer-Hübner, K.Brunnstein, "Opportunities and Risks of Intrusion Detection Expert Systems", Proceedings of the IFIP TC-9/GI Conference ORAIS'89, Hamburg July 1989.

**[GAO 81]** U.S. General Accounting Office, "Federal Information Systems remain Highly Vulnerable to Fraudulent, Wasteful, Abusive, And Illegal Practices", Report, Masad. 82-88, April 21, 1981.

**[Herschberg/Paans 85]** I.S Herschberg, R. Paans, "The High Mortality of Data", in: JB. Grimson and H.-J. Kugler (eds), Computer Security, the practical issues in a Troubled World, North-Holland, 1985

**[Holvast 91]** J.Holvast, "Vulnerability of Information Society, The Conflicting Demands of Security and Privacy", in: Clarke/ Cameron (Eds.), Managing Information Technology's Organisational Impact, North-Holland, 1991.

**[IDA 90]** E.Roskos et al., "Integrity in the Department of Defense Computer Systems", prepared for NCSC, IDA Paper P-2316, Institute for Defense Analysis, Alexandria, Virginia, July 1990.

**[Irving et al. 86]** R.H. Irving, C.A. Higgins, F.R. Safayeni, "Computerized Performance Monitoring Systems: Use and Abuse", Communications of the ACM, 1986, Vol.29, No.8.

**[ITSEC 91]** Information Technology Security Evaluation Criteria, Provisional Harmonised Criteria, June 1991.

**[NCR 91]** "Computer at Risk. Safe Computing in the Information Age, System Security Study", Committee Computer Science and Telecommunications Board, Commission on Physical Sciences, Mathematics, and Applications, National Research Council, National Academy Press, 1991.

**[von Neumann 56]** J. von Neumann, "Probabilistic Logics and the Synthesis of Reliable Organisms from Unreliable Components", in Automata Studies (ed Shannon / McCarthy), Princeton University Press, 1956

**[Nilsson 90]** P. Nilsson, "Information Quality - An analysis of quality aspects of information used in problem solving", thesis for licensium, Dept. of Computer and system Sciences, University of Stockholm and Royal Institute of Technology, Stockholm 1990.

**[SARK 79]** "The Vulnerability of Computerized Society", Considerations and Proposals, Liberförlag, 1979.

**[Schoderbek et al. 90]** P.Schoderbek, Ch.Schoderbek, A.Kefalas, "Management Systems. Conceptual Considerations", Business Publ. Irwing-Dorsey, London 4th ed 1990.

**[Solarz 1985]** A.Solarz: "Datateknik och brottslighet", Forskningsenheten, Stockholm 1985 (1985:3)

**[TDR 81]** "OECD Workshop Stresses Dependency on Computers",Transnational Data rep., Vol.4,May1981,3-4

**[Yngström 83]** L.Yngström, "Education in Safety Systems and Security Analysis - Suggestions for a one year university program in Fak", V (ed) Security, IFIP/SEC'83, North-Holland, Amsterdam, 1983.

**[Yngström 89]** L.Yngström, "Experiences from a one-year Academic Programme in Security Informatics", in: W. Caelli (ed): Computer Security in the Age of Information, North Holland, 1988.

**[Yngström 91]** L.Yngström, "Security Informatics 1985-1991, An Assesment", SIIS Report, Dept. of Computer and System Sciences, Stockholm University and Royal Institute of Technology, 1991

Education and Society / R. Aiken (Editor)
Information Processing 92, Volume II
Elsevier Science Publishers B.V. (North-Holland)


# Human Factors In Computer Security

Ibibia Dabipi, Husam Yaghi, and Issam Qasem[a]

[a]Electrical Engineering Department, Southern University, Baton Rouge, Louisiana 70813

## Abstract:

The problem of network security has existed from the inception of communication networks. While the objectives of computer networks were primarily resource sharing and the reduction of costs, there remained the problem of unauthorized access. For example, the threats to privacy of individual records become a great problem. These threats may originate from hackers, eavesdroppers or criminals whose intentions for whatever reasons probably will result in loss of data, falsification of records through fraudulent means and blackmail due to access to unauthorized information.

While managing a computer data center for several years, the authors investigated, monitored, and researched computer security of all possible forms. They played the roles of managers and hackers. At the end, they began to publish their findings. In this paper they will illustrate several important computer and computer network security issues which they encountered. Human factors governing these issues of concern are discussed.

Keyword Codes: K.4.0; K.4.2; K.6.5
Keywords: Computers and Society, General; Social Issues; Security and Protection

## 1. INTRODUCTION:

Computer Security can be broadly categorized into three major areas:

I. Physical Network Security:

While network physical security issues resolve around installation of barriers and other safety devices to prevent total loss of information and equipment, other measures or procedures to limit access by security managers are usually instituted. However for large networks these measures are isolated at the node sites where major equipment resides.

Transmission of data over the network could be via satellite disk, copper wire, coax cable, microwave link of fiber optic cables. Each of the above mentioned communication links have their drawbacks and as such pose a problem toward network security. For satellite communication, the satellite channel of interest is accessible to all points within the coverage area thus presenting itself as an easily interceptable target within the coverage area. The key to targeted interception of any given signal of interest is to know which satellite and transponder channel frequencies are of interception. For a microwave system, an interceptor needs only to know technical information about the transmitter and this is easily obtained through information made public by the United States Federal communication Commission or its equivalent agency in foreign countries. Cables such as coaxial cables and copper wires (twisted pair cables) are easily tapped into. On the other hand, fiber optical cable requires a more elaborate scheme before a signal can be intercepted. It is now possible to listen to communication through fiber without being able to interrupt the signal by using a simple device and knowledge oflightwaves technology. Physical access controls such as modems with call back features are used to verify callers identity and improve security. Some modems are programmable so that only authorized users can dial in.

II. Logical Access Control:

Logical access controls are usually software driven. Their role is to provide a method for identifying and verifying authorized users and may also be required to limit users to use only the resources required to perform the assigned job functions. Such access controls can effectively maintain network security by selectively providing grant/revoke authorization over all accesses and access levels, and document violations. In some cases, as in file encryption software, the host file encryption software transforms incoming information by using some mathematical algorithm, thus providing a ciphertext which is the protected form of the information. This process is accompanied by a secret key which is used to recover the information by the authorized party.

From an authentication view point, logical access controls work with the operating system to secure data and resources by evaluating the authorization code of the intended user through password validation. These software packages limit the number of trials and generate records to show number of trials and failures.

III. Network Organizational Security:

The broad area of management or organizational security include such things as operational control, application development, workstation control and personnel control. Issues such as error control and error recovery and input/output media control are functions that fall under the category of operational control. When not managed properly, the system and network reliability can be brought to question. Another aspect of the management security issue is the introduction of adequate measures such as organizational standards that will guide the application developers within the organization to acquire only tools that meet organizational standards. When products are locally developed, then a procedure for documentation will ensure that modifications can be easily accomplished even when the developer no longer works with the company.

Rigorous change procedures help ensure the verification of authorization, thus limiting the threat to security. Other issues such as data integrity requirements, auditing requirements and fault isolation requirements to name a few fall into the application development and operational control areas.

Personnel controls have been seen to mean controls such as appropriate hiring procedures, controlling vacations, job rotations, and restricting employee accounts and following complete termination procedures. Most of the functions are currently beeing performed using some form of artificial intelligence (AI) software which incorporates the security procedure preferred by an organization based on its application. These AI applications can be developed to perform intelligent dynamic analysis of system activity to detect infractions. Intrusion detection with AI is based on the fact that a security violation involves abnormal use of the system and this can be checked by detecting abnormal patterns of system usage. Reports generated by these methods are often studied by security officers or auditors whose task is to conduct a detailed study of those reports and point out issues of concern.

The human aspects of network security which have received little attention in the literature. Most often security issues have focused on technological advances in the physical and logical access control measures with little emphasis on the human interface. The assumption here is that once a system is intelligent and/or physically inaccessible, it presents a greater problem for an intruder. Usually, however, intruders originate externally or internally. Externally, most measures addressed in physical and logical access controls will suffice. However, a knowledge of the operating system and thus the pitfalls or security measures can be obtained mostly by an inside intruder.

## 2. HUMAN INTERFACE ISSUES IN COMPUTER SECURITY:

Recent studies have shown that the external threat to security is limited to about two percent while ninety eight percent come from within. Among the ninety eight percent, sixty percent are intentional intruders while thirty eight percent intrude out of negligence or misuse of the system and resources.

The motives for computer crime can be broken into two categories:

Category I:

This category includes motives such as self-challenge, game playing, curiosity, money, career criminology and a disgruntled employee to name a few. The issue of self-challenge comes into play when an individual challenges the limit of his/her understanding of computer systems. Usually, the motivation here is to either establish self-confidence or an awareness of capabilities. When applied to the security of the system, the person may not always be driven by malice or the desire to break a system, but by the desire to break and restore system security operation without detection. There are various reasons why such tasks are undertaken and the background of such attackers is not limited to software developers, writers, or any particular social group.

The underlying factor, however, is that the person or persons are proficient in their method of attack. The end result of these action usually is the acknowledgment of self-limitations or the establishment of self-confidence levels.

With game playing, the original intent of the intruder is to deceive the targeted system. This objective is achieved through various means, one of which is to first enhance one's knowledge of the system. This process takes the form of casual communication with the system users, execution of programs that would assist the system in revealing information that otherwise would not be possible to obtain. This may lead to a method of mimicking system operation, thus invoking unauthorized levels of clearance that will eventually lead to violation of network security. Another approach may deal with intentional change of passwords by legitimate system users who pretend then to have forgotten their new passwords such that the system revokes their privileges. They can then go back to revalidate their ID's since they are legitimate users and through the frequency of such occurrences determine the process of password validation and creation. One can also use an already logged-on system operator's privilege to command the system beyond one's authorization.

A curious intruder, on the other hand, starts off with finding alternate methods of doing things on the system to enhance his own productivity by means of shortcuts or modification of commands to achieve a desired objective. As one's proficiency increases, the person attempts to understand how and why events occur in a given manner. This action usually leads to accidental discoveries of system logical access control techniques and eventually, intentionally or unintentionally, violate system security. This type of computer criminal is psychologically a dreamer who is more interested in the "what if" situations. He is always in search of new knowledge whether it is constructive or destructive. The career criminal has only one intention and that is to destroy. This person is guided by only the desire to be a bandit. The motives for destroying systems or violating security could be just for fun, financial, or revenge. Such a person is usually never satisfied and can go to the extremes to achieve the objective. Incorporated in the one's personality are self-challenge, curiosity, game-playing, and greed. The danger of such a person is that he/she is very methodical and can evade most of the physical access control schemes. Since logical access controls are usually designed to deal mostly with abnormal activities, the career criminal normally exercises patience until a better understanding of the system is obtained before initiating an attack.

Category II:

In this category, we are dealing with indirect violations which are triggered accidentally, through negligence, software bugs and by the environment. An example of accidental would be the case where a user executes an authorized user command to perform an intended task without paying close attention to the associated parameters of access level. This may result in loss of data or corruption of part of the system. There could also be a question of data integrity or production of a wrong key for deciphering and encrypt information. Negligence can take the form of a user simply leaving the workstation unattended. This could influence/assist a hacker to gain access to unauthorized information which could be used to achieve a desired objective. Negligence also covers the act of disposal of information without taking the proper means of dealings with different classes of information (sensitive or ordinary information.)

Undetected programming errors are sources of software bugs which could lead to system corruption and loss of data. It could also be a logical error, thus affecting system utilization.

Finally, the environmental aspect of computer security violation covers all possible types of natural disasters and inadequate facilities that will affect computer performance or system software and data. While category II issues are important, they are easily resolved either through logical access or physical access controls and will not be the focus of this paper. Incidences in this category fall within the thirty eight percent of all network security violations.

## 3. MANAGERIAL ISSUES IN NETWORK SECURITY:

Designers of security systems usually analyze an adversary problem where the designer and the opponents think out independently their strategies. The focus of this section will be on the human factors as they affect an organization. Although the design of an optimum system requires relative measures which are cost dependent, the key is to consider the security threats of the sixty-eight percent of hackers who are usually within the organization. It is quite obvious that they are legitimate users and have a better understanding of the system function, organizational structure and access procedures. Therefore they are not limited by the physical access controls employed by the organization. We can now speculate on who they are and what could be and their degree of freedom and level of threat to the organization. Lets take the case of a dishonest system developer who will provide hooks or patches in the software to assist in later attack. These developers can in tern introduce viruses or modify the software to generate the desired effect regardless of the operating system. The severity of such hooks can be very great depending on the application of the developed software. As a financial package, it could lead to undetected fraud. In the case of a security auditor who is responsible for reviewing the reports generated by the logical access controls, if he is the attacker, then not only is he studying his success rate, but he is also not informing his supervisor about his findings concerning his personal activities. He may be acquiring new knowledge about the system and if left unchecked could be a great threat to the network. It is the basic assumption that people in such positions are honest and are therefore loosely managed.

Sometimes network security is compromised as a result of the value judgment of the managers. What he sees as a small risk may actually turn out to be a very big risk due to underestimation of other factors affecting such decisions.

## 4. RECOMMENDATIONS:

This paper is intended to bring attention to the human aspect of computer security and although the readers will come up with other preventive measures which would address their needs, here are a few recommendations.

First, consider everyone including the management as a possible threat to security and devise a scheme of checking the validity of your assumption. This process should include the management and security personnel. Identifying a check and balance system where management sees the security personnel as a threat while the reverse is true. It should be noted that the group must first consider the overall objective that such a technique is healthy to the reliability and integrity of the system. Therefore they can see their actions as not one of cooperation between management and security personnel but one of think, counter-think.

Secondly, there should be a randomization of security access levels such that they are geared toward maintaining minimum access required to perform a designated assignment at any given time. This provides for the withdrawal of higher level clearance when it is required by an individual in the organization. It also can be reissued when such clearance becomes necessary.

Thirdly, there should be distributed management scheme where pieces of the required information are not within a given location. Duplication should be minimized and the process should be such that the information can be system triggered. If the information is within a given location, then the identity and security responsibilities of the associated personnel should not be in the public domain. Furthermore this information should be cryptographic.

Finally with the possibility that the security auditor might be the hacker, there should be a random rotation such that the new officer can be in a position to detect previous patterns. As rotations occur, levels of access should immediately be modified accordingly.

## 5. REFERENCES:

1. Davies and Price, Security for Computer Networks, John Wiley & Sons, 1984.
2. Rein Turner, Advances in Computer System Security, Vol. I, II, III, Artech House, 1988.
3. NATO Advanced Study Institute on the Challenge of Advanced Computing Technology to System Design Methods, University of Durham, 1985.
4. William Perry, Management Strategies for Computer Security, Butterworth Publishing, 1985.
5. Lance Hoffman, Modern Methods for Computer Security and Privacy, Prentice-Hall, 1977.
6. August Bequai, Computer Crime, Lexington Books, 1978.
7. I. Douglas, Audit and Control of Systems Software, NCC Publications, 1983.
8. Denise Donnely, The Computer Culture, Dickinson University, 1985.
9. Thomas Logsdon, Computers and Social Controversy, Computer Science Press, 1980.
10. Jan Chaiken, Varieties of Criminal Behavior, Rand Co., 1982.

Education and Society / R. Aiken (Editor)
Information Processing 92, Volume II
Elsevier Science Publishers B.V. (North-Holland)



# HOW VULNERABLE IS INFORMATION SOCIETY ? A SOCIOLOGICAL APPROACH

Drs. Ryan Tewari

Managing Consultant of the Organization Consultancy Unit, Synergie Consultancy B.V., Amsterdam, The Netherlands.

**Abstract**
In this paper three dominant approaches in the study of information society are examined. These views have one assumption in common: their firm belief in technology as crucial to societal developments. The approaches prove that sociological analysis is urgent. Sociological theory provides us the mechanisms of social analysis. We also show how we come to the identification of the vulnerability of information society.

Keyword Codes: J.4;K.4.2
Keywords: Social and Behavioral Sciences;Social Issues

## 1.INTRODUCTION

Vulnerability defined as a potential weak spot can be found very easy in the information society. Some authors stress the danger of invading privacy and the brokerage of sensitive data (legal issues). Other stress the change in job structure due to factory and office automation technologies. Especially the strong influence of information technology colours information society just as the machine technology did in the rise of the industrial era. But vulnerability occurs on different levels of analysis and should be approached accordingly. After a brief expose on how we (do not) view the concept of information society, we discuss three leading approaches to information society and relate them to a framework of vulnerability analysis. The basic message is, that this analysis depends on the approach adopted to study information society, as will be illustrated in this paper.

## 2. INFORMATION SOCIETY: CHANGING SOCIETAL DEVELOPMENTS IN HUMAN HISTORY ?

Information society is a relatively new organizational concept in the analysis of society. There have been different explanations of how it started and how it developed. These are mostly discussions on historical and technical roots of this phenomenon. Several authors use various concepts to define a society in which information technology is dominant: computer age, global village, robot society, control society, information age and so on. Information technology undoubtly is the

key 'defining technology' of this era. One of the most biased definitions is the one posed by Masuda:
"A society that grows and develops around information, and brings about a general flourishing state of human intellectual creativity, instead of affluent material consumption" (Masuda, 1990). We propose the following definition: **information society is a societal type, in which a societal transformation has taken place, dominated by (the products of) information technology, giving rise to a changed set of social, political and economic relations.** Like every social phenomenon, there are mechanisms to cope with its specific problems.
Studying vulnerability also depends on the approach adopted to study information society ('idealism', 'technicism', or 'control'). In this respect David Lyon rightly posed the following question when discussing the information society (Lyon, 1991): "..Does IT bring about a new society without precedent, or does it rather help to intensify certain processes of today's society of which we are all too aware".

## 3. WHAT APPROACHES ARE THERE TO ASSESS THE VULNERABILITY OF INFORMATION SOCIETY ?

We present three dominant views: the technological Approach (Blauner, Ellul), the Control Approach (Beniger), and the Futurist Approach (Masuda).

### 3.1. The technological Approach

The concept of information society suffers from technological determinism. Advocates of this approach state that new technology will bring about a transformation in society. Technocratic planning and other 'technological guidance' will prevail in all aspects of life. Furthermore, technocratic evolution will further social progress and reform. Lyon refers to two common beliefs about social impact of IT from this point of view: (a) a total societal transformation is predicted; (b) this transformation is a generally good and progressive movement. Blauner sees automation as a efficient pattern of cooperation contrary to division of labour as one key element of social relations. "Automation restores meaningfullness" (Blauner in Francis, 1989). This technological determinism perspective is being strenghtened through the theory and practice of teleworking, datacommunications, networking with national and international databases etc. (See Beniger,1986; Lyon, 1991).

### 3.2 The Control Approach

This approach asserts, that there is a market for information as there is for capital or labour. It also asserts, that everything in societal developments has its origin in an urge for control (or power to manage). The control approach sees the control revolution as the latest struggle for control in society. Beniger introduces control society: "a complex of rapid changes in the technological and economic arrangements by which information is collected, stored, processed, and communicated, and through which formal and programmed decisions might effect societal control" (Beniger, 1986). He distinguishes 4 levels of control: (1) Life (Molecular programming); (2) Culture (Learning by imitation); (3) Bureaucracy (Commercial/Industrial revolution); and (4) Technology (Control revolution: computer, microprocessors, genetic programming technology. The control of societal forces in society will be supported by information technology and its control mechanisms.

### 3.3 The Futurist Approach

Finally, information society is seen from a **idealistic** and futuristic point of view (Masuda). In this view, information society will have its drawbacks, but will be proceeded by a voluntary community society: the voluntary community will be the core of the social structure. Technology facilitates new social relations and creates a global and open information structure with no conflict of interests.
"Information revolution will bring about not only the transformation of society, but the transformation of man himself, the genesis of human species." Masuda, associates the information society with "a society in which the cognitive creativity of individuals flourishes throughout society".

### 3.4 The approaches compared

When discussing these approaches we cannot refrain from relating the futurist approach as one that believes in progress through rationality and cooperation. Herbert Simon taught us an essential lesson: man suffers from 'bounded rationality' and 'opportunism'. People also do have conflicting interests and act accordingly when the occasion arises. History has shown us various examples of this type of human behaviour. Man will remain unperfect and dubious. According to Masuda, Simon's view was that of a homo sapiens (modern man). Masuda approaches man as a 'homo intelligens'. What these views have in common is their firm belief in technology and its centrality over human life. **My thesis is, that information society has been made possibble, beceause socio-cultural conditions facilitated this.** It is not technology that determines societal developments. It is culture that places fundaments of research and development boundaries in social and industrial life. Mankind exploits the fruits of technological advancement for several (un)legitimate purposes. It cannot be denied that technology has developed rapidly (see the practice of home-banking and teleworking). But technology is not the sole determining factor in society. The information society is the result of reinforced synergy between the social conditions of comtemporary society and technological innovations.
Still, the presented approaches reflect a different aspect of the 'truth' about information society . Therefore, when studying social and technical aspects, we prefer to follow the **socio-technical systems approach**. This paper does not go further into the theoretical backgrounds of this perspective. The socio-technical approach sees a social arrangement as an open system with social and technical subsystems, that should be studied together.

## 4. HOW TO ANALYSE THE VULNERABILITY OF INFORMATION SOCIETY

Vulnerability can be analyzed on 3 societal levels: (1) Macro (society as a whole),(2) Meso (institutional/ /organizational), and (3) Micro (individual or small groups). The three early-mentioned views on information society can be analyzed and put into this framework of analysis. This approach enables us to cope with existing findings on this topic and group them in a systematic way.

### 4.1 Macro-level vulnerablity

This level refers to the overall societal analysis of the information society. Although it refers to society as a whole, we also extend it to the views presented hereafter, whereby the international dimension is being considered. On this level all three approaches coincide with each other. According to the control approach, society will be shaped by "the progressive convergence of all information technologies - mass media, telecommunications, and computing-, in a single infrastructure of control at the most macro level. Masuda speaks of a global information utility: this is a (even international) global information infrastructure using a combination of computers, networking and satellites. The concept is based on complete and equal access to all types of data, one requires for personal and business uses. Lyon recognizes its vulnerability: such a global 'village' exists through domination and exploitation (or imperialism in Lyon's words). Furthermore, what about the imposed standards on or denied progress in the relations with the Third World ? Lyon calls this global information society a pathetically hollow concept. Like any other societal type, information society has its own 'haves', or should we state, 'know' or 'know nots' and persistence of class-based relations. As class struggle existed from the materialistic perspective, the chance of a struggle for information can also occur (Toffler,1990).

### 4.2 Meso-level vulnerability

Analyzing the organizational or institutional vulnerabilities of information society, we face the phenomenon of 'interorganizations': organizational networks of information transactions. This occurs on all institutional levels (both on state as private organizational level). Information increases in volume and size and result in a greater market share for organizations. Knowlegde of information is crucial. But knowledge is not power: as Lyon states, the knowledgable are not powerful. Control of and access to information is a crucial medium of domination. Beniger states, that one could associate the technocrats, technocratic rationality, and decison making with the thrive for control. But there are different types of control and therefore different types of organizational arrangements in society. Control problems therefore, depend on the type of control: metering, labour relations, union structure and power (how to meter individual efforts, avoid free rider problems, deviance from technocratic rules and procedures). There will always be people who employ others for their own benefit, conflict will exist and may vary from the control type exerted (Francis,1989).

What we face now is the rise of a new elite in information society. This is the group of **infocrats**: these are the fruits of the fact, that information is being strongly objectivated. The infocrats are mediators of information (products), serve as owner and broker in a information society with the following classes: information producers ( technocrats, scientists), information processors (consumers, clercks, analysts), information distributors (retailers of information), and those operating in the (service of) information structure (see 'Information Activities, Electronics and telecommunications Technologies, Impact on employment, Growth and Trade, OECD Report of 1980). Infocrats serve as the information (product) dominated society. We face them nowadays in the large data oriented corporations as Graydon, Dun & Bradstreet, Reuters, Heli View IDC etc.
Alvin Toffler has exposed some tactics, that any dominant group in the business of information can apply. The infocrats will use so-called infotactics (preprocessing or any kind of manipulation of information as Toffler calls it). They can also resort to metatactics or manipulating not the access but the contents of information. Of all kinds of elites in current society, infocrats are currently the **dominant elite**. The reason for this is the gradual shift in dominance from technology to information (partly its product) in the information society.

### 4.3 Micro-level vulnerability

An individual's life has always been 'treathened' by (technological) progress in time. But man cannot innovate himself continuously. Social deprivation will also occur here, as there will be social 'victims' of any social arrangement. As societal requirements change, new patterns of social relations emerge. Like computers, man cannot expand its capabilities with software and/or hardware. Man can respond differently to these effects. Also, man can opt out of the big system or even resort to violence or other forms of protests. In order to prevent this behaviour, private and state agencies will try to control the individual and thereby resort to store data on people's movements. Supporters of technological determinism argue that the 'electronic cottage' (e.g. homeworking/teleworking) will restore the individual's autonomy and give more free time to workers. They minimize the role of social contact even with advanced technology. The control approach argues that man will be used, for "the more objective capacity of their brains to store and process information". Thus, we face exploitation of man in a different way ! The futurists on the other hand, see man evolve from a homo sapiens to homo intelligens: cleverness and shrewdness were modern man's features. We can rightly ask ourself if man can adjust his social arrangements in dealing with information society? In a summary we group the preceeding levels into the following scheme:

| VULNER. LEVELS | SUBJECT OF ANALYSIS | TYPICAL FEATURES | VULNERABLE ASPECTS |
|---|---|---|---|
| MACRO | Society as a whole | Control society<br>Multi-centered complex society<br>Global networks | Dominant groups<br>Conflict of interests,only for advanced society |
| MESO | Organizations or Institutions | Voluntary communities, Functional relations, Information infrastructure | Exploitation<br>Problems of metering<br>Infocrats |
| MICRO | Individuals or Small groups | Autonomy<br>Homo intelligens | Deviant behaviour<br>Protest<br>'Know nots' |

This paper calls for thorough sociological analysis of the information society; not by simply embroidering on the existing approaches as demonstrated above. The paper serves as an eye-opener for those interested in the applcation of existing social theory concerning information society. In fact, this society as the object of sociological study calls for a interdiciplinary social science in which sociology and other behavioural sciences are part of. Further research is necessary into the social structure of the information society, thereby revealing its stratification, mobility aspects, power structure, social changes and aspects of vulnerability.

## 5. REFERENCES

1. J. Beniger, The Control Revolution: Technological and Economic Origins of the Information Society, Cambridge, Massachusetts, 1986.
2. P.A. Cornelis,J.van Oorschot, Automatisering met een menselijk gezicht (Automation with a human face),Deventer, 1986.
3. A. Francis, New Technology at Work, Oxford,1989.
4. Information Activities, Electronics and Telecommunications Technologies, Impact on employment, Growth and Trade, OECD Report of 1980.
5. H. Johnson, Social Problems of Urban Man, Illinois, 1973.
6. B.S. Kleinberg, American Society in the postindustrial age: Technocracy, Power, and the end of Ideology,Ohio,1973.
7. D. Lyon, The Information Society: Issues and Illusions, Oxford, 1988.
8. Y. Masuda, Managing the Information Society, Cambridge, Massachusetts, 1990.
9. S. Parker, R. Brown,J. Child,M. Smith, The Sociology of Industry, London, 1972.
10. A. Toffler, Powershift: knowledge, wealth, and violence at the edge of the 21st century, New York, 1990.
11. T. Treu, The Technology Debate (II), The Impact of New Technologies on Employment, working conditions and industrial relations, in: 'Labour & Society', Vol.9, nr.2, p. 109-135, April-June,1984.
12. T. Wentink, H. Zanders, Kantoren in Actie (Offices in Action), Deventer, 1985.

Education and Society / R. Aiken (Editor)
Information Processing 92, Volume II
Elsevier Science Publishers B.V. (North-Holland)


# Responsible scientists - a social-constructivist approach

Marc van Lieshout, Mieke Massink

Department of Informatics, Faculty of Mathematics and Informatics, University of Nijmegen, P.O. Box 9010, 6500 GL Nijmegen, The Netherlands

**Abstract**
Information technology is a prime mover of societal changes. The way we see and use information technology in bringing about these changes still reflects the ideology of the Enlightenment, which advocated an optimum control over our surroundings. The predominant moral position in judging these developments is best described by what is called the teleological attitude: we judge our acts by the effects they produce. In this paper this ethical position is compared with the current predominant scientific view of the world. The paper then continues with a critical confrontation of this view with contemporary insights, known as the social-constructivist approaches. It is argued that assessing the role of information technology in society from a social-constructivist point of view offers better opportunities for debate about responsible behaviour of scientists.

Keyword Codes: K.4.2; K.7.0
Keywords: Computers and Society, Social Issues; The Computing Profession, General

## 1. INTRODUCTION

Today, the scientific world experiences a revival of the debate about science and ethics. The past decade, characterized by unreflected technological and economical progress, has turned into a more critical stance towards the 'merits' of this progress. The computer revolution that started in the sixties, has not reached its end yet, and will without any doubt continue changing the world in unforeseen and unpredictable ways. The changes that occurred so far, certainly have not all been for the better. Computer scientists see a world that is changing as a result of their activities, while they seem to have lost control over the developments. Therefore there is a need to reconsider our responsibilities. Paraphrasing Paul Valéry, we should reflect on the following: "Can the human mind master what the human mind has made?" [1]

Sociologists and historians have developed new ideas about the functioning of science and technology within society. In this paper we will try to incorporate their views into the debate on responsibility, thus offering opportunities to tackle some of the dilemmas that surround the problem of responsible behaviour. We start this paper with two illustrations of well-known computer scientists that have taken position in this debate, and, after elaborating on the alternative approach to the backgrounds of the scientific enterprise, we shall return to the relevance of the different approaches for the debate about responsible behaviour of scientists.

## 2. PROFESSIONAL RESPONSIBILITY

### 2.1 Working for the military

David Parnas has become a well-known critic of the Strategic Defense Initiative. Though initially belonging to the inner circle of advisors to the Pentagon, Parnas decided to resign after having attended only one meeting of an advisory panel on software aspects of Star Wars. His very own views about professional conduct guided his decision to get off. [2] In short, Parnas, considers himself as fully responsible for his own actions. Secondly, tasks to be performed should be of benefit to society, and should solve real problems. Finally, it should be clear that the jobs to be done do not simply provide short term satisfaction of the contractor. With respect to Star Wars, Parnas considered this programme totally unrealistic, and he accused the other participants of using improper motives for judging otherwise. Parnas published his, technical, arguments against the feasibility of Star Wars in *American Scientist*, and with this deed ended his active career as a military advisor. [3]

### 2.2 Creating Frankenstein's monster

Seen by some as the 'eminence grise', by others as the 'enfant terrible', Joseph Weizenbaum without any doubt is one of the most prominent contributors to the debate on scientific responsibilities. His story is widely known: the creation of a rather modest programme to mimick Rogerian therapeutists (the name of the programme was *Eliza* after the principal female person in *Pygmalion*) lead to a boom in speculations about computer intelligent behaviour. Even his own secretary, having witnessed the development of the programme, was not able to discriminate between the inanimate computer and the impression of intelligent conversation. This lead Weizenbaum to a firm stance against the threats of computers. In his opinion the triumph of rationalism has lead to a new conformism which "permits us to say anything that can be said in the functional languages of instrumental reason, but forbids us to allude to what Ionesco called the living truth." [4]

## 3. THE TECHNOLOGICAL BACKGROUND OF WESTERN ETHICS

Parnas and Weizenbaum are well-known and highly esteemed scientists. Their status as scientists might even have increased because of their personal decision to withdraw from the work they were involved in. In making these decisions they partly relied on ethical 'guiding principles'. Their principles – like almost all our ethical considerations – can be traced back to two basic positions. These two positions are reflections of our Western way of thinking and acting. Both positions concentrate on what a person should *do* (in contrast for instance with approaches that concentrate on whom a person should be). Parnas clearly shows himself to be a *teleologist*, in that he judges his acts by their consequences (or by the consequences of omitting these acts). Weizenbaum's position is a mixture. He shows himself to be a teleologist, especially when he argues that we should be very cautious in undertaking activities with irreversible side-effects. [5] But he has something of a *deontologist* as well, by saying that "the good of an act inheres in the act itself", which is a very typical aspect of deontologist theory. [6]

### 3.1 The instrumental reason

Interestingly enough, there are parallels between the teleological position and the ideological backgrounds of scientific practice. The roots of this practice stem from the Enlightenment, when the human ratio became the instrument *optima forma* in the struggle against nature. This *instrumental reason*, or *technicism*, supplied the dominant intellectual motives for the development of science and technology. It can be described as "the pretension of man to master reality with technological-scientific means and to solve all possible problems with these means". [7] Science and technology are considered to be *instrumental* in the control of nature and society. Today we would say that scientific and technological practices are goal-oriented. They do not simply serve the holy quest for truth, but they are also used as strategic tools to guarantee material prosperity and control over society. [8] This description of the ideological backgrounds of science and technology fits computer science nicely: many of the activities in this field are in one way or another aimed at the realization of a practical goal.

### 3.2 Divide and Conquer

Another aspect of modern scienticific practice is its reductionistic character. In an attempt to master the reality that surrounds us, this reality is reduced to something that is comprehensible. The dazzling complexity of the real world is transformed to a reality that can be manipulated. Real world knowledge and experiences are substituted by relatively simple models that contain all parameters which are considered important to describe the situation under consideration. This reduction of complexity does not always lead to the desired results, as, for example, weather models show. In general however, the method of reduction is effective, in that it offers a reality that can be controlled to some extent. However, this leads to a tension between the artificially created reality and the real world: Weizenbaum's instrumental world versus Ionesco's living truth. People become strangers in their own world, in their own social reality. For scientists, the scientific method of reduction and abstraction leads to the problem of having to interpret the results of their activities in the context of the outer world. As a result, this may hinder scientists in taking a moral position in their own scientific practices.

### 3.3 The individuality of ethics

The imperialism of the instrumental reason has penetrated into our ethical judgements as well, since we judge our acts in terms of the consequences of these acts and not merely in terms of the motives for acting. As we stated above, this teleological attitude poses problems for scientists in taking a moral position.

The teleological attitude is further complicated by the fact that responsibility, in Western civilization, is seen as a personal, individual issue. We are not able to transfer our responsibility to someone else. In final judgement we are responsible for our own behaviour. (This is Parnas' first ethical guiding principle.) Most individuals however, are not in the position to fully control their own activities. Scientific work, for instance, is done within a social context, within a community of co-workers who together try to tackle cognitive 'puzzles'. How should an individual scientist, from a teleological point of view, judge his or her activities if these activities are restricted to a small part of the research programme, and other people decide on how the results will be used? Scientific knowledge can not be concealed. As soon as scientific information is published, anyone can use it for his or her own purposes. It is a delusion to think that precise control over the use of this knowledge is possible. Therefore new knowledge may produce applications that were not intended, not foreseen and maybe not desired by the original 'inventors'. Parts of mathematics, like numerical analysis and complexity theory, for instance, were not primarily developed within a military context, but turned out to offer interesting perspectives for specific military domains like cryptography. Simple statements in articles and theses, in which the author declares that he or she does not want the results to be used for military purposes do not guarantee that this wish will be respected. To escape from this problem some people propose to separate control over the application of knowledge from the pursuit of knowledge for its own sake. Pursuit of knowledge belongs to the responsibility sphere of the scientist, while control over its applications should be exercised by politicians, or democratic bodies. This position surely is attractive in that it relieves scientists of the moral responsibility for what happens with their scientific results. The separation itself however, is artificial and non-satisfactory, and can not be defended from a moral point of view. There is no simple solution to this problem. Weizenbaum offers a solution that is not very convincing as well. He argues that we should restrict our activities to those that we are able to control. We should not undertake activities that might lead to unforeseen consequences, especially if there are indications that these activities might lead to irreversible side effects. [9] But as we argued above, precisely the interfering externalities, that by definition are not under direct control, lead to unpredictable events.

An interesting option is proposed by some authors who suggest to broaden the notion of individual responsibility to a *collective* one. [10] This collectivity may follow from the social group one belongs to. Computer scientists, for instance, may organize themselves in special interest groups with a focus on specific domains. Parnas and Weizenbaum both embrace this notion of collectivity, with Parnas elaborating it in the direction of a code for professional conduct. [11] This notion of collective responsibility preconsiders that people are able to be touched (in a moral sense) by events they themselves clearly can not be held responsible for. Part of the community of physicists, for instance, feels responsible for the building of nuclear weapons, even when it is obvious that these particular physicists have not done anything to stimulate work on nuclear weapons, on the contrary.

We shall return to the usefulness of this notion at the end of this paper.

## 4. THE SOCIAL CONSTRUCTION OF SCIENCE AND TECHNOLOGY

Part of the world that we live in is the result of our scientific and technological activities. Some argue that the world is strongly determined by these activities. Ellul, the famous French philosopher of technique, advocates the lawlike behaviour of the resulting socio-technical systems, which in his view is best described by an attempt of these systems to organize the world in 'the one best way'. [12] This 'one best way' is equivalent with the most efficient way. From another perspective however, it may be argued that the social constraints that guide the construction of technical systems leave the possibility to adapt the design of the socio-technical systems to specific circumstances. To stimulate discussion on the responsibility of scientists we present a perspective that focuses on the social construction of science and technology, and we use this perspective to elaborate the notion of responsible scientists.

### 4.1 The rejection of the autonomy of science and technology

Contemporary studies of the dynamics of science and technology have shown the intrinsic socio-cognitive characteristics of scientific practice. Sociological studies have revealed Machiavellian struggles in the development of new scientific theories and applications. These studies have shown the need for making allies and for acting strategically to get one's ideas accepted. [13] The scientific enterprise is embedded in social struggles. However, it is not only the 'outer world' of science (for instance the continuing struggle with funding organisations) that is influenced by ordinary games of power, but these power games are part of the cognitive work as well. Knowledge itself is socially shaped, science and technology are in their cognitive core socially constructed. In its strongest form this social construction is defended by David Bloor, the 'founding father' of the Edinburgh Strong Programme of Scientific Knowledge, who claims that all knowledge is impartial to categories of truth and falseness. [14]

Interdisciplinary studies in the field of science and technology dynamics have opened the 'black box' of scientific and technological practices. They have shown the interaction between epistemological features and sociological ones. The strictly causal, linear models that are used to explain the development of scientific and technological developments are substituted by models in which success and failure are no longer obvious categories, but are precisely the features that should be explained: why has a successful scientific theory or technological artefact turned out to be a successful one? Success and failure need symmetrical explanations. All relevant social groups have their own definition of reality, in which perceptions of the future technological system are different. In general, technological trajectories cannot be predicted on grounds of technical arguments alone.

In an interesting study Bijker has shown how the typical form of the bicycle was shaped over a period of decades. [15] Different social groups advocated different design strategies, based on different opinions about relevant features. Air tires, for instance, were initially seen as highly dangerous, compared to wooden tires, untill bicyclists showed the speed advantage of these tires. In a similar vein, Elzen and MacKenzie have shown how the construction of supercomputers was shaped by different interacting opinions and views of the relevant actors, and that it is precisely the success of the Gray-computer that should be explained. [16]

### 4.2 The social shaping of science and technology

The above-mentioned studies support the notion that science and technology may not be seen as autonomous forces that impinge on society. Lawlike developments, that appear to be the result of purely internal dynamics, can be proven to follow from specific circumstances. The increase in the capacity of chips, for instance, seems to be governed by a law that leads to an apparently autonomous increase in capacity every few years (the so-called Moore-law). Closer inspection however, shows that the industries themselves have internalized this 'natural growth' and have made it into a law that must be realized. [17]. Other cases show how specific features are introduced into systems because of combined social and technological characteristics. David Noble, for instance, has shown how the design of computerized numerical control machines was decisively influenced by a choice the higher level management made to prevent the blue-collar workers from gaining a position of power. By transferring knowledge of how to operate the CNC-machines from the blue-collarworkers to software developers, the firm became less dependable on the workers' knowledge. [18]

Another example is given by the design process of an international communication infrastructure. In the mid-eighties the coming of ISDN (Integrated Services Digital Networks) was seen as the future backbone of the information society. Today, this 'integrationist view' is supplemented with the 'segregationist view' that, partly as a consequence of liberalization of PTT monopolies, foresees competition on all kind of netwerk infrastructures. [19] Two kinds of futures are possible: a future in which a centralised system – which by means of legislation is put in the hand of a central manager – controls all kind of information exchange activities, or a future in which a variety of intelligent networks is interconnected by intelligent gateways and offer a flexible degree of operability to different users.

A final example stems from the Dutch futurologist Fred Polak, who at the end of the sixties argued that the Soviet Union would presumably benefit most from the computer revolution, since its internal (centralized) structure would fit best the (centralized) character of the computer mainframes. [20] The implicit assumption that technical developments parallel social developments, (because they are based on the same rationality) has in this case seriously been flawed by the historical developments.

### 4.3 The rejection of the 'waterfall-model' of science and technology

Galbraith defines technology as the systematic application of scientific knowledge. [21] The scientific process of knowledge gathering precedes the technological application of this knowledge. This 'top-down' model, or waterfall model, in which scientific knowledge fills a source engineers can dip into to realize their practical goals, does not offer a correct description of scientific and technological practices. Scientific and technological practices cannot be that neatly discerned. They are interwoven, the community of practitioners consists of scientists and engineers whose tasks cannot be clearly separated. Research on artificial intelligence, for instance, has been guided by a combination of theoretical considerations and practical applications. Conceptual models, theoretical work on problem solving strategies, logical and psychological studies on representation of knowledge, and practical applications in specific domains influenced one another. At present, work on neural networks, partly stimulated because of failures in A.I. research to meet even modest claims, shows the same interdependency between 'pure' scientific activities and practical applications. [22]

This entanglement of scientific and technological practices can also be found in the military. Even 'strategic programmes', aimed at stimulating research on specific topics (for instance A.I. in the U.S. Strategic Computing Programme), has a very strong applied side as well. In the European context, the same orientation is shown by the many international research programmes. These programmes combine fundamental scientific research with practical goals, aimed at exploring the innovative potential of new technologies. European technology programmes like ESPRIT and RACE illustrate this trend.

## 5. CONCLUSION

In the previous section we gave a brief sketch of the social constructivist perspective on science and technology. In our opinion, this perspective adds interesting points of view to the debate about responsible behaviour of scientists. We drew attention to the ideology of control that underlies present day changes in society. The success of this ideology, in short described as Divide and Conquer, runs in parallel with a growing societal discontent with the technological culture, with increased feelings of alienation and impotence. These feelings contrast with the prevailing social image of our technological culture as if everything is perfectly under control. We experience the paradoxical situation that, while science and technology enable an unprecedented level of control, the development of science and technology themselves seems to escape every kind of control. Technological reality and personal reality do no longer match, resulting in problems with the 'implementation' of ethical (teleological) theory in practice. Usually, the results of science and technology are treated as 'black boxes'. These closed, stable, fixed entities can be used or not, and are tools in a toolkit, serving instrumental purposes, void of any moral values.

The social constructivists have opened these 'black boxes', and have shown a vivid activitiy inside. Elaborating on earlier findings on the cognitive relativity of scientific knowledge they have shown the relation between social and cognitive phenomena. They have shown micro-worlds of scientific activities, and the intrinsically social characteristics of knowledge. These social characteristics are found at different levels. First, previous notions about science and technology as autonomous forces that follow internal laws only (stemming from the attempt to present the best description of either a natural or a social reality) should be rejected. Secondly, a linear model, in which scientific knowledge preceeds technical applications, should be rejected as well. No demarcation between scientific and technological practices, with respect to both cognitive and social characteristics, can be made. Thirdly, though scientific and technological activities are aimed at realizing practical goals, the trajectories for reaching these goals are ambiguous and open to change, while the goals themselves are open to change as well. Constraints that guide these trajectories are a mix of social, technological and other interests.

### 5.1 Consequences for an ethical attitude

In our opinion these new insights in the characteristics of the shaping of science and technology have a drawback on the debate about responsible behaviour. An ethical attitude is hindered by the following problems: the impossibility to assess the consequences of one single deed; the problem of bearing an individual responsibility while being part of a group; the fragmented nature of the present 'puzzle-solving' activities; and above all, the instrumental reason which seems to guide any scientific or technological activity.

We think these problems show the failure of a teleological approach. Furthermore we think the teleological approach is based on a misconception of how scientific and technological practices really work. We have presented arguments for this misconception in the preceding paragraph.

This of course leaves the question "What could form the basis of responsible behaviour?" unanswered. Without the pretention to present a full-fledged answer, we will sketch a possible basis for an alternative ethical approach.

First, as will be clear, we need to reconsider the value of a deontological approach, in which more attention is paid to the *motives* of acting, instead of to the results. Secondly, though some have shown that we live in an age *After Virtue*, it is still open whether the social conditions for returning to ethics, based on whom we should *be*, instead of what we should do, are or will be met in the near future. [23] Thirdly, as the social constructivists have shown, it is possible to understand to some extent the motives for and limitations of scientific and technological activities. Though this does not mean that it will be possible to *aim* our activities at goals that are worthwhile (after all, we concluded that different trajectories are possible), the awareness of the intrinsic socio-technical conditions that shape these developments offers opportunities to escape a fatalist attitude, leading to indifference and apathy with respect to their responsibility.

Finally, the idea of a collective responsibility needs more elaboration. The mere fact that we somehow feel responsible for the acting or consequences of acting of our colleagues may form a starting point for reconsidering how we can deal with these feelings. This collective responsibility is related to what is called *tragic* responsibility: the fact that we feel responsible for (sometimes dramatic) events in which we feel involved without any possibility to influence the course of it (for instance the break down of a critical computer system in hospital environments that leads to loss of lives). [24]

### 5.2 What next?

In this paper we have tried to add to the debate about our responsibilities as 'constructors-of-the-future'. We offered another view about the social reality that surrounds scientific and technological activities. We think this view is important. It feeds the ethical debate with new arguments and insights. We need to counter-balance the apparent misconception of technological determinism. The approach of social-constructivism provides convincing arguments for this counter-balance.

Irrespective of the contents of the ethical dispute, we should pay more attention to the ethical debate as such. We need more debate on what kind of society we want and how science and technology can be committed to realizing this society. We should stimulate public discussions on certain issues. Professional organisations, like CPSR in USA, FIFF in Germany and SAIA in the Netherlands, deal with professional responsibility, and stimulate the debate amongst their members. They take positions in the societal debate. Members of these groups have developed ideas for ethical approaches. [25] Finally, all starts with educating people to make them aware of the social implications of their future work and to teach them to incorporate ethical aspects in their scientific and technological activities.

Both in debate and in education we think the new insights generated by the social constructivists may prove to be very valuable.

## 6. REFERENCES


1 L. Winner, Autonomous Technology. Technics-out-of-control as a theme in political thought, MIT Press, Cambridge Mass, 1977.
2 David L. Parnas, Why I won't work on SDI: one view of professional responsibility, The CPSR Newsletter, 2 (1986).
3 David L. Parnas, Software Aspects of Strategic Defense Systems, American Scientist, 9/10 (1985).
4 J. Weizenbaum, Computer Power and Human Reason, Penguin Press, London, 1976, 261.
5 J. Weizenbaum, 270.
6 J. Weizenbaum, 276.
7 E. Schuurman, Filosofie van de technische wetenschappen, ('A philosophy of the engineering sciences'), Martinus Nijhoff, Leiden, 1990, 81.
8 J. Beniger, The Control Revolution, Harvard U.P., Cambridge 1986.
9 J. Weizenbaum, 270.
10 P. van Tongeren, Kollektieve verantwoordelijkheid ('Collective Responsibility'), Algemeen Nederlands Tijdschrift voor de Wijsbegeerte, 78 (1986).
11 D. Johnson, Computer Ethics, Prentice-Hall, Englewood Cliffs, 1985.
12 J. Ellul, The Technological Society, Vintage Books, New York, 1964.
13 W. Bijker, T. Hughes and T. Pinch (eds.), The Social Construction of Technological Systems, MIT Press, London, 1987; M. Callon, J. Law and A. Rip (eds.), Mapping the Dynamics of Science and Technology, MacMillan, London, 1987; B. Latour, Science in Action, Milton Keynes, Open University Press, 1987; B. Latour and S. Woolgar, Laboratory Life. The Social Construction of Scientific Facts, SAGE, London, 1979.
14 D. Bloor, Knowledge and Social Imagery, Routledge and Keegan Paul, London, 1979.
15 W. Bijker, The Social Construction of Technology, Alfa, Enschede, 1990.
16 B. Elzen and D. Mackenzy, The charismatic engineer: Seymour Gray and the development of supercomputing, Jaarboek voor de Geschiedenis van Bedrijf en Techniek ('Yearbook for Corporate History and History of Technology'), NEHA, Amsterdam, 1991.
17 H. van den Belt, Kritiek op het technologisch determinisme ('A critique on technological determinism'), Wetenschap en Samenleving, 2 (1987).
18 David F. Noble, Social Choice in Machine Design: The Case of Automatically Controlled Machine Tools, and a Challenge for Labor, Politics and Society, 3/4 (1978).
19 R. Mansell, Rethinking the telecommunications infrastructure: The new 'black box', Research Policy (1990).
20 F. Polak, De nieuwe wereld der automatie. ('The new world of automation'), De Haan, Hilversum, 1966, 239.
21 J.K. Galbraith, The New Industrial State, Penguin Books, England, 1967, 31.
22 Tyler Folsom, The Search for an "Electronic Brain", The CPSR Newsletter, 1 (1989).
23 A. MacIntyre, After Virtue – a study in moral theory, London, 1984.
24 P. van Tongeren, *op.cit.*.
25 C. Floyd, The responsible use of computers. Where do we draw the line?, The CPSR Newsletter, 2/3 (1985); J. Ladd, Ethical issues in information technology, Paper presented at the conference of the Society for Social Studies of Science, Irvine CA, (1989); T. Forester and P. Morrison, Computer Ethics, Basil Blackwell, Oxford, 1990.

Education and Society / R. Aiken (Editor)
Information Processing 92, Volume II
Elsevier Science Publishers B.V. (North-Holland)


# ETHICS, VULNERABILITY AND INFORMATION TECHNOLOGY (IT)

**Julie Cameron*, Roger Clarke, Simon Davies, Agnes Jackson, Mark Prentice, Brian Regan.**
*Managing Director, Organisational and Technological Solutions Pty Ltd, Sydney, Australia

**Abstract**

This paper was based on discussions by delegates (including IFIP TC9 Chairman, Klaus Brunnstein, IT professionals, privacy advocates, University academics and management consultants) who attended the workshop on Ethics at the SOST'91 (Shaping Organisations, Shaping Technology) Conference held in Adelaide, Australia, 9-10 October, 1991. This paper considers who needs IT ethics; identifies the stages required to develop and effectively implement IT ethics; establishes performance criteria; considers options for the status of international IT ethics; and concludes that IFIP should develop IT Ethical Principles which could be adopted by member countries and incorporated into instruments as considered appropriate for each culture and legal structure.
**Keyword Codes:** K.1; K.4.m; K.7.m. **Keywords:** Computing Industry; Computers and Society, Miscellaneous (Ethics); Computing Profession, Miscellaneous (Ethics).

## 1. WHY DO WE NEED IT ETHICS?

Any discussion of Information Technology (IT) immediately poses the question of what do we mean by "IT"? For the purposes of this discussion IT is defined as "the use of computing, electronic and communications technologies to collect, process, store and retrieve data". And the "IT industry" comprises the organisations and resources involved in providing "vehicles" to enable "data" to be used for a variety of purposes or activities.

Like any other technology, IT can be used to assist or harm the individual and/or society. A car is an invaluable means of transport which has revolutionised our lifestyle. It makes travel over long distances possible and gives independence. However, when improperly used, it kills. So society has confined the use of the car to roads and controls its use by enforcing road laws. A large number of deaths still occur as a result of its use, but society has decided that the value and usefulness of the car outweighs the significance of the number of people killed by its use.

IT is still in the "Ford Model A period". The technology is cheap enough to be "driven" by "the masses". But we have not completed a road system. We have not yet predicted all the ways IT will be used. And the rules are very new and relatively untested, or totally inadequate, or do not exist. In the case of IT we are already finding that the "deaths" relate to issues like vulnerability and loss of privacy. (1) With datamatching, for example, we are experiencing "trial by database" where the citizen has to prove the "computer" wrong! (2) The challenge for the IT industry and the community, is to foster the benefits while identifying and minimising the "deaths".

We need IT ethics because:

* IT is a powerful and constantly evolving tool
* IT permeates all aspects of our lives
* IT dependency creates vulnerability on a large scale (3)
* IT evolution and use outstrips the formulation and implementation of policy and legal instruments
* Changing community values are likely to impose external regulation on the IT industry.

## 2. WHO NEEDS IT ETHICS?

Because of its pervasive characteristics most people have a variety of roles related to IT. Each roles can have some influence on the decisions, policy and laws concerning or impacting on IT design and use. Some roles, usually those of people employed in the IT industry, are directly responsible for supplying, developing, implementing or operating IT - these are the designers. Currently the designers have the major role in decision-making related to IT. The role of "user" relates to the use of IT for work or to obtain the benefits. Other roles relate to "usees" who are affected, but cannot directly influence either the design or the use. The responsibility these people have, is as citizens.

### 2.1 The Designers - The Information Technology Industry

The designers of IT are the hardware and software developers, vendors and their employees. The most influential designers are very large suppliers, which are usually multinational organisations with large research and development divisions, backed up by well-financed marketing and sales divisions. The main groups involved in designing IT are:

* *Organisations*

- Suppliers; organisations that provide "ready-made" hardware and software in "packaged" or "standard" forms or "customised IT products" to clients
- Developers; organisations or parts of organisations that are "contracted" to other organisations or individuals to design specified products usually on a project basis.

* *Investors*

- Investors; organisations and individuals that benefit, usually financially, from the activities of suppliers and developers
- Sponsors (eg, military), those that have a vested interest in, or have provided tangible input or resources or those that will benefit directly from the outcome or output if the designers succeed.

* *IT Professionals*

- Decision-makers; managers of IT professionals who are directly responsible for design or development decisions and outcomes
- Implementers (eg, engineers, programmers); IT professionals actively engaged in designing and developing IT products
- Controllers (eg, computer operators, network controllers); people who manage and operate the computing facilities, communication networks and other hardware.

### 2.2 The Users of IT

The users of IT can be organisations or employees. They are do not have the power to directly influence the design of systems, but they can influence the designers indirectly by their reaction to IT and the way they utilise it. Senior organisational decision-makers, through their financial and line responsibilities, may have the power to decide whether to purchase or introduce or to reject specific IT proposals. However, their decisions are dependent on the availability of accurate, objective information about the IT concerned. Currently, before a new system or technology is selected some organisations undertake cost/benefit analysis. Even fewer organisations attempt risk analysis. But the SOST'91 delegates believed it is becoming increasingly obvious that IT organisational impact studies should be carried out to assess the impact on the organisation. This would help to predict the expected level of vulnerability and the changes required to the staffing, skills, structure and other internal and external components of the organisation resulting from the IT proposal.

The main groups of users are:

* User organisations; organisations that are IT technology-takers, that may decide to accept or reject the use of IT products in order to carry out their business

* User employees; people who use IT products in their work, but who do not influence its design, development or implementation.

### 2.3 The Citizen User and Usee

The concept of the citizen "user" and "usee" embraces people, who in their private capacity as citizen, actively use IT, or are affected by other people using IT. This category of "usee" represents the most vulnerable group for whom a failure of ethical practice has the most impact. This is largely because those who are not direct users or paying customers of the system have no direct market power to challenge the system. Nevertheless, these people too, have a role in relation to the use of IT. They can either accept a specific use of IT or reject or ignore it. Examples of the influence of this type of behaviour was seen in Australia when banks failed in their initial attempt to introduce EFTPOS because of non-acceptance by consumers; and when the government was unable to implement the Australia Card system of identification for all citizens because of community opposition.

The main groups of "citizen user" and "usees" are:

* Users; individuals who actively use IT in their role as citizen (eg, a bank customer using an automatic teller machine)
* Usees; those affected without having a direct role (eg, a shopper at a supermarket that uses price scanning devises)

### 2.4 Public Policy

Public policy roles at national and state level can or could direct or influence the design and use of IT. Governments could refuse to allow the development, import or sale of IT considered unsafe or undesirable. Ideally public policy reflects community attitudes about "good" and "bad" design and use of IT, assuming that the community is aware and IT literate. Public policy lags behind IT design and use and the policy-makers are heavily influenced by investors, designers and developers.

International policy is increasingly important when dealing with the IT industry and IT because of the multinational characteristics of suppliers and developers. Most countries are dependent on IT imported from countries like Japan and the United States that may have very different value systems. Multinational companies, by their nature, are difficult to control. Small countries are IT-takers, and with the imported IT they import the values incorporated into the technology and implicit in its operation.

We need to realise the limitations and vulnerabilities of IT - preferably in advance of its introduction. Ideally, independent assessment should occur before development of new IT. However, for obvious commercial reasons, any assessment concerning the ethical desirability of the development must be undertaken by the "developers" themselves. In many countries, because of the possible risk to the environment, many new industrial or commercial developments are subjected to environmental impact studies. It has been recognised that the level of vulnerability likely to occur as a result of the use of natural resources should be assessed before approval to proceed is given.

The impact of IT on a community is becoming better understood. IT, in use, is not neutral. IT has the potential to be harmful or beneficial. Harmful affects can be permanently damaging to individuals and communities. For these reasons the potential application of any new technology should be subject to IT community impact studies, similar in concept to environmental impact studies. Conditions related to the use of specific IT could then be developed in advance. Communities could be proactive in ensuring that only beneficial uses and ethical behaviours and outputs are permitted.

### 2.5 Legal Instruments

Legal instruments are the most direct way of influencing the use of IT. And, in order to be effective, legal instruments need to have a consistent ethical basis. The limitations and challenges of legal instruments are the need for them to be applied to a single, specified jurisdiction.

The challenge at the national level, is to understand and predict the implications of the use of IT and to ensure that any legal instruments are enforceable and enforced. Lawyers, citizens and the courts need to understand the issues involved in cases concerning IT. What is needed is a clear understanding of ethical and unethical behaviours and outputs associated with IT. The complexities of the technology and the related issues require a high level of IT literacy.

International law related to IT is critical because IT is not confined to national boundaries. International communications networks and transnational dataflows are important and common components of trade and commerce. Internationally accepted IT ethics would simplify the development of international law and regulation.

## 3. WHAT PROCEDURES ARE NEEDED TO DEVELOP AND IMPLEMENT IT ETHICS?

There are four main stages that are necessary to develop IT ethics and implement effective regulatory mechanisms. These stages, which form an on-going cyclical process, are:

1. Development and introduction of ethics or codes of conduct incorporating extensive consultation between the industry and external groups.
2. Design and implementation of independent complaint handling and enforcement mechanisms.
3. Assessment and review by industry and external groups of the effectiveness of the ethics or codes of conduct and responsiveness of the review and complaint handling and enforcement mechanisms.
4. Development and implementation of recommendations resulting from the assessment and review process.

Many professional bodies use industry consultation to construct ethical principles or codes of conduct. (4, 5, 6) But for the development of IT ethics the other stages, incorporating independent complaints handling, enforcement, and assessment and review, are mandatory due to the nature of IT and the way it permeates all aspects of society. External consultation, the adoption of the other stages, and the acceptance of these stages as an on-going cyclical process, is essential.

### 3.1 Consultation

Extensive consultation with groups affected by IT, such as consumers, privacy groups, "users" and "usees" is essential. These groups see IT issues from a different perspective. They can provide a practical framework for principles or codes based on common sense and community values. In seeking external consultations, it is essential that not just the computer literate be involved in these discussions. Too much computer related decision making is dominated by those with either a vested interest in the technology or an enthusiasm which causes them to overlook reasonable reservations that should be expressed about IT-based proposals. IT Industry representatives and professionals have expert knowledge about the capabilities, use and potential use of IT but they may have a biased and a narrow vision of the way IT ethics could affect the industry and their own professional working lives.

Any code or principles developed need to build on the frameworks provided by the external groups. It is essential to ensure a fair balance between the legitimate self-protection of the industry groups and the rest of society. This balance may differ among societies and will change over time.

### 3.2 Enforcement

Education is a critical component of enforcement. This includes education of the community about what they should expect from IT use and the IT industry as well as intensive education of IT professionals. Ethics should be included as a part of the IT curriculum at schools and universities.

Responsibility for enforcement may range from self regulation of professional or industry bodies, to enforcement by legal instruments. There must be some form of pressure to conform and penalties for nonconformity. Consistency in enforcement is important. Compliance by individual professionals or industry organisations is often encouraged or enforced by the introduction of accreditation, certification or licensing requirements. Individuals may be required to adhere to ethical principles or codes of practise as a condition of retaining a licence to practice (eg, the medical profession). Industry or professional complaint and enforcement mechanisms are often established to enforce compliance. In a self-regulated environment, individuals and organisations can be called before a recognised body of peers to answer complaints concerning accusations of wrongful behaviour. Offenders may be disbarred from practicing. In addition to self-regulation, many countries retain legal remedies against malpractice under criminal and civil law.

The development of independent complaint handling and enforcement mechanisms is considered crucial because of the enormous impact and power of the IT industry. How this is done will need to vary in different countries. In situations where transnational and international transactions occur (eg. international use of EDI), some international monitoring and enforcement may be required. This has already occurred in the case of transnational flows of data in the European Community. The possibility of local organisations being excluded from trade and commercial dealings if standards are not adhered to is an excellent incentive for countries to conform to standards and guidelines.

### 3.3 Review

To assist with the assessment and review process, performance criteria for ethical principles and codes of conduct and the complaints handling and enforcement mechanisms need to be established. Performance criteria should be developed as a part of the initial consultation and development stage.

Independent assessment and review is necessary to ensure that there has been objective and impartial consideration by the complaints mechanisms of issues raised and consistency in enforcement procedures. The overall assessment and review process (stage 3) is critical to ensure adherence to ethical principles and codes, particularly when financial interests are involved.

In order to be effective and responsive, review mechanisms need to be permanent structures otherwise the effort required to initiate a review becomes so difficult that only extreme breaches of the principles will warrant the investment in time to lobby for a review. Reviews also need to be carried out at regular intervals and the results need to be published to assist other countries to assess the effectiveness of varying mechanisms in specific circumstances. It is also important to ensure that any recommendations arising from the review are incorporated into the complaints handling, enforcement mechanisms, future review processes or the principles or codes themselves.

## 4. WHAT ARE THE OPTIONS FOR THE STATUS OF IT ETHICS?

Some of the most obvious options for establishing IT ethics, listed in order of enforceability, are:

* Principles which are generally statements that may provide international guidance, or act as a reference document, or provide a basis for the development of legal instruments in particular jurisdictions (eg. the OECD Privacy Principles, which are widely recognised and have acted as standards for drafting and reviewing legislation and regulation).
* Public policies which may incorporate aspects of acceptable behaviours, practice and standards.
* Codes of conduct which usually incorporate ethical principles but tend to focus on behaviours, outputs and quality of service so that they are used to form the basis for the interpretation of substantive behaviours. Although they are usually used as standards for self-regulation by industries or professions, they may also be used as guidance in external regulation (eg, by courts assessing what comprises "negligent behaviour").
* Guidelines which may be legal within a single jurisdiction and used to provide guidance, legal meaning and relevance, even though they are generally not enforceable.
* Legal instruments which are generally enforceable, provided they are drafted correctly and the courts are sufficiently qualified to assess the matters bought before them.

## 5. IS IT PRACTICAL TO DEVELOP INTERNATIONAL IT ETHICS?

There has been debate within IFIP, TC9 and the IT community about the feasibility and practicality of developing IT ethics or codes of conduct. (7) The main issues of the debate relate to:

* the possibility of developing internationally applicable principles or codes because of differences in cultural and social values
* the possibility of developing internationally enforceable principles or codes because of differences in legal structures
* the practicality of developing rules because of the complexity of IT and its use and impact
* the difficulties in deciding the "type" and status of "rules" that should be proposed.

SOST'91 delegates who attended the workshop on Ethics discussed these issues but concluded that although these concerns need to be considered, they should not prevent the development of international IT ethics.

Ideally, IT ethics would be enforceable. However, SOST'91 delegates acknowledged the importance of international variations in cultural and social values and the practical constraints of differing legal structures. They therefore recommended that the status of IT ethics developed by IFIP should have the status of Principles. Although these Principles would remain outside particular legal jurisdictions and consequently would not have the status of legal instruments, they would be able to be adopted by member countries and could provide the IT ethical basis of the instruments considered appropriate for each culture. Even though IFIP IT Ethical Principles would not be enforceable, they would have a vital role internationally, and an important moral influence and practical usefulness in the:

* education of IT professionals
* assessment of role behaviour related to IT, particularly the behaviours of IT professionals and the IT industry
* risk and IT impact analysis of IT systems
* assessment of the design, output and use of real IT systems
* framework for national and international policy
* framework for legal instruments.

## 6. WHAT SHOULD BE INCLUDED IN IFIP IT ETHICAL PRINCIPLES?

Although the status of Principles would not allow IFIP to co-ordinate all of the four main stages that need to be completed in order to develop ethics and implement effective regulatory mechanisms, an IFIP Ethics Working Group would be able to initiate the industry consultation, referred to in stage 1, and establish a process for effective international external consultation. This Working Group should be established under the auspices of TC9, but should include a representative from each Technical Committee. Care should be taken to ensure diverse geographical membership. The IFIP Ethics Working Group would also be able to develop performance measures as a basis for discussion. In addition, once the Principles are developed, IFIP, in conjunction with the international external consultation process, would have an important role in monitoring international progress in adopting IFIP Ethical Principles and in helping member nations to assess the effectiveness of their complaints handling and enforcement mechanisms.

IFIP IT Ethical Principles need to address roles and behaviours and outputs related to those roles. This approach is necessary because behaviours and outputs are visible and measurable. Acceptable or unacceptable behaviours can be stated and associated with roles. The SOST'91 delegates considered that brief, practical, comprehensible and memorable statements setting out appropriate behaviours, outputs or standards for specific roles should be developed by an IFIP Working Group. The behaviours, outputs and or standards should be related to the specified roles of Designers, Users, Citizens,Public policy and Legal Instruments.

Performance criteria need to be established as a basis for measuring the effectiveness of the Principles. The SOST'91 delegates proposed that the critical characteristics and performance criteria for the IFIP IT Ethical Principles should:

* have a legal frame of reference incorporating governing texts (eg, the Universal Declaration of Human Rights, International Covenant on Civil and Political Rights, International Covenant on Economic, Social and Cultural Rights)
* conform to universally accepted conventions and have the consent of the general community and the IT profession
* assist in interpretation and application of the laws and values in a particular area (eg, liability laws)
* incorporate common sense principles and be easily understood and comprehensible to the general community
* reduce the vulnerability of the industry and the general community
* be relevant, practical and practiced

* incorporate measurable standards
* obviate unnecessary administrative restrictions.

## 7. CONCLUSIONS AND RECOMMENDATIONS

The main aims of developing effective IT Ethical Principles and regulatory procedures relate to the need to balance community interest with maximum independence for the IT profession and the IT industry so that it is free from unnecessary regulation. Abuse of the environment and concern about environmental vulnerability, combined with the failure of commerce and industry to heed community concern, has resulted in many countries introducing extensive legal and regulatory restriction on the industrial and commercial activities related to the use of natural resources and environmental impact. Concerns are now being raised about the use of IT. IT professionals and the IT industry have the choice of developing and enforcing effective IT ethics which are acceptable to the community or, as concern for individual and community vulnerability increases, regulation will be imposed. (8) And the IT industry could be excluded from the development and enforcement processes.

SOST'91 workshop delegates recommended that an IFIP IT Ethics Working Group comprising a representative from each Technical Committee, but also ensuring geographical diversity of membership, should be immediately established under the auspices of TC9. The initial role of the IT Ethics Working Group would be to:

* initiate the IT professional and IT industry consultation, and establish processes for effective international external consultation
* develop performance criteria and IT Ethical Principles utilising international external consultation processes.

The ongoing role of the IT Ethics Working Group, in conjunction with the international external consultation processes, would be to:

* monitor and report on international progress in adopting IFIP Ethical Principles
* assist member nations to assess the effectiveness of their complaints handling and enforcement mechanisms.

SOST'91 workshop delegates also recommended that IFIP IT Ethical Principles should address roles, behaviours, outputs and standards and be related to the specified roles of Designers, Users, Citizens, Public Policy and Legal Instruments. Performance criteria and Principles should be based on the existing work of IFIP TC9, including the SOST'91 workshop, and the Codes of Ethics of IFIP member countries.

## REFERENCES

1. J Holvast, "Vulnerability of Information Society: the Conflicting Demands of Security and Privacy" "Managing IT's Organisational Impact" R Clarke, J Cameron (ed.), North Holland, Amsterdam (1991).

2. D Campbell, S Connor, "On the Record: Surveillance, Computers & Privacy", Michael Joseph Ltd, UK (1986).

3. K Brunnstein, "Service Continuity Planning", R Clarke, J Cameron (eds), SOST'91 Proceedings (Oct 1991).

4. Australian Computer Society, "Code of Ethics Instrument, 1987".

5. British Computer Society, Code of Ethics.

6. New Zealand Computer Society, Code of Ethics.

7. H Sackman, "Toward an IFIP Code of Ethics Based on Participative International Concensus" in "Managing IT's Organisational Impact" R Clarke, J Cameron (eds), North Holland, Amsterdam (1991).

8. S Davies, "Elastic Vulnerability: the End of the Good Times for the Computer Industry", R Clarke, J Cameron (eds), SOST'91 Proceedings (Oct 1991).

Education and Society / R. Aiken (Editor)
Information Processing 92, Volume II
Elsevier Science Publishers B.V. (North-Holland)



# An IFIP Code of Ethics - Some of the Issues Involved

Richard Sizer

Independent Consulant in Risk Assessment and Computer Security. Past Chairman, BCS Professional Advisory Committee, Past Vice-chairman BCS Professional Board. Currently UK delegate to TC9 and Chairman of WG9.6 - IT Security and the Law.

**Abstract**
The paper first gives definitions of 'ethic' and decribes the problems inherent in the use of the term 'professional'. It is shown that 'chartered' is a more appropriate term. Criteria for chartered status are given. It is then argued that it is inappropriate for IFIP to have its own code of ethics; rather IFIP should produce guide-lines for use by national bodies in drafting their own relevant codes of conduct and practice.

## 1 DEFINITIONS OF THE TERM 'ETHIC'

It is necessary to define the term 'ethic'. Webster's definition is 'the discipline dealing with what is good and bad and with moral duty and obligation'. Roget's Thesaurus places ethic under morality - to incur a duty, to accept responsibility, to make oneself liable. Reference is also aptly made to a 'code of duty' in the context of 'professional status'.

## 2 DEFINITIONS OF THE TERM 'PROFESSIONAL'

The term 'professional' also needs to be defined for present purposes as it is used ambiguously in english-speaking countries. Its most common meaning is 'one who earns money for doing something' as opposed to the 'amateur' as 'one who would do the same thing, literally, out of love'. However, not all people who work for money in the context of the above meaning are necessarily regarded as 'professional'; there is clearly an implicit, albeit imperfect, distinction in english-speaking society as to what distinguishes one job from another so that one is professional, the other not so.

The problem lies in the imperfection: because there are no universally accepted criteria as to what might constitute a professional, it is assumed that one may become a professional in the more restricted sense merely by, say, changing a job to one which has had 'professional' attached to it to make it more attractive. This use of the term is rampant in the UK, particularly in IT, both in the way many jobs are advertised and titled at the place of work.

For present purposes, the 'true' professional is typified by those who are members of an organisation whose membership criteria define accepted standards of relevant academic achievement, practical experience and personal behaviour. In the UK such organisations are known as 'chartered bodies'; examples are the General Medical Council (GMC) for doctors, the British Computer Society (BCS) for information systems engineers, those engineering institutions which are part of the Council of Engineering Institutions (CEI), and the Institute of Chartered Accountants).

In brief, a charter is granted only when an organisation aspiring to chartered status has satisfied the Privy Council that its membership criteria are of the requisite standard and that it has the necessary means of controlling membership (including disciplinary procedures). For present purposes, therefore, 'chartered' is taken to be a more appropriate and meaningful term than 'professional' even though its use is confined to those countries which ascribe to the charter principle.

### 3 CHARTERED STATUS

The chartered individual is a member by definition of a chartered body and as such will:

systematically have acquired knowledge
have attained a specific standard
bear a responsibility for work done
maintain intellectual independence

In the UK, the BCS (now with the title 'Chartered Engineering Institution for Information Systems Engineers) is a member of the CEI which, in turn, is a member of the Federation Europeenne d'Associations Nationales d'Ingenieurs (FEANI). The BCS is responsible for relevant educational matters, disciplinary procedures, professional development, accreditation of certain academic institutions, and its codes of conduct and practice.

### 4 IFIP MEMBERSHIP

It is now appropriate to consider certain aspects of IFIP in the context of the above definitions. Membership of IFIP falls into a number of categories. These are, briefly:-

Full Membership - a national scientific or technical society, one per country. In the UK, the BCS is the relevant body.
Corresponding Membership - one organisation of a country (not already, a full member) interested in information processing.
Affiliate Membership - any organisation having relevant interests and a willingness to cooperate with IFIP.
Individual Member - one admitted in recognition of a relevant contribution to IFIP. There is a limit on numbers.
Honorary Member - awarded on the basis of exceptional merit for life.

Memberships, other than Honorary, may be terminated for a number of reasons amongst which is 'serious offence'. However, it is relevant to note that no guidance is given as to what constitutes such an offence and there is no immediately available record of any membership terminations.
It is argued, therefore, that IFIP is not, as a body, comparable with chartered bodies each of whose members meets the set of criteria given above. This is not, in any way, a criticism of IFIP. The point is made only within the context of the current argument as to whether IFIP should have a code of ethics: the essential point is that such a code is meaningful only in the situation where there are relevant and accepted behavioural criteria applying to all members backed by disciplinary procedures.

## 5 ETHICS WITHIN IFIP

By definition, IFIP is an international body which, under Article 1 of its Statutes 'does not take account of the political, social or economic aspects of its Member organizations because IFIP is totally dedicated to the transfer of scientific and technical information and experience.'

In practice there is evidence of both the letter and spirit of Article 1 being disregarded by members of IFIP when making parochial or personal interpretations of what constitutes unethical behaviour in attempts to frustrate the due processes of IFIP's activities. One example was the position taken by certain members during Technical Committee and Working Group sessions when issues involving South African membership and participation were involved. Such members were, on their own admission, either self-motivated or under pressure from political bodies within their respective countries to adopt ethical positions which countered the letter and spirit of Article 1. To other members who ascribed to the letter and spirit of Article 1, the frustration was the unethical behaviour and the members responsible should have been dealt with accordingly.

Also running counter to the letter and spirit of Article 1 are the wide variety of political, religious, moral and legal viewpoints contained within IFIP. Were IFIP to promulgate its own code of ethics realisable in practical terms it would need to embrace 'ethics' which are inherently mutually conflicting. A current example lies in the 'death threat' to Salman Rushdie. On the one hand, such a threat may well be regarded as moral, legal and ethically justifiable by certain countries who are represented within IFIP. On the other hand, there are other countries so represented who regard the death threat as immoral, illegal and ethically unjustifiable.

In the past, the BCS has faced similar predicaments over issues raised by members whose views of what constituted unethical behaviour in a given situation were not those embraced by the Society's charter. BCS policy is to regard a member as free, as an individual, to express personal misgivings in which he may state that he believes he is acting in accordance with his interpretation of, say, the BCS Code of Conduct. The extent of any BCS involvement is then limited to advising the member on a course of action if he is subsequently penalised because of his stance.

## 6 CONCLUSIONS

Because of IFIP's membership structure and criteria and the lack of a unified IFIP view of what is, or is not, ethical in given circumstances it is neither appropriate nor feasible to formulate an IFIP code of ethics. In particular, there could be no power of sanction which is an essential feature of chartered bodies. However, it would be both appropriate and invaluable on an international basis for IFIP to produce guide-lines to help its national member organisations to adopt the principle of a code of conduct (and possibly practice) and supportive disciplinary procedures.

Such guide-lines would, of course, need to be without prejudice to IFIP's Article 3 where section 3.3 'Termination [of membership]' could usefully be redrafted so that what constitutes a 'serious offence' is made clear.

## 7 RECOMMENDATION

IFIP should establish a working party to draft IFIP guide-lines on what form codes of conduct and practice should take. To help in setting the agenda for such a working party, extracts from the BCS Code of Conduct are given below:

### 2. CODE OF CONDUCT

1. Professional Conduct

   Member's conduct shall uphold the dignity, reputation and good standing of the profession.

2. Professional Integrity

   A member shall not by unfair means do anything that would harm the reputation, business or prospects of another member, and he shall at all times act with integrity towards the Society, its members and the members of other professions with whom he may be concerned in a professional capacity.

3. Public Interest

   A member in discharging his responsibility to his employer or client shall have proper regard to the public interest and to the rights of third parties and, in particular, shall ensure that the intellectual property rights of others are not prejudiced by him.

4. Fidelity

   A member shall discharge his obligations to his employer or client with complete fidelity. He shall not disclose confidential information relating to his employer or client.

5. Technical Competence

   A member shall offer only those services which are within his competence and shall declare to his employer or client the relevant level of competence he possesses when his services are being sought.

6. Impartiality

   A member, when acting for a client, shall inform his client in writing of any interest he may have which could prejudice the impartiality of his advice or could conflict with his client's interests.

### 6. DISCIPLINARY PROCEDURES

**All members of the Society undertake to abide by the Society's Code of Conduct. It will sometimes happen, however, that someone (member or non-member) wishes to lay a complaint against a member for infringement of the Code, and this note explains the Society's procedures.**

**First the complaint is laid by letter with the Secretary-General. In many cases, because of the knowledge and experience that is available to members of the Society in the several areas of computing practice, the grievance can be settled there and then, avoiding the time and effort of formal enquiry. These discussions are conducted in strict confidence.**

**When a more difficult problem is presented, the Society's Disciplinary Committee, the members of which are appointed by Council, will be called to look into the grievance. The Disciplinary Committee will set a date for a hearing and invite the complainant and respondent to be heard, giving due notice to both parties.**

**In the event of a complaint being found to be substantiated by the Disciplinary Committee, the sanctions which can be applied include reprimand, suspension and, subject to resolution by the Council, cessation of membership.**

Education and Society / R. Aiken (Editor)
Information Processing 92, Volume II
Elsevier Science Publishers B.V. (North-Holland)



# A PERSPECTIVE ON SOCIAL RESPONSIBILITY FOR THE COMPUTING COMMUNITY

K. A. Duncan

Health Information Systems
15 Parsons Way
Los Altos, CA 94022 USA

## ABSTRACT

Virtually every country is vulnerable because of inadequate social systems which can no longer cope with increasingly complex contemporary problems. Examples are found in arenas such as health care, education, economics (inflation and unemployment), and protection of the environment, and two arenas -- health care and education -- are discussed here. Approaches to solving problems in these arenas inevitably will involve computer systems, but these add further complexity. Computing professionals are well positioned to make significant contributions to solving complex problems, and this paper describes one experiment to do so. To study two barriers to progress on social problems: managing complexity and modeling reality, the Association for Computing Machinery sponsored the 1990 Conference on Critical Issues. The Conference Action Agenda is summarized and recommendations are made for further action.

Keyword Codes:K.4.2;K.7.0
Keywords:Social Issues;The Computing Profession, General

## 1. INTRODUCTION

Entire populations are faced increasingly with social ills such as pollution, recession, unemployment, homelessness, hunger, sub-optimal health, addiction, crime, and inadequate education. The major social institutions of our cities and countries are likewise increasingly unable to serve their intended purposes of alleviating these problems in contemporary society.

These kinds of socially pervasive problems affect both developed and developing countries in one form or another. They dominate the news, overshadowing the achievements of the Information Age. They play havoc with national budgets, cause us to mistrust our leaders, and cast doubt on our optimistic vision of a technology-based future. Motivation is indeed strong at local, national, and global levels to solve these problems.

In the past several decades, societies have turned increasingly to computing and communications technology, collectively called information technology, for help with previously unsolvable problems. So it is reasonable to consider how the technology might help alleviate these debilitating social problems as well, and why it has not done so yet.

It is difficult to imagine how information technology can contribute in a direct and concrete way. But an even more immediate question is how can computing professionals make a difference, and what are the first steps. As a step toward answering these, it may be useful to examine the relevant commonalities of these types of problems, and then to look in some detail at two of these socially significant arenas which will serve as models of how to approach these problems effectively.

In the next section, this paper describes the nature of complex problems where information technology has contributed to solutions, and the complex commonalities of social problems that make it difficult to use information technology. Then two social arenas where computing has clear potential -- health care and education -- are discussed as examples of how one might approach solutions. Finally, the contributions of one professional association are presented, along with a description of directions for additional contributions that could be make by other groups of computing professionals.

## 2. COMPLEXITY AND MODELS

Information technology has made it possible to solve many previously intractible large problems, and the results have transformed many aspects of society. The ability to acquire, store and retrieve on demand millions of airline fares and reservations underpins modern air passsenger service. The ability to execute billions of accurate financial transactions on a global basis every day underpins contemporary financial dealings such as the 24-hour stock exchange, options trading, currency markets, and the credit card industry. Today, also, ordinary people with TV sets can witness world events as they happen. These kinds of uses are <u>logically complex</u>, in that the processes to be automated have long been understood, but were beyond the power of humans to carry out before information technology became available.

Computing power has enabled contemporary imaging, weather prediction, space exploration, deciphering the genetic code, and weapons technology. These kinds of uses are <u>technically complex</u>, in that computing is a new tool that powerfully extends the capabilities of scientists and engineers in their domains. Again the underlying processes were either understood a priori or at least conjectured.

But many of the problems noted above which afflict societies today are not being solved by information technology because they are complex for entirely different reasons. On the surface, the sources of trouble and the ways in which the problems are growing seem to be clear and deceptively simple processes. No high technology or heavy science appears to be involved, and the volumes are manageable.

However, what these tough social problems uniquely have in common is that they are <u>conceptually complex</u>. They all involve underlying processes which are not understood, or are thought to be unimportant, or even not known to exist. That is, all require understanding human capabilities, motivations, relationships, impulses and thought processes, and their interactions with their environments. Thus, while we may be able to understand specific instances of homelessness, unemployment, hunger, or disease, the underlying elements and processes -- models -- of wide-spread malaise are not understood at all. Failed approaches to problem-solving in these arenas typically identify a small number of well-understood causes and assume these constitute an adequate model for the larger problem.

## 3. THE HEALTH CARE MODEL

Consider the example of health care -- a system abounding with human elements. In the United States health care currently consumes about 13% of the Gross Domestic Product (GDP), a ratio which is increasing every year. Further, about 1/3 of all Americans do not have any health insurance or government-sponsored health care. In fact, the health care system is now considered to be "in crisis".

Contemporary methods of medical education and practice have their roots in a model formulated early in the twentieth century -- before the discovery of antibiotics and almost all medical technologies, before the explosion of medical knowledge, before modern transportation and communications systems were known, and certainly long before the Information Age was even dreamed of. Since then, medical students have learned their craft by attending lectures, memorizing information, and practicing on patients who could not pay for private care. Health care was a privilege, not a right. The medical care delivery system was organized around the practices of individual physicians, and no policy-making body or standards for clinical practice existed. This is still the situation today in the United States and in most Western countries.

This model of health care was appropriate 75 years ago. But it is not appropriate in today's environment where the amount of medical knowledge is increasing at an unmanageable rate, where most people do not have access to even basic levels of care, where the simplest of problems must be diagnosed and treated by a person with ten years of higher education, and where diseases and treatment options can be so complex that they are poorly understood even by specialists.

New models are needed that take into account such diverse neglected <u>conceptual complexities</u> as the underserved segments of the population, the inadequate resource planning, the uninformed physician who does not know how to find and use effectively the constant stream of "new" information, the unused information in millions of hand-written medical records gathering dust in hospital basements, the unpracticed preventive care, the over-educated primary care provider, and the unknown effectiveness of many therapies. In an attempt to find a solution for the United States, leaders have focused on the only dimension of the health care system they understand -- changing the payment mechanisms, such as providing national health insurance.

Thus health care provides a concrete example of problems in a complex system that is spinning out of control, and of a leadership that ignores all but the one familiar dimension of cost in the search for a solution. Similar measures are being used in many other countries as well. [1] Even worse, the attention focused on possible payment mechanisms has obscured more fundamental problems, attention to which would have a much higher long-term payoff. Budget controls have been found to slow rising costs in some situations in the short term, but they will lead inevitably to compromised quality of care in the long term.

## 4. THE EDUCATION MODEL

Education hasn't changed much in the past several centuries. Children still gather around their teachers to receive information passed down orally -- supplemented by largely-ignored textbooks and little-used computer programs -- from generation to generation. Unfortunately, in the Information Age this approach is already failing. We now know that this approach does not equip children to deal effectively with the world in which they live -- a world in which events are moving faster and faster, and in which life is becoming increasingly complex.

Today citizens are being asked to make increasingly sophisticated decisions for which they are not equipped. The most important decision they must make in a democracy is choosing and judging their leaders. But increasingly it is clear that neither ordinary people nor their leaders understand the issues, how they affect our daily lives, and how to solve them. Worse, leaders do not understand the complex tangle of consequences their injudicious actions cause. This has depressing implications for public policy in all arenas of life.

Educational systems of today must prepare children, and especially future leaders, for a world of conceptual complexity in which there may be no right answers, but only differing viewpoints which must be weighed and acted on. Thus, children must learn to be effective acquirers and users of readily available information rather than memorizers of important but woefully inadequate information.

The need for the above is well-recognized; the path to achieving it is not. Some elements of the solution seem clear, such as creating knowledge banks and making them available through multi-media interfaces to individuals. But will tomorrow's citizens and leaders be able to use such tools? Learning today is structured so that only the most trivial cases of one or two variables for most classes of problems in almost all disciplines can be taught -- not a fertile background for coping with tomorrow's complex world. Currently proposed solutions in the United States, such as introducing competition among schools, paying teachers more, or establishing uniform knowledge criteria for graduation, seem sadly misplaced.

## 5. THE ROLE OF INFORMATION TECHNOLOGY

Information technology is used extensively in both health care and education. In health care many devices such as imaging or monitoring equipment use computers, but most applications of information technology are the same as those in business and manufacturing environments such as billing, inventory, and communications. Databases and clinical decision making are more recent, thus far limited, applications.

Information technology similarly had an early marriage with education. The benefits of such techniques as self-paced learning, drill and practice, and testing were obvious, and they were soon joined by fleeting recognition of the power of computing to extend the intellect with programs such as LOGO. More recently, computing has come into its own in schools as an applications tool for word processing, database access, and number-crunching.

However, none of these kinds of applications is going to help very much with the necessary problem solving which today is so seriously flawed in both health care and education. Rather, it will be necessary to look beyond applications that support traditional health care toward those that help us examine and understand underlying health maintenance and disease processes in humans and in populations. And it will be necessary to look beyond applications that support traditional methods of teaching toward those that will help us to examine and understand the very processes of teaching and learning.

The real power of computing lies in its use as a tool for modeling the complex systems of health care and of education. For it is only through understanding of the underlying processes that intelligent public policies in these arenas can be formulated. The greatest service computing can perform is to drive the understanding of such human processes.

Even in the short term there are more sophisticated uses for computing that would have high impact. In health care, for example, simple medical knowledge bases and record keeping systems could make it possible in both developed and developing countries to use a much lower-level health professional -- say, a high-school or a college-level graduate -- to deliver most health instruction, preventive and primary care, and to make referrals to appropriate specialists and agencies. The potential for cost savings and for bringing a basic level of care to all people is quite clear.

In education, computing could be used extensively in a variety of settings to help children learn concepts of complexity -- and therefore reality -- as applied to virtually all their studies. For instance, Biology could be extended and deepened to become Ecology, Mathematics and Civics to become Economics, and Family Living to become World Sociology. Lessons conveying these concepts may be beyond the scope of individual teachers to prepare, but they would be relatively simple for the computer to present at all grade levels. The tools for these extensions are those such as Intelligent Computer Based Instruction, modelling and simulation, statistics, information banks and search strategies.

## 6. BARRIERS AND SOLUTIONS

Even the relatively straightforward applications suggested above would probably be very difficult to achieve. Not the least of the barriers is the economic impact of making changes in entrenched systems which account for a substantial proportion of the GDP of almost all countries. For instance, making the changes that really need to be made ultimately could put tens of thousands of United States health insurance industry workers out of work, or render obsolete the skills of tens of thousands of teachers.

Many -- but not all -- aspects of these problems are beyond the scope of computing professionals to solve. But information technology is an essential tool in their solution, even though real barriers exist to using the technology effectively in these environments. It is in overcoming these barriers that the computing profession can contribute.

Although these arenas are inherently complex, introducing the necessary computer technology introduces even more layers of complexity. Thus the computing profession doubly has a contribution to make. That is, the kinds of contributions the computing profession can make to assist the sociologists, statisticians, and policy makers is toward an understanding of how to manage complexity and model reality. A similar case could be made for additional underlying issues.

The next section discusses the approach used by one element of the computing community -- the Association for Computing Machinery (ACM), an international professional society based in the United States.

## 7. THE ACM APPROACH

In November, 1990, ACM sponsored its first Conference on Critical Issues which examined the two factors of managing complexity and modeling reality in depth. Although the focus of the conference was specifically on complex projects that involved computing, it is worthwhile to examine the processes and outcomes of the conference as a model of how professional associations or other concerned groups could proceed.

At the conference, a multi-disciplinary group of computing professionals listened to expert viewpoints, discussed the underlying strategic problems, and in a workshop format created an Action Agenda designed to break down the barriers to progress in integrating information technology with socially significant problems. A significant element of the Action Agenda is that it points to which institutions, agencies, or individuals should be responsible for initiating each action.

Despite time pressures, participants were able to capture in each Action Agenda item the essence of a highly significant recommendation that might take months or years to act on.

Recommended action items for modeling reality fell into the areas of: education and curricula, public awareness, methodology, better understanding the role of people in systems, and modeling research. Key elements of that Action Agenda are summarized (unprioritized) in Table 1.

Recommended actions items for managing complexity fell into the areas of: education and awareness of complexity issues, capture and transfer of experience, development of an infrastructure, and complex systems research. Key elements of that Action Agenda are summarized (unprioritized) in Table 2.

Although the Action Agenda items were developed separately for managing complexity and modeling reality, the two groups had many concerns in common. Both groups' recommendations reflect concern for the public's ability to deal with a world in which many, if not most, important decisions would be based on interpretation of model outputs. Similarly, there was concern in both groups about the ability of scientists to create and use models appropriately, and about the preparedness of leaders and public policy makers to interpret model outputs. Both groups recognized the need for better tools and for an infrastructure within which significant research, development and validation could take place.

Table 1
Action Agenda Summary for Modeling Reality

-- Educators, professional associations, and vendors need to develop K-12 curriculum materials on understanding the use of models; government should provide funding.

-- Professional associations need to establish professional curriculum requirements for appropriate use of models in science and engineering, including the social perspective.

-- A multi-disciplinary group of professional associations should develop new professional graduate education programs in modeling (a new discipline).

-- Professional associations and universities should develop workshops for policy makers who need to understand the strengths and shortcomings of models.

-- Professional associations should provide examples of model development and application to the press for public education.

-- Professional associations should encourage sharing of information about modeling among professionals through provision of a network forum, encouraging publications, creation of a software repository for visualization and modeling tools, and offering workplace problem focus meetings.

-- Government, industry, and foundations need to work together to define a strategy for further research, development, training, and funding in modeling, to include a) establishing a unifying taxonomy and theory of modeling, b) understanding how to model the role of humans and social environments, and c) establishment of standards.

Table 2
Action Agenda Summary for Managing Complexity

-- Government should organize a multidisciplinary effort to address specification, design and operation of complex systems.

-- Planned government initiatives should include basic research on complex systems and include adequate investment in, and training for, software engineers.

- Government needs to establish a major new initiative focusing on software.

-- The research community should develop new methodologies oriented toward dynamic processes.

-- Universities and professional associations need to offer professional curricula for problem solving in realistic, complex situations, and recommendations for staff qualifications to develop and operate specific types of complex systems.

-- National repositories are needed for historical project data and for research into system development and behavior.

-- Government needs to enhance its programs on public understanding of science to include complexity of computer-based projects.

## 8. CONCLUSION AND RECOMMENDATIONS

The process of creating this Action Agenda has served to dramatize the work that needs to be done, from the perspective of computing professionals, for just two of the fundamental, critical cornerstones to progress in realizing the benefits of information technology in socially significant arenas. It bears repeating that this is a higly significant contribution for those professionals to make, because the burdens which complex social systems are placing on societies are enormous.

Although useful in and of itself, this exercise also points to a number of possible next steps which ACM and other groups such as professional organizations like IFIP, governments, industry groups, academic groups, or combinations of these, could take.

1. Facilitate this Action Agenda. The scope of this Action Agenda is beyond the capabilities of any single organization, but steps can be taken to: a) prioritize and select among the agenda items those items appropriate for action by a particular group, and/or b) act as a facilitator to bring together the relevant groups which could take action on the ACM recommendations.

2. Implement one or more agenda items. The first steps here might be to develop a multi-disciplinary consensus for a position paper on, say, justification and guidelines for curriculum changes, or a proposal for a Center of Excellence for Modeling.

3. Broaden the base of the recommendations. These recommendations were made by computing professionals. They could be strengthened/validated by taking the same issues to other groups (or combinations) such as sociologists, legal experts, public policy makers, health care providers, and educators.

4. Create a process for identification of critical issues. The two issues studied at the ACM Critical Issues Conference were identified by its Strategic Planning Committee as being particularly appropriate for ACM's consideration. A more broadly-based selection process might well identify "better" (higher visibility, more timely, more significant) issues.

5. Develop Action Agendas for other issues. Although Agenda development is an important action per se, there is also an important possible second effect. Agendas developed for a wide selection of critical issues could form the basis for a model that could lead to understanding underlying problem-solving processes.

The Critical Issues Conference report cited earlier, which is available from ACM Press, may provide useful guidelines to other groups interested in creating conference-based Action Agendas. The report contains all the papers presented at the conference, and it explains in some detail the processes used in arriving at the Action Agenda, including the intermediate output (such as positive and negative problem factors and strategic problems ) of the process. It also contains an extensive bibliography of the two issues of managing complexity and modeling reality.

## 9. REFERENCES

1 Health Care Spending Control: The Experience of France, Germany, and Japan, United States General Accounting Office, Washington, DC, 1991.

2 Frailey, Dennis J., Managing Complexity and Modeling Reality, Strategic Issues and an Action Agenda from the 1990 ACM Conf on Critical Issues, ACM Press, New York City, 1991.

Education and Society / R. Aiken (Editor)
Information Processing 92, Volume II
Elsevier Science Publishers B.V. (North-Holland)



# Ethics and Information Systems Practice

A. B. Morris

Information Systems Section, Department of Accounting, University of Cape Town, Private Bag, Rondebosch, 7700, South Africa.

e-mail: andrew@infosys.uct.ac.za

## Abstract

Ethics is a subject that should receive more attention from information systems (I.S.) practitioners than it does at present. This lack of attention, and in many instances total indifference, may be due to the nature of I.S. practitioners and their perceived role in organisations.

Technology continues to advance at a pace that leaves the I.S. practitioner little time to consider the broader picture. Increasing demand for networks, and software solutions create a vast range of ethical issues. I.S. practitioners faced the problems of balancing privacy against the demand for access, whilst ensuring accuracy and protection of information.

The combined effect of computers and data communications alters relationships between people and organisations, and the nature of this interaction has undergone a fundamental change. Conventional telephony and documentation allow both the initiator and the receiver sufficient time to make considered decisions, based upon a set of agreed facts. High speed networks make vast amounts of information immediately available, and large complex databases continually enhance available information. Together, these factors influence the nature of the decision-making process. Whilst the parties are better informed they are unable to devote sufficient time to making considered decisions.

General business policies and codes of conduct are seldom debated, let alone written down or enforced, and few attend to the issues surrounding information. The majority of I.S. executives leave such matters to senior management and this may contribute to the fact that the I.S. function remains relegated to a secondary role in most organisations.

It is the role of I.S. to find solutions, often asking, *Can we do this?* There is increasing pressure to ask the more searching question, *Should we do this?*

Keyword Codes: K.4.2; K.5.0; K.7.2.
Keywords: Computer and Society, Social Issues; Legal Aspects of Computing; The Computing Profession, Organisations.

## 1. Introduction

As we move into a new era of technological innovation the role of the computer is developing from a simple data processor to a corporate asset: *'Computers are rapidly becoming the primary repositories of negotiable assets which can only be viewed through automated means,'* **(20, p196)**.

This suggests that organisations are increasingly dependent upon information systems (I.S.) practitioners for the protection of a vital asset. It is therefore important that I.S. practitioners develop a sense of responsibility in applying ethics to their daily activities. The alternative is external pressures, to conform to a code of ethics, **(13)**. Despite the growing concern for ethics in the field of I.S., there seems to be little agreement about methods to overcome these problems. Legislation in most countries has focused upon the protection of information and intellectual property, rather than as a basis for the development of I.S. as a profession.

In South African, the proposed Bill of Human Rights and other legal activities are likely to bring information issues to the fore, as is happening in other countries **(23)**. This will continue to raise complex problems. State controlled information and the subordination of individual rights will become an increasingly contentious issue as the process of democratization continues.

There is also an urgent need for South Africa to adjust to again becoming a player in the global market. What was expedient during sanctions may no longer be acceptable. Many international software companies left South Africa and appeared to *abandon* their users. As a result, copying software was not only *justified* but seen as an act of almost patriotic zeal.

## 2. What is ethics ?

Ethics is defined in the Oxford English Dictionary as: *'the rules of conduct recognised in certain limited departments of human life'; 'the science of human duty in its widest extent, including, besides ethics proper, the science of law whether civil, political or international.'* This definition is extremely broad and may appear vague and insubstantial when applied to the provision of service. A more practical definition **(8)** and the one that is most applicable in the context of practice suggests that: *'any issue implying significant harm or benefit to others can be described as ethical.'*

## 3. Values and Responsibility

I.S. practitioners should strive for professional standing, but what constitutes a profession? Bennion **(4)** proposes that the following characteristics apply to professional practice:

- **Intellectual Basis.** An intellectual discipline, capable of formulation on theoretical, if not academic, lines, requiring a good educational background, and tested by examination.
- **Private Practice.** A foundation in private practice, so that the essential expertise and standards derive from meeting the needs of individual clients, normally on a fee basis.
- **Advisory function.** Often coupled with an executive function to carry out what has been advised, and full responsibility taken by the person exercising them.

- **Tradition of service.** An essentially objective and disinterested outlook, where the money motive is subordinate to service in a manner consistent with the public good.
- **Representative Institute.** One or more societies or institutes representing members of the profession, particularly those in private practice, having the function of safeguarding and developing the expertise and standards of the profession.
- **Code of Conduct.** A code of professional ethics, laid down and enforced by the professional institute or institutes.

Although many of these elements exist, I.S. cannot truly be classed as a profession. Industry bodies depend entirely upon influence rather than legal requirements, and have no power to control entry. The most severe sanction is withdrawal of membership, which has little effect, since membership is not a pre-requisite for practice.

The absence of strong representation is likely to see greater legislative control in the long term. However, raising concern for ethics in the field of I.S. is a means of minimising external control, and individually I.S. practitioners should strive to develop *professional* qualities **(1, 5)**:

- **Honesty.** 'Would I want this done to me if I were in the client's position.'
- **Candour.** The ability to deal with professional relationships in such a way as to ensure disclosure of all necessary information.
- **Competence.** Becoming and remaining proficient, but also knowing the limits of competence.
- **Diligence.** Avoiding carelessness or neglect whilst acting timeously.
- **Loyalty.** A strong sense of allegiance but which avoids concealment of illegal acts.
- **Discretion.** Protection of the underlying value of privacy.
- **Self-confidence.** Seeking different points of view to decide what is right at a given time and place in a particular set of relationships or circumstances.
- **Tough mindedness.** The willingness to make decisions when the facts are not, or can not be known, and questions arising have not established and definite solutions.

In assessing actual events to determine *right and wrong* it is necessary to consider:

- **Intention.** There must be intent for an act to be ethical. It has to be the result of a rational process, not simply an omission.
- **The act itself.** Consideration must be given to the act in isolation to assess whether it is ethical regardless of other considerations.
- **Relationship of parties.** Recognising relationships focuses duties of care and obligation.
- **Consequences for primary parties.**
- **Consequences for society as a whole or other parties.** Extending the scope of influence beyond the immediate ensures consideration of the ethical issues in their true perspective.

Ethical issues differ from legal issues since unethical behaviour requires intent and knowledge. In law, ignorance is no defence. Therefore responsibility is an essential ingredient: *'Responsibility is the only effective force because it breaks the common gridlock of interests, we must create responsibility,'* **(8)**.

This sentiment is echoed in much of the literature as the ability to accept the consequences of actions to be an effective decision-maker. The demands upon the professional are to be vigilant and to face conflicts: *'the price of success involves ethical pressures -- playing to win may involve hurting someone. Some say that 'business ethics' is a contradiction in terms,'* **(2, p132)**. This suggests that the simple process of commerce may create unavoidable conflicts of an ethical nature.

If we are to become a profession in the true sense, it has to be the result of an internalised drive for change. No amount of external pressure will assist the process of legitimising the professional aims. Probably external pressure would have a negative effect upon professional standing.

*'Rather than waiting for others to develop codes of appropriate behaviour, it behooves business and the professions to reexamine their behaviour. The mere process of developing and promulgating a code will itself sharpen the realisation of individual and group responsibilities and hopefully reduce the probable government interference in the freedom of enterprise and the professions,'* **(3, p167)**.

Although there is strong evidence to suggest that ethics is a subject that needs attention, it remains difficult to grasp: *'to generalise the ethical aspects of a business decision, leaving behind the concrete particulars that make it real, is too often to sermonise, to simplify, or to rationalise away the plain fact that many instances of competing ethical claims have no satisfactory solution,'* **(1)**.

## 4. Rights in the Information Age

Computer assisted misbehaviour is no greater nor less amongst I.S. practitioners than it is among the general public. However, the general availability of computer power has seen an increase in computer related crimes based upon usage, which is not confined to I.S. practitioners, **(5)**. There are numerous publications on computer crime **(6, 7, 15, 20)**, and sensational media coverage creates the impression that I.S. practitioners should be more accountable and honest than the general public. This implies a general concern that I.S. practitioners have a duty to act professionally.

The industry must tackle this problem, since the inevitable result will be a reduction of the freedom currently enjoyed by I.S. practitioners. Whether this is beneficial, there is a real danger that any such legislation must involve the industry if it is to be for the common good.

Commercial computing has only been in existence for about 30 years and the rate of change has outstripped the individual's ability to keep up to date merely on the technical issues. Unlike other professions, I.S. needs to react quickly as a result of the issues surrounding information as an asset. As the technology is increasingly available to all there is little time to wait before taking action.

Few academic I.S. curricula include ethics, and the emphasis remains primarily on technical requirements. As the focus moves more towards behavioural issues, ethics must become increasingly relevant to help practitioners to function in the industry of the future.

Does the I.S. practitioner have an adequate understanding of ethical issues?

A difficult question to answer, and quantify, but there is a need to develop comparative measures.

The most important factor is to sensitise the practitioner to the broader issues that will confront them in the execution of their duties **(12)**. By developing a questioning environment, more commonalty of resolution will emerge. The industry will then be able to develop the knowledge of how to manage these situations.

Recognising the rights of individuals concerning information provides a basis upon which to develop. The four basic rights that are relevant to the information age are **(16)**:

- **PRIVACY**
  Protecting information from unauthorised use.
- **ACCURACY**
  Decision-making requires high quality information if it is to be effective.
- **PROPERTY**
  Knowledge embedded in computers needs protection.
- **ACCESS**
  Information must be available appropriately, but strictly controlled.

It is essential to consider that only when technology is applied moral issues are raised. This suggests a need to establish a framework for the integration of technology. This is a vital step for the industry since significant ethical learning occurs primarily in social interactions with real consequences for real actors, **(18)**.

Being professional requires that practitioners take care when applying their skills and consider the effects of their actions carefully. *'The sphere of ethical prescription is coterminous with the possibility of persons to enhance lives ... cooperation, sharing, mentoring and teaching ... is part of what is meant by professional,'* **(8, p165 & 192)**.

The I.S. practitioner is becoming increasingly responsible as custodian for vital assets and over the years has created an aura of mystery around the subject. This is the basis of power that must be exercised *'with discretion, care, and concern for those less knowledgeable in our art form than we are ourselves,'* **(5)**.

## 5. Review of Prior Research

A number of studies **(10,19,22,24)** have aimed at eliciting responses to assess ethical standards. Although they provide a basic understanding of the current values, they do not create situations that can be realistically evaluated according to experience.

The first study into ethical conflicts conducted by Parker, developed an experimental approach to discussing ethical issues, referred to as scenario analysis. Ten years later, in 1987, the study was repeated. During the intervening years the nature of computing had changed considerably. Participants were selected for their known interest in ethics in the computer field and they represented a wide range of specialties. Some of the participants in the 1987 study also participated in the earlier workshop.

The scenarios cover a wide range of practical situations that exist in I.S., and although some categories received more attention than others, there are secondary principles in all scenarios that provides broad coverage.

Parker's research provides a practical method of introducing and developing awareness of, and concern for, ethics. Creating a questioning environment in which individuals assess scenarios, allows them to exercise their own judgment. There are no *right* or *wrong* responses. The study attempts to clarify general principles in the context of practical situations. These scenarios form the basis for other survey instruments **(24)** and remain the most referenced work in this field.

Some attempts to incorporate ethics into the course curricula **(9,12,17)**, utilise scenarios together with reported events and codes of conduct of professional bodies. Dejoie et al, incorporated scenarios in a recently published text designed for use in developing ethics material for academic courses.

Further research in this area should aim to build upon this framework to *personalise* the concern for ethics, which Couger suggests is an essential first step towards proper ethical behaviour, **(12)**.

## 6. Conclusions

Despite the difficulties in developing ethics programmes it is an area that needs to be addressed. Critical situations are arising which need to considered for the ethical issues involved. Failure to do this effectively will resulting in increased external pressure and curtailment of freedom.

There is a need to develop a sense of how ethics influences the I.S. practitioner, and to construct a generalised measurement. This framework provides a means of assisting the practitioner to develop a sense of responsibility and to assess the impact of actions on others.

Simply creating awareness will encourage debate and acute skills of criticism. Moreover, consideration of the issues may help to create a basis for professional status, which is commonly recognised to be lacking in the I.S. field.

As information becomes a global commodity it is critical for representative organisations to work towards a common understanding of the ethical issues concerning information.

In South Africa there is likely to be considerable activity in this area due to the current actions in the legal system, and the re-integration into world markets, where South Africa is recognised to be *the gateway to Africa*. This could prove to be an ideal opportunity for the I.S. profession to make a significant contribution.

There is some resistance amongst practitioners working towards *being ethical*, which has caused a number of individuals to remark that: *'if everyone else does it OK, but I'm not going to be the first,'* or *'being ethical only allows people to take advantage of you ... but I'm not a computer criminal,'* **(6)**.

## 7. Recommendations

There is a need to develop a common approach to identifying and addressing ethical issues. Scenario analysis provides a basis that sensitises participants to the ethical nature of everyday events. This approach is ideal since it allows participants to frame responses to scenarios as a substitute for real situations, without running the risk of actual unethical behaviour.

Studies are currently being conducted in South Africa, using scenarios to provide a measure of local understanding of general ethical issues. The studies also take into account local conditions, such as legal issues and representative Codes of Conduct **(11)**. These studies will create a suitable basis for comparative studies with other countries, whilst developing specific requirements for educational purposes.

## 8. References


(1) K.R. ANDREWS [1989], Ethics in Practice, *Harvard Business Review*; September-October, pp. 99-104

(2) J.A. BARACH [1985], The Ethics of Hardball, *California Management Review*; vol. 27(2), pp. 132-139

(3) J.N. BEHRMAN [1988], *Essays on Ethics in Business and the Professions*, Prentice-Hall

(4) F.A.R. BENNION [1969], *Professional Ethics: The Consultant Professions and Their Code*, Charles Knight & Co. Ltd.

(5) G.J. BOLOGNA [1987], The Ethics of Managing Information, *Journal of Systems Management*; vol. 38(8), pp. 28-30

(6) J.J. BLOOMBECKER [1989], Short-Circuiting Computer Crime, *Datamation*, October 1, pp. 71-72

(7) J.J. BLOOMBECKER [1989], Malpractice in I.S., *Datamation*, October 15, pp. 85-86

(8) F.N. BRADY [1990], *Ethical Management, Rules and Results*, Macmillan

(9) R.B. BRUNNER [1990], Intellectual Property Rights in Computer Education: Legal, Societal and Ethical Issues, *Computer Science Education*, vol. 1(4), pp. 355-368

(10) E. COHEN & L. CORNWELL [1989], A Question of Ethics: Developing Information System Ethics, *Journal of Business Ethics*; vol. 8(6), pp. 431-437

(11) COMPUTER SOCIETY OF SOUTH AFRICA, Code of Practice (September 1988)

(12) J.D. COUGER [1984], Providing Norms on Ethics to Entering Employees, *Journal of Systems Management*; vol. 35(2), pp. 40-42

(13) J.D. COUGER [1989], Preparing I.S. Students to Deal With Ethical Issues, *MIS Quarterly*, June, pp. 211-218

(14) R. DEJOIE, G. FOWLER & D. PARADICE [1991], *Ethical Issues in Information Systems,* boyd and fraser publishing company.

(15) T. FORESTER & P. MORRISON [1990], *Computer Ethics, cautionary tales and ethical dilemmas in computing*, Basil Blackwell

(16) R.O. MASON [1986], Four Ethical Issues of the Information Age, *MIS Quarterly*, vol. 10 (1)

(17) P.R. MORRISON & T. FORESTER [1990], Teaching Computer Ethics and the Social Context of Computing, *Australian Computer Journal*, vol. 22(2), pp. 36-42.

(18) A. MOWSHOWITZ [1981], On Approaches to the Study of Social Issues in Computing, *Communications of the ACM*; vol. 24(3), pp. 146-155

(19) D. NEL L. PITT & R. WATSON [1989], Business Ethics: Defining the Twilight Zone, *Journal of Business Ethics*; vol. 8, pp. 781-791

(20) D.B. PARKER [1983], *Fighting Computer Crime*, Charles Scribner's Sons

(21) D.B. PARKER [1988], Ethics for Information Systems Personnel, *Journal of Information Systems Management*; vol. 5(3), pp. 44-48

(22) D.B. PARKER S. SWOPE & B.N. BAKER [1990], *Ethical Conflicts in Information and Computer Science, Technology and Business*, QED Information Sciences Inc.

(23) P. SAMUELSON [1991], Is Information Property?, *Communications of the ACM*, vol. 34(3), pp. 15-18

(24) E.A. WEISS (Editor) [1990], Self Assessment Procedure XXll, *Communications of the ACM*, vol. 33(11), pp. 110-135

Education and Society / R. Aiken (Editor)
Information Processing 92, Volume II
Elsevier Science Publishers B.V. (North-Holland)


# Towards an IFIP Frame Code of Ethics

Bl.Sendov

Center for Informatics and Computer Technology,Bulgarian Academy of Sciences,Acad.G.Bonchev str.bl.25A, 1113 Sofia, Bulgaria

As a leading international organization of computer professionalists and all specialists in the field of data processing, IFIP is committed to the solution of all problems related to these professions. The maturity and social prestige of a profession is determined by its moral principles. Therefore we, as scholars and citizens,are keenly aware of the ethics problems of our walk of life - data processing. In the process of reflection and discussion on these problems naturally a constructive idea was born - the idea to work out "The IFIP Code of Ethics" or "IFIP Code of Good Conduct".

On the other side, the ethics of a society is closely linked to its culture in the broader sense of the word. Values and moral principles are not the same for all peoples, societies and individuals in the world .This fact makes it understandably difficult to find out these invariants that could possibly serve as a Frame Code of Ethics for all states members of IFIP.

Preliminary considerations on this issue, with the broadest possible participation of representatives of various countries and cultures is necessary point of departure. The most proper forum, for holding such a discussion is undoubtedly a World Computer Congress.

It is implicitly clear, that the problem of an IFIP Frame Code of Ethics is not devoid of contents. The crux of the matter is to define this contents, which is invariant for all countries and cultures, represented in IFIP. It is only natural that this contents should take shape through a wide and competent discussion.

Education and Society / R. Aiken (Editor)
Information Processing 92, Volume II
Elsevier Science Publishers B.V. (North-Holland)



# AIMS and SCOPE of the DRAFT IFIP CODE of ETHICS

Harold Sackman

California State Univ., Los Angeles, California

## PREAMBLE

The IFIP Code of Ethics has been constructed not only for individual Information Technology (IT) professionals, but also for multinational IT organizations, and the extended IT community concerned with international legal informatics and related public policy. This Code provides guidelines for individuals, international organizations, national societies, and those influencing international public policy. The guidelines are global and multi-cultural, and are not intended to reflect any particular ideology or creed. It is hoped that the evolving Code will contribute to the constructive development and application of Information Technology throughout the world.

1. <u>Individual Professional Ethics</u>: 1.1 Social Responsibility; 1.2 Protection of Privacy; 1.3 Individual Integrity; 1.4 Professional Competence; 1.5 Personal Accountability.

2. <u>International Organizational Ethics</u>: 2.1 High Performance Standards; 2.2 International Standards and Regulations; 2.3 International Legal Protection; 2.4 Employee Productivity and Quality of Working Life; 2.5 User Participation and Feedback.

3. <u>Ethics for International Legal Informatics</u>: 3.1 Intellectual Property Law; 3.2 International Public Law; 3.3 International Telecommunications Law; 3.4 International Criminal Law.

4. <u>International Public Policy Ethics</u>: 4.1 Freedom of Communication; 4.2 Privacy and Dignity of Individuals; 4.3 Humanized Information Systems; 4.4 International Computer Literacy; 4.5 Equitable Opportunity for Information Services; 4.6 Cultural Quality of Life and Human Choice.

Education and Society / R. Aiken (Editor)
Information Processing 92, Volume II
Elsevier Science Publishers B.V. (North-Holland)


John A. N. Lee[a]

[a]Department of Computer Science, Virginia Polytechnic Institute and State University, Blacksburg VA 24061-0106, USA
Ph: 1 (703) 231-5780, FAX: 1 (703) 231-6075
E-mail: janlee@vtcs1.cs.vt.edu (internet).

**Abstract**

The availability of the computer to a broad spectrum of the community has brought under its influence a number of individuals who may not be well disciplined in appropriate ethical behavior. In a curriculum lacking precedents and truly parallel paradigms as in driver and sex education, this presentation recommends that serious consideration must be given to introducing ethical concepts and case studies into secondary school classes as well as in professional school curriculum related to computing. Surveys have shown that the person most likely to have misused a computer or communication system is the employee of the system under attack. It is the responsibility of the computer community to reach as many of these employees during their formative years to divert them from inappropriate practices. The objective of this presentation is to consider the state of affairs in computing which leads to deep concerns about ethical behavior and to present proposals for the inclusion of ethical concepts in early computer related courses.

Keyword Codes: K.5.0; K.3.2
Keywords: Legal Aspects of Computing, General; Computers and Education, Computer and Information Science Education.

Education and Society / R. Aiken (Editor)
Information Processing 92, Volume II
Elsevier Science Publishers B.V. (North-Holland) 


# Efficacy of Ethics Codes for Computer Professionals

C. D. Martin[a] and D. H. Martin[b]

[a]Electrical Engineering and Computer Science Department, The George Washington University, Washington, D.C. 20052, USA

[b]Vice- President, Q-Systems, 1655 N. Fort Myer Dr., Rosslyn, VA, 22209, USA

## Abstract

To determine the ethical standards recognized by computer professionals, the existing codes of ethics from the Association for Computing Machinery (ACM), the Institute of Electrical and Electronic Engineers (IEEE),the Data Processing Managers Association (DPMA), and the Institute for Certification of Computer Professionals (ICCP) were compared[1]. A number of common themes emerged as the core of ethical behavior for all computer professionals. They are 1) personal integrity / claim of competence; 2) personal accountability for work; 3) responsibility to employer /client; 4) responsibility to profession; 5) confidentiality of information / privacy; 6) conflict of interest; 7) dignity /worth of people; 8) public safety, health, and welfare; 9) participation in professional societies; and 10) increase public knowledge about technology. It is encouraging that in all of the ethics codes of the computer professional societies there is an emphasis on the relationship and interaction of the computer professional with other *people*, rather than with *machines*. This places the focus of ethical behavior upon ethical or right dealings with people, rather than upon the technology.

With the recent efforts of the International Federation of Information Processing (IFIP) to undertake the ambitious task of developing an international code of ethics for information technology professionals, new areas of concern have been added to the code. In attempting to cut across international boundaries in a multicultural arena, the proposed IFIP ethics code goes far beyond ethics into the areas of international law and cultural values. At the individual level it covers some of the same issues of the four previous codes. With the exception of participation in professional societies, the common ethics themes from previous ethics codes are found, either directly or indirectly, in the new IFIP code. Eight additional themes raised in the IFIP code not found in previous codes are a specific statement of social responsibility, the establishment of standards, an emphasis on quality of life, equity, protection of intellectual property, consequences of networks, basic human rights, and the rights of users.

To judge the efficacy of the IFIP code of ethics we must ask whether it will be able to fulfill the functions of a professional code of ethics delineated by Frankel[2]. Will it be an enabling document for professionals, a source of public evaluation, a source of professional socialization, an enhancement of professional reputation and public trust, a deterrent to unethical behavior, a support system for members, and a source of adjudication?

[1]Martin, C. D. and Martin, D.H. "Professional Codes of Conduct and Computer Ethics Education." *Social Science Computer Review*, 8(1), Spring, 1990, p. 96-108.

[2]Frankel, M.S. "Professional Codes: Why, How, and with What Impact?" *Journal of Business Ethics*, 8(2&3), Feb. - Mar., 1989, p.110-115.

Keyword Codes: K.4.1, K.4.2
Keywords: Public Policy Issues, Social Issues

Education and Society / R. Aiken (Editor)
Information Processing 92, Volume II
Elsevier Science Publishers B.V. (North-Holland)


# LEGAL ASPECTS OF THE INFORMATION SOCIETY

Professor Bryan Niblett

5, Fairlawn Wharf, East Saint Helen Street, Abingdon, Oxfordshire, England

## ABSTRACT

The purpose of this paper is to highlight the significance of certain legal aspects of a developing information society. Such a society is founded on the representation of information as strings of binary digits. Representation in this most basic of forms makes possible new methods of transmitting and processing information which amount to a revolution in communications. Strings of binary digits may be conveyed at high speed and high volume to any point on the earth by terrestrial or satellite carriers; they may be reproduced without error any number of times at minimal cost; they may be transferred as ciphers using advanced cryptographic methods; they may constitute vast databases which can be searched simultaneously by many users at remote terminals; they may be disseminated over networks which are themselves interconnected; and above all these bit strings may be processed by digital computers in an immense variety of ways. So powerful and pervasive is this technology that it is inevitably accompanied by noteworthy legal consequences.

One distinctive feature of the information society is the emphasis it gives to proprietary rights in intellectual products. These intangible goods are the new wealth. The information society entails a market place for these products and the essence of a market is the transfer of property rights. Patents for novel circuit designs, copyrights in computer programs and compilations of data, and claims to trade secrets are examples of proprietary rights that may be exchanged in these markets to enable purchasers to express their choices in a way that guides further developments by suppliers. This paper affirms the view that well-defined rights to intellectual property are necessary for the effective development of a global information society.

Whilst property rights have been successfully created for computer products, both tangible and intangible, few proprietary interests exist in the heavily regulated telecommunications industry. This may well be the reason why the power of processing modes in digital networks is so much greater than the capacity of communication links to feed those nodes. This paper suggests that a new industry of digital interface design and manufacture is essential to allow effective communication between networks at all levels and that this industry can best be founded on proprietary rights in these interfaces. An even bolder step would be to create private rights in the electromagnetic spectrum to encourage an efficient market in telecommunications that would motivate more efficient use of the spectrum.

Among the torrent of bit strings that are processed automatically in an information society are those that represent personal details of living individuals. The new opportunities for high speed matching, searching, linkage and transmission of these sensitive data has become a major concern for legal systems. Intellectual property law provides some protection against improper use of personal data as do the laws of contract and of tort. Useful as these familiar laws may be they do not provide the special remedies required in response to new methods of automatic processing. Hence the active world wide interest in specific laws for data protection. This paper argues that data protection can best be achieved by methods similar to those for protection of intellectual property: the creation of private rights which enable actions to be brought by the private person rather than by public authorities.

The use of bit strings to represent valuable commercial information and to provide means for transmission of funds across digital networks is vulnerable to various types of computer misuse. Much of this misuse comes within the scope of conventional crimes of theft, false accounting, dishonestly obtaining property by deception and criminal damage. No doubt these offences will have to be extended to deal with the special characteristics of digital systems and new offences introduced to deal with novel acts of fraud or deception or damage. There is however a less serious type of activity which is classified as unauthorised access to computer systems. What is vital is that the technology of computer security be developed to enable private protection of computers and computer networks. This paper adopts the view that this technological development can be best achieved by providing remedies for unauthorised access by means of the civil law rather than criminal prosecution. The use of authoritarian law as a means of preventing unauthorised access is likely to be less effective than providing a remedy by way of civil actions brought by private persons.

The development of the information society inevitably results in the occurrence of commercial disputes which involve a complex mix of law and computer and communication technology. Many of these disputes are between parties from different jurisdictions and comprehend novel technical issues which lie beyond the leading edge of the law. The most effective method of resolving these disputes is not in the public courts of one specific jurisdiction but in private tribunals where arbitrators with an understanding of this technology can apply legal principles independent of any national legal order. Again this paper argues that the private resolution of these disputes is superior to the public remedy.

The generation, processing and transmission of information by means of bit strings supplies remarkable power to the private individual who at a processing mode in a computer network has immense intellectual resources at his fingertips. This shift of power from the public to the private, from a top down command structure to a bottom-up configuration, inevitably endows the private law with a role of immense significance in the healthy development of the information society.

Education and Society / R. Aiken (Editor)
Information Processing 92, Volume II
Elsevier Science Publishers B.V. (North-Holland)



# Legal Aspects of Data Security

Prof.Dr. iur. Wolfgang Kilian, Director, Institute for Legal Informatics, University of Hannover, F.R.G.

## 1. Data Security - a matter of legal concern?

Data security seems to be an area, where computer scientists are the actors and lawyers should keep off. This indeed happened in the past. But the increase of data transmission networks, the computer-to-computer exchange of data and documents, data based services and data processing of person related data created an urgent need for establishing a legal framework, which would serve as a guideline for the developing of standards and technical measures. As data transmission became a worldwide phenomenon, the demand for national and international rules increased. Computer systems are risky instruments, as Joseph Weizenbaum predicted many years ago[1]). Meanwhile, we have learnt a lot about systems failure, deficient software, technical errors, incompatible standards, human insufficency. Financial losses are caused by deficient software, personal harm results from defective computer assisted medical monitoring or expert systems. The demand for trusted operating systems is obvious. But who is responsible for nominating the level of security, establishing security categories, the introduction of nationally and internationally binding rules and standards? Who is held responsible to harmonize the interests of hard- and softwareproducers, service providers and consumers? Who is to prevent the externalization of risks caused by deficient data security? Computer scientists must expect the intervention of law and the lawyers in their work, it is only in this way that inadequate design in disregard of legal requirements may be avoided.

## 2. Threats

There are two major sets of threats affecting computer systems: Deficiencies and Misuse.

### 2.1 Deficiencies

One threat is that technical errors in data transmission and operation result in disturbed communication, financial losses, defective products or personal harm. The technical errors may be caused by wrong input/output data, deficient software or incompatible technical standards. The Open Systems Interconnection (OSI) reference model tends to reduce technical errors. The OSI-implementation is a successful step-by-step approach. But the technical standards developed so far by technicians do not reflect legal aspects like evidentiary value of electronic documents or the transmission of person related data.

## 2.2 Misuse

A second threat is that information and documents in computer networks could be secretly reproduced in their entirety or altered after their original creation or misused by disloyalemployees, trustees or recipients. Keywords in this context are: Penetrating, probing, hacking, lack of integrity, lack of confidence. One example is the "worm"-attack of 1988 in the U.S.A., when 6000 data processing systems were intruded and the losses exceeded 20 M US-Dollars[2]). The fixing of technical security measures has to be related to legally and economically reasonable security provisions.

## 3. Network Security and the Legal Model of Regulations

The legal issues involved in data security within computer networks come into focus as one examines the principles of risk allocation, the criteria for loss distribution and the requirements of data protection. Whereas for risk allocation and loss distribution the law may ultimately employ market oriented theories concerned with economic efficiency, in respect of protection of personal data it must consider the right, guaranteed by the constitution or special acts, of each individual to determine what personal data is being held about him.

There is no point in treating equally those communications networks differing from each other in both form and purpose. Because of the variable status of material and immaterial values, a higher level of protection is demanded by law whenever human life or health is at stake, as is the case with (for example) flight security, military warning systems and medical monitoring systems.

Legal issues involved in the security of communications networks can arise in three different elements of that system:

*In the network infrastructure
*In provision of network services
*In data communication

These elements are to be dealt with in the context of various levels of legislative authority and subjects of legislation.

## 3.1 The Network Infrastructure

In a number of states the network infrastructure is controlled by state monopoly: this is the case in Germany, France, the Netherlands and Japan. In Great Britain there is a 'double monopoly' [British Telecom and Mercury] and there are local monopolies in the USA. In respect of the German postal system the Direct-Dial network, the Datel networks, the Datex-L and Datex-P networks, the Telex network, the analogue telephone network as well as the Integrated Service Data network (ISDN) are administered as a monopoly by the German post office. The objective being to enable public and private networks should be able to communicate with each other in a sort of "non stop shopping" system[3]). This approach will entail additional problems when plans for public access are implemented.

The main focus of legislation is to be found in public law measures to the exclusion of private (contractual) arrangements.

### 3.2 Provision of Services

The operation of these networks is underpinned by standardized transmission services. As regards the German postal system these are (for example) Telex, Telefax, Telebox and Btx. Such services using the public networks must compete with each other. The competitors have the capacity to influence the security of their services. Offering a range of security standards could be an element of that competition.

The main emphasis of the legislation in this area is on contract, competition and commercial law. In the near future these areas of law must be reformulated and adapted.

### 3.3 Data Communication

Data communication encompasses every type of information which may be digitally formulated.

The legal emphasis is on contract law, but tort, insurance law and data-protection are also important. It is conceivable that a specific "Data Traffic Act" may come about along the same lines as the "Road Traffic Act".

### 3.4 A Technical Model for Network Security

The basic functions of a secure system from a technical standpoint are[4]):

*Identification and authentication of those persons and actions involved in the system of communication.

*Allocation and verification of authority to use the system of communication.

*Setting out the manner in which this authority is to be used.

*Recycling of network components.

*Safety-net in case of loss of function or data in the system.

*Guaranteeing the operation of the system.

*Protecting the means of transmission by authentication of the other party, by access-control, by maintaining the secrecy of the data, by directing the data to a specific destination, and by authentication of data flow according to sender and receiver.

All these basic functions in computer networks can be rated on a scale of very weak to very strong and arranged into appropriate performance classes. The safest possible system therefore would take the form of a data network very strongly influenced by all the basic functions mentioned and for evidential purposes, demonstrating those functions in the most formalised manner possible.

This ground model for a secure network from a technical standpoint begs the question whether, and to what extent, the basic functions mentioned could be acceptable as a legal model and (if they are acceptable) whether they could ever be enforced. This would then have an effect on (for example) software development, contract drafting, risk allocation and damages liability.

## 3.5 Consequences for the Legal Model of Network Security

In the technical model of a secure system just described it is to be noted that no mention is made of the rules applicable to a particular communication. Thus the technical model is abstracted from the roles and expectations of the parties, the contents of the data being transferred, the reasonableness of the security precautions taken and the effects of falsified or incomplete data on the individual or company concerned. It is, however, precisely these points which appear important to the legal model. It is true that as yet no legal model for network security has been explicitly formulated, but the inclusion of the latter elements are inferable from arguments which proved decisive for other arrangements involving similar risks. The technical model therefore forms only the basis of the legal evaluation but it fails to cover all the material points. Moreover it has its own faults: yet to be considered are databank security, risk management, harmonisation with other models and the interplay of various operators. Nonetheless further development of this technical model will contribute dynamism to the development of legal standards.

Defining international technical standards of data protection assumes a special meaning for the law. Such standards are an attempt to make legal requirements workable by means of criteria that are capable of being empirically tested. These criteria comprise not only an expert opinion but also a value judgement which sets a precedent for judicial decisions. More than 100 international norms exist for the OSI seven layer model alone[5]. In addition there are countless telecommunications standards for ISDN which will soon provide the nerve system of the European services market.

The most complex legal issue in relation to data security in computer networks may prove to be establishing the required level of protection for one particular technical measure. Since there can not be absolute security it will ultimately be a question of minimizing risks in a reasonable and economically acceptable manner. The state of scientific knowledge or technology at any one time can provide a basis, legal assessment is not rendered superfluous however.

# 4 A Summary of the Legal Debate

The legal issues concerning security in data processing networks have established themselves at different levels of legislative authority and in different areas of law.

## 4.1 Legislative Levels

The legislative levels of authority to be considered are:

*International treaties and administrative agreements
*Private international contracts
*European Community law
*National law
*Duties between individuals - contract law

### 4.1.1 **International Treaties and Administrative Agreements**

Data flow does not stop at borders. For this reason the legal framework for data security cannot be exclusively national, rather it must be supranationally regulated. Hence a number of international organisations are responsible for regulating the network infrastrusture or organizing services. The following are of note.

*The International Telephone and Telegraph Consultative Committee (CCITT)
*The European Commission for Postal and Telephone Communications (CEPT)
*The International Telecommunications Union (ITU)
*The General Agreement on Tariffs and Trade (GATT)
*The European Committee for Standardization (CEN)
*The European Committee for Electrotechnical Standardisation (CENELEC)
*The European Telecommunications Standards Institute (ETSI)

Various international organisations have in addition set up closed groups of data network--users and in doing so simultaneously regulate their conditions of use. Belonging to this group are:

*The data network of the World Meteorology Organisation (METEOSAT)
*The data network of the international maritime satellite radio organisation (INMARSAT)
*The data network of the police authorities (INTERPOL).

The United Nations is also dealing with legal problems arising from computer networks within several sub-organisations. Hence the UNCITRAL rules as to liability for electronic payment systems and the legal implications of computerized files.

### 4.1.2 **Private International Contracts**

Not to be overlooked are those private international contracts which contain legally relevant material on data security in computer networks. The closed network of the Society for Worldwide Interbank Financial Telecommunications (SWIFT), a company subject to Belgian law to which more than 3,000 banks from 70 industrialised countries belong, is regulated by privately agreed security mechanisms. The same is true of the network of the international aviation companies (SITA) or the European Academic Research Network (EARN).

However, most influential for the law are those security standards set out by the International Standardisation Organisation (ISO), an organisation based on private international contracts. The ISO seven layer model could be adopted as it stands as a basis at least for data security. There is now the ISO's comprehensive proposals for a set of standards allowing secure public access to networks[6]).

Legally speaking one should note in connection with the development of norms by private organisations that the norms set down cannot claim a general binding authority in the same way as democratically legitimated laws. Nevertheless, these norms have become a legal indicator of expected technological standards due to their incorporation into network user contracts, service contracts, software contracts and insurance contracts and due to their citation in judicial decisions[7]).

### 4.1.3 European Community Law

As yet the EC has done little to promote data security law within the common market. There are several grounds set out in the EEC treaty conferring legislative competence in this matter: Free flow of services within the common market (Art. 8a(2)), harmonisation of laws (Art. 100(1)), establishment of collective standards in the field of technological development (Art. 130(2)), or enactment of legislation for unforseen circumstances (Art. 235). Admittedly there is always the difficulty that data security law can be seen as limiting the free flow of data thus conflicting with the aims of liberalising the movement of goods and services (Art. 30, 31, 59 EEC treaty). The need for an equilibrium with other aims such as the protection of privacy or of trade secrets is not provided for in the treaty.

Nonetheless since the single European Act came into force in 1987 there has been a shift in technology policy within the EC. Worthy of note are the foundation and promotion of ETSI and the research project TEDIS, concerned with the legal requirements of electronic data exchange according to the laws of the member states.

### 4.1.4 National Law

To the extent that there are no legally binding supranational provisions for data security in computer networks, the national legislative may put forward legislation. In view of the huge extent of some group networks, the range of national measures is admittedly limited. A state's legislative competence applies only to domestic matters. For example a link could be made to the service provider's registered office within that state or access to the network within that state, alternatively that the data transmission occurred to or from that state.

In the context of the law of conflicts the more basic question arises as to which data security laws are to be applied to these cross-border group networks: The law of the state in which the service provider has his registered office? The law of the state in which the mistake occured? This can have a considerable effect on the scope of data security provisions, the quantum of damages upon breach of contract and the evidentiary problems involved.

### 4.1.5 Duties between individuals - Contract Law

The legal issues of data security are most frequently addressed in the sphere of private autonomy. Such self-regulation has its advantages and disadvantages: As an advantage one could point to the lack of state intervention, a disadvantage is the risk allocation, usually in favour of the party with the better bargaining power.

At present self-regulatory standards are being developed predominantly in sectors of industry (the chemical industry; automobile industry; transport; banks; insurance). The International Chamber of Commerce has drawn up a unified code for the interchange of commercial data by means of data transmission (UNCID-rules) which have been adopted by the United Nations Economic Commission for Europe (UNECE).

In the field of international payment transactions not only is the technical network highly developed but also its legal basis. In Germany the leading economic interest groups have struck the following agreements:

*An agreement for the inter-institutional cash dispensing systems.
*An agreement on the use of screen texts
*The conditions of use of screen texts
*A framework agreement for the completion of a system of automated cashless payments to trade and services businesses implemented on an inter-institutional scale.

All conditions of use for the customer entail inter alia liability clauses proportioning risk between bank and customer. The bank's customer is allotted all liability resulting from misuse or forgery under their general terms of business (for example inadequate safeguarding of his EC-card; failing to keep the personal identification number (PIN) or transaction number (TAN) secret; use of card subsequent to theft). Admittedly the banks may not free themselves entirely under German law, they must for their part take such organisational measures as are technically possible and economically viable. To this category belong, by way of illustration, security precautions in allocating PIN and TAN numbers and recording entries. This allocation of the risks is widely endorsed in the courts and literature.

SWIFT as the central organiser of international bank transactions has developed its own approach to data security. Deficiencies may be observed however: for example Belgium, where the company is registered, has no data protection law and has yet to ratify the convention on data protection. At the beginning of this year the US General Accounting Office on behalf of the House of Representatives was given the task of investigating the systems of electronic payment in the US from a security standpoint; in doing so it was established that there were also serious deficiencies in the SWIFT system.

## 5 Conclusion

Currently, almost all technical provisions and legal problems related to data security should be studied in the context of establishing transborder electronic data interchange (EDI). The United Nations Standard EDIFACT (UN\EDIFACT), in particular, will assist the transformation of paper based to paperless transactions and communications. The probative value of electronic documents, the acceptance of an electronic signature, the conclusion of a contract by computer-to-computer communication are disputed and have to be regulated on a private, national and international level. Lawyers have to think about functional equivalents to paper based correspondence and person-to-person declarations of intent. Adaption of the legal system to technical developments for the purposes of harmonizing the legal provisions in the member states is being effected by the European Economic Community (EEC) TEDIS project. An additional approach is being undertaken by the United Nations Economic Commission for Europe (UNECE): Many states are participating there in the formulation of a private EDI model agreement for electronic transactions. The UN-EDI model agreement will comprise not only provisions on electronic contracting and communication by means of computers; security aspects, risk management and rules on liability are also expected to become part of this model agreement.

## References

1. Computer Power and Human Reason, Boston 1976, Chap. 10.

2. German Government, Appendix 2, Kabinettsvorlage BMI, Oct. 25, 1989.

3. Roden, EDI-Aktivitäten der EG, EDI 89 Report, p. 12.

4. Information Technology Security Evaluation Criteria (ITSEC), Harmonised Criteria of France, Germany, The Netherlands, The United Kingdom, Version 1.2 June 28, 1991 (distributed by German Information Security Agency BSI)

5. See Tobergte, Standards und Normen, in: Computerrechts-Handbuch (ed. Kilian/-Heussen), München 1991, Chapter 401.

6. OSI-Security Architecture (ISO DIS 7498.2).

7. See BGHZ 59, 303 (308)-German Federal Civil Court.

Education and Society / R. Aiken (Editor)
Information Processing 92, Volume II
Elsevier Science Publishers B.V. (North-Holland)



# Legal Control of IT Misuse: The Limited Relevance of the Criminal Law

Martin Wasik

Reader in Law, Manchester University, Manchester, UK

**Abstract**

The Computer Misuse Act 1990, which became law in the UK in August 1990, created three new criminal offences. Two of these outlaw the gaining of unauthorised access to computer-held programs or data(1). The third offence criminalises the deliberate corruption or erasure of computer programs or data, including the circulation of worms and viruses. The new law has been considered in detail elsewhere(2). The purpose of this paper is to consider it within the general context of the criminal law's response to IT misuse. Is the criminal law the most appropriate tool in this area? This question has been little examined. It is argued that the criminal law should not be overused in this area.

## 1. A BRIEF SURVEY

In a helpful survey, the German expert Sieber(3) has noted a series of legal developments common to the countries which have criminalised IT misuse.

The first was the creation of data protection laws, in the 1970s and 1980s. The UK Data Protection Act 1984 in fact places little reliance upon criminal sanctions, but similar laws elsewhere contain quite severe criminal sanctions. This shows a different emphasis in the legal protection of privacy and different perspectives on the role of the criminal law. Other European data protection laws contain criminal offences with high maximum punishments, covering the unauthorised collection, storage and recording of data, the unauthorised obtaining of or access to or disclosure of data, or the unauthorised use of data(4). In the UK, in contrast, the criminal law is not widely used in the 1984 Act or in the protection of privacy generally. The Lindop Committee proposed that a breach of the data protection Codes of Practice should be a crime(5), but this proposal was not adopted in the legislation. The UK scheme is seen as educative and regulatory rather than punitive, with only "limited and complex criminal sanctions"(6) available only in the last resort.

The second development was new criminal laws in the early 1980s to cater for computer-related economic crimes. These took account of the fact that crimes were no longer necessarily directed towards tangible property, but towards intangibles, such as deposit money, computer programs, valuable or sensitive information held in computer records, and "computer time". Special problems of fraud have also been addressed, particularly the problem of deception of machines(7) and the gaining of unauthorised access to computers. A key issue has been whether these laws are best seen simply as updating existing criminal law concepts (redefining "deception" and extending "burglary" to include unauthorised electronic access, for example), or whether they should be seen as entirely new, requiring a fresh start in a comprehensive "computer crime statute"(8).

The third wave of amendments has been the improvement of intellectual property protection in the field of IT. Many countries now provide copyright protection for computer programs and special protection for the topographies of semiconductor products, backed by criminal sanctions. These vary in strength from one country to another(9). In the UK the criminal law, in s.107 of the Copyright, Designs and Patents Act 1988, is almost entirely confined to copyright infringements committed in a business context. Commercial copying of computer software is a crime, but individuals who copy data or programs for their own personal attract only civil liability(10).

Various bodies, such as the Council of Europe and the OECD, and many computer law experts, have urged the importance of harmonisation of these developments. For the moment, however, different countries, or even separate jurisdictions within a country, have chosen to deal with the problems in different ways. In Australia(11), for example, some states have taken special measures to criminalise computer misuse, such as hacking, and some have chosen to rely on the old law. Those which have legislated have taken different routes. This creates difficulties of jurisdiction, since such offences can easily be, and often are, committed across national and international boundaries. The Computer Misuse Act provides special rules of jurisdiction(12), so that UK courts will have jurisdiction whether the computer misuse originates in the home country or is directed against a computer located within it. A Law Commission Report on Jurisdiction(13) has recommended a change to jurisdictional rules in the UK in fraud or dishonesty cases, but the rules for computer misuse have already been changed in the Computer Misuse Act. Jurisdiction is subject to double criminality. So if the hacker is working from England, but the effect will occur abroad, the UK courts only have jurisdiction if the effect amounts to a crime (however defined) in that country as well as in the UK. Within the EC, rapid progress has been made in harmonisation of many areas of law, but criminal law and procedure has been largely unaffected so far. There are many differences between different countries about the proper aims and scope of the criminal law, and little attempt has been made to bridge those differences(14). IT and computer misuse must be tackled both on a national and international level, and so these underlying problems must be brought out into the open.

## 2. NEW CRIMES BY ANALOGY?

One approach has been to extend by analogy existing criminal law. This is a cautious approach, based on the principle that criminal law should be "reactive" rather than "proactive", and should follow behind societal change. It is better not to create legislation which may be unnecessary, or which may miss the mark(15). Some American states have been criticised for producing computer-specific criminal offences such as "causing physical damage to a computer"(16), or "using a computer to cause physical injury to a person"(17), which merely duplicate existing offences. A Canadian offence drafted to criminalise deliberate acts which delete or encrypt data, rendering them inaccessible to data users, is drafted so broadly as to cover the waylaying of a computer programmer on his way to work(18). The fact that so few prosecutions have been brought under these laws is some evidence that they were not needed, or have missed their mark. Five years elapsed before the first prosecution was brought under the much-vaunted Federal computer misuse legislation(19), and State computer crime investigation units state that very few cases are coming to light which could not have been prosecuted perfectly well under the earlier criminal law(20). Those who are cautious about extending the criminal law would restate the general principle that, so far as possible, the criminal law should be certain, and knowable in advance. The criminal law should be kept to an essential minimum. Even the identification of a genuinely new form of mischief need not entail the creation of new crimes to deal with it, for other responses, including development of the civil law, may be a better way forward.

The main focus of the UK legislation has been upon the unauthorised access to the computer. Unauthorisd access is criminalised, both per se (under s.1 of the 1990 Act), and when standing together with proof of some additional criminal intent (under s.2). This mirrors the two-tier legislation of other countries, such as some of the State computer crime laws in the US(21). This style of legislation is attractive to lawmakers. First, the new offences can be argued for and introduced on the basis of analogy. Hacking offences are similar to established offences, particularly burglary. In English law burglary is committed where a person enters premises as a trespasser with intent to commit a crime, such as theft or criminal damage(22). The new hacking offences can be seen as a necessary extension of an established concept to the modern environment, where entry to a computer can be effected electronically. A second advantage of this kind of law is that, by concentrating on the unauthorised access, there is no need to define precisely the conduct which was contemplated by the person making access. This avoids, or at least postpones, confronting the ultimate question whether the law should bring "information" within the definition of "property" for the purposes of theft and related offences(23). In the Computer Misuse Act the s.1 hacking offence is established by proof of the deliberate access alone, and the s.2 offence is satisfied by proof of a further intention to commit any offence which is punishable with more than five years imprisonment.

While the attractions of the "unauthorised access" approach to law reform are considerable, there are drawbacks to it. First, the analogy argument can only be carried so far. Certain special situations excepted, trespass is not a criminal offence in England. The basic hacking offence is, then, itself an anomaly in criminalising electronic access to a person's computer where physical access to that person's home would not amount to a crime. Neither is surveillance, even when accompanied by the use of specialist technical device, such as an electronic bug or an infra-red camera, a crime. This takes us back to the failure of English law to address issues of privacy in a systematic fashion, particularly within criminal law. The Younger Committee's proposal in 1972 that "surreptitious surveillance by means of a technical device" should be made a criminal offence(24) was echoed last year by the Calcutt Committee on privacy(25), but there is no prospect of legislative change. In 1979 a government minister stated in Parliament that the government was "not persuaded that it is practical to extend the criminal law to cover electronic or other surveillance or eavesdropping"(26). Second, there is a danger that developments in distributed processing may soon render the idea of unauthorised access to a "computer" outmoded. Current and future developments will make it more difficult to distinguish between computer systems and the telecommunication systems which link them together. To this extent, the attention of criminal lawyers may well have to shift away from the integrity of the computer towards the vulnerability of the information, and the enforcement of security and regulatory requirements with respect to that information.

## 3. A CRIMINAL INFORMATION LAW?

Sieber has suggested that the "change of paradigm" from corporeal to incorporeal objects means that a "criminal information law" must be developed(27):

> "(I)t is evident that a legal regime for information cannot be derived from an analogy with rules for corporeal objects, but must be founded separately."

In Sieber's view, future criminal laws must be addressed to the concept of "information" rather than the integrity of the "computer". Some early state computer crime legislation in the US took this approach. Theft laws designed to cover the taking of tangible property were extended by the legislature or by the judges to embrace any "thing of value", which was held to include computer programs and data, and computer time(28). This kind of criminal law development, particularly where put into effect by the judiciary, can be objected to on "constitutional" grounds of vagueness and uncertainty of scope. It flies in the face of the important principles mentioned above, that the criminal law should be clear and that its ambit should be rigorously defined in advance of its application to an individual case.

It is a mistake to regard information as just another species of "property" which can be "stolen", and to extend theft laws accordingly. Property normally implies an exclusivity of possession and ownership, while information normally implies a generality of access. While the English law of theft does extend to a number of items of intangible property, such as bank balances(29), and the category of intangibles does not appear to be closed for these purposes, cases have held that information, whether confidential, valuable or otherwise, cannot be stolen(30). Information is a quite different kind of commodity from the forms of intangible property which are capable of being stolen, such as a bank credit. Information is not a legal right or a claim. It does not exist by virtue of a relationship between the owner of the commodity and the person against whom it can be enforced. In Canada, the Supreme Court has confirmed that the position is the same in that country, reversing a Court of Appeal decision to the contrary(31).

The English Law Commission considered a related question in their Report on Computer Misuse: that of damage to or destruction of computer-held programs or data. Initially the Commission had been content to rely on a charge being brought under the Criminal Damage Act 1971, an Act confined to damage to tangible property, in respect of the physical medium upon which the program or data was stored(32). They subsequently accepted, however, that where data was housed in a computer memory, or was in the process of being transferred from one medium to another, its destruction or corruption would amount to the destruction or corruption of an intangible. A new offence was therefore required, and was provided by section 3 of the Computer Misuse Act.

We need to think much more carefully about rights and duties in respect of categories of information and, where appropriate, to enforce those rights and duties by providing redress through the civil and criminal law. This is in line with more recent US developments which reject the more static "property-theory" and instead favour the procedural "relationship-theory" and "entitlement-theory", looking at the relationship between the discloser and the recipient of the information(33). This approach would, for example, require the much more rapid development of trade secret laws in the UK, where the position is well out of line with other European and North American jurisdictions(34). Another aspect is to develop further the duties imposed upon software manufacturers and data users. Most jurisdictions, including the UK, now impose a duty to take adequate security precautions with regard to at least some categories of data. In some countries neglect of proper security measures is a crime(35). This is to enact a rule equivalent to making the householder criminally responsible for failing to lock the doors of his home, when this had allowed entry by a burglar. It is hard to imagine English criminal law extending so far. Some would argue for it, on the ground that management's failure to take simple computer security precautions is one of the most consistent findings to emerge from surveys of computer misuse. The response, from criminal law principle, must be that this is unacceptable, both in imposing liability for mere carelessness and by failing to have proper regard for the key causative factor in the loss, which is clearly the visit by the intruder. In their Report on Computer Misuse the Law Commission toyed with the idea of limiting the scope of computer misuse offences to cases where the hacker had overcome a computer security device which was in place. Despite similar laws in some other jurisdictions, the Law Commission concluded that, in effect, the failure of the householder to keep the door locked ought not to affect the potential liability of the burglar(36). Whether the carelessness of the data user or manager should be addressed by way of a code of practice, which might ultimately be enforced by the criminal law, is considered next.

## 4. CRIMINALISING OR REGULATING?

Should the criminal law, in the IT field, serve primarily a criminalising or a regulatory function? This is important, because the law's function is related to the proper level of fault required in the offences, the style of enforcement policies and the nature of penalties to be imposed. Many hundreds of existing offences in the UK deal with breach of regulatory codes, such as in health and safety at work, pollution regulation, consumer protection and environment conservation. In these cases the offences "cannot be regarded as "criminal" in any meaningful sense but merely as infractions of a technical nature, somewhat akin to an "offside goal" in football"(37). Often these offences have strict liability and are enforced by specialist agencies rather than the police. The agencies operate mostly by way of warning and education. They use prosecution as a last resort, for persistent and wilful infraction(38). One possible role of criminal law in the area of IT, then, is to focus on the reponsibility of the program manufacturers and data users instead of, or as well as, the perpetrators of misuse.

The offences in the Computer Misuse Act 1990, however, are not regulatory. They are of the more traditional type, designed to stigmatise the wrongful conduct. Hacking offences, as defined in the Computer Misuse Act, are in line with traditional mainstream offences in requiring proof of deliberate rather than negligent or inadvertent conduct. The Law Commission, in its Report, insisted on the importance of this, and the fault requirement was not watered down by Parliament. The Act may be compared in this respect to the criminal provisions in the Copyright, Designs and Patents Act 1988, where liability may attach to a defendant who "has reason to believe" that a relevant article is an infringing copy of a copyright work.

Criminalising hacking can be regarded as pursuing a number of objectives. On the one hand, the statute may stand as a marker (indeed this is one argument for legislating in the form of a computer crime statute), which may encourage more responsible use of computers and may (perhaps) also act as a deterrent. Advocates of deterrence claim that it has a short term impact and a longer term educative value. This may be true, given the uncertainty, not least among those who work with computers on a daily basis, over many central issues of computer ethics(39). On the other hand, if the curiosity of hackers outweighs the scruples of breaking the criminal law, the law itself may be brought into contempt by habitual flouting of its provisions. If it turns out to be virtually impossible to obtain the necessary evidence against hackers, and to prosecute them successfully, this damages the law itself.

The pace of development in IT is extremely rapid, and there are some who are anxious that the criminal law should keep up with changes, or anticipate them, to remain effective. On balance, however, while the criminal law undoubtedly has a role to play in this general area, its purpose and proper scope in this area is problematic. The criminal law is only one of a range of possible responses, and its routine overuse must be avoided.

## FOOTNOTES

1. An unreported decision in Sean Cropp (1991) would, if followed, undermine the Act. See (1991) 7 Computer Law and Practice 270.
2. M. Wasik, Crime and the Computer, Oxford, 1990.
3. U. Sieber, "General Report on "Computer Crime", 13th International Congress of International Academy of Comparative Law, University of Bayreuth, 1990.
4. eg French, Austrian and Swedish laws.
5. Lindop Committee, Report of the Committee on Data Protection, Cmnd 7341, London: HMSO, 1978, para 19.91.
6. Law Commission (1989), para 3.60.
7. Any offence requiring proof of an element of "deception" cannot be made out unless a human mind is deceived: see Re London and Globe Finance Corpn [1903] 1 Ch 728 and DPP v Ray [1973] 3 All E R 131. See also Moritz, unreported (1981), and Finance Act 1985, s.12(5).
8. See M.D. Scott, Computer Law, , New York, John Wiley, 1985
9. See U. Sieber, The International Handbook on Computer Crime, New York, John Wiley, 1986, pp.65-72.
10. Reid v Kennet [1986] Crim L R 456.
11. G. Hughes, "Disjointed Australian attack on hackers" (1989) 6 Computer Law and Practice 28.
12. Computer Misuse Act 1990, s.5-9; M. Wasik (1990) pp.215-221.
13. Law Commission, Report No. 180, Jurisdiction Over Offences of Fraud and Dishonesty with a Foreign Element, London: HMSO, 1989.
14. OECD, Information Computer Communications Policy No. 10, Computer-Related Crime: Analysis of Legal Policy, Paris: OECD, 1986.
15. C. Tapper, "Computer crime: Scotch mist?" [1987] Crim LR 4.
16. eg. California Penal Code, s.502(d).
17. eg. Va. Code s.18.2-152.7 (offence of "personal trespass by a computer") and Wis. Stat. Ann. s.943.70(2)(b)(4).
18. Canadian Criminal Code, s.387(1.1)(d) (mischief in relation to data).

19. Robert Morris, convicted under Computer Fraud and Abuse Act 1984 for introducing a worm virus into the Arpanet System.
20. National Institute of Justice, Computer Crime Units, 1990.
21. B.J. George, "Contemporary legislation governing computer crimes" (1985) 21 Criminal Law Bulletin 389.
22. Theft Act 1968, s.9.
23. Oxford v Moss (1979) 68 Cr.App.R. 183.
24. Younger Committee, Report of the Committee on Privacy, Cmnd. 5012, London, HMSO, 1972.
25. Calcutt Committee on Privacy and Related Matters, Cm. 1102, London, HMSO, 1990.
26. Hansard, 13 March 1989, Col. 187.
37. U. Sieber (1990), pp.15-16.
28. eg. Lund v Commonwealth 217 Va 688, 232 SE 2d 745 (1977); US v Sampson 6 Comp L Serv Rep (Callaghan) 879 (ND Cal 1978).
29. Kohn (1979) 69 Cr App R 395.
30. Oxford v Moss (1978) 68 Cr App R 183.
31. Stewart 63 C.R. 3d 305 (SCC, 1988).
32. Cox v Riley (1986) 83 Cr App R 54.
33. Sieber, p.18.
34. A. Coleman, "Trade secrets and the criminal law: the need for reform" (1989) 5 Computer Law and Practice 111.
35. eg Luxembourg and Danish privacy laws.
36. Scottish Law Commission, Report on Computer Crime, Cm. 174, Edinburgh: HMSO, 1987, para 4.15. French, Swedish and German computer misuse laws make just this distinction.
37. J. Rowan-Robinson et.al., Crime and Regulation, 1990, T & T Clark, Edinburgh.
38. See G. Richardson, "Strict liability for regulatory crime: the empirical research" [1987] Crim L R 241.
39. See T.W. Bynum (ed), Computers and Ethics, Oxford: Blackwell, 1985.

Education and Society / R. Aiken (Editor)
Information Processing 92, Volume II
Elsevier Science Publishers B.V. (North-Holland)



# Security measures, standardisation and the law

Prof.Dr. Henrik Kaspersen[a]

[a]Managing director of the Computer/Law Institute, Vrije Universiteit, De Boelelaan 1105, 1081 HV Amsterdam, The Netherlands

*Security is the mother of danger and the grandmother of destruction*
(Thomas Fuller, 1608-1661)

**Abstract**

The security and reliability of IT-products primarly seem to belong to the shared responsibility to producers and users only. However, because of the (side)-effects that the implementation or non-implementation of information security functions can have to the whole of our society or to individual members, laywers who give shape to the moral principles and organization of our society in the form of rules and regulations, should join the debate to about the ways information security can be advanced and ultimately achieved. This essay evaluates some solutions provides by the computer scientists from a legal point.

Keyword Codes: K.5.m; K.6.5
Keywords: Legal aspects of computing, miscellaneous: Security and protection

## 1. SECURITY AS A SOCIAL PROBLEM

Informatization (automation and computerization) of our society has brought us many benefits and offered great chances to the development of the individual but - o paradox - at the same time has put us in a situation of dependancy. Computer systems can have such a preponderant position within organizations, that a breakdown of the system, no matter whether it was caused deliberately and for malicious reasons or not, for a period of only a few hours can be enough to put such an organization out of business. Consequently, computer users are looking for defence mechanisms to arm their computer systems and data with. *Information security* combines the elements of correctness and the presence of such defence mechanisms against external threats that might endanger or disturb correct and steady operation. The user, for his own interest as well on behalf of the intrests of third parties, has a strong need for confidence in the correctness and effectiviness of the security functions of his IT-system and its software.

The daily practise shows that computer users do not take defend their interests as serious as they are expected to. Divers sources, e.g. insurance companies records and criminal records, provide alarming figures about the annual financial damage as a consequence of computer *in*security. In the Netherlands e.g., a survey of computer crime established that in the year

1986 69% of the questioned enterprises maintained security regulations, but in only 50% of the latter number the regulations was written down.[1] In 1990, a similar survey showed that one out of five organisations had to deal with computer crime cases but the percentage of organisations that had security regulations - written or not - was hardly better.[2] Of course, these figures are an average of the real situation and only provide an impression. Moreover, organisations do not strive for 100 % security but often base their security policy upon the results of an risk analysis, which comprises the balancing of costs and risk of damage. Given the fact that information security under circumstances can not only affect the interests of the individual computer user, but also the interests of a society as a whole, the question can be raised, whether and how the implementation and maintaining of security measures should be stimulated or even enforced by means of legal instruments.

## 2. ENFORCEMENT BY MEANS OF LEGAL OBLIGATIONS

Present legislation contains many examples of security prescriptions for special areas or special equipment, which among other things can be related to IT- products.[3] With regard to general purpose computers the legislator only in a few cases stipulated legal obligations to maintain security measures in relation to electronic data processing. E.g. art. 7 of the European Data Protection Convention states that *appropriate* security measures shall be taken for the protection of personal data stored in automated data files against accidental or unauthorized destruction or accidental loss as well as against unauthorized access, alteration or dissemination. The notion appropiate stands for "... adapted to the specific function of the file and the risks involved and based on the current state of the art ...).[4] In national Data Protection Acts this basic principle can be elaborated into concrete measures[5] or simply translated. Sometimes not taking security measures is made a criminal act[6] or a negligent organization becomes liable for damages.[7]

A second group of regulations that may contain security prescriptions are those concerning obligations to employ correct book-keeping or administration and preserving data of evidential value.[8]

A more indirect obligation to secure computersystems can be found in some computer crime provisions whereas the presence of security is a condition for punishableness of the perpetrator, e.g. the hacking provisions in Germany, France and the Netherlands.[9]

An important example of legislation in the field of computer security was the US Computer Security Act 1987[10], which made the National Bureau of standards responsible for development of cost-effective standards and guidelines and imposed an obligation to all operators of US Federal computer systems to have a security plan. The Dutch Computer Crime Bill orders the external auditor of a business firm to report about the reliability and continuity of automatic dataprocessing (i.e. indirectly about security) in the yearly account.[11]

However, one can infer from these examples that legal prescriptions at a general level are necessarily broad, not very flexible and vulnerable to obsolescence because of the lapse of time.

Development of standard tools and standard security functions may be a guarantee to achieve harmonization and necessary to develop further regulations. Given the fact that standardisation is already undertaken to a large extend[12], it is necessary to dispose of an independent instrument to test and evalute security functions.

Information security generally can be achieved by technical, logical or procedural means. It becomes effective by the combination of the three type of measures. *Procedural* security measures are left to the responsibility of the management of the organisation that runs the information system, *logical* security measures can be implemented both by the user or by the supplier of the software, *technical* measures have to be built in by the producer of the IT-system or IT-product.

Nowadays, a computer user does not have to invent all the security measures he wants to implement himself. IT-producers or security suppliers offer a wide range of technical security products. Moreover, at the other security levels too, the techniques to create security features are available with external experts, independant wether logical, procedural or technical security is wanted. However, the scope of the law or other regulations, is generally too broad and too less specific to provide accurate prescriptions with regard to the information security required, which non-observation can be checked and eventually can be given legal consequences. Of course they may constitute a means to make computer users more aware of their social responsibilities and they directly attract attention to the matter as a subject of public dicsussion. But it has to be feared that in this way only a lip service is paid to the societal interest of information security.

## 3. ANOTHER APPROACH

Whereas imposing legal duties legal duties upon computer users to provide for a certain level of security necessarily will have to fail, an alternative approach will be the development of procedures. By those one could raise the awareness amongst the latter group, create the market conditions under which an extended set of security tools will become disponible and create a control mechanism in order to maintain a certain quality of the security tools and the rate of implementation. The European Commission therefore prepares a directive under the name of INFOSEC[13], short for information security, containing a proposal to develop a general strategy for users of electronically stored, treated and transferred information, to protect information and information systems against accidental and deliberate threats.

Part of the program is to achieve specifications, standardisation and verification of information security. An example in this field is ITSEC a joint project by France, Germany, United Kingdom and the Netherlands. The general idea of standard evaluation criteria was developed in the United States under the uninforming title of Orange Book[14], edited and used by the US State Department of Defence. The United Kingdom in keeping with tradition prepared a Green Book on the matter[15], while France upheld national pride by the Blue-White-Red-book. Germany did not dedicate a colourfull name to the analogue publication by the German Security Agency. The latter two were both published in 1989. The best part of the national evaluation criteria system were passed onto the framework of the common approach and eventually adapted with respect to maximal applicabiliity and compatibility to already existing criteria, such as the Orange Book.[16] Nevertheless the system had to be supplemented and expanded. ITSEC had as a purpose to supply future users with a yardstick to compare security capabilities of IT-products, because users need to have confidence in the system they use.

ITSEC contains a number of standard evaluation criteria with respect to the security of security relevant components of computersystems. These components consist of IT-systems, an unique operational environment designed and built for the need of the specific user, and IT-products, hardware and/or standard software packages, "bought off the shelf". ITSEC evaluates the claim made by a sponsor of an IT-product with regard to the predifined level of security against certain threats. The evaluation is carried out by an independent body in accordance with defined security evaluation criteria.

ITSEC has its limitations. Because of the fact that the sponsor determines the security objects and threats and eventually the level of confidence the evaluation process does not lead to absolute results overall, but definitely to absolute results at the level specified by the sponsor. In literature other criticisms can be found.[17] On behalf with this paper I limit myself to refer to the fact that ITSEC does not provide any criteria to judge to what extent the interests of users and usees of the IT-products and systems are guaranteed. E.g. Security mechanisms often will have privacy-sensitive implications, because they use and produce personal data that can be misused or are open to access by unauthorized people. This can lead to internal conflicts between the use of security mechanisms as means to protect privacy intrests and their misuse causing privacy violations. Examples of security mechanisms with such a double-headed face are Authentication mechanisms, Discretionary and mandatory access controls, but also monitoring, auditing, and intrusion detection security mechanisms. Data protection legislation provides legal principles and standards to which human behaviour has to respond. Therefore, security functions should be weighed against the threats and security objects on one side and the privacy protection principles and ethics on the other side.

## 4. LEGAL STANDARDS

Systems like ITSEC will not provide technical specifications which can be incorporated in legal standards, because regulations usely have a higher level of abstraction and the criteria of ITSEC do not possess absolute value. Laywers therefore will create legal standards separately from technical standards. The questions is how legal standards fit in to the ITSEC-system. It is still discussed whether ITSEC should enable an evaluation with regard to legal obligations. It is obvious that such a test will be necessary to check whether specific security functions are in accordance with the legal prescriptions in the specific field.

A great deal of the possible security functions aim at the prevention of abuse by humans. E.g. those with regard to identification, authentication and access control. In addition, by creating accountability in a computer system it is possible to put human behaviour or results of it under surveillance. ITSEC provides criteria to evaluate the quality of the security functions, eventually it will allow to evaluate them by means of legal presciptions, but until now there is no room to test whether and to what extent the application of security functions is in accordance with other more distant and often contrary legal interests, especially human rights with regard the protection of his privacy.

The Conventions of Human Rights prohibit States to interfere with the private life of their citizens unless granted by law, similar provisions can be found in the Constitution. Constitutional rights may also affect the relations between the mutual citizens. What exactly has to be understood under a person's privacy is hard to tell, generally one discerns privacy in relation with locations, privacy with relation of behaviour and privacy with relation of personal data.[18] Separately should be mentioned the right of protection of the integrity of the body and the secrecy of communication.[19] Security functions, with regard their structure and operation can interfere with each of those basic rights, which on behalf with this paper I will denote as personality and privacy rights. In my opinion only such security functions should be developed and offered at the market which are not only formally in tune with the requirements of the law but also by their structure and use in an operational environment. Moreover, users who want those functions implemented in their IT-systems should be made aware of possible frictions or tensions that the use thereof can cause with individual rights of other persons. Therefore, with respect to that legal evaluation criteria will be needed in order to qualify security functions. Such an evaluation extends to all levels of a security system, to start with the individual basic elements.

ITSEC seems to provide a suitable platform for a legal evaluation. It will take a lot of time, effort and discussion before an appropriate set of criteria will be available. I will restrict myself to present a rough sketch of some basic principles of testing.

### 4.1 Legal standards

Security functions shall meet direct legal prescriptions, mostly concerning technical matters. Moreover, the structure and elements of security functions can be in conflict with other legal provisions in the sense of prohibitions. An example: a security function concerning the identification and authentication of a computer user based upon the recording of physical qualities of a person such as racial characteristics can be unlawful.[20]

### 4.2 Legal conditions

In most cases the previous test cannot plainly be answered, because the establishment of what is unlawful or not depends from the fulfillment of a number of legal conditions. E.g. the recording of a file containing data about persons in behalf of identification and authentication procedures in itself is not unlawful. At this level the test should show that the structure and elements of a security function at least enable the fulfillment of these legal conditions. The first question to be answered is whether the pass word data collection is a file of personal data in the meaning of the national law and who is in control of it? Furthermore, if it is organised in such a way that the relevant data can only be recorded by the computer user and are *de facto* not accessible to other users including the super user because of application of other security functions this function it is out of the scope of Data Protection Legislation. If organised otherwise, it should be tested how e.g. the data protection principles[21] can be met.

### 4.3 Environmental factors

Security functions will be used in a specific environment and in a specific way. It might very well be that a function passed gloriously the tests under 1. and 2. but that its implementation and factual use make it unlawful. E.g. the unattended monitoring of the activities of a computer user - a security function under the header of accountability - is unlawfull under most jurisdictions. This unlawfulness can be healed by the consent of the monitored person provided that a number of conditions will be met, e.g. when the person involved is aware of the consequences of his consent with regard to the use that will be made of the data, when a technical feature allows him to establish when he is actually monitored, when the monitoring does not reveal more information about the person than necessary for the execution of the security function and when the monitored data will be surrounded by the technical measures of due care as embodied in the data protection principles. A great deal of the latter conditions can be achieved by technical means, which in turn form part of the security function.

### 4.4 Ethics

A possible fourth level of evaluation is at stake when the legal framework, directly or indirectly, does not provide concrete standards to evaluate the acceptability of a certain security function. An example: the use of blood or human texture for identification and authentication purposes as such generally is not unlawful when the persons involved consented in such a procedure and voluntarily renounce the necessary materials for that purpose. Nevertheless, anybody will feel that such security functions are "over the edge" as far as ethical principles are involved. In exceptional cases only they still could be justified because of the protection of big (societal) interests. The implementation of security functions based on similar techniques deserves a critical mind and can in my opinion only be accepted when special interest are at stake and effective alternatives be absent.

These overall-criteria need further elaboration and refinement. They will enable to evaluate a security function with regard to its personality/privacy sensitiviness. The minimum standard should have to be that the security function at least passed the tests of the first two levels.

## 5. CONCLUSIONS AND RECOMMENDATIONS

5.1 National and Supranational bodies have a responsibility to stimulate the propagation and implementation of Information Security measures by developing a legal framework. Standardization of security functions and mechanisms can promote the operation of the Market and the transparancy of security products to potential customers.

5.2 There are so many aspects to Information Security that the enacting of explicit and specified legal obligations for computer users to have their systems and other IT-products secured is not workable and therefore not addressed.

5.3 The development and use of technical IT-security standards are a means to achieve an adequate level of IT-security, provided that the implementation of these standards can be evaluated not only with regard to its technical qualities but also with regard to the consequences to personality/privacy rights and ethical principles.

5.4 Legal evaluation criteria should be developed to be included in the ITSEC framework as an integrating part of the evaluation system.

## 6. REFERENCES


1 Informatietechniek en Strafrecht, The Hague 1987, Appendix C.

2 Computercrime in the Netherlands, The Hague 1990, p. 153, 154.

3 E.g. the Dutch Security Act 1934, Act with regard to Working Conditions 1983 and specific regulations with regard to Nuclear Power Plants, Electricity power-stations, Aeroplanes, etc.

4 Explanatory Report on the Convention for the Protection of Individuals with Regard to Automatic Data Processing to art. 7.

5 E.g. BDSG par. 9, France Loi 6 januari 1978, art. 29, UK Data Protection Act 1984.

6 (e.g. U.K., France, Luxembourg, Danemark).

7 E.g. Germany, The Netherlands.

8 Such as in tax law, commercial law and civil law. Under influence of new electronic applications (e.g. EDI) there is a trend towards including regulation concerning the security of these kinds of information as well.

9 Par. 202a StGB, art. 461-2 CP, resp. art. 138a Sr (Computer Crime Bill, TK 1989-1990, 21 551, not yet in force).

10 Pub.law 1987-235.

11 Art. 391:2 BW.

12 See e.g. Stuurman, IT-Standards Regulation, Computer Law and Security Report, Vol. 8, 1992, p. 2-11.

13 COM (90) 314 final 3 juli 1990.

14 Information Technology Trusted Computer System Evaluation Criteria (ITSEC), Europe, Luxemburg June 1991.

15 DTIEC, from the Department of Trade and Industry.

16 Department of defense Trusted Computer System Evaluation Criteria, 15 August 1983, Maryland.

17 See e.g. Martin Meijer and Kai Rannenberg, Eine bewertung der "Information Technology Security Evaluation Criteria", DuD 1991, p. 131-138.

18 See e.g. art. 17 Treaty of New York 1948, art. 8 Treaty of Rome. In the Dutch Constitution these principles are elaborated in art. 10 Gr (general privacy right), art 12 (locational privacy right, art. 13 secrecy of communication.
Par. 2 and 3 of art. 10 Constitution instruct the legislator to develop rules with regard the protection of personal data (See Wet persoonsregistraties, July 1 1989, S 665).

19 Art. 7, Treaty of New York 1948, art. 3 Treaty of Rome,bodily integrity.
Art. 17 Treaty of New York 1948 and art. 8 Treaty of Rome, locational privacy and secrecy of communication (see art. 12 resp. art 13 Dutch Constitution).

20 At least under future Dutch Law: art. 7 Data Protection Act and art. 1 of the related Statutory Instrument with regard to sensitive personal data (Besluit gevoelige gegevens).

21 OECD Recommendations of 23 September 1980, see also European Convention for the Protection of Individuals with Regard to Automatic Processing of Personal Data of 28 January 1981 (ETS 108).

Education and Society / R. Aiken (Editor)
Information Processing 92, Volume II
Elsevier Science Publishers B.V. (North-Holland)


# Network(er)s at risk
# The Fairy-Tale of Invulnerability of Computer Supported Work

Herbert Kubicek
Telecommunication Research Group
University of Bremen, Germany

## Abstract

Although the vulnerability of information systems was a subject of concern for a long time, it has not been picked up in the discussions about computers and work. Vulnerability so far has mainly been dealt with from the point of view of systems owners and occasionally with respect to the consequences for clients. Computer scientists and official authorities prefer to talk about information security and claim that secure systems are achievable by technical, organizational and personnel measures. But they do not consider that security measures like user control and monitoring get into conflict with privacy rights of workers. They are reducing the risks for networks by putting networkers at risk. Social scientists, analyzing the vulnerability of the emerging information society, point at the goal conflict between security and freedom on the societal level. But the procedures recommended are not easily transferable to the level of intra- or interorganizational work systems.

After reconstructing these different approaches a conceptual scheme for the analysis of the vulnerability of computer supported work is developed by showing that there are acknowledged workers' interests which also apply to security functions and that system designers are running into several dilemmas. Based on the assumption that computer supported work systems are coalitions of different interest groups a multi-actor model of vulnerability is suggested as an extension of present security concepts and handbooks and as a starting point for further interdisciplinary research and political discussion.

Keyword Codes: H.5.2; K.4.2; K.6.5.
Keywords: User Interfaces; Social Issues; Security and Protection.

## 1. INTRODUCTION

Reading the subtitle of this paper one might wonder who is telling the *fairy-tale* of invulnerability of computer supported work. There is a five-days-stream about vulnerability in this conference. There have been several IFIP conferences on computer security (e.g. CAELLI 1989) or security in information systems (GRISSONNANCHE 1989), there are official state authority guidelines such as the Orange Book by the US Department of Defense (DoD 1985) or the newly created German Agency for Information Technology Security (BSI 1991) as well as handbooks for company management (e.g. FINE 1986, KRALLMANN 1989, CAELLI et al. 1991), there is a proposal for a decision by the EC Commission and a suggestion for IT Security Evaluation (COMMISSION 1990a, 1991), there is an ISO standard (ISO 1988a) and there are studies by technology assessment institutions (NATIONAL RESEARCH COUNCIL 1989, OTA 1990) and research groups on the vulnerability of the emerging information society (e.g. ROSSNAGEL et al. 1989).

Nobody maintains that today´s computer systems *are invulnerable* - on the contrary: All this work contains lists of possible points of vulnerability, types of system failures, attacks and aggressors as well as procedures to identify the vulnerability and increase security. But these specialists claim that the risks of vulnerability can be *reduced* or *avoided* by measures of *information security*, starting from software development methods and including a lot of technical, organizational and personnel measures. The markets for IT security products are growing fast, new positions in organizations and new institutions for testing and certification are founded, thus creating a profession which lives by pointing to the risks of vulnerability and presenting the solutions at the same time. As in the *fairy-tales*: the evil is there and threatens people, but finally it will be beaten by the hero.

In order to go on with computerization politicians, managers and users are ready to believe in this fairy-tale or myth. However, from other risk areas, e.g. traffic or energy supply, we know that efforts to reduce one risk lead to creating other risks. But such an ecological view is not dominant in the IT security debate. One way to procede is to challenge the fairy-tale of invulnerability with another fairy-tale. I mean "The Emperor´s New Clothes". Let us try to challenge the information security tailors and tell the public what we see!

But who is "we"? As this session is organized by the working group "Computers and Work" I would like to take a worker´s point of view. However, there is no established view on questions of vulnerability from this perspective. The discussions on computers and work deal with a lot of aspects but not with the significance of vulnerability and the consequences of measures to achieve IT security. And on the other side the debate on IT security strictly takes the point of view of the owners of systems or information and mentions workers mainly as threats and objects of security measures. Social scientists dealing with the vulnerability of the information society mainly concentrate on the consequences for clients or the public at large.

With the emergence of computer networks the vulnerability of systems increases and actions taken from one point of view have effects on other participants. At the moment I see the danger that in order to reduce the risks for networks for the sake of owners and clients new risks for networkers are created. But developing an integrated or ecological view means bringing worlds together which so far have developed in splendid isolation. Therefore this paper can only show the differences in perspective, the interrelatedness of aspects and goal conflicts, develop a conceptual schema for an integrated multi-perspective approach and present questions which need further discussion and research.

## 2. PRESENT APPROACHES TOWARDS THE PROBLEM OF VULNERABILITY

In order to understand what is meant by vulnerability two very different approaches are described in this section.

### 2.1. IT security for the owners of information

From the large number of official programmes and documents I would like to look at two examples which, on different levels, will have great influence on what will be conceived as secure and what kind of system features will be installed in future computer systems.

#### 2.1.1. ITSEC: Certification of IT products to create trust by purchasing organizations

In 1991 the EC Commission published a recommendation for a decision of the EC Council for an action programme in the field of information security: Because almost two third of the economy depend on products or services applying information technology, integrity, security and trustfulness of information become a decisive factor for economic development. A coherent programme for the community shall create trust in the application of information technology and telecommunication services without putting up new boundaries between the member states and other countries due to divergent security requirements.

ITSEC is one line of action in this programme which employs harmonized IT security criteria for the community-wide *certification of IT products*, so that producers can sell trusted products in the whole community.

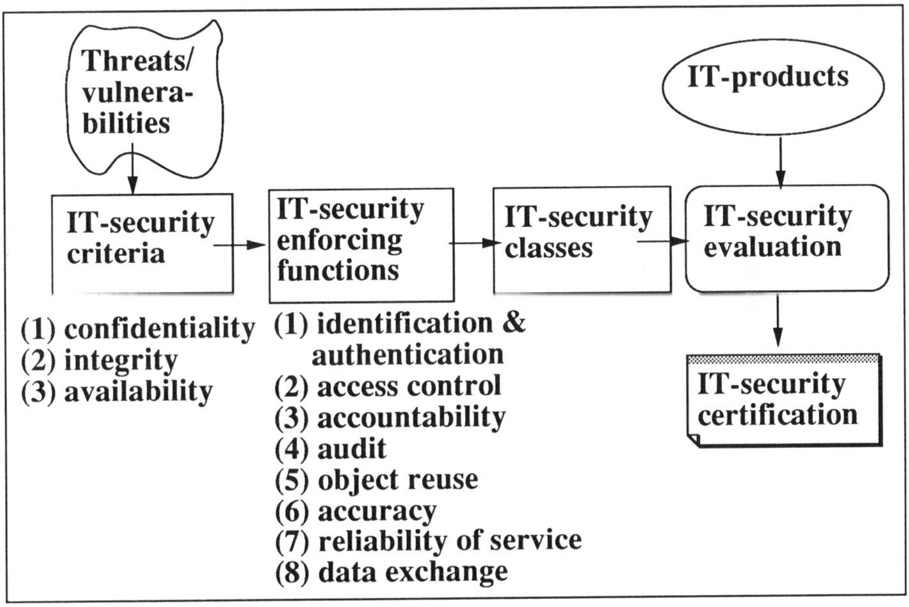


Figure 1: ITSEC framework and criteria (Commission ... 1991)

Figure 1 shows the ITSEC concept. The document does not try to define vulnerability or possible threats and risks in detail. The paper simply assumes that user organizations need confidence in the security of a system they are thinking of purchasing. And from that owner point of view IT security is defined by three requirements which are defined as the prevention of three general vulnerabilities or threats:

(1) *Confidentiality* - prevention of the unauthorized disclosure of information;

(2) *Integrity* - prevention of the unauthorized modification of information;

(3) *Availability* - prevention of the unauthorized withholding of information or resources (COMMUNITY 1991, p. 1).

These requirements shall be met by eight *security enforcing functions* or security targets provided by hardware or software products as mentioned in Fig. 1 (COMMUNITY 1991b, p. 2).

As Rihaczek notes in his *critical comment* this scope of functions is restricted to the military paradigm, assuming a system owner who defines who is authorized for which actions and who wants to protect his system against unauthorized actions taken by members of his organization or external hostile persons. Therefore these functions assume a centralized host configuration with central administration of rights, but do not apply to open communication systems where users have dialogues with other users whom they do not know where the requirement of authentication between users arises. He also misses the requirement of anonymity or unobservability as well as that of liability.

Whatever the history and motives may be, this selection of security functions will have severe consequences for computer supported work and workers by intruding into their *privacy*. But this is not mentioned in the document and does not easily become apparent, as it does not illustrate how the functions mentioned may work within IT products. However, another paper by the EC Commission with the title INFOSEC contains a lot of examples of available mechanisms and ongoing research (COMMISSION 1990b). For example identification and authentication may be realised by

- passwords,
- questionnaires, i.e. "the user is asked a series of questions chosen at random from a selection for which the computer knows the answer. Typical questions are:
  - What is your wife´s maiden name?
  - Where does your grandmother live?
  - When were you born?"
- token such as magnetic strip cards, active or smart cards,
- physical characteristics such as sound of voice, retina, handgeometry or finger prints analysis,

or for accuracy several cryptosystems are offered (pp 64ff).

### 2.1.2. The German IT security handbook: Guideline for public administration

The second example for approaches towards IT security does not concern single products but *operating IT systems in organizations* conceived as sociotechnical systems, especially in public administration organizations. Federal public administration organizations in Germany have to develop frame concepts for the application of information technology with a yearly update, which should include a *security concept*. In 1991 the Federal Agency for Information Technology Security (BSI) compiled a handbook published by the Federal Minister of the Interior which specifies the content of such security concepts and the procedures for their development. The IT security handbook adopts the same three security criteria as the ITSEC document, but speaks of *basic threats* (BSI 1991):

(1) loss of availability,
(2) loss of integrity,
(3) loss of confidentiality.

Federal user organizations have to develop their own security concept with a *procedure of 12 steps* for which a number of checklists and examples are presented in the handbook. Figure 2 shows these 12 steps and illustrates some basic concepts. The range of threatened objects and threats to be considered is much broader than in the ITSEC concept. It covers the infrastructure, the organization and persons involved. But again the whole evaluation procedure only takes the point of view of the *owner* of the system or the information in the system.

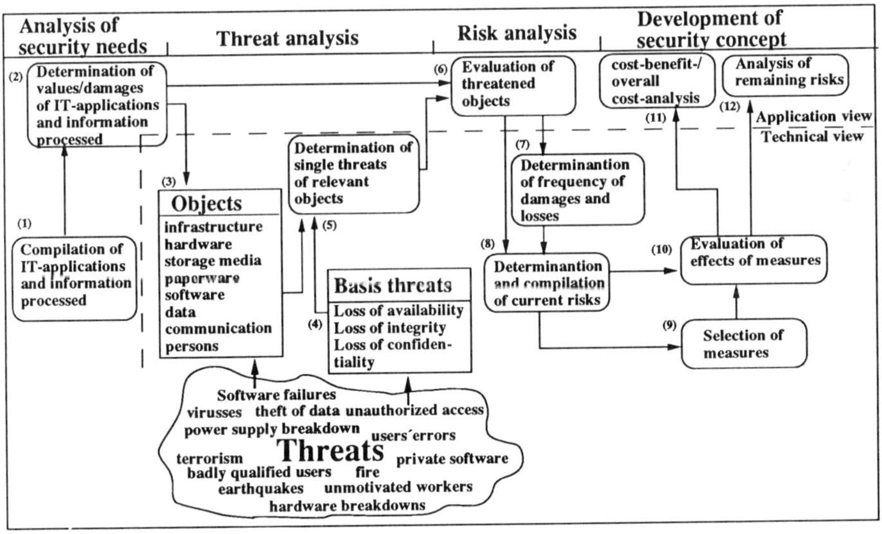


Fig. 2: Conceptual scheme for the development of security concepts in German federal public administration (BSI 1991)

Despite a rather comprehensive listing of *threats* in the appendix, regarding internal threats the main text simply states: "In statistical terms the users of the IT system including operating and administration personnel are the greatest threat. The causes are: errors, careless or malicious behaviour. Further sources of danger are software faults which cannot be ruled out" (p. 21). And regarding external threats the paper states: "External threats include unauthorized users who gain access by trial, faults of the system or by carelessness or cooperation of authorized users."

Accordingly the *security measures* mentioned do not only consider hardware and software aspects (like identification or access control), but also *organizational measures* (e.g. rules and orders accompanied by introduction, motivation and supervision in order that people behave according to the rules) and *personnel measures* (e.g. education, motivation, sanctions, monitoring and security checks) (p. 73). Possible restrictions due to workers´ rights are not mentioned at all. Although the handbook recommends the participation of a large number of experts of the user organizations (p. 39) the *participation of workers´ representatives* which is necessary due to workers´ legislation if monitoring is possible is not mentioned.

### 2.2. The vulnerability of the information society and the collision of basic civil rights

A broader view is presented by studies dealing with the vulnerability of the information society. As many societal institutions and functions become more and more dependent from information systems and telecommunication networks society as a whole has to be protected against disturbances of these systems. However, security measures which employ *supervision of people* might get into conflict with basic civil rights, in particular *privacy*, and gradually change the democratic structure of society (LUTTERBECK 1987). The most elaborate study dealing with this problem was undertaken by an interdisciplinary research group around the professor of constitutional law Alexander Roßnagel (see Fig. 3).

Their analysis starts from functions or services of the social and political system or societal subsystems, and looks at their dependency on information technology. While the kind of threats and the security measures considered are quite similar to the IT security handbook, the range of effects and the yardsticks for evaluation are quite different. Effects of disturbances are analyzed from the point of view of *owners* and *clients*, and the evaluation of security measures is derived from basic constitutional rights and takes into account *collisions with other basic rights*. Roßnagel et al. show that many IT security measures are aimed at the supervision of people occupied with the development,

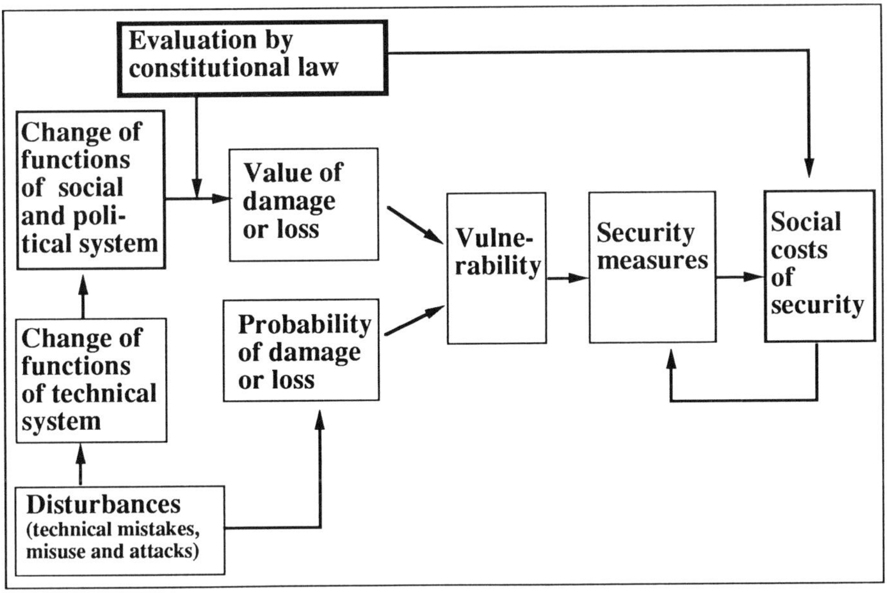


Fig. 3: Conceptual scheme for the analysis of the vulnerability of the information society by Rossnagel et al. (1989)

operation and maintenance of IT systems and of the endusers. In order to prevent vulnerability company security services, police and secret services try to *gather information about people* who might become a risk factor, including actions in private life and even data about family members and other people in the social environment. They get into *conflict* with the personal rights of these individuals as laid down in the constitutional right of informational self-determination, privacy legislation and workers legislation concerning electronic monitoring and surveillance thereby creating *social costs* in terms of restrictions of *freedom* and *democracy*.

The authors argue that all this legislation deals with *balancing* of rights and requirements. As the requirements for the security of vital societal functions increase privacy concerns get less weight in the balancing decisions. And although there are *codetermination rights* of shop stewards concerning electronic monitoring in Germany, they become more and more *restricted by legislation* enforcing security measures. Therefore they summarize that the greater the damage potential of IT applications, the more restrictions of civil rights are allowed by the present principles of constitutional law, the balancing of values and the appropriateness. And they argue that over the time there will be a shift in the judgement of which security measures are appropriate. If it is proved that speech or face recognition increase the security of access control the civil rights concerning the right of the own image and word will be reinterpreted and restricted. Although the evaluation of security measures is of greatest societal importance, Roßnagel et al. criticize that the secret services and security agencies have a *de facto monopoly* in defining which measures are efficient and necessary and thereby change the balance between freedom and security without democratic control and public discourse.

This approach by Roßnagel et al., although dealing with the societal level and aiming at a societal discourse to deal with the dilemma between freedom and security in society at large, might well help us to develop a conceptual scheme for the analysis of the vulnerability of computer supported work.

## 3. A CONCEPTUAL SCHEME FOR THE ANALYSIS OF THE VULNERABILITY OF COMPUTER SUPPORTED WORK

It is obvious that the dominating view in the IT security debate taking the perspective of system owners and dealing with workers mainly as security threats is not appropriate for an analysis of work systems. Rather it has to be considered that workers have acknowledged interests in work design.

### 3.1. Acknowledged workers´ interests in IT applications

The application of information technology in work processes means a change of *working conditions* for users and thereby touches their interests. This includes technical, organizational and personnel measures for increasing IT security. I will not go deeper into the long debate about workers´ interests in work design and systems design in general (c.f. BRIEFS et al. 1983, BRIEFS 1984, MIN TJOA et al. 1988) but rather concentrate on specific acknowledged rights and regulations.

For the incorporation of workers´ interests into work design there are general *participation or negotiation rights* due to legislation or agreements, and for particular issues there are special laws and national or international standards. Besides the health and safety hazards of visual display units there are two regulated issues which are of particular relevance in this context:

(1) <u>Software ergonomics and task design</u>: Besides national standards for the design of user interfaces (e.g. DIN in Germany) there are two

international directives and standards defining requirements. The *EC directive* on work places with visual display units (COUNCIL 1990) requires that software must be userfriendly, appropriate to the task, put no extra burden on the user and be transparent in all its functions to the user. And there is a draft for an *ISO standard* "Visual Display Terminals (VDTs) used for office tasks - ergonomic requirements" which demands that appropriately designed tasks should "facilitate task performance" and "provide an appropriate degree of autonomy to the user in deciding priority, pace and procedure", and that "overload or underload, which may lead to unnecessary or excessive strain or fatigue or to errors" as well as "undue time pressure" should be avoided (ISO 1988b).

(2) Electronic monitoring: In Germany electronic monitoring is an issue for a strong codetermination right of shop stewards. In the USA the Office of Technology Assessment published a report called "The Electronic Supervisor" in 1987, recommending legislative action in order to restrict electronic monitoring. In 1990 a draft for a "Privacy for Consumers and Workers Act" was introduced to the US Congress. And the directive of the EC Council mentioned above requires that no monitoring may be used without the knowledge of workers.

It is obvious that these regulations define *requirements for IT security* measures. But in the official documents on IT security I did not find a single hint. For example the ITSEC document of the EC Commission does not mention at all that software functions must correspond to the requirements of software ergonomics as laid down in the directive of the Council. The debates and regulations on *"IT security"* and *"workers´ security"* so far do not take notice of each other. This splendid isolation is not only a threat to workers interests but also to a viable and socially accepted IT security policy.

### 3.2. Security dilemmas with respect to workers´ interests

It is not possible to analyze the relationship between security measures and work design requirements in detail in this paper. However, as a starting point I would like to point to some dilemmas faced by system designers and management if the two spheres are brought together.

(1) The overload dilemma: System design shall avoid *work overload* and provide for *autonomy*. System breakdowns or the loss of data mean additional strain and a restriction of autonomy. But IT security measures do so either. They lead to more complicated work procedures bearing new risks for making mistakes. Often they do not meet the requirements of ease of use and transparency. And as

user qualification about the whole system often is quite poor stress is increased.

(2) The responsibility dilemma: According to the security guidelines users have to be made responsible for information security in their work area. Monitoring, audits and sanctions were mentioned above. Although in many cases it is not obvious whether a loss of data is due to an error of the user, an error of the programmer or a technical fault, users have the load of proving that it is not their fault, although they have not enough knowledge to prove that the cause is in the system. And the usual increase of work load and the increasing time pressure in combination with a high degree of division of labor even across the organization's boundaries does not allow for a deep and comprehensive check of any information received. Work organization design is based on the assumption that the computer systems work correctly.

In the case of decision support systems or socalled expert systems users usually are not able to reconstruct and evaluate the processes performed by the technical system. The tighter the coupling, the greater the responsibility in terms of possible damages, but the smaller is the possibility to behave according to this responsibility. Security measures promise to solve this dilemma. But this has to be examined in each case.

(3) The security-privacy-dilemma. Many security measures rely on the processing or gathering of user-related personal data. Obviously there are cases where users have an own interest that others do not get access to processes and files under their responsibility. And there are cases too where owners and users have a common interest in accountability of messages delivered, transactions performed etc., esp. if a third party is involved. But the existing regulations for privacy and monitoring demand that the kind and extent of security related controls, reports and audits must be necessary and capable of increasing security and only interfere with personal rights to an acceptable degree.

IT security measures leading to additional work load, responsibility and monitoring are only acceptable to workers if they *really* reduce the risks of breakdowns and losses and if they do not interfere with acknowledged rights. This can only be evaluated if security policy is integrated into the general *design of work organization* and *organizational design.* Often the dilemmas mentioned above may only be reduced by a redesign of work organization and systems. But reading the literature on

IT security one gets the impression that the intellectual frame of analysis and the options considered are mostly based on *tayloristic* or *hierarchical-bureaucratic* models of organizations and management: personnel selection, strict bureaucratic rules, and supervisions, sanctions etc. Organization and management theory for some decades, however, has recognized that these models are based on *two false premises*:

- The assumption that the behaviour in organizations can be influenced by *formal rules* has turned out to be an overestimation of the design power of managers. Recent management literature stresses the *limits of the designability* of organizations, emphasizing the importance of culture compared to structure. And it suggests that managers should not see themselves as captains of a battleship but rather as coaches of a football team.

- Tayloristic work design is based on a basic *mistrust* against workers and leads to a vicious circle of control and mistrust by enforcing strict control and supervision (CLEGG/DUNKERLEY 1980, p. 364). Analysing the success of *Japanese management* recent management literature stresses the need to build up an organization of trust and to employ mechanisms of self-organization. Trustful organization in this context means quite a different thing than trusted computer systems.

The recommended IT security measures, however, introduce *new bureaucratic rules* and monitoring and thereby *reinforce the elements of mistrust organizations*. From an overall management perspective, as distinct from a security management perspective, they are doubtful with respect to effectiveness and highly costly in terms of loss of motivation.

It might well be that IT security experts, who often come from the *military environment* in particular stick to buraucratic models of management. But they only can gain influence as long as their view is supported by *computer scientists*. And I think that their views converge though because of different reasons: They want to develop products and functions which can be built into technical systems. Hardware and software producers want to make profit with these products. As often in the computer field the problem is defined according to the solutions available. The redesign of organizations towards a culture of trust is not the business of computer specialists.

## 3.3. Types of computer supported work and vulnerability concerns

As workers´ protection regulation concerning task design and monitoring employs rather vague terms such as "appropriate" or "as far as possible" it is necessary to consider the context of *individual IT applications*. From the point of view of workers just as from the point of view of the owners the degree of perceived vulnerability depends on the functions of the computer supported work systems and the kind of computer support. And it is also accepted that vulnerability increases if networks are involved. In order to understand the design dilemmas better it seems helpful to use a rough classification of computer supported work systems, in particular net-work. I would like to suggest a typology along two dimensions (see Fig. 4):.

(1) The degree of sensitivity of information processed depending on the represented objects;

(2) the degree of coupling of processes depending on the mode of man-computer-interaction.

| Objects / Mode of interaction | **Misc. Information** | **Contractual information** | Information about **financial processes** | Information about **technical processes** | Information about **persons** |
|---|---|---|---|---|---|
| **Transfer systems** and **human mediated transaction systems** | announcements, messages<br>online databanks | orders, invoices | accounting | CAD | personell information systems<br>medical information systems<br>police information systems |
| **Decision support systems and semi-automatic controll systems** | | just-in-time-production delivery information | interbank clearing | production control systems (PPS)/ CIM<br>Flight traffic control | medical control systems in hospitals |
| **Automatic control systems** | | | EFTPOS-authorization | chemical plant control<br>subway traffic control | |

Fig. 4: Types of networking and vulnerability risks

Looking at the examples mentioned in the cells of the matrix one can get a first impression what vulnerability means. Security requirements from the owners´ point of view increase with the value of the information and the degree of coupling of the technical system. Of course this classification needs elaboration and may well be modified. But for heuristic purposes it should be noticed here that for the class of tightly coupled systems vulnerability includes risks to the health and lives of people as *clients* depending on the functioning of the system or simply as people living in the *neighbourhood* of the system under control (e.g. chemical plants or airports). As a consequence the question of what kinds of security measures are appropriate and tolerable for workers must consider these *concerns by other parties affected* and cannot be dealt with in the context of industrial relations alone. Rather the whole range of parties involved in and affected by the functions and dysfunctions of a system has to be considered.

## 4. A MULTI-ACTOR MODEL OF VULNERABILITY OF COMPUTER SUPPORTED WORK

For the development of an ecological, multi-actor approach towards vulnerability it seems appropriate to take up the approach of Roßnagel et al. which stresses the analysis of conflicting objectives. But there is no easy way to transfer their approach from the societal level to the organizational level or the level of work systems. In contrast to the societal level there are no highest common objectives for all parties involved in computer supported work. Most approaches in organization theory rather assume that an organization is a coalition of different interest groups or stakeholders (CYERT & MARCH 1963, MORGAN 1986) and that it is the main task of management to keep this coalition together. This does not lead to something comparable to a society´s constitution legislated by a parliament and a constitutional court, but rather to a kind of negotiated order which has to be renegotiated and adapted permanently according to shifting participants. Although this is obvious to organization theorists and managers it is not considered in the debate on IT security. Rather this literature assumes that there are no problems in defining the value of information and damages or losses.

A more realistic approach therefore has to start from the different interests of those groups involved in and/or affected by the functions of the organization or the work system as a part of an organization. Interests in this context mean a state of the work system or a single function which is desired by the respective group of people. Vulnerability of a work system following Roßnagel et al. means the possibility to disturb the functions of the system in such a way that it is transformed to a state which is against the acknowledged interest of at least one party as this state is not in accordance with legal rights or formalized standards developed by authorized bodies or collective contracts.

Taking this definition the conceptual scheme of Roßnagel et al. can be adopted to the organizational level or level of work systems (Fig. 5):

(1) <u>Identification of groups with acknowledged interests in the system and definition of system boundaries and functions in the perspective of these interests</u>. Adapting a multi-actor-approach there are no given functions and boundaries of a system, but these have to be defined from the perspectives of the different interest groups. Therefore, starting from a first rough definition of the computer supported work system, the interest groups have to be identified and included in the further steps.

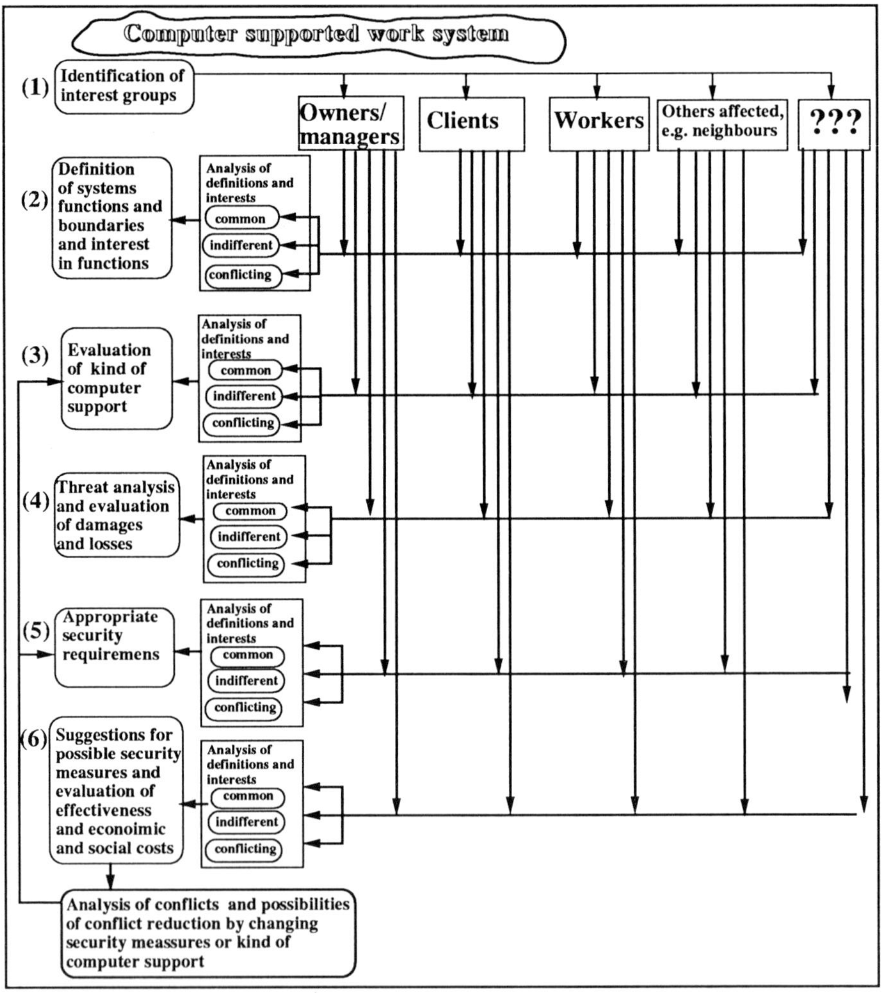


Fig. 5: Multi-actor approach to the vulnerability of computer supported work systems

(2) Definition of interests in function of the work system by each group: Each group may stress different functions of the work system as a sociotechnical system and might draw the boundaries of this system differently. And of course they have different interests in these functions. The relationship between these interests should be analyzed whether they are common to all groups, indifferent or in conflict.

For each of the following steps as shown in Figure 5 the definitions of these interest groups are to be analysed, whether they lead to common, indifferent or conflicting views or evaluations. Finally the analysis of conflicting requirements has to deal with possibilities of conflict reduction by changing security measures or the kind of computer support.

Of course this model raises a lot of questions. Who is to organize the whole process and to decide whether requirements are common or in conflict? How can the different groups participate, in particular, if several organizations are connected by computer networks? At this stage the model shows the restrictions of present approaches such as the IT Security Handbook, but still does not present a viable alternative. Rather it is meant as a suggestion for starting further research.

## 6. RECOMMENDATIONS FOR FURTHER RESEARCH AND ACTION

The main message of this paper is that the debate on IT security and that on work design so far have not taken notice of each other and that this splendid isolation leads to IT security strategies which are not viable, because they are based on wrong assumptions about organizational behaviour, or not tolerable because they intrude in acknowledged rights of workers. IT security means a change of sociotechnical systems and social organizations and therefore is too complex and too important to leave it to computer specialists and agencies with a secret service tradition. In the future these measures will concern millions of computer users as workers or consumers and therefore have to be put to a broader discussion based on an ecological, interdisciplinary approach. This affords changes on the conceptual level as well as with regard to the process of concept development.

### 6.1. Conceptual questions

The question of vulnerability of computer supported work has to be analyzed from an organization theory framework of reference. The responsibility dilemma mentioned above makes it necessary to check organizational structures as a whole as they often assign organizational responsibilities which do not fit to the kind of technical systems employed. Using complex computer networks therefore requires a change of organizationally assigned responsibility.

But most of all the kind of computer support must be appropriate to the desired organizational design resulting from requirements from the environment or the workers. Groupwork and self-organization are not compatible with a strict monitoring of individuals, rather accountability has to be established on a work group level. As another point the visions of more and more tightly coupled systems have to be examined critically. In industrial production control where disturbances directly lead to production breakdowns and quality costs former visions of Computer Integrated Manufacturing have been given up. Instead concepts of loosely coupled production isles with workgroups as coordinating entities are viewed to be more effective. The same shift of paradigms might well occur in other application areas and obviously has consequences for IT security concepts.

### 6.2. Need for an integrated debate

The questions raised can only be answered if the lines of discussion are brought together. This need has been mentioned for the case of the directive of the EC Commission. As the present IT security concepts pose new threats to workers, trade union officials and work-oriented researchers should articulate their critique on international and national level. As the situation in Germany shows there are realistic chances for such a dialogue: Due to political intervention of the Green Party and with the help of Alexander Roßnagel the law enacting the Federal Agency for IT Security (BSI) adopted a broader understanding of security in Germany. And within the office there is at least a small research staff which has to study the social consequences of security measures. On Sept. 21/22 this staff organizes the first meeting between security officials from federal ministries, computer scientists and social scientists.

Within IFIP a first step might be to start a discussion between TC 11 and TC 9, perhaps leading to a joint Work Group and a joint conference.

Considering that the IT security debate is going on for more than 10 years and due to a lot of research money has reached a certain state of the art one may argue that the critique from a workers´point of view is coming rather late. But I think that it is not too late if actions on different levels are started from this conference.

## 7. REFERENCES

BRIEFS, U.: Informationstechnologien und Zukunft der Arbeit. Köln 1984.
BRIEFS, U./CIBORRA, C./SCHNEIDER, L. (Eds.): Systems Design. For, With and By the Users. Amsterdam et al. 1983.
BSI: IT-Sicherheitshandbuch. Handbuch für die sichere Anwendung der Informationstechnik, ed. by the German Agency for Information Technology Security (Bundesamt für Sicherheit in der Informationstechnik - BSI). Der Bundesminister des Inneren/Koordinierungs- und Beratungsstelle der Bundesregierung für Informationstechnik in der Bundesverwaltung, Bonn 1991.
CAELLI, W.J. (Ed.): Computer Security in the Age of Information. Amsterdam et al. 1989.
CAELLI, W./LONGLEY, D./SHAIN, M.: Information Security Handbook. Basingstoke 1991.
CLEGG, S./DUNKERLEY, D.: Organization, Class and Control. London et al. 1980.
COMMISSION OF THE EUROPEAN COMMUNITIES: Proposal for a Descision of the Council Concerning Information Technology Security. Brussels 1990a.
COMMISSION OF THE EUROPEAN COMMUNITIES: INFOSEC. Background Material, Definitions. Conventions and References to on-going Work. DG XIII/Directorate F. RACE. Programme and Development of Telematics Services. Brussels 1990b.
COMMISSION OF THE EUROPEAN COMMUNITIES (Ed.): Information Technology Security Evaluation Criteria (ITSEC). Provisional Harmonized Criteria. June 1991. Luxembourg 1991.
COUNCIL OF THE EUROPEAN COMMUNITIES: Directive on Health and Safety of Work with Visual Display Units. Amtsblatt v. 21.6.1990, pp 14ff.
CYERT, R.M./MARCH,.J.G.: A Behavioral Theory of the Firm. Englewood Cliffs, N.J. 1963.
DoD: Trusted Computer Systems Evaluation Criteria. DoD 5200.28-STD. Department of Defense, United States of America. December 1985.
FINE, L.H.: Computer Security. A Handbook for Management. 2nd Ed., London 1986.
GRISSONNANCHE, A. (Ed.): Security and Protection in Information Systems. Amsterdam et al. 1989.
ISO: Information Processing Systems - Open Systems Interconnections - Basic Reference Model - Part 2: Security Architecture. International Standard ISO 7498-2. International Organization for Standardization, 1988a.

ISO: Visual Display Terminals (VDTs) Used for Office Tasks - Ergonomic Requirements - Part 2: Task Requirements. Draft International Standard ISO/DIS 9241-2. International Organization for Standardization 1988b.
KRALLMANN, H.: EDV-Sicherheitsmanagement. Integrierte Sicherheitskonzepte für betriebliche Informations- und Kommunikationssysteme. Berlin 1989.
LUTTERBECK, B.: Das Restrisiko der Informationstechnologie: Gefahr für Freiheit und Demokratie? In: Löwe, M. et al. (Eds.): Umdenken in der Informatik. Berlin 1987, pp. 43-58.
MIN TJOA, A./KOCH, M./REITERER, H./KOLM, P./MOSER, U.: Softwaregestaltung aus Arbeitnehmersicht. Gewerkschaft der Privatangestellten. Wien 1988.
MORGAN, G.: Images of Organization. Beverly Hills et al. 1986.
NATIONAL RESEARCH COUNCIL: Growing Vulnerability of the Public Switched Networks: Implications for National Security Emergency Preparedness. Board on Telecommunications and Computer Applications. Washington, DC 1989.
OTA: The Electronic Supervisor. New Technology - New Tensions. US Congress. Office of Technology Assessment 1987.
OTA: Critical Connections. Communication for the Future. US Congress, Office of Technology Assessment. Washington 1990.
RIHACZEK, K.: Die harmonisierten Evaluationskriterien für IT-Systeme. In: Datenschutz und Datensicherung 12/1990, pp. 628-634.
ROSSNAGEL, A./WEDDE, P./HAMMER, V./PORDESCH, U.: Die Verletzlichkeit der "Informationsgesellschaft". Opladen 1989.

Education and Society / R. Aiken (Editor)
Information Processing 92, Volume II
Elsevier Science Publishers B.V. (North-Holland)
1992 IFIP.



# Impacts of eletronic markets on work

Pertti Järvinen

University of Tampere, Department of Computer Science, P.O.Box 607,
33101 Tampere, Finland Email pj@uta.fi Fax +358-31-156 070

**Abstract**

The domain of electronic markets are increasing in relation to electronic hierarchies. Hence it is important to analyze possible impacts of electronic markets on a human being at work. A man can be in different positions concerning electronic markets: 1. a developer of an inter-organizational information system (IOS), 2. a user (a seller or a buyer) of electronic markets, and 3. an object of markets, i. e. a specialist whose services are sold on electronic markets.

First, to construct the IOS a developer has to perform particular tasks: requirements analysis, design, implementation and thereafter often also maintenance. Second, a user of electronic markets can do different things depending on whether she/he is working in a producer company, in a distributor firm, in a buyer company, in a network provider company or in financial services. Third, services offered by a human being on electronic markets should inform potential buyers about her or his service. On the other hand a buyer must describe which kind of service she or he needs.

In the first position, the idea of the IOS means that the production/ consumption chain is lengthened. The developer of the IOS must master this chain over two or more organizations. Hence, she or he must be more competent than nowadays. Concerning the second position, a user of electronic markets, by definition, will lose social contacts. Her variety to communicate will diminish, because she or he must use the standardized product/service description language and/or the information retrieval language at hand. In the third position, the services offered by a certain expert must be described as in detail as possible. But this creates a dilemma, if a a task can be described in elementary operations, it could be automated, i.e. the task is no more necessarily performed by a human being but by a computer or by an automaton.

Keyword Codes: K.4.2, K.4.3, H.1.2
Keywords: Computers and Society, Social Issues; Organizational Impacts; User/Machine Systems

## 1. Introduction

The innovations in information technologies of the past two decades have radically reduced the time and cost of processing and communicating information. These reductions have in turn brought many changes in the ways tasks are accomplished within and between firms. Progress in data processing may cause changes in how firms and markets organize the flow of goods and services through theis value-added chains [11].

Economies have two basic mechanisms for coordinating the flow of materials or services through adjacents steps in a the value-added chain: markets and hierarchies [13]. Markets coordinate the flow through supply and demand forces and external transactions between different individuals and firms. Hierarchies coordinate the flow of materials through adjacent steps by controlling and directing it at a higher level in the managerial hierarchy [10].

Malone et al. [10] estimated that information technology can cause an overall shift from hierarchies to markets. An example of the shift toward electronic market has already occurred in the airline industry. When airline reservations are made through a travel agent, the sale is made by the travel agent acting as an external agent for the airline. This selling process is coordinated by the market relationship between the travel agent and the airline. - Later Malone and Rockart [9] have showed many examples of new applications of electronic markets. To this end it is important to analyze potential social impacts of electronic markets.

Ciborra [4] was one of the first advocates for a transaction costs approach [13] to information systems. Gurbaxani and Whang [5] took the acency theory for sketching out internal coordination costs, and the transaction costs theory for external coordination costs. They considered the impacts of information systems on organizations and markets from the economic perspective. Malone et al. [10], Gurbaxani and Whang [5], and Malone and Rockart [9] have emphasized management or managerial aspects of electronic markets. But there are also other effects of electronic markets. We have not found any study of the impacts of electronic markets on work or on persons at operational level.

To this end our research problem can be stated: What are impacts of electronic markets on work? Our theoretical and conceptual analysis concerns three categories of persons: 1. IOS developers, 2. users of electronic markets and 3. experts offering their service via electronic markets. Concerning categories 1 and 2 we are going to analyze their job by using core dimensions, for category 3 we shall consider the characteristics of services offered by experts. We shall also study some examples of the integration, brokerage and telecommunication effects [14, 18]. An interesting dilemma between the description of electronic service and the properties of tasks will be thought over.

The rest of the paper has structured according to categories above: IOS developers are considered in Section 2, users in Section 3 and the tasks of experts in Section 4. Finally a (self-)evaluation of our approach will be performed in Section 5.

## 2. On jobs of developers of inter-organizational information systems

Malone et al. [10] very successfully predicted that the evolution of electronic markets from multiple starting points leads to a common evolutionary path from the biased markets to the unbiased and finally to the personalized one.

In this section we are interested in the job requirements of developers of an IOS. To start our analysis, let us take the most simple system, the IOS between two organizations. A certain firm has many possible connections with its environment, i.e. to banks, to insurance companies, to governmental bodies etc.. We shall here concentrate our attention on the most typical case of two firms. The former (firm 1) is assumed to be a manufacturer (producer, supplier) and the latter (firm 2) a buyer (procurer, consumer). In each firm, the total manufacturing process can be divided to three consecutive functions: acquisition or purchasing (A), production or service (P) and marketing (M). The P function characterizes a certain firm. In our case, firm 1 produces such products or services that firm 2 consumes.

To develop an information system supporting production planning in a particular firm developers must master all the functions A, P and M, although this system mainly contributes the P function. In our case, the developers of the IOS for firms 1 and 2 must master functions P and M (say P1, M1) in the first firm and functions A and P (say A2, P2) in the second firm. Hence, it is necessary, to a certain extent, to master two different production functions and two different organizational cultures. These demands especially concern the requirements analysis of the IOS.

In order to analyse the job of a developer we take the core job dimensions. Buchanan [3 p. 70] has collected theories and techniques for job design. He called them as the generations of job design. The fourth generation was ranked the highest one. The five core job dimensions [6] are:
D1. Skill variety is the extent to which a job makes use of different skills and abilities.
D2. Task identity is the extent to which a job involves a 'whole' and meaningful piece of work.
D3. Task significance is the extent to which a job affects the work of other organization members or others in society.
D4. Autonomy is the extent to which a job gives the individual freedom, independence and discretion in carrying it out.
D5. Feedback is the extent to which information about the level of performance attained is related back to the individual.

To evaluate the skill variety (D1) of the job of a developer, we can conclude, that knowledge requirements concerning the application domains and the environments of the IOS are higher than in the traditional information system (IS). The development of the IOS is normally organized as a project. In our case the project group consists of the representatives of two or more firms. This situation states higher demands for social skills and abilities for the developers of the IOS than in building the internal IS. The firms connected by the IOS may have different computers with different operating systems. The shift from the IOS, from the biased market to the unbiased market requires that the technical subsystem allows to join different computers to the network.

Hence the technical requirements of the network are higher than in the local area network of a particular firm. - We can conclude that the development of IS for electronic market states higher demands in the skill variety than the development of the traditional IS.

Concerning the task identity (D2) of the job of a developer we can say that the IOS is the clearly defined and rather concrete outcome of development process. Hence criterion D2 is satisfied.

The same can also be said about the task significance (D3) of the job of a developer. By referring to Malone et al. [10], the IOS and later the electronic market affects the work of other people in various organizations.

The autonomy (D4) of the job of a developer (or a systems analyst) cannot be easily evaluated. The different interested parties, at least firms 1 and 2, and the representatives of functions P1, M1, A2 and P2 may considerably restrict the freedom of a developer. We must, however, remember that the development process is a solitary project and its final outcome is the new part of reality. Hence, it therefore contains the more degrees of freedom that the traditional repetitive type of work.

The real feedback (D5) about the quality of the new IOS or of electronic markets can be received after the new system is used for a while. During the development process the steering committee will regularly give feedback to the project group.

The results of our analysis means that either we must have a super-analyst or we should more carefully than earlier compose the project group covering new and wider demands. The group members must then have enough social and communication skills. The lack of a super-analyst or the lack of the necessary skills is clearly full of risk.

## 3. Social effects of electronic markets on a user

Referring to Malone et al. [10] a user of electronic markets can work in companies with different role: manufacturer or producer, distributor, information technology, financial services and buyer. A user working in a manufacturer company tries to specify the attributes of the product in enough detail to allow potential buyers (whether acquiring production inputs for company 2 or acquiring goods for consumption) to make selection. Stocks and commodities, for example, have simple and standardized descriptions, while those of business insurance policies or large and complicated computer systems are much more complex. A buyer would like to maximize the number of alternatives considered and the ease of comparing them. She or he uses electronic markets to speed order processing and to apply just-in-time inventory management policy.

The jobs of a seller and a buyer contain many other tasks than the tasks joined with electronic markets and outlined above. Hence social impacts of electronic markets on the jobs of a seller and a buyer do not much differ from the impacts caused by traditional computing systems (cf. [2]): The standardized interfaces do not support the skill variety (D1); the introduction of a new computing system has sometimes produced narrow jobs (cf. D2, task identity), and task significance (D3) has therefore lessened; computing systems have also reduced autonomy at work (D4), but created new communication channels and to this end improved feedback (D5).

The distributor or the broker is an agent between producers and buyers. It helps producers to find suitable buyers, and buyers to find suitable producers. We claim that a brokerage can be a transient phenomenon, because it causes more non-productive additional subtasks.

When two consecutive subtasks ($\Omega$ and $\pi$) contributing the same final outcome are assigned to two different processors (either to man or to computer), this division of labour creates some *non-productive additional subtasks*: transportation, two inspections, communication, coordination and in connection with computers possibly also en/coding and conversion [7]. These additional subtasks are called non-productive, because they do not contribute finishing of the final outcome. If the same processor will perform both consecutive subtasks $\Omega$ and $\pi$, the additional subtasks mentioned above will be eliminated.

The market itself creates those additional subtasks once, because there is a division of labour between a seller and a buyer. The broker doubles those non-productive subtasks, because there then exists the division of labour between a seller and a broker, and between a broker and a buyer. This fact should be taken into account, when the pros and cons of brokerage are evaluated.The brokerage within electronic market may vanish, because on one hand it creates non-productive additional subtasks, and on the other hand sellers and buyers may learn transact business directly with each others.

## 4. On services offered by an expert

We here use term expert to represent human services which differ from products. They are based on different assets. An input used by a firm (or individual consumer) is highly asset specific ([13]), if it cannot readily be used by other firms because of site specificity, physical asset specificity, or human asset specificity. Malone et al. [10] characterize a human asset as follows: Highly specialized human skills whether physical (e.g. a trade with very limited applicability) or mental (e.g. a consultant's knowledge of a company's processes) - that cannot readily put to work for other purposes are human specific. Malone et al. also claim that information technology may reduce human specificity. We in this section ask: How far this is possible? What does characterize services offered by human being?

Kortteinen [8] differentiates work to two classes: understanding and operative work. The operative work can be divided into small simple and elementary steps and the object of work (material or data) behaves deterministicly. Understanding work differs from operative work that it necessitates *cultural competence*. Concerning service work the idea of automation is not human. The automation cannot concern such human processes which behave indeterministicly. We call such processes *self-steering systems* (cf. Aulin [1]).

Suomi [12] claims that electronic communication and coordination or IOSs can be used to reduce human asset specificity. To his mind the *integration effect* can help as follows: "In many repair operations, the service staff are a scarce resource. Many vendors of equipment that requires servicing have provided online help facilities to assist customers in their attempts to cope the problems they have encountered. When online assistance is of no use, these systems then locate and dispatch the nearest repair staff. Systems like these are common in, for example, the computer and elevator industries." "The *brokerage effect* can also minimize human asset specificity in, for example, systems that support employment authorities. With systems offering access to many different databases that comprise both vacant jobs and available labour, the best match between supply and demand can be attained." "The *telecommunication effect* has the strongest influence on the asset specificities of time and place. The problem of the time specificity of human assets is attacked, for example, in some airports by a room in which a doctor can be consulted by means of telecommunication links. In a room fitted with teleconference-like equipment, patient - doctor audiovisual communication can be achieved, despite the doctor being at some other location. In the locale, the only personnel required are those assisting."

In the repair example, the object of work is an equipment behaving deterministicly. For the similar purposes many automatic repairing systems, i.e. for equipments intended to space research, were built. If the repair task was not completed with electronic facilities, Suomi [12] recommends to move the equipment to to a repair firm. The electronic service is then reduced to an address service. In this example the human asset specificity problem and its site specificity version was only partially solved.

In the doctor example the patient's illness can concern either her physiological or biological processes or her total intellectual process. The former behaves deterministicly but the latter not. In an airport situations the former cases mostly exist, and this may explain the success of the service. The audiovisual communication organized between the patient and the doctor may support cultural understanding, because it magnifies the communication capacity compared with the traditional telecommunication cable. The latter is normally used on electronic markets. In mental illnesses self-steering aspects may play a dominating role and they could not therefore nurse with those arrangements. We can conclude that in this doctor example a human asset specificity problem is only partially solved and with exceptional arrangements.

In the employment example some kind of the greatest sum of match between jobs and unemployed persons is tried to find. To do that both the vacant jobs and all the candidates must be carefully described. We could now ask: How far we should go in details for achieving the best fit. To our mind that point cannot be stated. This example demontrates the main problem with electronic markets and human assets. The description of the services based on human assets is very difficult. If you can do that (in elementary steps), the task might be automatized.

We can conclude there is a dilemma: if you like to offer the services based on human assets, they must be described in very detail; and if the human task can be described in elementary steps, it could be automated. This dilemma stresses on the difference between a computer and a human being. The risk in offering human service is there that somebody may try to offer the service whose performance may require cultural competence.

## 5. Discussion

To our mind our main results can be divided to two categories: 1. predicted changes and 2. new classifications. From the former we would like to emphasize the dilemma concerning services based on human assets, from the latter we stress on non-productive additional tasks. Those models may "live" even longer than the predicted changes.

We have attempted to predict changes that have not yet occurred on a large scale, our forecats are based on a simple conceptual analysis than on systemic empirical studies. A conclusive test of our model and our predictions will, therefore, require further empirical and analytical work.

Other researchers may succeed to improve our results by taking “better” classification and models than we did. Another potential approach possibly leading better result is to divide some of our classes to subclasses and in that way to get more concrete results. Both empirical and theoretical studies are welcome, because electronic coordination via hierarchies and markets is continuously increasing [9].

## References


1. Aulin A. (1989), *Foundations of Mathematical Systems Dynamics: The Fundamental Theory of Causal Recursion and its Application to Social Science and Economics.* Book Series of Systems Science and Engineering, Pergamon Press, Oxford.
2. Bjørn-Andersen N. (1979), The impact of the computer systems in the five banks, In Bjørn-Andersen, Hedberg, Mercer Mumford and Sole (Eds.), *The impact of systems change in organisations*, Sijthoff & Noordhoff, Alphen aan den Rijn, 269-292.
3. Buchanan D.A. (1979), *The development of job design theories and techniques*, Saxon House, Farnborough.
4. Ciborra C.U. (1987), Research agenda for transaction costs approach to information systems, In Boland and Hirschheim (Eds.), *Critical issues in information systems research*, Wiley, New York, 253-274.
5. Gurbaxani V. and S. Whang (1991), The impact of information systems on organizations and markets, *Comm. ACM* 34, No 1, 59-73.
6. Hackman J.R. and G.R. Oldham (1975), Development of the job diagnostic survey, *Journal of Applied Psychology* 60, No 2, 159-170.
7. Järvinen, P. On structuring problems of job design met in the development and maintenance of information systems, *BIT* 20 (1980), 15-24.
8. Kortteinen M. (1987), *Hallittu rakennemuutos?* , Hanki ja Jää, Helsinki (in Finnish).
9. Malone T.W. and J.F. Rockart (1991), Computers, networks and the corporeation, *Scientic American* Sept., 92-99.
10. Malone T.W., J. Yates and R.I. Benjamin (1987), Electronic markets and electronic hierarchies, *Comm. ACM* 30, No 6, 484-497.
11. Porter, M.E. and V.E. Millar (1985), How information gives you competitive advantage, *Harvard Business Review* 63, No. 4, 149-160.
12. Suomi, R. (1991), Removing transaction costs with inter-organizational information systems, *Info. and Software Technology* 33, No 3, 205-211.

Education and Society / R. Aiken (Editor)
Information Processing 92, Volume II
Elsevier Science Publishers B.V. (North-Holland)


# Automation-Related Complacency: A Source of Vulnerability in Contemporary Organizations

S. Parasuraman[a], I. L. Singh[b], R. Molloy[b], and R. Parasuraman[b]

[a]Department of Management, Drexel University, Philadelphia, PA. 19104, U.S.A.

[b]Department of Psychology, Catholic University of America, Washington, D.C. 20064, U.S. A.

**Abstract**

The study examines the concept of automation-related complacency as a source of vulnerability in organizations using advanced automated technologies. The paper reports the results of empirical research using data from two independent sources to develop and validate a complacency potential rating scale (CPRS). Results indicate that automation-related complacency is a multidimensional construct that includes *general attitudes towards automation*, and four components: *confidence, reliance, trust,* and *safety-related complacency.*

Keyword Codes: K.4; K.4.2; K4.3.
Keywords: Computers and Society; Social Issues; Organizational Impacts

---

## Introduction

The extensive adoption of new technologies involving increased computerization and automation of operating systems has radically altered the nature of work in manufacturing and service industries. The increased use of automation has been motivated by the desire to: (1) control or constrain variability and unpredictability in various phases of manufacturing and service operations (Hulin & Roznowski, 1985); (2) enhance the technological strength and competitive position of organizations; and (3) reduce or obviate the need for human intervention and control (Adler, 1986; Buchanan & Bessant, 1985).

Many of the anticipated benefits of automation have been realized. For example, aircraft automation has led to better fuel economy, permitted flying in all weather conditions, improved flight control and navigation, and reduced cockpit crew size in commercial aircraft (Norman, Billings, Nadel, Palmer, Wiener, & Woods, 1988). Similarly, consistency, reliability, and cost-effectiveness have been cited as benefits accruing from automation in other areas of transportation (e.g., shipping), manufacturing, and in medicine, (Hirschorn, 1984).

However, advanced technological systems also increase the vulnerability of organizations to costly errors. Automated systems alter the human-machine interface in unpredictable ways (Adler, 1986; Hirschorn, 1984). The increased abstractness of tasks imposes additional cognitive demands on supervisors and operators, as well as increased need for coordination to manage the complex interdependencies among organizational roles (Adler, 1986; Weick, 1990). Wiener (1988) found that half of the commercial airline pilots in her study believed that automation had increased their mental workload, particularly at critical phases of flight such as takeoff and landing. Hulin & Roznowski (1985) suggested that excessive reliance on automation could to lead to an erosion in individuals' technical skills or "technological atrophy."

Weick (1990) argues that the greater prominence of stochastic events and system malfunctions in highly automated systems highlights the critical importance of human skills, especially diagnostic and monitoring skills. However, the problems encountered are less analyzable, and employees' role as passive monitors or "variance absorbers" fails to provide them with the information they need in handling exceptions (Hulin & Roznowski, 1985; Weick, 1990). Paradoxically, while the increased reliability of automated systems has reduced the incidence of or eliminated many kinds of error, new forms of error that did not exist formerly have emerged, with potentially serious if not catastrophic consequences.

Human factors researchers have identified "automation-induced complacency" as one potential source of these types of errors (Singh, Molloy, & Parasuraman, 1991; Thackray & Touchstone, 1989; Wiener, 1981). The purpose of this paper is to briefly review the phenomenon of complacency as a source of vulnerability in automated systems, to report the results of empirical research conducted to develop and validate a complacency potential rating scale (CPRS), and to discuss the implications of automation-induced complacency for the management of new technologies in organizations.

**The Concept of Automation-Related Complacency**

Operator complacency is thought to arise in highly-reliable automated environments in which the operator serves in a supervisory role but does not directly control the automated process. The operator also does not have ready access to the "inner workings" of the process, a phenomenon of "peripheralization" that is now thought to be a general characteristic of most automated systems (Adler, 1986; Norman et al., 1988). Although the term complacency has been associated largely with highly sophisticated and complex systems, the underlying phenomenon has been noted in older, less sophisticated automated systems as well.

Operator attitudes such as over-confidence in automation may not necessarily be reflected in complacent behavior, but may only indicate a *potential* for complacency. Singh et al. (1991) propose that complacency potential is a set of attitudes that arise in certain *contexts* and which subsequently *may* adversely affect performance (e.g., in a different context). The individual with a high potential for complacency may display *complacent behavior* under conditions of high workload, fatigue, or poor interpersonal communication.

**The Present Study**

Despite the growing research interest in the notion of operator complacency and its potential link to accidents and problems of industrial and aviation safety, little systematic research has been conducted to develop a reliable and valid measure of the concept of automation-related complacency or to identify the dimensions of the concept. Thus, the present study sought to develop a scale for measuring attitudes toward automation that reflect a potential for complacency. Such a scale would enable us to examine the prevalence of the phenomenon as well as its relationship to job-related behaviors indicative of operator complacency.

Our approach was that complacency is exhibited by certain individuals, under certain environmental contexts, particularly highly automated operating systems. Singh et al. (1991) define complacency as "a set of attitudes involving uncritical trust towards, over-reliance on, excessive confidence in, and other related attitudes towards automation technology. The condition manifests itself in certain environmental contexts and may adversely affect performance in different contexts" (pp. 4 - 5). Based on this, the present study conceptualized attitudes toward automation as representing an individual's predisposition to react in a certain way towards automated devices. It was expected that the attitudes toward automation assessed by the proposed complacency rating scale would reflect various dimensions of complacency concerning automated devices.

**Sample and Measures**

The sample for the first phase of the study consisted of 139 undergraduate students (50 men and 89 women) enrolled in a variety of arts and science programs in an eastern university who volunteered to participate in the research. The participants ranged in age from 17 to 38 years, with a mean age of 20 years.

The researchers generated an initial pool of one hundred general statements about the possible advantages and disadvantages of automation, as well as items related specifically to complacency potential. Four judges considered to be experts in the area reviewed the items, and based on face validity, selected 16 items including both positive and negative statements as representing dimensions of automation-related complacency. A questionnaire including these 16 items plus 4 "filler" items was pilot-tested with a separate subsample of 10 student volunteers. Respondents were asked to indicate their agreement or disagreement with each of the statements on a five-point scale ranging from (1) "strongly disagree" to (5) "strongly agree." A final version of the survey was then administered to the initial sample of 139 participants. The survey also included questions on demographic characteristics of the respondents, including sex, age, education, experience in using microcomputers, and familiarity with the use of a "mouse" in operating a microcomputer

## Results

### Factor Structure of the Complacency Potential Rating Scale

The negatively worded items were recoded such that high scores represented favorable attitudes toward automation. A total score was computed for each respondent by adding scores on all items except the filler items. Item analysis was conducted out to determine and select the best statements for use in a scale measuring complacency-potential. Results showed that all statements were highly intercorrelated ($r >.98$ ), indicating high internal consistency among the items. Item discrimination analysis revealed extremely low ($r < .22$) correlations, thus favoring the retention of all statements.

The 20 items on attitudes toward automation were then factor analyzed using the principal components method with varimax rotation in order to determine the existence of underlying homogeneous factors. Examination of the results revealed the presence of five factors with eigen values greater than 1, which accounted for 53.2 % of the explained variance. The criterion used in determining the inclusion of an item in a given factor was that it should load unambiguously on that factor and have a loading of .30 or higher.

Factor 1, General Attitudes toward Automation: This factor consisted of four items reflected general attitudes toward automation. The items and their respective loadings on factor 1 were: (1) People save time by using automatic teller machines (ATMs) rather than a bank teller for banking transactions (.73); (2) I do not trust automated devices such as ATMs and computerized airline reservation systems (72); (3) I often use automated devices (.68); (4) I do not like to use ATMs because I feel that they are sometimes unreliable (.61).

Factor 2., Confidence-related Complacency: This factor consisted of four items reflecting confidence about various aspects of automation. (5) I think that automated devices used in medicine, such as CAT-scans and ultrasound, provide very reliable medical diagnosis (.68); (6) Automated devices in medicine same time and money in diagnosis and treatment of disease (.55). (7) If I need to have a tumor in my body removed, I would choose to undergo computer-aided surgery using laser technology because computerized surgery is more reliable and safer than manual surgery (.54). High scores on this factor were interpreted as reflecting over-confidence in automation, and thereby indicative of a potential for complacency.

Factor 3, Reliance-related Complacency: This factor consisted of three items reflecting individuals' perception of the reliability of automation and their consequent reliance on automation. (8) ATMs provide a safeguard against the inappropriate use of an individual's bank account by dishonest people (.78); (9) Automated devices used in aviation and banking have made work easier for both employees and customers (.51); (10) Even though the automatic cruise control in my car is set at a speed below the speed limit, I worry when I pass a police radar trap in case the automatic control is not working (.35).

Factor 4, Trust-related Complacency: This factor included three items reflecting the individual's trust in automation. (11) Manually sorting through card catalogues is more reliable than computer-aided searches for finding items in a library (.69); (12) I would rather purchase an item using a computer than have to deal with a sales representative on the phone because my order is more likely to be correct using the computer (.68); (13) Bank transactions have become safer with the introduction of computer technology for the transfer of funds (.53).

Factor 5, Safety-related Complacency: This factor consisted of two items concerning the individual's perception of the safety afforded by automation. (14) I feel safer deposting my money at an ATM than with a human teller. (15) I have to tape an important TV program for a class assignment. To ensure that the correct program is recorded, I would use the automatic programming facility on my VCR rather than manual taping (.66).

The internal consistency reliability coefficients (alpha) of the five factors were: general attitudes toward automation (.97); confidence-related complacency (.82); reliance-related complacency (.85); trust-related complacency (.89); safety-related complacency (.95). The high alphas obtained for the five factors indicate acceptable levels of internal consistency reliability, and provide further confirmation of the homogeneity of the items comprising them. The overall reliability CPRS as a whole was .90.

**Construct Validation**

Developmental Study. As part of the construct validation process, we examined the relationships of selected demographic characteristics of the participants with their scores on the complacency-potential rating scale. The results showed that gender (coded women = 0; men = 1), age and education were negatively correlated with the scores on the CPRS. Computer experience, computer use, and mouse use were positively related to complacency potential, though the correlations were not significant. The pattern of relationships found is similar to those reported in studies of computer anxiety and attitudes toward microcomputer usage (Igbaria & Parasuraman, 1991), and provides some evidence of the role of key background variables as correlates of automation-related complacency. Although not as robust as expected, these results provide partial support for the construct validity of the CPRS. The low correlations between the antecedent variables and complacency scores are perhaps due to the restricted range of the individual variables within the student samples used in this study.

The stability of the CPRS was assessed by computing the test-retest reliability coefficients. Of the 139 subjects who participated originally in the development study, 44 students (10 men and 34 women) participated in a second administration of the questionnaire three months after the initial survey. The internal consistency reliability coefficient for the scale as whole was .87, and the coefficients of stability for each of the five factors were high, indicating further support for the psychometric adequacy of the complacency-potential rating scale.

Validation Study. In the final phase of the study, we tested the validity of the CPRS with data gathered from 175 students enrolled in a variety of business-related programs at an urban technologically-oriented university in the east. Respondents included 114 men and 61 women; their average age was 23 years.

Factor analysis using the principal components method of extraction and varimax rotation revealed a five-factor solution which accounted for 55% of the explained variance. The factor structure, and factor loadings of the items comprising each factor, were were very similar to those found in the developmental study. The internal consistency reliabilities of the five factors were: General factor (.69); Reliance factor (.61); Confidence factor (.64); Safety factor (.76); Trust factor: (.87). The scale as a whole had a reliability of .89.

Correlational analysis showed that gender, mouse use, and computer use were negatively associated with automation-related complacency, while age, education and computer experience were positively associated with it. These findings are similar to the pattern of correlations found in the developmental study, and provide further support for the reliability and validity of the CPRS as a measure of automation-related complacency.

Another indicator of the validity of a scale is its criterion-related or predictive validity (Schwab, 1980). In a companion study, we obtained behavioral evidence for complacency in a simulated flight control task carried out with partial automation (Parasuraman, Bahri, Molloy, & Singh, 1991). The performance index of complacency in this study could be used as a criterion measure for the complacency-potential scale.

**Discussion and Conclusions**

The study focused attention on the complexity, magnitude, and high cost of errors encountered in malfunctions of advanced technological systems, and the role of automation-related complacency as one source of vulnerability of organizations with highly automated operating systems. The study results indicate that the potential for complacency can be evaluated using attitude ratings of items related to everyday automation technology. The findings show that automation-related complacency is a multidimensional construct. It includes general attitudes toward automation as well as four components of complacency, i. e., *confidence, reliance, trust, and safety-induced* complacency.

Although the study results provide substantial evidence of internal consistency reliability, and test-retest validity of the instrument, the convergent and discriminant validity of the CPRS need to be evaluated. Additional research using samples of employed adults is also needed in order to determine the generalizability of the CPRS for use in a variety of occupations and organizational settings, as well as its utility and predictive efficacy in explaining task or job performance in highly automated systems. It is also necessary to assess empirically whether automation-related complacency is a situationally induced phenomenon as proposed by Singh et al. (1991), or whether it is an individual difference variable analogous to such constructs as risk propensity, uncertainty avoidance, and cognitive complexity.

### References

Adler, P. (1986). New technologies, new skills. *California Management Review*, 29, 9-28.

Buchanan, D. A., & Bessant, J. (1985). Failure, uncertainty, and control: The role of operators in a computer integrated production system. *Journal of Management Studies,* 22, 292-308.

Hirschhorn, L. (1984). *Beyond mechanization: Work and technology in a post industrial age*. Cambridge, MA: MIT Press.

Hulin, C. L., & Roznowski, M. (1985). Organizational technologies: Effects on organizational characteristics and individuals' responses. In L. L. Cummings & B. M. Staw (Eds.), *Research in Organizational Behavior*, Vol. 7 (pp. 39-86). Greenwich, CT.: JAI press.

Igbaria, M. and Parasuraman, S. (1991). Attitudes toward microcomputers: Development and construct validation of a measure. *International Journal of Man-Machine Studies*, 35, 353-373.

Norman, S., Billings, C. E., Nadel, D., Palmer, E., Wiener, E. L., & Woods, D. D. (1988). *Aircraft automation philosophy: A source document*. NASA, Ames Research Center: CA.

Parasuraman, R., Bahri, T., Molloy, R., & Singh, I. L. (1991). Effects of shifts in the levels of automation on operator performance. In *Proceedings of the International Symposium on Aviation Psychology, 6th Annual Conference*, Columbus,Ohio.

Schwab, D. P. (1980). Construct validity in organizational behavior. In B. M. Staw & L. L. Cummings (eds.), *Research in organizational behavior,* Vol 2, (pp. 3 - 43). Greenwich, CT.: JAI Press.

Singh, I. L., Molloy, R., & Parasuraman, R. (1991). *Automation-induced "complacency": Development of a complacency-potential scale*. (Technical Report No. CSL-A-91-1). Washington D. C: Cognitive Science Laboratory, Catholic University of America.

Thackray, R. I., & Touchstone, R. M. (1989). Detection efficiency on an air traffic task with control monitoring and without computer aiding. *Aviation, Space, and Environmental Medicine, 60*, 744-748.

Weick, K. E. (1990). Technology as equivoque: Sensemaking in new technologies. In P. Goodman, L.S. Sproull & Associates (1990). *Technology and organizations* (pp. 1-44). San Francisco: Jossey-Bass.

Wiener, E. L. (1981). Complacency: Is the term useful for air safety? In *Proceedings of the 26th Corporate Aviation Safety Seminar.* (pp. 116-125). Denver, CO: Flight Safety Foundation, Inc.

Wiener, E. L. (1987). Application of vigilance research: Rare, medium, or well done? *Human Factors*, 29, 725-736.

Wiener, E. L. (1988). Cockpit automation. In E. L. Wiener & D. C. Nagel (Eds.), *Human factors in aviation.* San Diego: Academic Press.Olsen (Eds), *Mental models, tasks and errors.* London: Taylor & Francis.

Education and Society / R. Aiken (Editor)
Information Processing 92, Volume II
Elsevier Science Publishers B.V. (North-Holland) 


# Vulnerability of computer systems: Establishing organizational accountability

Ina Wagner

Institut für Gestaltungs- und Wirkungsforschung, Technische Universität Wien, Argentinierstr. 8, A-1040 Wien, Austria

**Abstract:**

This paper discusses risks associated with human-computer-interaction and the complexity of safety work in organizations with the aim to lay grounds for an organizational discourse on risks.

Keyword Codes: K.4.3, K.6.1, K.6.5
Keywords: Organizational Impacts, Project and People Management, Security and Protection

## Introduction

Within the computer sciences discussion on risks has largely focussed on technical aspects (on how to increase the security of IT) with the study of legal provisions (for protecting privacy rights on information or guaranteeing access to information that should be "public") forming a side field. Experience has drawn attention to the practical problems of implementing technical security measures and legal norms. These are partly organizational, partly rooted in the complexity of human-machine interaction, with actors having little experience in identifying and analyzing social and organizational practices of the people who are designing, running, maintaining high tech systems and have to cope with emergency situations. A need to establish organizational accountability for risk assessment and safety measures and to define this as a major management task has been defined.

## 1. Complex systems - parallel technologies

Some largely discussed arguments within the computer sciences refer to the unreliability and untrustworthyness of software. Large real-time software belongs to those systems that Perrow (1986) classifies as high risk systems: they are characterized by high interactive complexity and strong coupling both of which are the source of multiple, unforeseeable errors and their spreading through the system. Even in highly structured software systems which are built upon a number of carefully structured modules and equally carefully designed interfaces, the incredibly large number of states and possible interactions makes it impossible to achieve a full understanding and full control of a program. Progress in programming methods and mathematical tools for describing complex programs is extremely slow, for systematical reasons, not for the lack of effort. Software technology is largely a trial and error craft. Testing for programming errors, and this is done extensively, usually stops when the rate of discovering new errors falls dramatically (Parnas 1985).

Two alternative conclusions are drawn from this type of analysis: To mimimize human intervention in anyhow highly complex systems is one answer. To develop distributed systems which build upon decentralized, linear, and only loosely coupled processes and give space for human intervention is the opposite answer (Roßnagel et al 1989). A clear decision between those two positions seems difficult if not altogether impossible.

Human intervention, though acting as a "buffer", may itself be a source of new and often unforeseeable risks. This can be illustrated by an example: computerized monitoring equipment in intensive care of patients. There can be no doubt that a continuous monitoring of the vital functions of high risk patients adds to their safety. But health practitioners know:

* False alarms may occur - that means the system needs competent human intervention.
* The system monitors selected variables, the information it collects and interprets giving only a partial picture of a patient's health condition. This makes personal monitoring indispensable, particularly in high risk situations.

An important risk-creating factor is the proportion of attention given to machine-related monitoring. Not only do additional tasks - reaction to and interpretion of signals, adjustment and calibration of apparatus, routine maintenance operations - absorb nurses' attention. Nurses admit that when they first learn to handle the equipment they tend to focus less on the experiential and interactive side of nursing. Reading the body and behavioural signs and paying attention to and interpreting machine alarms are based on different (and not necessarily complementary) competencies and procedures (Wagner 1991). Nurses need to learn to combine the interpretation of monitor signals with alertness to subtle changes in e.g. patients' respiration, colour of skin.

In a study of Airbus 320 pilots Gras (1989) has pointed to the difficulties of moving competently in "artificial territories". The pilot does not steer the aircraft with his hands. He administers data which inform him on the computer system´s ongoing decisions. Piloting the aircraft is transformed into an activity "téte basse" - from looking outside and maneuvering through "real" territory to looking at the computer screen.

Baudrillard (1982) has argued that one problem of working with "simulacra" ("coded" models of reality) is that these do not answer the question of how to achieve a meaningful interpretation of information - to decide "what is real and imagined, what has been repressed, manipulated, the illusions they represent, what they conceal, additional meanings - all this has been extinguished" (1982,90). The danger of a pilot misjudging machine signals or of the computer misinterpreting interventions or misreading "images" is rooted in the restrictions of "context" which seem typical of human-machine-systems and have stimulated a long debate on the formalization of knowledge (Polanyi 1968, Suchman 1990). As information is decontextualized (Raulet 1988) - transmitted in delocalized and coded form - inconsistencies between what actors perceive as "real" and what has been implemented in technological systems may arise. These form sources of uncertainty and risk.

Zmud (1991) builds upon this point when arguing that ITS multiply the possibilites of misunderstanding and manipulating data. His main argument is that the artificiality of information sources (which are nor influenced by "codes of conduct") and the existence of multiple "processor-nodes" which connect and interpret information make it increasingly difficult to judge the authenticity and "truth" of information and encourages actors to develop methods of strategic information behaviour

Organizational psychologists have pointed out a second type of risk associated with human-computer interaction. This interaction and therefore competent human intervention in high risk technological systems is made difficult by the fact that <u>different</u> representations of reality are interacting. The computer systems which guide the aircraft and give messages to the pilot and the pilot's perception and interpretation of ongoing events are in fact two parallel "technologies", involving a technology in the head and a technology in the machine. Each is self-contained. Each is coordinated with the other intermittently rather than continuously. Each corrects the other discontinously. One can never be sure that both systems - the technology and its mental representation in the pilot's head - are well coordinated (Weick 1990). If we add for example a third crucial element of an airport´s safety system - the tower which works with a totally different technology - radar - based on an analogous (and not a digital) form of representation - the sources of error contained in the interaction of those different ways of representing "reality" multiply.

The conclusion to be drawn is that creating space for human intervention requires careful consideration of those problems that occur when different systems of presenting and assessing reality - one or several technological systems on one hand, their mental representation in a person's mind on the other hand - interact. Using the example of electronic media, Mary Ferguson (1990) has pointed out that the trangression of temporal and spacial constraints may be more problematic for individuals and organizations than generally conceded, since new time-space realities usually do not entirely replace old ones. As a consequence demands on individuals' time elasticity and ability to cope with local indeterminacy increase and the individual has to actively engage in synchronizing new and old time-space structures. To the extent that time and space become a new region of experience, uncertainty, speculation, and exploration, "changes in the nature of language, of ordinary knowledge, of the very structures of awareness" (Carey 1988), are taking place.

## 2. Risk management in organizations

In complex organizations it is highly probable that people who belong to different departments and different professional cultures interact. The complex nature of safety work calls for much sharing and overlapping among the various services, departments and occupational groups within an organization. Airports, a nuclear power plant or an intense care unit - each one is run, maintained and supervised by a variety of highly specialized people. Each occupational (or professional) group creates its own modes of perceiving and interpreting risks and of coping with them.

This has drawn attention to those technological risks that are rooted in specialization and the problems of establishing interdisciplinary communication between different groups of safety workers within an organization. The example of time management in organizations can serve as an illustration of this point. In complex organizations a plurality of time reckoning-systems can be found (Egger/Wagner 1992). Individuals and groups differ widely in how they react to time pressure, how they make use of gaps of time, or how they evaluate time loss. The willingness to give time for specific tasks, to share it with others as well as the power to dispose of the time of others and to withdraw time are unequally distributed. This makes the synchronization of people and activities extremely difficult. Failure to synchronize temporal resources is a source of risk in organizations with consequences for the management of emergencies.

Many problems of mishandling errors and failures in technical systems can be traced back to the closedness of professional cultures and their difficulties to interact efficiently, not only in emergency situations. Renn (1991) in his analysis of risks in organizations translates cultural diversity into the distinction of "cultural types" (such as the loner, the burocrat, the autonomous person, the entrepreneur, the equalizer) each of which represents a different approach to the assessment of risks.

Organizations are not only characterized by a plurality of interpretation systems (Gioia 1986) or cognitive maps (Weick/Bougon 1986). They are usually segmented, the stable units being small units: "Organizations built of small stable segments make sense over shorter spans of time, involving fewer people than we thought. Once these temporal and spatial boundaries are exceeded, orderliness, predictability, and sensibleness decline" (Weick 1985, 118). Risks in such organizations can be understood as a consequence of a lack of explicit responsabilites and rules, minimal agreement on the interpretation of existing rules and poorly developed feedback mechanisms. Informal relationships and with them status and power will gain influence and an immediacy unmodified by rules and procedures will develop.

From their investigations in hospitals Fagerhaugh et al (1987) have worked out policy suggestions that seek to improve risk management in organizations; such as:

* the need for stable, trained staff working together for a long period of time whose collective experiential knowledge about safety issues eventually evolves into accepted norms of work;
* open discussion of errors within an organization;
* developing negotiation skills, learning ways of improving interdisciplinary communication.

Establishing norms of work

Scientists and engineers are socialized into practices and a corresponding world view which can roughly be characterized as being:

* limited to the analytical solution of well defined problems;
* not suited to an analysis of problems such as the nature and operation of complex human organizations and their interactions with a technical system.

They tend "to look for abstract orientations in the form of generalizable, empirical data as a basis for decision-making" (Wolf 1988, 165). This is also reflected in their practices of dealing with questions of safety and risks.

For many engineering professions "codes of conduct" are being defined through the development of technical norms. Such norms are based on "an immanent logic of quantification, standardization and focus on detail" (Wolf 1988, 173) Grudin (1991) discusses some of these norms, that guide software development such as design simplicity, consistency with a real-world analog, or anticipation of low-frequency events. Other types of norms (technical as well as legal ones) can be found in the field of data security and data protection.

Such explicit normative regulations can act as some kind of guarantee for minimal social standards to be taken into account. In their analysis of technical norms Ekart and Löffler favour those types of codes of conduct which "strongly accentuate the regulation of procedures in addition to material criteria of rightful vocational practice and ... which require the practitioner to consciously connect a cognitively elaborate analysis of a problem with a differentiated moral-practical judgement" (1990, 14). If the consequences of normative regulations are to be understood and evaluated, norms have to be applied to and interpreted within a specific context. They may be in conflict with competing norms and of limited generalizability. This is why Ekart and Löffler formulate two requirements such norms would have to fulfil:"Their formulation should make clear the consequences of an adequate, responsible attitude to the task for the relationships between all participants (in the design). ... Such ethical codes should clearly express the difference and unsuspendable tension between the obligation to watch legal and quasi legal norms on one hand and to take distance from these norms if other principles or the situation make this necessary" (1990, 20f).

The problem poses itself that as many different people and occupations have to interact efficiently to minimize risks, there will be a plurality of competing norms within an organization, representing different values and interpretations of risks. Occupations, especially professions, tend to build collective defenses against outsiders. They insist on the right to define their own standards of practice and their own mistakes.

Error work

Developing efficient practices of coping with errors presuppose that errors have already occured, been evaluated, controlled and corrected. This is partly, because many different and unforeseeable errors may occur within complex organizations using complex technologies, partly because the type of error often changes with the history of the organization, the technology and the environment (e.g. client´s responses). In this sense errors are "epochal", they reflect processes of change and learning.

Different sources of errors can be distinguished:

* Some types of errors can be labelled as predominantly "human failure" - due to lack of knowledge, to neglect and forgetfulness, to lack of concentration.
* Other types of errors are organizational, rooted in lack of control mechanisms, wrong methods, a wrong distribution of competencies and knowledge within working groups, temporal constraints.

Error work, as defined by Strauss et al (1985), refers "to the various tasks involved in preventing, minimizing, defining, detecting, covering up, rectifying, estimating the consequences of, and so on, mistakes" (242). This means that risk management needs to be based on a careful assessment of the organization of work, of working conditions, of workers´ skills, their belief systems and social practices, their interactions with others. This is made difficult by the fact that errors are often kept secret, unless they are already visible. It involves identifying the sources of an error (including person-related reasons such as responsability, skill, stress, fatigue and their organizational sources), evaluating its consequences and defining measures for error prevention.

Establishing a discourse on risks and safety

Senghaas-Knobloch et al (1990) have elaborated the idea of an interdisciplinary dialogue and tested it in a variety of groups. They conceptualize such a dialogue as one of lay-persons (non experts) whose aim it is to develop a shared "language game" (in the sense of Wittgenstein). Participants in such a "project" face the two-fold task of creating the conditions for "normal" communication through problematizing mutual misperceptions and prejudices, surmounting communication blocks; of revolutionizing communication through "pulling down the limits of communication within communication or making them permeable" (Leithäuser 1990, 203). The authors have developed methods for monitoring such a communication process (e.g. through agreeing on goals for learning and communication, the systematic changing of perspectives) and for analyzing the process as well as the issues that have been dealt with (e.g. analysis of "core sentences").

A particular problem stems from the fact that different groups of actors within an organization represent different forms of knowledge and that this knowledge is not equally valued. Theoretical, empirical, practical as well as analytical and more associative knowledge compete with each other. The resulting communication barriers often clearly reflect internal organizational hierarchies (such as between computer scientists and non-engineers or between experts and e.g. maintenance people who vastly differ on what e.g. makes a statement "vague" or "exact", what counts as a valid argument, who can possibly have relevant knowledge of an event).

As a consequence, the possibility of such an intercultural dialogue on risks and safety largely seems to depend on actors´ role definition: That they do not act as promoters of issues or as experts in such a dialogue They are viewed as participants in a process for which they do not have any specific expertise. They are expected to examine their own individual and professional one-sidedness, including the implicit cultural norms inherent in the practice of their discipline. One main task for such an interdisciplinary and intercultural dialogue would be to develop ways of representing the tools and methods of different types of safety workers (e.g. software developers, maintenance people) through images and concepts to which all actors within an organization are able to relate to (Wagner 1992). This means that risk management in organizations needs to be based on a "common knowledge" in oder for actors to be able to share experiences with a technical system, to develop a common understanding and to coordinate action.

## 4. Conclusions

There is a need for a much more integrated approach to issues of risk and safety in high tech systems. More specifically, I should like to point out:
* the necessity to achieve a fuller understanding of different representations of reality and their interactions;
* the need to build into the human organization which is monitoring and supporting a high tech system arrangements that make safety more visible, precise and cooperative.

With this I am advocating a more disciplined and responsible approach to risk assessment and safety without challenging the basic argument that some technologies might be too unreliable and too risky to be used at all.

### Bibliography


Egger E., Wagner I.: Time Management. A Case for CSCW. Manuscript. Wien 1992.

Ekart H.P, Löffler R.: Organisation der Arbeit - Organisation der Profession. Workshop *Technikforschung an hessischen Universitäten*, 15.12.1989, TH Darmstadt. ZIT Publikation 4 (1990).

Fagerhaugh S.Y., Strauss A., Suczek B., Wiener C.L.: *Hazards in Hospital Care. Ensuring Patient Safety.* San Francisco 1987.

Ferguson M.:Electronic Media and the Redefining of Time and Space. *Public Communication. The New Imperatives,* London: Sage 1990, 152-172.

Gioia D.A.: Symbols, Scripts, and Sensemaking: Creating Meaning in the Organizational Experience. Sims H.P., Gioia D.A. (ed): *The Thinking Organization*, San Francisco 1986, 49-74.

Grudin J.: Systematic sources of suboptimal interface design in large product development organizations. *Human-Computer Interaction* 6(1991): 147-196.

Leithäuser T.: Exkurs: Sprache und Wissen im interdisziplinären Technikdialog. Senghaas-Knobloch E., Volmerg B.: *Technischer Fortschritt und Verantworungsbewußtsein.* Opladen: Westdeutscher Verlag 1990.

Parnas D.L.: Why software is unrealiable. University of Victoria 1985.

Perrow C.: *Normale Katastrophen. Die unvermeidbaren Risiken der Großtechnik.*Frankfurt 1987.

Renn O.: Risikokommunikation. Bedingungen und Probleme eines rationalen Diskurses über die Akzeptabilität von Risiken. Schneider J. (ed): *Risiko und Sicherheit technischer Systeme.* Basel 1991.Roßnagel A., Wedde P., Hammer V., Pordesch U.: *Die Verletzlichkeit der 'Informationsgesellschaft'.* Opladen: Westdeutscher Verlag 1989.

Strauss, A., Fagerhaugh S., Suczek B., Wiener C.: *Social Organization of Medical Work.* Chicago: The University of Chicago Press 1985.

Wagner I.: Caught in a Web of Fuzzy Problems. Confronting the Ethical Issues in Systems Design. Paper submitted to the *PDC'92 Conference* Cambridge, MA,November 1992

Weick K.E., Bougon M.: Organizations as cognitive maps. Charting ways to success and failure, in: Sims H.P., Gioia D.A. (Hg): The thinking organization, San Francisco 1986, 102-135.

Weick K.E.: Sources of Order in Underorganized Systems: Themes in Recent Organizational Theory. Lincoln Y.S. (ed): *Organizational Theory and Inquiry.* Beverly Hills: Sage 1985: 106-136.

Whipple C.: Dealing with Uncertainty. About Risk in Risk Management .*Hazards: Technology and Fairness.* Washington: National Academy Press 1986: 44-59.

Wolf R.: 'Herrschaft kraft Wissen' in der Risikogesellschaft .*Soziale Welt* 39/2 (1988), 164-187.

Zmud, R.W.: Opportunities for Strategic Information Manipulation Through New Information Technology. Fulk J., Steinfield C. (ed): *Organizations and Communication Technology.* Newbury Park: Sage Pub. 1990, 95-116.

Education and Society / R. Aiken (Editor)
Information Processing 92, Volume II
Elsevier Science Publishers B.V. (North-Holland)



# Perspectives in Information Technology Security

**Dr. Harold Joseph Highland, FICS**

Distinguished Professor Emeritus, *State University of New York* and Editor-in-Chief Emeritus, *Computers & Security*. 562 Croydon Road, Elmont, New York 11003-2814, USA.

**Abstract**
Information technology security has concentrated on hardware and software over the past few decades. The results have been far from heartening. We have overlooked the most important component in information security -- *wetware*, a term used for about a decade to mean the human brain, possibly because it is moist when removed from the cranium. It is the term used by neuroscientists to differentiate the working of the human mind from the software used by computers. We must pay more attention to information security education and awareness training if we are to succeed.

## INTRODUCTION

We live in an age of computer insecurity. We live in an age in which too many people lie about the status of information security in their organization. Although aware of the shortcomings, they rationalize their lies. Some unfortunately even believe their own lies. As a dinosaur, having been commissioned more than a half a century ago, I have witnessed the growth of computer security. If you are confused and disturbed about computer security, you are not alone.

It was the use of computers by the military and for intelligence analysis in many countries that prompted the growth of computer security as we know it today. As computers became more widely used in industry, the computer manufacturers who installed the systems for the military transferred those "security features" to the commercial environment. Few people in industry had any idea of what was needed and relied heavily on the computer manufacturer's specialists to guide them.

For years computer security was an after-thought, an add-on after a system was designed and installed. The failure to develop meaningful computer security measures has to be shared by three communities.

- The academic community has always been lax in its acceptance of computer security. In the early days we freely exchanged information and programs. We were an elite community of computer scientists who shared in an effort to promote the use of computers among scholars. Today many feel that even the low level of computer security impinges on their freedom.

- The business community, even when they recognized the need for computer security, was unable to specify its needs. Instead they blindly accepted the military model created by the computer manufacturers. It is only within the last few years that the existing model has been challenged.

- The military has been guilty of developing a security model, necessary for them, but unsuitable for the real world. Their models have been designed as if there is an endless supply of money. The problems of human compliance have been overlooked because military protocol and procedure make it easy to overlook human compliance.

## THE CHANGING WORLD

The information technology explosion of the past several years make it necessary to radically change our concepts, principles and implementation of computer security. Unfortunately most computer security directors and computer security consultants are ill prepared to deal with the critical problems we face today in computer security.

Many of them lack the necessary background to solve the rapidly emerging problems. This not an animadversion of these individuals. They learned their trade in a mainframe environment. I feel that it is not possible to solve the current problems by transferring the procedures used with mainframes to microcomputers, even minicomputers.

It was fairly simple when we dealt with computer professionals in a computer center. It was easy to impose some level of computer security when we had systems analysts, programmers and even keypunch operators in a single confined center. But now we now have to deal with practically every employee in an organization. These are employees not versed in computing. Their microcomputers have replaced their typewriters, adding machines, and record books. To them the computer is a tool somewhat like the slide rule was to engineers year ago.

Even in the best of times, computer security has never been more than temporary. The more one studies attempted solutions to computer security, the more one has the impression of well-meaning, often gifted, people wearing out their ingenuity at an impossible task. They are trying to get computer security into neat and permanent packages without regards to their interaction and the *human* element.

### The Leaders We Count On

I foresee a bumbling through in the solution of current problems in computer security because many of the current leaders are not up to the task. For more than a decade since my retirement, I have meet hundred, perhaps thousands, of computer security directors and computer security consultants in business, industry, government and the military/intelligences agencies in all parts of the world. Over the years many of them have become close friends. Computer security directors today have a difficult, and often frustrating, administrative job. Many of them are capable, knowledgeable, dedicated administrators. Yet from my viewpoint, most security directors are technical illiterates.

Although comprehensive industry data are not readily available, I believe that the turn-over rate for computer security specialists is higher than for any other group of computer specialists.

- A Deloitte-Touche study in 1990 indicated that directors of computer information have an average tenure of three years. And a third of these did not leave voluntarily.

- Several years ago Bob Courtney, the computer security specialist who served as IBM's interface with U.S. government agencies, often notes that the average tenure of computer security specialists in these agencies is about seven months.

There appears to be a constant stream of new entrants into this field. Unfortunately from a technical viewpoint of computing and computer security, the average member of the computer security community has only, what I call, *catalogue knowledge* of the field.

Aside from their own field of expertise [which many have not practiced for years and are undoubtedly now obsolete], their knowledge of many areas of computing is based on [1] literature they receive from vendors, [2] information (often incomplete and at times inaccurate) they receive from colleagues, and [3] a smattering they remember from listening to speeches at conferences. Many security directors do not have the time, and some unfortunately do not have the backgrounds, to learn much beyond the computer security buzzwords.

Generally they know about risk analysis, access control, audit trails. Some have heard about the *Clark-Wilson Integrity Model* and its superiority over *The Orange Book*. Some have somewhere heard about baseline security concepts. Others read about the utopia promised by biometrics. Some might even know the difference between FIPS and IFIPS, between TCSEC and ITSEC, and even between CHIPS and CHAPS. Some probably know the details about the *Bell La Pudula* algorithms. Others are even versed in DES transposition and substitution along with P-boxes and S-boxes.

## IMPLEMENTATION FAILURES

Although some organizations have implemented security programs, some options are only partially, or possibly even inefficiently, used. Let us examine two: passwords and access control.

### Password Size

Most password software modules used on mainframes and minicomputers are obsolete and inadequate. These are, at best, rewrites of modules used on systems back in the 1970s and early 1980s. Even password software modules used on microcomputers are frequently poor copies of those found on larger systems. The software producers can be faulted, but security directors are equally to blame. In speaking with security administrators I am constantly amazed as to how few of them know the *minimum* number of characters in a password that will be accepted by their systems. Most reply by telling me the *maximum* number of characters. Unfortunately some do not even know this.

About five years ago I posed this question to a security administrator who was a guest at my home. His government agency supervises security programs used by defense contractors. He admitted that he was not certain about the answer. Upon his return an analysis was made of the number of characters in the passwords used by some 1,500 employees in his agency. Here are the findings:

[1] only 4% used six characters [the maximum accepted by the program],
[2] less than 3% used five characters,
[3] about 5% used four characters,
[4] slightly less than 10% used three characters [possibly their three initials],
[5] some 43% used only *two characters* [probably two initials], and
[6] over 21% used only a *single character*.

Several months later I was able to compile a character frequency list based on reports from six commercial companies in the United States. Both six and eight character systems were studied involving more than 14,000 users. The report highlights showed:

[1] between 2% and 12% used the *maximum* number of characters
[2] between 22% and 26% used a *single character*

Early in 1990 I secured the cooperation of three companies with nationwide facilities. They had about 50,000 users. All the companies reported that their systems would accept a single character as a password. Somewhat over 10,000 or 20% of the users had passwords of *one character*.

Each company indicated that it was possible for the security director to set a minimum number of characters. Two directors had not known that it was possible to set a minimum. The other security directors had not taken the time to implement this option.

**Access Control**

In many organizations an audit trail is maintained of system log-ons. Because these reports are so lengthy, they are printed but no one looks through them. They are maintained for 30 days and then discarded.

In examining some 16 systems internationally we found that their audit program permitted the company to printout a list of unsuccessful log-ons. Many of the companies, some 11, took advantages of this option.

The reports were usually scanned by a secretary in the department who took no action unless there were seven or more attempts to use the same password. The action taken was to notify the manager of the department in which the attempt was made. In most cases the investigation stopped there; the action the other managers took pathetic.

Last year one of our close friends overseas evaluated several companies using Novell-secured LANS. In only one of six companies did he find that the LAN administrators had implemented the option to limit the number of attempts a user can make to access the system.

**THE PROBLEMS THAT FACE US**

The basic security problems of fraud, access control, etc. will not disappear. Vendors will continue to offer the same products but some will come up with packages to plug existing holes. I do not expect much change in the availability of computer security software and hardware until the users, the computer security directors, rebel and ask for better.

A number of years ago when network intruders first appeared, there were some who believed that if the press did not write about them and the professional community did not discuss the problem openly, the intruders would disappear. We could then return to our peaceful world of yesterday.

Note that I have not used the term, *hacker*, to describe the network intruder. I belong to the old school in which hacker referred to a knowledgeable, dedicated and inquisitive computer science student. *Crackers* are the bad guys. Some security specialists have coined special new words to associate intruders with criminals. But names alone will not solve this problem.

When you permit someone to enter a mainframe network using an ID as "*anonymous*" or "*guest*" you are not providing network security. Instead you are inviting trouble. At one extreme we can have a user-friendly system -- enter your first name as ID and your cat's name as the password. At the other extreme you can have a rigid system with a sign-on screen that is totally blank. What do you enter? Your name? An ID number? A password? A system connect command?

When computer viruses surfaced late in 1987 we heard an earlier refrain -- do not give them publicity and their writers will soon tire and write no more. Yet neither network intruders nor computer viruses have disappeared. If anything they are more of a problem today than they ever were.

## New Issues Must Be Faced

The basic security problems will have to be viewed in a different light. We have a radically changing computer environment. For example, in 1990 the dollar value of computer shipments in the United States showed that more dollars were spent on small systems than mainframes. Considering the price per unit, it is obvious that there were many, many more small systems, particularly microcomputers, sold than mainframes. This trend will be accelerated in the next several years.

There are a number of old and new issues that will have to be addressed in a new light. We have failed to do anything even though the handwriting was on the wall for almost a decade. Many security specialists have looked the other way, hoping that the problems and issues would disappear. Again in the computer security field we must play "catch-up" instead of preparing for the future. Unfortunately, the future was here yesterday.

## Small Systems Security

One important security issue that must be solved since time is rapidly running out involves microcomputers. It is obvious that microcomputers are less secure than mainframes. Gone are the good old days when only an anointed few could enter my university's computer center and run their programs themselves.

- In many companies the information stored on microcomputers is as critical and confidential as that on the mainframes. Because the cost of security for a microcomputer is so high as compared with the cost of the machine, do we walk away from the problem?

- To operate efficiently we often most permit interfacing the mainframe with microcomputers. Are the security measures on the mainframe sufficient to deal with the threat of downloading sensitive data? Some organizations have introduced measures so that no one can download a mainframe data file but they permit viewing the file on the microcomputer. With a simple freeware product I can capture anything that appears on my screen to a disk.

- Do the LAN products written by companies in the communication field really provide meaningful security? Are many of their features "tinsel" that can be easily defeated by a user with really little technical knowledge? One LAN security specialist has already demonstrated how a LAN user with read/write privileges can download the system's password list.

- Are microcomputer users adequately trained to make necessary backups? Should we not seek backup programs that are not user dependent?

■ Should we use virus scan programs which notify the user that the action they are about to take is disastrous to the system? Can they truly answer the question with *Yes* or *No*?

■ Much has been made about purchasing software from reliable sources in order to reduce the virus threat. Does that mean we can use that software without checking it for virus infection?

■ What procedures have been introduced to prevent a company virus infection from a disk an employee takes home to work on? In one case the chief financial officer of an organization took disks home and he used his daughter's microcomputer without shutting it down before he inserted a disk. His home machine was infected and when he returned to the office that disk infected not only the administrative LAN but also the company's financial LAN.

**Privacy, Confidentiality and Property Rights**

These are not a new issues but an important ones now that almost everyone has access to a computer. Forty years ago when developing a computer *laboratory* at a leading university, I learned about data privacy and confidentiality. One of my student assistants, updating faculty files, which were on punched cards, noted the birthdate of one of his teachers. He loudly announced to his classmates who were in the laboratory: "Florence's birthday in next Tuesday; let's bring her a cake with 44 candles - it will light up the room." Florence was not married and very aware of her "advanced" age.

■ What information about one's self or associates must be kept confidential? What safeguards are in place? What data may an organization not request from an employee? What about personal data an individual keeps on his/her microcomputer?

■ Is an employee's e-mail confidential? Does the company have the right to read it? Can the company maintain a log of to whom and from whom an employee receives e-mail?

■ Who owns the information? Does an employee who writes a program on his/her own time on a company computer own the program?

■ May an employer access an employee's password-protected file without the employee's permission? Can an employer demand that an individual provide the password for files for which the employee is responsible?

**Data Integrity**

■ Who is responsible for data accuracy and integrity?

■ Who is accountable for errors in information when several people has read/write access?

■ If personal damage results from a data error what is the company's responsibility? What efforts must be made to correct the damage?

■ Are audit trails maintained to track entry and/or modification of data?

■ If integrity checks are used to assure accuracy of information, can the information be transmitted in cleartext? What is the economic value of the information?

## AN OVERLOOKED RESOURCE -- PEOPLE

One aspect of computer security, wittingly or unwittingly, that has been overlooked is the *user* - the people who interface with the system. Without a clearly defined user policy and an educational program we will never be able to implement a successful computer security program.

Most companies do not have any policy statement regarding computer use and misuse that is provided to its employees. Among the larger corporations, many of the documents are vague, fail to address current issues and sometimes read like military orders. There are far more people today using the computer in industry than there were users of typewriters only a few decades ago when there were no written policy statements.

Many industry, and even government, user education programs are conducted in a rote manner. There is little attempt to obtain user understanding and cooperation in making the security program a success. Some of the training aids reminder me of the military films shown to troops during World War II to warn them about venereal disease.

We are dealing with a new generation of users and must adapt our educational programs. Most users have a Sesame Street approach to learning -- snapshot capsules that change frequently. Attention span is shorter; the need for hype in presentation is greater. We have the multi-media tools available and should use them. It probably would be far better to prepare individualized instructional material for presentation on a microcomputer than to use our traditional company lecture approach.

I am chairman of *IFIP/WG 11.8* on information security education and training. The major focus of this committee is on improving computer security education and training. We will address the problem at the university, in business and in the government on a world-wide basis. For more information communicate with me by mail or e-mail [*Highland@dockmaster.ncsc.mil*].

## THE FUTURE

When I first started in computing some 35 years ago, our only concern about security was to keep the hardware from being damaged. When microcomputers were first introduced more than a decade ago, physical security was the main concern -- preventing people from stealing boards or even the microcomputer itself. We have come a long way since then.

We must address the issues of information security quickly and in a meaningful manner. This can be done, if and only if, we concentrate much more effort on security awareness training. It starts with more emphasis on computer security education at the university level. Courses should be aimed at non-military needs [cryptography and trusted systems]. Concurrently we must mount an intensive program in security awareness training in industry, universities and non-military government agencies.

Although I am a dinosaur, I do not expect to be around when the key issues are resolved. I am least concerned with getting top management to recognize the need for information technology security. I was around decades ago when we tried to get top management to accept modern analysis techniques made possible by the computer -- break-even analysis, linear programming, modeling and simulation, non-parametric sampling, game theory. Over the years as the older top managers retired or died, the newer ones, trained in these areas, readily accepted them. Maybe by the year 2020 top management will not only readily accept information security but will *insist* on it.

Education and Society / R. Aiken (Editor)
Information Processing 92, Volume II
Elsevier Science Publishers B.V. (North-Holland)



# DASS: Distributed Authentication Security Service

M. Gasser[1], C. Kaufman[1], J. Linn[1], Y. Le Roux[2], J. Tardo[1]

[1]Digital Equipment Corporation, 550 King Street, Littleton, Massachusetts 01460-1289 U.S.A

[2] Digital Equipment, Imperial Way, Reading RG2 0TE U.K.

**Abstract:**

In a distributed environment, authentication is particularly challenging. This paper will present the authentication service component of the Distributed System Security Architecture (DSSA)[1]. The Distributed Authentication Security Service DASS has been proposed to Internet as a potential standard[2]

After positioning the problem, we will explain the choice of the central concepts behind this service:

After this conceptual approach, we will present according to the six phases described in the OSI Authentication Framework, a DASS walkthrough .

Keywords Codes: K.6.5,D.4.6,C.2.4

Keywords: Security and protection, Distributed Systems

## 1 WHAT IS DASS?

Authentication is a security service. The goal of authentication is to reliably learn the name of the originator of a message or request. The classic way by which people authenticate to computers (and by which computers authenticate to one another) is by supplying a password. There are a number of problems with existing password based schemes which DASS attempts to solve. The goal of DASS is to provide authentication services in a distributed environment which are both more secure (more difficult for a bad guy to impersonate a good guy) and easier to use than existing mechanisms.

In a distributed environment, authentication is particularly challenging. Users do not simply log on to one machine and use resources there. Users start processes on one machine which may request services on another. In some cases, the second system must request services from a third system on behalf of the user. Further, given current network technology, it is fairly easy to eavesdrop on conversations between computers and pick up any passwords that might be going by.

DASS uses cryptographic mechanisms to provide "strong, mutual" authentication. Mutual authentication means that the two parties communicating each reliably learn the name of the other. Strong authentication means that in the exchange neither obtains any information that it could use to impersonate the other to a third party. This can't be done with passwords alone. Mutual authentication can be done with passwords by having a "sign" and a "counter-sign" which the two parties must utter to assure one another of their identities. But whichever party speaks first reveals information which can be used by the second (unauthenticated) party to impersonate it. Longer sequences (often seen in spy movies) cannot solve the problem in general. Further, anyone who can eavesdrop on the conversation can impersonate either party in a subsequent conversation (unless passwords are only good once). Cryptography provides a means whereby one can prove knowledge of a secret without revealing it. People cannot execute cryptographic algorithms in their heads, and thus cannot strongly authenticate to computers directly. DASS lays the groundwork for "smart cards": microcomputers sealed in credit cards which when activated by a PIN will strongly authenticate to a computer. Until smart cards are available, the first link from a user to a DASS node remains vulnerable to eavesdropping. DASS mechanisms are constructed so that after the initial authentication, smart card or password based authentication looks the same.

Today, systems are constructed to think of user identities in terms of accounts on individual computers. If I have accounts on ten machines, there is no way a priori to see that those ten accounts all belong to the same individual. If I want to be able to access a resource through any of the ten machines, I must tell the resource about all ten accounts. I must also tell the resource when I get an eleventh account.

DASS supports the concept of global identity and network login. A user is assigned a name from a global namespace and that name will be recognized by any node in the network. (In some cases, a resource may be configured as accessible only by a particular user acting through a particular node. That is an access control decision, and it is supported by DASS, but the user is still known by his global identity). From a practical point of view, this means that a user can have a single password (or smart card) which can be used on all systems which allow him access and access control mechanisms can conveniently give access to a user through any computer the user happens to be logged into. Because a single user secret is good on all systems, it should never be necessary for a user to enter a password other than at initial login. Because cryptographic mechanisms are used, the password should never appear on the network beyond the initial login node.

DASS was designed as a component of the Distributed System Security Architecture (DSSA) [1]. It is a goal of DSSA that access control on all systems be based on users' global names and the concept of "accounts" on computers eventually be replaced with unnamed rights to execute processes on those computers. Until this happens, computers will continue to support the concept of "local accounts" and access controls on resources on those systems will still be based on those accounts. There is today within the Berkeley rtools running over the Internet Protocol suite the concept of a ".rhosts database" which gives access to local accounts from remote accounts. We envision that those databases will be extended to support granting access to local accounts based on DASS global names as a bridge between the past and the future. DASS should greatly simplify the administration of those databases for the (presumably common) case where a user should be granted access to an account ignoring his choice of intermediate systems.

## 2 CENTRAL CONCEPTS

### 2.1 Strong Authentication with Public Keys

DASS makes heavy use of the RSA Public Key cryptosystem. The important properties of the RSA algorithms for purposes of this discussion are:

- It supports the creation of a public/private key pair, where operations with one key of the pair reverse the operations of the other, but it is computationally infeasible to derive the private key from the public key.

- It supports the "signing" of a message with the private key, after which anyone knowing the public key can "verify" the signature and know that it was constructed with knowledge of the private key and that the message was not subsequently altered.

- It supports the "enciphering" of a message by anyone knowing the public key such that only someone with knowledge of the private key can recover the message.

With access to the RSA algorithms, it is easy to see how one could construct a "strong" authentication mechanism. Each "principal" (user or computer) would construct a public/private key pair, publish the public key, and keep secret the private key. To authenticate to you, I would write a message, sign it with my private key, and send it to you. You would verify the message using my public key and know the message came from me. If mutual authentication were desired, you could create an acknowledgment and sign it with your private key; I could verify it with your public key and I would know you received my message.

The authentication algorithms used by DASS are considerably more complex than those described in the paragraph above in order to deal with a large number of practical concerns including subtle security threats. Some of these are discussed below.

### 2.2 Timestamps vs. Challenge/Response

Cryptosystems give you the ability to sign messages so that the receiver has assurance that the signer of the message knew some cryptographic secret. It is important that the message I send you only be accepted by you and only once. I can prevent the message from being useful at any other server by including your name in the message. You will only accept the message if you see your name in it. Keeping you from accepting the message twice is harder.

There are two "standard" ways of providing this replay protection. One is called challenge/response and the other is called timestamp-based. In a challenge response type scheme, I tell you I want to authenticate, you generate a "challenge" (generally a number), and I include the challenge in the message I sign. You will only accept a message if it contains the recently generated challenge and you will make sure you never issue the same challenge to me twice (either by using a sequence number, a timestamp, or a random number big enough that the probability of a duplicate is negligible). In the timestamp-based scheme, I include the current time in my message. You have a rule that you will not accept messages more than - say - five minutes old and you keep track of all messages you've seen in the last five minutes. If someone replays the message within five minutes, you will reject it because you will remember you've seen it before; if someone replays it after five minutes, you will reject it as timed out.

DASS uses the timestamp-based scheme. The primary motivations behind this decision were so that authentication messages could be "piggybacked" on existing connection establishment messages and so that DASS would fit within the same "form factor" (number and direction of messages) as Kerberos.

### 2.3 Delegation

In a distributed environment, authentication alone is not enough. When I log onto a computer, not only do I want to prove my identity to that computer, I want to use that computer to access network resources (e.g. file systems, database systems) on my behalf. My files should (normally) be protected so that I can access them through any node I log in through. DASS allows them to be so protected without allowing all of the systems that I might ever use to access those files in my absence. In the process of logging in, my password gives my login node access to my RSA secret. It can use that secret to "impersonate" me on any requests it makes on my behalf. It should forget all secrets associated with me when I log off. This limits the trust placed in computer systems. If someone takes control of a computer, they can impersonate all people who use that computer after it is taken over but no others.

Normally when I access a network service, I want to strongly authenticate to it. That is, I want to prove my identity to that service, but I don't want to allow that service to learn anything that would allow it to impersonate me. This allows me to use a service without trusting it for more than the service it is delivering. When using some services, for example remote login services, I may want that service to act on my behalf in calling additional services. DASS provides a mechanism whereby I can pass secrets to such services that allow them to impersonate me.

Future versions of this architecture may allow "limited delegation" so that a user may delegate to a server only those rights the server needs to carry out the user's wishes. This version can limit delegation only in terms of time. The information a user gives a server (other than the initial login node) can be used to impersonate the user but only for a limited period of time. Smart cards will permit that time limitation to apply to the initial login node as well.

### 2.4 Certification Authorities

A flaw in the strong authentication mechanism described above is that it assumes that every "principal" (user and node) knows the public key of every other principal it wants to authenticate. If I can fool a server into thinking my public key is actually your public key, I can impersonate you by signing a message, saying it is from you, and having the server verify the message with what it thinks is your public key.

To avoid the need to securely install the public key of every principal in the database of every other principal, the concept of a "Certification Authority" was invented. A certification authority is a principal trusted to act as an introduction service. Each principal goes to the certification authority, presents its public key, and proves it has a particular name (the exact mechanisms for this vary with the type of principal and the level of security to be provided). The CA then creates a "certificate" which is a message containing the name and public key of the principal, an expiration date, and bookkeeping information signed by the CA's private key. All "subscribers" to a particular CA can then authenticated to one another by presenting their certificates and proving knowledge of the corresponding secret. CAs need only act when new principals are being named and new private keys created, so that can be maintained under tight physical security.

When authentication is to be used in a global context - between companies - the concept of a single CA is untenable.

DASS addresses this problem by creating a hierarchy of CAs. The CA hierarchy is tied to the naming hierarchy. For each directory in the namespace, there is a single CA responsible for certifying the public keys of its members. That CA will also certify the public keys of the CAs of all child directories and of the CA of the parent directory. With this cross-certification, it is possible knowing the public key of any CA to verify the public keys of a series of intermediate CAs and finally to verify the public key of any principal.

DASS uses the X.500 directory hierarchy for principal naming.

### 2.5 User vs. Node Authentication

In concept, DASS mechanisms support the mutual authentication of two principals regardless of whether those principals are people, computers, or applications. Those mechanisms have been extended, however, to deal with a common case of a pair of principals acting together (a user and a node) authenticating to a single principal (a remote server). This is done by having optionally in each credentials structure two sets of secrets - one for the user and one for the node. When authentication is done using such credentials, both secrets sign the request so the receiving party can verify that both principals are present.

## 3 AN AUTHENTICATION WALKTHROUGH

The OSI Authentication Framework characterizes authentication as occurring in six phases. This section attempts to describe DASS in these terms.

### 3.1 Installation

In this phase, principal certificates are created, as is the additional information needed to create claimant and verifier credentials. OSI defines three subphases:

- *Enrollment.* In DASS, this is the definition of a principal in terms of a key, name and UID.

- *Validation,* confirmation of identity to the satisfaction of the CA, after which the CA generates a certificate.

- *Confirmation.* In DASS, this is the act of providing the user with the certificate and with the CA's own name, key and UID, followed up by the user creating a trusted authority for that CA. A trusted authority is a certificate for the CA signed by the user.

Included in this step in DASS is the posting of the certificate so as to be available to principals wishing to verify the principal's identity. In addition, the user principal saves the trusted authority so as to be available when it creates credentials.

### 3.2 Distribution

DASS distributes certificates by placing them in the name service.

### 3.3 Acquisition

Whenever principals wish to authenticate to one another, they access the Name Service to obtain whatever public key certificates they need and create the necessary credentials. In DASS, acquisition means obtaining credentials.

Claimant credentials implement the representation of a principal in a process, or, more accurately, provide a representation of the principal for use by a process. In making this representation, the principal delegates to a temporary delegation key. In this fashion the claimant's long term principal key need not remain in the system.

Claimant credentials are made by invoking the get credentials primitive. Claimant credentials are a DASS specific data structure containing:

- a name
- a ticket, a data structure containing
  . a validity interval, . UID, and
  . (temporary) delegation public key, along with a
  . digital signature on the above made with the principal private key
- the delegation private key

Optionally in addition, there may be credential information relating to the node on which the user is logged in and the account on that node. Verifier credentials are made with initialize_server. Verifier credentials consist of a principal (long term) private key. The rationale is that these credentials are usually needed by servers that must be able to run indefinitely without re-entry of any long term key.

In addition, claimants and verifiers have a trusted authority, which consists of information about a trusted CA. That information is its:

- name (this will appear in the "issuer" field in principal certificates),
- public key (to use in verifying certificates issued by that CA), and
- UID.

Trusted authorities are used by principals to verify certificates for other principals' public keys. CAs are arranged in a hierarchy corresponding to the naming hierarchy, where each directory in the naming hierarchy is controlled by a single CA. Each CA certifies the CA of its parent directory, the CAs of each of its child directories, and optionally CAs elsewhere in the naming hierarchy (mainly to deal with the case where the directories up to a common ancestor lack CAs).

Even though a principal has only a single CA as a trusted authority, it can securely obtain the public key of any principal in the namespace by "walking the CA hierarchy".

### 3.4 Transfer

The DASS exchange of authentication information is illustrated in Figure 1. During the transfer phase, the DASS claimant sends an authentication token to the verifier. Authentication tokens are made by invoking the create_token primitive. The authentication token is cryptographically protected and specified as a DASS data structure in ASN.1. The authentication token includes:

- a ticket,

- a DES authenticating key encrypted using the intended verifier's public key

- one of the following:

. if delegation is not being performed, a digital signature on the encrypted DES key using the delegation private key, or

. if delegation is being performed, sending the delegation private key, DES encrypted using the DES authenticating key

- an authenticator, which is a cryptographic checksum made using the DES authenticating key over a buffer containing

. a timestamp

. any application supplied "channel bindings". For example, addresses or other context information. The purpose of this field is to thwart substitution and replay attacks.

- additional optional information concerning node authentication and context.

As a side effect, after init_authentication_context, the caller receives a local authentication context, a data structure containing:

- the DES key, and

- if mutual authentication is being requested, the expected response.

In order to construct an authentication token, the claimant needs to access the verifier's public key certificate from the Name Service (labeled CDC, for Certificate Distribution Center, in figure 1).

Note that while an authenticator can only be used once, it is permissible to re-establish the same local authentication context multiple times. That is, the ticket and DES key establishment components of the authentication token may have a relatively long lifetime. This permits a performance improvement in that repeated applications of public key operations can be alleviated if one caches authentication contexts, along with other components from a successfully used authentication token and the associated verified principal public key value. It is a relatively inexpensive operation to create (and verify) "fresh" authenticators based on cached authentication context.

### 3.5 Verification

Upon receipt of an authentication token, the verifier extracts the DES key using its verifier credentials, accesses the Name Service (labeled CDC for Certificate Distribution Center) to obtain the certificates needed to perform cryptographic checks on the incoming information, and verifies all of the signatures on the received certificates and the authentication token. Verification can result in creation of new claimant credentials if delegation is performed.

As part of this process, verified authenticators are retained for a suitable timeout period.

### 3.6 Unenrolment

This is the removal of information from the Name Service. The only other form of revocation supported by DASS is certificate timeout. Every certificate contains an expiration time (expected in ordinary use to be about a year from its signing date). DASS does not currently support the revocation lists in X.509.

## 4. CURRENT STATUS

A full description of DASS has been submitted to the Common Authentication Technology Working Group of the IETF.

DASS has been implemented and is currently in use on ULTRIX platforms at Customer sites.

## 5.REFERENCES

[1] "The Digital Distributed System Security Architecture" by M. Gasser, A. Goldstein, C. Kaufman, and B. Lampson, 1989 National Computer Security Conference

[2] "DASS Distributed Authentication Security Service" by Charles Kaufman Common Authentication Technology Working Group of the IETF

FIGURE 1- AUTHENTICATION EXCHANGE OVERVIEW

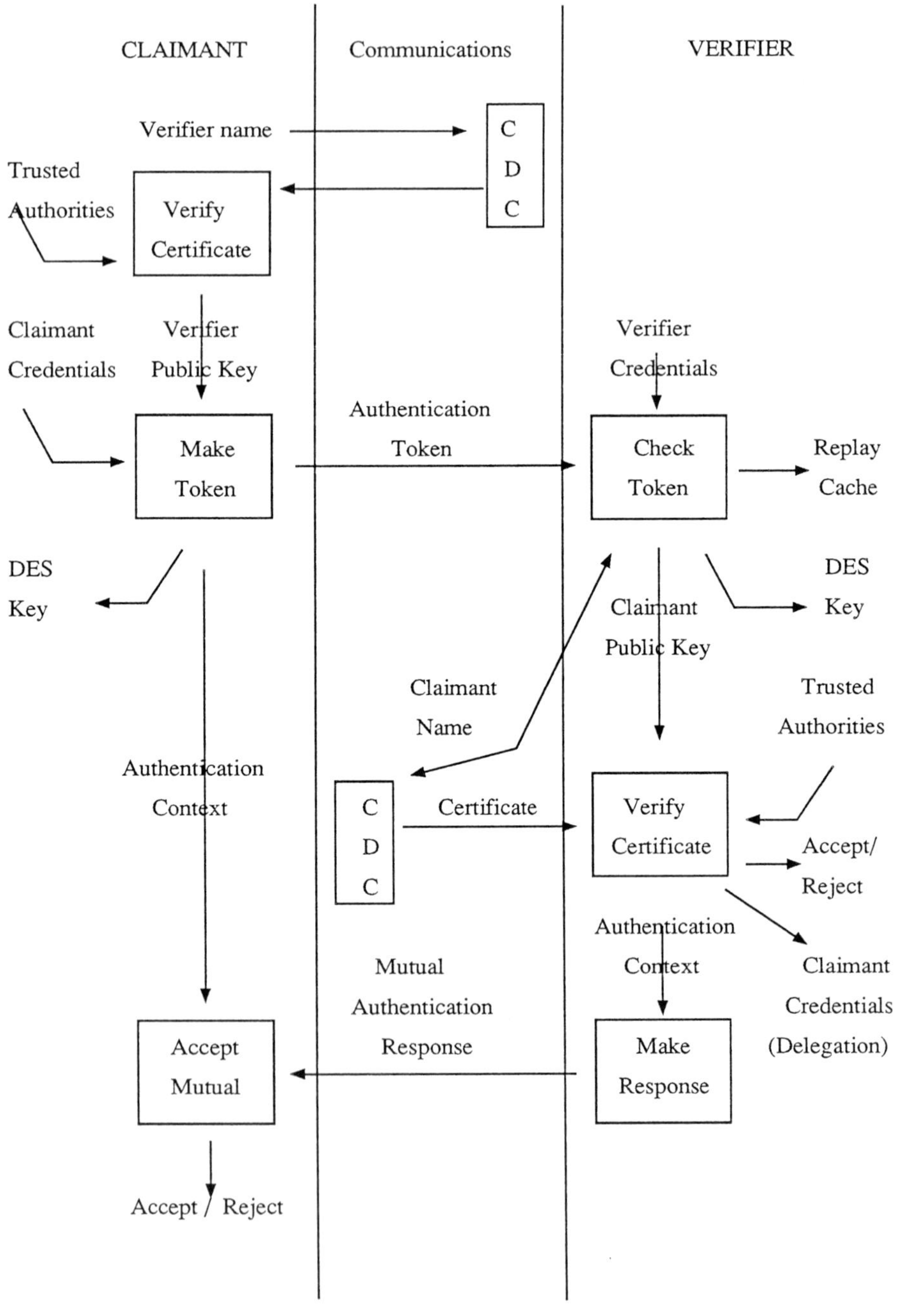

Education and Society / R. Aiken (Editor)
Information Processing 92, Volume II
Elsevier Science Publishers B.V. (North-Holland)



# Security Issues in EDI Environment

Snehamay Banerjee[a] and Damodar Y. Golhar[b]

[a]Department of Management, College of Business and Administration, Drexel University, Philadelphia, PA 19104, U. S. A.

[b]Department of Management, Haworth College of Business, Western Michigan University, Kalamazoo, MI 49008, U. S. A.

**Abstract**

Electronic Data Interchange (EDI) is the newest frontier of communication technology which can virtually eliminate paper flow between trading partners. Use of this technology is expected to grow at an annual compounded growth rate of more than 23% in USA and by more than 40% in Europe during next three years. This high growth in a potentially paperless environment presents a variety of security risks. We examine potential EDI security risks associated with different trading partner agreements, and create a framework to synthesize current and future research in this field. Such a framework also presents a foundation for classification of the related literature.

Keyword Codes: H.4.3; K.6.5
Keywords: Communications Applications; Security and Protection

## 1. INTRODUCTION

To remain globally competitive, businesses around the world are seeking ways to increase productivity and reduce operating cost. Developments in computer technology are helping businesses to achieve these goals. Availability of user-friendly software and affordable computer hardware increased the use of computers in business during the last decade. Computer technology is now routinely used for effective communication within and between organizations. Messages are created at a point in time and forwarded to one or many recipients. These messages are discrete objects and the communication is not in 'real time'. These communication usage of computers can be broken down into four general types: person to person (using computer as a medium), person to computer, computer to computer, and computer to person. Recently, a specific type of computer to computer communication namely, Electronic Data Interchange (EDI), has received significant attention from the business community.

EDI is the newest frontier of communication technology. It involves an automated exchange of business documents between computers. According to Hansen and Hill (1989), "EDI is the movement of business documents electronically between or within firms in a structured, machine-retrievable, data format that permits data to be transferred, without rekeying, from a business application in one location to a business application in another location". In the EDI environment, a computer can directly use the data sent by other computers in electronic form. Other communication technologies such as facsimile (FAX) and E-mail are not considered to be a part of EDI because they do not support automation facilities and the information sent using such communication technologies has to be rearranged or rekeyed into a computer for further use. The three basic functions of EDI include:

(a) data transfer between trading partners (actual transmission),
(b) data transformation between proprietary formats (as used by sender or receiver) and standard formats as required to meet transmission protocol, and
(c) directing the data to, and gathering it from, different computer applications.

It should be noted that data can be transmitted between trading partners either by establishing a dedicated link between them or by using one of the existing communication networks. The expected benefits of EDI include better and faster communication between trading partners, reduced overhead cost, increased data accuracy, improved information about suppliers, and reduced inventory [Hansen and Hill 1989]. If properly implemented, EDI virtually eliminates paper flow in the order/delivery/invoice/payment cycle because manufacturers, carriers, buyers, and suppliers can electronically exchange such documents as purchase orders, invoices, freight bills, and payment advice.

Although the concept of EDI has been around for about 20 years, only recently has the use of EDI increased significantly for exchanging routine business documents. In manufacturing and service sectors, the use of EDI is expected to grow at an annual compounded growth rate of more than 23.2% during 1990-1994 in USA [EDI Research 1991] and by more than 40% during 1991-1995 in Europe [Kutten 1991]. This growth in the use of EDI has given rise to problems that have not been faced before and are unique to this technology. The problems associated with using EDI include security issues, lack of signature or authorization for transactions, lack of audit trails, and lack of universally acceptable standards for data transmission [Hansen and Hill 1989, Powers 1989]. Considering an organization's sensitivity regarding the security related issues, the success of future EDI implementation will depend on the effective resolution of these issues.

Only a few studies examine security related problems of EDI [Crawford 1989, Hansen and Hill 1989]. These studies either investigate a very specific technical issue related to EDI or describe in general the need for such work in future. EDI being a new field, not surprisingly, there is a lack of a comprehensive examination of the security related issues and a common framework to synthesize the reported research. In this paper we summarize potential security risks and present a framework to classify future work in this field.

The rest of the paper is organized as follows: Section 2 provides a discussion on security risks associated with EDI. Section 3 investigates electronic contract related risks for EDI. Finally, the paper concludes with a discussion on future work.

## 2. SECURITY RISKS IN EDI

EDI can be implemented either through a dedicated network between trading partners or by using one of the existing value added networks (VANs). In a dedicated system the trading partners may or may not have their own communication channel. But the trading partners must use identical communication protocols, the same transmission speeds, and must have compatible hardware. A VAN can solve these problems by providing services to enhance the offerings of the network. VAN can also offer mailboxes to temporarily store messages. Security risks are reduced if EDI transactions are carried out over a dedicated network between the trading partners. However, such a dedicated network reduces the flexibility of trading partners and also increases the cost of EDI implementation. On the other hand, security risks increase if a VAN is used for communication purposes but it also increases flexibility in implementing EDI. Therefore, management must evaluate the risks associated with potential EDI systems prior to deciding on EDI implementation plan.

EDI changes the way transactions are input into an application system. Hence, to ensure completeness and accuracy of input by authorized parties only, appropriate audit and control procedures are needed. Such procedures have been discussed in the literature [Powers 1989, Hansen and Hill 1989]. This manuscript focuses on communication related risks associated with EDI which are not directly under the control of the organizations where the transactions originate. Some of these risks are not even detectable by audits and cannot be controlled by the control procedures specified in such audits. However, these security risks can severely damage an organization's effectiveness in communicating with the trading partners and can jeopardize the trading partner relationships. The security risks associated with EDI communication system can be grouped into the following categories: (a) disclosure of messages, (b) modification of message contents, (c) modification of message sequence, (d) sender masquerade, (e) repudiation of message origin or receipt, and (f) denial of services. These six problems are common with other form of electronic messaging e.g., electronic mail [Simpact Associates 1990]. However, the impact of such problems and laws related to such problems are expected to be different between electronic mail and electronic data interchange. Table 1 summarizes these six security risks, potential solutions to such risks, and impact of these risks on an organization:

Table 1
Risks associated with EDI transaction

| Security Risks | Description | Potential Solution | Impact on Organization |
|---|---|---|---|
| Disclosure | Unauthorized access to message | Data encryption, Password | Undue advantage to competitor |
| Message modification | Alter the content of message | Password, Multiple copies of message. Network keeping copies of transmission | Delivery of unwanted or incorrect material disrupting both buyer & supplier schedule |
| Sequence modification | Delaying message or altering the sequence of message | To be protected by network security | Schedule disruption, repeated message transmission generating duplicate work. |
| Sender masquerade | A party attempts to appear as another party | Password confirmation of message | False trigering of orders generating excess inventory |
| Repudiation of message origin | Denial of receipt of the origin of message | Network keeping backup copies | Cash flow interruption, production schedule disruption |
| Denial of service | Denying access to legitimate user | To be protected by network security | Immediate action by network will minimize impact |

*Disclosure* is the most common security problem. Disclosure occurs when an unauthorized party gains access to a message. Such disclosure can reveal the nature of transaction between trading partners to a competitor. *Modification of message contents* is another security violation that is directly related to the security of the system as a whole. Such modification usually involves either an user who has system privileges to alter the message or someone (possibly a computer hacker) gaining an illegal access to the system and changing the message contents. *Sequence modification* involves changing the order in which the messages are received or repeating the same message. Delaying a message (say a purchase order) can cause disruption in the production schedule of the buyer. *Masquerading* occurs when a phony user acts as a legitimate sender or receiver of messages. By masquerading, any party can either send for an order, or schedule transportation of non existing orders. Such disruptions can affect the schedules for both buyers and sellers. *Repudiation of message contents* involves a receiver denying the receipt of an original message. An example of repudiation is denial of issuance of instructions to release funds or the disclaimer of knowledge of a message. *Denial of service* occurs when the user either gains unauthorized access or uses existing privileges in a manner that is denying use of the system resources to legitimate users. Since denial can be easily detected and reported by the system, this poses a lesser risk in the EDI environment.

It is clear that communication related risks in an EDI environment can pose significant threat to trading partner agreements. Internal audit and controls of a company have very little capability to reduce these risks. Such risks are to be covered in the EDI contracting agreement. EDI transactions, because of its very nature, are conducted between close trading partners. Therefore, legal aspects of EDI contracting is yet to draw much attention from the business community [Kutten 1991]. However, security and contracts related issues for EDI are expected to draw significant attention in the near future.

## 3. TYPES OF ELECTRONIC CONTRACTING IN EDI

A key assumption in electronic contracting is that EDI message duplicates documentary functions. Therefore, laws applicable to other forms of documents are also applicable to EDI transactions. However, current legal interpretations on contracts are based on written, signed documents. Interpretation of such laws for electronic documents is yet to be established. EDI agreements, therefore, are expected to substitute any gap in the existing law. A recent survey of EDI users in Canada shows that a thorough and complete EDI agreement is necessary for effectively dealing with contract related security issues [Crawford 1989]. To facilitate development of an effective EDI agreement, it is important to identify the type of agreement that is right for a given organization. Table 2 summarizes the characteristics of five basic trading partner agreements and the involvement of network carriers in each of these categories [Kutten 1991]. The five categories are: (i) private bilateral, (ii) private unilateral, (iii) private multilateral, (iv) private third party carrier, and (v) common carrier multilateral agreements.

Table 2
Types of EDI trading agreements

| Type of EDI agreement | Current Status | Type of Network | Network Responsibility | Type of Communication |
|---|---|---|---|---|
| Private Bilateral | Used by many organizations | Private & dedicated between two parties | None because the trading partners can handle the problem directly | Established, mutually agreed upon protocol between two parties. |
| Private Unilateral | Not a common system | Multi-party network | None. It acts as a carrier only. | Offeror established protocol available to any one who agrees to it. |
| Private multilateral | Typical hub & spoke arrangement | Private & dedicated between one buyer and multiple supplier | None. Protocol & security established by buyer | Suppliers communicate with a single buyer and cannot communicate among themselves. |
| Private third party carrier | Used by many organizations | Multi-party value-added network | Depends on carrier. But should take care of access control, message back up etc. | Multiple parties communicate with each other using same transmission protocol. |
| Multilateral common carrier | Potential future system | Multiparty - dedicated for EDI only | Everything for transmission including translation facility | Different parties using different protocol. Network takes care of responsibility & other issues. |

*Private bilateral* systems are the typical current systems with highly individual contracts which provide direct communication of EDI messages between trading partners, with no other party substantially involved. These systems are relatively risk free from outside interference. *Private unilateral* systems do not have prior agreements between parties. The offeror establishes a protocol and any party that uses the protocol can do business directly with the offeror. This arrangement requires multi-party communication network but the network only serves as the means of communication and has no record keeping or other duties. *Private multilateral* is a typical hub and spoke arrangement where a large manufacturer, using a dedicated network, implements an EDI system with many of its suppliers. The suppliers do not communicate among themselves using this system. *Private third party carrier* is currently a common arrangement which requires the use of a third party network. The network is responsible for delivering messages to recipients. The network provides the facility for storing information. It also retains copies of the messages for some period to settle any disputes regarding the actual contents of the messages. *Common carrier multilateral* requires the carrier to be the dedicated EDI clearinghouse that can perform "translations" between different EDI standards and makes it difficult for an EDI organization to control the carrier. Hence, record keeping of the carrier is less likely to be fraudulent. However, the carrier will have to accept the responsibility of separating the messages of different customers. Like the private third party carrier, the network will have to keep documents of the messages transmitted.

## 4. CONCLUSION

The set of potential risks in an electronic contracting environment and the potential types of trading partner agreements provide a basis for developing a framework for attributing legal and fiscal responsibilities in the EDI environment. Such a framework will help an organization to evaluate the type of EDI agreement it should have with its trading partners. This categorization will also help to organize current and future research work, both legal and technical, in a manner that will foster easier dissemination of information to the user community.

## 5. REFERENCES

Crawford, B., "Strategic Legal Planning for EDI," *Canadian Law Journal*, Vol. 16, 1989, pp. 66-77.

EDI Research, Inc., The State of US EDI: 1991, EDI Group Ltd.,Chicago, 1991.

Hansen, J. V., and Hill, N. C., "Control and audit of Electronic Data Interchange," *MIS Quarterly*, Vol. 13, No. 4, 1989, pp. 403-413.

Kutten, L. J., Reams, B. D., and Strehler, A. E., Electronic Contracting Law: EDI and Business Transactions, Clark Boardman Callaghan publishers, NY, 1991.

Powers, W. J., EDI Control and Audit Issues, TDCC/EDIA Monograph, The Electronic Data Interchange Association, Alexandria, VA, 1989.

Simpact Associates, Security in Electronic Messaging: Things You Should Know, San Diego, CA, 1990.

Education and Society / R. Aiken (Editor)
Information Processing 92, Volume II
Elsevier Science Publishers B.V. (North-Holland)


# SECURITY POLICY

S H Banks.

Computer Audit, The Royal London Insurance, Royal London House, Middleborough, Colchester, ESSEX, CO1 1RA, UK.

## INTRODUCTION.

It is a well accepted fact that it is important to protect information (both held electronically and otherwise) critical to an organisations operation, as indeed we are all aware of the importance of not polluting the earth sea or air. Not unlike the pollution scenario the controls required, in our case to ensure the security of data, are all too often left up to individuals judgment.

Like the pollution problem, we **all know** what the solutions are (that is why this country still believe that, dumping raw sewage into the sea does no harm and others have banned this practice). As you can see we will all have our own ideas as to what is required and what we can get away with. Identifying the requirements is, therefore, not good enough on its own.

In order to enforce the controls over the data it is necessary to have a formal policy as a base for the controls, (that is why the government introduced regulations covering; the burning of coal to reduce smog and the acceptable levels of discharge into rivers and the sea to reduce pollution). The need for a formal policy and the introduction of controls must be recognised and endorsed at the highest level of management, preferably the policy statement should be issued by the board of directors as a Company Policy. Anything less and it is likely to be viewed as the concern of a few eccentric cranks. Only if it has top support will it be possible to enforce the controls necessary to protect the data.

It is also important to remember that once a policy has been introduced it must be distributed to **ALL** members of staff, with special attention being paid to ensuring that all staff that join the Organisation after the initial distribution of the document are made fully aware of its presence and their role in ensuring that the data is kept safe.

What follows is an outline of the areas that I believe a Security Policy should address. While this may not be a definitive statement of all the requirement it should provide a sound basis on which to work.

Keyword Codes: K.6.5
Keywords: Security and Protection

## 1. POLICY STATEMENT.

In order for staff to take notice of the security policy it is important to point out the benefits to be gained and the danger is not ensuring that the information is secure. The policy should therefore state that;

> The ORGANIZATION and its subsidiaries are heavily reliant on data & Computer systems to meet its operational, financial, and information needs, in fact the computer systems are crucial to the day-to-day operations.
>
> This reliance is such that the group will begin to incur extra costs and/or reduced revenues if the information is not produced on schedule, or is incorrectly processed, contains inaccurate data, or is just unavailable. It is therefore essential that the equipment, systems and data must be maintained in a controlled environment. The cost associated with partial or complete loss of key resources, software, data and procedures in extreme cases could be catastrophic.
>
> The policies defined in this document aim to ensure that the requisite level of security is applied in order to provide for the integrity and continuity of processing. This policy will apply to **all** information used within the Group whether held on Mainframe, mini and personal computers, word processors, any other device which holds data electronically or in any other format.

## 2. MANAGEMENT.

For the policy to work it is essential that the implementation and ongoing management is clearly defined and handled correctly. The policy must be seen as a top management decision, therefore a Director should be made responsible for ensuring that all aspects of the policy are adhered to.

Effective management and control systems should be in place to ensure that;

a) there is compliance with the legislation that pertains to the processing of data or the operation of computer equipment, such as;
   i) the Data protection act, the eighth principle of which states;-

      Appropriate security measures will be taken against unauthorised access to, or alteration, disclosure or destruction of, personal data and against accidental loss or destruction of personal data.

   ii) LAURTO & IMRO etc.

b) Data will be made available on a regular basis as to the effect faults and errors have on the provision of services to users. A formal problem management system will be in place to reduce error incidence and avoid recurrence of problems.

c) Effective management and control systems are in place to ensure applications are developed in accordance with user departments plans, and that losses to the business do not accrue.

d) Effective management and control systems are in place to monitor performance according to standards, procedures and service levels.

e) An area is made responsible for Data Security, and this area should be responsible for ensuring the Groups business is protected against fraud and misuse of information in connection with computer based system. It would therefor:-
   i) Assist Line Management in the design of control procedures,
   ii) Control, monitor and test the operation of security procedures and systems,
   iii) Investigate to determine the extent of any actual or potential case of computer abuse, misuse or fraud.

f) Internal Audit Department in accordance with its charter undertake an Independent appraisal of operating performance. It may therefore conduct selective evaluations of the effectiveness and efficiency of controls in operation.

g) Adequate insurance cover is taken out for failure of computer hardware and resultant emergency costs.

h) A list of all systems is maintained along with users responsible for the integrity of the data, (hereafter called the data owners).

i) In order to determine the appropriate level of security a Risk evaluation is carried out on all data and systems.

j) Line Managers (see Appendix n) define and enforce proper control and security procedures within their areas and enforce the procedures embodied in the Policy statement.

k) Breaches of the policies defined in this statement are reported to the Director responsible for issuing this policy and are dealt with as a disciplinary offence.

l) Effective measures are in place to ensure the continuation of processing in the event of a disaster.

m) No area of expertise is the sole responsibility of one person and there must be separation of responsibility for sensitive functions.

n) Any enquiries with regards to data security are be addressed to the Director responsible for issuing the policy.

## 3. SOFTWARE AND DATA.

Software and data are of course the backbone of the Policy, without them there would be no need for the Policy. It is, therefore, essential that the policy should define;

a) Who owns this information ie. that the intellectual property rights on all software and data will be vested with the Group.

b) The restrictions associated with access to Live data eg. Auditors and Computer staff will not be permitted to update Live data. Knowledge about systems and data will be restricted only to those who have a genuine need to know.

c) That there will be a formal change control procedure for acceptance of ALL software and processing procedures on operational Libraries and data.
d) That copying of programs or data is only carried out in accordance with contracts, agreements, leases and licences.
e) That Contracts, Agreements, Leases and Licences with suppliers of computer software should include a provision (approved by the Company Secretary) advising vendors of the Groups retained property rights.
f) That Software requirements will be completely documented prior to being developed and an effective method of software configuration control will be applied to the requirements both during development and the life cycle of the software.

## 4. INTEGRITY.

What use is the data if it can't be relied upon to be accurate, or perhaps worse still if confidential information becomes widely available. What would the C.G.M think if he new that his Email box was open for all to view. The policy must therefore ensure that;

a) A procedure will be in place to ensure all documents submitted for processing are properly authorised and that all sensitive documents remain confidential.
b) Sensitive information is identified and that procedures will be in place to ensure its confidentiality and security until it is disposed of.
c) Suitable methods of disposing this information is provided.
d) Controls and audit trails will be designed into software applications to ensure the integrity of the data and processing in them.
e) All staff will be instructed on their role in confidentiality.
f) Adequate training will be provided to insure authorised accurate and timely processing takes place.

## 5. PHYSICAL SECURITY.

The first line of security is probably the easiest to implement in theory but the hardest to undertake in practice. After all who is going to close the security door in the face of the C.G.M. It is important, therefore, that the policy should define the requirements for;

a) Buildings access (to protect against unauthorised access).
b) Restricted areas. ie areas where key resources are cited which would be at risk from accidental or malicious action. The minimum number of staff necessary for effective and safe working should have access to restricted areas.
c) Staffing in restricted areas.
d) Supervision of Non-company staff or temp authorised staff in a restricted area.

f) Installing the appropriate means of securing restricted areas against unauthorised access and that the level of security will be installed according to the levels of risk.
g) The prevention of the outbreak of a fire and the means of containing an outbreak should this happen.
h) Alternative forms of lighting and power supply.

i) Identifying staff / visitors and their access to restricted areas by badges and the display of these badges.
j) Dealing with Access cards that are lost, stolen or damaged.
k) Code numbers eg. Where code numbers are used, (eg. in the case of digital locks), no person may divulge to another any security code or combination Number without specific authority from the security officer.

## 6. TERMINAL ACCESS.

The next line of defence it that which restricts access to the systems and data from a terminal, the policy should therefore, include statements to the effect that;

a) Access to computer systems via terminals will be permitted only to staff so authorised by the data owners.
b) Appropriate methods of preventing access to computer systems by unauthorised staff will be in place for all systems.
c) Security logs will be maintained and examined regularly for breaches or attempted breaches in security and failures reported to the security officer and data owner.
d) Any attempted or actual violation of any security system will be treated as as misconduct and may result in disciplinary proceedings being taken.
e) Staff with terminal access authority will receive appropriate instructions regarding security matters.
f) Staff who leave the employment of the group will have their access revoked as soon as their intention to leave is known unless otherwise authorised by a senior official. When staff change department or section their terminal access should be reviewed and amended as appropriate.

## 7. PASSWORDS & SIGN-ON.

### 7.1 PASSWORDS.

Passwords are the bane of every DP users life but are readily accepted when we reffer to them as PIN numbers. They are, however, a key factor in maintaining security of access to computer data. It also provides a means by which an audit trail can be maintained. The policy should ensure that;

a) All passwords must be chosen by the individual user.
b) Passwords must be kept confidential and never be divulged to any other person.
c) Each user must be responsible for the privacy and security of their own password.
d) Obvious passwords such as 1111AAAA, personal name and date of birth must not be used.
e) Passwords must be of the maximum size allowed by the appropriate system or application security software.
f) Passwords should be regularly changed and at a maximum of 90 days though more frequent changes should be made whenever it is necessary because of the sensitive nature of the data being accessed.

### 7.2 SIGN-ON

a) Signing-on must be effected by a user only by means of his/her own password. Under no circumstances must any deliberate attempt be made to sign-on using a different, unauthorised, password.
b) Signing-on, or attempting to sign-on, whilst already signed-on elsewhere is prohibited.
c) The signing-off procedure must be effected immediately upon completion of the task requiring access to a computer system.
d) Signing on to enable another individual to gain access to data is prohibited.

7.3 Staff with terminal access authority will receive appropriate instructions regarding security matters and to the consequences of not conforming to the security policy.

## 8. BACK UP.

For all critical data it must be possible to recover the information in the event of loss, damage, corruption or any other problem.

### 8.1 Electronically held data.

a) All electronically held data and software will have on and off site copies taken regularly enough to minimise disruption when faults occur during processing. Back-up copies will be tested for viability at regular intervals.

b) If off-site copies are used for restore, they will be copied before any further use is made of them.

c) The frequency of and levels of on-site and off-site back-up copies of data and software will be carried out to defined standards sufficient to ensure recovery is possible in any circumstances.

8.2 **Other data.**

a) All critical data will have on and off site copies taken regularly enough to minimise disruption when faults occur during processing. Back-up copies will be tested for viability at regular intervals.

b) If off-site copies have to be used in the event of the master copy being lost/destroyed a further copy will be made before any further use is made of them.

c) The frequency of and levels of on-site and off-site back-up copies of data will be carried out to defined standards sufficient to ensure recovery is possible in any circumstances.

## 9 <u>CONTINGENCY.</u>

What happens if the unthinkable happens,eg. the flood or storm occurs, the building catches fire or becomes unsafe to work in or even something as simple as a key member of staff not turning up to work one day. To cover these circumstances and many more besides the policy should define that:-

a) appropriate levels of hardware and communications back-up must exist.

b) contingency plans must make provision for all key resource, and that appropriate fall back procedures will be identified and documented. Copies should be stored off-site.

c) acceptable levels of service in contingent circumstances must be agreed and documented.

d) appropriate contingency plans must be in place to maintain essential continuity of service in the event of the loss or partial loss of any facilities within the group, the objective being to maintain all the groups data, applications and system software; and applications, technical systems and operations documentation intact. also to provide appropriate processing capability to meet contingent levels within an acceptable and agreed timescale.

e) such contingency plans will be integral with overall company contingency plans, and will be documented in multiple copies and held off-site.

f) contracts of employment for key staff will permit working at a contingency site.

g) as far as practicable, contingency plans will be tested at appropriate intervals.

h) to support a contingency plan, off-site security copies must be regularly taken of all software and data. Procedures must be in place to sample that such copies are viable, both prior to, and after storage.

i) Operations procedures, user procedures, systems reference manuals, program specifications and contingency plans are key documentation resources and will have off-site copies stored.

j) Key personnel should be identified and their role in instigating and carrying out the contingency plan must be clearly documented.

## 10. GENERAL.

A statement covering general security matters such as the following should also be included in the policy.

a) Any violation of security procedures established pursuant to this policy statement will result in the instigation of disciplinary procedures.

b) Staff leaving the Groups employment shall return all property and equipment used in conjunction with the computer systems and installations. Items such as keys, identification badges, and card entry badges, portable computer and communications equipment, manuals, documentation and other materials shall be returned to the individual employee's Manager prior to the last day of active employment.

c) Theft, Fraud, damage or misuse of the Groups property, including programs and data may give rise to criminal and civil proceedings through the courts.

d) Deviations from procedures laid down in this policy document may only be made with the written permission of the Director Responsible for this policy document.

e) Any unauthorised use of computer equipment or time is not allowed.

f) Line managers are responsible for computer equipment under their control and for its proper utilisation.

When issuing the policy a signed receipt should be obtained and retained on file.

## 11. PC PROBLEMS

The power available on the PC in use today is equivalent to that which was in use on the Mainframe computer ten years ago. It was seen fit then to keep this power the data behind locked doors. It must therefore be appropriate to provide security on PC systems but this could be the subject of another paper.

Education and Society / R. Aiken (Editor)
Information Processing 92, Volume II
Elsevier Science Publishers B.V. (North-Holland)


# ATTRIBUTE BASED DATA MODEL AND POLYINSTANTIATION

T. Y. Lin

Department of Mathematics and Computer Science, San Jose State University, San Jose, California 95192, U. S. A.

**Abstract**

Analysis of polyinstantiation shows that the ratio between real data and total data is near zero. This leads us to conclude that real data (real world entities) and imaginary data (cover stories) have to be properly controlled. SeaView stores different levels of data in different locations (base relations). Here, we require further that real and imaginary data should also be stored separately. To formalize this, we use Hsiao's Attribute Based Data Model (ABDM). ABDM is essentially a relational model plus some architectural modeling. Interestingly, it appeared earlier than the relational model. It consists of two relations: a Base Data (universal relation) and a Meta Data (relation of equivalence classes; its tuple is called a cluster). Using ABDM, we can smoothly specify that the data of the same security level should be stored in the same cluster (as in SeaView), further the real data and the cover stories should be stored in different clusters (our proposal). This separation also settles the conflict between integrity and secrecy constraints. We will call our model Secure ABDM (SABDM). We believe that SABDM gives the correct formulation for multilevel database security that includes polyinstantiation.

Keyword Codes: K.6.5; H.2.4
Keywords: Security and Protection; Database Management, Systems

## 1. INTRODUCTION

In database security, SeaView is one of the most courageous and outstanding endeavor. There are many outstanding contributions by SeaView [Denn87]. Here, we are interesting in its

(1) Architecture, and
(2) Polyinstantiation

Seaview's architecture requires that data with different levels of classification should be stored in different locations. This requirement is vital important in secure database systems. Using its architecture, SeaView can avoid the using of trusted subjects (in the sense of Bell Lapadula Model). Its architecture is an integral part of its secure data model. From general data modeling point of view, SeaView's data model is lying between Attribute Based Data Model (ABDM) and Relational model. Our analysis on the effect of Polyinstantiation forces us to extend SeaView Model to some form of ABDM.

Polyinstantiation leads to a "multivalued mathematical modeling". Mathematically this is a revolutionary thinking, in fact, implicitly we have adopted similar idea in topological and fuzzy modeling [Lin91]. That is, to each real world entity, there are several corresponding data, in which we have no precise information about which is the real data. These multiple data are called polyinstantiated data; One of them represents real event (called real data), others are cover stories (called imaginary data). In our analysis, we show that the percentage of real information among total information is negligible. So in a secure database system, it is not only important that different levels of data should be stored in different clusters, it is also important that the real data and imaginary data should be stored in different clusters. For example, in case of insufficient storage, we should give up imaginary data instead of real data. Such storage organization will make the retrieval of real data much more efficient.

## 2. POLYINSTANTIATED DATA

As usual, let TS, S, C, U be the security classes representing Top Secret, Secret, Confidential and Unclassified. An element is polyinstantiated if a lower user try to update a null value which in fact is a higher data. So Given an X-data, there is a corresponding Y-polyinstantiated data for every $Y < X$. So to a Top Secret data, there are three polyinstantiated data, to Secret data, two, and to Confidential data, one. Thus there are more imaginary data than real data. A piece of information is represented by a collection of data. And a piece of

*Information is accurate iff each individual primitive data is accurate.*

So a tuple is a noise if one of its element is a noise. A relation instance is a noise if one of its tuple is a noise.

Let us assume that there are 10 elements for each security class. After polyinstantiation, in worst case, there are 40 accurate data and 60 polyinstantiated data. Therefore the ratio between accurate and total information is $2^{40}$ to $2^{100}$, a near zero figure. So an accurate account of real data is essential in any multilevel database. A new data organization is needed to manage such a potentially huge amount of imaginary data. We propose to use Attribute Based Data Model (ABDM) [Hsiao70], [Wong71].

## 3. A REFORMULATION OF ABDM

### 3.1. Base Data and Meta Data

Let F = {A1,A2,...Aj,...} be a family of sets Aj's, called attribute domains. Then a Cartesian Product P is a set P which consists of all possible mappings t from F to the attribute domains such that t(Aj) is an element of Aj, for all j. t is called a record or tuple.

Definition 3.1. A Base Data is a subset of P.

A binary relation is an equivalence relation iff it is reflexive, symmetric and transitive. A relation is said to be discrete equivalence relation, if the relation is identity. A relation is said to be indiscrete relation if the relation is a constant. For every equivalence relation there is a partition and vice versa. If a relation is discrete equivalence relation then every equivalence class is a singleton. If the relation is indiscrete then the only equivalence class is the whole set itself. Let R be a given equivalence relation over A. The family of all equivalence classes is a set, it is called quotient set and denoted by QA or A/R. Let u be an element in A. The equivalence class containing u will be denoted by [u].

Let Rj be an equivalence relation on Aj, its quotient set is QAj. Let QF be the family of the quotient sets QAj. Let QP be the Cartesian Product of QAj's. Elements in QAj are called clusters. Elements in QP are tuples of clusters. Each tuple of Base Data determines uniquely a tuple of clusters:

(u1,u2,u3,...) ----> ([u1],[u2],[u3],...)

where [uj] is the cluster (equivalence class) of uj. A tuple in QP, which is an image of a tuple in Base Data, is called a cluster tuple of Base Data.

Definition 3.2. The Meta Data consists of cluster tuples of Base Data. It is a mathematical relation over the quotient attributes (its domain is the quotient set Domain(Aj)/R). Meta Data may also be called the Relation of Clusters.

In traditional ABDM, Meta Data is expressed by two tables: one table, called DDIT, essentially defines the equivalence relation (or partitions) of each attributes, another, called CDT, defines the Meta Data and its corresponding tuples in Base Data. We also would like to point out that in the traditional ABDM attributes Aj in Meta Data is actually our quotient attributes QAj(=Aj/R); however, they have same name, Name(Aj)=Name(QAj).

Let t=(u1, u2,...) be a tuple of Base Data, then it determines a cluster tuple [t]=([u1], [u2],...) of Meta Data. Several distinct tuples of Base Data could determine the same Meta Data (a cluster tuple). Note that a primary key value uniquely determines the tuple t and hence its cluster tuple [t]. If Name(Aj) = Name(QAj), then the primary key is the same for Base Data and Meta Data.

Let R be the base data, and Q be the Meta Data, then there is a natural projection (called Natural Quotient)

NQ: R ----> Q

defined by

NQ(t) = [t]

where t is a tuple (u1,u2,..) of base data and [t] is a cluster tuple of Meta Data ([u1],[u2],...). The complete inverse image of [t]=NQ(t) is called a cluster. A cluster should be stored together physically.

## 4. MULTILEVEL WORLDS AND THEIR SABDMS

A mathematical model reflects users' view of real world. User's view is represented by an actual one to one correspondence between the entities in the structure of mathematics and objects in the real world. In a multilevel world, such simple correspondence needs a major modification. Users with different security classifications have different views of the real world, and hence have different models and different correspondences. A multilevel data model is a conceptual integration of these multilevel views. Each level is represented by a relational SABDM model.

Definition 4.1. A multilevel SABDM consists of
(a) A multilevel base data scheme is a finite set of attributes names

{A1,C1,TR1,A2,C2,TR2,..., An,Cn,TRn}

where (1) Ai denotes the attribute name over Domain(Ai), (2) Ci is the name of security classes for Ai values. The domain of Ci is the Security Class Lattice SCL, and (3) TRi is the name of truth values for Ai values. Each TRi value represents whether the data is real or not.

Occasionally, we may denote the Base Data relation by

BD(A1,A2,...,An, C1,C2,...,Cn, TR1,TR2,...,TRn)

or, suppressing the Ci's and TRi by,

BD(A1,A2,...,An)

(b) A multilevel Meta data scheme is a finite set of quotient attributes names

{QA1,C1,TR1,QA2,C2,TR2,..., QAn,Cn,TRn}

where (1) QAi denote the attribute name over Domain(Ai)/R, (2) The equivalence relations on Ci and TRi are the discrete equivalence relation, and (3) the security class of an element in QAj is the g.l.b. of the security classes of all data in the equivalence class. Namely, the security class of Name([u]) is the g.l.b of security classes of x for all x in [u].

Occasionally, we may denote it by

MD(QA1,QA2,...,QAn, C1,C2,...,Cn, TR1,TR2,...,TRn)

or, suppressing the Ci's and TRi by,

MD(QA1,QA2,...,QAn)

(c) A key (directory keyword) for Base Data scheme is a collection {A1,A2,..Am}, (m =< n) whose values can identity a tuple [more precisely, Name(A1), Name(A2), ..., Name(Am)]. This implies that {QA1,...QAm} is a key for Meta Data. Note that Name(Aj)=Name(QAj).

There is no Seaview type assumptions on primary keys [Denn87].

Corollary. A SeaView type multilevel model is a multilevel SABDM in which all attribute Aj has indiscrete equivalence relation and the primary key (directory keyword) satisfies SeaView assumption [Denn87].

Definition 4.2. Let X be an element in the lattice of security classes SCL. A multilevel SABDM of X-World, X-model for short, is a multilevel SABDM in which Base Data scheme

BD(A1,A2,..., An, C1,C2,.....Cn, TR1,TR2,..,TRn)

satisfies Ci =< X for i=1,2,..n, and Meta Data scheme

MD(QA1,QA2,..., QAn, C1,C2,.....Cn, TR1,TR2,..,TRn)

satisfies Ci =< X for i=1,2,..n.

For each world, there is a corresponding multilevel X-model. We will prefix any data model concept with X- to mean the corresponding notion in X-world. For example, X-relation means the relation viewed at X-world and etc.

Let X, Y be two security classes. Let YX-World be the common world of X- and Y- worlds, and YX-Model be its Model. There are some Y-data which are real to Y-users, but are known to be imaginary for X-users. The collection of these data is denoted as YXL-World and its model is YXL-model that is the common world of Y-World and X-Lie, where X-Lie is the world (cover stories) that X-users know that they are imaginary data.

For simplicity, we assume that there is only two security levels: U and S. For each real world object there is one corresponding "correct" data, and one mis-represented (imaginary) data. These misrepresented data are called S-Lie in SSL-Model, because S-users know that they are imaginary data.

In multilevel worlds, X-Models interact among different worlds, via XY-maps and YX-maps. Intuitively, XY-map is a Y-view of X-World. We would like to caution the readers that the obvious inclusion is not accurate.

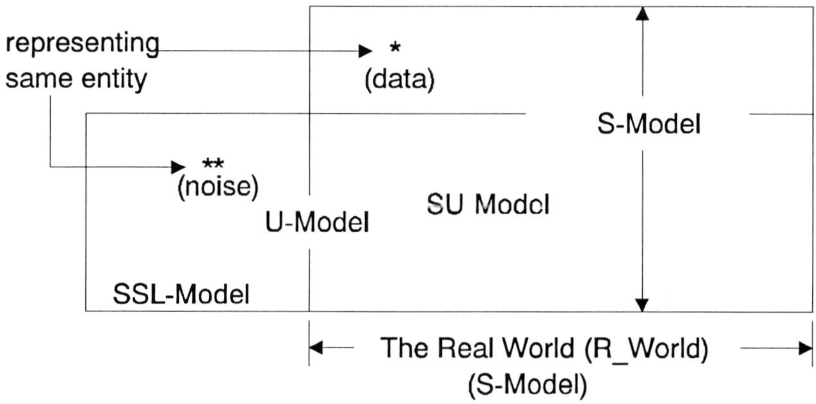


Let us summarize what we have so far.

Definition 4.3. A MultiLevel SABDM Model is a mathematical structure such that

(M1) A set of X-Models for each security class X,

(M2) XY-map from X-Model to Y-Model, and

(M3) X-Model and Real-Model (the real data) are ordinary ABDMs that satisfy the usual constraints.

## 5. CONCLUSION

Polyinstantiation is invented for closing up signaling channel. However, polyinstantiation potentially can generate a large amount of imaginary data, therefore it is important to manage the real data wisely. Traditional approach in polyinstantiation results in multivalued correspondence between the real world entity and data [Denn87]. In this paper, we proposed to add a mechanism to maintain the one-to-one correspondence between data and real world entities.

The security requires that each cluster contains only those data which have the same security level (SeaView did that). Our analysis of polyinstantiation suggests that real data (real world entities) and imaginary data (cover stories) should be stored in different clusters. The separation of real and imaginary data allow us to require the integrity within real data and within each X-world. So the conflict of integrity and secrecy constraints is settled [Burns90].

**Acknowledgements**

This research was supported by a research grant MDA904-91-C-7048. The author is gratitude for the support. Also he would like to thank David Hsiao at Naval Post Graduate School and Teresa Lunt at SRI for many helpful conversations.

## 6. REFERENCES

[Burns90], Rae Burns, "Integrity and Secrecy: Fundamental Conflicts in the Database Environment", Proceedings of The Third RADC Database Security Workshop, June 5-7, 1990, pp. 37- 40.

[Date81,86,90] C. Date, Introduction to Database Management Systems, Addison-Wesley, 1981,86,90.

[Denn87] D. Denning, T.F. Lunt, R.R. Schell, M. Heckman, and W.R. Shockley, "A Multilevel Relational Data Model," Proceedings of 1987 IEEE Symposium on Security and Privacy, 1987.

[Hsiao70] D. Hsiao and F. Farary, "A Formal System for Information Retrieval from Files", Communication of ACM Vol. 13, 2(February 1970), pp. 67-73.

[Hsiao88] D. Hsiao and G. Hoppenstand, "Secure Access Control with High Access precision: An Efficient Approach to Multilevel Security", Database Security, II: Status and Prospects, 1989.

[Lin91] T. Y. Lin, "Topological and Fuzzy Rough Sets", Kluwer Academic Publishers.

[Wong71] E. Wong and T. C. Chang, "Canonical Structure in Attribute Based File Organization", Communication of ACM Vol. 14, 9 (September 1971), pp. 593-597.

Education and Society / R. Aiken (Editor)
Information Processing 92, Volume II
Elsevier Science Publishers B.V. (North-Holland)




# Zero-knowledge based identification: from a theoretical concept towards a practical token

M. Burmester[a] and Y. Desmedt[b]

[a]Department of Mathematics, University of London – Royal Holloway and Bedford New College, Egham, Surrey TW20 OEX, United Kingdom

[b]Department of Electrical Engineering & Computer Science, University of Wisconsin, Milwaukee, P.O. Box 784, WI 53201, United States of America

**Abstract**

We overview various attacks on identification systems based on zero-knowledge proofs, and measures to prevent them. We also consider the efficiency of zero-knowledge proofs and overview protocols with a low communication and computation complexity. We conclude that with today's technology it is possible to make identification tokens which are secure and efficient.

Keyword Codes: D.4.6; E.3; K.4.2
Keywords: Operating Systems, Security and Protection; Data Encryption; Computers and Society, Social Issues

## 1. INTRODUCTION

Identification is an important security issue with numerous applications. Passports, identity cards, drivers' licenses, credit cards, are all examples of identification mechanisms. These are an essential means for granting access to most services in an organized society, and their origin goes back to the beginning of civilization. One of the oldest methods of identification is the password. This is based on secret knowledge. The prover is identified by revealing a secret password. However he may be identifying himself to an adversary who could later use the password fraudulently. So this method is insecure. Other methods of identification rely on the assumption that it is hard (expensive) to copy certain types of credit cards (*e.g.*, those with a hologram). However even these can be copied by resolute criminals. Recently, systems relying on physical features (*e.g.*, fingerprints, etc) of the users have been proposed. Such systems can have a very dubious security and are, in many instances, either too expensive, too impractical, or unacceptable to the users [1].

Feige, Fiat and Shamir proposed to use zero-knowledge proofs for identification [2,3,4]. With such systems, individuals are identified by proving that they know a secret without revealing it, or, any information that could help a would-be impersonator compute it. However, if the protection of the identification system is not adequate, several frauds are possible. For example, we can have a real-time attack in which an individual's proof of identity is diverted by a corrupted party (the Middleperson fraud), or in which the prover deliberately helps an impersonator (the Terrorist fraud).

Our objective is to overview ways to thwart attacks which would otherwise undermine the security of identification systems, and to further improve the complexity of such systems. We believe that most threats, except Rental, can be dealt with, and that therefore identification based on zero-knowledge is not only a theoretically elegant concept but also leads to practical and efficient identification mechanisms.

This paper is organized as follows. In Section 2. we explain what zero-knowledge proofs are and in Section 3. we discuss the Feige–Fiat–Shamir model for identification. In Section 4. we overview various threats to identification systems, and in Section 5. we consider countermeasures for these. In Section 6. we discuss the efficiency of zero-knowledge protocols. Conclusions are drawn in Section 7.

## 2. INTERACTIVE ZERO-KNOWLEDGE PROOFS

Goldwasser, Micali and Rackoff introduced the concept of interactive zero-knowledge proofs [5]. They considered a setting in which a 'powerful' prover $A$ wants to convince a verifier $B$, with limited (polynomial-time) computer power, that an input $x$ belongs to a language $L$ (*i.e.*, that a theorem is true). With interactive proofs, $A$ and $B$ exchange messages (strings) and can privately (outcome is unknown to other party) toss coins (use randomness). When $A$ sends a message to $B$ we call this a *move* and similar for $B$ sending to $A$. So $B$ is allowed to ask (random) questions, and is convinced only with a certain probability. For an *interactive proof of membership in L* we require that: when $x \in L$ then the verifier will (almost) always accept, whereas when $x \notin L$ the verifier will (almost) always reject, whatever a dishonest prover attempts to send the verifier.

Intuitively a proof is zero-knowledge if it reveals no more than is strictly necessary, *i.e.*, that the theorem is true. A dishonest verifier $B'$ may deviate from the protocol in an attempt to gain some additional knowledge. The *view* of $B'$ is everything that $B'$ 'sees' during his interaction with $A$. That is, the messages exchanged and the randomness that $B'$ uses (the coin tosses). Clearly $B'$ will gain no further knowledge if this view can be simulated *with no help from* the prover. A proof is *perfect zero-knowledge* [5] if, when $x$ belongs to $L$ (the theorem is true), for any verifier $B'$, there is a simulator with limited (expected polynomial time) computer power, which will generate a distribution which is identical to the view of $B'$.

For the formal definitions the reader is referred to [5].

## 3. IDENTIFICATION BASED ON ZERO-KNOWLEDGE

Feige, Fiat and Shamir proposed two identification systems [2,3,4] based on zero-knowledge proofs. With the first, which has been called a *public-file-based* system, the users select their own secret key and publish the corresponding public key in a directory.

With the second, which has been called an *identity-based* system, a Trusted Authority gives each user a secret key partially based on their physical description. For both systems, individuals are identified by proving with an interactive zero-knowledge proof that they know the secret key. Since no information whatsoever is leaked, the identification system is not degraded however many times it is used.

Identity-based systems are secure if the physical description of the users is adequately tested. The Trusted Authority must check the identity *ID* (name, etc) of each user and his/her physical description. Observe that with identity-based systems it is not necessary to use a zero-knowledge proof since a signature scheme [6] will suffice [7]. Indeed if *SID* is the Trusted Authority's signature of *ID*, the pair (*ID, SID*) will identify the user *ID*. There is *no need* to keep *SID* secret. The verifying party must check that *SID* is a valid signature of *ID*, and that *ID* properly describes the individual. For a practical implementation one can use Rabin's signature scheme [8], which only requires one modular squaring for verification. For more details consult [7,9].

Public-file-based identification systems are subject to many security risks. We discuss these in the following section.

## 4. SECURITY PROBLEMS

We overview some of the major threats to identification based on zero-knowledge. Threats are due to either weaknesses in the zero-knowledge protocol, or the way in which the system is implemented. The first type of threat is discussed in [10] and can easily be dealt with. Here we are concerned with the second type, which includes the Middleperson fraud and the Terrorist fraud [9,7]. Other threats are Theft and Renting. These apply only if the physical description of the individual is not used in the identification process. Finally we discuss the abuses of identification systems.

### 4.1. The Middleperson fraud

Four parties are involved in this fraud [7], $A$, $B$, $C$ and $D$. $A$ and $D$ are 'honest' and are not aware of a fraud in which $C$ masquerades as $A$. $B$ helps $C$ by relaying messages. $D$ is the verifier. Let us describe this in more detail.

$B$ and $C$, the 'dishonest' parties, wait until $A$ decides to prove his identity to $B$. When this happens, $C$ initiates the identification procedure with $D$. In response, $D$ sends $C$ a challenge. $C$ cannot answer this by himself because he does not know the secret of $A$. $B$ helps him by sending this challenge to $A$. Unsuspectingly, $A$ answers the challenge, because he thinks that he is being identified by $B$. $B$ then sends the answer to $C$, who in turn sends it to $A$. This procedure is repeated as many times as required. At the end $D$ is convinced that $C$ is $A$.

This fraud must be performed in real time. Some means of communication between $B$ and $C$ is also required (*e.g.*, a secret radio link). We remark that the fraud can only perpetrated if there is no secure check of the physical description of $A$. However, many systems that check the physical security are not very secure against a malicious adversary.

### 4.2. The Terrorist fraud

This is a variant of the Middleperson fraud for which the prover $A$ is willing to collaborate with $C$ ($B$ has no role here) [9]. Again $C$ (the terrorist) masquerades as $A$.

### 4.3. Other frauds

With public-file systems the users select their own secret keys and then register the corresponding public keys (which are not related to their physical description) in a directory. So criminals can choose several secret keys and register the public keys under fake names. Well known frauds in which individuals have several identities can be perpetrated, and these are untraceable [11]. An obvious way to prevent such frauds is to have a Trusted Authority check the true identity of each user before granting an entry (one only) in the directory. A user should not know his secret key, otherwise he could share it with others who could then impersonate him [7] (*e.g.*, chairpersons might wish to 'copy' themselves so that someone else can represent them). Worse, a user could deliberately allow his secret key to be leaked in order to deny a previously signed document [12]. Such frauds can be prevented by letting the Trusted Authority choose the secret keys of the users, and then issue tamper-free ID Smart Cards which contain these keys. The Authority should then destroy the secret keys and keep only a directory of the public keys. This solution is not very satisfactory because it makes it possible for a corrupted Authority to misrepresent users. However, using commitment protocols, it is theoretically possible to overcome this last problem.

Another fraud is Renting. Even if the owner of an ID Smart Card does not know his secret key, he may be willing to hire his ID card. This would allow a criminal to commit crimes with a perfect alibi. Several possible scenarios are discussed in [11]. Evidently this is also possible with ordinary ID cards (*e.g.*, by replacing the photograph). It is very hard to prevent the Renting fraud if the physical description of the user is not used or tested adequately. Finally frauds can occur (and it do occur all too frequently) because of Loss or Theft. One can easily protect against such frauds by using a black list.

### 4.4. Abuses of identification systems

A procedure is *abused* if it is used for a different purpose than that intended. The Fiat–Shamir identification system (or any system based on the proof in [4]) can be used to send secret information which cannot be detected by traffic analysis. This would allow a country sponsoring terrorism to send up to 500 new words of secret information each time a passport is verified [9].

### 4.5. The significance of the frauds and consequences

One may have reservations about the significance of such frauds. The Middleperson fraud is easy to set up. One only needs two people who conspire. The fraudulent benefits could be substantial if one takes into account how frequently ID cards are used (*e.g.*, to access information or other services). The same applies for the Terrorist fraud. Thefts of ID cards (and passports) are already a major problem. Finally, abuses of the type described above can be used to implement mechanisms helpful for espionage.

# 5. SOLVING SECURITY PROBLEMS

## 5.1. Thwarting the Middleperson fraud

A method to avoid this fraud is presented in [9]. With this, the individual uses a one-time-valid authentication system to sign a message which includes the time, his/her name and *exact* location. This method is very practical for secure remote login, however it does not protect against the Terrorist fraud. Another solution that protects against the Terrorist fraud is presented in [7], but because it is theoretical it is not discussed here. A more practical solution is presented in [13] which we presently discuss. This method only works when prover and verifier 'see' each other.

To prevent this fraud prover and verifier agree in advance on a *fixed* playing time for their moves, and make each move precisely when the time runs out. This leaves no time to relay the moves. For this purpose the prover and verifier measure independently their *relative* distance and compute an appropriate time length (the accuracy required will depend on the crowdedness of their environment [13]). Inexpensive quartz technology will give sufficient precision.

## 5.2. Solving the terrorist fraud

For a practical implementation we let a Trusted Center issue each user with an electronic tamper-free ID card (credit card, etc.) which can make the necessary distance measurements and identification calculations [13]. The distance measurement and all calculations are carried out by the device and *not* by the user.

## 5.3. Countermeasures for abuses

The solution proposed in [11] uses an *active eavesdropper* as a *warden* to restore the independence of the messages exchanged in the zero-knowledge protocol (where appropriate). For more details about the abuses of zero-knowledge proofs and countermeasures, the reader is referred to [11].

# 6. PRACTICAL ZERO-KNOWLEDGE SCHEMES

Practical zero-knowledge proofs have been proposed recently [2,14,4,15,16,17]. The Fiat–Shamir protocol is similar to the Goldwasser–Micali–Rackoff proof of quadratic residuocity [5], but has $k$ input numbers. For efficiency it is desirable to choose a large $k$ and a small number of iterations $t$, (one iteration is 3 moves). We cannot have $t$ constant (for 'black-box' zero-knowledge simulation [18]), unless the quadratic residuocity problem can easily be computed. For the same reason we must have $k = O(\log|n|)$, where $n$ is the modulus. So $k = \Theta(\log|n|)$ seems to be the best bet, but then the length of the input $(I_1, \ldots, I_k; n)$ is unnecessarily long.

Guillou and Quisquater [16] proposed a proof for which the secret numbers are modular $v$-th roots, where $v$ is a prime greater than 2. For each user there is only one secret/public number. Again for ('black-box' simulation) zero-knowledge, $v$ must be polynomial in $|n|$. If $v$ is constant, then there is no asymptotic advantage over $v = 2$. By choosing a $v$ such that $|n| < v < 2|n|$, we have a zero-knowledge proof [21] provided that $t = t(|n|)$ is not constant, for example $t = \lfloor\log^*|n|\rfloor$ [19]. We call such proofs *almost-constant* round.

Because of the result in [18] quoted earlier, these proofs are very efficient. In Table 1 we compare the efficiency of this protocol with some other well-known protocols.

Table 1
Complexity of some zero-knowledge identification schemes. $|x|$ is the length of the input.

| Zero-Knowledge schemes | Number of iterations | Bits communicated | Multiplications |
|---|---|---|---|
| Fiat-Shamir [2] | $\log^{1+\varepsilon}\|x\|$ | $\|x\|\log^{1+\varepsilon}\|x\|$ | $k\log^{1+\varepsilon}\|x\|$, $k = O(\log\|x\|)$ |
| Guillou-Quisquater [16], Ohta-Okamoto [17] | $\log^{1+\varepsilon}\|x\|$ | $\|x\|\log^{1+\varepsilon}\|x\|$ | $\log^{1+\varepsilon}\|x\|$ |
| Chaum-Evertse-van de Graaf [14], Beth [15] | $\log^{1+\varepsilon}\|x\|$ | $\|x\|\log^{1+\varepsilon}\|x\|$ | $k\|x\|\log^{1+\varepsilon}\|x\|$, $k = O(\log\|x\|)$ |
| Schnorr [20] (not zero-knowledge) | One | $\Theta(\|x\|)$ | $O(\|x\|)$ (without preprocessing) |
| Burmester [21] | $\log^{\varepsilon}\|x\|$ | $\|x\|\log^{\varepsilon}\|x\|$ | $\log^{1+\varepsilon}\|x\|$ |

A proof for the discrete logarithm problem was presented in [14]. This problem deals with finding an integer $s$ such that $I = \alpha^s$, where $I$, $\alpha$ are elements of a group. If $\alpha$ is in $Z_p^*$, then the problem is to find an $s$ such that $I = \alpha^s \bmod p$. The discrete logarithm *decision* problem deals with the *existence* of $s$. A very efficient identification protocol based on this problem has been presented recently [22].

## 7. CONCLUSION

We have discussed state of the art identification methods based on zero-knowledge. We overviewed various threats which apply to identification systems based on zero-knowledge proofs, and discussed measures which, if adopted, will make the identification secure. We also considered the efficiency of zero-knowledge protocols. Even though the Fiat–Shamir protocol is very efficient, it can be improved. We mentioned a variant of the Guillou–Quisquater protocol which requires much less interaction (almost-constant round) than the Fiat–Shamir protocol for the same level of security. The number of bits communicated is also lower than that of the Fiat–Shamir protocol. The computer power required is comparable with Fiat-Shamir. There are similar protocols based on the discrete logarithm (however they need more computer power). Combining these results we see that identification based on zero-knowledge has evolved from an elegant theoretical concept, towards a practical and efficient token. The only (known) remaining security issue is Renting.

## 8. REFERENCES

1 D.W. Davies and W.L. Price, Security for Computer Networks. John Wiley and Sons,

New York, 1984.
2 A. Fiat and A. Shamir, Advances in Cryptology, Proc. of Crypto '86 (Lect. Notes Comp. Sc. 263), Springer-Verlag, (1987) 186.
3 A. Fiat and A. Shamir, Securicom 87, Paris, (1987) 147.
4 U. Feige, A. Fiat, and A. Shamir, J. of Cryptology, 1 (1988) 77.
5 S. Goldwasser, S. Micali, and C. Rackoff, Siam J. Comput., 18 (1989) 186.
6 D.E.R. Denning, Cryptography and Data Security. Addison-Wesley, 1982.
7 S. Bengio, G. Brassard, Y.G. Desmedt, C. Goutier, and J.-J. Quisquater, J. of Cryptology, 4 (1991) 175.
8 M. Rabin, Digitalized signatures and public-key functions as intractable as factorization, tech. rep., Massachusetts Institute of Technology Technical Report MIT/LCS/TR-212, Cambridge, Massachusetts, January 1977.
9 Y. Desmedt, Securicom 88, Paris, (1988) 147.
10 M.V.D. Burmester and Y.G. Desmedt, Electronics Letters, 25 (1989) 1509.
11 Y. Desmedt, C. Goutier, and S. Bengio, Advances in Cryptology, Proc. of Crypto '87 (Lect. Notes Comp. Sc. 293), Springer-Verlag, (1988) 21.
12 J. Saltzer, On digital signatures, ACM Operating Syst. Rev., 12 (1978) 12.
13 T. Beth and Y. Desmedt, Advances in Cryptology — Crypto '90, Proc. (Lect. Notes Comp. Sc. 537), Springer-Verlag, (1991) 169.
14 D. Chaum, J.-H. Evertse, and J. van de Graaf, Advances in Cryptology — Eurocrypt '87 (Lect. Notes Comp. Sc. 304), Springer-Verlag, (1988) 127.
15 T. Beth, Advances in Cryptology, Proc. of Eurocrypt '88 (Lect. Notes Comp. Sc. 330), Springer-Verlag, (1988) 77.
16 L. Guillou and J.-J. Quisquater, Advances in Cryptology, Proc. of Eurocrypt '88 (Lect. Notes Comp. Sc. 330), Springer-Verlag, (1988) 123.
17 K. Ohta and T. Okamoto, Advances in Cryptology — Crypto '88, Proc. (Lect. Notes Comp. Sc. 403), Springer-Verlag, (1990) 232.
18 O. Goldreich and H. Krawczyk, Proc. $17^{th}$ Intern. Colloq. Automata, Languages and Programming, (1990).
19 G. Brassard and P. Bratley, Algorithmics — Theory & Practice. Prentice Hall, 1988.
20 C.P. Schnorr, Advances in Cryptology — Crypto '89, Proc. (Lect. Notes Comp. Sc. 435), Springer-Verlag, (1990) 239.
21 M.V.D. Burmester, An optimal class of interactive zero-knowledge proofs. Accepted for publication in Inform. Process. Letters.
22 M. Burmester, Y. Desmedt, and T. Beth, Computer J., 35 (1992) 21.

Education and Society / R. Aiken (Editor)
Information Processing 92, Volume II
Elsevier Science Publishers B.V. (North-Holland)


# Security in Local Area Networks

Dr. Peter Lipp

Technische Universität Graz
Institut für Angewandte Informationsverarbeitung und Kommunikationstechnologie
Klosterwiesgasse 32/I, A-8010 Graz

**Abstract**

local area networks are currently widely implemented. During the first stages technology was the driving factor, any other important aspects, as security threads imposed by such new technology were of minor importance or even deliberately ignored. Nowadays security has become playing a much more important role in the network-community (at least concerning experts). There is a certain gap between available security and security needs. This paper tries to give an overview on security problems in local area networks and their connection to the wide area networks and to present possible solutions. It concentrates on an environment, in which local area networks, a mixture of computers including personal computers and workstations, and Internet-Protocols (TCP/IP) are primarily used.

Keyword Codes: K.6.5, C.2.2, C.2.5, K.8.0
Keywords: Management of Computing and Information Systems, Security and Protection; Computer Communication Networks, Network Protocols, Local Networks; Personal Computing, General.

## Security Problems in local area networks

To be able to judge security problems in local area networks, there are a few details to be discussed. First, there is the technology used, which is largely responsible for many of the problems. Second, there are organizational aspects, which also contribute to security problems and solutions in this area.

### Technology

Local area networks nowadays are mainly based on two technologies: CSMA/CD and Token Ring. These technologies have certain inherent properties, which is the reason for many of the problems discussed here.

1. CSMA/CD is based on a Bus-structure and has a broadcast-type transmission characteristic. Therefor any station is able to receive any traffic on the media and any station can transmit any packet on the media. In principle, the same holds for Token Rings.
2. The address-structure used does not allow any identification (or even authentication) of source and destination of packets.

This enables attacks like

- *Masquerade*: One station pretends to be another station simply by sending packets with the other station's source address. Because of the broadcast-type, this cannot easily be detected; and because of the address structure, even random-addresses are not recognizable. So masquerade can only, if at all, be recognized at higher layers.
- *Unauthorized Disclosure*: Any station can receive all packets on the net. Most controllers discard packets not containing their address as the destination address and not being broadcast-type packets. But: One can usually program them to receive all packets. This is used to build bridges or monitoring stations using these cards. Even a personal computer can be used for these purposes.
- *Data Modification*: In local networks using a ring topology, like a token ring, all packets pass all controllers of all other stations. Therefore it should not be impossible or complicated to have one of these stations modify packets passing by. In CSMA/CD, modification is not directly possible, but can be accomplished on higher layers using design-weaknesses of the protocols involved.
- *Denial of service:* a single station can block all traffic on the net simply by broadcasting packets continuously. This can be done by malicious intention or by malfunction of hard- or software components. In wide area networks, a single host cannot disable the whole network as it is the case in local area networks.

Beside the technological basis, these problems have different influencing factors as well. These are protocols, equipment, software bugs and general security aspects.

**Protocols**

The deficiencies mentioned above could be solved to some extend or even totally by higher-level protocols. As it was the case for the Local Area Network-Technology, security aspects have been neglected in the protocol-specifications for a long time too. Even now, where solutions have been defined (e.g., Internet-Security-Option, Privacy Enhanced Mail, OSI-Security Architecture), these standards or definitions have not been implemented into most of the products available on the market and are not available to the customers. This situation is improving, but we will have to live with lots of insecure systems for some time still.

**Equipment**

The situation would not be as bad (as it is), if there were no additional aspects contributing to the overall LAN-(In)Security. First, there it the kind of machinery connected to the Networks, that can create problems. In many environments and networks the personal computer plays a very important role. Personal computers are very cheap, there is lot of excellent software available and so they are very attractive to be used especially in organizations like universities, where money still plays a very important role in decision making. Personal computers allow fraudulent users to penetrate the network and to launch attacks very easily. The user needs some knowledge about the machine and the network, of course; but this is not a big task for some bright student. He just needs to write a small program, may be one page long, to be able to paralyze the network -- and with another page he can easily intercept and modify traffic on the network.

**The Super User**

Doing the same with workstations (e.g., running the UNIX-OS) is of course feasible as well, but the situation can be different. Most workstations in most environments are being controlled by a trustworthy "superuser," a person who has no interest in bad things happening and thus is trying to keep his system safe. Only the superuser should be able to do things on a workstation that are possible on a personal computer. Workstations seem to solve the problem -- but they don't. First, who can trust the superuser? There are sites (again universities are an excellent example) where there is a single user owning a certain workstation, who is his own superuser as well and has total control over the operation of his machine as if he had a personal computer available. Even if you can trust the superuser, there still are chances that somebody else guesses his password. As long as identification and authentication of users are done by passwords, all the other security measures available are not worth much.

**Software bugs**

Even if there would be better authentication mechanisms available, you still can not be sure of having secured your system. As with all software, there is a chance that there are some yet unrevealed flaws in the operating system that can enable access to an intruder giving him the rights of the superuser . With operating systems like UNIX, where source code is available relatively easy, the intruder has the opportunity to study the source code to find out programming-weaknesses he then can use to exploit for his goals, instead of using the trial-and-error-method. This is even more true for network-protocols, where specifications are published as a standard or quasi-standard (RFC in the internet-environment). If there is a flaw in the protocol-specification it should be relatively easy to find out; and all implementations follow this specification. Even if the software is working properly, there is the possibility that the configuration of the system allows intruders to attack the system. Modern operating systems are quite complex to manage and in many cases the strategy of the manufacturers of these systems is to deliver the software configured "loosely secure."

**The influence of the network**

As has been shown above by a few examples, there are lots of possibilities to attack machines. Many of these security problems can be handled well, if the systems can be physically protected and access to the system is under tight control. In a networked environment, this is no longer possible or at least much much harder to do. Network access increases the possibilities and decreases the risks of being caught.

For local area networks, the situation might be a little different. Traditionally, local area networks have been defined as networks that are installed in a locally restricted environment, like a building, where all property belongs to one organization. If this is the case, it might be possible to restrict access to components of the network and machines connected to the network (the situation corresponds to stand-alone-systems to some extend). If the Local area network belongs to a department, which is small enough, this could too be accomplished by tough regulations and surveillance. If the organization is too big, spreads over different sites in a city (like universities in Europe, which often have not enough space in their traditional campuses), and if the structure is quite heterogeneous, if departments are not that controllable (again like in universities), the situation might become dangerous. local area networks often are connected by backbone-networks; so big local area networks are created, which have similar physical and security characteristics but are not restricted to the local environment any more. These structures then additionally connect to wide area networks to enable cooperation with the world wide community, like the internet. Then dangers are increasing while security possibilities remain the same.

## Strategies

While this is happening, users are quite often no aware of the risks, but happy of being offered that many possibilities. So one of the most obvious and important, but still quite often ignored strategy in improving security is to **improve the security-awareness** of all users of the system. This is again true generally, but especially important in a vulnerable environment like local area networks. As already has been mentioned above, if the attitude of the users towards security, which is for instance, expressed in choosing and handling of passwords, does not meet the needs, any other measures will be inefficient. There are several organizational things that can be done to improve security; some of these are:

- setting up rules to choose passwords and enforcing their implementation,
- setting up acceptable-use-policies which users have to accept and stick to,
- setting up a security policy which has to be followed,
- engaging a responsible person for handling security related incidents (if the organization is big enough),
- improving physical access control to all components (including the wire) and
- improving the overall security of the systems.

In the following we want to concentrate on the latter, especially concerning improvement of security in an environment, where personal computers and local area networks are main components.

## Improving overall security

The first thing to be done is to identify the components that can be attacked, how they can be attacked and how they can be protected. In this paper we will concentrate on the protection of data in transfer between any two stations in a Local Area Network. If we can protect the communicating computers and the ongoing communication sufficiently well, all would be won. It is of course not that easy. One of the main problems is the openness of the network. If you cannot restrict yourself to a certain class of machinery with one single operating system; if you want to communicate with any machine connected to the network somewhere else; finally: if you do have security requirements for your communication, then you have only a limited choice of possibilities:

1) *Use standardized protocols for security services.* This usually means that the security services provided will automatically cooperate with any partner using the same protocols. The functions would be in the right place, providing services for the applications. The problem here is the availability of products. So there is often no choice than to use option
2) *Use security functions implemented into your application.* This is contrary to the OSI-Idea. In many circumstances, this is the only way you can do it at the moment. Lower layers, which could be the place to put security functions in, usually do not have this functionality implemented.

One good example, to clarify this position, is electronic mail. This broadly used feature is one of the most attractive features of international networking and is very widely used worldwide. There are lots of possibilities to attack electronic mail systems. If the right security services would be available, the electronic mail users would have the possibility to

a) make sure that the message came from the partner who is shown as the sender;
b) make sure that nobody else can read the mail;
c) make sure that the message has been delivered unmodified;
d) get a chance to register mail;
.....

The risks involved into electronic mail have been recognized, and there is a method to add privacy to electronic mail under development: PEM, privacy enhanced mail [PEM-1,PEM-2,PEM-3,PEM-4]. This proposal puts security functions into the mail-user-agent, the program used for sending and receiving mail. This of course is not the ideal solution, but currently the only practical possibility to achieve any advance in this area.

Contrary to this, in local area networks there are other possibilities that can be implemented to add security to the network without the need to change all the application programs.

1) *Do not connect your local area network to the outside.* This (obvious) solution can be necessary in very critical environments. There remains of course the need to check security within the network. If this method is to extreme, the next step is to have a look on the connection points of the local area networks to the outside world.
2) *Control traffic between networks.* This option is often called *building a firewall.* Here we have to deal with different connection-types differently. The most dangerous types are
   a) *Bridges.* Most of them are adaptive, self learning bridges that can easily be tricked to forward traffic they should not forward. In certain configurations, bridges function as the connection between local subnets and a high-speed backbone-network, these bridges play an important role in communication. Pure bridges do not add any security to the network.
   b) *Gateways and Routers* are a little better than bridges, because they deal with more structured addresses than bridges and thus automatically stop a number of threads only possible without them. There are more possibilities to check traffic for security-related events than on level 2. Modern routers offer several possibilities to specify, which hosts are allowed to communicate with other hosts. To make it clear: gateways and routers offer more possibilities, but the not all off them do and they do not offer them automatically. There are known attacks to gateway- and routing protocols, so they are no solution on their own.
   c) *Firewalls* restrict all access to your local network through a single system. That is, all access to and from the local network must be made through a dedicated host, which then is called firewall. The security of the local network then depends on the security of the firewall system.
   d) *Special Security Devices* can be used to connect stations to the network and to encrypt all outgoing and incoming traffic. These stations have to communicate themselves for key-exchange and other organizational purposes and allow secure traffic between any two stations using these devices. Traffic between stations using this device and others, who do not, is still possible, but without security (of course).

## A possible configuration

In this section we want to present a possible configuration, that provides for additional security in a local area network environment. Technische Universität Graz is a non-campus type university. The university consists of buildings spread all over the city with a concentration on three sites. All of the sites are connected by fiber-optic-media and the backbone is formed by an FDDI-Ring. To this backbone several local area networks are connected. Some of these are connected via star-couplers, which work like a repeater and thus directly form a bigger LAN out of several physically independent local area networks. These networks are usually situated in different departments and are not centrally controlled. There is a coordination center that knows about all installed machines and the responsible persons. Further on, there exist connections to the Universität Graz and local research centers.

This situation is ideal for intruders. There are lots of possibilities to get access to the net; by using one of the connected stations or simply by connecting another station to the network. If one department has the need to protect their subnetwork from the network, we are proposing the following scheme:

The connection is formed by a personal computer, which contains two (or more) network-controllers and runs a software, which protects the subnetwork from influences of the outside world. The following functions can be activated:

- **Securing internal communication:** this is achieved automatically, because the bridge cannot be forced to transmit packets from one subnetwork to another, if the destination is known to be on the local side. There are static lists of addresses; others can be learned; this feature has dangers, so it can be disabled or enabled at will separately for each subnetwork connected to the bridge.
- **Restricting communication:** the personal computer, which performs bridge-functions, can be forced to filter packets, according to the conditions set by the network manager. These conditions are formulated as

  $$\left(t_i-\left(t_i+\Delta t_i\right)\right),\left(S_{A_i},S_{B_i}\right),P_i$$

  where $S_{A_i}$,$S_{B_i}$ are stations in subnetworks $A_i$ and $B_i$, specified by their hardware address; $P_i$ is a protocol like DECNET or TCP/IP and $t_i$ is a time specification, which restricts connections to certain times of day.

  A router is a key component of our network, and many stations want to communicate to the outside world; so we simply allow all local stations to communicate to this machine. On layer two this reduces the security added to the net by using the filtering method. Therefor we had to add another filtering type, for certain layer two connections: we can check packets on layer three (currently only IP-packets) for certain conditions. Thus we can restrict traffic through the router as well. We simply check outgoing packets sent to the router if the final destination is in the list of allowed partners.
- **Connection management**

  These restrictions make a flexible, dynamic management scheme necessary. While we tend to decentralize as many management-tasks as possible, there is the need of centralized management in controlling the functions of the bridge. This is done remotely using encryption for transmission of commands to the bridge. Status information can be retrieved using SNMP.

As we want to protect our net from the outside, we think of giving users the possibility to set up filters themselves, for instance if they want to communicate with a certain machine which is not in the list. So management could be made a little more decentralized.

- **Securing external communication**
  There is no general possibility to add security to end-to-end communication automatically by the bridge. What we can do is to protect communication between two "secure" subnets connected by an insecure network, if each is protected by such a bridge. We are assuming however, that there are no threads to be feared in the subnets themselves.
  What we want to achieve is
- *Confidentiality*
- and *Integrity* on selected connections. Three choices are possible:
  1) *Asymmetric encryption* is used for exchanging keys, symmetric encryption for Data Transfer. Key management is provided by a special security server.
  2) *Using asymmetric encryption* for data transfer. Currently there are no efficient Hard- or software components available. Encryption rates of less than 10kbit/second represent a factor of 1/1000 compared to the transmission rate in the ethernet environment. So it can only be used rarely and for a low amount of data. We expect to have solutions available in the near future, that can achieve encryption rates of about 500 kbit/second by using parallel mechanisms. This could then provide meaningful possibilities for certain applications.
  3) *Using a Vernam-Type Cipher*, which is known as being very secure and fast. To solve the key-transmission problem, we think of generating keys in the bridges. One station transmits a starting value n; the vernam key is then calculated as
     where e is a secret RSA-key, shared by the bridges. This calculation can be done

$$f_0(n)^e, f_1(n)^e, f_2(n)^e, \dots\dots\dots$$

  either during idle times or in an external unit, like a transputer board. The generated key can of course then only be used for relatively short streams of data and not for all communication passing the bridge.
  These security functions can be provided by two bridges involved in a communication of two stations on request of any of the communicating partners. As an integration into used protocols is not possible, these functions have to be turned on by the applications or, if they too cannot be adapted, by their users via a special management program.
- **Authentication of bridges**
  In this case data-blocks transmitted have to be signed by the sending bridge. Asymmetric methods cannot easily be used, because even if the amount of data to be encrypted is low, a minimum size of data is necessary. This can be handled by calculating the signature for more than one packet transmitted. Packets would become valid after receiving the delayed signature. The bridge has to store the packets until the correct signature validates them. We are currently studying these mechanisms for practicability. This may extend to upper layers, where these layers or the application could accept the packets under the assumption, the packet was valid. This should be the case most of the time. If not so, the software has to be able to declare these packets as invalid and roll

back all processing that has been started. These concepts are found in principle in database applications, where transactions can be aborted and undone.

## Conclusions

In this paper we presented a possible configuration, that adds security services to an environment, where several local area networks are connected by a possibly insecure backbone network. The secure bridge, connecting the networks, offers the users of network-applications several possibilities to enhance the security of communication using unmodified existing software and network-protocols. These solutions do not fit too smoothly into the environment, but they are not intended as ideal solutions anyway; it will be replaced by better integration of security mechanisms and services into standard protocols and products. Currently it seems that we will have to wait for this to happen, so the proposed solution is only meant as one way of intermediate immediate help to all those, who need such functions. Standardized methods and protocols will penetrate the network-environment during the following years and might void these and all similar attempts to add security to local area networks.

## References


[BERSON 89] Berson, T.A. (Ed.) *Local Area Network Security.* Workshop LANSEC '89. European Inst. for System Security <E.I.S.S.>. Lecture Notes in computer science 396. Springer (1989).

[BRAND 1990] Brand, R., *Coping with the Thread of Computer Security Incidents: A Primer from Prevention to Recovery.* June 1990. Available online from cert.sei.cmu.edu:/pub/info/primer.

[CURRY 91] Curry, D., et al., *Site Security Handbook.* RFC 1244, July 1991.

[IEEE 88] *IEEE Network,* The Magazine of Computer Communications, Vol. 2, No. 1, January 1988, Special Issue on Bridges and Routers.

[PEM-1] Linn, J., *Privacy Enhancement for Internet Electronic Mail: Part I: Message encryption and Authentication Procedures.* Internet-Draft 1113E, April 10 1992

[PEM-2] Kent, S., *Privacy Enhancement for Internet Electronic Mail: Part II: Certificate-Based Key Management.* Internet-Draft 1114F, March 23 1992

[PEM-3] Balenson, D.: *Privacy Enhancement for Internet Electronic Mail: Part III: Algorithms, Modes and Identifiers.* Internet-Draft 1115C, April 1992

[PEM-4] Kalisi, B.: *Privacy Enhancement for Internet Electronic Mail: Part IV: Key Certification and Related Services.* Internet-Draft FORMS-E, 15. April 1992

[PFLEEGER 1989] Pfleeger, C.: *Security in Computing.* Prentice Hall, Englewood Cliffs, NJ., 1989.

[X.509] CCITT Recommendation X.509 (1988), *The Directory - Authentication Framework.*

Education and Society / R. Aiken (Editor)
Information Processing 92, Volume II
Elsevier Science Publishers B.V. (North-Holland)


# Perspectives on Home-Oriented Informatics and Telematics

Felix van RIJN[a], Kresten BJERG[b] and Gisela FRERK[c]

[a] Vakgroep Communicatiewetenschap, Universiteit van Amsterdam, Oude Hoogstraat 24, 1012 CE Amsterdam, The Netherlands

[b] Psykologisk Laboratorium, Københavns Universitet Amager, Njalsgade 88, 2300 København S., Denmark

[c] Gesellschaft für Mathematik und Datenverarbeitung mbH, Postfach 1316, D 5205 Sankt Augustin 1, Germany

**Abstract**

This paper is written on behalf of IFIP's Working Group 9.3 on Home-Oriented Informatics and Telematics (HOIT). After a short introduction of the subject we give an outline of the scope of HOIT referring to the main constituents of HOIT: home automation, home information systems and home telematics. Reflections on historical, economic and social perspectives on HOIT converge to vulnerability aspects of HOIT and the conclusion that benevolent developments of HOIT are dependent on the proper choices to be made by the involved parties.

Keyword Codes: K.4.2; K.4.m; K.8.0
Keywords: Computers and Society, Social Issues; Miscellaneous (home information systems, home telematics, economic aspects); Personal computing, General

## 1. INTRODUCTION

In today's homes people live who sleep, eat, work, relax, study, have fun, attempt anything and communicate with people outside. Or they go out for study, work, shop, have fun, eat and to do many other activities or just to meet people. These activities are integrated in life-styles and have to do with everyday functioning, information processing and communication.
Looking at the future 'electronic habitat' we can imagine a highly automated house or flat, equipped with electronic information systems and with all means for communicating with the outside world. (We prefer the concept of *electronic habitat* rather than 'electronic cottage' as a more universal indication for all kinds of places people live in.) Very probably, people living in the electronic habitat will sleep, eat, work, relax, study, have fun, attempt anything and communicate with people outside. Or they go out to study, work, shop, have fun, eat and to do many other activities or just to meet people.

Indeed, the generic nature of human activities will not change as it has not changed since the prehistory of mankind. However, several of these activities have changed drastically with regards to appearance, context, place and time with tremendous consequences for individuals' everyday lives, for societies and for cultures. In this, 'new technologies' have always played a significant role, like the wheel, the art of printing, electricity, steam engine, telephone, phonograph, radio, television, videorecorder and so on. Sooner or later all these technologies will have had their impacts on everyday and domestic life.
Today we are facing the increasing invasion of information technology into the home like automation of domestic functions, home computers and telematics services. The braid of home automation, home information systems and home telematics is called *Home-Oriented Informatics and Telematics (HOIT)*, which deals with features of the emerging electronic habitat. We may expect that HOIT will affect people's everyday lives as other technologies did earlier. Also their adaption may change social structures and cause shifts in culture.
In order to assess the effects of HOIT on daily life and households we have to sketch the scope of HOIT and to consider HOIT in various perspectives.

## 2. The scope of Home-Oriented Informatics and Telematics (HOIT)

### 2.1. The emerging electronic habitat in its environment.

When will the common home have been transformed into an electronic habitat and what will it look like? Most existing prototypes of the 'house of the future', the 'smart house', the 'intelligent home' or whatever they are called basically look very much like traditional houses, although there are significant exceptions. Many of the demonstrated electronic equipment can be installed in existing houses rather easily. As a matter of fact the turning of common houses into electronic habitats will take place gradually and has indeed already started.
Already today we find many examples of *automation of domestic functions and activities*. People are getting used to *process information* which has been stored on electronic media. No longer is the telephone only used for personal voice-to-voice *communication*, but also for datacommunications and a scala of new applications of *home telematics*.

Until recently home automation, information processing at home and communication between the home and the outside world were rather distinct areas. This distinction is fading rapidly. Let us illustrate this by giving a simple example.
From the home computer connected to an electronic network one can make reservations and payments for theatre tickets. After (electronic) confirmation of the reservation for the theatre, the personal calendar and the budget scheme in the home computer can be updated. In addition information about date and time of the performance automatically could be fed to the heating control system for the purpose of energy saving during the visit to the theatre.
The integration of home automation, information processing at home and communication with the outside world will be one main feature of the electronic habitat. Another important feature will be that less and less 'home' will be confined to domestic activities and the physical house. In the electronic habitat many non-domestic activities can be executed electronically from the home, like banking, shopping, learning, consulting, working, etcetera. One can 'get the whole world at home'. The ultimate consequence could be that on the one hand people do not leave their homes

and communicate with the outside world via electronic networks only. On the other hand it offers opportunities to diminish the social isolation of less mobile, home bound people.
Home telematics also offer opportunities for performing home activities from anywhere outside the house. Domestic activities will not necessarily be restricted to the physical house. From a distance the house can be 'tele'-monitored and -controlled, from a distance lights, heater, microwave oven can be switched off and on, people do not have to be at home to receive and answer phonecalls and they may, from far, pick up text, images, video and sound documentations from their very private domestic multimedia-database-bureau. With the advent of laptops and mobile communication, while permitting a more extended and prolonged nomadism, the domestic nucleus may paradoxically be increasingly reflected along our extradomestic trail.

## 2.2. Home automation

Today we are used to machines in the household like clocks, washing and drying machines, vacuum cleaners, refrigerators, central heaters and many others. The nature of these devices has been changing steadily from (electro)mechanical automata into computer controlled equipment. Some apparatus would not even have existed without computer technology like microwave ovens and CD players. Many of these devices are equipped with integrated, dedicated microprocessors and if we make an inventory of all computer controlled equipment in the home, the ubiquity of 'hidden' information technology in daily life may come as a surprise.
With the introduction of the general-purpose personal computer in the home a device became available which can be programmed by the users not only to automate various functions in the house but also to combine functions. As an example, for the purpose of climate control and energy savings, information from temperature sensoring devices can be used to open or to close curtains and windows automatically and to control the heating in different parts of the house. Of course this implies a communication channel in the house. Today some devices in the house are already interconnected, for example the temperature controller which is connected to the central heater by twisted pair cables. X10 is an existing standard for remote control of devices via the electric network in the house. It is expected that a digital home area network - home bus - will be developed to which electronic equipment can be connected at any place in the house. This home bus should finally replace the different cables in the house. Some see the future electronic habitat or 'smart house' controlled via this home bus by a central computersystem like the 'House Brain' in the Xanadu house (Mason, 1988). This concept would lead to an increased vulnerability of the everyday life environment. If the central system breaks down all controlled functions will be paralysed.
The more desirable - and likely - scenario for the future home is distributed intelligence in dedicated appliances which communicate together, with the outside world and with the users. Failure of one device may have consequences for the functioning of some other but not for all. The home bus could even get totally out of order without preventing all appliances to work properly.

## 2.3. Home information systems

To orient ourselves adequately relative to home information systems, it is necessary to take a few steps back in order to gain some historical perspective.
Remember the broadest perspective of predominantly oral, face-to-face culture. Then think of the long historical transitions from belonging to tight congregations,

attending interpretation of authoritative text from the pulpit, into becoming, as we, actors and participants in a growing textreading and handwriting literate public with its 'Gutenberg galaxy': the massive output of newspaper-, journal- and book-mass-markets. Add the parallel transformations of our lives brought about by the telephone and the advent of 'radio days'. Then think of how we have domesticated a whole lot of older and newer tools and tokens of literacy: paper, pens and pencils, the ball-point pen, rulers and scissors, glue, clips and stapling machines, folders, drawers, book-shelves and even typewriters. And do not forget the sedimentation of cameras and photos, of phonographs and records.
Our world was already divided in *text, picture and sound*, when TV days arose, with their audiotapes, videotapes and now even compact discs, with their portable video-cameras and home-computers. An avalanche of increasingly complex and multipurpose apparatus is now piling up in our homes, as is also generation upon generation of storage media.
In the midst we see persons and families in love and care, often overloaded by attractive and imperative information in all these media, and often overwhelmed by demands and obligatory commitments to a workplace and a multitude of extra-familial relationships. To gain a valid perspective on the further steps of transition we will have to detail the multitude of input, output and storage media and software.

INPUT MEDIA
We have been using input media from generations of typewriters to keyboards on computers. From pens, pencils and easels to joy-sticks, mice , track-balls, electronic drawing pads and datagloves. From pianos to electronic music-keyboards. Micro-phones, soon wireless, not only to audiotape, but also to sound-digitalizing, - *and voice and word-recognition!* Wireless telephones, portable videocameras, and TV and video-picture frame-grabbing for digitalizing. Optical scanning devices (as in telefax-machines, and hand-scanners and flatbed-scanners), - *and Optical Character Recognition.* Add to these: sensors for monitoring of indoors and outdoors climate and sensors for monitoring body states.

OUTPUT MEDIA
The process of transition of output media, which started with gramophones and radios, telephones and typewriters and suddenly swelled into black-and-white TV, then into colour TV, is going to continue, as old and new generations of audio visual display equipment are spreading in the homes across the continents: various types of liquid crystals displays. screens (e.g. calculators and notebook-computers) and smaller and larger computer-screens, increasingly with colour and sound. Further: matrix printers, ink-jet and laser printers and telefax-machines.
With computers sound, images and text, which have been inputted by different media can be transformed into - and mixed with - each other, and can be outputted via diverse media.

STORAGE MEDIA
Spread in millions of homes are today:
- several standards and generations of homemovie and video formats
- several standards and generations of media for living sound and speech
- several standards and generations of computer-storage medias for text, numbers, and graphics (and remember, that they almost all fit into only one kind of machine).

We are talking of varieties of actual informative objects piling up, and - for the oldest - travelling away from their potential decoding or use, because they, unlike the book or the painting, take working electronic equipment to access or - for the last category - even to identify. Old machines are ever becoming obsolete and rare, and the knowledge of their operative systems is even becoming hard to retrieve. To restore a sense of continuity we must give the utmost consideration to the transition-problems, instead of blindly heading towards the Ultimate Intelligent Home of our nightmares. The imminent merging of storage technologies for text, sound and images may open new horizons for home information systems and put users in control of information at an entirely new level.

SOFTWARE

At present the main use of home information systems is for fun, leisure, household management and personal interest. For this a multitude of programmes and packages are available as commercial products, as so-called share-ware or as public domain software. Much of this software is an advance to business software with regard to animation and sound processing.

We may envisage home information systems which are capable of recognizing hand written text and voice, which have the capacity for speech-synthesis and which will be able to read aloud to us any text from any input medium in its original language, or in translation. Creating 3-dimensional animated screen dolls and letting them move and speak in a simulated 3-dimensional living space is no more just futuristic science fiction. Already gloves and helmets are sold as play tools for moving around in a 'virtual' world. Finally we will be able to create in our homes a 'realistic' simulation of any real or imaginary environment.

## 2.4. Home telematics

People have always been intrigued with conquering time and distance. Home automation as such mainly deals with time. Telematics is the new vehicle to bridge time *and* distance.

Telephone, radio and television in their first appearances can be considered to be ancestors of home telematics. With the progressing digitalizing and use of information technology they have become useful to transport not only sounds and pictures but other information too. They form the backbone of home telematics, which from a technical point of view can transport virtually all information of any kind faster and more reliable than any other means of transportation. But, independent of what is feasible technically, important questions concerning home telematics are of what information will be communicated, why and by whom?

In accordance to their functionality diverse types of so-called new services can be distinguished.

- *Information services* for consulting directories, catalogues, timetables, agenda's for events, product information files, governmental information files, etcetera.
- *Transaction services* for electronic shopping, banking, paying fines, acquiring personal documents from the government.
- *Conversation services* for electronic communication, interactive distance education, interactive consulting of a physician or a fortune-teller, collaborative decision-making processes.
- *Registration services* for theatre reservations, subscriptions to periodicals, applying for membership of an organisation, give notice of address changes, registration to the public authorities.
- *Monitoring and control services* like alarm and security systems, remote control of devices, safety systems for elderly people.

- *Facilities services* to support the use of remote resources - like using from home the computer and/or printer in the office - and to support new organisational structures: teleconferencing, telecommuting, teleworking, etcetera.

It will be clear that new services often will have a combined functionality as in the example of simultaneously electronic reservation and payment of theatre tickets.

Relating to vulnerability it is important who takes the initiative for communication and who controls the information stream.
If the communication is *initiated from the home* by the user then he takes the initiative for communication, decides what service to use and mainly controls what information he will receive. However he cannot be sure that the wanted information will not be accompanied with unwanted information e.g. advertisements.

If the communication is *initiated from outside the home* in general the addressee can decide to respond to it or not. In the case of non-individual, one-way communication (broadcasting) the response is receptive only. One can decide to turn on the radio or TV and to tune into the desired channel. The receiver has no influence on the contents and he has to take unwanted information, like advertisements, for granted.
In the case of an incoming phone call or fax, a delivered letter or electronic mail message the recipient, after he has decided to answer the phone or to read the message, can decide how to continue or discontinue the communication. This gives at least some control over the information stream, but does not prevent the reception of unsolicited messages and of 'junk' mail (by letter, fax or electronic) and calls.

Other applications for communication initiated from outside the home are *monitoring and control services*. All automated functions in the home can be accessed from anywhere if the devices are connected to external communications networks. From a distance people can interrupt and change programs of devices at home or ad hoc switch functions on or off. Examples of applications are the remote controlled answer machines, security and alarm systems, safety systems for elderly people.
However, communication to the home is not necessarily controlled by the occupants of the house. As is the case with tele-metering of the use of energy supplies, which is accomplished by the companies.
Setting up systems at home for responding to incoming communications initiatives, makes the home vulnerable to risks of unwanted and malevolent electronic intrusion.

## 2.5. Context and contiguity

HOIT has to fit in the existing contexts of personal lifestyle, domestic and family life, inter-domestic relations and social life. This means that people should experience that and experience how the use of HOIT applications can assist them in everyday activities at those different levels. Or that they recognise that it enables them to perform activities in another way resulting in time or money savings or in more convenience or fun.
On the other hand HOIT can establish new contexts for daily life activities. HOIT can offer new opportunities to set up very personalised, integrated databases, diaries, climate control and home automation systems. It gives opportunities for enlarging people's individual lifespaces, to create new forms of domestic coexistence, to add a new dimension to the existing structures between families, friends and social groups for mutual support and help, for sharing and recycling of cultural resources.
These contextual concepts of HOIT imply that home information systems and telematics have to be contiguous to the mental, social and cultural reality of people and

to other artefacts which have found their place in this reality. However in very few households the computer computer has a significant role in the domestic setting as it is disconnected from any wider communicating or informing network which would provide it with another function than a games machine (Silverstone, 1991). Unless the computer will be domesticated, information technology may become an alien phenomenon and even a threat to the personal and domestic level. Therefore, working with a computer as *a component of* a home information system or using a telematics service has to be in keeping with other forms of information processing and service using and with the other media and equipment used at home. The consequence is the merging of different media (speech, written text, drawings and paintings, sound, (moving) pictures) into interactive multi-media creating an integrated 'information environment' (Vitalari, 1990). Tying together existing cultures for expressing, superposing a meta-level for information storage and processing and for communication, integrating the means for relocating thematic contents of engaged, responsible personal life (Bjerg, 1992). Keeping in mind that the main feature of the electronic habitat will be its continued persistence and value as a home for people who perform human activities and that HOIT has been considered to be no more than a means to serve people's needs and actings.

## 3. PERSPECTIVES ON HOIT

### 3.1. HOIT in historical perspective

We have already discussed that HOIT must be considered in a long history of continuous transitions. In this perspective the own history of new technologies in the households is very short. These days common conveniences like electric lights, washing machines, food processors, thermostatic controlled central heating, telephone, radio and television, audio equipment, and other technologies for home automation, home information and home telematics 'avant la lettre' only entered the home in this century. The history of HOIT is even shorter.

The introduction of information technology in the home started less than twenty years ago. The first computers for home use (i.e. games) came on the market in the late seventies. About the same time a new mass communications medium, viewdata (videotex), was introduced (Fedida & Malik, 1979). It is seen as the first public system for a broad range of services based upon telematics, the integration of information technology and telecommunications networks. In 1981 the ambitious 'Plan Télématique' for a large scale introduction of videotex was launched in France. Other countries started in the early eighties with public videotex experiments at a more modest scale, but with optimistic speculations about wide acceptance and use by the public.

These assessments may have been sustained by the euphoric visions on the 'electronic cottage', the electronic marketplace and the real global village which came to life around 1980 (a.o. Martin, 1978, Toffler, 1980; Williams, 1982).

Others were less optimistic and warned for a potential demise of the freedom of information and the growing gap between the information rich and the information poor (Wicklein, 1981; Moscow, 1982).

In fact the penetration of computers in the home and the development and acceptance of home telematics services occurred at a much lower rate and smaller scale than predicted. The total number of installed Minitel terminals in France by the end of 1989 was about 5 million, while the original target was 30 million.

In 1988 the number of subscribers to videotex in the USA was only 1 million and no more than 21% of all US households was estimated to have a home computer early 1990 (De Sonne, 1990). It seems reasonable to assume that this number will not be significantly higher in other countries.

It can be concluded that the majority of private homes is still far away from being converted into an electronic habitat. This should not really be surprising only about one decade after the introduction of home information systems and home telematics, if we realise that the 'incubation' time for the telephone to become a basic feature in private houses was over fifty years. On the other hand information technology has already penetrated everyday life on a wide scale, concealed in 'ordinary' household equipment as we have pointed out before.

### 3.2. HOIT in economic perspective

The relevance of HOIT from a economic perspective starts at the 'working place' of private household production. This approach involves a shift in emphasis as regards the economic function of private households. According to private household work the significance of private households for economic development is not confined to its role as a demand agency for consumer goods and to its significance as a supplier of 'wage labour' for business but also involves the labour input in the private household production. In terms of the New Home Economics (Becker, 1975; Schulz, 1974), private households are regarded as a decision-making unit by allocating time and market goods between consumption and private household production. According to Becker, the private household production is defined as the production of 'more basic' commodities - such as seeing a play or having a meal - and whose inputs are market goods and time. In the theory of the more advanced New Home Economics, market goods are just one input factor in private household production. Another important factor of home-production is 'unpaid labour'. Households are assumed to combine both unpaid labour (measured in terms of time) and market goods (i.e. domestic capital equipment) to produce instead of buying commodities that enter their utility function. Similar to the rationalisation effects of the use information technology in business and enterprises, we can expect effects in private households as well as at a macro-economic level, as is discussed hereafter.

#### Household production costs

We can assume that the new forms of use of information technologies in private households affect the organisation and content of domestic work and yield a variety of saving effects. Technical progress in the form of new information technologies adds up to a major rationalisation potential in private household production. This is because information technologies are likely to change both unpaid labour input plus the share of domestic capital equipment needed (Seel, 1988). In this respect, transaction costs which cover primarily the costs of inconvenient travel, waiting and transportation times, as well as time spent for searching and gathering information, can be reduced. In this context the use of information technology can change the production and transactions costs of private households.

#### Costs of information processing and decision-making

If we consider household management as a decision-making process, information is derived, processed and passed on. However, since the procurement and processing of information may involve considerable cost and time inputs, there is a trend toward minimizing such informational costs (Szyperski, 1980). New information technologies offer options for accessing a virtually unlimited amount of information from ones own living room without any restrictions to time of day or location. The resulting better market transparency (comparison of vendors and prices) can improve decision-making processes and will lead to increases on household production level (Presvelou, 1986).

### Allocation of time

Because the family time budget is restricted to 24 hours per day, households want to optimize allocation of time to paid work, housework and leisure activities. Thanks to the use of new information technologies, many tasks can be performed inside the home that used to be performed outside, enabling the household to dispose of inconvenient travel, waiting and transportation time (Miles, 1988). A better information access will shorten lengthy searching and information-gathering time.
Starting from the assumption that the use of information technologies in private households save time for unpaid housework these time units saved can be used either for additional wage-labour, or more unpaid housework or 'do-it-yourself', or for more leisure activities.

### Flexibility and lifestyle

We may propose that resulting from the use of information technologies in private households, a qualitative and quantitative structural change of private household production can be forecasted (Frerk, 1990). New information technologies are aimed at a greater self-determination about time and location (Biervert & Monse, 1992). Therefore, they offer new opportunities for new ways of private household production. Relaxation of time restrictions enables broader time flexibility and time budget management. The normal working hours of those engaged in 'wage-labour' are used to being adjusted to business and consulting hours of big service operators. Due to this overlap, people who are in regular employment are able to go shopping or banking or visit public authorities only within their own effective working hours. New information technologies help to bridge space and time. Private households can create additional leeway in free time and relocate activities that were previously tied to specific opening and consulting hours.

### Effects on the labour market

If we regard the private household as the final link in a production chain, the use of new information technologies in private households is likely to have an impact on previous production stages (Gershuny, 1985). If we follow the so-called machine production argument (, a positive impact on employment is likely to be triggered by the family's demand for information technologies investment goods (i.e. hardware, software, networks that have to be produced in the business sector). Also the expansion of time for leisure activities could increase the demand for leisure-goods having a positive impact on employment. These gains in employment, however, must be compared to losses in employment if the new investment goods in demand merely replace products formerly traded on the market.
The preferences of the members of the family to allocate time savings by the use of information technologies to wage-labour, leisure or household activities have consequences for the labour supply function of private households. If private households take over certain activities formerly carried out on official labour markets (insourcing) or will integrate certain activities from the business sector into home production, this probably will have lay-off effects. Replacing of paid work by unpaid work and substituting 'own-production' for purchases can be expected to have a negative impact on employment in the tertiary sector, especially in banking, insurance and the retail trade. For example, electronic banking and shopping may become a serious substitute

for some activities performed by counter and sale staff (Dostal, 1986). Furthermore, the process of 'learning by doing' will lead to a growth in the human capital of private households. The productivity of private household production increases, and unpaid house work will be more efficient and effective (Krüsselberg, 1986). This means a greater incentive to increase household work based upon the use of information technology.
In general it is likely that the use of HOIT will change the division of labour between market, public and private sectors.

OTHER EFFECTS ON THE MACRO-ECONOMIC LEVEL
The constraints on the length of the article inhibits us to discuss in details other effects on the macro-economic level (Zameck, 1988). Therefore we will restrict ourselves to mention some major macro-economic aspects of household economies
- value added to gross national product by household production
- fiscal interest for informal labour and household production
- allocation of formal/informal labour/economic activities
- possible beneficial impacts on environment.

### 3.3. HOIT in social perspective
Social aspects on a *global level* include unequal access to information and services for large populations with potential consequences for political and economic power relations (Moscow, 1982). This unequality is being reinforced by the basic infrastructure of hard-wired, two-way communication networks on which telematics services are developed, although one of the oldest datacommunication networks (ALOHANET) was based upon communication by radio. Therefore in the near future home telematics will probably be of marginal importance in developing countries and thin populated rural regions where no telecommunication infrastructure exists.
It must be emphasised that discussions on social implications of home-oriented informatics and telematics seem of relevance to the industrialised part of the world, as long as home automation, home computers and teleservices are luxuries which go far beyond the essential needs of everyday life in developing countries.
The potential impact of home telematics at *national and international level* was recognised in the French telematics programme which was intended to stimulate telematics for political and macro-economic reasons, namely to resolve the French crisis in economic stability, social consensus and national independence (Nora & Minc, 1980). In practice however it has been reduced to a technology and economics programme.

At the *level of private households* it is observed that in 'traditional' households patterns of buying automatic household equipment are related to the household labour division between women and men. If a man is going to be more active with household activities the purchase of automatic apparatus is stimulated. Or after a machine has been acquired for a certain task the man is inclined to take over that task, at least partly. What he does not take over is the imbedding of such, now 'automated', household tasks in the total organisation of housekeeping. For this reason domestic electronic equipment sometimes is characterised as 'toys for boys'. It seems that this attitude is reflected in existing prototypes of 'homes of the future' - mainly designed by males - where the focus is upon automation of domestic functions like temperature and environment control, energy savings and security. Very little attention is paid to basic household work like cleaning and washing (Berg, 1991).
While the use of new technologies - like information technology - in the home can

lead to time savings for specific activities and for the household as a total, it does not mean that it will necessarily reduce the total time spent for all kinds of household activities. Studies show that over more than half a century the time spent for housekeeping and household management was not reduced in spite of the increasing numbers of machines in the houses (Hagelskjær, 1988). The increased flexibility of lifestyles, made possible by new technologies, often increases also the demands for more flexibility and more variety of 'basic' household tasks like cleaning, washing cooking. Even if this does not lead to an increase of physical household tasks, someone has to organise it, to care for time schedules and to operate the machines.
Home automation should go beyond mere automation of domestic functions. It should take into account the connection between these functions and the organisational structure of housekeeping. This is an imperative for future 'smart houses' to make people feel at home in it.

At the *personal level* HOIT affects personal lives of people living alone or together, relations between people and the functioning of people in society. Home telematics allows people to perform activities from home which before required people to leave the home thus saving time for travelling, waiting and transportation. The reverse side of the coin is that communications between or with computers differs substantially from communication between human beings.
For many people going out to a shop or a bank and face-to-face communication with the people there is an essential part of daily life. If this would be replaced by *electronic transactions* it could increase their social isolation. On the other hand people who cannot easily leave their homes could find new opportunities to communicate with the outside world. But, as they would become more self supporting, others (family, welfare workers) could conclude to reduce their visits.
*Telelearning* could be a solution for people who cannot go to schools at regular hours. But education is more than learning facts and skills. It is a social process which includes communications between the students and the teachers and between the students mutually. To what extent can this be replaced by electronic communication?
Experiments with *telework* have shown that for most people regular physical contact with colleagues is an important element of their working situations. In this context advertisement of telework at home as an 'opportunity' for people who have to take care of children at home is rather ironic.

Dehumanisation of communications and impoverishment of social contacts may be a serious risk of wide-scale use of home telematics (Mettler-Meibom, 1988). Home telematics may also have consequences for the privacy of people. Technically it is rather simple to trace and record what services people are using and when. It makes it possible to build profiles of individuals' and whole families' private lives.

## 4. VULNERABLE PEOPLE LIVING IN THE ELECTRONIC HABITAT

Undoubted HOIT can be a menace to people who will have to live in the electronic habitat. We have to admit that man is about the most vulnerable mammalian species with its dependency on artefacts to survive. The more complex these artefacts - i.e. technologies - are, the more they are susceptible to failures and unexpected functioning. The increasing vulnerability of systems increases the vulnerability of people relying on it. A simple disruption of the electric power supply could paralyse the electronic habitat and its automated functions. The home information system would

become inaccessible and the electronic communication channels with the outside world would be cut off.
But a well-functioning HOIT can also increase the vulnerability of people being overloaded with information, non-information, persuasive marketing, to unwanted and even malicious electronic intrusion into the home, to social unequality and social isolation, to reduced diversity of products and services and market monopolism, etcetera (see f.e. Ölander, 1988).
The access to and use of HOIT is only partly a matter of economics: costs versus savings. It depends also on education, abilities and cultural background. This brings serious risks to an increasing gap between haves and have-nots, between the information-rich and the information-poor, between cultural majorities and minorities. The electronic habitats might become new, elitist ghettos for people who can financially afford to live in it and who are qualified to use the technology and the new services. The other perspective is that HOIT can contribute to make the home more comfortable to live in and to free people from burdening and boring tasks. It can help to save time and money and to increase the mobility of people in time and distance. It can reinforce the independency of individuals and families, open new horizons to communications between people and support social networking. It can be a tool to improve the social positions of vulnerable individuals and groups.

## 5. CONCLUSION: A MATTER OF CHOICES

We should not let HOIT befall and wait and see how it will contribute to whether a decrease or an increase of vulnerability of people, groups and society.
Until now choices for development of HOIT technologies, products and applications have been made by industry, information suppliers and service organisations. Also choices are made by government and public authorities who decide about stimulating measures for experiments and introduction of new services. It may be doubted if these choices are always made for the benefit of the intended users.
The development of HOIT mainly occurs from a techno-economic perspective and applications of HOIT are developed to offer solutions for non-existing or luxury problems. Socially benevolent applications are disregarded if there is no prospect of financial revenues in the short term. Basic principles of genuine user-friendliness are neglected. The lack of standardisation and compatibility with regard to interfaces and storage media looks like an attempt to erect a new, electronic tower of Babel.

The public, in particular consumer organisations and pressure groups, should exert more influence on the other parties to make better choices in research and development and in implementation and stimulation strategies. Choices for a consumer-oriented policy, for a more humane design of applications of HOIT, for consulting users about their wants and needs, for social design of HOIT, for a bit more accountability for benevolent Home-Oriented Informatics and Telematics (van Rijn, 1991). Finally, people who will live in the electronic habitat must always retain the choice if, how and to what extent they will utilize HOIT besides and complementary to other media and artefacts.

## References


Becker, Gary S.: A Theory of the Allocation of Time, Economic Journal, Vol. 75, No. 229, 1965, pp. 493-517.

Berg, Anne Jorun: Gender and the smart house. Paper presented at the GRANITE seminar 'New information technologies and the changing nature of domestic', Amsterdam, 1991.

Biervert, Bernd & Kurt Monse: The Creation of Information Technology Applications in the Service Sector. In: M. Dierkes & U. Hoffmann (eds.): New Technology at the Outset. Social Forces in the Shaping of Technological Innovations. Boulder, Colorado, 1992.

Bjerg, Kresten: Hjemmets informationsdynamik, University of Copenhagen, 1992. (Home information dynamics)

De Sonne, M.L.: Spectrum of new broadcast/media technologies, National Association of Broadcasters, Washington, 1990.

Dostal, Werner: Telearbeit - eine neue Arbeitsform, IBM Nachrichten, Vol. 36, No. 284, 1986, pp. 7-13.

Fedida, S. & R. Malik: The viewdata revolution, Associated Business Press, London, 1979.

Frerk, Gisela: Economic effects of the use of new information technologies in private households, International Journal of Information and Library Research, Vol. 2, No. 1, 1990, pp. 11-21.

Gershuny, J.I.: Economic Development and Change in the Mode of Provision of Services, In: Beyond Employment, 1985.

Hagelskjær, Elin: Bringing modern times into households. In: Felix van Rijn & Robin Williams (eds), Concerning home telematics, North-Holland, Amsterdam, 1988.

Krüsselberg, Hans-Günter et al.: Verhaltenhypothesen und Familienzeitbudgets - Die Anhaltspunkte der "Neuen Haushaltsökonomik" für Familienpolitik (Schriftenreihe des Bundesministeers für Jugend, Familie und Gesundheit, Bd. 182), Stuttgart, 1986, p. 36.

Martin, J.: The wired society, Prentice Hall, Englewood Cliffs, 1978.

Mason, Roy: Living in tomorrow's electronic home today. In: Felix van Rijn & Robin Williams (eds), Concerning home telematics, North-Holland, Amsterdam, 1988.

Miles, Ian: Home Informatics, Information Technology and the Transformation of Everyday Life, Pinter, London, 1988.

Mettler-Meibom, Barbara: Communication at stake? In: Felix van Rijn & Robin Williams (eds), Concerning home telematics, North-Holland, Amsterdam, 1988.

Moscow, V.: Pushbuttons fantasies, Ablex, Norwood, 1982.

Nora, S. & A. Minc: The Computerization of Society, MIT Press, Cambridge, 1980. (Originally published as L'Informatisation de la Societé. La Documentation Française, Paris.)

Ölander, F.: The impact of the new electronic media on the consumer situation. In: Felix van Rijn & Robin Williams (eds), Concerning home telematics, North-Holland, Amsterdam, 1988.

Presvelou, C.: Households, the home computer and related services in the Netherlands: Attitudes, trends and prospects, FAST (Forecasting and assessment in science and technology), Occasional Paper, No. 94, Brussels, 1986.

van Rijn, Felix: Interactive telematics comes home: a long way. In: J. Berleur & J. Drumm, Information Technology Assessment, North-Holland, Amsterdam, 1991.

Schultz, Theodore W. (ed): Economics of the family, Chicago/London, 1974.

Seel, Barbara: Hausarbeit und Wertschöpfung, Jahrbuch für Nationalökonomie und Statistik, Vol. 205, No. 2, Stuttgart, 1988, pp. 97-115.

Silverstone, Roger: Beneath the Bottom Line: Households and Information and Communication Technologies in an Age of the Consumer: PICT Policy Research Papers, No. 17, London 1991.

Szyperski, Norbert: Computergestützte Informationssysteme. In: Erwin Grochla (ed), Handwörterbuch der Organisation, 2nd edition, Stuttgart, 1980, pp. 920-933.

Toffler, A.: The third wave, William Morrow, New York, 1980.

Vitalari, N.P.: Information technology in daily life. In: J. Berleur et al., The information society: evolving landscapes, Springer Verlag, New York/Heidelberg & Captus Press Inc., North York, 1990.

Wicklein, J.: Electronic nightmare, Viking, New York, 1981.

Williams, F.: The communications revolution, Sage, London, 1982.

Zameck, Walburga von: Im Schatten der Schattenökonomie: Die Hausarbeit, Jahrbücher für Nationalökonomie und Statistik, Vol. 205, No. 4, 1988, pp. 289-300.

Education and Society / R. Aiken (Editor)
Information Processing 92, Volume II
Elsevier Science Publishers B.V. (North-Holland)


# Vulnerability in the Electronic Cottage - Electronic Data Interchange and the Electronic Cottage

A Sloane

School of Computing and Information Technology, University of Wolverhampton, Wulfruna St, WOLVERHAMPTON, England, WV1 1SB
Fax (+44) 902 322680, Email cm1950@uk.ac.wolves.a

Keyword Codes: H.4.3; K.8.0
Keywords: Information Systems Applications, Communications Applications; Personal Computing, General

**Abstract**
The use of electronic data interchange (EDI) using structured messages has long been a tool of business and commerce. The extension of these EDI services to the home is investigated, along with the expansion of services to include some that are more relevant to the individual user. The corresponding use of other data types is also included to give added functionality to message types and provide new structures for further applications.

## 1. Electronic Data Interchange (EDI)
EDI can be defined as 'The transmission of information between computer applications, using structured messages, without human intervention.' In other words it involves the automatic transfer of information from one computer to another. The applications that currently use EDI are all associated with the business world; mainly invoices and orders that can be exchanged automatically between suppliers and customers.

## 2. The electronic cottage
The extension of EDI systems to the level of the home requires a change in the applicability of the messages that are used in EDI. There needs to be new message types and forms for use in the home that differ from the commercial messages in a number of ways. The EDIFACT standard allows the combination of messages into functional groups that allow the inclusion of many messages. This is unlikely to be a required feature in the use of EDI in the home. The main requirement for home systems will be the individual message to one supplier or service provider.

## 3. Application areas
Home Information systems, Home Banking, Home shopping, Administration of personal documents and database records.

## 4. Future extensions
New message content types to include more complex data such as pictures and graphics. New structures to incorporate database query techniques.

## 5. Conclusion
The concept of EDI is simple, but to extend it beyond the office or business into the home will provide the electronic cottage of the future with a system of transaction messages which will provide simpler, more secure and more accurate information transfer in an environment that is diverse and unstructured, i.e the home.

Education and Society / R. Aiken (Editor)
Information Processing 92, Volume II
Elsevier Science Publishers B.V. (North-Holland)



# Reducing the vulnerability of women in an information society: Enlarging information systems perspectives

Andrew Clement

Faculty of Library and Information Science, University of Toronto,
140 St. George Street, Toronto, Canada M5S 1A1, clement@flis.utoronto.ca

The vulnerability of women in an information society derives not only from their historically disadvantaged position in the occupational hierarchy, but also from fundamental misunderstandings about the nature of information systems and how they should be developed. Women make up a very large proportion of those whose working days are spent tied to computers rapidly performing routinized, low status, service tasks. At the same time, women are seriously under-represented among those who design these computer systems and manage their development. It is not just the individual workers who suffer from this disparity, but the values widely recognized as characteristically 'female' - attention to interpersonal relationships and caring over the details of service to others.

There are three principal approaches to redressing this gross imbalance. The most obvious of these are attempts to encourage women to enter conventionally male-dominated, higher level technical and managerial occupations. A second approach is to expand systems development processes to include the active participation of users, and indirectly, more women. To achieve this fully also requires that the fundamental nature of information systems development (ISD) be made much more compatible with female modes of understanding the world and acting within it.

The dominant ISD methods are based on a scientific model that celebrates rationalized formal descriptions of phenomena. Standard methods for analysis focus on the creation of abstract data models in which crucial features of the physical and social world are deliberately removed or simply not recognized. Techniques amenable to rigorous mathematical treatment enjoy the highest status from this perspective. Learning such techniques requires specialized training and fosters an elite corps of experts with its own exclusionary language and culture.

However, despite the authoritative status of this ruling paradigm, it is increasingly recognized that it alone is not adequate for producing practical, usable computer systems. Often it proves to be tacit skills of working with others and situated "tinkering" processes lying outside the system-centred world view that are vital to the successful application of computer technology. These are precisely the forms of knowledge and ways of working that women especially can bring to system development. A major challenge for information systems researchers and practitioners now is to break the dominant grip of rationalism and enlarge our understanding of information systems to see the human and social aspects as central. In this way all may benefit from including women and women's values in an increasingly computerized world.

Education and Society / R. Aiken (Editor)
Information Processing 92, Volume II
Elsevier Science Publishers B.V. (North-Holland)


# Vulnerability and gender issues in Information Systems Design seen in a Euro-business perspective.

by Siv Friis
Dept. of Information and Computer Science, Lund University, Lund, Sweden.
e-mail: siv.friis@ibadb.lu.se

This statement is based on a talk I had with Joan Greenbaum, New York University, on gender and/or class issues in information systems design, and on the risks and vulnerability of white collar workers due to the design. The discussion developed very much the way it is written below.

Most workplaces are managed with the aid of organizational information systems. Today some of these are automated by means of information technology. The technical tools of information technology are computers. In information systems design research we quickly discovered that information technology tend to preserve the current hierarchical work organization.

Many studies on gender issues and information technology focus on the way women loose jobs and/or skills with the introduction of information technology. This tends to confuse the class and gender issue and end up in the downward spiral of saying that we can't do anything about technology. Scandinavian systems literature on the other hand tries to point to ways that design projects can be developed so that more groups can be empowered (cf. Greenbaum 1991, Friis 1991). Sometimes the literature tends to assume that the right systems approach can result in a system that enhances work (cf. Mumford 1983).

Both schools of research need to be seen within the context of what feminism sees as both class and gender. It is certainly a fact that many organizations, particularly large multinationals use class, and race and gender and technology to divide a work force. Within this framework, particularly as it applies to bureaucratic type organizations, technology is usually introduced and redesigned to enforce existing divisions of labor. Thus, there are many circumstances where women begininning on the bottom - either end up there or off the ladder entirely (Friis 1991).

Certainly within the EC, this issue should be a central one as the charter of the EC is for open labor mobility. Given the large number of bureaucratic organizations that currently discrimate against women and use technology to divide workers, this open labor mobility may result in the use of systems that further oppress groups on the bottom.

To effectively talk about Cooperative Design and a Feminist perspective it is necessary to integrate these ideas into an understanding of organizations and the economic reasons surrounding labor mobility. Of course it is possible to talk about and show that participatory design can bring about systems that enhance and empower people in lower levels within organizations (cf. Friis 1991, Mumford Enid 1983).

We need to find a way to put this in both an organizational and human context within the EC discussions. A method to analyze the vulnerability and risks of white collar workers in Europe due to information technology. To find a way to reduce the vulnerability and alleviate the consequences.

REFERENCES:

*Friis Siv*, "USER CONTROLLED INFORMATION SYSTEMS DEVELOPMENT - problems and possibilities towards Local Design Shops", Lund University, Information and Computer Science dept, Lund, Sweden 1991.

*Greenbaum Joan*, in "DESIGN AT WORK", Greenbaum Joan & Kyng Morten eds: Lawrence Erlbaum Ass. Publishers, Hillsdale, New Jersey, 1991.

*Mumford Enid*, "Designing Secretaries", Manchester Business School, Manchester, UK 1983.

Education and Society / R. Aiken (Editor)
Information Processing 92, Volume II
Elsevier Science Publishers B.V. (North-Holland)



# Checksumming Techniques for Anti-Viral Purposes

Y. Radai

Computation Center, Hebrew University of Jerusalem, Jerusalem 91904, Israel

**Abstract**

This paper describes one type of anti-viral technique popularly called **checksumming**. Criteria are presented for choice of a good algorithm. Emphasis is placed on the distinction between two environments, U (inter-machine integrity; transmission of files) and V (intra-machine integrity; the viral problem). The claim that forging is more of a threat when CRC is used than when a cryptographic algorithm is used (which is true in U) is shown to be false in V, provided certain conditions are satisfied.[1]

Keyword Codes: D.4.6
Keywords: Operating Systems, Security and Protection

## 1 INTRODUCTION

A computer virus is a section of code which replicates when the program which contains it is executed. While not part of the definition, it should be noted that a typical virus performs some type of damage after it has had a chance to spread to many computers, but that until this time it tries to be as inconspicuous as possible. Among the various anti-viral techniques, the one which will be discussed here is known by several names, particularly **Integrity Checking**, **Message** or **File Authentication**, and **Modification Detection**. The basic principles behind this technique are as follows:

1. The distinguishing feature of a virus is that it *replicates*.
2. In order to replicate, a virus must attach itself to executable files (or other regions containing executable code).
3. This necessarily causes some modification in the file.
4. Almost all viruses postpone their damaging effects for a long time (typically months) in order to give themselves a chance to propagate as widely as possible without being noticed.
5. Therefore to detect all infections, it suffices to examine all such files, either periodically or just before execution, to determine whether they have been modified. If a file has not been modified, one can be certain that it is not infected (assuming it was not infected to begin with).

The advantages of this technique are that *if it is properly designed and implemented*, (1) it seems capable of detecting *all* viral infections which occur after its installation, even by viruses which have never been encountered before, (2) it cannot be fooled, neutralized, or circumvented by stealth viruses or other hostile software, (3) it is not affected by polymorphism, variable encryption techniques or compression, (4) in principle, the program does not require updating.

[1] A greatly expanded version of this article is available (for those with access to PostScript-reading printers) by writing to the author at e-mail address *radai@vms.huji.ac.il*.

It should be noted that this type of program will indicate mismatches in certain situations which are not due to viruses. In other words, if an alarm is sounded, it means only that a file has been modified, not necessarily that it is infected. The modification could also be due to replacing a program by a new version, modification of configuration (''setup'') information within a file, etc., but the user should be able to identify such situations and exclude them from consideration.

## 2 CHECKSUMMING IN GENERAL

The almost universal way of implementing integrity checking is to compute, for each file $F$, a small fixed-sized value $H(F)$ (typically 2 to 16 bytes in size) such that if any modification is made to $F$ – call it $F'$ – then $H(F')$ will be different from $H(F)$; or to be more precise, the probability that $H(F') = H(F)$ when $F'$ is different from $F$ will be negligibly small. Then modifications can be detected by changes in $H(F)$ instead of in $F$, and it suffices to store only these small original values $H(F)$ (instead of the entire original files $F$) for comparison.

The most common names for the value $H(F)$ and the process of computing it are **checksum** and **checksumming**, resp. Some people, feeling that the word ''sum'' is inappropriate, prefer an alternative term to ''checksum'', such as **hash value**, in which case $H$ is called a **hash** function. In any case, whenever I use the term ''checksum'' it will always be in the *broad* sense described above, unless it is qualified by the adjective ''simple''.

## 3 CRITERIA FOR CHOICE OF ALGORITHM

Three obvious requirements on the algorithm or hash function $H$ are:

1. **The length of the hash values should not be too great, so as not to take up too much disk space.**
2. **For any given file F, computation of H(F) should be fast.**
3. **The probability of two files having the same hash value should be very small.**

Now while a small probability is necessary for preventing *random* cases of two files having the same hash value, it is not sufficient when a forger attempts to mount a *directed attack.* In this case, a more important question is how difficult it is (knowing the checksum algorithm and checksum length) to modify a file deliberately without altering its checksum. But how shall we express this condition in a form similar to the above three conditions?

Anyone familiar with the cryptological literature will immediately suggest the condition that the function $H$ be computationally ''non-invertible'', i.e. for (almost) any given hash value $h$, it must be computationally infeasible to find an $F$ such that $H(F) = h$. However, this condition is insufficient for our purposes since even if it is satisfied, it might still be possible, given a file $F$, to find a different file $F'$ such that $H(F) = H(F')$, and this would constitute a type of forgery which must be guarded against. We therefore formulate our condition as follows:

4. **Even if the hash function H is known, for any given file F it should be computationally infeasible to find another file F' such that H(F') = H(F).**

(Of course, finding an *arbitrary* $F'$ satisfying the above condition is not sufficient to create a *virus*, but we wish to prevent even arbitrary modifications because a virus might, as a ''side effect'', corrupt data files.)

By ''computationally infeasible'' is meant that the amount of time (or of storage) which is required to find such an $F'$ is too large to be practical. How large is ''too large''? That depends on the application. In the viral environment, where the computation must be performed on the target computer, it may be as little as 5 seconds because of the risk of being noticed by the user.

Unfortunately, no hash function has ever been *proved* in an *absolute* sense to satisfy our fourth criterion. The best that has been done so far is to show *relative* intractability, i.e. that the function is non-invertible under the assumption of intractability of some well-researched mathematical problem such as factoring very large integers or computing discrete logarithms using very large moduli. Despite notable advances in the last 20 years, factoring an arbitrary 200-digit number still requires hundreds of thousands of years using the fastest known general-purpose algorithms (currently PPMPQS and GNFS) on the fastest present-day computer.

Actually, for use in the viral environment the fourth criterion should be rephrased to take into account the desirability of $H$ being key-dependent. However, I shall defer this to a later section.

# 4 THE CRC ALGORITHM

Many authors of integrity checking programs use the algorithm known as **CRC** (Cyclic Redundancy Check), although this algorithm was originally designed for a somewhat different purpose, viz. to detect whether a message has become corrupted because of noise picked up over a communications line.

The hash value or checksum using the CRC algorithm of a given file is computed as follows: Let $r$ be the number of bits in the checksums we wish to generate, and let $G$ (the **generator**) be a string of bits which consists of a 1-bit followed by $r$ additional bits. Treat both the file $F$ and the generator $G$ as binary numbers, append $r$ 0-bits to $F$, and divide the result by $G$ using ''long division'', except that ''polynomial arithmetic modulo 2'' is performed instead of ordinary arithmetic.

If we express the bit strings as vectors of bits, the CRC algorithm can be expressed in just a few lines: Let $F$ be the given file and $G$ the generator *without* the leading 1-bit. Let $m$ and $r$ be the lengths of $F$ and $G$, resp. Let $C$ be an auxiliary vector of length $r + 1$. Then the algorithm (written in a pseudo-high-level language) is simply:

```
For j=1 to r+1 do C(j)  := F(j);
For i=1 to m do {
  K := C(1); For j=1 to r do C(j)  := C(j+1) XOR (K AND G(j));
  If i < m-r then C(r+1)  := F(i+r+1) else C(r+1)  := 0        }
```

and the $r$ bits of the checksum are given by the first $r$ bits of (the final value of) $C$. (Remark: The first statement of the algorithm assumes that $m > r$; if this is not the case, $C$ must be padded with zeros.)

The CRC algorithm is much more secure than a simple checksum. It is also quite fast. In practice, the bit operations are implemented by shifting and masking instructions. The process can be speeded up considerably by generating in advance a table based on the user's generator.

In general, the larger $r$ is, the smaller the probability that a different file will have the same checksum. However, if the checksums using a given algorithm are $r$ bits long, then the probability of two files having the same checksum attains its ideal value of $1/2^r$ only if the algorithm distributes its values uniformly. In the case of CRC, if the number of trailing zero bits of the generator is $k$, then this probability is actually $1/2^{r-k}$. Hence in order to prevent non-uniform distribution of checksum values when using CRC, the last (low-order) bit of the generator should always be a 1.

# 5 IS CRC SECURE FOR ANTI-VIRAL PURPOSES?

You will often hear it said that while the CRC algorithm is useful for detecting random modifications when a file is being transmitted from one node to another, forging is possible and therefore this algorithm is insecure when an intelligent agent is attempting a "directed attack", as may be the case when viruses are unleashed, and only a cryptographic algorithm (e.g. ANSI X9.9) can be secure. Could such a widespread opinion be wrong?

The answer is that it is correct ... *relative to certain environments*, but that *the viral environment is a very different one*, and *what is true in one environment is not necessarily true in the other.*

I shall return to the subject of "environments" later. Meanwhile, let us examine the specific argument behind the claim that CRC is insecure. As above, let $r$ be the length of the checksum, let $G$ be the generator, and let $H(F)$ be the result of applying the CRC algorithm, using this generator, to the file $F$. A forger replaces $F$ by $F'$, and $H(F')$ is different from $H(F)$. It can be shown that the forger, knowing $F$, $F'$ and $G$, can then make a small ($r$-bit) modification to $F'$, yielding a file $F''$ such that $H(F'') = H(F)$. Moreover, this modification *can be computed directly, without need for trial and error.* (In general, it is necessary to compute $r$ checksums using $G$ and then solve a system of $r$ linear equations in $r$ unknowns in which the right-hand sides of the equations are based on $H(F)$ and $H(F'')$.) The forger has succeeded when he replaces $F$ by such an $F''$.

There is only one little catch in the above forgery scenario: In order for it to work, the particular generator $G$ which is being used by the victim *must be known by the forger*. Now when CRC is used for communications purposes, everyone on the network must use the same generator. But what many people seem to overlook is that when CRC is used for anti-viral purposes, the generator can and *should* be chosen *differently for each user* (either randomly by the checksum program or personally by the user), so that no one other than the user knows his generator. If this is done, the above attack cannot succeed.

True, it is possible for a forger to determine a given user's generator if it is stored unencrypted in some file which is accessible to an enemy program, or if the forger has access to the user's CST (CheckSum Table, i.e. table of file names and their corresponding checksums). For from only a few such file-checksum pairs it is possible to *compute* that user's generator (using the fact that the generator must be a divisor of all differences $F - H(F)$). However, the CRC algorithm is *perfectly secure* against forging (see definition in next section), provided that the following two conditions are satisfied:

1. **Different users use (in general) different generators and each user's generator is unknown to others.**

2. **The generator and the CST are inaccessible to a hostile program.**

Of course, the CST and generator have to be accessible by the checksum program itself. It is only necessary to ensure that it is accessible *only when it is certain that memory is uninfected.*

There are some who claim that memory can be ensured clean even after booting from the hard disk, but this has never been proven. The surest way to guarantee a clean system is to perform a cold-boot from an uninfected bootable diskette. It is best to keep the checksum program, along with the CST and generator, "offline", i.e. on a diskette which is never left in the drive except when the checksum program is being executed and which is always write-protected except when it is necessary to update the CST, and to execute the program only from that diskette and only immediately after cold-booting from it.

## 6 IS FORGING EVER A REAL RISK IN THE VIRAL ENVIRONMENT?

By "forging" I mean either (1) replacing a given file $F$ by another file $F'$ such that $H(F') = H(F)$, or else (2) replacing $F$ by any desired $F'$ and also replacing $H(F)$ in the CST by $H(F')$. In either case a subsequent application of the algorithm will show that $H(F')$ equals the value in the CST even though $F$ has been replaced by $F'$. (Note that the term "forging" is used only when this is done by a technique *specific to a particular function* $H$.)

Now I have shown that CRC cannot be forged if a certain pair of conditions is satisfied. But it is often claimed that users find working from diskettes too inconvenient, thereby making my second condition unrealistic. That being the case, it is argued, CRC is insufficiently secure and a cryptographic checksum is required.

First of all, even if the second condition is not satisfied, there are too many obstacles for forging to be worthwhile, except perhaps in certain special environments. Secondly, in any environment in which forging *is* feasible, there are *much greater dangers than forging*. Let us discuss each of these points.

Suppose the user ignores our recommendations and keeps his CST on his hard disk. In principle, a hostile program could then read the CST and perhaps discover the key or the checksum corresponding to a target file. But even then, forging would almost certainly be impractical for the following reasons:

1. There are many different algorithms in use, and any technique for forging with respect to one of them would be useless against any other algorithm.
2. If the forging process depends on trial-and-error rather than on direct methods, it is likely to be very time consuming.

The only situation in which forging *might* be worth someone's time and effort would be if he is satisfied with attacking a limited environment, such as an office or a student lab, in which many computers use *the identical* program, CST format, etc.

But even in this environment he has much better options open to him. For in order to perform forging on these computers he would have to get his program activated on them, and to do this, it would presumably have to be a resident program. But if a virus can get into memory when the checksum program is activated, then the virus writer can do something far *simpler, faster, and surer* than forging, something which is *completely independent of the checksum program used*, and which *does not require any computations* (of checksums, keys, etc.): he could launch a *stealth* virus. The surest way to prevent this is by executing the checksum program only when memory is clean. But *this same measure will also prevent forging*. Thus *forging within the viral environment is either infeasible or pointless.*

## 7 ENVIRONMENTS U AND V

We have discussed the mistakes of assuming that CRC must be used with a known generator and that forging is a significant risk. But what often lies behind these mistakes is a *confusion between two entirely different situations or contexts or "environments"*. Distinguishing between them can save much misunderstanding.

Consider first the following environment U: The author of a file uploads it to a BBS or file server. From here, the sys-op of another BBS transfers it to his BBS, and so on. Eventually, copies of the file are downloaded by thousands of end-users all over the world to their respective disks. How can we be certain that it has not been altered somewhere along the way?

Now this is a very important problem. But the environment V with which we are dealing here is quite different: Instead of being concerned with the possibility of replacement of a file during *transmission* from one computer to *other* computers, we are concerned with detection of modification of a file which takes place *on a given computer*. The question here is not whether the file has been altered or replaced *en route*, but whether, *after* installation on a given user's disk, it has been modified by a virus on the *same* machine. Thus U describes a form of *inter*-machine integrity, whereas V describes *intra*-machine integrity.

What is so different about these two environments? For one thing, in Environment U, it is not sufficient to have file authentication, since even if a file has not been altered, it may have been uploaded by someone other than the presumed author. Thus *sender* authentication is relevant in U, but not in V.

But even if we restrict our attention to *file* authentication, there are many (at least seven) important differences. The two most important of them are:

1. In Environment U, the same algorithm must be used by the recipients of the file as was used by the sender, whereas in V each user can use a program of his own choice. There is no one program which is in use by more than a tiny percentage of users, and any technique for forging which works against one algorithm won't work against the great majority of other algorithms.
2. In V, even if many users use the same algorithm, it can be implemented in such a way that each of them uses a different key, unknown to anyone else. This is impossible in Environment U. Thus in V, but not in U, the checksum for any given file differs (or at least should differ) from user to user, and cannot be known to a forger without access to the particular machine. Moreover, in V the checksums can be made inaccessible to hostile programs.

These differences between Environments U and V are crucial in avoiding incorrect claims about the security of various algorithms. Much pointless argument to which I have been witness could have been avoided if the participants had been aware that one of them was assuming U while the other was assuming V, and that *what is true in one environment is not necessarily true in the other.*

# 8 CRITERIA FOR THE ALGORITHM IN ENVIRONMENT V

We can now return to the promised amendment to the fourth criterion. For despite the fact that we are unable to prove of a single function that it satisfies our fourth criterion, we have a practical solution in Environment V which is not available in Environment U, namely to make the hash function dependent on a **secret key**, i.e. a parameter which is unknown to anyone other than the user, by having it selected randomly by the checksum program or personally by the user.

While there are cryptologists (e.g. Merkle) who recommend a keyless algorithm even for anti-viral purposes, requiring the algorithm to be *key-dependent* has several advantages in Environment V:

a. No matter how secure an algorithm may *appear* to be, in the absence of proof it is possible that a way of forging will be found. However, making the algorithm dependent on a secret key gives complete security provided the CST is inaccessible.

b. Suppose a user (ignoring our recommendations) keeps his CST on a disk to which a hostile program has read access, and that it knows how to interpret the information which it reads. In this situation, forgery becomes theoretically possible, i.e. the forger's program may be able to compute the user's key from information on his disk, and then to compute an $F'$ such that $H(F') = H(F)$. However, any computation based on this key is likely to require a lot of time. The fact that the function is key-dependent generally means that the computation must be done on the *victim's computer*, and this results in a significant restriction on the amount of time available for the computation, since a computation of more than a few seconds is likely to be noticed by the user.

c. Again, assume the forger has read access to the CST on the hard disk. But under DOS, if there is read access to a hard-disk file, then anyone capable of writing a virus surely knows how to obtain write access to that file also (unless hardware protection, which is rather expensive, is used). This raises the possibility of a *different* kind of forging: If there is no secret key, then even if the forger cannot modify the file to fit the hash value, he can easily modify the hash value to fit the modified file and then write the new hash value into the CST. Under DOS, if the former type of forging is possible, then so is the latter. And it is much simpler and faster than the above type, since there is never any need to use trial and error.

Because of these three considerations, it is very desirable in Environment V to use a *key-dependent* algorithm. Therefore in the case of this environment we rephrase the fourth criterion above as the combination of the following two criteria:

4a. **The hash function should depend on a key k specific to each user (or computer or disk) which is unknown to anyone other than the user. In order to emphasize this dependence, we write $H_k(F)$ instead of $H(F)$.**

4b. **Even if the hash function H is known, for any given file F it is computationally infeasible (without knowledge of the key k) to construct a different file F' such that $H_k(F') = H_k(F)$.**

# 9 LOOPHOLES IN DOS

At the beginning of this paper we stated that among other things, integrity checking was predicated on the assumption that viral infection necessarily causes some modification in an existing file. This is not always correct. Under DOS (for PC-compatible computers), there are several ways in which a virus can spread without any existing file getting modified. I call these ''loopholes'' in the system.

Only one of these loopholes has been exploited in any actual virus so far. It's usually called a ''companion'' or ''spawning'' virus. The ''target'' file is any EXE file, say FOO.EXE. However, the virus does not modify it in any way. Instead it creates a COM file having the same name, FOO.COM. When the user types FOO, he thinks FOO.EXE will be executed, but because of DOS's precedence rules, it is actually FOO.COM which gets executed. After doing whatever the virus writer wishes, FOO.COM passes control to FOO.EXE, so that the program FOO seems to behave normally. What is important for our discussion is that what gets executed (first) is the infected file FOO.COM, even though nothing in the FOO.EXE file is modified, so a checksum reveals nothing to notify the user about.

Such viruses can be detected by a properly constructed checksum program. Some programs keep, in addition to the names and checksums of all files to be checksummed, a list of *all* currently existing files, so that files which have appeared (or disappeared) since the last run of the program will get spotted and a warning will be given to the user. This is a good idea. However, for purposes of detecting the above type of virus, it is sufficient to check whether for each program of the form FOO.EXE in the CST there exists another program named FOO.COM, and to sound a warning if there does.

There are other loopholes in DOS which could be exploited to fool a checksum program, but since they have not yet been used, I shall not describe them here. The point is that it's easy to modify a checksum program to catch this and other such holes ... provided one is aware of what the holes are. Unfortunately, the great majority of checksum program authors don't bother themselves with such considerations until a virus which implements one of them is encountered.

Education and Society / R. Aiken (Editor)
Information Processing 92, Volume II
Elsevier Science Publishers B.V. (North-Holland)


# Generation of secure passwords by the user

Ernst PILLER

Institute for Softwaretechnology, Vienna University of Technology, Resselgasse 3/188
A-1040 Vienna, Austria

**A b s t r a c t**

Almost everybody remembers passwords or PINs today. The two most important features in a password are its security and simplicity. However, usual secret passwords can be find out from a hacker, observer (e.g. over the shoulder looker), maskerade and line eavesdropper. Improvements can be achieved by using passwords based on algorithms. The results of the use of password algorithms by the user are either one-time passwords (for instance through the completion of a secret-word or through selection of signs on the screen or an addition with the help of mathematical methods or a question and answer game) or very long *relative static* passwords, which the user remembers through a special technique (for instance reconstructed passwords or word combinations with veiling). In this article password algorithms (inshort PWA) are being introduced. Starting point of all studies are todays usually secret passwords which are only rarely changed by its user.

Keyword Codes: K.6.5
Keywords: Management of Computing and Information Systems, Security and Protection

## 1. INTRODUCTION

Almost everybody remembers passwords today, whether it be a lockcode of their bikes and suitcases or the code of the safe or the door openers either to computer rooms or military and other security places, the ATM (Automatic Tellery Machine), POS-terminal (Point of Sale Terminal) or the password to computers. The password is a character string (often even only a series of numbers) used by men with the help of an input device (mostly keyboard or number-wheels). In this paper there is no different between password and PIN (Personal Identification Number). The two most important features in a password are its security and simplicity. Passwords are easy to use and to work with. The disadvantages of passwords are: you have to remember them, you can pass them on unauthorizedly and you can find them out (e.g. by looking somebody over the shoulder who types in a password or by trying out).

The disadvantage of remembering a password can easily be eliminated through *reconstructed passwords* as in example 7. The possibility of passing on passwords even over large distances need not be a disadvantage; e.g. if somebody is absent the password can be passed on over the telephon if necessary. The disadvantage of finding out a password can in most cases be eliminated with the help of password algorithms (inshort PWA) which are named below. The passwords *competition* - the biometrical data - are not as secure to use as many people think. You also need expensive systems for the input and processing of biometrical data. That is why the password is going to keep its place even in future times; on condition that one does not ignore new developments with the password.

A password may be chosen by the user or assigned. Assigned passwords can be more secure than user selected passwords, but they are easy to forget. Therefore they are often written down by the user or are taken from a list which is discovered.

More and more people have to remember at least one password. Many use two or more passwords all the time. For example, as owner of a ATM/POS-card, a credit-card with password, a lock-code for a bike and a briefcase and as user of videotex and a host computer I have to remember all together six different passwords.

For security reasons passwords should be: long (as many characters as possible), without meaning (no well known names of persons, countries, firms etc., first names, birthdates, house numbers, street names, city names, words as "test", "demo" etc. and also these words spelled backward), changed regularly (for instance once a month; but not too often, since the password can be easily forgotten or written down or because of the frequent change become too easy), various (several equal passwords for different applications should be avoided), be put into the terminal (keyboard) quickly, not written down anywhere and only stored in the user's brain and under protection in the computer.

You cannot force people to remember many different and long passwords without meaning, however. That is why we use short passwords and passwords which have a meaning (e.g. one's birthdate, names of friends and relatives or words like "demo", "test"), which in addition are changed only rarely. Short passwords, but especially passwords with special meanings, can be found out by trial and error method or by looking over someones shoulder while he is putting the password into the keyboard. One way out of this dilemma is the use of special algorithms (password algorithms, inshort PWA). It is simpler and more secure, to remember a password algorithm with, for instance a simple secret-word, than to try to remember a long password without any meaning and to change this regularly. The results of the use of password algorithms are either one-time passwords (for instance through selection of signs on the screen) or very long *relative static* passwords, which the user remembers through a special technique (for instance reconstructed passwords).

## 2. USED CHARACTERS AND DEFINITIONS

P = passwords $P=p_1.....p_q$
G = secret-words $G=g_1.....g_h$
K = cleartext-words $K=k_1.....k_l$
E = complementary-words (extension-words) $E=e_1.....e_f$
M = complementary-masks or selection-masks $M=m_1.....m_n$

For the single characters of a word lower case letters are used. The alphabetical successor of the letters shows the length of of a word (e.g. $G=g_1g_2...g_h$). The actual characters of a word are specified through inverted commas (e.g. $G=g_1.....g_h$ = "Charles").

$p_i, g_i, e_i, k_i, s_i \in \Omega$ $m_i \in$ {"0", "1"}

$\Omega$ contains all characters of a character-set (e.g. ASCII-character-set), at least all digits {"0", .... ,"9"} or all capital letters {"A","B", .... ,"Z"}. The Mathematics-PWA (see below) has the restriction $p_i \in$ {"0","1", .... ,"9"}.

A password $P = p_1p_2 .... p_q$ can contain parts which are not considered by the password checking software. These parts are called *blank-words*, the other parts *effective-words*. The basic information (input data of the PWA) which leads to the password is called *basic-word*.

The part of the *basic-word* which the password user can see is called *cleartext-word*, the invisible part is called *secret-word*. If a person has to add to an usually secret numeric password a random number - which is shown on the screen at the password input call - the usual password is called *secret-word* and the random number is called *cleartext-word*. Both words together represent the *basic-word*.

## 3. PASSWORD ALGORITHMS

### 3.1. Supplement-PWA

With the Supplement-PWA the secret-word $G=g_1g_2 \ldots g_h$ is supplemented with characters $E=e_1e_2 \ldots e_f$ whereby the complementary-mask $M=m_1m_2 \ldots m_n$ shows at which points the additional characters are placed. Within the password $P=p_1p_2 \ldots\ldots p_q$, $E=e_1e_2 \ldots e_f$ represent the blank-word and $G=g_1g_2 \ldots g_h$ the effective-word. The complementary-mask has to be kept secret.

Example 1: The secret-word consists of the usually secret password G = "BORA". The complementary-mask contains the binary sequence M = "00001111000....0". That means, the user has to enter first four senseless characters (random characters), after that the secret-word "BORA" and then an unlimited number of senseless characters. E.g. the following passwords are given: P = "RQPCBORAJRXOKI" or P = "YQJLBORASKAIGOSIXJIUDLBSIVIO" etc.

The passwords are relatively secure from observers through its additional characters (random characters). This example shows how easily a usual secret password can be improved.

#### 3.1.1. Different Supplement-PWA

Depending on the complementary-word E there are e.g. following PWA:

| | |
|---|---|
| a) Random-Supplement PWA | E = random characters (see example 1) |
| b) Date-Supplement PWA | E = actual date |
| c) Time-Supplement PWA | E = actual time |

Example 2: ad b) E = day, month (each two-digit)
ad c) E = minute, hour (each two-digit)
With G = "2719" and S = "00110011" at 16.03 the password P = "03271619" is given.

The single Supplement-PWA can easily be combined with each other, too. With G = "MOLI" and the complementary-mask S="000011001100....0" $e_1 \ldots e_4$=(four digit time) and $e_5 \ldots e_f$ (senseless character string through playing with the keyboard) following effective password can be given at 16.09: P = "0916MOERLIQZFWJGVSYLORSGWUHFO"

Comments: The password always changes (one-time password), as with all Supplement-PWA the complementary-word E is new at each password calculation. With the Random-Supplement-PWA the complementary-word is a blank word; with all others the complementary-word is part of the effective-word of the password. The complementary-mask should be easy. With the Random-Supplement-PWA, masks without certain length are advisable (see example 1).

With the above mentioned Supplement-PWA the password is generated from a secret-word (usually secret password), a complementary-mask (complementary rule) and a complementary-word. The secret-word is veiled with the complementary-word and therefore, the *password find out* gets much harder for an observer. Especially easy and effective is the supplement with an unrestricted number of random characters. With the directly following PWA the password is generated with an information - which the user gets over screen or headphones before the password input - through application of the chosen PWA. This information represents a clear-text-word and is generated before each password input. The following PWA, therefore, are completely opposite to the above mentioned PWA.

### 3.2. Selection-PWA

With the Selection-PWA a cleartext-word $K=k_1 \ldots k_l$ is displayed on the screen. The password $P=p_1 \ldots\ldots p_q$ is calculated from this displayed word based on selection criterias (e.g. selection-masks, starting-characters, selection characters). The selection criteria depends on the single PWA. In this paper one important algorithm of this class is described [1].

#### 3.2.1. Lettermatrix-PWA

The user takes note of the usual secret password $G = g_1 g_2 \ldots g_h$. When the password is requested (log-on phase), a lettermatrix with 24 rows and 24 columns will be displayed on the screen. Each of these 24 rows and columns contains all 24 letters of the alphabet from "a" to "x", i.e. individual letters appear only once in a row or column. The user now searches for his password by going through the lettermatrix. This way has h positions (changes of direction) resulting from the letters $g_1$ to $g_h$. Since the lettermatrix is changed at each log-on, the user constantly receives a new password.

| U | X | W | G | I | V | K | N | P | E | O | H | B | R | T | A | L | F | Q | M | S | C | D | J |
|---|---|---|---|---|---|---|---|---|---|---|---|---|---|---|---|---|---|---|---|---|---|---|---|
| I | L | K | S | U | J | W | B | D | Q | C | T | N | F | H | M | X | R | E | A | G | O | P | V |
| G | J | I | Q | S | H | U | X | B | O | A | R | L | D | F | K | V | P | C | W | E | M | N | T |
| W | B | A | I | K | X | M | P | R | G | Q | J | D | T | V | C | N | H | S | O | U | E | F | L |
| D | G | F | N | P | E | R | U | W | L | V | O | I | A | C | H | S | M | X | T | B | J | K | Q |
| A | D | C | K | M | B | O | R | T | I | S | L | F | V | X | E | P | J | U | Q | W | G | H | N |
| V | A | X | H | J | W | L | O | Q | F | P | I | C | S | U | B | M | G | R | N | T | D | E | K |
| T | W | V | F | H | U | J | M | O | D | N | G | A | Q | S | X | K | E | P | L | R | B | C | I |
| S | V | U | E | G | T | I | L | N | C | M | F | X | P | R | W | J | D | O | K | Q | A | B | H |
| C | F | E | M | O | D | Q | T | V | K | U | N | H | X | B | G | R | L | W | S | A | I | J | P |
| M | P | O | W | A | N | C | F | H | U | G | X | R | J | L | Q | D | V | I | E | K | S | T | B |
| R | U | T | D | F | S | H | K | M | B | L | E | W | O | Q | V | I | C | N | J | P | X | A | G |
| X | C | B | J | L | A | N | Q | S | H | R | K | E | U | W | D | O | I | T | P | V | F | G | M |
| F | I | H | P | R | G | T | W | A | N | X | Q | K | C | E | J | U | O | B | V | D | L | M | S |
| J | M | L | T | V | K | X | C | E | R | D | U | O | G | I | N | A | S | F | B | H | P | Q | W |
| O | R | Q | A | C | P | E | H | J | W | I | B | T | L | N | S | F | X | K | G | M | U | V | D |
| K | N | M | U | W | L | A | D | F | S | E | V | P | H | J | O | B | T | G | C | I | Q | R | X |
| H | K | J | R | T | I | V | A | C | P | B | S | M | E | G | L | W | Q | D | X | F | N | O | U |
| L | O | N | V | X | M | B | E | G | T | F | W | Q | I | K | P | C | U | H | D | J | R | S | A |
| P | S | R | B | D | Q | F | I | K | X | J | C | U | M | O | T | G | A | L | H | N | V | W | E |
| Q | T | S | C | E | R | G | J | L | A | K | D | V | N | P | U | H | B | M | I | O | W | X | F |
| N | Q | P | X | B | O | D | G | I | V | H | A | S | K | M | R | E | W | J | F | L | T | U | C |
| E | H | G | O | Q | F | S | V | X | M | W | P | J | B | D | I | T | N | A | U | C | K | L | R |
| B | E | D | L | N | C | P | S | U | J | T | M | G | W | A | F | Q | K | V | R | X | H | I | O |

Figure 1: Lettermatrix Example

The user starts searching for his password by looking for the first letter of his secret-word ($g_1$) in the first row of the displayed lettermatrix. The position of $g_1$ in the first row indicates the column, in which the second letter of the secret-word ($g_2$) is to be found. The position of $g_2$ in this column indicates the first final position. The letter following horizontal (in the row) this first final position makes up the first character ($p_1$) of the password. The position of the third letter of the secret-word ($g_3$) in the first row of the lettermatrix indicates the column, in which the fourth letter of the secret-word ($g_4$) is to be found. The position of $g_4$ in this column indicates the second final position. The letter following horizontal (in the row) this second final position makes up the second character ($p_2$) of the password. This algorithm is to repeat until the last character ($p_q$ with $q = h/2$) of the searched for password has been found.

Example 3: The user chooses as his secret-word the letters "KRILER" and then gives this data to the computer-system. This secret-word are valid until the next change is made. The computer-system generates randomly a combination of letters to make up a lettermatrix which is then displayed on the screen (see Figure 1).

This results in the password P = "UAD". The next time a password is requested, another lettermatrix is displayed on the screen and therefore by using the same secret-word another password results. An observer and an eavesdropper cannot find out the current secret-word then, and a hacker without actual lettermatrix also fails because of the many possiblities which exist, since every password represents a random character string.

**3.3. Mathematics-PWA**

A PWA $\alpha$ is called Mathematics-PWA if $P = \alpha(K)$ $\alpha$... simple mathematical function

Example 4: $\alpha: P = (k_1 + k_2 + k_3 + k_4)\ k_5\ k_6$

Addition of $k_1 + k_2 + k_3 + k_4$ and concatenation of the result with $k_5$ and $k_6$

From K="5389297" follows the password P = "2529", from K = "2158093" follows P = "1609"

Comments: The basic-word can also be a secret-word and a cleartext-word and the PWA is the sum of these two words. With a Mathematics-PWA the password is mostly short and consists of digits only. The security, therefore, is relatively small with this PWA.

**3.4. Question/Response-PWA**

With this PWA (see [2]) the user defines a Question/Response-matrix (table) containing at least 15 questions along with the response that the user associates with each question. The contents of the matrix must be specified by each individual user and the preparation takes 10 to 25 minutes. The user has to remember reliable the table (the key for guessing responses lies in the context), but has to avoid obvious associations as "Albert - Einstein".

Example 5: Part of a Question-Response-Matrix:

| | | | | | | |
|---|---|---|---|---|---|---|
| Stockholm | Cologne | Frankfort | Zurich | Amsterdam | Vienna | etc. |
| Lidingövägen | Dürener Str | Seiler Str | Seebahn Str | Kerk Straat | John Str | etc. |

With the cleartext-word K = "Vienna" the password is P = "John Str".

**3.5. Secretword-PWA**

With a Secretword-PWA the password $P = p_1p_2 \;.....\; p_q$ is calculated exclusively from a secret-word $G = g_1 g_2 \ldots g_h$.

As this PWA generates a password exclusively from a secret-word a dynamic (e.g. one-time) password without the help of the password user can hardly be realized. With Secretword-PWA, however, very long passwords can be generated. It is possible to define several classes of Secretword-PWA. In this paper two important classes are described:

- word combinations with veiling
- reconstructed passwords

### 3.5.1. Word combinations with veiling

The user chooses a secret-word (e.g. a sentence) consisting of several words. With this PWA the user joins (concatenates) these single words and supplements/deletes/shifts some characters. The user defines the rules to construct the password.

Example 6: Secret-word G = "groenland is the largest island"
a.) single combination: P = "groenlandisthelargestisland"
b.) as a.) but deletion of the final letter of each single word: P = "groenlanithlargesislan"

### 3.5.2. Reconstructed passwords

The password is mentally constructed by the user by means of certain personal knowledge (see [1] and [3]). Knowledge of one‘s private life and hobbies are suited best for the reconstructing of passwords. For example, a music lover, who doesn‘t want to remember a 8 letter long password - respectively forgets it easily, can use his knowledge of music. He remembers 8 notes of his favourite song for sure. And at the password input he can *play* 8 notes of this song on the keyboard. In the same way can somebody who loves to knit remember 8 stitches of his favourite knitting pattern and he can use this sequence with the help of a slight codeing as password. Sport-fans remember, for a certain point of time, the listing of a championship with the scores of their teams. This number of points can now, for example, in reversed order, be typed in. For someone, who observes this sequence seems to be accidental and does not remind him of something special.

Example 7: $P = p_1 p_2 \ldots p_{10}$ G = (Song "Eurovision", see Figure 2)

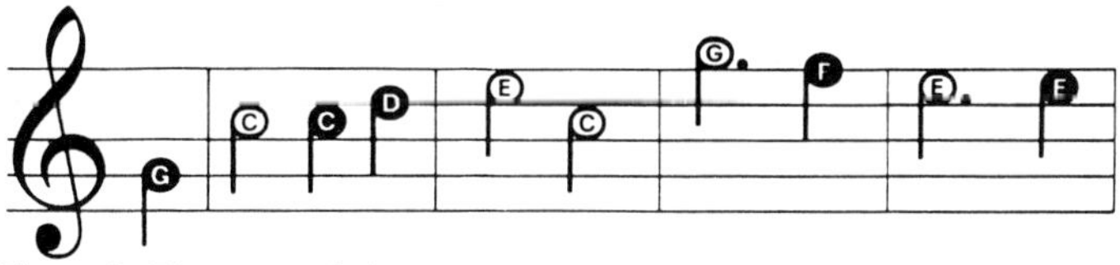


Figure 2. First part of the song *Eurovision*

From this song many different passwords can be made:
a) From *10 following notes of G as letters* ==> P = "GCCDECGFEE" (see Figure 2)
b) the same as a) but G has a different key.

### 3.6. Time-Interval-PWA

With this PWA the basic-word is identically with the password and represents the result of another PWA (e.g. Supplement-PWA), but this password must be entered within a certain time interval (e.g. 5 - 8 seconds). Outside of this interval the password is rejected.

This PWA lead to total confusion at practical security tests. As no testing person knew this algorithm and everybody made the password input immediately after the call, no one succeeded in the right password input. Though many testing people were sure that they knew the password through watching. They actually knew the character string but no one realized the time interval.

## 4. CONCLUDING COMMENTS

PWA can be applied wherever passwords are used today. They grant a higher security, however. With some applications only special PWA can be used; e.g. with the lockcode for a bike or a suitcase you can practically only use the Random-Supplement-PWA. Then the lockcode for a bike or suitcase - up to now mostly three to six digits - can for example have ten *number-wheels* with four effective and six uneffective wheels. The user only has to remember where the effective wheels are (e.g. 3, 5, 7 and 9) and a four digit number. An observer has to remember all ten wheels and for a *tryer* a ten-digit-number-wheel is frustrating.

With some PWA you have to note additional rules. E.g. a password input with Supplement-PWA, especially Random-Supplement-PWA, has to be made constantly fast (the single characters of the complementary-word and of the secret-word have to typed in almost at the same speed). With Random-Supplement-PWA the secret-word has to have at least four digits or three characters, as only the secret-word is checked and the security against tryers would be too little. With a Random-Supplement-PWA with many random characters (e.g. at least 15 characters) and a constantly fast password input the security against observers is extremely high.

With a PWA with a cleartext-word the refusal of a password need not mean that the password will be refused at the next try, too. The best Selection-PWA is the Lettermatrix-PWA. For this PWA an encryption of the password (or cleartext-word) is not necessary. A combination of this PWA with another PWA (e.g. Random-Supplement-PWA) may be the optimum of all described PWA. Unfortunately, some users have problems in using the Lettermatrix-PWA in that they cannot always find their way through the lettermatrix.

An acceptance examination has shown that the Random-Supplement-PWA is the best. With this PWA problems only occurred with the demand after a constantly fast password input. Another good acceptance was given to the Lettermatrix-PWA and Secretwort-PWA. No good valuation was reached for Mathematics-PWA and Question/Response-PWA.

The password algorithms require more work to be done at the log-on phase. Since any *unnecessary* extra effort is always regarded as being inconvenient, the user should be briefly informed as to the dangers of using conventional password systems and the advantages of the described methods. Additionally, if the user no longer needs to change his secret-word (i.e. his conventional password) so often (e.g. annually instead of monthly) then, as a rule, no important acceptability problems should arise. Generally it can be taken for granted that a considerably higher degree of security should be more important for certain users than the fact that the log-on phase is somewhat more complicated.

All described PWA have been realized in different program-libraries under MS-DOS and UNIX.

## 5. REFERENCES


1 E. Piller, Paßwörter, Oldenbourg Verlag, 1992, in German.

2 S.L. Smith, Authenticating Users by Word Association, Computers & Security 6 (1987) 464.

3 J.A. Haskett, Pass-Algorithms: A user validation scheme based on knowledge of secret algorithms, Communications ACM 27 (1984) 777 - 781.

Education and Society / R. Aiken (Editor)
Information Processing 92, Volume II
Elsevier Science Publishers B.V. (North-Holland)



# Reducing the Proliferation of Passwords in Distributed Systems[1]

Ralf C. Hauser, M. Sc.[a] and Prof. E. Stewart Lee, Ph. D.[b]

[a]Institut für Informatik, Universität Zürich, Winterthurerstr. 190, 8057 Zürich, Switzerland, +41/1/257-4315(11), Fax +41/1/363-0035, hauser@ifi.unizh.ch

[b]Department of Computer Science, University of Toronto, 10, King's College Road, Toronto, M5S 1A4, Ontario, Canada, (416)978-5035, Fax (416)978-4765, stew@hub.utoronto.ca

**Abstract**
Remote commercial applications like databases, telebanking, electronic mail systems run security mechanisms based on passwords. Too many passwords per user become a security problem. The goal of this research is to design systems allowing "password-less" user access to network services while improving the security of existing password mechanisms.

A system relying on one primary login with one password is proposed. A "guard" functionality on the user login host's side relays the application service suppliers' password requests to a password server which satisfies these requests with strong "machine" passwords. To the user, this system appears to be password-less. Application providers do not have to give up their current password security.

Variations of this architecture and its protocols for three levels of increasing security are described, employing complete message traffic encryption, public key cryptography, trusted hardware and software and strong authentication devices like chipcards.

Keyword Codes: C.2.2; D.4.6/K.6.5; C.2.4.
Keywords: Computer-Communication Networks, Network Protocols; Security and Protection; Distributed Systems

## 1. INTRODUCTION

Password security relies on the assumption that the human brain is the only trustworthy password storage area. In reality people tend to relieve their memory by employing paper, etc. to make reminders which risk to be inadvertently revealed to intruders. This questions the current system architectures and leaves the users in a weak position because they remain liable to the service provider for what happens with their passwords.

This work proposes a solution so that once users have authenticated themselves to one trusted system-component, all subsequent authentications are automatically executed. That trusted component is, for example, the user's workstation.

---

[1] The work for this paper was done as a thesis for the degree of a Master of Science in Computer Science in the University of Toronto.

## 2. PREVIOUS WORK

**BAN: Authentication Protocols and a Logic for their verification.**

In "Using Encryption for Authentication in Large Networks of Computers", Needham and Schroeder [1] proposed an authentication protocol which is the basis for many implementations. This protocol uses encryption to exchange authenticating secrets over a network which is possibly subverted and unreliable. Under the assumption that the employed encryption is unbreakable, mutual trust in the communicating principals' identity can be established. After discovering some flaws in this protocol, in 1989 a systematic analysis tool was published: "A Logic of Authentication" [2]. A Prolog verifier has been built on an improved BAN-logic which was used to automatically check the viability of the distribution of competencies and items of the proposed protocols.

**Kerberos**

The Kerberos Authentication Service [3] is the first widespread protocol that doesn't transmit plaintext passwords over the network and encrypts the whole subsequent conversation with DES based session keys.

Bellovin/Merritt [4] suggest in their in depth analysis of the protocol several extensions to increase its generality which we partly cover with the proposed variants. Also, the initial request should authenticate the requester to the session-key/password server to force an intruder to at least passively wiretap to obtain data for an off-line password guessing attack. In the current version, intruders can obtain any tickets they know the login names of.

**Lomas et al.: Protocol for Poorly Chosen Keys**

Instead of Diffie and Hellman's Exponential Key Exchange [5] to overrule passive wiretappers' password guessing attacks as suggested above [4], Lomas, Gong, Saltzer and Needham [6] put this in a more general framework and introduce "*verifiable plaintext attacks*".

They pragmatically state that making passwords stronger against guessing attacks is infeasible because normal users can neither remember them nor are they willing to carry trusted hardware authentication devices. Therefore they tolerate relatively easily guessable passwords called *poorly chosen keys*, but make the password crackers unable to detect a successful guess by employing one public key encrypted message.

Further related work is Clifford Neuman's Proxies [7] which might solve the problem for systems where a global and only authentication service providing access to homogeneous remote resources can be designed from scratch.

## 3. APPROACH TO FEASIBLE ARCHITECTURES

Feasible architectures for protocols to avoid multiple passwords will be described which determine the minimal assumptions that must hold to achieve password-free authentication.

The main distinctions among the three scenarios are whether users must provide hardware tokens to authenticate themselves and within the token-less scenarios, if public key cryptography is assumed to be feasible.

The different scenarios must always be evaluated against a hypothetical hostile intruder. This intruder is assumed to perform every malign action except those excluded by explicit assumptions. As the intruder might wiretap the communication lines, modify and insert messages at will, every message disclosure is by default assumed to be a *broadcast*.

Furthermore the intruders have the power of the most modern available technology at their disposal and they don't forget nor miss the slightest information they can obtain.

### 3.1. The Assumptions of Present Practice

The analysis of authentication protocols is dependent upon the assumptions about the system's parts. Variations in these assumptions result in significant changes in system behaviour.

These variants evolve along the axis of gradually refining the following set of status quo assumptions given as reference below to approximate present reality:

- Assumption I: *Communications Security*
  The communication channels are secure: In open networks, all hosts must consider the network as public. After establishing user connections to hosts are considered as trustworthy such that plaintext passwords can be transmitted.
- Assumption II: *Server trustworthiness*
  The application server is trusted: Providers are responsible for whatever happens within their application servers. The users are only responsible for consumed services and pay according to agreed rates. The problem becomes critical if the provider's accounting database has doubtful integrity and the users lack the proofs of not having used specific services.
- Assumption III: *Local trustworthiness*
  The users' host is trusted: The users are responsible for all actions initiated with their passwords. If passwords are compromised, either: (i speed) be faster than the intruder, authenticate yourself and change the password or (ii out-of-band communication) phone the service providers and block your "account" and send a new password using some communications medium other than the network.

**Evaluation**:
These reference assumptions either imply arbitrary trustworthiness of system components, which is very expensive, or don't live up to the expectations they raise. Unfortunately, the second is usually true, and therefore the status quo must be considered as highly disadvantageous.

### 3.2. Systems for Users Without Hardware Identity Proofs

Variant 1: Intruder Controlled Network and Trusted Path without Public Key Cryptography

**Architecture:**
The new architecture (fig 1) consists of an additional third host functioning as a *password server* and two processes called "guards" on the already existing hosts which perform encryption and some functions of the authentication protocol.

**Protocol:**
We propose the following three party authentication protocol which is inspired by the improved Needham/Schroeder Protocol. Notation:

The two acronyms connected by → state origins and destinations of messages. `ulh` = user login host, `as` = application server, and `ps` = password server. The desired server i = `dsi`. The user password to access this service = `pdsi`, `Kpu` is the shared key between `ulh` and `ps` resp. `as` and `ps` (`Kpa`). `ga` is the guard on the `as` side, `gu` for the `ulh`, `nu/na/np` are nonces of the `ulh`, etc. and `kau` is the shared session key between the `as` and the `ulh`.

| | | |
|---|---|---|
| i) | ulh → as : | ulh, nu |
| ii) | ga → ps : | ulh, nu, na, dsi |
| iii) | ps → ulh: | {{pdsi,na,kau}Kpa, nu, kua }Kpu |
| iv) | ulh → ga : | {pdsi,na,kau}Kpa |

**Explanation and justification of the properties of this protocol:**
First, the reference assumption I about Communications Security, must be adjusted to the described intruder:

- Assumption I-1: Total exposure of the communication subsystem to intruders:
  There is no communications security: Intruders have complete control over all in and out connections of every host.

An authentication providing the aspired level of security is realistic only if the subsequent service operations are protected too, i.e. with session keys. Thus, the guard must be split and reside on the `ulh` as well as on the `as`. The guard encrypts with this session key the entire session message traffic which follows the authentication. Therefore, *Local Trustworthiness* (III) must be refined as follows:

- Assumption III-1: There are trusted hardware parts that are unalterable by intruders. They protect trusted code with specific properties.

The `ulh` must now be seen in a hostile environment with even physical threats. No software (e.g. operating system) is trusted per se. Software can even be attacked during execution through networks. This problem can be avoided by declaring strategic parts of the operating system unalterable and by protecting them with tamper proof hardware during storage- and execution-time. These software parts could encompass the entire operating system kernel which then would be called a Trusted Computing Base TCB (see [8] p. 200 for a definition).

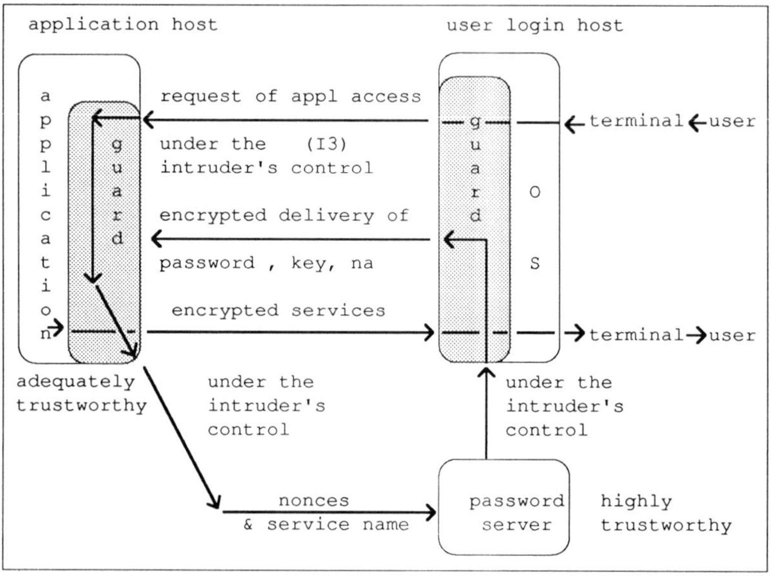


Figure 1: Architecture scheme of variant 1

The primary login process is not part of this figure. The interactions of the guards with the existing operating system should be minimized to be adaptable to existing services. Adaptations of existing operating systems like patches should only be minor. The guards work like transparent filters encrypting the messages, they only become active when they detect password requests from application servers and answers from password servers.

The above protocol requires at least the following behaviour properties of this TCB (i) the system must not leak any secret information to other users and (ii) both guards can store well-chosen keys (i.e. `kau` temporarily during the sessions and the `ga Kpa` permanently). The protection of the TCB could rely on two specific hardware parts:

- a trusted path button (hardware) to avoid spoofing login (=attack against initial authentication).
- an augmented boot ROM, which has enough capacity to store all code for booting by the trusted path or is capable of verifying the code to be loaded. In the case of alteration the system would (i) require booting from a trusted (external) source or (ii) authenticate itself to a trusted file server to boot remotely or (iii) decrypt the code from the permanent storage.

The described *password server* must not increase the risks of the original authentication process. This adds the following assumption to the scenario:

- Assumption IV-1: Universal trustworthiness of the password server:
  The password server is universally trustworthy at the highest level of the system.

Password servers/key distribution centres `ps/kdc` are hosts with the following features: (i) they are able to create well-chosen keys and (ii) they have a database containing an authenticating secret per validated `ulh` on the network. `ps/kdcs` are network security authorities.

The following *cryptosystem* assumptions must hold:

- Assumption V-1: Cryptosystem Security: The used encryption keys are unbreakable.
- Assumption VI-1: Cryptosystem feasibility:
  Public key cryptography in software is assumed to be computationally infeasibly expensive, thus slow and dedicated encryption hardware is not considered.

With the cryptosystem security assumption, intruders can't attack the ciphers themselves. Consequently, they will concentrate on obtaining passwords, and keys, etc. Therefore the usage of encryption techniques is only adequate, if these secrets are protected with the same care. This leads to the goal of never transmitting a plain key/password/ticket.

The "permanent" key `Kpu` is built as in Kerberos [3]: the users' initial login passwords are expanded by a one-way function as users preferably provide only one authenticating secret. It is expanded because not all passwords give good keys and the user's initial password is never stored on the `ulh`, only it's "digest". The drawback pointed out by Bellovin and Merritt that intruders not even have to wiretap to accumulate the equivalent of the UNIX /etc/passwd file can be resolved with two extra messages and some adaptations.

Even this protocol doesn't protect against wiretapping intruders guessing poorly chosen passwords [6]. Intruders always can calculate `Kpus` off-line from password guesses and verify it with wiretapped messages or a challenge to the `as`, if the `pdsi` is not "verifiable plaintext".

**Evaluation:**

Intruders can disturb the three principals by creating denial of access situations, or exhaust the `as`'s password utility, but they are unable to obtain real services without being noticed.

This configuration depicts the minimal assumptions for a system without public key cryptography and without specific hardware identification tokens to achieve trustworthy authentication. The possibility of password guessing attacks is the weakest spot of this variant. Therefore, either the initial login must be performed with a strong password or one of the following, more expensive variants must be chosen.

### 3.3. System Allowing Public Key Cryptography

Variant 2: Poorly Chosen Passwords With Public Key Cryptosystem

Updated Set of Assumptions: Still assumed are:

- Total exposure of the communication subsystem to intruders (I-1)
- (Application) Server Trustworthiness (II)
- Trusted, unalterable hardware and a TCB (III-1)
- Universal password server trustworthiness (IV-1)
- Cryptosystem security (V-1)

The changed assumption is:

- Assumption VI-2: Full Cryptosystem Feasibility:
  Cryptosystems of the computational complexity of the RSA algorithm are feasible.

This protocol is derived from Lomas et al.'s proposal [6]. It requires only one message encrypted with public key encryption, thus assumption VI-1 can be abandoned. The users may only remember poorly chosen secrets, because intruders can't detect hits in guessing attacks.

In the following **protocol**, `rulh` is a high quality random string generated by `ulh`, `c` is a confounder of high randomness with confounding impact on every bit of messages encrypted with block ciphers, `Ks` is the public key of `ps`, `pulh` is the poorly chosen password authenticating `ulh` to `ps`:

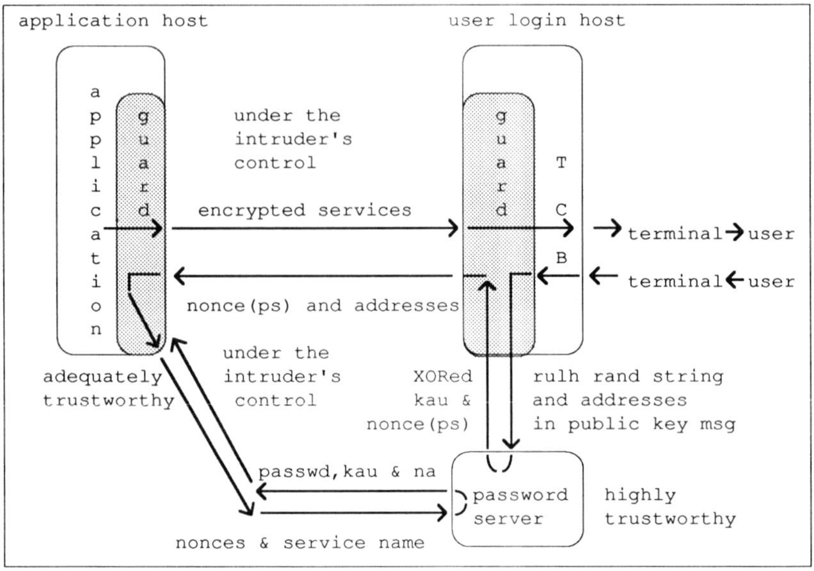


Figure 2: Architecture scheme of variant 2

| | | |
|---|---|---|
| i) | ulh → ps : | {pulh, dsi, rulh, c}Ks |
| ii) | ps → ulh: | {kau, np}XOR rulh |
| iii) | ulh → ga: | np, ulh, dsi |
| iv) | ga → ps: | np, na, ulh, dsi |
| v) | ps → as : | {pdsi,na,kau}Kpa |

`rulh` serves simultaneously as key and nonce for `ulh`. Every above message is *non-verifiable*

**Evaluation:**
These are the assumptions for systems without hardware tokens to achieve trustworthy authentication with strong protection against password guessing attacks.

### 3.4. System for Users With Hardware Identity Proofs

Variant 3: Hardware Identity Proof for Non Public Key Systems.

Updated Set of Assumptions:
- Total exposure of the communication subsystem to intruders (I-1)
- Server trustworthiness (II)
- Universal password server trustworthiness (IV-1)
- Cryptosystem security (V-1)
- The previous Cryptosystem feasibility (VI-1)
  There is no need for public key cryptography because this variant requires chipcards which store well-chosen secrets.
- The Local Trustworthiness assumption (III-1) now must encompass a smartcard system.

Here, users must not only know a secret, but also provide a hardware device like smartcards (chipcard), etc. It stores at least strong keys for the initial login authentication with the `ps`. User passwords are still necessary to assure the smartcard against theft, but they can be a poorly chosen because the number of challenges to the system is limited.

The **protocol** is essentially the same as in variant 1 with the now smartcard stored key `Kpu` which is well-chosen. Thus password guessing is hard even without public key cryptography.

**Evaluation:**
The problem is relatively trivial to solve with Hardware Identity Proofs because these tokens can be equipped with powerful devices capable of trustedly storing large amounts of data, performing encryption and executing entire protocols or even booting the `ulh`.

Future chipcards are imaginable with that much functionality that the `ps` becomes unnecessary for every authentication and only is consulted for periodic updates to determine expired keys and obtain new keys almost like of out-of-band communication.

In the future, biometric identification of users could add another layer of security, but such devices are presently neither at reasonable prices nor convenient and only a thorough analysis could answer the question whether user identification is still the weakest entity in the system.

The presented protocols have all been proven with the BAN based Prolog Verifier.

## 4. SUMMARY, CONCLUSIONS AND FUTURE WORK

This research started from the observation that the present efforts to improve the security for services in heterogeneous Distributed Systems can decrease the overall security through a multiplicity of passwords.

The three proposed architectures rely on one primary login with one password and use password servers and some kind of a trusted path combined with a trusted computing base and encryption modules. The additional measures taken in the three variants improved not only the overall system security, but also the security of single authentications significantly.

The amount of necessary changes to existing systems to achieve the largely improved security of the proposed solutions can be kept to a minimum.

**Directions for Future Work:** Personnel management and physical access policies for example to terminals must be taken into consideration to achieve an even broader foundation of the described solutions.

## 5. REFERENCES


1 R. M. Needham, M. D. Schroeder, "Using Encryption for Authentication in Large Networks of Computers", CACM vol. 21, # 12, Dec. 1978, pp. 993-999.

2 M. Burrows, M. Abadi, R. Needham, "A Logic of Authentication", Operating Systems Review, Dec. 3-6, 1989, Vol. 23, #5, pp 1-13.

3 J. G. Steiner, C. Neuman, J. I. Schiller, "Kerberos: An Authentication Service for Open Network Systems", Proceedings of the USENIX 1988 Winter Conference

4 S. Bellovin, M. Merritt, "Limitations of the Kerberos Authentication System", Computer Communications Review, vol. 20, #5, October 1990, pp. 119-132.

5 W. Diffie and M. E. Hellman, "New Directions in Cryptography", IEEE Transactions on Information Theory, November 1976, vol. 6, pp. 644-654.

6 T. M. Lomas, Li Gong, J. H. Saltzer, R. Needham, "Reducing Risks from Poorly Chosen Keys", Proceedings of the 12th ACM Symp. on OS Principles, Dec. 1989, pp 14-18.

7 B. Clifford Neuman, "Proxy-Based Authorization and Accounting for Distributed Systems", University of Washington, Seattle, Tech Rep 91-02-01, March 1991

8 E. S. Lee, P. Boulton, D. Lewis, M. Stumm, B. Thompson, "A Trusted Network Architecture", Tech Rep., CSRI, University of Toronto, Oct. 1988, pp. 97.

Education and Society / R. Aiken (Editor)
Information Processing 92, Volume II
Elsevier Science Publishers B.V. (North-Holland)


# An efficient public key distribution system

N. Alexandris[a], M. Burmester[b] and V. Chrissikopoulos[a]

[a] University of Piraeus, 80-86 Karaoli & Dimitriou Str., Piraeus 185 34, Greece

[b] RHBNC-University of London, Egham, TW20 OEX, U.K.

**Abstract**

We present a public key distribution system based on the Okamoto-Tanaka scheme. We consider a general setting which makes use of a one-way group homomorphism. The key exchange protocol has one-round and offers mutual authentication. The main feature of our system is its efficiency. Users select their own secret keys and register with a Key Authentication Center.

## 1. INTRODUCTION

Security is a major issue in an open computer network environment, where data is readily available through distributed processing and distributed data bases. Various types of security mechanisms have been proposed to prevent information being disclosed, destroyed, altered or copied by unauthorised users in a computer network (LAN or WAN).

Since the publication of the seminal paper by Needham and Schroeder [1], many practical authentication schemes for computer networks have been implemented. Some use secret key encryption, such as Kerberos [2,3] which uses the DES algorithm. Others, such as Selane [4], use public key encryption. For these, the users can make their own session keys with a key exchange protocol, so that the role of the Authentication Server is reduced to that of a key issuing authority. Some public key exchange protocols use the RSA scheme, e.g., [5]. Others, use the EI-Gamal [6] scheme, e.g., [4]. The choice of encryption depends on the requirements of the system. If secret key encryption is used (Kerberos) then an Authentication Server is required to manage the (secret) keys of the users and the authorisation. With an identity-based public key encryption scheme (Selane) only a Key Authentication Centre is needed to select the parameters of the system and to issue secret keys. However the public key encryption schemes which are currently available are computationally rather slow. Nevertheless, because of their flexibility and (provable) security, their use is gradually extended with the advent of faster hardware/software implementations.

A secure authentication and authorisation network should offers the following:

- protection against unauthorised and erroneous access,
- protection against attempts to disable its security,
- an appropriate support for access control policy,
- flexibility and efficiency.

Ideally such systems should cope with an environment in which there is little or no trust; users (and servers) should not trust each other, or the Key Authentication Centre. The users and servers of an authorization system must be correctly identified. Feige, Fiat and Shamir propose two systems for public key identification [7]. An *identity-based system* for which the public keys of the users are related to their *physical description* and the secret keys are obtained from a trusted centre, and a *public-file-based* system in which there is no such relation and the users choose their own secret keys and publish the public keys in a public. Identity-based systems offer better security provided that the physical description of the user can be tested adequately [8]. However such testing could limit the flexibility of a Local Area Network, and furthermore, there is the threat of a corrupted center managing the secret keys. For our purpose therefore public-file-based systems seem to be an appropriate alternative.

We shall describe a public-file-based key echange system. We envisage a hybrid setting which combines the attributes of single key and public key authentication systems. The secret keys of the users are encapsulated in tamper-proof Smart Cards which serve as a login device.

## 2. KERBEROS - SELANE - IDENTITY BASED KEY DISTRIBUTION SYSTEMS

### 2.1 Kerberos

Kerberos is an authentication scheme for distributed systems [2] (here we consider version 5 [3]). It employs a symmetric encryption scheme, the DES, and uses two types of data structure : Tickets and Authenticators. A Ticket contains information which identifies the user, a time-stamp which determines the lifetime of a practical session, and a session key. An Authenticator validates the use of the Ticket and prevents replays. Kerberos has two control system components : The Key Distribution Center (KDC) and the Ticket Granting Server (TGS). The KDC is a trusted party holding the secret keys of all the users of the network. The TGS issues the session keys. The key distribution protocol is described below where $K_X$ ($K_{Y,Z}$) is the secret of X (Y,Z) and (•)K means encryption under key K. U is the user's name and $T_1$, $T_2$, $A_1$, $A_2$ are Tickets and Authenticators.

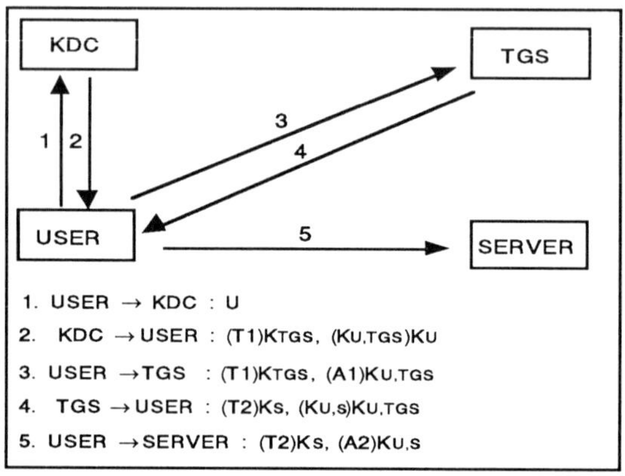


One basic restriction of Kerberos is that it requires an on-line Key Distribution Center. Each time a user wants to access a server he has to get authorization from the KDC. It is essential that the KDC is trusted and cannot be corrupted. Indeed the manager of a corrupted KDC can impersonate any user.

## 2.2. Selane

Selane [4] is an identity-based key distribution system in which the user only needs to know the identity of the server. A Key Authentication Center, KAC, generates and manages the public and private keys of the users. Selane uses the El-Gamal signature scheme [14]. The KAC generates a (large) prime number p, a number $\alpha \in Z_p$, $\alpha \neq 0$, a number $x \in Z_{p-1}$ and publishes: p,α, and $y=\alpha^x \bmod p$. It keeps x secret.

For each user the KAC creates an identity ID based on the name and physical characteristics of the user. Then it computes the El-Gamal signature (r,s) of ID,y. That is, the KAC chooses a random $k \in Z^*_{p-1}$ (i.e., gcd(k,p-1)=1), which should not be reused, and computes $r \equiv \alpha^k \bmod p$ and $s \equiv k^{-1}(ID - xr)(\bmod (p-1))$. The signature (r,s) can be verified by checking the congruence $\alpha^{ID} \equiv y^r r^s (\bmod p)$. The KAC gives the user (ID,r,s). The user may publish ID and r, but must keep s secret. The key exchange protocol is given below. This is a variant of Selane due to Gunther [9], and offers two way authentication. As with Kerberos, a corrupted KAC can misrepresent any user.

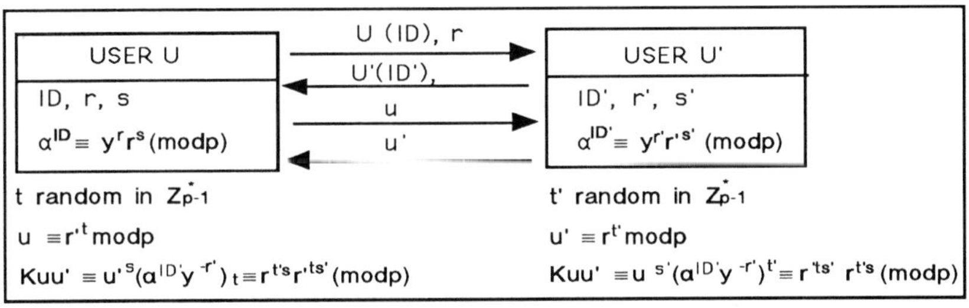


## 2.3 The Okamoto-Tanaka identity based Key distribution system

This system [10] is similar to Selane, but uses the RSA scheme. A key Authentication Center (KAC) generates two primes p and q, and determines a prime e and an integer d such that $e.d \equiv 1(\bmod (p-1)(q-1))$. Then it determines a number g which is a primitive element of GF(p) and GF(q). For each user U whose identity is ID, the KAC computes $s \equiv ID^{-1}(\bmod n)$ . The KAC issues the user with (n,g,e,s). This system authenticates indirectly the users.

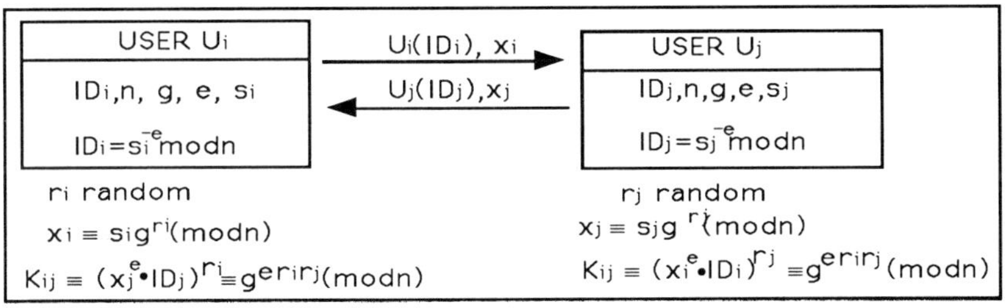

## 3. A PUBLIC KEY DISTRIBUTED SYSTEM

Of the three systems described earlier, only with Kerberos do we have immediate revocation of rights. The others do not have an on-line server, and the revocation of rights must be done on a server basis.

We shall describe a public-file-based key distribution system in which users select their own secret keys and the role of the KAC is reduced to choosing the parameters of the system and to managing a directory of authorized users. The KAC has an on-line connection with the users, which is used to revoke rights and to update the directory.

### 3.1 A general setting

Let G, H be groups and $f : G \rightarrow H$ be a group homomorphism, that is $f(x.y)=f(x).f(y)$ for all $x,y \in G$. Formally, $f_n : G_n \rightarrow H_n$ is an infinite family of group homomorphisms indexed by a binary string n. For a secure scheme f must be a one-way function.

The KAC chooses the parameters of the system and an element $\alpha \in G$ which it publishes together with a description of the algorithm for the function f. Each user $U_i$ selects a random $s_i \in G$ and computes $I_i$ which is such that $f(s_i).I_i=1$. The public and secret keys of Ui are $I_i$ and $s_i$. User $U_i$ sends $I_i$ together with his/her name (and other identity details) to the KAC, but keeps $s_i$ secret.

To establish a session key, users $U_i$, $U_j$ select random numbers $r_i$, $r_j$ and compute $x_i = s_i.\alpha^{r_i}$, which they exchange. Each user can now compute the session key $K_{ij}$. User $U_i$, computes $K_{ij}=(f(x_j).I_j)^{r_i}$. Because f is a homomorphism,

$$f(x_j).I_j = f(s_j.\alpha^{r_j}).I_j = f(s_j)f(\alpha^{r_j})I_j = (f(s_j)I_j)f(\alpha^{r_j}) = f(\alpha^{r_j})$$

since $f(s_j).I_j=1$. Therefore $K_{ij} = f(\alpha^{r_j})^{r_i} = f(\alpha^{r_i r_j})$. Similarly $U_j$ can compute $K_{ji} = (f(x_i).I_i)^{r_j} = f(\alpha^{r_i r_j})$.

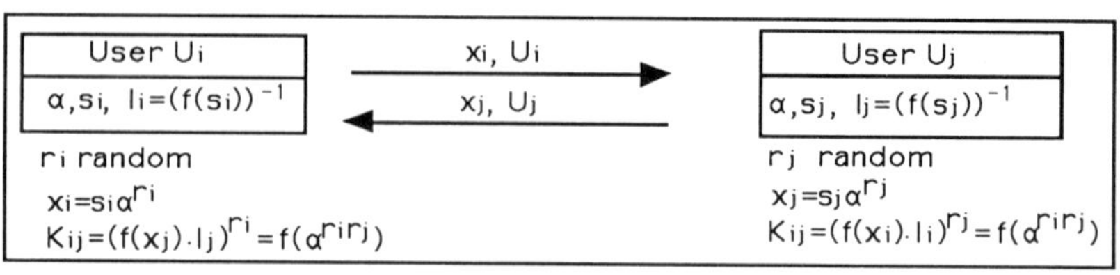

### 3.1.1 Security

If a user $U_K$ can find integers x,r which satisfy $f(x).I_i = f(\alpha)^r$ then he can impersonate $U_i$ [12], by sending x to $U_j$ and by using the session key $K_{ij} = (f(x_j).I_j)^r = f(\alpha)^{r_j r}$. To find x with r fixed requires the inversion of f (we are assuming that f is a one-way function). To find r with x fixed requires finding the discrete logarithm of $f(x).I_i$.

In the final paper we shall show that the security of the general protocol can be reduced to the intractability of the "derived Diffie-Hellman" problem. We shall show that if $si=\alpha^{\sigma i}$ , then the protocol reveals no information about the secret keys of the user which can be of any use to a masquerader.
Our system is based on the public-file model of identification of Feige-Fiat-Shamir. The users select their own secret keys and compute the corresponding public keys.

## 3.2 Particular cases

### 3.2.1 A key exchange protocol based on an RSA setting.

We take G = H = $Z_n$, n = pq, where p,q are appropriate primes and α is a number which generates both $Z_p$ and $Z_q$. The homomorphisms of f: $Z_n \to Z_n$; $r \to r^e \bmod p$.

This is similar to Okamoto-Tanaka system (Section 2.3) except that in this case the users select their own secret keys. Observe that in this setting it is not necessary that gcd(e,(p-1)(q-1))=1. In particular we can take e=2 to get a key exchange protocol based on the square root problem.

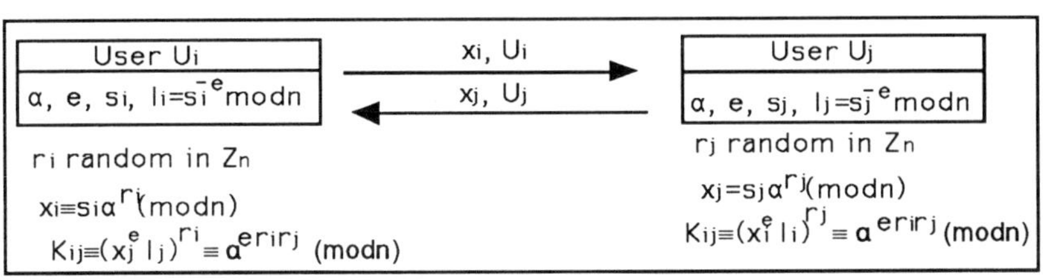


### 3.2.2 A key exchange protocol based on the discrete logarithm

In this case $G=Z_{p-1}(+)$, $H=Z_p^*(\cdot)$, p prime, and α=1 (which is a generator of G).

So $\alpha^r$ can be written 1+1+...+1 (r-times)≡r modp. Therefore f: r → $\beta^r$(modp), where $\beta$=f(1)∈ $Z_p^*$ ($\beta$ must be either primitive, or has "large' order). User $U_i$ selects his secretkey $s_i \in Z_{p-1}$. The public key is $I_i \equiv \beta^{-s_i}$modp.

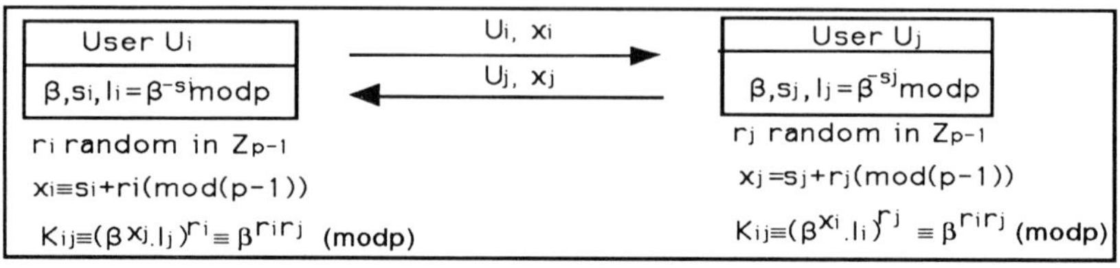


The efficiency of this protocol can be improved by adopting some of the modular reductions proposed by Schnorr [11] and implemented in the DSA [12]. For example, we can take $\beta$ to have order q, a prime factor of (p-1) which is not "too large' (but superpolynomial in logp) and then reduce $r_i$,$r_j$, modulo q.

## 4. CONCLUSION

We have reviewed some of the currently available authentication systems for computer networks. Our objective is to investigate such systems in an adverserial environment. We have described a public key distribution system which has a two-way, one round, key-exchange protocol with a low communication and computation complexity. The system is designed to protect the user, and is based on the public-file model of identification of Feige-Fiat-Shamir. It is ideally suited for Smart Card implementation. We envisage a hybrid system which can be used to extend the functionality of Kerberos. The Key Authentication Center has diminished control and responsibility and can revoke the rights of any user. To prevent misrepresentation of users, the public key of a user (even if his rights are invoked) must remain the same for the lifetime of the system. Ultimately some form of trust must always exist in a distributed system. The features of our system are summarized below.

- public key encryption
- one-round, two-way authentication, key distribution protocol with low communication and computational complexity.
- on-line server, used occasionally; immediate revocation of rights.

## 5. REFERENCES


1 R.M. Needham and M.D. Schroeder. Using Encryption for Authentication in Large Networks of Computers. *Commun. ACM,* 21, 1978, pp.993-999.

2 S.P.Miller, C. Newmann,J.I. Schiller and J.H. Saltzer. Kerberos Authentication and Authorization System. *Project Athena Technical Plan,* MIT, 1987.

3 J.T. Kohl. The Evolution of the Kerberos Authenitcation Service. Proceedings EurOpen Conference, Tromse, Norway, 1991.

4 T.Beth and H.J. Knobloch. Open Network Authentication Without an Online Server. Proceedings CS90, Symposium on Computer Security, Rome, 1990.

5 E. Okamoto. Key Distribution Systems Based on Identification Information. *Advances in Cryptology-Crypto'87, LNCS#293,* Springer-Verlag, 1988, pp. 194-202.

6 T. El Gamal. A Public Key Cryptosystem and a Signature Scheme Based on Discrete Logarithms. IEEE Trans. Inform. Theory S1, 1985, pp. 469-472.

7 U. Feige, A. Fiat, and A. Shamir. Zero knowledge proofs of identity. In *Journal of Cryptology,* 1(2), pp. 77-94, May 25-27, 1988.

8 S. Bengio, G. Brassard, Y. Desmedt, C. Goutier, and J.-J Quisquater, Secure implementations of identification systems. Journal of Cryptology, 4(2), 1991, pp. 175-184.

9 C.G. Günther. An Identity-Based Key Exchange Protocol. *Advances in Cryptology-Eurocrypt '89, LNCS #434,* Springer-Verlag, 1990, pp. 29-37.

10 E. Okamoto and K. Tanaka. Key Distribution System Based on Identification Information. *IEEE J. Selected Areas Commun,* SAC-7, 1989, pp.481-485.

11 C.P.Schnorr. Efficient Identification and Signatures for Smart Cards. *Advances in Cryptology-Crypto "89, LNCS #435,* Springer-Verlag, 1990, pp.239-252.

12 Digital Signature Standard, Federal Register, Vol. 56, No 169, 1991.

Education and Society / R. Aiken (Editor)
Information Processing 92, Volume II
Elsevier Science Publishers B.V. (North-Holland)


# Group-Oriented Key Management and Authentication Method

Yasushi Mutoh, Kazuyuki Takagi, Ken-ichi Okada, and Yutaka Matsushita

Department of Instrumentation Engineering, Faculty of Science and Technology,
Keio University, 3-14-1 Hiyoshi, Kouhoku, Yokohama 223 JAPAN

**Abstract**

A cryptographic scheme can be used for controlling access to various information, since no user without a proper key can not decipher encrypted information. On the other hand, attention to the computer supported cooperative work has increased recently. Therefore, we propose a key management method supporting cooperative work, "Group-oriented Key Management method (GKM)", and an authentication method based on it,"Interactive Authentication Method based on GKM (IA/GKM)."

In GKM, each user manages data for generating communication key (we call them "pieces".) instead of keys themselves. For a cryptographic communication with other users, users can generate communication keys generated from a common key and adequate pieces. Since users do not hold communication keys that is used to encipher and decipher, this method raises key security. In IA/GKM, a prover can be authenticated by a verifier who can be any user else.

Keyword Codes : E.3; H.4.3; K.6.5
Keywords : Data Encryption; Information Systems Applications, Communications Applications; Management of Computing and Information Systems, Security and Protection

## 1. Introduction

A cryptgraphy is a scheme to secure security, authenticity, or integrity of data. In addition to these, it can be used for controlling access to information, for no user without a proper key can not decipher the encrypted data. In local area networks or communication satellite networks equipped with broadcast facilities, secure communication such as an encryption system controlling access to information is generally needed, since each user can pick up all information easily[1].

On the other hand, attention to computer supported cooperative work has increased recently[2][3]. Since a member of a group in cooperative work needs to communicate with other members of his groups frequently, it will be desireble that members of a same group can access freely each other. In an organization, there may be many members who belong to several groups, since we usually have several works at a same time. In the case of managing groups we will have to consider the change of group structure, since new working groups may be organized frequently and some groups may be re-organized with some flexibility. Practically such changes of group structure mentioned above can be seen very often in our organization.

It is a typical coventional cryptographic key management method for group communications that keys are assigned to the members of each group and the members make cryptgraphic communications with these keys ( Copy Key method : CK.). But this method has serious problems in terms of key renewal and re-distribution[4]. In order to change the structure of groups such that a new member is added, a member is removed, or a new group is organized, keys for the members of the changed (or new) group must be renewed and re-distributed. Since these changes seem to occur very often in an organization, renewal and re-distribution of keys are thought to be some troubles for a key manager. Therefore a key management scheme is required so that keys can be changed easily according to the change of group structure.

In order to satisfy this requirement, we propose " Group-oriented Key Management method (GKM )", where multiple keys are generated from a common key and some data for generating communication key . GKM has the following effective features :

(1) Renewal and re-distribution of keys are not necessary whenever the structure of groups changes.
(2) It is not necessary to make a distinction between group communications and individual communications, because an indivisual communication is regarded as a group communication of two members.
(3) Since each user uses communication keys generated from only one common key, communication keys can be renewed easily by changing the common key.
(4) Since each user holds a common key and pieces instead of communication keys used for encryption and decryption, it is difficlt for attackers to disclose communication keys.

When we construct a secure communication system, we need not only a secure key management scheme but also a secure authenticaton scheme in order to keep security. Therefore we propose an interactive authentication method based on GKM, "Interactve Authentication Method based on GKM (IA/GKM)". This method satisfies an important requirement that a prover can be authenticated with any member else.

## 2. GKM : Group-oriented Key Management Method

### 2. 1 Common key and Pieces

We consider a communication system where many groups are formed and each user belongs to one or more groups. When let n be the number of all users, there are specified n pieces $\{P_1, P_2, \ldots P_n\}$ and each user holds a common key and unique sets of pieces obtained by combinations of n pieces taken n-1 at a time, then a member Mi and another member Mj can share an unique set of n-2 pieces without fail. An example of distribution of the common key and pieces to an each member is illustrated in fig.1, where n equals to 6. In fig.1 the members of a group $\{M_1, M_2, M_4\}$ have $P_3$ , $P_5$ and $P_6$, on the other hand, the non-members $\{M_3, M_5, M_6\}$ do not have all of $P_3$ , $P_5$ and $P_6$. Since $M_1$, $M_2$ and $M_4$ can generate a communication key from the common key K0 and $P_3$ , $P_5$ and $P_6$, they can make a secure cryptgraphic communication with each other.

| | P1 | P2 | P3 | P4 | P5 | P6 | K0 |
|---|---|---|---|---|---|---|---|
| * M1 | | ○ | ● | ○ | ● | ● | ○ |
| * M2 | ○ | | ● | ○ | ● | ● | ○ |
| M3 | ○ | ○ | | ○ | ○ | ○ | ○ |
| * M4 | ○ | ○ | ● | | ● | ● | ○ |
| M5 | ○ | ○ | ○ | ○ | | ○ | ○ |
| M6 | ○ | ○ | ○ | ○ | ○ | | ○ |

**Mi** : Member i
**Pi** : Piece i
**K0** : Common Key
* : A member of the group {M1,M2,M4}
● : A common piece for a group communication
○ : A distributed piece

**Fig.1 An example of piece distribution .**

When a user wants to broadcast to all users, the common key K0 is used for a broadcast communication among all users of the organization. It is because that a common piece of all users does not exist, and the only common key is shared in common.

### 2. 2 Key generation

In GKM, users do not hold communication keys used for enciphering and deciphering, but hold a common key and pieces instead of keys themselves. Each user gets a communication key generated from a common key and some pieces held by himself, when a cryptographic communication. Communication key K can be generated from a common key K0 and a piece P as follows:

$$K = f(K0, P) \qquad (1),$$

where f( ) is an appropriate encryption function in order to generate a unique K from an unique set of P and K0. If multiple **P** {P1, P2, . . . Pi} are used to generate a communication key K, it will be generated as follows:

$$K = f(\ldots f(f(K0, P1), P2), \ldots\ldots, Pi) = f(K0,\mathbf{P}) \qquad (2),$$

where **P** is substituted in the ascending order of the subscript number of **P**. If f( ) is one to one mapping, a unique key will be generated from a unique set of **P**. Communication keys are generated from the combinations of n-1 pieces taken r (2<=r<=n-1) at a time. Therefore the total number of keys which can be generated from n-1 pieces is as follows:

$$\sum_{r=1}^{n-1} {}_{n-1}C_r = 2^{n-1} - 1 \quad (3).$$

Consequently a user can manage $2^{n-1}$ keys ( one common key and $2^{n-1}$- 1 communication keys) by holding one common key and n-1 pieces.

## 3. IA/GKM : Interactive Authentication Method based on GKM

### 3. 1 Requirements for authentication scheme

For a secure communications or access control in a broadcast environment with a cryptography, not only key management scheme but also authentication scheme are needed. Then we propose a prototype authentication scheme based on GKM proposed above,"Interactive Authentication method based on GKM (IA/GKM)". A.Fiat and A.Shamir said that an authentication scheme must meet the following condition : a prover (A )can only prove to the verifier (B) that he is A, but someone else cannot prove to B that he is A[5]. Therefore our method is designd to meet this condition by utilizing the feature of GKM .

### 3. 2 Authentication procedure

STEP 1: A prover Mi generates a random number r, and generates a proof Fi from r and all pieces except Pi, as follows:

$$Fi = g( \ldots g( g( r, P1),P2), \ldots ,Pn ) \quad (4)$$

where g( ) is an appropriate one-way function, which is independent of its operation order. An example of g( ) is as follows,

$$g( x, y ) = x^y \bmod n \quad (5)$$

STEP 2: Mi sends Fi and his identity number i to a verifier Mj.

STEP 3: Mj sends his identity number j back to Mi.

STEP 4: Mi generates a credential Cj from r and piece Pj, as follows:

$$Cj = g( r, Pj ) \quad (6)$$

STEP 5: Mi sends Cj to Mj.

STEP 6: Mj generates the proof Fi' from Fi and Pi, and the credential Cj' from Cj and all pieces except Pj, as follows:

$$Fi' = g( Fi, Pi ) \quad (7)$$

$$Cj = g( \ldots .g( g( Cj, P1 ), P2 ) \ldots ,Pn ) \quad (8)$$

STEP 7: If Fi' is equated with Cj', Mi is authenticated.(shown in fig.2)

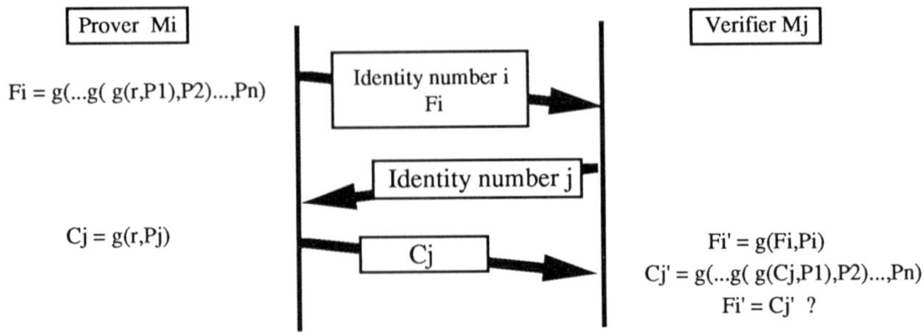


**Fig.2 Authentication procedure**

## 4. Evalution

### 4. 1 Group-oriented key management method

**(1)Key security**

In this section we discuss about a ratio of risk with which other keys are disclosed when some keys are disclosed to an attacker in some ways such as an exhaustive search. It is very difficult for an attacker to get pieces, for they are not used directly for encryption and decryption. Though he may be able to get a few keys in some ways if possible, it will be the fatal problem whether he can infer other keys from keys which he has disclosed. Since f( ) of formula (2) is one way function, he can not infer pieces which are used to generate disclosed keys. Therefore, if one key is disclosed (but none of pieces at the same time), other keys will be kept in safety .[6]

On the other hand, since the common key K0 is directly used for encryption in the case of broadcast communication, it should be changed periodically in order to keep the system more safe[7].

**(2) The number of keys**

Here we consider an evaluation for GKM and Copy Key method (CK) in assigning keys to members of groups. It is because that CK is conventional among key management methods for the secret-key cryptosystem. Assume a communication system that supports individual, group and broadcast communications. And assume that there are n users in a organization and each user belongs to g groups($0<=g<=2^{n-1}-n-1$).

If there are only two members in a group, group communications between them will be regarded as an individual communication. And if the function f( ) of formula (2) is the same encryption function as that used for text encryption, pieces could be regarded as keys. In GKM method, the number of keys required for each user is n, that is one common key and n-1 pieces mentioned in section 2.2. On the other hand,in CK the number of keys required for each user is g+n, that is g keys for group communications, n-1 keys for individual communications and one key for broadcast communications. Therefore,in the case that the number of group is very many, it can be said that our method is more effective than CK .

**(3) Re-distribution of keys for group changing**

When the struture of groups changes, it will be serious problems to make new group keys and distribute them to all members in CK. On the other hand, it is not necessary to re-distribute either a common key or pieces in GKM , because each member of a group can get an unique group key generated from a common key and pieces which are shared by all members of the group. Since these changes may happen frequently, GKM will be highly effective from the viewpoint of key management.

**(4) Renewal of keys**

Since using a same key many times reduces key security, keys must be renewed in a certain term[7]. In CK, since all keys must be renewed, all transmissions must be kept safe from illegal members. However, it is time-consuming to renew and re-distribute all keys. On the other hand,in GKM the renewal of only a common key can serve the same purpose, for the common key is used for all key generation. It is very easy way and the system is kept safe unless the common key is disclosed. But all pieces need be renewed in order to make the system more safe. So it can be said that GKM has two levels of key renewal.

**4. 2 Authentication**

In this section, we discuss about the features of our authentication method. GKM is designed for the secret-key cryptosystem, because the secret-key cryptosystem has the advantage of speed, security and group communication. IA/GKM also is designed for the secret-key cryptosystem, since it is based on GKM. The condition that a prover can be authenticated with a same proof by any member else can be realized in authentication schemes based on the public-key cryptosystem[8],[9] like as RSA[10], but it cannot be realized in conventional ones based on the secret-key cryptosystem generally. Therefore, the fact that IA/GKM satisfies the condition that a prover can be authenticated with a same proof by any member else is a very remarkable feature.

Since IA/GKM is designed basically to satisfy the condition memtioned above,it has some expansivility of higher level of authentication. For an example, a two-way authentication method may be designed. If in STEP 3 of authentication procedure the verifier Mj performs as the prover Mi do in STEP 1 and STEP 2, Mj also can be authenticated by Mi. Moreover, since all members of any group share a common key and an unique set of pieces in GKM, by utilizing this feature a membership authentication method may be designed. If in STEP 1 of authentication procedure Mi generates a proof from the pieces which is used to generate a group key, he will be able to prove that he belong to the group.

## 5. Conclusion

We pay an attention to networks equipped with broadcast facilities, so in this paper we have proposed a cryptographic key management method for broadcast communications and an authentication method based on it. Since GKM generates various group communication keys from a common key and pieces, each user can communicate with others without making a distinction between group communications and individual communications. Furthermore, re-distribution of keys is not necessary when the structure of groups changes . Moreover, we consider to apply GKM to key management in a hierarchical group structure[11].

Since IA/GKM is designed for an authentication scheme utilizing GKM, it has the feature that the prover can be authenticated by any member else with a same proof. Moreover IA/GKM has some expansivility of higher level of authentication such as two-way authentication and membership authentication etc.

## REFERENCES


[1] S. J. Kent, "Security Requirement and protocols for a Broadcast Scenario", IEEE Trans. Commun., COM29, no. 6, pp. 778-786, June 1981.

[2] Kum-Yew Lai and Thomas W.Malone,"Object Lens : A Spreadsheet for Cooperative Work",Proc. CSCW '88,1988.

[3] S.Ichimura,N.Matsuura,K.Okada and Y.Matsushita,"I-CEM : an Intelligent Communication System for Collaborative Work",Proc. 1st International Conference on Parallel and Distributed Information System,December,1991.

[4] Y. Desmedt, "SOCIETY AND GROUP ORIENTED CRYPTOGRAPHY: A NEW CONCEPT", Lect Notes Comput Sci, 293, pp. 120-127, 1988.

[5] A.Fiat and A.Shamir,"How To Prove Yourself: Pratical Solutions to Identification and Signature Problems",Proc CRYPTO '86,LNCS 263,Springer-Verlag,pp.186-194,1986.

[6] Merkle,R.C. and Hellman,M.E., "On the Security of Multiple Encryption", Commun. ACM, vol.24, no.7, pp.465-467, July 1981.

[7] E.Okamoto and K.Nakamura,"Limitlife of keys in cryptographic key management systems"Lect. Notes Comput. Sci.,218,pp.246-259,1986.

[8] W. Diffie, and M. Hellman, "New Directions in Cryptography", IEEE Transactions on Information Theory, Vol. 22, No. 6, pp. 644-654, Nov. 1976.

[9] S.Goldwasser,S.Micali and C.Rackoff,"The Kowledge Complexity of Interactive Proof Systems,Proc. of STOC '85,pp.291-304,1985.

[10] R. L. Rivest, A. Shamir and L. Adleman, "A method for obtaining digital signatures and public-key cryptosystem" Comm. ACM, vol. 21, No. 2, Feb, 1978.

[11] H.Nakamura,K.Takagi,K.Okada and Y.Matsushita,"Hierarchical Group Oriented Key Management Method : HGK",Computer Security Applications Conference,6th Annual,pp.44-49,1990.

Education and Society / R. Aiken (Editor)
Information Processing 92, Volume II
Elsevier Science Publishers B.V. (North-Holland)



# Implementation of Security Functions into File Transfer, Access and Management Protocol

Hua Chang, Ostap Monkewich and William A. McCrum

Systems Interconnection Research, Department of Communications, Canada, 300 Slater Street Ottawa, Ontario K1A 0C8

**Abstract**
In the ISO/IEC 8571 standard, File Transfer, Access and Management (FTAM), filestore-password and initiator-identity of the F-INITIALIZE-request Protocol Data Unit are exposed to the lower layers and public networks during the initial association establishment. In the scheme of access control, the file create-password and the eight access-type passwords for read, insert, replace, extend, etc. all face the same problem. To enhance the protective service of authentication and access control in FTAM, a set of security functions were implemented and positioned within the FTAM constructs. The implemented security modules were added to FTAM without modifying the standard.

Keyword Codes: K.6.5; C.2.2; H.4.3
Keywords: Security and Protection; Network Protocols; Communications Applications

## 1. BASIC RESOURCES FOR THE IMPLEMENTATION

This work was carried out to study security issues within the framework of the seven-layer Basic Reference Model for Open Systems Interconnection. Relevant protocols and security features were developed on a VAX/VMS system in the Division of Systems Interconnection (DSI) Research in the Department of Communications. The objectives of the work were to provide first-hand experience with implementation of selected security enhancements for upper layer applications and to serve as a basic resource for future implementation and testing of specific security requirements. As part of the research program, DSI has developed a full seven-layer implementation of OSI. At each incremental phase of the development, the implementation was interoperability tested with a number of international partners. The class 0 component of the OSI Transport protocol was demonstrated during a joint experiment between Sweden and Canada at the Second International Conference on the Introduction of OSI Standards, Ottawa, 1984 [1] and the Third International Conference on the Introduction of OSI Standards, Cambridge, 1985 [2]. The Class 2 and 4 Transport protocols and the Session protocol were subsequently implemented semi-automatically from formal specifications in ESTELLE [3]. The Session protocol includes the Session kernel functions, two-way alternate and simultaneous data transfer functions and release functions. During a demonstration with Japan, South Korea and Canada at the Fifth International Conference on the Application of Standard for OSI, Tokyo, 1989, FTAM protocol was used to transfer North American Presentation Level Protocol Syntax (NAPLPS) files. The resulting seven-layer OSI system will serve as a framework for interworking operations and conformance testing of security functions.

## 2. CONSIDERATION ON SECURITY ENHANCEMENTS IN FTAM

The document ISO/IEC 7498-2, Basic Reference Model - Part 2: Security Architecture specifies the relationship of security services, mechanisms and layers. ISO/IEC 7498-2 is not an implementation specification and does not indicate what security features should be implemented for a particular security problem. Representatives of JTC1/SC21 WG5 FTAM and WG1 groups on security [4] considered several FTAM security issues in the context of Upper layers: Should FTAM continue to pass names and passwords in its protocol (both encrypted and unencrypted)? Should FTAM consider the use of public key mechanisms? The FTAM group reviewed the framework and recommended a number of ways to achieve the security enhancements. The priority was given to the enhancement of the management of Access Control Lists and to better peer authentication. Several amendments to the ISO/IEC 8571 were subsequently issued. This work is based on the current OSI environment and indicates where and how security functions can be placed in FTAM.

## 3. THE POSITIONING OF SECURITY FUNCTIONS IN FTAM

The basic architecture of FTAM can be described in terms of the Virtual Filestore, the File Service and the File Protocol. The Virtual Filestore defines a reference model dealing with a filestore, its files and file properties in a unified view across machines. It includes a set of file attributes, a rooted tree structure of the file's contents and the number of constraint sets and document types. The operations, such as read, insert, delete and replace are actions on files. Constraint sets define restrictions on file access structures. These include sequential flat constraint set, ordered flat constraint set and ordered hierarchical constraint set. Document types define file structures as well as the data types forming the data units. The File Service definitions are based on the characteristics of the virtual filestore rather than any real filestores that contain actual files. These characteristics are system independent. The responsibility of FTAM implementors is to rewrite mapping functions for each local system. These functions should map the virtual filestore descriptions and operations into local file descriptions and operations. The file service defines the operations on the virtual filestore. Operations may be taken on a whole file or a data unit. Typical operations are create, select, open, read, insert, replace, and delete. These operations are implemented as service primitives. The file protocol specifies the valid service primitive sequences and the detailed form of the protocol data units that carry the semantics of the request and response primitives. The basic structure of the file protocol reflects the nesting of the file service regimes. The behaviour of the file protocol is usually described as a finite state machine.

Let us take an example to show the sequence for a file transfer. Suppose that there exist an

FTAM Initiator and an FTAM Responder to carry out a file transfer. The Initiator starts from F-INITIALIZE request and waits for an F-INITIALIZE confirmation, the Responder waits for an F-INITIALIZE indication and sends an F-INITIALIZE response. To send a file, the Initiator and the Responder communicate using the following phases:

- FTAM service initialization phase,
- File selection phase,
- File access phase,
- Data transfer phase,
- File access termination phase,
- File deselection phase,
- FTAM Service Termination Phase.

At the FTAM Service Initialization Phase, F-INITIALIZE-request Protocol Data Unit (PDU) is encoded and enclosed as user data in the ASSOCIATION request service primitive of Association Control Service Element. It passes User-Identity, Account and Password data values of F-INITIALIZE-request PDU down to the lower layers and public networks. Suppose that Password is encrypted, then the readable octet string or graphic string representing the password is then an encrypted "pattern". The encryption does not prevent an intruder from locating the encrypted "pattern" in the PDU stream on the public networks. This "pattern" need not to be decrypted to break into the system. For example, a Password "k1r6w7" of a User is encrypted as "YGVA3NQ1qDY02". There is no semantics between Password and User-Identity. Their decryption is not necessary for an intruder to break a system. Passwords of a closed system are not accessible to public, but are fully exposed in an open system. In certain cases, lower layers may be used to provide security service. Also, when Application protocol control information is exchanged between open systems, the provision of security service may be achieved within the Application Service Element (ASE). For the purpose of this work, security procedures were placed within FTAM. Some security features may be implemented to be invoked during the File selection phase to protect the Access-Passwords in the F-SELECT-request PDU visible to the lower layers and the public networks. Depending on the chosen type of Access-Request, there may be eight optional passwords involved corresponding to the read, insert, replace, extend, erase, read-attribute, change-attribute and delete operations. There is a similar mechanism associated with the Access-Control-List at the File access phase.

## 4. SECURITY ENHANCEMENTS WITH AUTHENTICATION SERVICES

The FTAM standard, ISO/IEC 8571, defines only unilateral authentication service at FTAM regime control. Three services are associated with FTAM regime control: regime establishment service, regime termination service and regime abort service. The F-INITIALIZE primitives are used only to create an FTAM regime. The F-INITIALIZE request primitive is issued by the file transfer initiator. In the F-INITIALIZE request, the initiator identity parameter identifies the calling user. If this parameter value is unacceptable to the responder, the responder generates a state result indicating failure to establish the FTAM regime. The filestore password parameter of the primitive conveys a password which is used to authenticate the initiator to the responder. This parameter is a GraphicString or an OCTET STRING defined by Abstract Syntax Notation One (ASN.1) [5].

To improve the unilateral authentication service, an encryption algorithm was used with a time dependency (timestamp) to code Filestore Password as a function of its plaintext, Initiator Identity and a timestamp. The timestamp was derived from the generation and expiring times of the encrypted filestore password using year, month, day, hour and minute. An instance of a coded Filestore Password is valid only for a period of few minutes. The steps involved are depicted as: (1) FTAM Initiator submits his identity and filestore password to a local security manager (physical or logical). (2) The local security manager uses a software module to encrypt the filestore password as a mathematical function of plaintext of the submitted initiator identity, filestore password and the time (timestamp). Clocks are logically synchronized by bilateral agreements. (3) FTAM initiator sends the encrypted filestore password through an F-INITIALIZE-request PDU to an FTAM responder. (4) The FTAM responder extracts the filestore password from F-INITIALIZE indication and submits it to a local security manager. (5) The local security manager decrypts the filestore password and verifies the time-stamp. If the received initiator identity and the filestore password are correct, then a positive answer is sent back to the FTAM responder.

The coding functions and its algorithms contained in a separate module can be changed from time to time. Thus, changes to the module as a result of future advances in cryptography, mathematical techniques or computational capabilities can be supported. This module can be integrated with an FTAM implementation. The danger from direct attack and replay may be reduced without the need to supply or distribute encryption keys through networks. It solves the problem of the exposure of user's password raised by WG1 SECURITY and WG5 FTAM RAPPORTEUR GROUPS in 1989 [4]. The FTAM standard does not define mutual authentication service. Unilateral authentication provides assurance of the identity of only one principle, the FTAM Initiator. There is a possibility of opportunistic attacks. An intruder may tap in the middle of an authentication exchange, intercept the authentication information and take over the role of the responder. There is no verification of authentication information of FTAM responder.

At FTAM regime control, the filestore password used for authentication and association establishment is not used to set any activity attributes into the next file service regime - file selection regime control.

## 5. SECURITY ENHANCEMENTS WITH ACCESS CONTROL SERVICES

In FTAM, access to files is managed by the Virtual Filestore. The access control scheme is based on access control lists. Access control lists are sets and sequences of entries, such as requested access, concurrency access, user identity, access passwords and application entity title. There are eight types of elements in the requested access parameter: read, insert, replace, extend, erase, read attribute, change attribute and delete. When a file is selected by the use of F-SELECT, F-CREATE, or F-RECOVER, the requested access parameter is used to state the access types. These access requirements may be password protected by the access control file attribute which is matched to the access passwords parameters. The access passwords provide passwords associated with the actions specified in the requested access parameter. The access control decision is made on the basis of whether or not a match is made between the requested access and its access passwords. The parameter of the access passwords is a major component in the access control for validation of the requested access.

When FTAM passes access passwords down to the lower layers and public networks, simple encryption of the access passwords may not prevent intruders from replaying the encrypted passwords. If we use timestamp encrypted password mechanism as implemented for the authentication part, it would not increase the security level with access control.

FTAM has an asymmetrical initiator-responder relationship, similar to a client-server model. From the security point of view, servers are necessarily trusted. Initiators must be subject to a security check. After initial connection establishment, the initiator should request a security check for file access. The responder may provide a random number to the initiator. The initiator must send the received random number and his identity to a security manager to compose a time-dependent access password. Initiators are not eligible to compose any access passwords. The module for composing access passwords resides outside FTAM. The access passwords obtained from a local security manager is valid only for a very short time, for example, five minutes. It cannot be reused by the same initiator or anyone else. Anyone with the intention to trace the secrecy of the password algorithms, has to repeatedly request passwords and immediately become a suspect recorded by the security manager. This represents one solution to the problem of password exposure in FTAM. The password generation mechanism can be updated from time to time. It is independent of any FTAM implementation and its standard. The steps involved are depicted as: (1) an FTAM initiator asks an FTAM responder for a random number; (2) the FTAM responder sends a random number to the initiator; (3) the initiator submits the received random number, his identity, and access passwords to a local security manager; (4) the security manager uses the received data to encrypt access passwords with a timestamp; (5) the initiator sends the encrypted access passwords to the FTAM responder through an F-SELECT request. (6) the FTAM responder extracts the access passwords and submits to a local security manager. (7) the security manager decrypts and verifies the received access passwords and sends back the result. If it is a positive result, then the FTAM responder sends a positive F-SELECT response. These steps may be included in an FTAM implementation without modification of the standard.

In Annex E of ISO/IEC 8571-3, File Transfer, Access and Management - Part 3: File Service Definition, the state transition diagrams define the sequences of service primitives in the external file service. These diagrams can be decomposed into several directed subgraphs. The diagrams for the initiator and the responder applicable at the initiating and responding file service access points are provided separately.

Let us analyze the state transition diagram of the file regime establishment service (initiator) Figure 13 of ISO/IEC 8571-3, Annex E. In Figure 13, there exists a directed subgraph whose arcs compose a closed circuit. It represents a sequence of six service primitives: (1) F-SELECT request, (2) F-SELECT confirm (positive), (11) F-READ-ATTRIB request, (12) F-READ-ATTRIB confirm, (4) F-DESELECT request and (5) F-DESELECT confirm.

For comparison, the sequence numbers shown in parentheses were kept the same as in Figure 13. Before file access and read attributes, an initiator may execute the above sequence an arbitrary number of times. Normally the sequence is executed only once. The initiator may use the above sequence to request a random number from the responder. On first execution, the access password parameter of F-SELECT request may take on the value of the password for authentication. For a real file access, the initiator has to use the received random number to compose the access password parameter to execute F-SELECT request and subsequently the other service primitives. A similar procedure is used for the execution of the respective sequence of service primitives on the responder side. The respective algorithms may be stated as follows:

Initiator:
1. Send F-SELECT request to access a random number generator as a resource with the filename attribute of encrypt.txt which is under the control of a security manager on responder side.
2. The access passwords of F-SELECT request take the same value of the password for authentication. The access password(read) of this F-SELECT request instance is valid only for access to the random number generator of responder.
3. If receive F-SELECT confirm (positive), send F-READ-ATTRIB request with read-filename and read-encryption-name attribute-names.
4. receive F-READ-ATTRIB response.
5. Extract the actual values of encryption-name as a random number assigned from the security manager of the responder side. 6. Deliver the received random number and initiator identity to the security manager to compose access password for subsequent file access.

Responder:
1. Receive F-SELECT indication. Verify whether its filename attributes is encrypt.txt and its access password(read) is the same as the password for the authentication at the association establishment, then send positive F-SELECT response otherwise send negative one.
2. If a positive F-SELECT response was sent, then wait and receive F-READ-ATTRIB indication .
3. If there read-filename and read-encryption-name were in the received F-READ-ATTRIB indication instance, then send F-READ-ATTRIB response with encrypt.txt filename and a random number as encryption-name actual value.
4. wait for second instance of F-SELECT indication, verify whether the received password satisfy an encryption function of the above random number, initiator identity and the access time instance, otherwise gobo step 1.

Applying the algorithms to reading a file, the Initiator and the Responder communicate through the following phases:
- FTAM service initialization phase,
- (File selection phase, F-READ-ATTRIB phase, and File deselection phase)
- File selection phase, - File access phase,
- Data transfer phase, - File access termination phase,
- File deselection phase, - FTAM Service Termination Phase.

Similarly, for creating a file, the Initiator and the Responder communicate through the following phases:
- FTAM service initialization phase,
- (File selection phase, F-READ-ATTRIB phase, and File deselection phase)
- File create phase, - File open phase,
- Data transfer phase, - File close phase,
- File deselection phase, - FTAM Service Termination Phase.

The sequences of phases enclosed in parentheses are inserted for getting a random number to compose access password for a real file access at the second File selection instance. The described mechanism demonstrates a new way to achieve security enhancements in open systems. The flexibility allows the selection of any valid sequence of protocol service primitives to realize the security requirements while avoiding modifications of the standard.

## 6. CONCLUSIONS

To protect FTAM initiator identity and password from exposure to public networks, an encryption with time stamp function was implemented to encode the initiator password. The encoding/decoding modules can be updated from time to time. They are used only by the security manager. To enhance security service for access control, a procedure for mutual exchange of a random number to compose the access passwords was designed and implemented. The procedure uses a directed subgraph constructed by F-SELECT and F-READ-ATTRIB service primitives on the state diagram to achieve the implemented security service. It can execute a closed circuit sequence of service primitives one or more times without violating the FTAM protocol machine and standard. Our experience in the implementation of the security functions indicates that there are several ways to achieve security enhancements using FTAM state diagram. Many optional FPDU parameters can be used to carry and exchange information for security management.

## 7. REFERENCES


1 O. Monkewich, M. Maksud and S. Weckner, "International Interconnection using OSI Transport Protocol", The Second International Conference on Introduction of OSI Standards, Ottawa, Canada, 1984.

2 K. Suzuki, T Kato and Y. Urbano, "Implementation and Testing of OSI Protocols",The 3rd International Conference on the Introduction of OSI Standards, Cambridge, UK, September, 1985.

3 G. v. Bochmann, "Semi-Automatic Implementation of Transport and Session Protocols", Computer Standards & Interfaces 5:343-349, 1986.

4 ISO/IEC JTC1/SC21 N4184, Request for National Body Comment on Security Enhancements to FTAM, 1989.

5 ISO/IEC CD8824, Information Technology - Open Systems Interconnection - Abstract Syntax Notation One (ASN.1), Parts 1-4, 1991.

Education and Society / R. Aiken (Editor)
Information Processing 92, Volume II
Elsevier Science Publishers B.V. (North-Holland)


# Reducing society's vulnerability as computers and networks proliferate

Lance J. Hoffman
Department of Electrical Engineering and Computer Science
The George Washington University
Washington, D. C. 20052 USA
hoffman@seas.gwu.edu

**Abstract**

After a review of previous work on the vulnerability of society to computer systems, we consider briefly what computer systems will look like in 2010 and the potential vulnerability of society of such systems. We enumerate some technical and policy issues which need to be resolved, and end with a suggestion of modeling work which may shed light on the problem.

Keyword Codes: K.4.1; K.5.1; K.6.5
Keywords: Computers and Society, Public Policy Issues; Legal Aspects of Computing, Software Protection; Management of Computing and Information Systems, Security and Protection

## 1. INTRODUCTION

As the world becomes increasingly dependent on computers and communications, significant system failures -- events which damage a significant segment of the populace or weaken social stability -- will occur from time to time. The frequency of these may increase as more and more systems are interconnected together.

### 1.1. Previous Vulnerability Studies

As early as 1979, the Swedish government concluded that "societal vulnerability is ... unacceptably high." [SARK 1979]. In 1981, the Organisation for Economic Cooperation and Development (OECD) explored the issue at a workshop at which sixteen nations were represented [OECD 1982]. In 1982, computer specialists disagreed at the United States National Computer Conference whether the society was being made more vulnerable or resilient due to the widespread use of computer systems [Hoffman 1982, Turn 1983]. A similar discussion took place at the 1983 International Federation of Information Processing Ninth World Computer Conference in Paris. Also that year, a group dominated by strategic thinkers, policy analysts, and lawyers (as opposed to technological experts) considered the topic at a workshop at Georgetown University [CSIS 1984]. The (electronic) Forum on Reliability and Risks to the Public, sponsored by the Association for Computing Machinery (ACM), has been the scene of a discussion of related topics since 1984. It was established by the ACM to question the risks in existing and new computer systems and to examine the consequences of failures in these systems.

**1.2 Security Problems in Today's Systems**

There has been an increasing number of publications related to safety and security of computer systems, for example [COMPASS 1991, Leveson 1990, RISKS 1989]. Several real-life computer system problems were described in the landmark report by the U. S. National Academy of Sciences [NAS 1991]. Examples included:

- Software design errors freezing much of the long distance telephone network of American Telephone and Telegraph Co. (ATT)
- An algorithm error in a radiation therapy machine which caused at least three separate patient deaths
- Thousands of attacks by computer viruses [Hoffman 1990, Denning 1990, Ferbrache 1992]

As computer applications reach into more and more domains, there are increased likelihoods of programming or logic errors. In safety-critical applications, faulty programming may mean lost lives. Intentional (as opposed to accidental) attacks also pose a threat. And intentional transnational attack threats may increase in an unstable international political environment, such as we have today [NAS 1991]. Already, we have reports of "computer virus factories" in some countries with a small number of computer-literate people who have little better to do than write viruses and try to propagate them. Personal computers have been delivered from the manufacturer with preformatted fixed disks, each containing a computer virus [Neumann 1992]. Shrink-wrapped software from legitimate companies has also been delivered with a virus [Stefanac 1988].

Decentralized networks of computers found in many organizations have fostered a situation in which (often part-time) system managers who are technically weak pay inadequate attention to security [Montz 1989]. Indeed, at some sites on the Internet key management personnel do not know who their system managers are. And organizations are linked to nontraditional users and other organizations [Clarke 1992]. This makes it difficult to install or control software and security upgrades.

**1.3. Network Vulnerabilities**

Networks complicate system security, even in nonelectronic systems. For example, in the New York City power blackout of 1977, the Consolidated Edison control room operator, confused by the complexity of rapidly occurring failures, called his off-duty supervisor for help. But the supervisor had lost electric power at home, and thus had to interpret complex network diagrams by the soft glow of a kerosene lantern. When the supervisor finally determined some corrective action, the harried operator carried it out improperly, plunging the entire New York metropolitan area into Stygian darkness.

Consider next the telephone network. Figure 1 shows just some telephone outages in 1991 in the United States, and their effects.

| | DATE | LOCATION | HOMES WITHOUT SERVICE | OTHER IMPACTS |
|---|---|---|---|---|
| F | Jan 4 | New York City | 6 000 000 | N.Y. mercantile exchange and commodity exchange shut down |
| S | June 10 | California | 2 000 000 | |
| S | June 26 | Baltimore | 10 000 000 | U. S. Government phones affected |
| S | June 26 | California | 3 000 000 | |
| W | June 26 | South Carolina | 150 000 | |
| S | July 2 | Pennsylvania | 1 000 000 | |
| P | Sept. 17 | New York City | 2 000 000 | 3 major New York airports shut down 6 hours |
| F | Sept. 23 | Miami | | Miami airport shut down |

(F= fiber cut, S = SS7 failure, S = switch failure, P = power failure)

Figure 1. Some U. S. Telephone Outages in 1991 and Their Effects

When it is remembered that the telephone in 1992 will be replaced by the computer in 2010, it is clear that more work must be done in software engineering and quality assurance.

Computer networks pose even greater challenges. Currently, at least 200,000 hosts and 1,300 networks are connected by the Internet, yet much of the programming controlling the network is somewhat out of date and not well-understood. To successfully launch a denial of service attack on either a host or the entire network is quite possible, as demonstrated by the Internet Worm of 1988 [Rochlis 1989, Spafford 1989]. Even since that attack, many of the network hosts have not been reconfigured to prevent that same attack from happening again. As Dennis Hall lamented in [Stoll 1989], "The agreements are informal and the networks are overloaded. Our software is fragile as well -- if people built houses the way we write programs, the first woodpecker would wipe out civilization."

By proactively taking security measures, vulnerability can be reduced significantly. Some of these measures might include:

- Building in survivability as a design requirement
- Requiring minimal safeguards for authentication, encryption, and transaction logging
- Requiring emergency and backup planning

Unfortunately, there is a lack of experience and education about high-tech vulnerabilities and networks. Many managers tend to be of the "if I ignore it, it will go away" school. And there is little constituency for crisis avoidance; careers tend to be made by resolving crises rather than avoiding them.

## 2. COMPUTING IN THE WORLD OF 2010

By 2010, the number of networked hosts and networks will have grown enormously. And by that time, computing will have likely subsumed other media. It's probable that the telephone, television, and computer will all be in one device carried in one's pocket or worn on one's wrist. Conversations will routinely include photographs and digitized audio and video recordings, and automatic natural language translation may be built in. There will be many more telephone-based (i.e., computer-based) services, and there will be massive data and program sharing using these telephone-based (computer-based) services. A person's personal telephone (computer) will be linked to nearly all the other telephones (computers) in the developed world.

## 3. ELECTRONIC TERRORISM AND WARFARE

We have already seen some instances of what could be called electronic terrorism, e.g., the Internet Worm incident and the Michelangelo and other viruses. For under $US600, anyone can now purchase an "electronic Saturday night special" -- a computer system along with the appropriate literature to construct and launch computer viruses. And virus incidents seem to be growing every year.

There is a potential military use of computer viruses [Cramer 1989] to remotely introduce computer viruses to enemy systems using radio frequency atmospheric signal transmissions. There has already been speculation that the United Nations forces secretly implanted viruses or rogue programs in certain Iraqi computer-based military systems for use during the Persian Gulf war in 1991 [Karn 1992, Slade 1992]. But there is a strategic question here as well: Would a country purchase weapons of war from another country that has been known to implant rogue programs in their electronic warfare systems?

Of course, the ultimate vulnerability is that of nuclear war. Could a computer system be improperly designed or coded such that false alerts, compound stimuli, a launch on warning policy, or other problems would inadvertently trigger a nuclear attack? This is a complex and detailed question, and has been treated in a long and excellent article [Borning 1987] elsewhere.

## 4. DAY TO DAY VULNERABILITIES

A good sampling of other vulnerabilities today can be seen in the small extract in Figure 2 of subject line postings from the ACM Forum on Reliability and Risks during the period July 1, 1991 to April 15, 1992. Computing professionals will have to work on both policy and technical issues to ameliorate some of these problems.

## 5. TECHNICAL ISSUES

The traditional and widespread von Neumann architecture is inappropriate for systems shared by a large number of users, not all of whom trust each other. Current personal computers are relatively easy to implant with a virus, and this will remain the case until most users upgrade to versions of their application programs which use later, more secure operating systems. However, many users never upgrade the version of an application program they are using.

Recent work in effectively changing the architecture of personal computers promises a "clean boot" from a smart card carried by the legitimate user [Clark 1992] or via other mechanisms [PC 1991]. But until these schemes are in widespread use, the threat of computer viruses continues. The technical community will have to produce changes in the basic architecture of personal computers to avoid the threat of expensive product liability suits. We will probably also start to see built-in backup hardware systems as the volume and importance of data in personal or networked computer system grows.

CNN Nearly Reported Bush Death, due to rapidly shared computer data
MacNeil/Lehrer Report on Phone System Risks
Re: Military uses for viruses
Not quite anonymous FTP
Virus breaks security of Italian Judicial System's computers
Cryptography used by Terrorist Organisation
Computer "error" blamed for murder?
Bell Atlantic 26 June Failure
Dutch Phreaks and Chaos Congress 90
Bay-Area Long-Distance Service Disrupted (again!)
Index of Known MsDos Malware: 998 viruses/trojans
Re: Smart cockpit with no backup
Licensing of Software Engineers
Virus Implants in DoD Weapons
Risk of Power Failures in Computer Controls: 9 Mile Point
TRW Wrong on Credit Reports for Entire Town
Misuse of computerized auto registration info
Re: "locking" DoD smart weapons
Automating commodities markets
Risks to Computers from Coup Attempt
RISKS of using electronic mail, and universal addressing
Radiation therapy machine dose rate doubled by configuration error
Re: Security Software Bug Locks Up System
Re: Security in software distribution
MCI Friends & Family & anyone else with a touch-tone phone
Risks of ''record'' and ''replay'' terminal capabilities

Figure 2. EXTRACTS FROM RISKS-L, July 1, 1991 through April 15, 1992

## 6. POLICY ISSUES

It has been noted previously [Hoffman 1986] that there are a number of policy issues related to vulnerability: Are there specific groups at risk? Who? Why? Should this be accepted or changed? Are alternatives available to persons not choosing to use a specific computer system? Should there be? Are some countries or regions more vulnerable than others? What are the differences and similarities between the post-industrial and developing countries? Is "vulnerability" just a codeword for broader concerns (privacy, equity, etc.)?

### 6.1. Encryption

One issue which has received a good deal of attention recently is the role of encryption in a free society. There are a number of uses of encryption which are desirable and, indeed, necessary in this electronic age. They include digital signatures, notarizing, creating "indelible" date/time stamps, and guaranteeing effective nonrepudiation of message receipt. Possibilities for "untraceable" electronic money have also been advanced [Chaum 1985].

Governments have always been concerned with communications because they put a multiplicity of economic agents into contact with one another, they aid information exchanges, and they are an instrument of power [Nora 1980]. The United States International Traffic in Arms Regulations (ITAR) require licensing for export of all modern cryptographic methods. In practice, this means that certain restrictions apply: the Data Encryption Standard (DES) can be exported to certain "friendly" countries but not to "Soviet bloc" or most Third World countries [Weissman 1991].

Since the DES algorithm [NBS 1977] is public and hardware devices to carry it out are manufactured and freely sold outside the United States, many observers believe that the U.S. only hurts its economic competitive position by clinging to these regulations. Indeed, despite society's best efforts to get it, one can hide data if one works hard enough at it [Diffie 1992]. The Advisory Board on security and privacy issues to the U. S. National Institute of Standards and Technology (NIST) has recommended a public debate on the topic. Among the questions to be discussed in such a debate would probably be these:

- Should government be permitted to restrict the use of cryptography? To restrict export of products that use cryptography?
- What legal protection should exist for encrypted communications?
- Who will issue keys, and how will users recover lost keys?
- Who will be trusted to authenticate messages? What will their legal status be?

Recently, the U. S. Federal Bureau of Investigation (FBI) suggested that the U. S. public telephone system be altered to allow tapping of digitally encrypted messages [Sessions 1992]. This was disputed by the major American civil liberties organization [Goldman 1992], as well as numerous telecommunications organizations, which pointed out that there are an increasing number of legitimate users for cryptography which should be of no interest to criminal justice organizations. For example, without digital signature techniques, false news stories could be fabricated, transmitted over unprotected RF links, and published, and have significant effects. In an almost-blunder recently, Cable News Network (CNN) came within ten seconds of falsely reporting the death of President Bush after his illness on a trip to Japan. A lively debate ensued among computer scientists on the digital telephone tapping issue [RISKS 1992] and at this writing, the fate of the FBI suggestion is still unknown.

### 6.2. International Computer Security Standards

The Japan Information Processing Development Center has noted that we now have a borderless society in information processing. It contends that social stability cannot be maintained in an age of global information unless all countries uniformly adopt the same level of minimum security measures.

Currently, there are a number of competing security standards: the Trusted Computer System Evaluation Criteria (Orange Book) from the United States [DOD 1985]; the Information Technology Security Evaluation Criteria (ITSEC) from France, the Netherlands, Germany, and the United Kingdom; and the MITI Computer Systems Security Standards from Japan. The OECD is expected to issue computer security guidelines later in 1992.

### 6.3. Barriers to International Harmonization

Harmonizing these will not be easy. "The protection of information within computer networks continues to be addressed from a wide variety of inconsistent perspectives by uncoordinated groups often working at cross purposes. ... none gives the total perspective required to understand the situation. ... the advocates of individual measures ignore the others for ... technical.../doctrinal reasons." [Walker 1989]

Justice Michael Kirby of Australia has pointed out that while technology is universal, laws and institutions are national or even local, and that international institutions are relatively weak; when the chips are down, economically and politically powerful persons make the vital decisions, usually keeping their national interests in mind. Altruism and true internationalism are rare. There are few votes in international data protection law and policy.

BloomBecker [BloomBecker 1982] has noted that international agreements on the locus of liability and a uniform definition of "computer crime" within each country is necessary before much progress can be made in prosecuting electronic terrorism. Stein [Stein 1992] has asked whether the United Nations should create an international technology agency that will monitor non-compliant and criminally predisposed nations so they can't launch teraflop weapons of electronic terror.

### 6.4. What Regulation Looms for Computer Professionals?

The use of computers and the actions of computer professionals will be under increasing scrutiny as the systems developed become more important and as they have the potential to make society more vulnerable. For that reason, several regulation mechanisms have been proposed.

#### 6.4.1. Self-Regulation

Computer professionals could regulate themselves, using ethics codes. Several attempts [Martin 1990] have been made in this direction. But there seems to be a general reluctance or indifference by the great majority in the field to put these into place [DeLoughry 1988].

#### 6.4.2. Licensing

Recently, some have pointed out that licensing might be appropriate for those developing certain kinds of programs or data bases [Kocher 1989, Hoffman, 1989]. Again, perhaps because of the many challenging technical problems ahead of the field, there has been little interest in this.

#### 6.4.3. Accountability

With the increasing complexity and importance of many computer applications, there must be some international agreement and clarification soon of responsibilities and liabilities of program creators, transmitters, and users. Some have likened this to populating the "electronic frontier" and to agreeing on the rules for civilizing cyberspace [Moore 1992].

## 7. A MODEL OF VULNERABILITY

By developing a simple abstract model of a problem, we can often isolate its salient features and thus obtain a better understanding of what to work on first to solve the problem. Some previous work [Hoffman 1982] used a tree-structured model in attempt to lay a foundation for understanding the breadth and depth of the problem of the vulnerability of society to computer systems. But the reality and richness of network connections today suggests that a network model is necessary. Very recently, a model for computer network security which incorporates costs and can make use of the impressive armada of graph theory has been developed [Fitch 1992]. It should be applicable to network vulnerability, and thus may be able to help us focus on the most vulnerable components of any computer network.

## 8. SUMMARY

After a review of previous work on the vulnerability of society to computer systems, we considered briefly what computer systems will look like in 2010 and the potential vulnerability of society to such systems. We enumerated some technical and policy issues which need to be resolved, and ended with a suggestion of modeling work which may shed light on the problem.

## REFERENCES

[BloomBecker 1982] BloomBecker, Jay, "International Computer Crime: Where Terrorism and Transborder Data Flow Meet", *Computers and Security 1* (1982), 41-53.

[Borning 1987] Borning, Alan, "Computer System Reliability and Nuclear War", *Communications of the ACM 30*, 2 (February 1987)

[Chaum 1985] Chaum, David, "Security Without Identification: Transaction Systems to Make Big Brother Obsolete", *Communications of the ACM 28*, 10 (October 1985).

[Clark 1992] Clark, Paul C. and Lance J. Hoffman, Using Smart Cards to Guarantee Boot Integrity and Enforce Access Control, Report GWU-IIST-92-11, Department of Electrical Engineering and Computer Science, The George Washington University, Washington, D.C., March 1992.

[Clarke 1992] Clarke, Roger, "Extra-Organisational Systems: A Challenge to the Software Engineering Paradigm", Proc. 1992 IFIP Conference.

[COMPASS 1991] *Proceedings of the Sixth Annual Conference on Computer Assurance (COMPASS '91)*, National Institute of Standards and Technology, Gaithersburg, Md., June 24-27, 1991.

[CSIS 1984] Center for Strategic and International Studies, Georgetown University, *America's Hidden Vulnerability: Crisis Management in a Society of Networks: Reinforcing the Fragile Fabric of Our Nation*, Panel on Crisis Management, Report No. 6, October 1984.

[Cramer 1989] Cramer, Myron L. and Stephen R. Pratt, "Computer Virus Countermeasures -- A New Type of Electronic Warfare", *Defense Electronics*, October 1989 (reprinted in [Hoffman 1990]).

[DeLoughry 1988] DeLoughry, T. J., "Failure of colleges to teach computer ethics is called oversight with potentially catastrophic consequences", *The Chronicle of Higher Education*, February 24, 1988, page A15.

[Denning 1990] Denning, Peter D., *Computers Under Attack*, ACM

Press/Addison-Wesley.

[Diffie 1992] Diffie, Whitfield, *Proceedings of the Second Conference on Computers, Freedom, and Privacy*, ACM Press, to appear.

[DOD 1985] U. S. Department of Defense, "Trusted Computing System Evaluation Criteria", DOD5200.28-STD, December 1985.

[Ferbrache 1992] Ferbrache, David, *A Pathology of Computer Viruses*, Springer-Verlag, 1992.

[Fitch 1992] Fitch, John A., A Network Security Model Based on the Resource-Constrained Shortest Path, D.Sc. dissertation, Dept. of Electrical Engineering and Computer Science, The George Washington University, Washington, D.C., to appear.

[Goldman 1992] Goldman, Janlori, Keeping an Ear on Crime: Why Cater to the Luddites?, *New York Times*, March 27, 1992.

[Hoffman 1982] Hoffman, Lance J., "Impacts of Information Systems Vulnerabilities on Society", *Proceedings of the 1982 National Computer Conference, Vol. 51*, AFIPS Press, Arlington, VA, 461-467.

[Hoffman 1986] Hoffman, Lance J. and Lucy M. Moran, "Societal Vulnerability to Computer System Failures", *Computers & Security 5* (1986), 211-217.

[Hoffman 1989] Hoffman, Lance J., Testimony before the Subcommittee on Criminal Justice, Committee on the Judiciary, U. S. House of Representatives, November 8, 1989.

[Hoffman 1990] Hoffman, Lance J., *Rogue Programs: Viruses, Worms, and Trojan Horses*, Van Nostrand Reinhold.

[Karn 1992] Karn, Phil R., "Gulf War Virus?", *RISKS-L, (Electronic) Forum on Risks to the Public in Computers and Related Systems, Vol. 13*, No. 4 (January 20, 1992)

[Kocher 1989] Kocher, B., "President's column", *Communications of the ACM 32*, 6 (1989).

[Leveson 1990] Leveson, N. G., *Software Safety*, Addison-Wesley, 1990.

[Martin 1990] Martin, C. D. and David H. Martin, "Professional Codes of Conduct and Computer Ethics Education", *Social Sciences Computer Review, 8*, 1 (Spring 1990) (reprinted in [Hoffman 1990].

[Montz 1989] Montz, L., U. S. General Accounting Office, "Internet Worm Difficulties", U. S. General Accounting Office, GAO/IMTEC-89-5F.

[Moore 1992] Moore, W. John, "Taming Cyberspace", *National Journal*, March 28, 1992.

[NAS 1991] U. S. National Academy of Sciences, *Computers at Risk: Safe Computing in the Information Age*, National Research Council, 1991.

[NBS 1977] National Bureau of Standards, "Data Encryption Standard", *FIPS PUB 46*, Washington, D. C., January 1977.

[Neumann 1992] Neumann, Peter G., "Leading Edge Distributes Michaelangelo

| | |
|---|---|
| | Virus", *RISKS-L, (Electronic) Forum on Risks to the Public in Computers and Related Systems, Vol. 13*, No. 7 (January 25, 1992). |
| [Nora 1980] | Nora, S. and Minc A., *The Computerization of Society*, MIT Press, 1980. |
| [OECD 1982] | Vulnerability of Computerised Society", *OECD Observer*, No. 114, January 1982. |
| [PC 1991] | "Safe Stations for Networks", *PC Magazine*, October 15, 1991. |
| [RISKS 1989] | "Risks: Cumulative Index of Software Engineering Notes", *Software Engineering News 14*, 1 (January 1989). |
| [RISKS 1992] | *RISKS-L, (Electronic) Forum on Risks to the Public in Computers and Related Systems, Vol. 13*, No. 41 (April 16, 1992) |
| [Rochlis 1989] | Rochlis, Jon A. and Mark W. Eichin, "With Microscope and Tweezers: The Worm from MIT's Perspective", *Communications of the ACM 32*, 6 (June 1989) (Reprinted in [Hoffman 1990]). |
| [SARK 1979] | Sweden Ministry of Defense, Committee on the Vulnerability of Computer Systems (SARK), *The Vulnerability of the Computerized Society*, December 1979. |
| [Sessions 1992] | Sessions, William S., Keeping an Ear on Crime: The F.B.I. Needs Industry's Help, *New York Times*, March 27, 1992. |
| [Slade 1992] | Slade, Rob, "Desert Storm Viral Myths", *RISKS-L, (Electronic) Forum on Risks to the Public in Computers and Related Systems, Vol. 13*, No. 6 (January 24, 1992) |
| [Spafford 1989] | Spafford, E., "The Internet Worm Incident", *Proc. 1989 European Software Engineering Conference (ESEC 89), Lecture Notes in Computer Science #387*, Springer-Verlag. (Reprinted in [Hoffman 1990]). |
| [Stefanac 1988] | Stefanac, Suzanne, "Mad Macs", *Macworld*, November 1988 (Reprinted in [Hoffman 1990]). |
| [Stein 1992] | Stein, Richard, "Open Channel", *IEEE Computer*, March 1992, p. 128. |
| [Stoll 1989] | Stoll, Clifford, *The Cuckoo's Egg*, Doubleday, 1989. |
| [TDR 1981] | "OECD Workshop Stresses Dependency on Computers", *Transborder Data Report 4*, 5 (May 1981). |
| [Turn 1983] | Turn, R. and Novotny, E. J., "Resiliency of the Computerized Society", *Proc. 1983 National Computer Conference, Vol. 52*, AFIPS Press, Arlington, VA, pp. 341-349. |
| [Walker 1989] | Walker, S., "Network Security: the Parts of the Sum", *Proc. IEEE Symposium on Security and Privacy, 1989.* |
| [Weissman 1991] | Weissman, C., "A National Debate on Encryption Exportability", *Communications of the ACM*, October 1991. |

Education and Society / R. Aiken (Editor)
Information Processing 92, Volume II
Elsevier Science Publishers B.V. (North-Holland)


# Extra-Organisational Systems: A Challenge to the Software Engineering Paradigm

Roger Clarke

Department of Commerce, Australian National University, Canberra ACT 2600, Australia

**Abstract**

Vulnerability is discussed in the context of data processing and information management applications. It is argued that a new class of information technology applications must now be recognised, in which one or more organisations cooperate with small enterprises and private individuals. The term 'extra-organisational systems' is coined for such applications.

Using illustrations arising from studies in the field of consumer EFTS, it is shown that members of the public are generally regarded as 'usees', beyond the system and affected by it, rather than being perceived as part of the system. It is argued that conventional systems life-cycle notions and techniques are inappropriate to extra-organisational systems. Rather than the software engineering, artefact-oriented philosophy inherent in existing techniques, such systems demand an alternative, organically-based paradigm.

Keyword Codes: D.2, J.1, K.4, K.6
Keywords: Software Engineering, Consumer EFTS, Organic Paradigm

## 1. INTRODUCTION

It is conventional to define vulnerability as "the possibility of loss, injury or denial of equal rights to a significant segment of the population, the weakening of social stability, or risks to national sovereignty due to dependency on computer-based information-technology" (TDR 1981). A variety of sources of risk arising from information technology (IT) have been classified, and a variety of dimensions identified, including individual, organisational, economic, social and national sovereignty (SÅRK 1978, 1979; Hoffman & Moran 1986; Holvast 1989; Berleur 1992).

Parallel with the literature on vulnerability, a number of related areas have developed, especially safety-critical systems and system- and software-safety. Systems engineering defines safety management as the measures taken to reduce the risk of accidents and of hazards, where the term 'hazard' means a set of conditions that can lead to an accident. Other relevant areas include software quality assurance, trusted systems, risk management, information systems failures, disaster recovery planning and service continuity planning.

Vulnerability is usually discussed in the context of artefacts which manipulate the environment, such as process control, transportation control and weapons guidance systems. Vulnerabilities also arise, however, in respect of quite banal IT applications. Employees' interests are threatened by inadequacies in a payroll system, and by insensitively designed features of a personnel or human resource management system. Affluent people rely on the convenience and consistent availability of banking systems. Social welfare clients are highly dependent on the systems used by government welfare agencies, and in countries in which welfare payments are now made into clients' accounts with financial institutions rather than by cash or cheque, welfare beneficiaries too are heavily dependent on banking systems.

This paper focusses on human vulnerabilities in such more conventional, unromantic and seemingly harmless data processing and information management applications. Its thesis is that:

- an increasing number of systems have a character quite different from the stereotyped administrative data processing system;
- this character embodies very important and easily overlooked vulnerabilities, at least of an individual and social nature; and
- conventional methods and techniques, and the philosophy underlying them, are inappropriate to such systems.

The paper commences by reviewing classes of systems previously identified in the literature, and the vulnerabilities associated with them. It identifies the need for a new class of system, for which the term 'extra-organisational' is coined. Subsequent sections identify weaknesses in conventional approaches to the conception, development and operation of extra-organisational systems, and suggest how the social vulnerability inherent in such systems can be significantly reduced. The argument is more fully developed in Clarke (1992b).

## 2. INTRA-, INTER- AND MULTI-ORGANISATIONAL SYSTEMS

Early applications of computers within organisations were oriented toward the automation of hitherto human tasks. Subsequently, rationalisation was undertaken, as it was recognised that the computer offered an opportunity to re-define the functions being performed. As the capacity of computing equipment grew, systems increased in scope, and integrated what had previously been separate business functions. The boldness and the capabilities of the new breed of programmers increased, and the seeds were sown for the technological self-confidence of contemporary systems designers. During this period, which we may retrospectively dub the **'intra-organisational systems'** era, computers were regarded as a productivity tool. By the end of the 1980s, the sophistication of IT had reached a point at which the long-promised staff reductions were becoming measurable, particularly in information industries such as banking, and particularly in middle-managerial ranks.

A variety of vulnerabilities arose in relation to intra-organisational systems, including job-displacement issues, dependence on the 'priestly caste' of computing specialists, new forms of crime, substitution of new forms of tedium for old ones, automated monitoring of worker performance, and enhanced bureaucratic obstructionism in the forms of blaming 'the computer' for errors, and investing 'the computer' with authority.

Maturation in systems life-cycle thinking has been apparent during the 'intra-organisational' era, in that it has become more widely appreciated that systems cannot be viewed only from the perspective of the system owner. The interests of 'users' have been increasingly recognised, not for altruistic reasons, but because lack of 'user involvement' has been shown to undermine systems' acceptance, and hence payback on the investment. To date, however, the interests of people affected by the system but <u>external</u> to the organisation, referred to within the IFIP TC9 community since the mid-1980s as 'usees', are seldom reflected.

The marriage of computing and telecommunications has been under way since the 1960s, and has brought the power of the computer to organisational units remote from the central site. Some applications of the emergent 'information technology' passed beyond the organisation's boundaries, and ushered in new forms of information systems commonly referred to as **'inter-organisational systems'**. Some of these involve terminals on the sites of an organisation's primary business partners. More sophisticated arrangements involve direct links between mainframes and/or front-end processors, or inter-networking via third-party communications facilities. A considerable degree of trust must exist between the business partners.

Inter-organisational applications continue to emerge, to increase in power and complexity, and to be used as the basis for implementing organisational strategies, and for realising competitive advantage through corporate collaboration and alliances (Kaufman 1966, Malone, Yates and Benjamin 1987, Wiseman 1988, Johnson and Vitale 1988, Rockart and Short 1989, Konsynski and McFarlan 1990, Oesterle 1991).

The increase in sophistication and prevalence of inter-organisational systems has resulted in the emergence of **'multi-organisational' systems**. These can be distinguished from inter-organisational applications in that they are designed to support multiple linkages with many organisations, and, in principle, with any other organisation with which there is a need to communicate. Particular forms include electronic mail (e-mail), electronic funds transfer systems (EFTS), electronic data interchange (EDI) and on-line trading. Many different flavours of multi-organisational system have emerged. Some of them essentially automate existing relationships and flows, while others represent wholesale revolution. Some have been used as instruments of competitive aggression, and some to protect the existing industry configuration. Some are organised along industry-sectoral lines, whereas others cut across industry boundaries (Clarke 1991).

The creation of multiple, linked intra-organisational systems had created inefficiencies, because data captured into machine-readable form in one organisation was being printed, sent by physical means to another organisation, and then re-captured. This was not only inefficient in terms of unnecessary data capture steps, but also because it involved significant error-levels, expensive consequences, and detection, investigation and re-work. Most such errors are in principle avoidable, and well-designed inter- and multi-organisational systems are in the process of removing these inefficiencies. This is part of what Wiener (1949), Forrester (1961) and Beer (1975) had in mind when they proposed the application of cybernetics to industrial organisation. The removal of inefficiencies is, of course, a cause for rejoicing, because it means that society can produce more goods and services for the same amount of labour input. There is, however, an inevitable negative impact on those employees who are displaced, and on their dependants. Multi-organisational systems also raise significant data protection, informational privacy and personal self-determination issues, all of which will clearly require a great deal of attention during the coming years (Dunlop and Kling, 1991).

The following section distinguishes a related class of IT application which has not to date received attention in the literature.

## 3. EXTRA-ORGANISATIONAL SYSTEMS

Implicit in the notions of inter- and multi-organisational systems are the assumptions that each of the nodes of the network is professionally managed, and that the facilities are used in an organisational context, with all of the discipline and cultural constraints that entails. These assumptions are important, because business partners depend on one another's professionalism in relation to such matters as security and control (e.g. physical access constraints, password management and backup), data quality, the reliability and responsiveness of decision and action, and the preparedness to take legal and moral responsibility for their decisions and actions.

There is an increasingly large number of systems which transcend the boundaries of an individual organisation, but for which these assumptions do not hold, such as:

- Automated Teller Machine (ATM) services;
- Electronic Funds Transfer at Point of Sale (EFT/POS) services;
- electronic home and office banking services;
- digital telephone call routing;
- public database access, such as electronic yellow pages;
- public transaction services, including:
    - tele-shopping;
    - public entertainment and travel reservation services; and
    - the sale of information-based services such as insurance; and
- electronic lodgement services for official submissions (such as taxation returns, statistical summaries and registration forms).

In these cases, many of the organisation's 'business partners' are small, single-site (and in many cases single-person) enterprises, such as retail outlets and service agents, or are members of the public. These partners do not have professional IT managers with an understanding of such arcane arts and technologies as systems analysis and communications protocols. Despite this, some of them will reliably and consistently perform the intended functions, and interpret their interaction with the facility in the way the designer intended. It would be a highly idealistic designer, however, who relied upon all, or even a large percentage of these partners to do so.

The following section draws on prior research relating to one particular form of extra-organisational system, to identify some specific instances of vulnerabilities, and trace the origins of those weaknesses to the philosophy and methods of contemporary systems life-cycle thinking.

## 4. THE CASE OF CONSUMER E.F.T.S.

Consumer electronic funds transfer systems (EFTS) includes automated teller machines (ATMs) and EFTS at Point of Sale (EFT/POS) services. This section is based on studies of consumer EFTS in Australia (Walters 1989, Clarke and Walters 1989, Clarke 1990a and 1990b, APSC 1990); and in Switzerland (Clarke 1992a). Australia has been among the world leaders in the rate of adoption of consumer EFTS.

ATMs were adopted very quickly when they were introduced in the late 1970s and early 1980s, but most other forms have achieved much slower growth rates. Factors which retarded progress included attempts by financial institutions to establish a dominant, proprietary system, followed by an attempt by the cartel of major banks to marginalise the non-bank financial institutions; slow commitment to EFT/POS by the large retail chains; and the unwillingness of the major players to recognise that a large-scale collaborative system is unlikely to be successful unless all parties stand to gain from it. On the basis of successful EFT/POS implementations, it appears that the system architecture needs to have the characteristics of 'business openness' (i.e. all terminals need to accept all cards), 'architectural openness' (either a common infrastructure, or interoperability between networks), and 'technical openness' (i.e. commitment to international telecommunication standards).

Once these corporate difficulties had been overcome, there remained the question as to whether consumers would actually use the resulting system. Too little attention was paid to the interests of the consumer, indicating a failure to appreciate the extra-organisational dimension of consumer EFTS. In particular:

- consumer education was overlooked;
- the confusion arising from the initial multiple, unlinked systems was underestimated;
- where terminals were installed on a pilot basis, there were too few of them, or they were inconveniently located;
- establishment of fair conditions of card use was tardy;
- the reporting of transactions on bank statements lacked detail which many consumers valued;
- the importance to the customer of being able to check the balance available prior to committing to the purchase was not understood;
- the importance of the 'cash-out' facility was not appreciated; and
- there was a lack of direct incentives (such as short-term, promotional rebates, bonuses or lottery-prizes for EFT/POS terminal usage), and of imaginative, EFT/POS-linked schemes (such as volume-discounts and frequent-buyer plans).

It is apparent that the success of EFT/POS systems depends on a strong affinity between the designers and the point-of-sale environment and consumers.

The conclusions drawn from these studies of consumer EFTS are that the major players made costly mistakes as a result of conceiving of the consumer and his actions as being outside the system boundaries. They treated the system as (at best) a multi-organisational system, when it was really an extra-organisational application. It was only when external pressure was brought to bear that the financial institutions were forced to reflect consumers' interests in their system designs.

Organisations have a clear motivation to reduce their costs by transferring tasks to other organisations, and to their clients. For relatively high one-time capital costs and relatively very low recurrent costs, organisations can arrange for their clients to themselves perform data capture, acquire the organisation's services, and/or access stored data. For such arrangements to be effective, however, a number of requirements from the perspectives of all parties must be satisfied.

These requirements are not readily analysable, because they are subject to interpretation by a wide variety of players, and are subject to ongoing change. The following section proposes a shift in the framework within which extra-organisational systems are brought to fruition, which will enable vulnerabilities to be reduced, and at the same time the likelihood of success to be increased.

## 5. TOWARDS AN 'ORGANIC' PARADIGM

The prevalent approach to information systems conception, development and operation reflects the attitude of the engineer, confident in his ability to harness the forces of nature to build bridges across yawning chasms. The primary concern is with the artefact, comprising hardware, network, electronic traffic and systems and application software. This paper is not concerned with the efficacy of that approach to intra-, inter- and multi-organisational systems. It argues that the software engineering paradigm is inapplicable to extra-organisational systems, and that an alternative 'organic paradigm' is needed, based on a less deterministic interpretation of general systems theory and cybernetics than has been common in recent decades.

The basis upon which the argument rests is that:

- it is pointless defining extra-organisational systems to be bounded by the human-machine interface, because the system's purposes and performance can only be measured in terms of its service to its clientele;
- extra-organisational systems are highly complex, not only because of the large number of participants, but also because of the heterogeneity of those actors, and the lack of a common organisational culture to imbue in them a common ethos and attitudes;
- the dimensions along which the heterogeneity exists are many and subtle, including educational background, religious/moral persuasion, political attitudes, cultural traditions, linguistic heritage, etc.;
- the individuals involved in the system make significantly different interpretations of the system's meaning, both initially and over time; and
- the marketing imperative is operational: if the people don't use it, it won't achieve its objectives, and thereby repay the large investments involved.

As far as I am aware, the term 'organic paradigm' is original. The concept, however, is well-established. Precursors include 'sociotechnical systems' (Emery & Trist 1960, Mumford 1983), Beer (1972, 1975), Miller's 'living systems' (1978), Checkland's 'soft systems methodology' (Checkland 1981, Checkland & Scholes 1990), the Multiview approach (Wood-Harper et al 1985), and the stream of thought emerging at the less mechanistic end of the cognitive science community (Winograd & Flores 1986).

Winograd and Flores argue:

- for the "rejection of cognition as the manipulation of knowledge of an objective world";
- for recognition of "the impossibility of completely articulating background assumptions"; and
- for recognition of "the primacy of action and its central role in language" (1986, p.11).

With them, I am arguing not for the rejection of rationalism and science in favour of holism, vitalism or some other a-scientific framework, but rather for the re-direction of the rationalistic tradition.

## 6. CONCLUSIONS

Vulnerability has been considered in the context of data processing and information management applications, and intra-, inter- and multi-organisational systems discussed. It has been argued that a new class of system must now be recognised, which is referred to in this paper as 'extra-organisational'. By this is meant systems in which one or more organisations cooperate with other entities which are not organisations, but rather are small enterprises and private individuals. Experiences in consumer EFTS have illustrated ways in which members of the public are still generally regarded as 'usees', beyond the system and affected by it, rather than part of the system. It has been argued that conventional systems life-cycle notions and techniques are inappropriate.

Extra-organisational systems are different and important. Conventional approaches will not work, and their inadequacies are deep-rooted. The artefact-orientation of contemporary methods must be mediated by a fuller appreciation of the environment of application – rather than 'technology', the focus must be on 'technology-in-use'. The dominant engineering credo must be replaced by a paradigm which owes more to organic conceptions of information systems.

## REFERENCES


APSC (1990) 'Report on EFT Security Survey' Australian Payments System Council, Reserve Bank of Australia, Sydney (November 1990)

Beer S. (1972) 'Brain of the Firm' Allen Lane, London, 1972

______ (1975) 'Platform for Change' Wiley, New York, 1975

Berleur J. (1992) 'Assessment of Risks and Vulnerability in an Information and Artificial Society' Working Paper on behalf of IFIP WG9.2, available from Facultés Univ. Notre Dame de la Paix, Namur, Belgium, January 1992

Checkland P. (1981) 'Systems Thinking, Systems Practice' Wiley, Chichester, 1981

Checkland P. and Scholes J. (1990) 'Soft Systems Methodology in Action' Wiley, Chichester, 1990

Clarke R.A. (1990a) 'Consumer EFTS in Australia – Part II – Security Issues' Comp. L. & Sec. Reporter (1989-90) 5 CLSR (Jan/Feb 1990)

______ (1990b) 'Consumer EFTS in Australia – Testing Times for Guided Self-Regulation' Comp. L. & Sec. Reporter (1989-90) 6 CLSR (Mar/Apr 1990)

______ (1991) 'Towards a Framework for the Study of EDI's Impact on Industry Sectors' Proc. 4th Int'l Conf. EDI, Bled, Yugoslavia (June 1991)

______ (1992a) 'Case Study Cardomat/Migros: An Open EFT/POS System' Austral. Comp. J. 24,1 (February 1992)

______ (1992b) 'Extra-Organisational Systems: A Challenge to the Software Engineering Paradigm' Working Paper, available from the author

Clarke R.A. and Walters M. (1989) 'An Introduction to Consumer EFTS With Particular Reference to Australia' Comp. L. & Sec. Reporter (1989-90) 4 CLSR (Nov/Dec 1989)

Dunlop C. and Kling R. (Eds.) (1991) 'Computerization and Controversy' Academic Press, 1991

Emery F.E. and Trist E.L. (1960) 'Socio-technical systems' in Churchman C.W. and Verhulst M. (Eds.) 'Management Science Models and Techniques Vol. 2' Pergamon, Oxford, 1960

Forrester J. (1961) 'Industrial Dynamics' MIT Press, Cambridge Mass, 1961

Hoffman L.J. and Moran L.M. (1986) 'Social Vulnerability to Computer System Failure' Computers & Security 5 (1986) 211-217

Holvast J. (1989) 'Vulnerability of Information Society: The Conflicting Demands of Security and Privacy' in Clarke R. and Cameron J. (Eds.) 'Managing Information Technology's Organisational Impact' Elsevier/North-Holland, 1991 pp.411-424

Johnson H.R. and Vitale M.R. (1988) 'Creating Competitive Advantage with Interorganisational Systems' MIS Qtly 12,2 (June 1988) 153-165

Kaufman F. (1966) 'Data Systems That Cross Company Boundaries' Harv. Bus. Rev. (Jan/Feb 1966)

Konsynski B.R. and McFarlan F.W. (1990) 'Information Partnership – Shared Data, Shared Scale' Harv. Bus. Rev. (Sep/Oct 1990) 114-120

Malone T.W. and Yates J. and Benjamin R.I.(1987) 'Electronic Markets, Electronic Hierarchies' Commun. ACM 30,6 (June 1987) 484-497

Miller J.G. (1978) 'Living Systems' McGraw-Hill, New York, 1978

Mumford E. (1983) 'Designing Human Systems', Manchester Bus. Sch., 1983

Oesterle H. (1991) 'Generating Business Ideas Based on Information Technology' in Clarke R. and Cameron J. (Eds.) 'Managing Information Technology's Organisational Impact II' Elsevier / North Holland, 1992 pp. 117-129

Rockart J.F. and Short J.F. (1989) 'IT in the 1990s: Managing Organisational Interdependence' Sloan Mngt Rev. (Winter 1989)

SÅRK (1978) 'The Vulnerability of Computerised Society: Preliminary Report' Ministry of Defence, Sweden, 1978

______ (1979) 'The Vulnerability of Computerised Society: Considerations and Proposals' Liberförlag, Stockholm, 1979

TDR (1981) 'OECD Workshop Stresses Dependency on Computers' Transnational Data Report 4, 5 (May 1981) 3-4

Walters M. (1989) 'EFTPOS – National Asset or White Elephant?' in Clarke R. and Cameron J. (Eds.) 'Managing Information Technology's Organisational Impact' Elsevier / North Holland, 1991 29-58

Wiener N. (1949) 'The Human Use of Human Beings' Avon Books, New York, 1949, 1974

Winograd T. and Flores F. (1986) 'Understanding Computers and Cognition: A New Foundation for Design' Ablex, Norwood NJ, 1986

Wiseman C. (1988) 'Strategic Information Systems' Irwin, 1988

Wood-Harper A.T., Antill L and Avison D.E. (1985) 'Information Systems Definition: The Multiview Approach' Blackwell, Oxford, 1985

Education and Society / R. Aiken (Editor)
Information Processing 92, Volume II
Elsevier Science Publishers B.V. (North-Holland)



# Artificial Intelligence Systems and Patents - the Challenge

Y. Skulikaris

European Patent Office, Erhardtstr. 27, 8000 Munich 2, Germany

**Abstract**
This work attempts an analysis of problems in the context of patent protection for industrial applications of Artificial Intelligence (AI). Since patent protection creates a status of monopoly associated with economic and legal implications, both AI involved industry and the public have a vital interest in an efficient patent system. The analysis focuses on AI systems based on inductive inference and systems involving connectionist architecture. The problems arising when patent protection is sought for such systems are pointed out and the shortcomings of the established patent examination practice with regard to such systems are briefly discussed. Special attention is given to crucial patent requirements with regard to the definition of an AI system, such as establishing clarity, avoiding monopolization of algorithms, and making functional interrelation explicit. Possible solution approaches are proposed.

## 1. INTRODUCTION

Industrial applications of AI(1) lead to systems that differ in essential aspects from deductive/deterministic information processing systems. Especially in the case of systems based on inductive inference and systems incorporating neural networks, it appears that a qualitative leap is established even with regard to analytic/ symbolic AI. By implementing an inductive inference (or connectionist) learning component in an AI system, not only the tedious task of thorough problem analysis and symbolic representation can be circumvented, but also robustness and fault tolerance can be achieved, both attractive factors for industrial applicability. Moreover, it appears that the verbalization bottleneck(2), from which symbolic AI methods suffer, can also be avoided. These systems, while being far from competing with human cognition, nevertheless offer industrially applicable performance in solving cognitive tasks in an adequately narrow domain. However, such systems prove to be problematic when it comes to patent protection, which creates a legal right of monopoly, i.e. exclusion of competitors from exploitation of a certain subject-matter. Owing to the commitment of AI to problems pertaining to human cognitive performance, such systems usually perform simulation of mental acts (for instance learning) by means of highly complex algorithms. However, certain subject-matter, for instance mental acts and mathematical methods, are excluded from patentability [EPC 91], so that patent protection for such a system necessarily leads to problems.

A further problem is that, particularly in the case of inductive inference systems or neural networks, non-predictable system configurations and non-predictable functionality can emerge. In this latter case of adaptive systems, the well defined input-to-output correspondence known from conventional information processing cannot be taken for granted any more(3). In such a context, where the subject-matter that has to be analysed with a view to patent protection inherently prevents complete analysis down to the lowest level of abstraction, any attempt to establish clarity and explicate functional interrelation (both primary concerns in the context of patents) will necessarily result in contradictions.

This work intends to demonstrate these problems and propose an approach to possible solutions. The statements made herein reflect the current status of problem analysis within the European Patent Office and should not be understood as an official policy, since the latter is subject to a permanent evolution process. It is however the author's assumption that such aspects will play a crucial role within the context of intellectual property protection in the near future.

## 2. BACKGROUND INFORMATION ON PATENTS

A **patent** is a right of monopoly in the sense that it prevents others (than the patentee) from exploiting a certain, technical subject-matter for a restricted time. In return, the patentee discloses the invention in the interest of technical progress.

The main lines along which current patent practice is exercised by most Patent Offices are similar to one another, both in the administrative and substantive fields [WIPO 88]. In the following, the European Patent Office is considered a typical example.

The **European Patent Office** (EPO) provides protection for inventions by granting patents valid in up to 16 European countries, which participate in the **European Patent Convention** (EPC). A European patent is granted (or refused) after examination of the corresponding patent application (consisting of a written description, drawings and claims) for compliance with various requirements including novelty, inventive step and industrial applicability. **Novelty** means that the subject-matter under examination must not have been disclosed to the public by anybody prior to filing the application. **Inventive step** means that the subject-matter must be non-obvious in the light of the relevant prior art[(4)]. Finally, **industrial applicability** in the field of computers is almost always taken for granted. After filing of an application, the relevant prior art is extracted during a data base search in the corresponding technical field. Following the search, substantive examination is performed by the Examining Division, a three member body of experts in the field. If an application is found not to fulfil the above mentioned requirements, it can possibly be amended (within the framework of the original disclosure) in an interactive procedure between the Examining Division, the applicant, and usually the applicant's representative (patent attorney). During this procedure, the patentable subject-matter (if any) is extracted, clearly formulated in the so-called claims, and a patent is granted. Otherwise the application is refused.

An appeal can be filed against a decision to refuse an application, and the case is decided before the Board of Appeal, a second instance body consisting of members having a technical and/or legal background and qualifications.

Within a certain time after the grant of a European patent, an opposition can be filed by anybody who thinks that the patent is invalid for any justifiable reason (e.g. prior art not found during search and examination). The parties involved are heard before the Opposition Division, a technically (and potentially legally) qualified body. The patent can be maintained in the same or in amended form, or revoked.

The **claims** are a short statement of the subject-matter for which protection is sought. They should be a clear and concise definition of the technical features of the system or the steps of a process carried out with such technical features. Thus, additional requirements of the European Patent Convention (EPC) include clarity in terms of unambiguous wording of the claims, resulting in unambiguous definition of the subject-matter put under protection. Moreover, the EPC requires "that the invention be of a technical nature", in the sense that no protection can be granted e.g. for mathematical methods, schemes and rules for performing mental acts, or computer programs[(5)]. The concept underlying this attitude is that algorithms cannot be monopolized since their public use is necessary for technical progress. With regard to computer programs, the prevailing opinion states that programs **per se** do not cause technical effects, since they can also be studied as a work of literature. However, the notions of "technical effect" or "mathematical method" cannot be sharply defined; they can be either very broadly interpreted, or even depend heavily on context, particularly within systems where software interacts with specially designed hardware (like neural networks). The problems thus arising affect not only the AI involved industry, but also the public, since the whole patent system is grounded on a consensus between these three parties as to the clear definition of what is protected (and consequently preempted from public use and possibly subject to negotiations and financial transactions) and what is not. Thus, the EPO has to find a viable solution in cooperation with AI involved industry, furthermore constantly evaluating (and possibly revising) its attitude in the light of current AI research results.

## 3. CLARITY - HOW TO VERBALIZE EXACTLY WHAT IS MEANT

In the context of patents it is essential to formulate the subject-matter for which protection is granted in a way that excludes (or at least minimizes) uncertainty. This is so because industry has a right to know exactly where rightful use ends and infringement begins.

A particular problem arises in the case of subject-matter that covers a wide spectrum of abstraction levels, as is the case in AI systems[(6)]. Undoubtedly, clarity increases when descending to lower abstraction levels. This fact implies that the technical description of an AI system necessarily will have to realize a trade-off between clarity and conciseness.

A second problem related to clarity arises from the fact that some AI systems are not subject to thorough analysis, i.e. analysis down to the lowest abstraction level. This is so simply because unpredictable configurations and functionality of such systems are very likely (if not certain) to emerge, since those factors belong to the concept underlying such systems.

Although establishing clarity in the sense of linguistic disambiguation is a known problem, existing efforts in the field of natural language processing usually rely on syntactic, grammatic and semantic regularities formalized by some means of representation. However, such analysis in the context of written description of complex subject-matter like an AI system has to rely heavily on context information and imaginative power, as demonstrated by the following example.

Consider the following claim wording, which, although imaginary, appears very realistic in the light of current research:

"**An image processing and pattern classification system**, comprising the following features:
- an x-ray apparatus arranged for making x-ray images
- a digital image processing apparatus for digitizing, processing and storing said images,
said image processing and pattern classification system characterized in that said processing apparatus further comprises:
- means for extracting similarity features from a predetermined plurality of digital images and for determining criteria of similarity to said plurality of images
- means for comparing a further digital image with said similarity criteria in order to determine whether said image meets the similarity criteria, thus classifying said further image within or outside said image plurality
- means for selectively integrating said further image within said predetermined image plurality".

Understanding the scope of said system-claim can be facilitated by the corresponding method-claim (claims usually are submitted in pairs of system and method claims):

"**A method of image processing and pattern classification** with a system according to the foregoing claim, characterized by the steps of:
- providing to the system a plurality of digital images belonging to the same class, and determining by said extracting means said similarity criteria for use as classification criteria for further images
- comparing by said comparing means a further image, in order to automatically classify said further image in respect of inclusion in said class
- in the positive case, selectively integrating said image in said plurality of images belonging to said class".

It is clear that the main cause of the unclarity problem is rather the high abstraction level of the terms used than their ambiguity in a linguistic sense. Speaking in terms of logics, the terms have a wide extension[(7)], so that the subject-matter subsumed under such wording goes beyond any reasonable limit. A practical way to determine the meaning (extension) of these claims is to match their wording with known systems, expressed in a more concrete way, and finding out whether these systems are covered. In other words, the various abstract means above should be expressed in terms of concrete features on a deeper level of abstraction within a semantic hierarchy. Thus, the extracting means and the similarity criteria referred to can be interpreted as a learning component based on inductive inference, i.e. learning from examples, and eventually providing some prototype representation of the exemplary class inclusion features. Further, it could be also interpreted as the procedure for building the components of an expert classification system, i.e. a knowledge base containing knowledge about class inclusion, and the inference engine applying the inference rules. Finally, it can be directly read onto a pattern recognition system possibly extended by a neural network trained to classify feature vectors as belonging or not belonging to said class. In any case, an unambiguous semantic interpretation is not possible without further information, extracted from sources different from the claim wording itself.

However, this trial-and-error procedure works only in the case of systems readily suggesting such extensional interpretations. Thoroughly novel systems, not lending themselves to such matching procedure, will necessitate a new approach. A hierarchically organized taxonomy of information processing terminology would be of great help in this case. Such taxonomies are for instance available for learning techniques in neural networks [Diederich 90]. Even if in a rapidly evolving field ongoing research and development tends to blur the borders of classes within such taxonomies or even render them obsolete, such a measure, as for instance already practiced by the World Intellectual Property Organization in the patent classification field, has been valuable also from the point of view of information dissemination.

## 4. THE PROBLEM OF TECHNICALITY - TRYING TO PREVENT MONOPOLIZATION OF ALGORITHMS

Another crucial problem is that of judging **whether there exists a technical effect in the system**. The requirement of a technical effect is essential to the whole patent system, and patent offices have developed strategies to judge this criterion [Holzwarth 87], [Laurie 91]. The notion of technical effect in general has been the subject of many debates. One tends to believe that technicality presupposes some kind of tangible mechanical apparatus or electronic device. Furthermore, technicality is assumed to reside within changes of some physical entity perceivable by the senses or understood by the intellect or indicated by means of instruments. Another interpretation requires use of a law of nature to manipulate some entity. However, none of these "definitions" captures for instance the notion of knowledge acquisition within an expert system, (such as the accumulation of experience within the pattern classification system presented above), or the effect of predictive classification on new images. Furthermore, is it a technical effect or not to adjust the input weights of signals in a neural network in such a way that the network solves a particular problem (e.g. written character recognition, which admittedly is a technical problem)?

Practically, the requirement of technical effect results from the principle that algorithms (which **per se** do not cause technical effects but rather explicate in a step-by-step manner manifestations of human cognitive performance) may not be preempted from public use. The standard attitude towards patentability requires that the algorithms used manipulate physical entities, like for instance the algorithms implemented in a cache arrangement. However, the algorithms encountered in AI applications (as for instance low level vision edge detection, disambiguation in a phrase, or synaptic weight adapting during neural network training) establish a qualitative leap in comparison with algorithms in conventional (non AI) information processing systems. Although such algorithms admittedly eventually manipulate physical entities (in the sense of electrical values within computer hardware), such algorithms are often conceived of in order to manipulate entities of a symbolic nature, bearing particular meaning (for instance application of inference rules in an expert system or syntactic/semantic analysis of a phrase to extract its meaning), or even of a sub-symbolic nature as in the case of neural networks.

One could say that the effect of algorithms should be considered in the system of abstraction levels involved in their concept and implementation. Thus, the effect of an algorithm should be judged only to the limit of direct entity manipulation intended by the algorithm's originator. In other words, an algorithm should be correlated to the inventor's primary intention. The term "intention", as used here, does not refer to the desired result, but rather to the conscious influence effected upon entities (i.e. the cause) necessary to render the desired result. If the inventor's intention can be recognized to involve conscious, direct, purpose driven manipulation of entities other that clearly notional ones, hence generating new functionality, (the result) by means of these entities, then technicality is given.

In other words, technicality is given in those cases where the "**direct manipulative influence**" of the inventor extends to entities not primarily notional. Notional entities in the sense mentioned above would be for instance semantic interpretations of a phrase (and their computer representations), inference rules in a knowledge base or fuzziness coefficients in an inference rule. Entities having a technical relevance would be for instance synaptic coefficients in a neural network, gray scale values in a digital image or rotational invariants in pattern recognition.

The notion of intentionality[8], already known from the context of natural language processing, appears to be appropriate in order to clarify the causal relation between manipulated entities and the resulting effect. If we accept that the primary focus of an information processing system can extend only to the limit of intentionality of its creator, this criterion should be able to discern the system's "intentional" effect from possible side effects that might appear to provide the system with a technical flavour[9]. Furthermore, this notion can be directly associated to the intended scope of protection, thus providing an objective judgement of whether protection is sought for an algorithm **per se**, or for a system producing a technical effect achieved inter alia by using such algorithm.

From a social/ethical standpoint, system implications outside the intentionality limit cannot be disregarded. However, this aspect is not within the scope of this work.

From another viewpoint, one could hardly avoid monopolizing an algorithm in the case of dedicated algorithms, i.e. algorithms that can be conceived of and used only in connection with a particular system. If protection is provided to such a system, then the algorithm is de facto preempted, since its use does not make sense with any other system ("induced preemption"). In such a case, as long as the algorithm under question remains dedicated in the light of current research, its induced preemption makes no difference. If the algorithm is proved to be useful for other systems as well, then its formerly induced preemption is no longer existent.

## 5. THE PROBLEM OF EXPLICATING FUNCTIONAL INTERRELATION - ESTABLISHING REPRODUCIBILITY

Another requirement of the patent system is that of reproducibility of the claimed functional interrelation. This is a kind of "raison d'être" for the patent system, since protection is offered in return for the disclosure of the invention. Thus, when assessing the effect of an algorithm within an AI system, the functional interrelation of system components subject to manipulation by that algorithm must be explicated in order to secure reproducibility. However, if such explication is prohibited by non-deterministic system nature, as for instance in the case of neural networks or in the case of systems based on inductive inference, an adequate substitute has to be found.

The main problem goes beyond inadequacy of pure verbal definition to explicate such complex functional interrelation. The crucial point is that non-determinism appears to exclude exact reproducibility in the first place. Thus, even if additional support is provided in the sense of formal definitions such as mathematical formulae, reproduction still takes place in a "fuzzy" way. Consider for instance the following "imaginary" claim:

"**An associative recall memory system**, comprising:

- a memory for storing input, weight, output and reference data
- a weight adapting means for adaptively determining weight data by evaluating the relationship between input, output and reference data".

An interpretation as a learning neural network suggests itself readily. However, even if layer structure, signal paths, neuron transfer function and weight adjustment function are additionally disclosed, network functionality is still insufficiently defined (and reproducibility inhibited), since performance still depends e.g. on the nature and contents of training data.

It appears that a viable solution in this case has to rely on going down the levels of abstraction until a level providing sufficient explication in comparison to the relevant prior art is encountered. Even on such a low abstraction level, system components will inevitably be defined, at least partly, in functional terms. Thus, no other solution to this problem can be envisaged at present, except for a more generous interpretation of the reproducibility requirement in the context of AI systems in general. Nevertheless, the process of descending along abstraction levels converges with the clarity requirement discussed already.

## 6. FUTURE PERSPECTIVES

The current status of consideration focuses on the problem rather than on a systematic solution approach. However, this is reasonable since the problem itself has been recently realized and its nature does not lend itself to a straightforward solution approach. It is expected that some still poorly understood cognitive functions like abstraction, intentionality, or even learning, creativity and imagination will play an important role as constituents of the problem and hence should be intensively studied in the effort to solve it. It appears that a viable solution will rather depend on novel ideas than replicate existing ones.

## NOTES

(1) The term Artificial Intelligence (AI) is used in this paper as for instance outlined in [Barth 91]. In a descriptive, analogy-based manner, one could say that AI is the electron microscope of cognitive science.

(2) Symbolic AI approaches (e.g. an expert system or a natural language processing system) necessarily have to verbalize knowledge in order to attach meaning to the symbols used [Becker 90].

(3) It is for instance predictable whether a spelling checker will "recognize" a certain misspelled word in a text. But it is not predictable whether a trained neural network will recognize a distorted version of a written character.

(4) Since the notion of non-obviousness cannot be formalized, EPO has developed a problem-and-solution oriented approach to help judge this criterion in a uniform manner.

(5) Protection of software **per se** is currently the subject of controversial debates, conducted along three primary directions: copyright (supported by the majority of software industry), patents (which appears to be the policy of the United States Patent and Trademark Office, which has recently granted patents on

substantially software-related subject-matter, and a "sui generis" (of its own art) solution, advocated mainly on the argument of inadequacy of the previous two.

(6) This is typical in computer science in general, as compared for instance to applied electronics, physics, chemistry and mechanics.

(7) "Extension" of a term means here the class of entities for which the term is applicable or which the term refers to (e.g. "flower" --> rose, tulip, ..). Usually, these are the contents of all levels below the term in a hierarchical taxonomy.

(8) The term "intentionality" is used (as usual in the context of natural language processing) in the sense of a consciously pursued goal of a human agent. It is not used in the sense of the property of mental states (such as for instance beliefs), to be about other entities (physical or notional), as e.g. usual in philosophy [Bechtel 89].

(9) If for instance iterative reprogramming of a recursive function in an application program results in memory economy, the application programmer cannot claim "direct manipulative influence" on the memory allocation involved, since the application program itself abstracts from direct memory allocation. Even if the programmer is aware of that property of iterative programming as compared to recursion, and implements an iterative algorithm with a view to memory economy, such influence is in this case "indirect".

## REFERENCES

**[Barth 91]** G.Barth et al., AKI: "Künstliche Intelligenz: Perspektiven einer wissenschaftlichen Disziplin und Realisierungsmöglichkeiten", in INFORMATIK SPEKTRUM, 14, 201-206, Springer-Verlag, August 1991

**[Bechtel 88]** W.Bechtel: "PHILOSOPHY OF MIND. An Overview for Cognitive Science", Lawrence Erlbaum Associates, 1988

**[Becker 90]** B.Becker, "Die Veränderung von (Experten-)Wissen durch den Prozeß der Wissensakquisition", KI 2/90, Oldenbourg Verlag, 1990

**[Diederich 90]** J.Diederich, Ed., "Artificial Neural Networks: Concept Learning", IEEE Computer Society Press, 1990

**[EPC 91]** European Patent Convention, European Paten Office Publication, Munich, 1991

**[Holzwarth 87]** A.Holzwarth, "Richtlinien für die Prüfung im Europäischen Patentamt", in W.Killian, P.Gorny, (Eds.), "Schutz von Computer-Software / Technische und rechtliche Aspekte", stmv Verlag, 1987

**[Laurie 91]** R.S.Laurie, "The Patentability of AI under US Law", lecture given in WIPO Worldwide Symposium on the Intellectual Property Aspects of Artificial Intelligence, Stanford University, March 1991

**[WIPO 88]** "Background Reading Material on Intellectual Property", publication of the World Intellectual Property Organization, 1988

Education and Society / R. Aiken (Editor)
Information Processing 92, Volume II
Elsevier Science Publishers B.V. (North-Holland) 


# Information Technology Security Evaluation Criteria (ITSEC) – a Contribution to Vulnerability?

Michael Gehrke[a], Andreas Pfitzmann[b], and Kai Rannenberg[c]

[a]Institute for Applied Informatics, Sekr. FR 5-9, Technical University Berlin, Franklinstr. 28/29, W-1000 Berlin 10, Germany, E-Mail: micky@cs.tu-berlin.de

[b]Institute for Informatics, University Hildesheim, Samelsonplatz 1, W-3200 Hildesheim, Germany, E-Mail: pfitza@informatik.uni-hildesheim.de

[c]Institute for Applied Informatics, Sekr. FR 5-10, Technical University Berlin, Franklinstr. 28/29, W-1000 Berlin 10, Germany, E-Mail: kara@cs.tu-berlin.de

**Abstract**

On initiative of the Commission of the European Communities, the Information Technology Security Evaluation Criteria (ITSEC) are designed to provide a yardstick for the evaluation and certification of the security of IT systems. To improve the usefulness of resulting evaluations and certificates for procurers, users, and manufacturers the ITSEC are intended to undergo further extensive review. We discuss weaknesses, remaining questions, and possible improvements concerning the current version 1.2 of ITSEC. Our criticism focusses on the intended scope, the functionality aspects, the assessment of effectiveness and correctness, and problems arising after the evaluation of IT systems. Additionally, the ITSEC development and the accompanying discussion are criticized and improvements are proposed.

Keyword Codes: K.7.3; K.6.5; D.4.6
Keywords: The Computing Profession, Certification, and Licensing; Management of Computing and Information Systems, Security and Protection; Operating Systems, Security and Protection

## 1 INTRODUCTION

The information society becomes more and more dependent on information infrastructures like telephone or data exchange networks. This trend is advanced by the permanent technological development and growing power of computer equipment. New applications like multimedia systems, computer-based medical systems, or electronic mail increase the needs of flexible, powerful, and secure information exchange.

Two threats have to be pointed out. First, with the expansion of information technology (IT) the dependency of society on the reliable operation of this technology is rising. Secondly, increasing information flow enhances the possibilities for misuse, e.g., by eaves-dropping, modification of information, or information flow analysis. In the following, we understand "security" as the property of IT to withstand accidental and intentional threats. To increase the security of IT systems the ITSEC [CEC 1991_1] have been developed.

This paper deals with weaknesses, remaining questions, and possible improvements found during review of the current version of ITSEC. Its purpose is to stimulate the discussion about the intended scope, the functionality aspects, assurance of effectiveness and correctness, and post-evaluation problems of ITSEC. Sect. 2 gives a short overview over aims, history, and approach of ITSEC and discusses related evaluation criteria. Sect. 3 briefly summarizes former criticism. Sect. 4 treats additional weaknesses, remaining questions, and possible improvements of ITSEC, and Sect. 5 discusses possibilities for further development.

## 2 THE ITSEC

The ITSEC shall provide a yardstick to measure the security of IT and to make users confident thereof. They are harmonized evaluation criteria of and by four nations (France, Germany, the Netherlands, and the United Kingdom). The ITSEC ought to be used within an evaluation process resulting in a certificate stating the degree of confidence that can be placed in an IT product or system. This section gives an overview over the history and the approach of ITSEC.

### 2.1 History of ITSEC

The first version of ITSEC (V1.0) was published in May 1990 and was reviewed and discussed on an international conference with about 500 participants in Brussels in Sept. 1990. After the discussion V1.1 was published in Jan. 1991 together with a paper of the 4 nations working group answering to the major issues of the discussion. In April 1991 about 50 experts who contributed substantially to the review of V1.0 were invited to a second workshop. The current version (V1.2) was issued in June 1991 and is intended to be used in evaluation and certification for two years. The experience gained shall then be used to further develop ITSEC.

As is indicated by the participation of four countries in publishing ITSEC several documents preceded and provided input to the ITSEC. These documents are:

- Catal. de Crit. Dest. à évaluer le Degré de Confiance d. Syst. d'Info. [SCSSI 1989]
- UK Systems Security Confidence Levels [CESG 1989]
- DTI Commercial Computer Security Centre Evaluation Manual [DTI 1989_1]
- DTI Commercial Computer Security Centre Functionality Manual [DTI 1989_2]
- IT-Security Criteria (ZSISEC) [GISA 1989].

Additionally, the Netherlands contributed to ITSEC. The U.S. catalogue, the "Trusted Computer Systems Evaluation Criteria" (TCSEC) of the Department of Defense [US_DOD 1983, 1985], is a predecessor which influenced all documents above. Despite several similarities between different national evaluation criteria a couple of main differences can be extracted. For readers familiar with the above evaluation criteria the differences are compiled in Table 1.

Table 1: Evolution of Security Evaluation Criteria

| | TCSEC | ZSISEC | ITSEC |
|---|---|---|---|
| Dates of Publication | 1983/85 | 1989 | 1990/91 |
| Security Approach | confidentiality | confidentiality + integrity + availability | confidentiality + integrity + availability |
| Functionality & Quality | linked | separated | separated |
| Classification | 7 Functionality-Quality-levels (F-Q-levels) | 8 Q-levels<br><br>10 F-classes as guidelines in the document | 7 E-levels<br><br>10 example F-classes in the annex<br>Recommended generic headings for own definition of F-classes |
| Certification Bodies | 1 | 1 | ≥ 4 |
| Evaluation Bodies | 1 (certification body) | ≥ 1 | ≥ 1 |
| Bandwidth of Covert Channels | ≤ 0.1 bit/s | ≤ 1 bit/s | the annex specifies "not unacceptably high" |

The harmonization of evaluation criteria by the four nations was generally applauded as a first step in the right direction. In 1990 the standardization project "Evaluation criteria for IT security" was initiated in ISO/IEC JTC1/SC27. The project consists of 3 subprojects "Introduction and model", "Functionality" and "Assurance". The ITSEC are expected to be the basis for this standardization project. This is obvious by a textual comparison of the current working draft of the "Assurance" document with chapter 3 and 4 and the description of "E-levels" in the ITSEC. Hence it is very important to stimulate discussion about weaknesses, open questions, and possible improvements of ITSEC.

## 2.2 The ITSEC Approach

The ITSEC shall be used as a guideline for evaluation and certification of the security of IT. "Security" in the ITSEC context means confidentiality, integrity, and availability. It is supposed that some threats to security can already be excluded by non IT measures like physical access control. Remaining threats are countered by IT measures which are the subject of evaluation.

**Systems and Products:** ITSEC differentiate between systems and products. A "system" is a combination of hard- and software tailored to the needs of a specific operational environment. A "product" is a piece of standard hard- and/or software that can be incorporated into systems. The main difference regarding security is: For a system the operational environment is known, for a product usually not. Systems and products are commonly referred to as "targets of evaluation" (TOEs).

**Evaluation and Certification:** The basis of an evaluation is the "security target" that consists of specific security objectives, threats, a definition of security enforcing functions, and all security mechanisms employed by a TOE. Additionally, the desired evaluation level is specified (see below). Security enforcing functions may be either specified individually or by referencing one of 10 predefined "functionality classes" [CEC 1991_1, Annex A]. If security enforcing functions are individually specified it is recommended to present them under the following "generic headings":

(1) Identification and Authentication
(2) Access Control
(3) Accountability
(4) Audit
(5) Object Reuse
(6) Accuracy
(7) Reliability of Service
(8) Data Exchange

The sponsor of an evaluation provides the security target together with the TOE to an independent evaluator and pays the evaluation. The main task of evaluation is to give assurance that the security objectives are achieved by the selected security enforcing functions.

Assurance is divided into confidence in the "correctness" of the implementation of security enforcing functions and mechanisms and confidence in their "effectiveness". Thus, evaluation has two phases that may proceed interleaved.

1) Assessment of Correctness: The TOE lifecycle for the security enforcing functions from their top-level specification down to operation including the development process is investigated. The result is a (preliminary) evaluation level between E0 ("no confidence") and E6 ("highest confidence").

2) Assessment of Effectiveness: It is checked whether the security enforcing functions satisfy the security objectives. Additionally, assessment of effectiveness deals with the strength of mechanisms of the TOE. Three strength ratings classify mechanisms: "basic", "medium", and "high". If during assessment of effectiveness the security enforcing functions turn out not to satisfy the security objectives the whole TOE is degraded to evaluation level E0.

As result of the evaluation the evaluator forwards a report to the national certification authority, which will provide a certificate to the sponsor at least stating the evaluation level reached.

# 3 SUMMARY OF FORMER CRITICISMS ON ITSEC

This section summarizes criticism already published and hence not repeated in detail.

### 3.1 Criticism by Karl Rihaczek

Karl Rihaczek [Rihaczek 1991] pointed out that standardization of evaluation criteria despite all advantages has the drawback that manufacturers will try to adhere to a standard because of marketing reasons. Vulnerabilities that are not covered by the criteria could be detected and systematically exploited by an attacker. This would be especially severe after the evaluation criteria gave rise to a security monoculture. He criticizes that ITSEC mainly takes into account closed systems where the interests of a system's management dominate over interests of single users. He states that non-repudiation, which can be seen as a fourth basic security property at the side of confidentiality, integrity, and availability, is not really covered. This makes ITSEC unsuitable for Open Systems. Moreover, he raises the question of the legal relevance of evaluation certificates. Although [Rihaczek 1991] is related to ITSEC V1.0, at the level of its treatment, all critical remarks remain true for V1.2.

### 3.2 Criticism by Rüdiger Dierstein

Although Rüdiger Dierstein does not mention ITSEC at all (since [Dierstein 1990] has been written before the first publication of ITSEC), this is an implicit, but especially severe criticism. He derives six functions as a possible set of basic security functions:

(1) Authentication (identification and verification)

(2) Administration of rights (assignment of rights and administration of rights)

(3) Verification of rights (= control of rights = control of authorization)

(4) Registration (protocolling for audit and recovery)

(5) Error Recovery (error detection and error compensation)

(6) Supervision (recursive application of the above).

This means at least two kinds of criticsm: Basic functions are *derived* (and not just stated) and his set differs from the corresponding set of ITSEC, i.e., the generic headings, cf. Sect. 4.2.

## 4 OUR ADDITIONAL CRITICISM ON ITSEC

This section summarizes our criticism on ITSEC V1.2. The first 4 subsections are oriented along the structure of the ITSEC dealing with the title and scope (4.1), the functionality aspects (4.2), and the two aspects of assurance – effectiveness (4.3) and correctness (4.4). Post-evaluation problems are addressed in 4.5, weaknesses of the ITSEC development and discussion process in 4.6. More detailed criticism [Pfitzmann 1991] can be obtained from the authors.

### 4.1 Title and Scope

The ITSEC do not address the scope suggested by their title and their scope section and needed in an information society. They tend to define a criteria framework and they do not take into account different kinds of potential attackers and decentrally managed IT systems. Moreover, the definitions of confidentiality and integrity are insufficient. An appropriate title for V1.2 of ITSEC might be: *A Framework of Security Evaluation Criteria for hierarchically managed IT Systems*.

**Criteria or Criteria Framework?** During the revisions the criteria became more and more general: ITSEC V1.2 are even less security evaluation criteria than V1.0. They define a *framework* to formulate security evaluation criteria, as the sponsors can define the functionality of their TOEs by themselves. This is less obligatory than criteria would be.

**Different Kinds of Potential Attackers:** The ITSEC do not cover problems of different kinds of potential attackers. This is obvious by reading, e.g., §2.37 of ITSEC V1.2 (p. 25):

> *In many TOEs there will be requirements to ensure that users and processes acting on their behalf are prevented from gaining access to information or resources that they are not authorised to access or have no need to access. Similarly, there will be requirements*

*concerning the unauthorised creation or amendment (including deletion) of information.*

There and in the following two paragraphs on access control only "users" are mentioned. Not only users, but also designers, manufacturers, and operators can cause threats to a system (the same has to be considered for development tools, too). Additionally, even in centrally managed systems a difference has to be made between potential attackers of different parts of the TOE.

Especially risks caused by the operator of the system are not considered or are not considered any longer. An example is §E4.35 of ITSEC V1.2 or V1.1 in comparison with the associated paragraph in V1.0 (p. 62): "Unrecognized loss of functionality of the security functions" caused by errors of the system operator is treated in V1.0 but left out in V1.1 and V1.2.

**Decentrally Managed IT Systems:** The ITSEC do not address *decentrally managed* IT systems, i.e., connected IT systems with multiple administrations with potentially conflicting interests. There are at least two deficits which show that decentrally managed IT systems are not covered: Different kinds of attackers are not covered (cf. Sect. 4.1); the aspect "Non-repudiation" is neglected. Reference to "Non-repudiation" under the generic heading "Data Exchange" is by far not enough and raises problems of systematics (cf. Sect. 3.1 and Sect. 4.2).

**Definitions of Confidentiality and Integrity:** These definitions are insufficient for 2 reasons:

(1) The best – and at least against strong attackers in today's systems, only – way to keep information confidential in a provable way is to avoid that it can be gathered. In theory nearly any application can be realized that way [Chaum 1990 and references there] and in practice many essential applications can, e.g., communication networks, payment systems, authorization systems or value exchange systems [Chaum 1985; Pfitzmann, Pfitzmann, Waidner 1991; Bürk, Pfitzmann 1990].

(2) In distributed systems one cannot prevent unauthorized modification of data, e.g., in transit on a network, but one can detect unauthorized modification with cryptographical means.

Therefore, the following definitions (changes in italics) are proposed:

| | |
|---|---|
| confidentiality | prevention of the unauthorized disclosure of information*, or, if possible, avoidance of unnecessary information.* |
| integrity | prevention of *undetected* unauthorized modification of information. |

Additionally, the changed definition of integrity provides for a cleaner separation of integrity and availability. Without that change, unauthorized overwriting of data would be both an integrity and availability violation. Changing the definition of integrity makes integrity correspond to the well established notion of *partial correctness* in program verification, and integrity and availability together correspond to the well established notion *total correctness.*

## 4.2 Functionality

The ITSEC divide the functionality aspects of secure systems in two levels of abstraction – generic headings and functionality classes – but do not treat the aspects of user protection in IT systems. The generic headings do not give an adequate structure to the issue of computer security. The example functionality classes cover a smaller range than they seem to do at first sight.

**Protection of Users in Communication Systems:** Neither the generic headings nor the proposed functionality classes give guidance for the adequate classification and certification of TOEs which provide anonymity, pseudonymity, and freeness from observability to their users [Chaum 1985; Pfitzmann, Pfitzmann, Waidner 1991; Bürk, Pfitzmann 1990]. ITSEC V1.2 do not give any help for evaluation and certification of TOEs which work without the need or enforcement of any gathering of unnecessary person-related information. TOEs which protect users by keeping their data confidential can only be classified by negating the generic headings. The same is true for TOEs which protect usees by making them users operating their own individual computers [Chaum 1985] ("Usees" are people, whose data "users" are working with, potentially putting them at risk). So the ITSEC seem to be focussed neither on the issues of the users nor of the usees.

**Generic Headings:** The 8 generic headings for the security enforcing functions are incomplete and unsystematic. They are incomplete as essential counterparts to the given classes are missing. For some services, *Identification* and *Authentication* are wanted, for other services, one needs the corresponding counterparts *Anonymity* and *Pseudonymity*, cf. [Chaum 1985]. The same relationship exists between *Audit* and its counterpart *Freeness from observability.*

The generic headings are unsystematic as "Data Exchange" is no generic heading at the same level of abstraction as the other 7 generic headings given, e.g., there is no generic heading "Data Storage". The unsystematic approach is obvious as "Authentication" and "Access Control" which are subissues to "Data Exchange" are issues treated as generic headings as well. Assigning to that eighth generic heading such important aspects as non-repudiation makes this unsystematic approach even worse, cf. Sect. 3.1.

**The Example Functionality Classes:** The 10 example functionality classes leave out the aspects of anonymity, pseudonymity, and unobservability and so give the false impression every relevant security problem is covered. Even the possibility to define additional functionality classes does not solve the following problem: Without guidance by the ITSEC themselves users, customers, and procurers will not be supported in specifying their security needs.

### 4.3 Assurance of Effectiveness

The effectiveness of security functions is strongly dependent on the strength of the mechanisms used. Therefore a well-contrived scale to classify mechanisms according to their strength has to exist. Additionally, for an international rating of security mechanisms to be objective, algorithms should be published. If they are secret this should become distinct in the rating. Third, determinations of acceptable bandwidths of covert channels are missing.

**Strength of Mechanisms:** "Beyond normal practicality" as the highest rating for the strength of mechanisms is too low. This is a trivial condition and only suited to characterize *basic* and not at all *high*. The highest rating has to be called, e.g., "unbreakable". One gets it from the highest rating in [GISA 1989], "virtually unbreakable", which "prevents all violations of the security policy and according to the present state of the art it is practically impossible to overcome. [...]". Omitting "according to [...] art" results in a time-independent definition for "unbreakable". Examples of mechanisms rated "unbreakable" are the one-time pad [Shannon 1949] or information-theoretic authentication codes [Simmons 1988].

The discrimination between strengths of mechanisms in only three ratings (basic, medium, or high) is very poor and not adequate. There must be more ratings, see, e.g., [GISA 1989] for more ratings and good definitions. Few ratings imply relatively big rounding errors which stimulates subjectivity. With many classes one can handle the problem of subjectivity by giving one class as expectation and two further classes as an upper and lower bound. This accords with confidence intervals which have a good tradition in engineering.

**Public Discussion of Cryptographic Mechanisms:** Opposed to ITSEC V1.2 §3.23 (p. 39) and §E6.32 (p. 106), the rating of cryptographic mechanisms has to be international and as objective and reproducible as possible. An open and international discussion increases the probability to detect possible weaknesses in an algorithm. It requires that all mechanisms be published in any detail. Any secret mechanisms are not suitable for certified secure systems. This has to be stated in the rating of cryptographic mechanisms to avoid national attitudes to employ secret cryptographic mechanisms.

**Covert Channels:** The use of covert channels can circumvent every security policy dealing with confidentiality and therefore has to be considered as an aspect of effectiveness. It is also an aspect of the correctness as Covert Channels can be introduced into a system during the implementation. Neither in the Chapters 0-6 of ITSEC, nor in the proposed functionality classes, there are limits imposed on the bandwidth of covert channels. Compared with [US_DOD 1983, 1985] and [GISA 1989] this is a large step backward.

To protect people from risks caused by information leaks the highest security class has to restrict the bandwidth of all covert channels together well below $4 \cdot 10^{-10}$ bit/s as the following example shows: One can imagine a database including information on the attribute "AIDS, yes or no". This bit of information has to be kept secret for the lifetime of the patient, e.g., 80 years. This yields an upper bound of the bandwidth of 1/80 bit/year $\approx 4 \cdot 10^{-10}$ bit/s. An acceptable bandwidth should be considerably lower.

The very least is that higher evaluation levels require a determination of the bandwidth of covert channels. It is then for the accreditor or procurer of a TOE to decide whether the possible bandwidth is acceptable or not. If the ITSEC do not require to evaluate this bandwidth for, e.g., products, many procurers will have to do that which is a multiplication of effort.

## 4.4 Assurance of Correctness

Considering the vulnerability of software development tools through, e.g., Trojan Horses six evaluation levels are not enough. Further on the current definition of E4 might restrict the evaluation of all TOEs of the near future to only three levels.

**Evaluation Levels beyond E6 – Consideration of Tools:** As in [GISA 1989], it must be stated clearly that evaluation levels beyond E6 are possible, very desirable, and might be defined in the future. One reason for this is the existence of transitive Trojan Horses [Thompson 1984]. Examples for evaluation levels beyond E6 are E7 (Verified design history of all tools used to develop the TOE) and E8 (Verified design history of all tools used to develop tools used to develop the TOE). The ultimate level would require verified design for all used tools (recursive definition!), i.e., one needs some form of secure bootstrap in generating these tools.

Even if the suggested levels E7 and E8 might be not achievable considering today's "state of the art" [CEC 1991_2] criteria should define or at least mention possible targets. What the criteria makers believe to be "the state of the art" might be more a matter of expense than "art". Even if it was "art" hopefully the "state of the art" emerges faster than (hopefully stable) criteria. Not mentioning what some users of ITSEC might desire because it is deemed not to be "state of the art" is very dangerous as it gives them a false impression of security.

**TOEs without Formal Specification:** A formal security policy for *all* aspects of security has to exist for the levels E4 and above (§E4.2 ITSEC). This is a major (at least short term) weakness of ITSEC because at present only 3 evaluation levels are possible for nearly all relevant TOEs (the argument of Sect. 4.3 that 3 ratings are much too less applies).

## 4.5 Post-Evaluation Problems

Evaluation and certification of TOEs do not stay valid forever and evaluated TOEs are going to be connected. This subsection addresses the problems after a TOE has been evaluated.

**Re-Rating and Re-Evaluation:** The re-rating and re-evaluation have to be harmonized internationally. The current document presents no concept to solve this problem. Reference to national certification bodies or a statement that this task is "beyond the scope of these criteria" as stated in §1.34 of V1.2 is a bad excuse for not addressing that issue.

**Security Flaws in Certified Products:** There are no concepts in the ITSEC, what shall happen if someone discovers – and possibly publishes – a security flaw allowing a break of security for a certified TOE. Maybe the certificate becomes invalid by discovery of a security flaw but there are no concepts to inform all users (not to speak about usees) of the TOE.

**Rating of TOEs consisting of Evaluated Components:** Evaluated TOEs often are not used stand-alone. An example is the connection of two computers by a network. ITSEC do not contain concepts what functionality class and evaluation level should be assigned to systems consisting of evaluated TOEs. Is in this case a complete, partial, or no re-evaluation required?

### 4.6 Development and Discussion of the ITSEC

The organization of ITSEC development and discussion must be improved to enable a public review and a constructive scientific discussion adequate to a project of this size and importance.

**Need for a Rationale:** To stimulate a constructive discussion it is not enough to publish the criteria themselves, but necessary to publish a detailed rationale, e.g., all options and suggestions and the reasons for their selection. This has been asked for unanimously at VIS'91, an international scientific conference on dependable computer systems organized by the GI (German IFIP Full Member) in March 1991 [Rannenberg 1991]. [CEC 1991_2] and its predecessor are only a first step as they do not contain all critical points and give very few answers.

**Avoidance of Critical Points:** The comparison between ITSEC V1.1 and V1.2 gives the impression that critical points are neither discussed nor clarified but left out in the course of the document's development. Examples are:

§4.24 in V1.1 was criticized because it did not cover the need for configuration control for tools to ensure that insecure functionality is not added. As a result in V1.2 the aspect of additional insecure functionality vanished from §4.24.

§E6.5 and §E6.11 in V1.1 were criticized as the vulnerability analysis mentioned there covered the circumvention of the security of a TOE only with respect to users and left out the risks caused by operators and designers. As a result in V1.2 the vulnerability analysis is not mentioned any longer.

Risks caused by the operators are left out since V1.1 of ITSEC (see Sect. 4.1).

## 5 CONCLUSIONS

The ITSEC and their use could both increase and decrease the vulnerability of society. Vulnerability increases if the ITSEC are used by unexperienced persons as certain threats are ignored without any documentation of this fact. An example are the recommended generic headings in combination with the 10 example functionality classes derived from the ZSISEC [GISA 1989] which can give the false impression every security issue is covered. A decrease of vulnerability caused by ITSEC is only possible if experienced people knowing the weaknesses of ITSEC use the criteria. Besides this aspect the criteria amplify the trend to systems which need a centralized and trusted instance sometimes called "big brother systems“.

At least the following measures are needed to make ITSEC a real contribution to security instead of vulnerability.

(1) The title and the scope section have to be narrowed or much more and much broader work is required. In any case, it does not help to re-define "evaluation criteria" in a way that the ITSEC title becomes correct.

(2) Functionality classes useful for a democratic society must be developed. They have to reflect the complex relations between the individual, the society, and the state, i.e., they must consider citizens rights on data protection and privacy in general and on unobservable communication in particular. The definition of functionality classes by independent bodies has to be sponsored to promote the consideration of human rights.

(3) The problems and risks of computer aided software engineering (CASE) have to be considered in the field of assurance. Especially the risks of transitive Trojan Horses in CASE tools, e.g., editors and compilers should be treated.

(4) A complete and detailed synopsis of the criticism and a rationale for the reaction to it have to be published.

(5) The criteria have to be tested by IT users in public administrations needing open systems.

(6) Only cryptographic mechanisms whose complete construction and design decisions are internationally known and discussed are eligible for high ratings.

The development process of the criteria, also in the standardization has to be organized publicly and openly and with a public rationale. The process must empower the issues of "usees" who normally lack the ability to appear for their interests. During the classical ISO standardization process "usee" representatives must be sponsored to visit *and* prepare the meetings.

Further on, concepts for at least the following problems are needed additionally to the ITSEC:

(1) TOEs must be re-evaluated continuously, e.g., to cover new arising threats.

(2) The evaluation and certification instances have to be evaluated, too. If many instances will evaluate and certificate TOEs a common basis for the legitimation and evaluation of these instances is needed.

(3) The public and international rating of cryptographic mechanisms has to be *organized* internationally.

## 6 REFERENCES


[Bürk, Pfitzmann 1990] Holger Bürk, Andreas Pfitzmann: Value Exchange Systems Enabling Security and Unobservability; Computers & Security 9/8 (1990) 715-721

[CEC 1991_1] (Informal) EC advisory group SOG-IS: Information Technology Security Evaluation Criteria (ITSEC) – Provisional Harmonised Criteria; Version 1.2, 28 June 1991, 163 pages (obtainable free of charge from CEC; Directorate XIII/F; SOG-IS Secretariat; Rue de la Loi, 200; B-1049 Brussels; Belgium)

[CEC 1991_2] (Informal) EC advisory group SOG-IS: ITSEC V1.1 Revision: Adressing the Main Issues, June 1991, 9 pages (obtainable free of charge like [CEC 1991_1])

[CESG 1989] UK Systems Security Confidence Levels, CESG Memorandum No.3, Communications-Electronics Security Group, United Kingdom, January 1989

[Chaum 1985] David Chaum, Security without Identification: Transaction Systems to make Big Brother Obsolete; Communications of the ACM 28/10 (1985) 1030-1044

[Chaum 1990] David Chaum: The Spymasters double-agent problem: Multiparty computations secure unconditionally from minorities and cryptographically from majorities; Crypto '89, LNCS 435, Springer-Verlag, Heidelberg 1990, 591-602

[Dierstein 1990] Rüdiger Dierstein: The Concept of Secure Information Processing Systems and their Basic Functions; IFIP/Sec'90, Helsinki, May 1990; North-Holland; Amsterdam 1990

[DTI 1989_1] DTI Commercial Computer Security Centre Evaluation Manual, V22; DTI, UK, February 1989

[DTI 1989_2] DTI Commercial Computer Security Centre Functionality Manual, V21; DTI, UK, February 1989

[GISA 1989] IT-Security Criteria, Criteria for the Evaluation of Trustworthiness of Information Technology (IT) Systems, ISBN 3-88784-200-6, German Information Security Agency, FR of Germany, January 1989

[Pfitzmann 1991] Andreas Pfitzmann: Statement of Observations concerning the Information Technology Security Evaluation Criteria (ITSEC) Version 1.2, 28 June 1991; Institut für Informatik, University of Hildesheim, Germany, November 29, 1991

[Pfitzmann, Pfitzmann, Waidner 1991] Andreas Pfitzmann, Birgit Pfitzmann, Michael Waidner: ISDN-MIXes – Untraceable Communication with very small Bandwidth Overhead; Proc. IFIP/Sec'91, Brighton, UK, May 1991; North-Holland; Amsterdam 1991; 245-258

[Rannenberg 1991] Kai Rannenberg: VIS'91: IT-Sicherheit – Bewertungskriterien; Computer & Recht 7/11 (1991) 699-701

[Rihaczek 1991] Karl Rihaczek: The Harmonized ITSEC Evaluation Criteria; Comp. & Sec. 10 (1991) 101-110

[SCSSI 1989] Catalogue de Critères Destinés à évaluer le Degré de Confiance des Systèmes d'Information, 692/SGDN/DISSI/SCSSI, Service Central de la Sécurité des Systèmes d'Information, Juillet 1989.

[Shannon 1949] Claude E. Shannon, Communication Theory of Secrecy Systems; The Bell System Technical Journal 28/4 (1949) 656-715

[Simmons 1988] G. J. Simmons, A Survey of Information Authentication; Proc. IEEE 76/5 (1988) 603-620

[Thompson 1984] Ken Thompson, Reflections on Trusting Trust; CACM 27/8 (1984) 761-763

[US_DOD 1983, 1985] DoD Standard: Department of Defense Trusted Computer System Evaluation Criteria; December 1985, DOD 5200.28-STD, Supersedes CSC-STD-001-83, dtd 15 Aug 83, Library No. S225,711

Education and Society / R. Aiken (Editor)
Information Processing 92, Volume II
Elsevier Science Publishers B.V. (North-Holland)


# Perspectives of the Vulnerability of IT-based Societies

Klaus Brunnstein
Faculty for Informatics
University of Hamburg, Germany

**Abstract**
This papers attempts to relate essential aspects covered in sessions and contributions to the World Congress stream "Diminishing Vulnerability of Information Society" in perspective from different views. As Information and Communication Technologies (IT) continue to rapidly evolve, new balances are needed to make optimum use of the opportunities and and to minimize the risks for societies, economies, cultures and individual in their international dimensions.

Keyword Codes: K.4; K.5; K.6.5
Keywords: Computers & Society; Legal Aspects; Security/Protection

## 1. Introduction: Information Technologies in Historic Perspective

500 years ago, Cristobal Colon alias Christopher Columbus and his Spanish marines opened the restricted European views to a global earth with different societies, cultures and economies. In Columbus' wake, the view opened further with the settlement of North America and Australia, to form today's understanding of the globe. In historical perspective, **opportunities and risks associated with the detection of "Las Indias"** (as Columbus misunderstood his detection) have been very differently experienced and analysed from the views of the detectors and those of the detected cultures. Even the detectors' heirs admit today that the exploitation of resources and the transfer of goods was rather one-directional.

The **development of industrial technologies**, starting 230 years ago from England to spread over the globe, seemed to present a new chance for more universal distribution of new opportunities. Again, the opportunities and risks associated with this development were rather unequally experienced as the distribution of wealth (which is verbally split into "4 worlds" depending on their economic behaviour) proves today. On the other side, the risks from ecological consequences and other effects of the industrial technologies as visible all over the globe bind the different economies and societies together. The continuously aggrevating problems may only be solved in a rational, joint approach.

The **advent of Information and Communication Technologies**, only 50 years ago, is often regarded as an even better chance for more equal interaction and cooperation of the different economies, cultures and societies. In such views, Information Technologies extend Columbus' detection of America as they assist in overcoming distances and (in a restricted sense) time and thus intensifying global cooperation of economies, cultural exchange and social interaction in some sort of **"global village"**. Moreover, these technologies are said to be fundamentally based on "rationalism" as they implement and extend human reasoning into machines. Following such arguments, adequate tools may be constructed to overcome many of the problems generated in the past and to develop a globe of economic cooperation, social development and cultural exchange.

## 2. Opportunities and Risks of Information Technologies

Generally, an **assessment of the opportunities and risks** of a new technology in it's initial stages of fast developments is rather difficult. As contemporary developments of new Information Technologies show, opportunities for new products, methods and services materialize within relatively short time. Personal and Portable Computers, connected to Local or Global Networks, provide for new goods and change existing ones, e.g. by integrating services into "older" technologies to enrich and diversify their use, as in Computer-Integrated Manufacturing. Generally, the velocity and the degree of integration and penetration of Information and Communication Technologies into economic and scientific, public and social applications has far exceeded the impact of other technologies.

Even now, slightly more than 50 years after the advent of the first computers and roughly 40 years after the first economic applications, the **risks gradually become more evident**, even to the public. Media reports about incidents related to computer or user malfunction increase the **public awareness that economies, states, groups and individuals have become highly dependent** on the proper work and functions of these technologies. Accidents such as system malfunctions, insecure design (e.g. the THERAC-25 therapeutic radiation system which killed two patients) and inadequate behaviour of vendors or users (e.g. in importing malicious software such as Trojan horses or computer "viruses") clearly demonstrate the **relative immature status** of these technologies' design, production, distribution and usage.

To diminish the vulnerability of IT-based economies and societies, a **fundamental understanding** of the nature and reasons of malfunctions, misuse and accidents is needed. The manifold aspects range from basic concepts - **paradigms** inherent in contemporary IT architectures, methods of system analysis and problem solving - to **insufficient understanding** of applications and **inadequate user behaviour**. While human "components" often enlarge the vulnerability of technical systems, it is too often overseen that malfunctions of critical IT-users - e.g. of pilots and other persons with responsibility for highly computerized, complex control systems - may not only come from insufficient education or training, but also from system interfaces constructed in a way as not to allow easy or otherwise adequate control (as in the AEGIS case where a military system assisted in shooting down a civilian airplane, killing over 280 passengers).

## 3. Concepts of Secure and Safe Systems

Consequently, one major means to diminish the vulnerability of IT-based societies must be the **development of secure and safe systems and tools** which behave with a given degree of trustworthiness, integrity of programs and data, availability and reliability. In the developing world of local, regional and global networks, distributed databases and processes as well as cooperative IT work, new methods and tools must be developped to preserve the secrecy of confidential information even during it's transport over insecure networks. Moreover, new methods of access control and authentication (e.g. using smartcards) are needed to reject any misuse of essential processes and any illegal access to confidential data. Unfortunately, it must be admitted that the **contemporary scientific understanding of IT security and safety is only rudimentary**; but there is some hope that the development of IT Security Criteria may enhance this understanding and help, at least in some future, to diminish IT vulnerability.

On the other side, improvements in design and implementation of secure and safe technologies may also affect and even endanger **essential user interests.** Enhanced access control (e.g. with Intrusion Detection and Avoiding Experts Systems) may be achieved by extensive control (auditing) of user behaviour, by which manifold personal data may be gathered even about non-malicious users, even at the price of vulnerating guaranteed legal rights (privacy, informational self-determination). For reasons of human control, it must be avoided that secure and safe systems suspect any user accessing it to be as an intruder: no wo/man could be made legally responsible for her/his actions with such tools and methods in control.

## 4. Vulnerability in Work, Organisation and Social Environments

Growing vulnerability also may develop when Information technologies are used in economic and social environments which are not well prepared or badly adapted to IT use. Many examples of **IT use in work environments** demonstrate the inadequacy of traditional approaches. New ways to organise IT work as well as to use IT tools and methods are needed to fully use the potential benefits from new products and methods, such as **Electronic Markets** and their expansion into **"Electronic Cottages".** One means to establish **organisational accountability** may also be to let users influence the design and organisation of newly developped IT products. Systems produced in some rational cooperation of designers, implementers and users may, with some probability, behave more reliably and may easier be controlled by the users than contemporary systems. Moreover, due to the global nature of Information and Communication technologies as well as of international production and trading systems, such developments should be worldwide, including also the "Developing Countries".

Evidently, it must als be discussed whether **traditional social standards and behaviour** are adequate to optimize the opportunities and minimize the risks of IT work. Here, **gender issues** play an essential role. Among others, the technical design of human-computer interfaces which probably has enhanced the vulnerability of society may be related to their designers' experiences incorporated in their age as young boys with technical toys, whereas young girls learn social behaviour often with less technically equipped toys. Such experiences may subsequently dominate also adult behaviour and therefore may be responsible for the fact that women rarely become system designers and implementors. Even if some arguments for a possibly (evidently?) difference in the "wiring of the brain" of men and women are not taken into account, an evidently unequal distribution of women and men in processes of IT design and IT use should be changed.

## 5. Legal and Ethical Aspects of IT Vulnerability

With the advent of **computer incidents and computer crime**, IT based societies also look for adequate and and effective means to develop and control standards of legal behaviour. Unfortunately, the continuous development as well as the difference between traditional technologies and Information Technologies makes it difficult, to develop consciousness among law-makers and law-practitioners. How to transfer the concept of theft (=taking away some material thing) to illegally copying a file (where the original file remains intact)? How to prove the damage produced by a malicious attacker or some software ("virus") without understanding the technology? Moreover, in a world where goods, tools and decision making growingly cross the boundaries of national legislations, worldwide agreement must be sought how to adress such legal problems. Evidently, continuous lack of international cooperation in the development of joint legal procedures would immediately enhance the problems of vulnerability, by further enabling international criminal organisations to work without restriction or control.

The continuous rapid development of Information and Communication Technologies evidently will have further impact in many new areas. As the public understanding and some new, broadly accepted legal, technical and social standards very probably will only develop slowly, the responsibility of IT professionals grows significantly with the complexity of their systems. This has been clearly understood by some respected IT organisations, such as the British Computer Society (BCS) and (based on US experiences)

Association for Computing Machinery (ACM) which develloped and published the **"BCS Code of Good Conduct"** and the **"ACM Code of Ethics"**. Other member societies of the International Federation for Information Processing have meanwhile adopted or are presently discussing their own Code of Ethics.

In engaged discussions, attempts are discussed to develop some **universal form of Code of Ethics**, such as the "Draft IFIP Code of Ethics". Such an approach assumes that the use of Information and Communication Technologies in some form of "global village" also should lead to some global values, which might be uniformly notified and obeyed though not enforced. Such an approach must be aware of the historical, cultural, social and economic backgrounds before which the value systems ot the respective partners have been developped. Evidently, any attempt to apply such differing views to essentially differing cultural and social value systems, might be seen as another attempt of superimposing traditional values with imported ones, which in analogy to the history of international economic and political relations might be named **"IT Imperialism"**. Unfortunately, there are some evident examples of inappropriate technology transfer from industrialized into developping countries. On the other side, international approaches to jointly minimize IT risks and optimize the opportunities would demand for some basic rules, in some sort of "frame of reference for Codes of Ethics".

## 6. Establishing Awareness among IT Professionals

Ideally, the organised IT community could try to **optimize the benefits** from its technology and at the same time to **minimize the risks and limit or diminish the vulnerabilities** developing from their growing distribution. **Historical consciousness** (e.g. understanding benefits and shortcomings of other technical developments) as well as **awareness** for the different societies' traditions should guarantee a high degree of respect for other value systems. Until now, human kind often learned in historical cases only by strong negative impact: wars, accidents, criminal attacks. As IT risks and the vulnerability of societies, economies, groups and individuals grow, there is a demand to prevent IT accidents. At least on a few tracks, there are attempts to adapt organisation, behaviour and technology.

# SYMPOSIUM 2: INFORMATICS FOR ENVIRONMENTAL PROTECTION

## Bernd Page
## Organizer

Peter Bollerslev, *Chair*
Ministry of Education
Copenhagen, Denmark

Robert Aiken
Temple University
Philadelphia, Pennsylvania, USA

A. Balasubrahmanian
Madras - 600 004, India

Antonio Vaquero Sanchez
Universidad Complutense de Madrid
Madrid, Spain

Ivan Stanchev
Bulgarian Academy of Sciences
Sofia, Bulgaria

Education and Society / R. Aiken (Editor)
Information Processing 92, Volume II
Elsevier Science Publishers B.V. (North-Holland) 


# Environmental Protection as a Challenge to Applied Informatics A Workshop Introduction

B. Page
University of Hamburg, Department of Informatics,
Vogt-Kölln-Str. 30, D-2000 Hamburg 54, Federal Republic of Germany

**Abstract**

Environmental problem solving is very much an information processing activity handling a wide range of environmental data. In this introductory paper five different categories of environmental processing systems are classified (monitoring and control systems, conventional information systems, computation and analysis systems, planning and decision support systems as well as integrated systems). Environmental informatics as a new discipline is introduced with some potential research fields in a number of applied informatics branches. In some detail knowledge-based approaches for assisting ecological system simulation are discussed. Finally an outlook on this workshop is given.

Keyword Codes: H.4.2, I.2.1, I.6.7
Keywords: Informations Systems, Types of Systems; Artificial Intelligence, Applications and Expert Systems; Simulation and Modeling, Simulation Support Systems

## 1. INTRODUCTION

The manifold problems in environmental protection, environmental planning and environmental research can be only solved on the ground of a comprehensive and reliable information basis. State and dynamics of the environment are described by biological, physical, chemical, geological, meteorological or socio-economical data. This data is time and space related and addresses past or current states. The processing of information on the environment, on its stress factors and mutual influence mechanisms are fundamental for any kind of environmental planning and preventive measure. Solution approaches to our environmental problems are highly dependent on the quality of accessable information sources.

In Fig. 1 (adopted from [1] with some modifications) it is shown schematically, how human caused environmental burdens and damages can be couteracted with computerized environmental data and information for the public, the economy, the administration and politics by means of feedback effects. Apparently, environmental problem solving is mainly an information processing activity handling a wide range of environmental data.

Information technology has become absolutely essential for contemporary environmental protection in providing the required environmental information on the appropriate level of detail, completeness, accuracy and speed. Computer applications in environmental protection, however, are often lacking a sound conceptual and scientific basis [2]. This is of course not only a matter of applied informatics, but an interdisciplinary task where many scientific disciplines should be involved (e.g. geo- and bio-sciences, environmental engineering, economics and law, measuring technology, admistrative sciences, etc.). However, **informatics** as the science of the **fundamental methodology** of **information and knowledge processing**, its **applications** and **implications** has the capability - and should therefore take over the responsibility - to play a central role in this interdisciplinary research. Applied informatics cannot only provide a number of well established techniques and tools, it can also push forward the extension of its own methodology by making use of the complex and manifold environmental problem area as a challenging test field for an application and public needs oriented research.

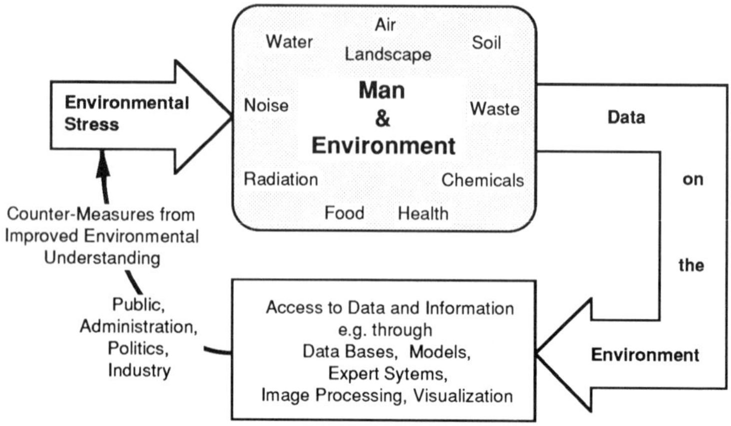


Figure 1: Feedback Effects from Environmental Information Processing

## 2. CLASSIFICATION OF ENVIRONMENTAL INFORMATION PROCESSING SYSTEMS

Information processing systems in the environmental field can be ideally classified into four main categories depending on the level and type of information aggregation or analysis:

- *Monitoring and Control Systems:* Information processing systems for the automation of monitoring measurements (including remote sensing) in water, air, soil, noise and radiation control, as well as for process control systems. Computerized process control is either directly employed in environmental technology such as in air or exhaust gas cleaning, sewage, sludge or refuse processing, or used in production process automation with secondary effects for environmental protection (i.e. energy conservation, emission reduction).
- *Conventional Information Systems:* Information processing systems for the collection of environmental data (e.g. measurements, facts such as chemical substance attributes or refuse class, documents like environmental laws and regulations, or literature abstracts), their storage, organization, structuring, integration and reproduction as environmental information. The deduction does not reach much beyond the selection and combination of environmental data. Here, conventional environmental data base and query systems fit in.
- *Computation and Analysis Systems:* Information processing systems for complex synthesis and scientific analysis of environmental data by means of powerful mathematical, statistical and graphical analysis methods as well as

analytical and simulation modeling such as pollution dispersion computations, smog forcasting, ecological simulations or environmental scenarios (e.g. alternative emission limit assumptions). The deduction deals with the quantitative statement of solution steps, alternatives, and causal relationships (e.g. causal models in forest damage research or graphical output of immission load over time and region). Also, image processing and analysis systems for environmental remote sensing data can be classified here.

- *Planning and Decision Support Systems:* Information processing systems for the assistance of decision makers in decision preparation and problem solving, the selection and assesssment of alternatives and the foundation of decisions such as in the evaluation of location alternatives in environmental impact analysis or in handling hazardous substances. In this context, methods of deduction are the combination, aggregation, analysis, and evaluation of quantitative and qualitative information and to some extent logical inference mechanisms. Expert systems, or more generally speaking, knowledge based systems, as well as model-based decision support systems fall into this category.

Typically real world environmental information processing systems will be often of an integrated nature, i.e., they will contain components of more than one system category just defined. An example for this class of *integrated systems* would be an air pollution information system with an automatic monitoring subsystem, a measurement data base or complex statistical analysis and graphics programs.

## 3. THE ROLE OF APPLIED INFORMATICS

**Environmental Informatics** is a rather new specialty in applied informatics dealing with the **collection, storage, retrieval and processing of complex environmental data.** Data on the environment show a number of specific characteristics typically not found in conventional information processing (i.e. business or administrative data processing or even in many engineering computer applications). First, we have many different, rather inhomogenious information sources in environmental information systems such as text data on environmental laws or research projects, measurement data from monitoring networks, structural data on chemical substances, formated engineering data on enviromental technology, just to name a few. In particular, environmental data is often **geographicaly coded,** i.e. information is attached to a particular point or region in space. Secondly, some of the data objects are **multidimensional** and have to be represented by means of complex geometric objects (e.g. polygons or curves). Third, the processing of **statistical data** and **methods** as well as of **vague**, **uncertain** and **incomplete knowledge** is a major concern in environmental informatics. Fourth, a comfortable user access on **heterogeneous distributed environmental data bases** should to be supported. And fifth and last, environmental data must be presented and evaluated in a **domain overlapping way**. As a requirement, this information has to be often deducted from a domain specific primary data base beforehand.

These characteristica result in different requirements on information processing in environmental protection. First of all, environmental informatics has to address aspects of geometric data structures and algorithms as well as of modern geographical information systems. Knowledge-based systems are of importance in dealing with uncertain environmental knowledge. Method base system architectures are useful for statistical and mathematical modeling or simulation approaches. Beyond that, there are many links to heterogeneous data bases, to natural language processing as well as to many neighbouring disciplines such as remote sensing, measuring technology or ecosystem analysis [3].

To provide a more systematic and structured view we will return to the classification scheme of environmental information processing systems given above. Environmental information processing as classified in section 2 offers a variety of complex applied research problem areas which are of principal interest in a number of informatics partial fields . In Table 1 the most relevant informatics branches are summarized for the different environmental information processing system classes. We will now base our discussion on this structure.

| Systems / Research Fields | Monitoring and Control Systems | Information Systems | Compution and Analysis Systems | Planning and Decision Systems |
|---|---|---|---|---|
| Data Bases | | ● | ● | ● |
| Man-Machine-Interaction | ● | ● | ● | ● |
| Measurement Data Collection &Processing | ● | | ○ | |
| Process Control | ● | | ○ | |
| Computer Networks | ● | ● | | |
| Computer Graphics | ● | ○ | ● | ● |
| Image Processing | ○ | | ● | ○ |
| Knowledge-based Systems | ● | ○ | ○ | ● |
| Modelling and Simulation | | | ● | ● |

Table 1

**Data base and information system technology** belong to the fundamental tools in environmental information processing. **Environmental information systems** (EIS) can be considered as special geographical information systems because of the common **spatial** reference of the data stored. In addition, they hold **thematic** data (i.e. **environmental facts** such as measurement values or substance data) or environmental documents as **text data** on research projects, laws, or literature) as well as data with **temporal** reference (e.g. usage alteration of restoration areas). According to the different types of environmental data, an EIS should be able to store information in different forms of representation. Future EIS should be seen in the context of **multi media information systems**, designed for the storage, retrieval and display of multimedia environmental objects (i.e. of different representational form such as text, facts, graphs, time series, maps, images). It is obvious, that EIS would cause serious difficulties if attempts were made to implement the concepts just mentioned with standard relational data base technology. Two open questions demanding more research are, to what extent typical EIS applications can be supported by today`s DBMS architectures and which DBMS concepts (e.g. data models) should be provided by future systems in order to give adequate support to EIS applications [4].

Beyond that, there is a challenge to applied informatics research in providing an **easy access to environmental data bases** for anyone, e.g. to receive information on the state of the environment, on environmental nuisances or rehabilitations, respectively. New EC regulations allow for a free access to environmental information for common people. Implementation of these regulations requires a substancial information system support. New easy to use (e.g. **natural language** ) **query languages** for environmental data bases have to be developed. **Meta data bases** are necessary to support user orientation within comprehensive environmental information systems with probably up to one hundred very heterogeneous specialized environmental data bases.

Another central topic is the **integration** of different **heterogeneous data sources** in **distributed applications**, which has to be solved as a prerequisite for truly comprehensive environmental information systems including also the strategic level in environmental politics and administration.

A general requirement for a wide use of environmental information systems is the application of modern concepts in designing comfortable **user interfaces**. In particular, the utilization n the very common group of occasional users in environmental information systems can be increased significantly ([5], pp. 47 f.).

**Process control systems** are first of all relevant for technical environmental protection (measuring technique, environmental technology for environment adapted production processes [6], pp. 237 f.). **Measurement data collection and processing techniques** including **remote sensing** (e.g. for forest damage mapping) play an important role because of the manifold measurements monitoring state and devolopment of the environment as mentioned above. Problems of **computer networking** have to be solved in the design of regional and national measuring networks (e.g. smog alarm systems [1], pp. 442f.). **High speed computer networks** are required for mass data exchange between distributed locations in global change (i.e. climatological, meteorological, hydrological, etc.) or environmental research, respectively [7]. **Distributed EIS** also demand powerful computer networks to transfer complex mass data (e.g. images) to different remote sites.

**Computer graphics** has been a very helpful instrument in the **visualization of environmental data** in environmental research, in decision making and comprehensive reporting ([1], pp. 799f.). Methods of **image processing** are used more frequently for the analysis of aerophotos in forest damage surveys ([8], pp. 335f.). Other potential applications are the spoting of oil pollutants on sea or the monitoring of emission sources in air pollution.

More recently attempts are made of applying **knowledge-based concepts**, in particular **expert system technology** to the construction of environmental information processing systems (e.g. for decision support in environmental impact analysis, for the handling of hazardous waste substances and contaminated sites or as advice tool in disturbance and crisis situations with environmentally dangerous chemicals [9]). However, most projects did not advance much beyond the prototype state.

The utilization of conventional expert system technology in environmental protection has been limited todate, because

- the spatial and temporal reference of most environmental problems require substancial advances in **spatial** and **temporal reasoning methods**,
- the **realtime capability of expert systems** is not yet sufficient for environmental monitoring and environment adapted process control applications,
- the **integration** of **expert system techniques** with **conventional system components** (i.e. data bases, geographical information systems, simulation models) has to be improved,
- **knowledge aquisition techniques** and tools for **interdisciplinary knowledge domains** such as environmental protection have to be refined. In this way, domain knowledge from experts of different disciplines have to be aquired and synthezised ([9], [6], pp. 491f.).
- **model-based reasoning** is more promising for some environmental domains ( e.g. technical diagnosis for wastewater treatment plants [1], pp. 197f. , or ecosystem analysis [10], pp. 193f.), than straigthforward rule-based

techniques, found in most conventional („flat") expert systems, however at the expense of a lower maturity degree.

**Modeling and simulation** is playing an important role in many science and technology disciplines and has a long tradition in the environmental field as well (up to a norm status in environmental laws, e.g. **dispersion models** for air or water pollution substances). It is a matter of applied informatics to develop powerful **software tools** for the **construction** and **utilization** of **environmental models** (i.e. environmental simulators) . In the following paragraph a new concept for an effective user support in environmental modeling and simulation is sketched mainly founded on the introduction of knowledge-based techniques.

## 4. KNOWLEDGE-BASED APPROACHES FOR ASSISTANCE IN ENVIRONMENTAL MODELING AND SIMULATION

Modeling and simulation methods have reached different significance in various environmental fields . It was argued in a recent study [6] , that next to a number of sections with a rather high acceptance level of modeling and simulation techniques (e.g. simulation of pollutant dispersion), there are other sections with a lower record of successful applications (e.g. ecosystem reseach). There are a number of reasons for this application deficit. First of all, the **great effort** in manpower required for a simulation study in different modeling stages (i.e. from systems analysis, model design, over simulation program implementation up to simulation experiments) is an important obstacle. Another problem is the **wide range of knowledge** in several disciplines necessary for the correct execution of a simulation study. Typically, scientists working on a simulation model have competence in their own discipline (e.g. air pollution or water quality), however limited qualification in simulation methodology and computer utilization, respectively.

Also, simulation model building is hindered by the **heterogeneity of the environmental domain with regard to the contents**. Many times, several disciplines are relevant for solving an environmental problem difficult to be covered by a single modeller. Although the models should reflect their interdisciplinary contents, working groups are not always sufficiently interdisciplinary. Heterogenity is the reason for missing a generally applicable simulation methodology in the analysis of environmental problems. Depending on problems involved and basic knowledge available different simulation methods are suitable. **Methodological diversity** is characteristic for the environmental domain.

Beyond that, problems arise from the type of knowledge typically found in the environmental sector. In many cases, it is not well suited for transformation into customary simulation models. Usually these consist exclusively of a mathematical or numerical description, respectively. Everything taken into the model has to be described in an exact, formalized notation. Against that, **knowledge on environmental processes** and their relations (e.g. in ecosystems) are rather **inprecise,** more **qualitative** and **descriptive**.

In applied informatics a wide range of software for modeling and simulation purposes has been developed for a long time already, including simulation languages, packages and simulation systems. Simulation systems are not only tools for model implementation, but provide functions for user assistance in different phases of the model building cycle. Modern, object oriented user interfaces take care of a high degree of user friendlyness, in particular for novices with limited computer experience [11]. These **conventional support concepts** are, however, not yet adequate for the environmental sector in many respects. User friendlyness as well as functionality are still insufficient. All appraoches have in common that they do not offer any support in providing required **modeling and simulation knowledge**. The user has to know himself how to apply the available functions in a sensible way. All approaches are based on the traditional (i.e. restricted) model notion missing a sufficient **representation** capability for **nonmathematical** and **nonnumerical** information. Another problem of traditional modeling software is the apparent contrast between level of support and system flexibility. The higher the comfort of the support functions, the more specialized (i.e. restricted) is the application domain of the modeling software. However, the combination of both properties would be required for an adequate application of modeling and simulation software in the environmental field.

On basis of the critical analysis of conventional modeling and simulation support software in the environmental field as mentioned above a concept for a new simulation system was designed [12]. The aims of this approach were the increase of user friendliness by advanced concepts for graphical modeling, to provide special knowledge (e.g. on a methodically correct model building) to users, to raise model representation capability, and to offer improved (i.e. knowledge-based) support functions for instance for modular model construction or the utilization of existing models as submodels). The latter is in particular helpful for building heterogeneous models with regard to the contents. The utmost aim, however, is the largely suspension of the contrast between comfortable support functions and system flexibility, characteristic for traditional support system concepts. The conceptional aims mentioned address some of the most essential limitations of modeling and simulation in the environmental field.

Flexibility as primary goal is achieved by a system architecture with three different layers, each incorparating respective functionality of a given type. First, there is an external lawer with all functions serving for user interface generation and in particular for model presentation in diagram form. Those functions are attached to the internal layer describing the model contents independently from from their external presentation form. On the knowledge-based layer model contents can be described as declarations and rules. Declarations and rules are integrated into knowledge bases, whereas the required knowledge-based layer functionality is provided by a connected expert system shell. In Fig. 2 the general system architecture with the different layers is shown. It is indicated that own elements exist for the expert system shell at the user interface level, which are, however, completely embedded into the homogeneous user interface from the user point of view. A vertical flexibility is realized by the system partition into different layers. In this way, the related diagram formalism could be exchanged for a simulation method without requiring modifications on the internal or knowledge-based layer.

A basic functionality is offered in a system kernel on any layer with all relevant system functions independently of a particular simulation method. In this way a **simulation frame system** is generated, which can be extended for support of concrete simulation methods by minimal supplements. To allow for an easy extension an **object oriented** apprach was chosen for the system design. The concrete layer formation in the system kernel therefore consists of an object class hierarchy with related methods. There are object classes for the generation of system components (e.g. dialog boxes) as well as object classes whose instances are used for building up the models managed by the simulation system. The extension of the frame system with objects and methods required for supporting a special simulation method can be realized by refering to the available object classes and their methods making use of the **inheritage principle**.

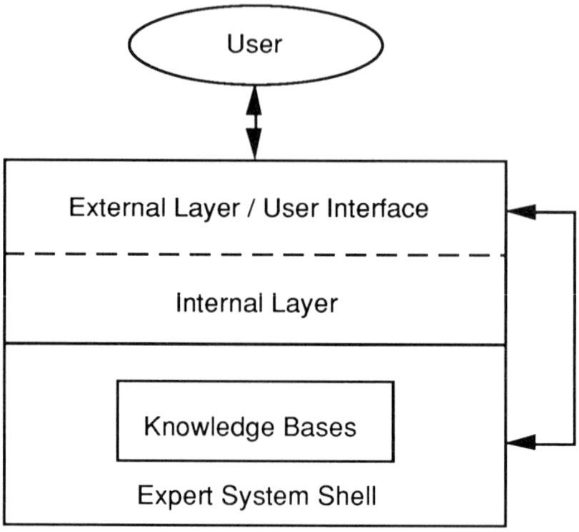


Fig. 2: General Architecture of the Simulation System

Thus replenishments of object classes and methods are only necessary, if a special simulation method to be integrated into the frame system is requesting deviations from the provided constructs. The flexibility arising from the object oriented view is even raised by the use of a knowledge-based system component. In particular, any kind of knowledge on a special simulation method (i.e. knowledge on methodically correct model construction) is stored in a knowledge base as far as it can be represented there adequately. The system is configurable for the support of another simulation method by a simple internal exchange of the resepective knowledge base to be loaded. In this way, the advantage of a consequent separation of knowledge and its processing in knowledge-based systems is exploited for system flexibility improvement.

The combination of the object oriented and the knowledge-based approach is also for the benefit of increasing the **expression power of simulation models**. On one hand, information can be kept in the model object attributes, on the other hand for every model a **model specific knowledge base** is generated , where declarations on the model and its components can be registered. Some of the entries ensue implicitely from the system at model construction, others are explicite entries by the users. This information can be reproduced by means of simple queries or used for deducting new knowledge depending on the available methodogical rule set. In this way, it becomes feasible to make early use of information already present in the model for **inferences** without a complete mathematical, numerical model specification.

Another aspect of system flexibility is the support of a **modular, hierarchical**

**model construction** very helpful in the environmental field for building integrated environmental models. Each model can be imbedded into another model as a submodel. A model interface is generated for each submodel, where its external relations to the higher level model are described. In this way, a model can be constructed from other models over any number of aggregation levels. Beyond that, the utilization of already existing models is promoted. Any model under construction with the simulation system can be classified by the user. This classification is then employed for assisting other users at the selection of appropriate models. **Model classification and selection** is also realized by the knowledge-based system component.

The flexibility and support function concepts just mentioned concern the inner system functionality, whereas concepts for the improvement of graphical modeling are directly visible at the system surface. Any user without special computer knowledge can profit from the high degree of fashioning freedom in individual model diagram construction. Some of the new facilities are the definition of background pictures for the modeling diagram for illustration purposes , the assignment of user defined images to the individual model symbols as well as the selective fading in and out of symbols.

A prototype implementation of the ecological simulator concept just introduced - with a high degree of adaptivity to varying requirements in the environmental domain as its main asset - is under way using a object-oriented *CommonLisp* environment and an expert system shell on a Macintosh PC.

## 5. CONCLUSIONS AND OUTLOOK

The solution of the versatile, very much interlaced and highly interdisciplinary tasks in the environmental field require more than ever the intensive employment of modern information processing methods and techniques. Computer utilization in environmental protection practice (as well as in many areas of environmental research) has not yet taken sufficient advantage of the methodical potential of applied informatics. Hereat the scientific discipline of applied informatics could help by dedicating more research effort to this challenging and socially significant application field in the sense of an inter-disciplinary and practical research orientation. A specialized applied informatics branch for the environmental field („Environmental Informatics“) has been maturing since the start of the yearly conference series organized by the working group „Informatics in Environmental Protection“ in the German Society for Informatics (GI) (see [5], [8], [13], [1], [10]) with a growing number of projects and publications (e.g. cited in [14] or collected in an appropriate bibliography [15], respectively.)

The purpose of this workshop as organized by the newly installed IFIP working group as the first activity is to present and discuss state-of-the-art applications of informatics in the environmental field on an international scale. It mainly deals with environmental data bases and information systems, with GIS, monitoring systems, decision support systems in environmental protection, environmental modeling software as well as knowledge-based systems for the environment.

We hope that this workshop will stimulate the international research community to intensify the work in this new field in order to let applied informatics take its adequate share in the solution of our urgent environmental problems.

## 6. REFERENCES

1 W. Pillmann, A. Jaeschke (eds.), Informatik für den Umweltschutz. Proc. 5. Symp., Vienna, Sept. 1990. Informatik-Fachberichte 256, Springer, Berlin-Heidelberg 1990.

2 B. Page, Environmental Computing - Status and Research Perspectives. In: P. Zanetti (ed.), Computer Techniques in Environmental Studies. Proc. ENVIROSOFT 88, 2nd Intern. Conf., Porto Carras, Greece, Sept. 1988, Computational Mechanics, Southhampton-Boston, 1988, pp. 597-607.

3 O. Günther, et.al. (ed.), Workshop Umweltinformatik, Research Institute for Applied Knowledge Processing, Univ.of Ulm, Oct. 1990. FAW-Rep. 91002/I, II, Ulm, 1991.

4 N. Fuhr, An Information Retrieval View of Environmental Information Systems. In: DEXA 91, Proc. 2nd Intern.Conf. on Data Base and Expert System Applications, Berlin, Aug. 1991, Springer, Berlin 1991.

5 A. Jaeschke, B. Page (eds.), Informatikanwendungen im Umweltbereich . Proc. Coloq. Nuclear Research Center Karlsruhe, Oct. 1986, KfK-Rep. 4223, Karlsruhe 1987.

6 G. Angerer, H. Hiesel , Umweltschutz durch Mikroelektronik - Anwendungen, Chancen, Forschungs- und Entwicklungsbedarf. vde , Berlin-Offenbach 1991.

7 M. Stonebreaker, J. Dozier, SEQUOIA 2000 - Large Capacity Object Servers to support global Change Research. The Regents of the University of California, College of Engineering, Berkeley, California 1991.

8 R. Valk (ed.), Vernetzte und komplexe Informatiksysteme. Fachgespräch „Informatik-anwendungen im Umweltbereich". Proc. GI- 18. Jahrestagung, Hamburg, Oct. 1988. Informatik-Fachb. 187, Springer, Berlin 1988, pp. 187-380.

9 B. Page, An Analysis of Environmental Expert System Applications. Environmental Software, Vol. 5 (1990), No. 4, pp. 177-198.

10 M. Hälker, A. Jaeschke (eds.), Computer Science for Environmental Protection. Proc. 6th Symp. Munich, Dec. 1991. Informatik-Fachb. 296, Springer, Berlin 1991.

11 K. Brunnstein, A. Häuslein, B. Page, DYNAMIS: A System for the interactive Support of Simulation Modelling and Experimentation. Proc. 2nd European Simulation Congress, Antwerp, Belgium, Sept. 1986, Simulation Councils 1986, pp. 297-301.

12 A. Häuslein, B. Page, Knowledge-based Approaches to Modelling and Simulation Support. Systems Analysis, Modelling and Simulation 8 (1991), 4/5, pp. 257-272.

13 A. Jaeschke, W. Geiger, B. Page (eds.), Informatik im Umweltschutz. Proc. 4. Symp., Karlsruhe, Nov. 1989. Informatik-Fachberichte 228, Springer , Berlin 1989.

14 Umweltbundesamt (Ed.), Bibliographie Umwelt-Informatik. Erich Schmidt, Berlin 1989.

15 B. Page, A. Jaeschke, W.,Pillmann, Angewandte Informatik im Umweltschutz. Part 1 and 2, Informatik Spektrum 13 (1990), pp. 6-16 and 76-87.

Education and Society / R. Aiken (Editor)
Information Processing 92, Volume II
Elsevier Science Publishers B.V. (North-Holland)



# The Evolving Technology For Environmental Decision-Making — Towards the Environmental Decision Support System

Dr. Ian K. Crain

The Orbis Institute, P.O. Box 4115, Station "C", Ottawa, K1Y 4P3, Canada

Fax: 1-613-725-0643 E-mail: Crain@arc.ab.ca

## Abstract

The environmental protection decision-maker wrestling with such problems as climate change, deforestation, loss of bio diversity, water pollution, and loss of sustainability, is faced with an enormous variety of potentially incompatible information sources from which to extract key indicators and forecast consequences of action. Decision-support technology is evolving to assist in this process, but there are many challenges to overcome. The challenges include the sheer size of the data banks, the geographic distribution of the information, hence need for spatial information systems technology, the difficulty of reconciling information collected by different methods and the needed integration of multisectoral data (including environmental, social and economic factors). Some of the principal tools for managing global environmental information include geographic information systems (GIS), data acquisition technology (satellite and ground based), metadatabases, advanced distributed databases and spatio-temporal modelling and forecasting systems. A number of important new technological tools are now available, but environmental decision-makers must continue to articulate their requirements to ensure that the continued evolution to meet future requirements.

Keyword Codes: H.2.5; J.2
Keywords: Computer Applications, Physical Sciences and Engineering; Information Systems, Database Management Systems, Heterogeneous Databases.

## 1. INTRODUCTION

The environment surrounds us as we move through life; it affects our personal health and prosperity, as well as the well-being of regions, nations and the globe. "Environmental Information" therefore has an equally encompassing scope. Of primary importance to decision-making is quantitative information, derived and integrated from measurement and observation which can tell the decision-maker how much, how many and how fast changes are occurring, and whether established standards are being met. The subject-matter scope extends well beyond the obvious of ecology. The World Commission on Environment and Development noted "The environment does not exist as a sphere separate from human actions, ambitions and needs...the environment is where we all live; and development is what we all do in attempting to improve our lot within that abode. The two are inseparable." (WCED,1988) And so, through this inseparability comes a package of environmental information which must include development and human information - that is economic, and social factors.

A list of contents of the information package for the environmental decision-maker must include:

- **ecology** (encompassing climate, wildlife, vegetation, soil)
- **economic activity** (inputs, products, wastes, wealth and resource stores)
- **social information** (including population, and health )
- **abiotic condition** (including the shape of the land)

More simply put, environmental information encompasses anything which affects the state of the lithosphere, the biosphere and the atmosphere - and humans, who are the principal factor in environmental change, are included as inhabitants of the biosphere.

Given this vast scope, an inconceivable volume of data exists. Much of it is collected locally for operational purposes far removed from policy decision-making. Recent advances in satellite remote sensing enable the daily capture of vast amounts of new data on the atmosphere, biosphere and lithosphere - far too much to ever be seen by humans or refined into "information".

Thus there are two characteristics which distinguish environmental information from most other classes of information - a broad multi-disciplinary scope and an apparent staggering overabundance, at the local to global scale. In spite of this information abundance, information which is appropriate for policy decision-making is apparently sparse.

## 2. INFORMATION NEEDS OF ENVIRONMENTAL DECISION-MAKERS

The establishment of a modern theory of decision-making is often attributed to Herbert Simon (see for instance, Newall et al, 1958) who postulated a three stage process - Intelligence, Design, Choice. In the Intelligence stage, the decision-maker gathers the information relevant to the subject or problem at hand. In the Design stage, alternative courses of action or choices are identified. Based on the available information the consequences of the alternatives are then forecast. Finally a Choice is made where the optimum outcome, and thus the preferred course of action is selected. The decision-making is usually considered to be rational if the choice is made based on objective (usually qu2(itative) criteria, such as cost-benefit or the maximization of some other sought-after benefit. This requires an appropriate model in the Design stage. Brookes et al (1982) point out that rationality becomes difficult when subjective concepts or measures such as love, family, happiness, or culture play a part in the choice. Environmental policy decision-making certainly invites this subjectivity through concepts such as "quality-of-life" and the introduction of religious and cultural values (such as equity). Important components of the decision-making process are the information base, the models necessary to predict outcomes of the choices, and the feedback loop ensuring appropriate re-adjustment of the objectives. In some form or another, computerized or not, modern policy decision-making utilizes this process. It is logical to assume that the quality of the resulting decisions depend on the quality of the information base and the quality (or realism) of the models.

The nature of the policy decision-making process and the enormous scope of environmental information certainly require both **summarization** and **abstraction** to a relatively high level.

Abstraction is reductionist, ie. it reduces the volume of information by selecting a few classes of observation as proxies for the behaviour of entire systems. These proxies or indicators can have many instances, ie., be measured at many locations of the world at frequent intervals. The search for a single indicator which would reflect the health of the environment in the way that the Gross National Product (GNP) is supposed to indicate the health of a national economy, is fruitless. Many environmental phenomena are spatially non-homogeneous and so, the needed indicators must be multivariate and spatially distributed.

Summarization reduces the information overload by grouping large numbers of observations and representing them by a simple quantitative value. Time-series may be summarized by annual averages, eg., mean annual temperature and spatially distributed data averaged over large regions. One common framework for spatial summarizing is by administrative region. For environmental information, however, there are disadvantages to this approach. Administrative boundaries seldom align with the natural boundaries which encompass ecological zones. National or regional summarization of statistics can dilute or mask the magnitude of change. The ideal framework for summarization from an environmental viewpoint would use natural boundaries defined for instance by watersheds, or eco-climatic zones. An important corollary of this approach is the need for information management tools which can integrate, correlate and transfer information to/from the administrative frameworks familiar to decision-makers from/to the issue oriented frameworks.

**Abstraction** and **summarization** are two separate dimensions (Fig.1) and how far to go with each is problem dependent. One rough rule of thumb would be that the summarization should be at one level below the primary subdivision, (for example, nations subdivided into provinces, river systems divided into basins, etc.). Regional decision-making requires one level below that, and local decision-making needs again one or more lower levels. The degree to which abstraction can be employed to reduce information to a few indicators is also highly problem dependent. Complex issues need complex information and over-simplification does not help.

## 3. STATUS OF TECHNOLOGY FOR ENVIRONMENTAL DATA GATHERING

Three important new tools for environmental measurement have matured in the last decade. The first, remote sensing, permits the rapid and frequent acquisition of imagery of the Earth's surface. Remotely sensed information is now used routinely in weather forecasting and marine navigation, and for generalized vegetation mapping. Data volumes are extremely high, and the entire earth's surface is scanned by a variety of sensors daily. Thus data management and summarization are major problems. Application to global change decision-making is non-routine as yet, and models and abstraction methods are just evolving. Information analysts now have a wide variety of

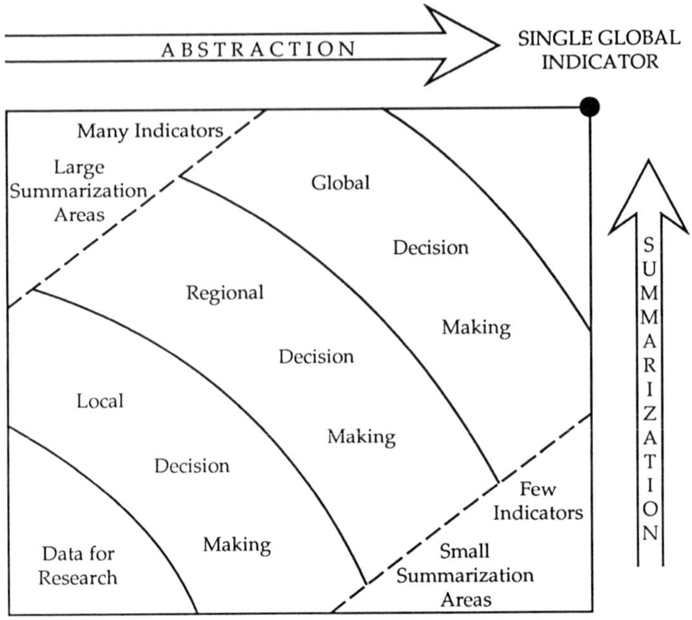


Figure 1. Summarization vs Abstraction

data sources from which to choose, including cloud penetrating radar imagery (airborne). Remotely sensed information is to be an important cornerstone of the IGBP Global Change Database Project (Ruttenberg et al, 1990).

A major limitation to remote sensing is the fact that it essentially only observes radiation (solar, radar, etc.) reflected from the surface. Therefore, while its value for determining land cover, including vegetation type, is undoubted, all other information (such as land use) can only be inferred. Considerable ground observation is required for such inference to have value. Characteristics of the soil more than a few millimetres below the surface, of wildlife, of human condition or economic activity are unobservable.

The second important technology advance is in ground based automated observing stations. These un-manned, unattended mini-observatories record local quantitative data digitally for later collection, or automatically transmit to a central location. These stations are most useful for gathering meteorological, air quality, and water quality data. Their major advantages are relatively low cost, ability to provide consistent standardized measurements, and ability to be placed ideally, permitting appropriate location in remote areas. The result is much more systematic and standardized data which can be summarized more easily and interpreted with confidence. Such automation is now used extensively in the UNEP/WMO BAPMON Program (United Nations Environment Program/World Health Organization Background Air Pollution Monitoring).

The third tool of significance to environmental information comes from laser and computer vision technology, giving greatly improved methods for the conversion of paper maps of resource information to digital form. Using laser scanners and artificial intelligence aided software, such information can be accurately and rapidly converted to digital files for integration and analysis.

The implications of these advances for decision-makers are:

- lower cost of information collection programs
- data are more consistent and comparable
- increased flexibility in the design of information gathering programs
- increased ability to integrate historical non-digital information into modern information banks.

## 4. STATUS OF INFORMATION TECHNOLOGY TOOLS FOR ENVIRONMENTAL DATA MANAGEMENT

It is clear that the environmental policy decision-maker needs to deal with large volumes of information of varying quality, on various media from various sources. To make wise decisions, in a realistic time frame, the modern decision-making team now must make use of modern tools to help in this task. These include facilities to manage information (store, organize, update, preserve), to transfer information and to analyze the information. These tools include aspects of computer technology, telecommunications, database technology, mathematics and statistics, artificial intelligence, and so on, commonly referred to collectively as "information technology".

### 4.1 Database Management Technology

It is obvious that environmental information for policy decision-making will be voluminous, even given considerable abstraction. Data management technology has had a number of recent advances of potential beneficial application to environmental decision-making. Until the mid 1970's database management systems (DBMS) were commonly either of a hierarchical or network structure. These data models are restrictive and so database structures lack the flexibility needed by decision-makers.

Recent years have seen the development of "relational database management systems". RDBMS organize the information as a set of tables or "relations" linked by relational keys. Relationships between files are implicitly determined by common values in the "related" tables. Thus the RDBMS offers a flexible database structure which is easy to define, expand and change. Dynamic relations are created at query permitting considerable exploration of relationships, typical of the needs of environment informational analysis.

Associated with RDBMS, has been the creation of "Structured Query Language" (SQL). This is an English-like retrieval language which adopts a mathematical set theory concept and uses the same symbols in query definition. This allows for easy use of various models independent of the brand-name of the RDBMS, thus considerable improvement in the potential for information integration.

The Object-Oriented Database Management System (OO-DBMS) is a relatively new approach which could give improved capability in dealing with groups of data items (objects) and connecting between objects (Premeriane et al, 1990). This technology is immature and therefore suffers from poor performance and lack of standards as did RDBMS a decade ago. The policy decision-maker can look to the future for the potential of this technology to allow for information compatibility on a broad base.

There have been recent developments, as well, in distributed database systems. A distributed database management system (DDBMS) is a single logical database that is physically distributed on several computers, communicating through a network. It provides multiple access to the database and mechanisms to avoid conflict in update, retrieval and backup of data. DDBMS can be very useful for very large databases where most users are concerned with only a small subset of the database, while permitting access to the user with broader needs. In reality, existing databases are hard to link in a DDBMS because of differing technology at each site. A solution to this which is now developing is the "Federated" database management system. It shares the advantages of the DDBMS, while additionally allowing data communication among DBMSs of different data models, brand-names and access methods. Each local DBMS is autonomous in that it preserves its own characteristics as viewed by the local user. The environmental policy decision support system of the future will no doubt use this technology, to link heterogeneous information collections in various countries and agencies. The technology is expected to mature in the next 5 to 10 years.

### 4.2 Geographic Information Systems Technology

Geographic Information Systems (GIS) technology has been used to manage environmental information and aid decision-makers since the inception of the Canada Geographic Information System (CGIS) in Canada in the mid 60s (Tomlinson,1987).

The basic advantage of a GIS is its ability to manage and perform complex processing on the spatial component of the data as well as the statistical aspects. In that way the actual geographic boundaries of regions defined on the earth's surface can be manipulated. This allows for the integration and summarization of environmental information using natural units -- such as watersheds, natural forest areas, soil units and so on, and to combine these effectively with man-made administrative data collection units. Thus it can provide the link between the decision-maker's viewpoint and the natural boundaries of the problem.

Several global data compilation projects are underway which will produce GIS compatible information - World Digital Database for Environmental Sciences (WDDES), Soil and Terrain (SOTER) and the Digital Chart of the World (DCW). All of these will produce complete global coverages of generalized baseline digital data, ready for analysis and integration with thematic time-series. Presently, the only truly international GIS used for environmental information are the European CORINE project and UNEP's GRID, although an earlier UNEP global desertification project used GIS technology.

In spite of the growing interest and demand, there are some problems with current GIS technology which limit its applicability for environmental decision-making. The primary problem is that regional spatial databases are frequently very large (Crain,1990), and exceed the capacity of existing systems. Commonly it is necessary to store and process in excess of 100,000 spatial objects (eg. soil units) requiring millions of coordinate pairs or raster cells to define. These two factors -- sheer data volume, and the need to perform repeatedly complex geometrical computation on spatial objects - are the cause of the practical upper limit on the useable size of spatial databases in GIS. Even with moderately large databases, users commonly note "lack of user friendliness", "slowness" and "unreliability" (Kalensky,1988). A further restriction on usefulness is the lack of standardization of internal structures and access methods. No standard spatial access protocol like SQL is yet on the horizon, so it may be some time before the heterogeneous distributed GIS needed for decision support is a reality.

**4.3 Other Evolving Tools**

A number of other areas of information technology which are evolving rapidly may have potential benefit to environmental decision-making. The two most relevant are advances in telecommunications and in knowledge-based systems for modelling.

The former now permits the transfer of very high volumes of digital data between locations globally. This permits in theory, a global distributed database, although none as yet has been implemented. In practice, at the least, it allows for the efficient movement of bulk information for integration and summarization at the decision-making location.

Knowledge-based or "expert" systems are intended to imbue the decision-maker with the effective reasoning power of a large group of experts who individually have contributed their knowledge. The applications for the environmental decision-maker are both to help locate the appropriate information (where the complexity of the data is too great for any one person to "know") and to provide the expert reasoning in the decision-support models. Considerable research is underway, but such systems for environmental decision-making are at the moment only experimental, or limited in scope, eg. local forest management.

## 5. THE ENVIRONMENTAL INFORMATION MANAGEMENT SYSTEM OF THE FUTURE

A review of the history of information technology shows that it is application demand that has driven the new developments. The information needs of complex business **required** the DBMS; multinational finance **required** automated funds transfer by telecommunications; and now today the environmental policy decision-makers require the Environmental Information Management System (EIMS). Some aspects of this evolution are shown in Figure 3, which illustrates its episodic nature — pauses in development of the EIMS awaiting breakthroughs in the enabling technology. One approach, therefore, to analyzing the need for environmental information for decision-making is to speculate on the characteristics of the EIMS which appear to be required.

The Environmental Information Management System (EIMS) of the future must have many of the following characteristics.

- Data holdings physically distributed on heterogeneous databases, but with a uniform appearance to the decision-maker.
- Extremely fast geo-processing calculations to provide on-line response.
- Extensive modelling and forecasting capability (eg. knowledge based) to enable scenario building and rapid response to "what if?" questions.
- Provision of a user perceived object-oriented view independent of the internal data structure and representation.

Conceptually, the EIMS of the future (Fig.2) must contain several new components not found in existing systems.

- The **spatial integrator**, including spatial superstructures and other metadata required to find, and integrate data from the distributed sectoral environmental databases.
- The **modelling engine** which provides for complex scenario building and evaluation of alternatives from the user viewpoint (likely with the aid of artificial intelligence).
- The **intelligent interface** which uses knowledge-based techniques to effectively optimize and translate user queries.

The past has shown that it is application demand that drives new technology developments. In order to ensure that the needed tools are soon available, environmental decision-makers must articulate these needs to the information technology community in clear terms. This will require the analysis of decision making processes and criteria and their organization and presentation in a rational framework.

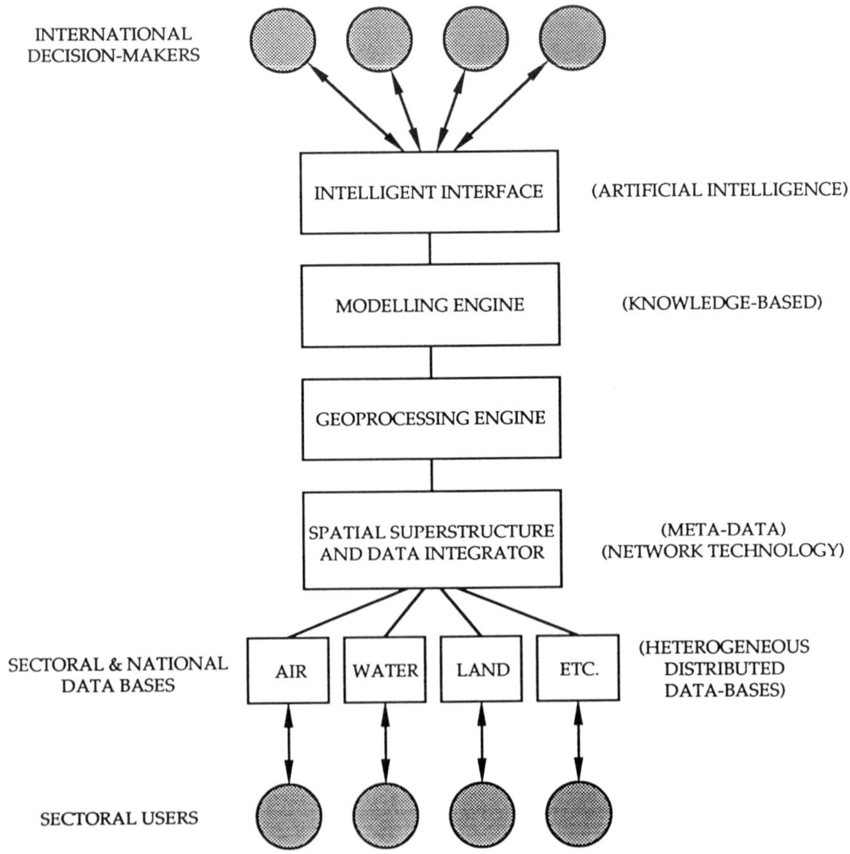


Figure 2: The EIMS of the Future

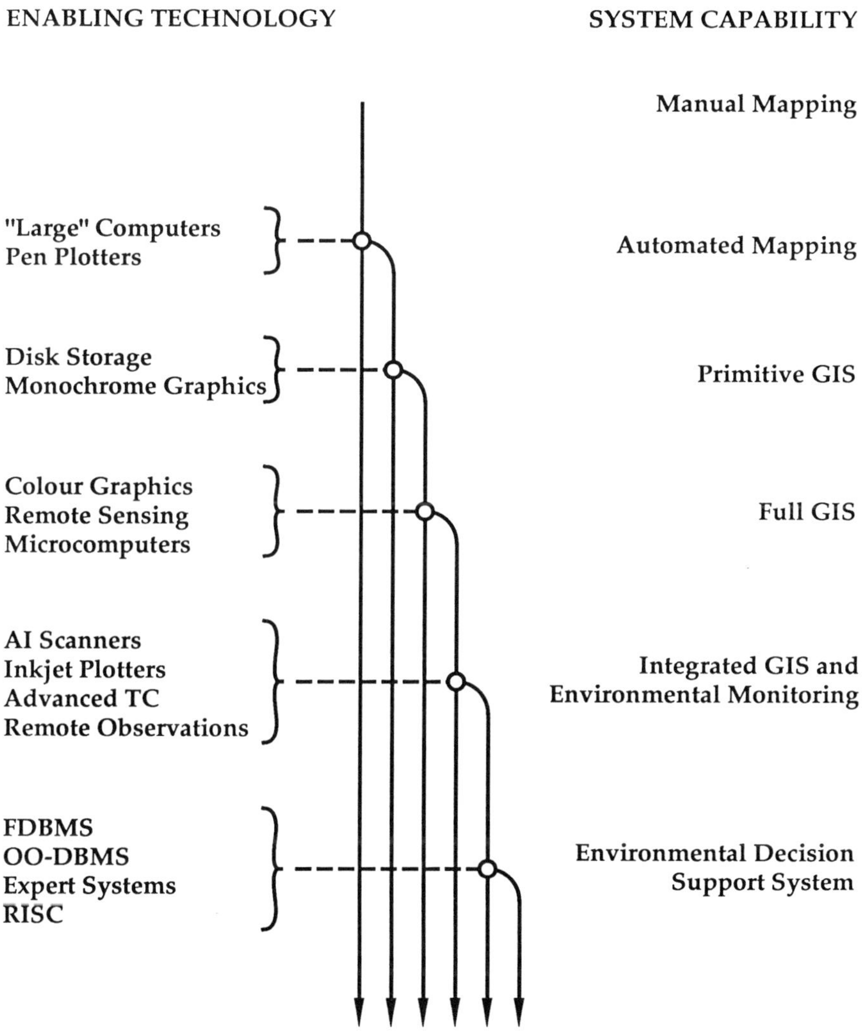


Figure 3: The Evolution of EIMS Technology

## 6. REFERENCES

Brookes, C.H., Grouse, P.J., Jeffery, D.R. and Lawrence, M.J., 1982, Information Systems Design, Prentice-Hall of Australia, Sydney, pp.477.

Crain, I.K.,1990, Extremely Large Spatial Information Systems — A Quantitative Perspective, Proc. 4th Intl. Symposium on Spatial Data Handling, Zurich, July 23-27, IGU/IGA, p.632-641.

Kalensky, 1988, Some Views on Georeferenced Digital Databases, in Building Databases for Global Science, H. Mounsey and R. Tomlinson, eds., Taylor and Francis, London, p.307-314.

Newall, A., Shaw, J.C., Simon, H., 1958, Elements of a Theory of Human Problem Solving, Psych. Review, May 1958, p.151-166.

Premeriane, W.J., et al, 1990, "An Object-oriented Relational Database", Communications ACM, Vol. 33, #11, p.99-108.

Ruttenberg, S., Kinneman, J.J., Eastman, R., 1990, The Global Change Database Project (GCDP), Science International, Vol. 41, September 1990, p.16-18.

Tomlinson, R.G., 1987, Current and Potential Use of Geographic Information Systems, The North American Experience, Int. J. G.I.S., Vol. 1, No. 3, p.203-218. WCED (World Commission on Environment and Development), 1988, Our Common Future, Oxford University Press, Oxford, pp.400.

Education and Society / R. Aiken (Editor)
Information Processing 92, Volume II
Elsevier Science Publishers B.V. (North-Holland)



# Distributed Environmental Data Compendia

## Connecting Information Sources between Central and Eastern Europe through CEDAR

W. Pillmann [ab], D.J. Kahn [b]

[a] *Austrian Institute for Public Health , Stubenring 6, A-1010 Vienna, Austria*
[b] *International Society for Environmental Protection, Central European Data Request Facility, Marxergasse 3, A-1030 Vienna, Austria*

**Abstract**

In several countries the availability of environmental data are very different and subsequently, information on sustainable development often has been unavailable. To assist in the development of environmental programs in Eastern Europe, the Austrian Ministry of Environment, Youth and Family provided a grant for the creation of the Central European Environmental Data Request Facility (CEDAR). Through CEDAR, an additional link between West and East will be established. Environmental issues, examples of emission control and waste management and the role of compter applications for environmental data integration are described in this paper.

*Keyword Codes:* *C.2.4; H.4.m*
*Keywords:* *Computer Communication Networks; Information Systems Application for Environmental Protection*

## 1. Introduction

Industrialized nations are generating a growing amount of compendia which describes the state of the environment. Additionally, there is a need for more detailed data in interdisciplinary environmental research activities. To address the handling requirements of this information, electronic data processing -- in the form of tools, methods, and user interfaces -- is being developed. Characteristic of these applications is the widespread, seldom coordinated gathering and distribution of data, and the different hardware utilized by research institutes, companies, and governments.

Since the beginning of environmental protection activities, computers have played an increasingly important role in the preparation of data for printed reports, particularly in industrialized countries [1]. The information is generated by various sources in different formats (eg. labor equipment, measurement stations, questionnaires, maps, imaging systems), and is often a prerequisite for environmental planning and economic management decisions at the administrative and political level.

A systemic view of the state of the environment is necessary and essential for international agreements and risk reduction decision making. Such an analysis is based on the quantitative identification of environmental subsystems using computers. Models and simulation systems are then tools for advanced applications in electronic data processing for systems analysis. In general, quantitative formulation of subsystems and the visualization of results provide a more effective means of decision-making support for experts.

Sources of environmental data are often widely dispersed, produced by various individuals and institutions. This is true on an international scale, less so at the local level. Additionally, countries afflicted with economic problems do not have the financial resources to pursue growth with an environmental mandate. As a result, little environmental information is available from these countries, which undercuts attempts at stressing the importance of long-term environmental protection activities. The effort to establish computer-based information systems also in such countries is a prerequisite for comprehensive environmental protection. The completion of information necessary to effectively address environmental protection is an urgent task. Therefore, raising the awareness of environmental issues in the hierarchy of scientific, political, and economic needs, while developing information integration and expert know-how, is essential.

## 2. The Role of Environmental Information

Activities which examine single aspects of environmental issues, vis a vis systemic investigation, can be of little utilitiy or may lead to negative effects in other subsystems. A more cybernetic-oriented approach to the environment, with system-wide relevant sets of variables, makes it more likely to initiate environmentally-sound processes. A control loop illustrating, in a simplified form, the subsystems involved in the process of environmental protection is shown in figure 1.

A quantitative approach to environmental measures (the output of the system "environment" in fig.1) can be obtained using measurement techniques, questionnaires, calculations, and simulation software. For studies involving complex systems like biotopes, more sophisticated scientific approaches are required. This environmental data, which describes impacts to human health and ecosystems, can be processed by means of computer hardware and software [2]. Analyzing this data provides decision makers with information necessary to create and implement preventive measures.

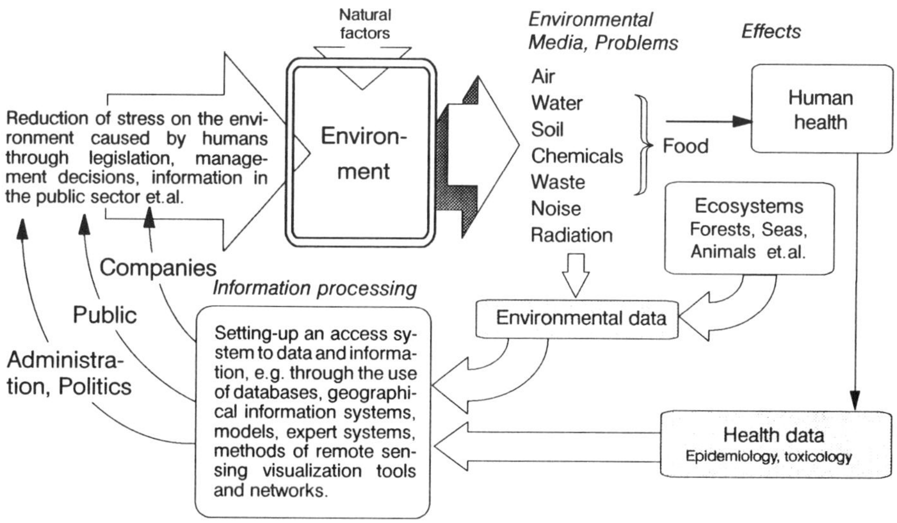


Fig. 1 : Environmental data processing systems:
outlining control actions for environmental protection.

The control system in figure 1 which reduces the stress placed on the environment acts to monitor different elements, providing necessary support both at the national and international scale. Furthermore, each subsystem in the environmental data processing system can be viewed in relation to other subsystems, helping to coordinate the development of all elements in the loop.

## 3. Tools and Methods of Computer Application

Trends in computer hardware development, software systems application, measurement techniques, and improved connectivity between computers have led to effective environmental data processing [3]. This processed data plays an important role in scientific evaluation, policy development and management. Some examples of environmental informatic applications are shown in table 1.

The complex structure of environmental information poses some problems. Spatial characteristics of data -- for example, point-, line- and area-sources in air quality research -- at the local, regional, and national level must be integrated. Geographic Information Systems and non-standard databases try to remedy this difficulty. Data influenced by time can be examined using simulations. Such computer applications help to investigate dynamic and statistical characteristics of systems. Overall there is a lack of software handling temporal and spartial distributed, multidimensional data.

Tab.1: Environmentally relevant computer applications

| | |
|---|---|
| Measurement Techniques | Automatization and process control<br>Computer-controlled labor measurement equipment<br>Measurement networks (air and water quality)<br>Remote sensing (land use, forest diseases, climatic changes) |
| Methods and Tools | Databases, non-standard databases, statistics<br>Geographic Information Systems<br>Models and simulation<br>Computer graphics and vizualisation; image processing<br>Hypertext |
| Computer and Communication Networks | Literature databases<br>Information systems for hazardous substances<br>Mailboxes and university (scientific) networks<br>Environmental information systems in administration<br>Expert and decision-support systems |

## 4. Information Requirements for Emission Control and Waste Management

What desirable results from an integration of environmental information could be expected, should be illustrated with two examples. Figures 2 and 3 present the elements of the air quality and industrial waste management webs.

In figure 2, emissions are divided into public and private categories. The classical substances under investigation are oxides of sulphur and nitrogen, carbon monoxide, and particulate matter. Recent concern has focused on chlorofluorocarbons, large hydrocarbons, volatile organic compounds, human-made ozone, and carbon dioxide and associated "greenhouse gases." These pollutants are injected into the atmosphere and, through physical, chemical, and photochemical processes, produce negative impacts in the environment.

Computer-related applications for emission reduction control include air pollution measurement networks (spatially distributed process control systems), graphic representations for immission levels, smog monitoring and warning systems, and satellite / air remote sensing and image processing for ecological research (eg. forest decline). Additional emission and immision measurement- and research results as well as evaluation of effects can be incorporated into inventories and databases and local or regional air quality information systems. This environmental information output will be used to evolve appropriate measure instruments and give the reasons for emission reduction control.

A system-oriented view of industrial waste management is presented in fig. 3. Waste management is affected directly by the production and consumption of goods. Recycling and circular processes are incorporated during the production, transport, treatment and deposition to curb the generation of wastes [4].

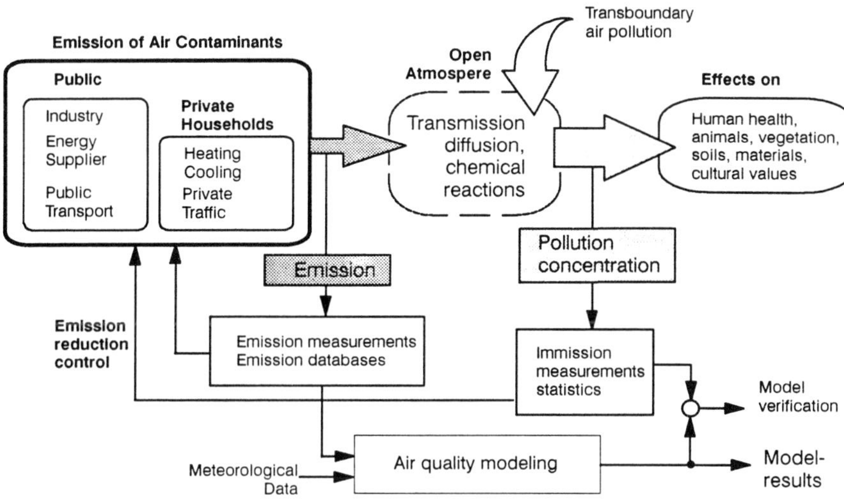


Fig. 2: Air quality improvement
Measurement and modeling system with emission sources and receptors

Hidden in figure 3 is the significant role of energy throughout the process, and the impact of these wastes on environmental media and human health [5].

Waste management computer applications utilize database information sets - e.g. on waste toxicity - and Geographic Information Systems for both site identification and sanitation of contaminated sites [6]. Computer-assisted analyses of waste production, treatment and effects of residuals are essential for risk management assessment and handling requirements at all stages of planning, development and construction [7,8]. Such feedback mechanisms will be used by decision makers to enact policy and legislative measures.

In a market economy, emissions as well as waste production are affected by demand-driven products and services. Economic incentives were originally left to self-regulation, but increased awareness of environmental and public health concerns have sought to modify behavior in both the public and private domains.

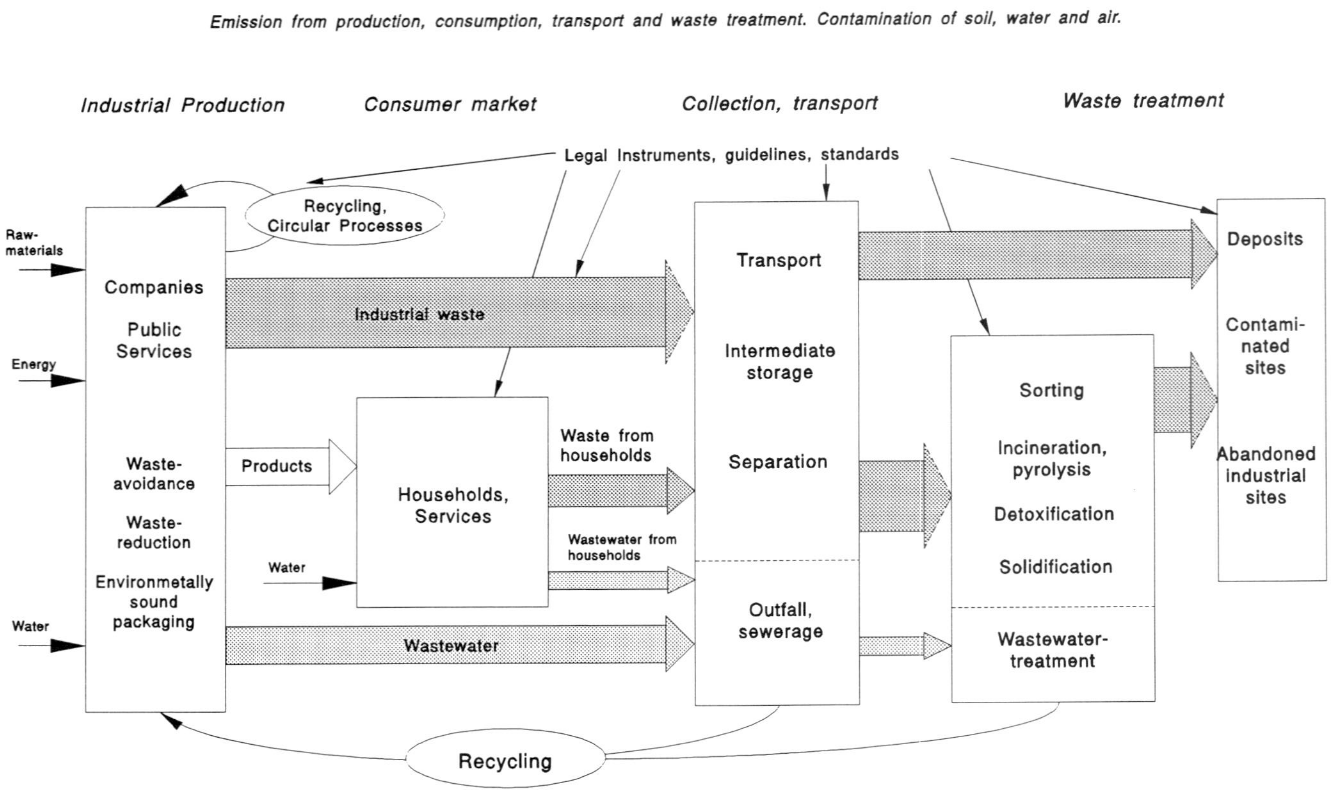


Fig 3: Industrial waste management - a system oriented view

## 5. Distributed Environmental Data: Compendia Versus Computer Networks and Metainformation

Several countries have developed reports on environmental statistics, and many international organizations, institutes, foundations and non-governmental groups have compiled information on environmental themes. For example, the Council on Environmental Quality in the United States produces an annual report providing an overview of the health of the environment [9]. The member governments of the Organization for Economic Cooperation and Development (OECD) have developed a questionnaire on the State of the Environment in order to "exchange and publish internationally comparable data on environmental conditions" [10]. The Federal Office for the Environment in Germany (Umweltbundesamt) has written "Daten zur Umwelt 1988/89", [11] a comprehensive presentation of environmental data that visualizes the spatial aspect of the data in the form of maps. The Austrian Federal Institute for Public Health has published a nine volume collection covering the synergistic relationship between complex of problems (noise, waste, chemical production), environmental media (air, water, soil), complex organisms (animals, vegetation) and landscape [12].

None of these printed materials can describe the *actual* state of knowledge about the environment in a given country or on an international scale. The time delay between data collection, information processing, an author's "work in progress," and the publication and distribution of finished papers and books often exceeds one year or even more.

Computer programs for environmental data are less static in nature since, optimally, data is continually fed into the system, providing a more accurate "snapshot" of a situation at a point in time. Two problems that systems designers attempt to address are the wide dispersion of environmental information in several institutions and the harmonization of environmental data. Therefore the Commission of the European Communities is developing the Catalog of Data Sources / CORINE Information Access System - a metainformation system. This pilot program's primary objectives are to compile the European collections of environmental data, harmonize the production of environmental data through the adoption of standardized methods and avoidance of replication, allows an easy access to distributed data and improve information transfer among member countries. In 1989, the United Nations Environment Programme (UNEP) started its Harmonization of Environmental Measurement Project (HEM) under the auspices of the Global Environmental Monitoring System (GEMS) [13]. The HEM Project is intended to coordinate the standardizartion of data from multiple fields to promote information compatibility.

*International Society for Environmental Protection (ISEP), Vienna*

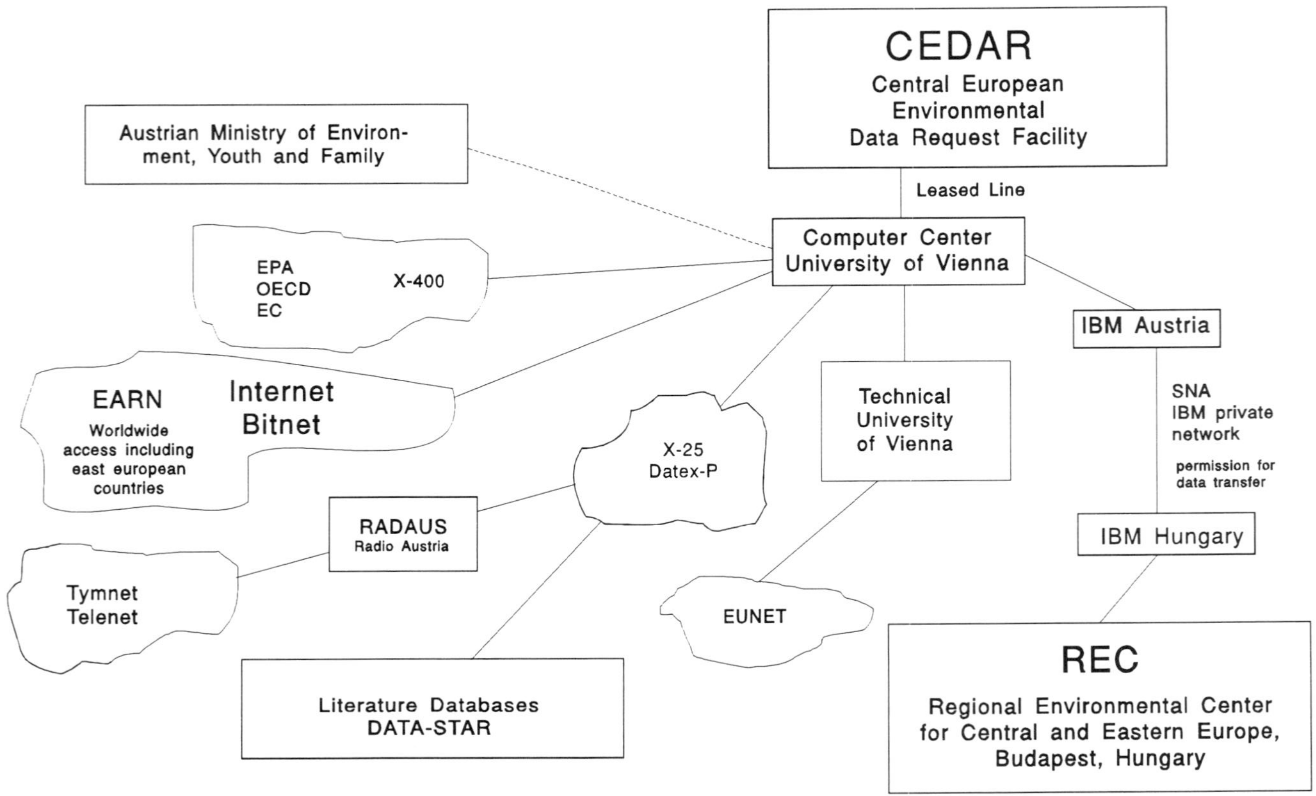


Fig. 4: Central European Environmenal Data Request Facility (CEDAR) - Status May 1992

## 6. CEDAR: An Expert-supported Communication Link for Integration of Electronic Environmental Data

CEDAR, the Central European Environmental Data Request Facility, is sponsored by the Austrian Ministry of Environment, Youth, and Family. Based in Vienna, CEDAR was designed to assist Central and Eastern European countries in environmental information and technology transfer (fig. 4), [14]. The primary users of CEDAR will be the Regional Environmental Center for Central and Eastern Europe (REC), REC's outreach offices in Bratislava, Bucharest, Sofia, and Warsaw, and the Pentagonale countries.

Additional working relationships with governments, institutes, and non-governmental organizations will be established in the east and west. To foster increased environmental knowledge in the region, CEDAR will:

- o assist in environmental information transfer by providing users with access to environmental databases
- o provide a platform for training programs and seminars for environmental experts in database information set up and retrieval
- o coordinate environmental activities with various international organizations and
- o pursue environmental projects that will allow partners in the region access to an advanced computing and software system.

CEDAR will have access to literature databases (eg. DATASTAR in Berne, Switzerland). The Center currently accesses information available on the EARN/Bitnet and Internet networks, and will install in-house databases from different research and environmental protection organizations. CEDAR is fortunate to have the technical support of the University of Vienna's Computer Center.

## 7. References


1 Page B., Jaeschke A., Pillmann W., Angewandte Informatik im Umweltschutz, Informatik Spektrum (1990) 13: Teil 1 6-16, 14: Teil 2 86 - 97, Springer Verlag 1990

2 Computer Science for Environmental Protection, 6 th Symposia 1991, Hälker M., Jaeschke A. (eds.), Informatik Fachberichte 296, Springer Verlag Berlin, New York, 1991, 5 th Symposia 1990, Pillmann W., Jaeschke A. (eds.), Informatik Fachberichte 256, Springer Verlag Berlin, New York, 1990, 4 th Symposia 1989, Jaeschke A., Geiger W., Page B. (eds.), Informatik Fachberichte 228, Springer Verlag Berlin, New York, 1989

3 Bibliographie Umwelt-Informatik, erstellt von B. Page unter Mitarbeit von A. Haeuslein und V. Matusall, unter Nutzung von UMPLIS (Informations- und Dokumentationssystem Umwelt), im Auftrag des Umweltbundesamtes Berlin, Erich Schmidt Verlag, 1989

4 Industrial Waste Management, Waste Reduction and Treatment, Site Remediation and Water Purification, 3 rd Conference Envirotech Vienna 1992: Pillmann W. (ed.) International Society for Environmental Protection, Vienna, 1992

5 Energy Resources and European Market Economy, W. Pillmann, S. Burgstaller (eds.), International Society for Environmental Protection, Vienna, 1990

6 Information Technology in Waste Management, Computer Application in Planning of Waste Reduction, Site Remediation, Monitoring and Education, Workshop on Envirotech Vienna 1992: Pillmann W. (ed.), International Society for Environmental Protection, Vienna, 1992

7 Pillmann W., Holzleithner H.: Modell der Abfallwirtschaft, Envirotech Vienna 1989, Vol. 2, International Society for Environmental Protection, Vienna, 1990

8 Computer Applications for Environmental Impact Analysis, Proceedings of the Computer Workshop on Environmental Information, Systems, Pillmann W. (Ed.), Internationale Gesellschaft für Umweltschutz, Wien, 1990

9 Environmental Quality - Twentieth Annual Report, The Council on Environmental Quality an the Executive Office of the President, Washington D.C., USA, 1989

10 OECD Environmental Data - Compendium 1989, Organisation for Economic Co-operation and Development (OECD), Paris, 1989

11 Daten zur Umwelt 1988/89, Umweltbundesamt Berlin, Erich Schmidt Verlag Berlin, 1989 Environmental Data Report, prepared for UNEP by the "GEMS Monitoring and Assessment Research, Centre, London, UK in cooperation with the World Resource Institute, Washington DC, UK Dep. of the Environment, London, Blackwell, 1989

12 Umweltbericht (Environmental Report in nine volumes), Abfall - Boden - Chemikalien - Landschaft - Lärm - Luft - Tierwelt - Vegetation - Wasser Österreichisches Bundesinstitut für Gesundheitswesen, Vienna, Austria 1989

13 Keune H., Theisen A., Environmental Databases and Information Management Programmes of International Organizations in: Hälker M., Jaeschke A. (Hrsg.) Computer Science for Environmental Protection, 6 th Symposium Munich, 1991, Informatik Fachberichte 296, Springer Verlag Berlin, 1991

14 CEDAR - Central European Environmental Data Request Facility, International Society for Environmental Protection, Vienna, 1992

Education and Society / R. Aiken (Editor)
Information Processing 92, Volume II
Elsevier Science Publishers B.V. (North-Holland) 


# Global environmental change data and modelling

A. M. Din

International Academy of the Environment
C.P. 81, CH-1231 Geneva, Switzerland

**Abstract**

The problem of assessing global environmental change in general and climate change in particular is a truly interdisciplinary enterprise. Basic data from the natural and socio-economic sciences must be acquired and integrated in one common methodological approach in order to predict potential impacts on ecosystems and society, e.g. sea level rise and migration.

Geographic Information Systems (GIS) are well adapted to organize the basic data and to present impact scenarios on regional, national and sub-national scales. However, standard GIS do not yet have adequate modelling capabilities and it is therefore necessary to combine them with techniques from dynamic simulation and expert systems.

GIS and modelling techniques may be developed together so as to create dedicated decision support systems which provide an interactive approach to informing decision makers and the general public, as well as a practical management tool for implementing strategies for responses to global environmental change.

Keyword Codes: H.1.1; I.2.4; I.3.2; I.6.5; K.4.1
Keywords: Public policy; Information systems; Simulation and modelling

## 1. THE PROBLEMS OF GLOBAL ENVIRONMENTAL CHANGE

Environmental management on the urban and country scale involves serious problems which already call for considerable efforts on the part of local and national governments. Why then is it absolutely necessary that attention must be focussed on problems of global environmental change and that appropriate action must be planned on an international scale?

The answer is that we are living in a global community with finite extent and limited resources where the activities of one group of people may have important consequences on all others through effects on the global environment. The example of transboundary pollution caused by industry exhausts is but one of many which shows that certain activities, e.g. energy production, may have negative environmental consequences, i.e. acid rain and soil acidification, at quite distant locations.

In recent years, climate change has come to be seen as the potentially most serious threat to our global environment with possible considerable increases in global temperature, changing rainfall and wind patterns and sea level rise. The impacts on countries and people, particularly in the developing world, might be dramatic. The origins of climate change are also of global nature, e.g. countries around the world with energy sectors injecting large quantities of $CO_2$ and other greenhouse gases into the atmosphere or with activities such as deforestation influencing negatively the global $CO_2$ exchange mechanisms.

Other problems of global nature involve hazardous and toxic waste, water and air pollution, desertification, ozone depletion and loss of biodiversity. The relevant data concerning all these different problems are to be found in both natural and socio-economic sciences. Since the bulk of the data is spatially referenced, GIS represents a convenient framework for organizing the information.

While the data coming from earth sciences have routinely been incorporated in GIS, the same is not quite true for socio-economic data and, in some sense, GIS may be seen as a common language which will permit researchers from natural and social sciences to approach the problems of global environmental change with similar methodologies. The intergovernmental programmes IGBP (International Geosphere/Biosphere Programme) and HDGECP (Human Dimensions of Global Environmental Change), which represent the natural and socio-economic science concerns respectively with the problems, therefore have the possibility of developing together in a methodological harmony not existing in most other areas where different scientific mindsets are confronted.

GIS is not only a convenient framework for integrating the basic data of global environmental change but also for displaying the results of various types of data processing. GIS has the capability of graphics and data presentation on scales required by the issue and so may be perfectly in line with the IGBP effort placing the global problems in a regional context, i.e. using 14 main regions of the world.

However, GIS do not yet have adequate capabilities of actually transforming basic data into information and options of direct use for the general public and decision makers concerned by global environmental change. There is therefore a need to combine GIS with modelling techniques of different kinds, e.g. simulation, optimization, game theory, expert systems. Furthermore, research and development of global change modelling paves the way for creating genuine decision support systems which incorporate all the relevant data and knowledge about the problems and which are of great value in understanding and evaluating the nature of environmental impacts as well as the range of policy options.

The management of global environmental change, and other environmental issues as well, may therefore be seen as composed of elements constituting a triad: GIS, modelling and decision support systems (see the diagramme). The input to these three methodological elements is also threefold: basic natural resource and socio-economic

# SYSTEM TRIAD
# OF
# ENVIRONMENTAL INFORMATION MANAGEMENT

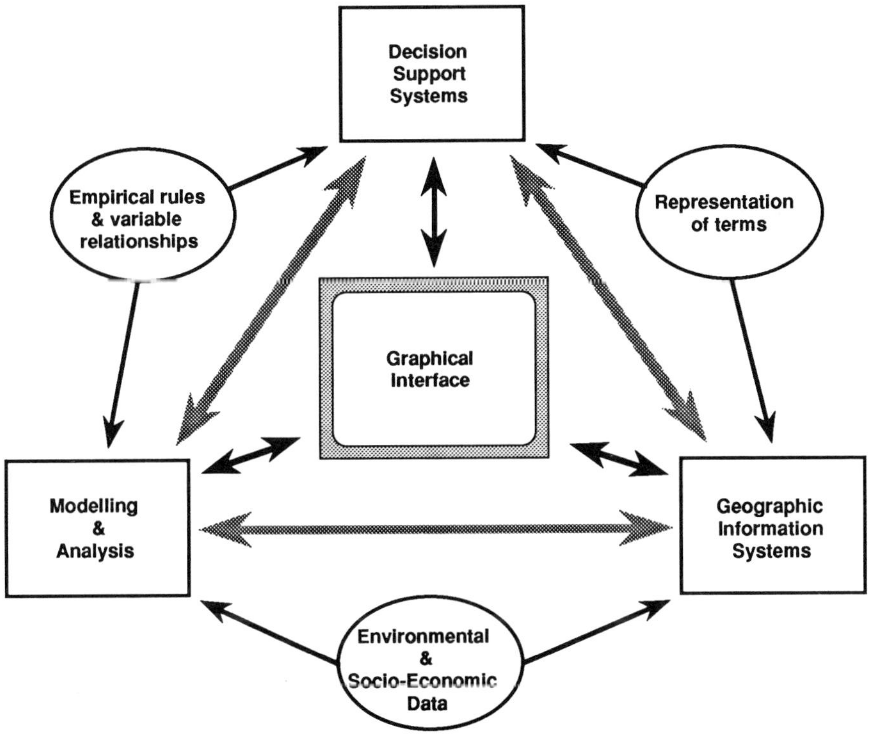

data, formal representation of basic terms, and a knowledge base of rules and relationships.

Modelling is already fundamental in earth sciences for understanding the development of the global climate system, i.e. through the so-called General Circulation Models (GCM). Given basic physical parameters, GCMs are able to estimate climate patterns on a grid scale of the order of hundred kilometers and developments in computing power, in particular concerning parallel processing, may soon be able to produce more refined predictions.

The modelling techniques for using results from GCM models and other atmospheric and earth science models in a regional context taking into account socio-economic factors are, however, not yet well developed. Below, some of the important data requirements and existing modelling frameworks are described.

## 2. NATURAL SCIENCE DATA AND GIS

The monitoring of earth and atmospheric processes proceeds through the use of a large of number space and ground based sensor systems. However, the natural science data are still in need of great efforts in order to establish a global database and associated GIS which cover the 14 major world regions with a sufficiently fine resolution (say of the order of a few hundred meters). Such detail is needed in order for environmental scientists to develop models for replicating in reasonable detail the earth processes.

The natural science processes of relevance to climate change may be depicted diagrammatically, in the so-called Bretherton diagramme. Different atmospheric and earth science processes are put in relation and they are the subject of the range of sub-programmes which constitute IGBP.

Natural resource data and GIS are used frequently in a wide range of applications, from simple inventories to complex development planning. The following are typical examples of environmental database contents, which are also of relevance for global change:

- land use
- erosion
- groundwater flow
- soil productivity
- soil conservation maps
- vegetation
- surface geology
- elevations
- roads and railroads
- streams and lakes

Global databases are principally constituted from remote sensing platforms (i.e. satellites and aircrafts) and land based techniques involving surveys and statistics. Satellites are particularly well adapted for delivering repeated coverage which allows the constitution of time series. Currently meteorological and atmospheric science satellites provide large scale, low resolution coverage while earth observation satellites like LANDSAT and SPOT provide smaller scale, higher resolution coverage.

The Earth Observing System (EOS) of NASA will be a major new source of remotely sensed data of global scale and of a hitherto unmatched data volume and detail. Polar platforms from NASA, Japan, and from the European Space Agency will from 1998 be producing more that 2000 GByte per day (i.e. data of the order of the total holdings of the major libraries of the world). It will be a comprehensive information system with data processing, international access and analysis capabilities.

Existing large scale databases include the Global Resource Information Database (GRID) of UNEP and 27 data centers around the world coordinate the global collection of data from meteorology, geophysics, atmospheric physics and oceanography. The World Meteorological Organization (WMO), in particular, collects and provides UN member states with data for meteorological forecasting through the World Weather Watch programme.

CORINE (Co-ordinated Information on the European Environment) is the European Economic Community effort on a regional environmental database for the member states are a territory of more than 2 million sq. km. The following database themes are included:

- topography
- soils
- climate
- nature reserves and other sites of scientific importance
- water resources
- atmospheric pollution

Several problems have been encountered in setting up this database, e.g. the merging of datasets of different scales and projections from individual member countries and the integration of these with remotely sensed data of lower resolution.

In general, natural science global databases of use for modelling are characterized by heterogeneous sources, frequent updates, high data volumes, big storage problems, and common georeferencing. All of these requirements indicate that the obstacles to making good models for global change are very substantial, but certainly not insurmountable.

## 3. SOCIO-ECONOMIC DATA AND GIS

The socio-economic processes of relevance to global change may also be described diagrammatically, although the break-down of flows and relationships is not as detailed as in the Bretherton diagramme. The diagramme includes social factors such as population, political system, preferences, production, technology and economic system. Data from these areas are very heterogeneous and, moreover, are rarely organized using GIS. The major database themes for inclusion in GIS are:

- demographics
- land use
- agriculture
- housing
- migration
- transportation
- employment
- occupations
- industry growth

Sources of socio-economic data may be found in government statistics, i.e. on population census, and in other administrative records. The integration of these data into GIS requires of course that appropriate locational data, i.e. digital information about census tract boundaries, city and commune boundaries, etc. If the basic geographic boundary data is available, then aggregation and merging of statistical and administrative alpha-numeric data is a simple, although maybe time consuming matter.

Some areas may already have a tradition for use of information systems in their management, e.g. concerning land records, facilities, transportation and agriculture. Land records may contain land parcel descriptions, demographics and land use planning; facility and transportation agencies have information about roads, power lines, gas and water networks; agricultural agencies have data on crops, yields, livestock etc.

In the context of global environmental change, the above socio-economic data are of particular relevance for regions which are specially exposed to climate change, e.g. coastal areas threatened by sea level rise, arid and semi-arid areas receiving less precipitation, mountain regions subject to increased temperature and changing wind patterns. The effects on human settlements and economic activities, such as migration and modification in agricultural practices, may only be assessed if these data are available but, in addition, the assessment requires modelling techniques.

## 4. GLOBAL CHANGE SCENARIOS AND MODELLING

In global change research, the concern is less about making precise predictions than to consider various type of future scenarios taking into account the current trends of ecosystem and socio-economic development. Thus, for example, climate change may be studied under a number of hypothesis, e.g. a business-as-usual scenario where greenhouse gas emissions continue as before, and various reduction scenarios involving energy taxation, for example.

Given such scenarios based on physical parameters (e.g. GCM data) and socio-economic factor, it is possible to invoke a number of modelling techniques to provide evaluations of impacts of climate changes as well as feed-back mechanisms involving policy responses. Modelling approaches must therefore be capable of dealing with a complex system evolving dynamically in time and subject to different constraints. The kinds of approaches which may be considered in the global change context correspond to three paradigms:

- Mechanical
- Metric
- Semantic

The mechanical modelling paradigm is typically based on differential equations describing the dynamical evolution of the system, as mostly done in science and GCMs. The metric approach is used extensively in econometrics and GIS (with its current limited modelling capabilities) may be considered to be part of this paradigm, e.g. through representation of time series of data. Finally, the semantic paradigm is based on the use of artificial intelligence and expert system techniques which logically lead to development of decision support systems.

Below a few examples of existing models of relevance to the GIS approach and global change research will discussed briefly. Given the importance of the energy sector in greenhouse gas emission, it is not surprising that the world energy model of Edmonds and Reilly have been incorporated as a module in global models. The first versions of this model focussed on particular aspects of the emission problem without regard to how the activity interacted with other humans and natural activities. For example, forecasts of radiative forcing were made without regard to the interaction of emissions and atmospheric processes.

In models such as IMAGE (Integrated Model for the Assessment of the Greenhouse Effect), the basic emission module of Edmonds-Reilly has been combined with other modules on atmospheric chemistry, carbon cycles, climate models and sea level rise. The IMAGE model considers a global climate change as a dynamic system evolving in time as a non-stationary Markov chain with discrete time steps of half a year and a simulation time of 200 years, from 1900 to 2100.

As such, the approach is a mechanical and deterministic computer simulation involving interlinked modules which describe aggregated global change effects. It is, however, easy to see how the model could be developed further in terms of a description of regional, and eventually even local effects by applying GIS techniques. The basic modules. e.g. the Edmonds-Reilly module, must be represented through regionally referenced emission data and the model output will be impact forecasts on corresponding regional levels.

Another interesting model, which is concerned with regional problems of acid rain, the RAINS model (Regional Acidification INformation and Simulation) also has a potential of further development using GIS. This model takes into account emissions of $SO_2$, $NO_x$ and $NH_3$ from industries and follows their transboundary propagation in Europe and subsequent deposition in nature with serious consequences on the acidity of soil, forests, lakes, and groundwater.

The model is based on a very coarse raster, a 150 km x 150 km grid for emissions and atmospheric processes and a 0.5° latitude x 1.0° longitude for environmental impacts. Instead, it is perfectly feasible to use input data in a more localized GIS format and also to present the environmental impacts on the same scale.

## 5. DECISION SUPPORT SYSTEMS

The need for presenting global environmental change issues (i.e. input scenarios, impacts, policy options) in an interactive way can hardly be underestimated. This is required both as an element in decision making for managers and politicians as well as in simple presentation graphics for a more general public. The further development of the analysis and display functions of GIS and the fusion with modelling techniques lead to the decision support systems which may fulfil such a role. The semantic modelling paradigm, involving artificial intelligence and expert system techniques, is particularly relevant in this respect.

The practical development of decision support systems (DSS) and specifically spatial decision support systems (SDSS) is not a straightforward matter. It encounters several problems, previously noted in expert system developments, related to the fact that most issues are neither well structured nor unambiguous. Goals and objectives are most often not clearly defined and therefore multi-criteria methods of decision may not be adequate.

SDSS are designed to help decision makers solve complex spatial problems through an integration of the following capabilities:

- database management
- graphical display
- tabular reporting
- analytical modeling
- expert knowledge

of which GIS normally provide the first three.

The SDSS architecture consists of several software modules: a GIS database management module designed to support cartographic display and spatial query (locational. topographic and thematic), a model base management module incorporating models in the form of analytical sub-routines, report generators for graphics and tables, a user friendly interface convenient for decision making. As with expert systems, a key module is the inference engine which incorporates the knowledge and rule base extracted from real life decision making contexts.

So far few practical examples exist for SDSS in the global environmental change application domain. One example is the CLIMEX prototype for climate impact assessment developed at IIASA. It is designed to perform assessment of regions such as river basins for a given climate change scenario. The GIS subsystem of CLIMEX incorporates datasets concerning climate data, vegetation and carbon fluxes, food and agriculture statistics, as well as basic topographic and elevation data.

The display system offers several tools and features for visual interpretation of the data sets. In addition, they are the input to the analysis component of CLIMEX which relies on a combination of simple models and rules. The models are called upon to provide specific estimates for key variables, e.g. irrigation water, and run in a distributed parallel computing scheme as an integrated part of the expert system inference mechanism.

The symbolic analysis rules are derived from literature or domain experts. The rule base and the alternative chains of reasoning form the basis of assessments, the conclusions of which may be queried using "why options". As a further explanatory feature, all the concepts used may be linked to a hypertext system providing interactive glossary and background information.

## 6. REFERENCES

J. Alcamo et al., The RAINS model of acidification, Kluwer, Dordrecht, 1990

M.B. Beck, Forecasting environmental change, Journal of Forecasting, vol.3, (1991) p.3 .

J.A. Edmonds and J.M. Reilly, A long-term global energy-economic model of carbon dioxide release from fossil fuel use, Energy Economics, April (1983) p. 283-297

K. Fedra and R.F. Reitsma, Decision support and geographical information systems, IIASA RR-90-9, 1990

J. Rotmans, Image: An integrated model to assess the greenhouse effect, Kluwer, Dordrecht, 1990.

Education and Society / R. Aiken (Editor)
Information Processing 92, Volume II
Elsevier Science Publishers B.V. (North-Holland)



# Artificial Intelligence and Environmental Protection: A Survey of Selected Applications in France

L. Buisson[a], R. Martin-Clouaire[b], L. Vieu[b], J.-L. Wybo[c]

[a] CEMAGREF (Nivologie) - Domaine Universitaire - BP76 - 38402 St. Martin d'Hères, France

[b] INRA (Laboratoire d'Intelligence Artificielle) - BP27 - 31326 Castanet-Tolosan, France

[c] Ecole des Mines de Paris (CEMEF/EII) - BP207 - 06904 Sophia Antipolis, France

**Abstract**

This paper surveys recent works carried out in France about the use of artificial intelligence (AI) techniques for environmental protection. On the application side, the problems addressed range from avalanche assessment and path analysis, to forest fire prevention, soil erosion prediction, management of hydroecological processes, landslide prevention and weather nowcasting.

From this survey it appears that a body of AI methodological features can greatly benefit to environmental protection. Of particular interest are the explicit representation of various kind of knowledge, spatio-temporal reasoning and uncertainty management capabilities that can be embedded in AI systems. Some future works outlined in the paper precisely aim at developing generic methodological capabilities for environmental simulation systems.

A national structuring programme has recently been set up in France to promote and monitor environment-related research. As one of its basic actions concerns modelling issues, a brief presentation of this programme is provided.

Keyword Codes: I.2.4; I.6.3; J.m
Keywords: Artificial Intelligence, Knowledge Representation Formalisms and Methods; Simulation and Modelling, Applications; Computer Applications, Environmental Protection

## 1. INTRODUCTION

Environmental protection involves limiting damages caused by humans to their environment, as well as and more generally, protecting the whole natural system, human beings included.

Environmental protection typically requires solving tasks such as diagnosis, forecasting, planning and designing. For a computer assistance in handling these tasks in this particular context, we must first have a sufficiently good understanding of the underlying natural phenomena, and second, be able to model them as faithfully as possible. In addition, this modelling helps improving knowledge of these phenomena, not only because it forces the formalisation of the implicit knowledge some experts may have, but also because some hypotheses may then be tested by simulation.

It is well-known that environment-related phenomena exhibit a high level of complexity. They are numerous, diverse and greatly interdependent. They occur at different spatial and temporal scales. What is more, the current modelling techniques show deficiencies in dealing with imperfect knowledge and data, which is what is to be done for most of the phenomena at stake. First, even though we understand the basic physical and biological principles, the available knowledge may still be incomplete. Some parameters or some relations between variables may be known imprecisely or even vaguely. The most suitable level of granularity in a hierarchy of sub-models composing a global one may not be reachable. Second, in the environment setting the models must work on input data that are often pervaded by imprecision and uncertainty. The imperfection on data may be due to the random variability inherent to some parameters as well as the difficulty to observe a fact or measure accurately a given quantity. In particular, a common characteristic of the environment-related tasks is that they rely heavily on climate data; meteorological predictions are often needed in forecasting and planning problems. Meteorological research is thus usually considered as part of environmental protection research.

This survey of environmental protection works in France reviews the application of the classic Artificial Intelligence (AI) paradigm. Basically, it consists of a body of techniques particularly suitable to solve problems requiring empirical human know-how and, more generally, problems not lending themselves to fully algorithmic approaches. Moreover, AI is classically considered as a way to solve problems in an intelligible (explicable) fashion.[1]

In the setting of modelling natural phenomena, a primary force of AI comes from what lies at its core: the explicit representation of knowledge of different kinds and some specific reasoning mechanisms adapted to the nature of the information to be processed. The so-called knowledge-based approach precisely embodies these two points. Its main asset is the representation of knowledge in a declarative form. The clarity of the representation so obtained makes alterations or refinements easier; moreover, models of several phenomena can be co-operatively integrated. The power of knowledge-based systems may benefit from specific AI research on the various types of knowledge. In particular, AI domains such as temporal and spatial logics and uncertainty management theories are of great interest for environment-related issues. Indeed, most of natural phenomena are dynamic and/or spatialized and, as was already pointed out, only imperfect knowledge and observations are likely to be available to characterise them.

The above-mentioned features of AI that can greatly benefit to environmental protection applications are present (at different degrees) in the examples provided in the remaining part of this paper. Only recent and published research works carried out in France (either under development or as a completed software project) are considered. The next two sections refer to the authors' own contributions. A brief description of other realisations and projects that we are aware of is then given.

In the last section, we outline the main objectives of a project to be undertaken by the authors of this paper. We will also briefly touch upon a recently set-up national structuring programmes, namely the "Programme Environ-nement" of CNRS (Centre National de la Recherche Scientifique). It aims in particular at promoting and organising research efforts in the domain of modelling (theories and tools) for environment-related problems.

## 2. REVIEW OF SELECTED AI PROJECTS

### 2.1 The EXPERTGRAPH system applied to forest fire prevention

EXPERTGRAPH is a knowledge based system designed for real time monitoring and analysis of spatial data; it has been developed in the "Ecole des Mines" in Valbonne (France) and applied to forest fire prevention [11]

### *Context of the problem*

Operators in charge of situation monitoring on a geographic area manage information mostly conveyed by maps. The two major kinds of maps are photographic documents and data maps giving the distribution of values of a parameter on the area of interest.

Monitoring of photographic documents is easily done with video or movies, but the problem is less obvious with data maps, due to the need of spatial and value evolution display. Data maps used by operators are very often the result of processes applied on incoming data; if the situation varies, these processes have to be triggered again, in order to update the maps.

[1] Another trend is concerned with solving problems through modelling brain-like behaviour and is exemplified by works on neural nets.

To validate the EXPERTGRAPH design, the research has focussed on an important problem of decision making about varying situations and related to environmental protection: prevention of forest fires in the French Riviera, on the Mediterranean coast. Critical aspects of this problem include:

- the multiplicity and unpredictability of causes;
- the fast and dangerous evolution that may occur under some conditions;
- the difficulty and cost of fighting fires.

To face this problem, two solutions are used: increase the number of means (planes, trucks, firemen) and enhance prevention. To enhance prevention, the best way is to have a good evaluation of risk over the area of interest, in order to put appropriate means on most dangerous areas and so decrease potential danger.

The study of forest fires shows three main kinds of risk, associated to knowledge-based evaluation methods, related to different processes:

- start-up (under equal conditions of ignition, is fire going to start ?),
- propagation (at what speed will the fire spread ?),
- fighting (how long does it take to reach the fire ?).

The decision making problem faced by operators can be divided into three main tasks:

- receiving and processing data from the environmental context,
- analysing the situation on the basis of empirical knowledge and synthesizing information,
- dynamically displaying information to operators.

These tasks represent the main goals of a decision aid tool for operators.

The EXPERTGRAPH shell has been designed around a real time kernel in charge of monitoring, analysing and displaying data. It is associated with a set of tools for creating and updating specific applications (see Figure 1). EXPERTGRAPH is based on the methodology of map processing used in GIS (Geographic Information Systems), on the declarative representation of knowledge used in expert systems, on monitoring methods used in process control, combined with a graphic user interface for data display.

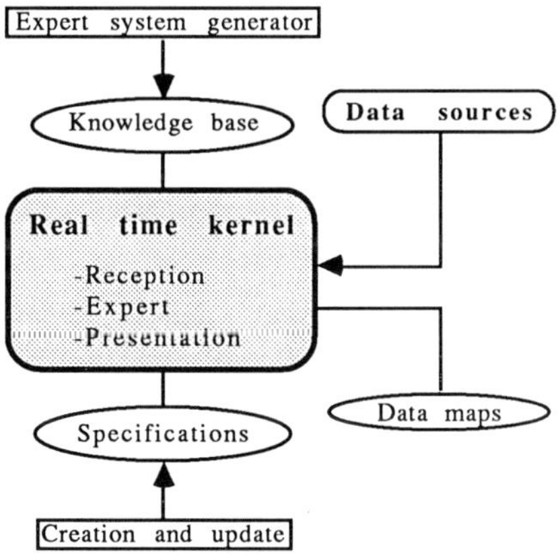


Figure 1. Architecture of EXPERTGRAPH shell

## *The Real Time Kernel*

The kernel is composed of three elements, dedicated to the three tasks: reception module for pre-processing of incoming data, expert module for analysing situations and synthesizing information, and presentation module for dynamically displaying information maps to the user.

It is assumed that the knowledge involved in the analysis task, and specifications used for data processing are available (experts have tools for creating and testing them). Sources of data are considered as external to the kernel, and they send data in an asynchronous way.

In designing this kernel, the following constraints have been taken into account: autonomous behaviour, generality and fast processing time (versus speed of evolution).

### *Development tools*

Applying the EXPERTGRAPH shell first requires to collect knowledge and transform it into a knowledge base. For this purpose, a specific expert system generator has been developed. Its inference engine differs from the one used in the expert module: the nature of data is scalar instead of spatial and the user interface is screen-oriented. In addition, input is done through typing and output values are updated on screen as on a spreadsheet. This inference engine carries out a testing of the knowledge base before the real time kernel is used.

Knowledge is represented through a propositional logic formalism possessing embedded arithmetic calculation capabilities. Backward and forward chaining modes are used.

The process of creating and updating specifications also exploits some knowledge: classes of values of a parameter are created with the list of values referred to in the rules and completed if necessary with new values to increase precision; default values for associated colours are also fixed.

The experts have also to part processes between reception module (algorithms) and expert module (rules); this choice is generally governed by libraries of algorithms, or by the need of explanation about processing, in order to enhance existing knowledge.

### *Results*

The EXPERTGRAPH shell is running since spring 1990 in a Firemen Operational Centre in Nice, and is daily used as a decision tool for risk assessment; it is also used to estimate the potential danger of a starting fire and decide on the means for fighting. It allows situation monitoring in real time: with a 3 mips workstation, update speed is 200 to 400 pixels per second, with 55 rules and 21 maps (512x512 pixels). It gives an aid to experts during creation of applications and allows mixing of complementary techniques: algorithms, knowledge management and graphic presentation.

EXPERTGRAPH is a generic application and will be used for other environmental protection problems and combined with complementary decision aid tools [10].

## 2.2 The ELSA system for avalanche path analysis

ELSA is a knowledge-based system dedicated to avalanche path analysis. ELSA is developed in CEMAGREF in Grenoble, France [2].

### *Avalanche path analysis*

Facing an equipment project, avalanche path analysis must answer the following questions: Is there any avalanche hazard on a path ? Which kind of avalanche can occur ? In which conditions ? What are the properties of this avalanche (magnitude, velocity, extension, pressure fields) ? This analysis will give criteria to choose the most adequate protection strategy.

Snow specialists have several tools to analyse an avalanche path. First of all, they can use their experience. They can make comparisons between this particular avalanche path and some others already studied or well-known. They can make assumptions based on terrain and vegetation features. But more and more, especially to give building rules, they need magnitude of flowing parameters. For that purpose, they can use simulation methods based on mechanical equations.

ELSA is a computer tool dedicated to avalanche path analysis. It tries to provide a snow specialist, not only with these classical simulation methods, but also with some empirical methods developed by using the experience of snow specialists.

### *Description of the terrain*

Obviously, the features of the terrain play an important role in avalanche path analysis. Topography, vegetation and soil nature are often the parameters which, associated with meteorological conditions, explain the characteristics of the avalanche. This is the reason why ELSA is provided with an accurate description of the terrain.

The natural terrain is assumed to be composed of triangular and plane facets. Each triangle is defined by the coordinates of its vertices.

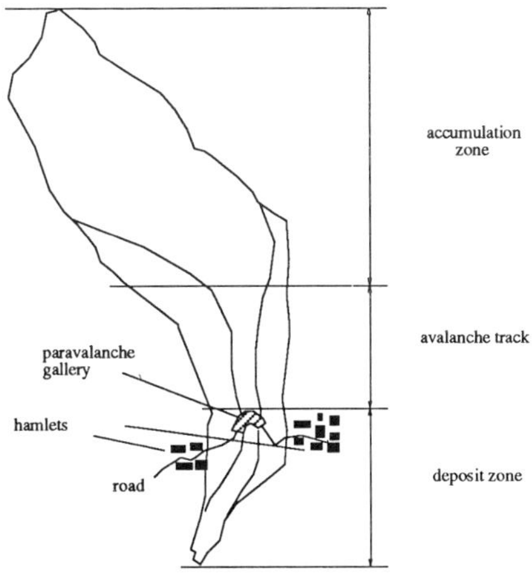


Figure 2 : Avalanche path of Drayre in Vaujany
Région Rhône-Alpes, France.

In order to use knowledge of specialists, ELSA must refer to the same decomposition. ELSA uses the same unit of terrain called *small panel*. A small panel is considered as homogeneous according to the criteria of the avalanche path analysis: slope, exposure, vegetation, soil and distance to the main ridges.

## *Meteorological conditions*

An avalanche occurs when a particular scenario takes place on an avalanche path. A *scenario* is described through an *initial condition* and a sequence of *events*. An initial condition is a description of the distribution of the snow cover on the accumulation zone. The last event is called *critical event* and it ends with an avalanche release.

## *Modelling several phenomena*

During an avalanche occurrence, several phenomena (Figure 3) take place on the avalanche path. For the analysis, specialists must deal with some of them. ELSA takes into account four of them:

- snow-drift,
- snow-cover stability,
- release propagation,
- avalanche flowing.

The first three are located mainly on the accumulation zone, the last on the avalanche track and on the deposit zone.

Snow drift and release propagation are coped with by symbolic simulation. ELSA drives a spatial reasoning. For snow-cover stability and avalanche flowing, ELSA uses numerical methods.

## *Integration*

Some of the methods involved in ELSA are well-known (especially the last ones). Some of them are new and need further work to be validated. Note, however, that these methods are not only "put together in the same tool-box". They are integrated in the same computer system: ELSA. The knowledge base approach allows the development of such systems called *problem solving environments* [6].

One of the main ideas on which ELSA is based, is the share of data between several methods. The best example is the topography. All the different methods use the same representation of terrain:

the triangulation. Moreover, the first three make an intensive use of the decomposition in small panels. The main advantage of such a share is in consistency and in time-sparing.

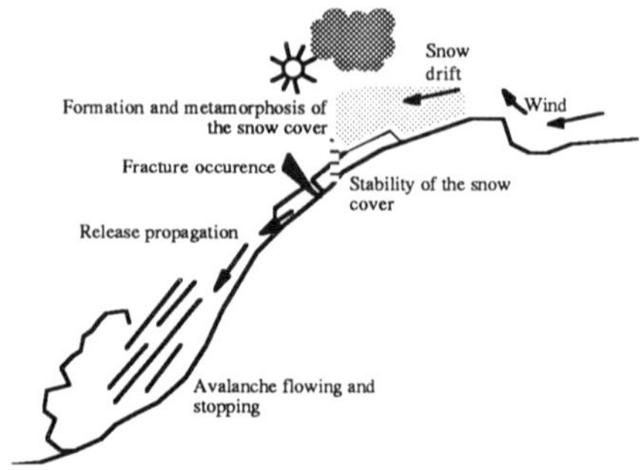


Figure 3 : Some phenomena involved in avalanches

Output of symbolic simulation can feed numerical simulation and conversely. As a results, all the phenomena described above are linked one with another in the process of the analysis [2]. Above all, the interactive interface allows non-computer specialists to use ELSA. The user-friendly interface based on a mouse and a bitmap screen lays emphasis on important parameters.

### *Conclusion*

The ELSA project is not completed yet. Beside the abilities which have been briefly presented in this paper and which are already implemented, further developments are considered. ELSA is built on SHIRKA, an object-centred knowledge representation system written in Le-Lisp.

### 2.3 AI research applied to erosion simulation

The work reported in this section [8] is conducted in the Artificial Intelligence laboratory of INRA (Institut National de la Recherche Agronomique).

### *The problem and its methodological context*

In recent years, damages due to concentrated flow erosion have increased in NW Europe on cultivated lands that are distinguished by moderate topographic and climatic conditions. Environmental protection in this area should start with a thorough understanding of runoff (generation, concentration and circulation) and erosion processes to make risk assessment possible. Choosing a cultural mode and designing equipement is then facilitated [1].

This work undertakes the modelling of the erosive behaviour of small ($\leq 1km^2$) watersheds with no permanent channel, which are the elementary functional units to be taken into account for the phenomena considered. The main purpose of this modelling is the designing of a runoff and erosion simulator in order to test various land division or cultural mode configurations under numerous climatic scenarios. Subsequently and advancing toward full hydrologic modelling, the simulator will quantify the risks (volumes of water and soil flowing out) in order to help hydraulic engineers in designing appropriate reservoirs and drainage where necessary.

Existing numerical models of watershed hydrologic behaviour do not take into account data characterising crop lands. And yet, a number of experimental results do show that erosion damages are strongly related to the spatial distribution of each kind of surface state (depending on the types of soil and crop, cultural operations and previous rainfalls) within the watershed [1]. As a matter of fact, current numerical models reveal incapacities in accounting for the observed variability of small watershed hydrologic behaviour (i.e. the relation rainfall-outflow).

More generally, it should be noted that existing numerical models are rough and non explanatory. The absence of explicit causality makes them look upon a watershed as a "black box", which is hard to adjust to new conditions; as a consequence, those models cannot be used as a research tool for agronomists and geographers developing theories and management rules. As was already mentioned, AI methods are useful to get round these difficulties, especially because of the declarative form given to knowledge.

### *The approach adopted*

Concentrated flow erosion modelling addresses two AI domains: spatio-temporal reasoning and qualitative reasoning.

Assessing the risks associated to a given configuration of a watershed isn't just a matter of evaluating some global variables characterising the watershed (as percentages of each soil type and each crop, slope mean value...). What is fundamental is the spatial combination of the collecting channels' location with the distribution of the various types of surface. Computing the hydrographic network generated in a given watershed by a given rainfall at a given period is achieved by a spatial reasoning involving the topography (direction of slope, talweg line, plot boundaries, furrows, rugosity...) and the actual state of infiltrability of the patches. Strictly speaking, this is a spatio-temporal reasoning: the temporal evolution of the water flow is relevant for erosion and flood issues (local speeds and length of time to reach the outlet); however, for the moment the temporal aspects of the phenomena are not mastered well enough to be dealt with.

The space-time representation chosen here [9] allows an easy and efficient representation of the various components of the watershed (patches, channels...) as well as the moving units (water). Moreover, it enables as directly as possible the above-mentioned reasoning processes.

Geometric data is directly represented in a symbolic manner (i.e. by relations), and does not depend on numeric representations (such as Geographic Information Systems —GIS— or Digital Elevation Models —DEM) which would be both too precise (the exact shape and elevation of every plot are not needed) and too poor (the range of spatial scales from a furrow to a talweg is not covered by a DEM). The representational structure is a "correct" spatio-temporal logic, that is, the definitions and axioms given for the spatial and temporal relations integrate space and time's specific constraints. For instance, two touching objects are necessarily at a null distance (spatial constraint) and contemporaneous (temporal constraint); relations like "upslope", "upstream" or "before" do not admit cycles... A major benefit is that many reasoning properties automatically ensue from these constraints (e.g. transitivities of inclusion, "upslope" and "before"). Moreover, a relational structure is flexible and presents an ability to cope with a large range of spatial and temporal scales: the structure may be very detailed in some places or periods and imprecise where data is missing or where precision is not necessary.

As already mentioned, the simulator will also be used to evaluate the water and soil quantities circulating in each channel. It has been said that, so far, knowledge is inadequate to perform every reasoning step. More specifically, the estimation of flow rates and flow speeds is difficult. Still, it is possible to evaluate by an empirical reasoning the volume of washed-away soil from: the rainfall, the actual state of every patch's top soil, the patches' area, the connections between patches and channels, and the length of potentially erodible channels. Because of this present imperfection, the simulator is made modular to allow for any knowledge improvement.

The methods used to model this type of reasoning suit the data available. For instance, the state of surface soil being a qualitative information, the soil infiltrability is an imprecise value. Any reasoning or computing based on such data must take into account their imprecision, vagueness, or uncertainty. So-called qualitative reasoning methods can be applied, along with an appropriate calculus.

However, the need to deal simultaneously with quantitative and qualitative data, the inherent gradual nature shown by continuous relations between factors, as well as the need for interpolation make the purely symbolic approaches of qualitative physics inadequate. A rigourous reasoning approach that deals with qualitative or quantitative knowledge, and which is compatible and coherent with numerical representations of the real-world has been developed. It takes advantage of the concept of fuzzy-set and possibility distribution for representing and reasoning with qualitative knowledge on numerical parameters. The evaluations requiring arithmetic operations are performed by calculus on fuzzy numbers, by means of an extension of the interval calculus.

*Conclusion*

In this application, AI methods, and more specifically, spatio-temporal logic and uncertainty management theories show their usefulness precisely where the classical approach using numerical models meets its limits.

It should be noted that spatio-temporal reasoning and qualitative reasoning will be more interconnected in the future. This is needed because, among other things, runoff stays in the furrows depending on their orientation, but also depending on the flow rate. For the moment, interactions of this kind are minimized, but their existence implies to carry out as explicitly as possible the reasoning processes.

## 2.4 Other AI projects

*Qualitative reasoning for hydro-ecological process management*

In order to monitor and control a complex living system one must frequently interpret various data from sensors, sample analysis or human observations. Due to the nature of such information and the incomplete knowledge that relate it to the underlying biological processes the interpretation task requires a strong experience which is hard to model using conventional mathematical tools.

Guerrin's approach [4], which has also been developed at the Artificial Intelligence laboratory of INRA, consists in identifying the important domain variables and their cause-effect relationships in a qualitative way. Each variable takes its value in a five symbol set (QS) made of qualifiers like: very low, low, medium, high, very high. Some empirically defined operators are used on QS for increasing, decreasing or taking the antonym of a value, combining additive influences, representing aspects of inhibition, permissiveness and activation.

His approach has been implemented in PROLOG as a rule-based system. Some rules aim at translating the numerical inputs and the observations into qualitative values. Some express how to perform the propagation of values in the causal network of the variables. The control of the reasoning process is also stated explicitly in rules. The system provides short-term predictions and causal explanations of what is happening in the biological processes.

It has been applied to an ecosystem composed of ponds aimed at exploiting the biological production of domestic sewage treatment lagoons (phytoplankton and zooplankton) through the aquaculture of cyprinid fish (larvae and juveniles).

*The MEPRA system*

MEPRA is an expert system developed by the "Centre d'Etude de la Neige" (CEN) in Grenoble, France [3]. CEN is in charge of the estimation of avalanche hazard in time. It provides the general public with avalanche warning bulletins adapted to a mountain region. CEN depends on the national meteorological service. The specialists in CEN take into account the meteorological conditions, the snow cover and their evolutions in time. Practically, for each region, they do not work on an actual accumulation zone of an avalanche path but on a theoretical (or virtual) slope. As a matter of fact, the warnings delivered do not cope with one single path but with all the paths of the region.

The main aim of MEPRA is to provide a snow specialist with decision support abilities for this job. The development began in 1985 through a research work in the framework of a computer science master thesis.

MEPRA must take into account the temporal aspect of data. Its inference engine has been chosen in accordance with this need. MEPRA manipulates a description of the snow cover as several snow layers. Unlike ELSA MEPRA does not take into account the spatial features of the accumulation zone such as ridges, vegetation, snowdrifts. MEPRA is written in Le-Lisp and is provided with a graphic user interface.

*Slope stability and landslides*

Dealing with landslide problems mainly consists in:

- analyzing slopes according to geology and hydrology viewpoints;
- estimating slide hazard;
- designing appropriate equipments when possible.

Several knowledge-based approaches of such problems have been investigated.

A system, called X-Pent, is currently under development at the "Ecole Nationale des Travaux Publics de l'Etat" (ENTPE). X-Pent deals with a representation of the terrain which is decomposed into several geological layers. X-Pent is then able to apply numerical models based on soil mechanics, or to use expert knowledge. X-Pent is written in Le-Lisp and is provided with a graphic user interface.

Prevention of landslides assisted by an expert system approach [5] has been considered by the "Bureau de Recherches Géologiques et Minières" (BRGM). Beside a study of the nature of the expert knowledge involved in this application, BRGM investigates the connection between expert systems and a geographic information systems.

Actually the above two projects are getting closer to each other.

*Weather nowcasting*

The "Centre National de Recherches Météorologiques" (Météo-France, Toulouse) has an AI team specialized in nowcasting (predictions up to 9 hours). The goal of their work is to assist forecasters in the symbolic data interpretation aiming at the construction of representations of observed or predicted situations, and their real-time monitoring.

The data are either directly observable, and sometimes measurable, parameters (e.g. surface and upper-air data, satellite and radar images) or obtained through numerical models (e.g. digital fields). The human capabilities in forecasting satisfactorily at short-time range and fine scale has never been reproduced by the application of numerical approaches. Actually, their main defect is inherent to their inability to cope effectively with the interactions among physical processes that are accessed to at different scales, along with the cost of the necessary observation network and the necessary computational power. The scale interactions are particularly important in the phenomena of air disturbances, caused by the ground roughness, on a thin layer of the atmosphere which is of primary interest for many human activities.

The nowcasting team already applies AI techniques [7] for helping expert forecasters in interpreting surface data and numerical model fields with respect to the so-called "frontal conceptual model". A more general tool providing computer-aided analysis is currently under development. The system first performs morphological image analysis on remote-sensing data and digital fields. It then elaborates synoptic and meso-scale representations in accordance with conceptual models using a knowledge-based approach for describing symbolically the models and their semantics (or, more specifically, what experts know about them).

## 3. PERSPECTIVES

Until recently, the French community concerned with the use of AI for environmental protection was unstructured and thus, composed of people working independently in particular fields of application. As a consequence, the review carried out in this paper cannot pretend to be exhaustive although we believe that the main realisations have been presented.

A bigger and more fertile research production can be expected in the close future, as research efforts will be carried out in a more organised and concerted manner.

The authors of this paper will continue their involvement in this domain and plan to set-up a joint research project that is briefly described next. From our respective experiences related to information processing within environmental protection problems, it comes out that simulation tools are quite often needed. The aim of our project is to develop the basic methodology that would confer such simulation tools some desirable generic capabilities. More specifically, key features that most applications require (though not simultaneously) are the ability to:

- identify the appropriate spatial entities by analysing and abstracting from maps;
- reproduce the spatial evolution of environmental phenomena;
- exploit faithfully the available knowledge and data that, as emphasized in the introduction section, are inherently incomplete, imprecise and uncertain when dealing with such matter;
- let the global phenomenon be decomposed clearly into feasible sub-phenomena (that may be specified in different ways depending on the precision and certainty of information

characterizing a particular starting or incoming situation) and find out efficiently which composition of sub-phenomena (each embedded in a model) correspond to a particular instance of the global phenomena;
- explore efficiently what happens in the simulated phenomenon when one switches from an initial situation to another one close to it; simulators are often used in this way to evaluate sensitivity or to search for optimum.

To achieve these requirements, some methodological AI issues are raised. They concern the choice or development of knowledge representation frameworks that lend themselves to sufficiently powerful spatio-temporal and uncertainty reasoning implementations. In addition, two important questions justify research investment. Uncertainty-guided hypothetical reasoning must be developed in order to find out the most appropriate composition of sub-models that matches an observed situation. A revision process needs to be mechanized efficiently, so as to allow an intelligent exploration of the consequences of close situations, thus making it possible to exploit inferences that remain valid.

Among the structuring initiatives appearing now in France in the field of environment-related research, the main programme is undoubtedly the interdisciplinary "Programme Environnement" coordinated by CNRS (Centre National de la Recherche Scientifique).

The purpose of this programme is to lead fundamental research on environment-related issues and to initiate and coordinate some pluridisciplinary projects within this research framework. The "Programme Environnement" promotes communication activities (symposiums, publications), relationships between public research institutes and various organisations. It gives financial aid to research projects selected through "calls for proposals" focussed on important subjects.

For 1992, five topics were identified. One of them is called "Methods, Models and Theories"; its creation was motivated by the lack of a strong methodological background for modelling complex phenomena appearing in the environment context. Within this theme, AI plays an important role along the lines that we have sketched in this paper.

## 4. REFERENCES


1 Auzet V., Boiffin J., Papy F., Ludwig B. & Maucorps J. Rill erosion on cultivated catchments in the North of France, Catena, to appear in 1992.

2 Buisson L. ELSA: a problem solving environment for avalanche path analysis, SCS Symposium on "Artificial Intelligence in Numerical and Symbolic Simulation". Lyon, March 1989.

3 Giraud G. Intelligence Artificielle et prévision du risque d'avalanche, in *Neige et avalanches*, N. 50, Grenoble, 1987.

4 Guerrin F. Biological process interpretation using a qualitative reasoning approach, in *Mathematical and intelligent models in system simulation*, R. Hanus, P. Kool, S. Tzafestas (eds.), J.C. Baltzer AG, Scientific Publishing Co., 1991, pp. 513-518.

5 Ke C. Système expert de prévention de mouvements de terrain, BRGM, October 1987.

6 Pavé A. & Rechenmann F. Computer-aided modelling in biology: an Artificial Intelligence approach, Artificial Intelligence and Simulation, SCS Series, 1986.

7 Sénési S. Automatic Symbolic Description of Synoptic Situations, Fourth AIRIES workshop, Québec, September 1990.

8 Vieu L. & Martin-Clouaire R. Spatio-temporal and qualitative reasoning in erosion simulation, submitted to AAAI'92 workshop "AI in Natural & Agricultural Resource Development", San Jose, CA, July 12-17, 1992.

9 Vieu L. Sémantique des relations spatiales et inférences spatio-temporelles, Ph.d thesis, Université Paul Sabatier, Toulouse, 1991.

10 Wybo J.L. & Carréga P. Implication de l'informatique avancée à la prévention des feux de forêt et à la gestion des espaces menacés, Revue forestière Française, XLII, fall 1990.

11 Wybo J.L. Expertgraph: Knowledge based analysis and real time monitoring of spatial data; application to forest fire prevention in French Riviera, SCS symposium on "Managing Risk With Computer Simulation", Orlando, April 1992.

Education and Society / R. Aiken (Editor)
Information Processing 92, Volume II
Elsevier Science Publishers B.V. (North-Holland) 


# The XUMA Expert System "Environmental Hazards from Contaminated Sites"

## Example of an Environmental Application Experience Gained from Development and Practical Use

A. Jaeschke, W. Geiger, M. Reißfelder, R. Weidemann

Kernforschungszentrum Karlsruhe (KfK)
Institut für Datenverarbeitung in der Technik
Postfach 3640, D-7500 Karlsruhe
Federal Republic of Germany

**Abstract**
Within the framework of the remediation of contaminated sites, the environmental hazard of the sites has to be assessed. Furthermore, it has to be decided upon the safeguarding and sanitation measures to be taken. The XUMA expert system, developed by the Karlsruhe Nuclear Research Center (KfK) and the State Institute for Environmental Protection (LfU) of Baden-Württemberg, is to support the authorities to plan the chemico-physical analyses, to evaluate the analysis results.and to deduce the environmental risk of the sites corresponding to the risk assessment procedure generally applied in Baden-Württemberg. The system is now in operation at the LfU. In this paper, it is reported about the functions of XUMA and about the experiences gained from development and practical use of the system.

### 1. Introduction

The objective of implementing computer systems capable of substituting a human expert in his activities had certainly been a motivation in the early days of development of the expert system methodology. However, at the latest when the techniques and tools developed with this objective were handed over to system designers this kind of pretensions lost in importance. The objective 'substituting an expert' was reduced to 'assisting the expert'. The most pragmatic system designers at present consider the methods as being hardly more than a novel technique of implementation (declarative instead of procedural), which offers advantages for certain classes of applications compared to the conventional techniques. Here planning, configuration and diagnostic tasks are in the foreground for which decision-support systems are being developed with such objectives as:

- relief of routine work,
- preservation and dissemination of expert knowledge,
- standardization of decision making,
- reproducibility and consistency of decision making,
- full utilization of information available,
- consideration of all alternative solutions and the like.

Early fields of application for expert systems had been medicine, geology, chemistry and technical configuration. The field of environmental applications and the methodology of the expert systems gained in importance in applied computer science at about the same time. In a number of survey articles dealing with the use of expert systems in environmental applications [1,2] it was investigated already which potential applications exist for the methodology, where the centers of development work lie and which tasks had already been tackled successfully. Synchronously to the general development in the expert systems sector, in an initial phase the attempt was made to demonstrate the suitability of the methodology for a broad spectrum of environmental applications. Only in a second phase, in a realistic assessment of the potential of expert systems, the implementation of practice-oriented systems followed for selected application tasks. In the environmental sector the following problem areas have emerged inter alia:

- environmental impact assessment,
- risk assessment of waste and contaminated sites,
- accident and crisis management.

Projects pursued within this framework have produced mature systems which justify to strike an interim balance. In this report some experience gained and trends arising from the development of expert systems will be discussed. The actual background for the discussion are experiences accumulated in development and application of the XUMA expert system 'Environmental Hazards from Contaminated Sites'.

## 2. The XUMA Expert System

### *2.1 The Task*

At present, in Germany there are nearly 100,000 sites suspected to be contaminated; these are dumping sites for domestic and industrial wastes, abandoned sites of industrial and trade firms and the like. They might constitute a major risk to man and the environment which, from case to case, calls for different countermeasures to be taken. The responsible authorities must decide whether the suspected site must be considered as hazardous and has to be cleaned up, safeguarded, surveyed, explored or whether it can be released from further consideration as a site constituting no risk to the environment. For this, the suspected site has to be fitted into an evaluation/assessment scheme which allows uniform and consistent decisions concerning the kind and urgency of actions to be taken.

The XUMA expert system developed by the authors in cooperation with Landesanstalt für Umweltschutz, LfU, (State Institute for Environmental Protection) has been developed as a decision-supporting toolkit which is to aid the expert in the individual activities resulting in a risk assessment procedure. The system is based on the evaluation method developed by LfU and introduced in Baden-Württemberg. It comprises the following steps:

- evaluation,
- chemical/physical investigation,
  - establishing a plan for analytical investigation,
  - compilation of analytical results,
- assessment.

The XUMA system assists the expert in the working steps listed above, and, in addition, makes available the functions for knowledge acquisition and explanation. The following description of the XUMA functions can reflect only incompletely the functionality and complexity of the system. A detailed description of the system is contained in [3,4,5].

*2.2 XUMA-function: evaluation*

In the evaluation the contaminated site is considered as a site potentially discharging pollutants into the environment taking into account the environmental resources ground- and surface-water, soil and air. From information available about the dumped pollutants and based on hypothetical standard site conditions for the waste in a first step the 'hazard in a reference situation' is estimated with XUMA. In a second step information about the actual conditions of the site are included and, by means of XUMA, the numerical value R for the 'decisive hazard' is determined which is referred to in order to fix the type and priority of the necessary actions.

*2.3 XUMA-function: elaboration of an analyses plan*

It is the objective of this XUMA-function to define the optimum measurement program for the further chemical/physical exploration of the contaminated site which guarantees a maximum of gain of information while necessitating a minimum of expenditure. The attempt is made to obtain concrete indications about any substances possibly present on the suspected site and to derive from them a plan for an optimal measurement program. Such indications might e.g. be the former use of the site, the origin of the dumped waste or the type of waste involved. To be able to elaborate the measurement program from this information, knowledge is necessary of the waste typical of an *industrial branch* as well as knowledge of the *substances* contained in the wastes.

Knowledge of the waste typical for each industrial branch is represented as a 'branch tree' in the knowledge base. The branch tree breaks down into main branches, sub-branches, plant components and production techniques and gives the relationships among these objects. Associated to each object of the tree informations are stored on the wastes typical for each branch, their quantities, their concentrations, their distribution and inheritance in the industrial branch tree as well as further, additional properties.

The term *substances* in XUMA comprises all kinds of material processed in the system, beginning with elements via compounds, mixtures up to and including products and types of waste. The knowledge base has stored the relations existing between these substances, their features and analytical parameters belonging to the materials.

The user can make his choice by which access he wishes to elaborate the analyses plan: via the industrial branch from which the waste originates, via a substance supposed to be contained in the waste or via a standard plan. Elaboration of an analyses plan may also be done in repeated runs at different phases of the assessment procedure, each run supplementing the preceding plan. Separate analyses plans are established for the media soil, eluate, water and air.

*2.4 XUMA-function: compilation of analyses results*

By this function sample- and analysis- descriptions and the measured results for the individual analytical parameters are recorded. The analytical data associated to one case, sample or analysis are stored in a hierarchical data structure. For each case there are one or several samples. For each sample there is one sampling protocol and one or several laboratory analyses (waste, soil, eluate, ground water, seepage water, surface water, air analyses).

*2.5 XUMA-function: assessment*

On the basis of the analytical results in the assessment function the environmental hazard caused by the contaminated site, indications regarding further need of exploration as well as other information (e.g. indications of inconsistencies in the analytical data, statistics) are derived.

For this task, the system has stored knowledge about limit value tables and rules implementing the assessment method. Approximately 25 tables containing limit values and reference values about some 100 analytical parameters are being used. Supplementing these tables rules are stored which specify in what cases the tables can be used, which qualitative data can be derived from the comparison of measured values with these tables and how the assessment should proceed in case the comparison with various tables yields different results. The rules of assessment comprise rules deriving statements from individual analytical parameters and from combinations of analytical parameters as well as rules summarizing these data into a general assessment of the analysis. Furthermore, there are rules which concentrate the assessment of different analyses to an assessment of the sample and of the case as a whole.

The user may choose whether he wishes to have output the assessment of an analysis, the concise assessment of a sample or the summarizing assessment of a case. The user may also have output statistics about the parameters, analyses and samples.

*2.6 XUMA function: knowledge acquisition and explanation facility*

The knowledge acquisition facility enables the authorized users to include new objects and rules in the knowledge base and to modify existing objects and rules without necessitating knowledge of programming. Such objects and rules are above all industrial branches, substances and analytical parameters, tables of limit values and the rules implementing the assessment of analyses results. The objects defined in the system are recorded and edited in a conventional way in display forms which are specific to the respective object type. To facilitate the acquisition of rules different groups comprising rules of the same type and same structure are defined in the system. During knowledge acquisition the system predefines the structure specific for each group on the display which then can be parametrized and edited by the user.

The explanation facility serves to explain to the user the derivation of the statements. The user may choose whether he wishes to obtain the local or the global explanation. In case of a local explanation the last rule which has led to that statement and the premises satisfied are listed. In a global explanation the entire derivation tree of the statement is shown.

*2.7 Status of the Project*

During the last four years a first version of the expert system suited for practical application has been elaborated. Knowledge acquired in the knowledge base presently covers the branches of coal refinement industry (gas works, coking plants, coal-tar distillations), electroplating shops, tanneries and foundries.

XUMA has been implemented in LISP using the ART expert system development environment and it runs on an EXPLORER computer supplied by Texas Instruments. The system presently contains approx. 1.000 ART rules and 80.000 lines of LISP and ART code.

About ten man-years have been spent so far on the development of the system. The expenditure additionally incurred by the user is difficult to quantify. Since June 1990 XUMA has been subjected to trial operation at LfU. In parallel to this, the extension of the system functions is being continued and the knowledge base is being supplemented by the expert users with regard to additional industrial branches.

## 3. Discussion

### *3.1 System Development*

In principle, there exist two alternatives for the development of an expert system: elaboration of the system on the basis of programming languages or profiting from an expert system development environment or shell. The latter provide the means of rapid prototyping with the objective of working out a version of the future application system with which the feasibility can be proved and the capabilities and features of the solution can be demonstrated. However, in practical application doubts have been raised regarding its benefits.

In the beginnings for environmental applications (as in other fields too) many 'mini-prototypes' were developed with a minimum amount of knowledge and functions and disregarding the complexity of the practical problem. These systems did not allow reliable extrapolations to be made to the desired target system and were capable of solving trivial problems only. These prototypes failed because they were not capable of either serving as demonstration system or as a nucleus for further development. Quite a number of discontinued projects are attributable to that failure.

A prototype suitable for scaling up which can provide information about the problem solving capability, the performance and the applicability in practice has to include already the architecture/structure, the major hardware/software features and a certain scope of functions. Consequently, the elaboration of a prototype which can be scaled up calls for considerable expenditure in systems/requirement analyses and in concept design.

The XUMA prototype development was mainly concentrated to the function 'elaboration of an analyses plan' which had been almost completely implemented for application in the field coal refinement industry. In prototype development three man-years were spent within two years (i.e. 30 % of the actual total expenditure).

The prototype has been essentially maintained as a nucleus in the present system and thus has provided the basis for further development. However, the extensions of the system were made primarily in LISP so that in the final system the relative fraction of the software implemented in ART is clearly smaller than in the prototype.

The prototype was handed over to the users for in-depth testing. Also all further stages of completion were installed and tested on the user system. In parallel the knowledge base was extended by the expert user to include major domains of knowledge for practical application. The system assumed a significant part as a supporting tool in knowledge acquisition. It showed up gaps, inconsistencies and limits of the evaluation method and provided indications concerning the further development of the assessment methodology.

*3.2 Acquisition of Knowledge and Explanation Facility*

The knowledge acquisition facility is of primary importance to the extension and modification of the knowledge base by the user. It serves to transform knowledge from the natural, not-formalized representation easy to understand and to manage by the user into internal knowledge representation. For this generally applicable concepts are still missing. In the majority of projects therefore application specific techniques are being developed, most of them, however, very restrictive in respect of a free formulation of knowledge.

The method selected for XUMA has proved its efficiency in practical application. It is restricted however to that sector of the knowledge base which is most frequently subjected to modifications. Specific modifications must be done by the systems engineer.

The capability of self-explaining is considered as an indispensable characteristic of expert systems and a major advantage for practical application and acceptance. However, this is not reflected in the actual system implementations. For lack of useful concepts many of the implemented systems do not offer an explanation component while others provide tracing functions only which allow to reproduce the problem solving process although they do not furnish a real explanation. For the expert user responsible for knowledge acquisition the central importance of the explanation facility lies in system testing, in building up and extending the knowledge base or in modifying it as soon as unexpected results are indicating errors in the knowledge base. Regarding this function, the explanation facility becomes indispensable to complex systems because practical testing is at present the only technique for testing consistency and completeness.

*3.3 Integration in the User Environment*

In the whole history of expert systems the development of stand-alone systems has so far been in the foreground; only recently, a tendency can be recognized towards expert systems as integrated components of more complex EDP systems. This tendency grows in importance, especially in environmental applications. In most cases the demand to integration is a direct consequence of the application structure in which the expert system solve subtasks only within the framework of a complex problem (e. g. environmental impact assessment within the general planning process or contaminated site assessment in the process of upgrading). It is decisive for the efficiency and acceptance of the expert systems in practical use to which extent optimum integration into the organizational frame and the EDP environment is successful. The integration in systems for environmental applications is impeded by the fact that, on the one hand, data and information of very heterogeneous structures, frequently originating in very different sources/systems have typically to be evaluated and that, on the other hand, processing of this heterogeneous information on the basis of interdisciplinary knowledge leads to expert systems of high complexity which, as e.g. XUMA, can be implemented only in special hardware/software environments. Shells and tools of the expert systems do not yet support concepts for integration which are of general applicability. Application specific concepts for integration have to solve individually the problems of communication, consistency and compatibility among the knowledge- and databases.

If the components are only loosely coupled with the environment, inclusion of the component together with its special hardware and software into a network might constitute an efficient concept of integration. It avoids portability problems and likewise the expenditure associated with a transfer but it is readily accompanied by communication and interface problems and, dependent on the degree of coupling, with performance problems.

The environment in which XUMA has to be integrated consists of user systems (stand-alone or interlinked) of the various users (environmental authorities, engineering offices, etc.) which have access to XUMA functions and desire to have processed their own practical cases. Integration of XUMA into the various user systems is automatically excluded because of the high expenditure for software transfer which is incurred repeatedly and the mostly insufficient resources of the user systems. A network concept as shown in Fig. 1 is planned for integration.

The expert system computer is integrated here as a server (XUMA server) into the network. The XUMA manager organizes the access to the XUMA functions which can be addressed by a local dialog system (on the server) or via remote dialog systems on the user systems (XUMA clients). The remote dialog components of the XUMA clients provide interfaces (DB-IF) to the user specific databases. Via these interfaces the case data needed in an operation may be taken from the user databases, converted into the structure required by XUMA and transferred into the XUMA database. During the processing time these data are, protected against access from outside, kept ready for use. Finally the results are retransferred to the XUMA client, when the case has been processed.

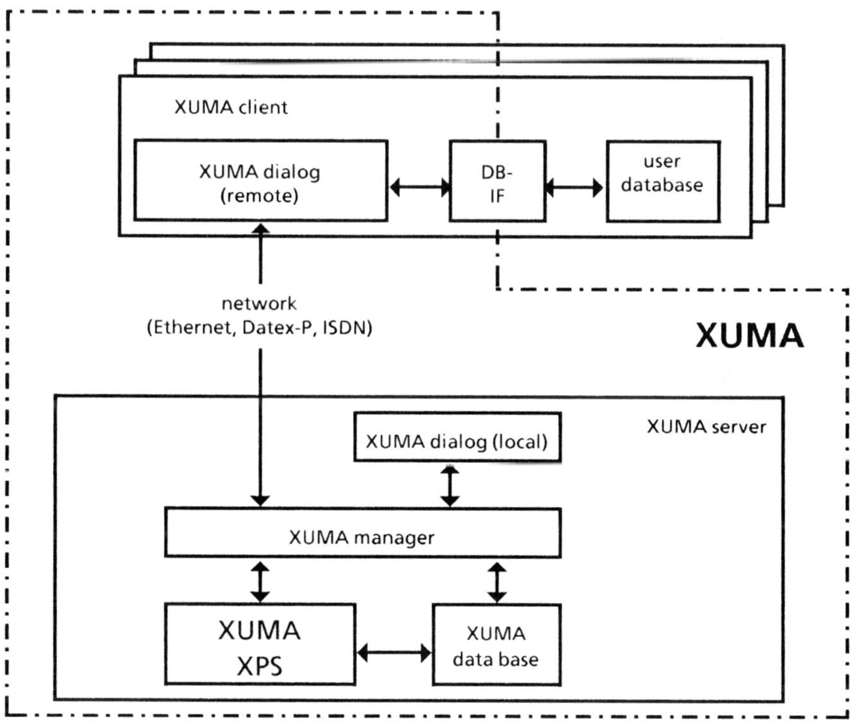


Fig. 1: Concept for Integration of XUMA

As in the example of XUMA (weak coupling) practicable solutions for integration can be found by means of the techniques available. However, for tightly cooperating components the problem remains essentially unsolved in spite of recent developments and progress made. A solution can be anticipated only if the methods of the expert systems can be combined with the conventional methods into one uniform concept.

## 4. Concluding Remarks

The project described here demonstrates that with the present state of the art expert systems can be implemented for solving complex tasks in environmental applications. However, development work has still to be done, both as regards the expert system methodology and the tools. Regarding the project under consideration, there has been a demand above all in the area of knowledge acquisition and systems integration. In other projects, problems of knowledge presentation are in the foreground. Systems relying exclusively on rules have nearly disappeared from practical application. However, mixed techniques in knowledge presentation are more difficult to keep transparent in practice than homogeneous structures. Also here adequate concepts and tools are lacking.

## References

[1] Page, B.; Jaeschke, A.; Pillmann, W.
Angewandte Informatik im Umweltschutz.
Informatik Spektrum, 1990, Vol. 13/1, S. 6 ff (Teil 1); Vol. 13/2, S. 86 ff (Teil 2).

[2] Page, B.
An Analysis of Environmental Expert System Applications.
Environmental Software 5 (1990), No. 4, pp. 177-198.

[3] Geiger, W.; Osterkamp, G.; Weidemann, R.
XUMA - An expert system assisting environmental protection authorities in the assessment of contaminated sites.
In: Zarri, G.P. (ed.), Operational Expert System Applications in Europe. Pergamon Press, pp 81-97.

[4] Eitel, W.; Geiger, W.; Weidemann, R.
Experiences gained when assessing contaminated sites with support of the XUMA expert system.
Arendt, F., et al. (ed.), Contaminated Soil '90, 3rd Internat. KfK/TNO Conference on Contaminated Soil, Karlsruhe, December 10-14, 1990, Kluwer Academic Publ., Dordrecht, 1990, Vol. 1, pp. 543-548.

[5] Geiger, W.; Weidemann, R.
The XUMA expert system for contaminated sites: functions, explanations and knowledge acquisition.
Proc. of the 10th Internat. Workshop on Expert Systems and their Applications, General Conference Avignon '90, Avignon, F, May 28 - June 1, 1990, Vol. 2, pp. 951-961.

Education and Society / R. Aiken (Editor)
Information Processing 92, Volume II
Elsevier Science Publishers B.V. (North-Holland)



# A Cooperative, Natural Language Environmental Information System

R. Becker[a], D. Küpper[b], M. Strobel[ab], D. Rösner[b]

[a]IBM Deutschland GmbH, Institute for Knowledge Based Systems (IKBS), Postfach 103068, D-6900 Heidelberg 1, Germany
Tel.: ++49 6221 404-288, e-mail: STROBEL@DHDIBM1.bitnet

[b]Research Institute for Applied Knowledge Processing (FAW), Postfach 2060, D-7900 Ulm, Germany
Tel.: ++49 731 501-530, e-mail: <Lastname>@faw9370.faw.uni-ulm.de

**Abstract**

This paper describes the extension of a natural language interface to relational databases with respect to its cooperative behavior. We argue that cooperative behavior is especially important for a complex domain such as environmental protection. In order to enrich traditional database reports our system[1] provides dialog-oriented features such as over-answering and handling of presupposition failure, as well as presentation-oriented features such as natural language responses and geographical maps.

Keyword Codes: H.1.2; I.2.7
Keywords: User/Machine Systems; Natural Language Processing

## 1. INTRODUCTION

Having the right information at the right time is an important topic in the field of environmental protection, e.g. in case of emergency. More and more information is being stored in databases which are becoming highly complex. Consequently, fast and easy access to required information for humans can only be achieved, either if they are database experts or if they are supported by a powerful access tool.

With this in mind, we are working on a system which allows a user to access a relational database with written German. For demonstration purpose restricted speech input is possible using a speech recognizer.

---

[1] The system has been developed within the project NAUDA (NAtürlichsprachlicher Zugang zu UmweltDAten) in the research area Human-Computer Interaction and Assisting Systems at FAW, headed by Dr. D. Rösner as senior scientist. The project was jointly funded by the state of Baden-Württemberg and IBM Germany.

We are using the water and waste management database from the Baden-Württemberg Ministry of Environment as a realistic application. The relevant concepts in this domain are buildings, areas, bodies of water, and plants (together with their relationships). Currently anticipated users are employees at the local environmental departments and at the Ministry of Environment.

We assume that the users are familiar with the domain, but unfamiliar with the structure of the database. Therefore, assistance is needed in bridging this gap. Natural language is one means of closing the gap, since users may express queries in their own terms. The translation process from natural language to a formal database language requires a model of the database structure and the mapping of natural language concepts onto database expressions. This may help users to some extent, but they must know what concepts and relations have been modelled. Furthermore, they must be aware of the formal character of the translation process, i.e. their queries are answered literally. More cooperative systems try to give an answer which considers the assumed intentions of the user. NAUDA's cooperative behavior focuses on the correction of presupposition failures and over-answering. In addition, tables as traditional output forms are replaced and/or enriched by natural language and graphics.

## 2. MOTIVATION

The need for a cooperative natural language interface for complex databases can be best motivated by a short comparison with the normal methods for accessing databases. There are two main alternatives available, namely

```
SELECT DISTINCT
X2.OBJ_ART,X2.OBJ_NR,X1.OBJEKTNAME,X3.BEZEICHNUNG
FROM
  BECKER.WWAO X1,BECKER.VABWASSREINANL X2,BECKER.AW04 X3,
  BECKER."ABWREIN-BAUWDAT" X4, BECKER.ABWASSERBAUWDATEN X5
WHERE X3.BEZEICHNUNG
 IN (SELECT X6.BEZEICHNUNG
  FROM BECKER.AW04 X6
  WHERE X6.SCHL_ID
  IN (600,120,100)
   AND X6.BEZEICHNUNG IS NOT NULL)
   AND X3.BEZEICHNUNG
   IN (SELECT X7.BEZEICHNUNG
    FROM BECKER.AW04 X7
    WHERE X7.SCHL_ID = 600
    AND X7.BEZEICHNUNG IS NOT NULL)
    AND X5.ABWASSBAUWDAT_ID = X4.ABWASSBAUWDAT_ID
    AND X5."BEREICH/STUFE" = X3.SCHL_ID
    AND X4.ABWREINANL_ID = X2.ABWREINANL_ID
    AND X2.OBJ_NR = X1.OBJ_NR
    AND X2.OBJ_ART = X1.OBJ_ART
```

Figure 1: SQL-statement corresponding to the sentence below

access via menus or via a formal database query language such as SQL. Menu-driven techniques are easy to use, but are not flexible enough for addressing more complex problem solving tasks. Unrestricted access to a database is currently possible with a formal language only. However, formulating a query with such a language is often time consuming and susceptible to errors. It requires proficient data processing skills and knowledge about the syntax and semantics of the language, as well as the names of the tables, columns, datatypes and possible join paths. To illustrate this, Figure 1 shows the SQL-query to our database which corresponds to the natural language sentence:

*Which sewage treatment plants have a chemical purifying stage?*

Natural language provides a means for unrestricted access, which does not require data processing skills or knowledge of the internal structure of the database.

The benefit of a natural language interface will increase, however, if the system provides cooperative behavior.

## 3. THE NAUDA SYSTEM

### 3.1 Cooperative Behavior of the NAUDA System

Although the notion *cooperative* is frequently used in the context of user interfaces to computers, the concept is not formally defined. Very often, only counterexamples of uncooperative behavior are given. Grice ([Grice 75]) gives a definition of cooperative behavior within the scope of a natural conversation. His definition is not concrete enough to be implemented in a straightforward manner, but may be used as guidance for further work. Grice claims that a cooperative agent must make its contributions to a dialog 'such as required' by the *purpose* of a dialog. A cooperative natural language system must recognize this purpose, and especially the goals of the user, because they are often not mentioned within a dialog. In addition to a comprehensive knowledge of the domain, an explicit model of the user's assumptions and goals provides a good basis for this task. A system which updates this model after each of the user's (and its own) statements has the best chance of understanding the user's goals and, consequently, of being able to react cooperatively. But a slight amount of uncertainty will usually remain, in which case the system may make a false assumption regarding the goals of the user. A system response which is based on this false assumption might be regarded as uncooperative by the user.

On the other hand, even without an explicit user model, several kinds of support for the user may be provided within the scope of an information system. We have focused on this type of cooperative behavior. Therein we distinguish between two major branches. One is related to the use of natural language, i.e. to the cases in which an information system should provide more information than required by a literal interpretation of a query. The other deals with an adequate form of a system response, i.e. presenting the information in a way which is comprehendable and avoids syntactically ambiguous sentences in generated system output.

### 3.1.1 Presentation of Results

In order to reach a high degree of user-friendliness, the form of the output should be appropriate for the type of information. Various phenomena may be fairly well expressed in natural language, whereas for others, graphics or combinations of language and graphics are more suitable. In addition to properties concerning the contents, aspects such as the amount of data play a crucial role in the mode of presentation. Texts produced by humans are often combined with non-linguistic representations (diagrams, pictures, maps, etc.), and database management systems usually have a graphics facility to support presentations in graphic form.

In the NAUDA Sytem different forms of presentation are chosen depending on the type and amount of information:

- The standard form of an answer to a wh-question (i.e. a question containing "which", "where", "when", etc.) is a table. The result from the database manager remains unchanged for tables containing a large amount of data. But the presentation of tables consisting of a single column heading and a single data value seems to cause an information overload. Instead, the result should be provided in natural language – either as a sentence or a noun phrase – or simply as a value.
- Yes-no questions are not simply rejected or confirmed but are – if appropriate – answered as full sentences. This is salient and can, in the context of over-answering, be seen as a useful technique for directing the user's attention to the fact that s/he received more information than explicitly requested.
- The system has been enriched by a facility for the display of topographical maps which show sections of the area in question, an aspect which is especially relevant in our domain. Spatial relationships between objects should be visualized for the following reasons: (a) expressing spatial relationships with linguistic means or as a table is rather inefficient and inadequate and can often be done much better visually. Moreover, theories about human information processing assume that humans use two different representation formalisms for processing spatial aspects [Paivio 71a/b]: a propositional (i.e. logic-oriented) and an analogous one (i.e. depictional); (b) the underlying assumption that a human often knows what s/he is interested in only when s/he sees it (as found in discussions about graphic interfaces, cf. [McDonald 86]) seems to be justified, at least for more complex spatial phenomena.

### 3.1.2 Over-Answering

Within information-seeking dialogs between humans, the informant often provides more information than explicitly required if it is relevant for the information seeker. This cooperative behavior is called *over-answering* [Wahlster et al. 83]. The problem of adapting this technique for an information system lies in adequately constraining the amount of additional information given to the user, i.e. avoiding the presentation of irrelevant facts. We have identified two cases in which we believe additional information is generally relevant and can be offered even without explicit user modelling. The first one is the presence of wrong presuppositions within the user's question; this will be discussed in the next section. The other deals with a user's yes-no question about a property value of a certain object when this question must be answered with "No". In this case, the system will assume that a) the user does not know the actual value of this attribute and b) the user is interested in this value. Consequently, the system should give the user the valid attribute values. Our system, for instance, will give the actual value of a numerical attribute if a corresponding yes-no question from the user must be answered with "No".

### 3.1.3 Handling presupposition failure

Within the scope of natural language interfaces to databases, frequently used types of questions are "how-many" and "which/who" questions [Lehmann et al. 78]. These questions usually contain an object description where the user is interested in the number of such objects or s/he requests more information about them. Such queries presuppose that these objects are in the database and, consequently, that they are legal in the domain. However, it cannot be expected that users are familiar with every detail of the contents and structure of the database. This is especially true for databases dealing with a complex domain such as environmental protection.

For instance, the question

*Which simple sewage treatment plants have a chemical purifying stage?*

contains the presupposition that the database stores at least one *simple sewage treatment plant with a chemical purifying stage*. This implies (among other things) that the database may store simple sewage plants, purifying stages, that a (possessive) relation between simple sewage plants and purifying stages exists, and that the range of this relation subsumes purifying stages of type 'chemical'.

If one of these conditions fails the database answer will be "No (empty set)" or something similar. In contrast, within normal cooperative dialogs the failure will be noticed and explained if possible. On the other hand, this means that presuppositions which are not rejected explicitly might be regarded as confirmed. Because users of a natural language interface expect that this kind of interaction is comparable to normal situations where natural language is used (see [Joshi 83]), a presupposition failure must be noticed to prevent the user from assuming that the system agrees with his presupposition. At least two levels of presupposition failure can be distinguished (cf. [Kaplan 83], [Mays 80], [Joshi 83]), namely extensional and intensional failures, i.e. failures with respect to the contents of the database, and failures with respect to the model of the domain, as determined by the structure of the database. Additionally, Marburger ([Marburger 88]) identifies the conceptual level, which is related to failures with respect to the domain itself, e.g. asking for objects which cannot exist in the domain.

To be most informative, a system should inform the user about the level of a presupposition failure. For instance, answering the above question with

*Simple sewage treatment plants with a chemical purifying stage are not known*

is insufficient, because it does not make clear whether the information (or parts of it) are not stored in the database at the moment, whether it cannot be stored in that database, or whether the objects in question cannot exist in the domain. In the case of a presupposition failure with respect to the structure of the database or to the domain, the user implicitly states that he is not familiar with this topic. Because this knowledge is relevant for exploiting the database, the system should provide additional (meta-) information. Within our domain, *simple* sewage treatment plants cannot have *chemical* purifying stages, but they may have at least a *biological* one. NAUDA provides this information with the answer:

> *Purifying stages of simple sewage treatment plants are by definition biological.*

### 3.1.4 Dialog Aspects

Up to now we have discussed phenomena which are related to a single question. Usually the users' questions are related. Two important kinds of relation are reference (e.g. with pronouns) and ellipsis, for instance, a follow-up question which is shortened to a phrase which only expresses the difference from the previous question. These phenomena, which may significantly shorten a dialog sequence, are handled by most of today's natural language interfaces (cf. [Küpper et al. 90]).

Furthermore, considering a question within the dialog's context may lead to a disambiguation or to an interpretation which cannot be justified without regarding the context. For instance, the question

> *Which sewage treatment plants have 3 purifying stages?*

can be interpreted in two different ways: the user may want to know which *types* of sewage treatment plants have 3 purifying stages, or he may want to see the corresponding individual database objects. If a presupposition failure with respect to similar objects is detected in the previous question, NAUDA presents the *types* of sewage treatment plants. Without a context like that the question is answered by querying the database.

### 3.1.5 Representation and Processing of Spatial Knowledge

Queries concerning environmental data often comprise spatial phenomena, since geographical aspects play an important role in this domain. This requires techniques for knowledge representation and knowledge processing which are adapted to the specific nature of the problem. NAUDA must be able to handle linguistic phenomena which express spatial relationships. Statements containing spatial prepositions (e.g. *nearby, around, near, along*) or expressions like *south of, in the environs of* must be mapped onto geographic regions. This means that vague expressions must be related to concrete database objects or computations on database objects.

We have investigated both representational formalisms for spatial aspects such as cell matrices [Khen 91], multidimensional search trees, methods from computational geometry, and Voronoi diagrams, as well as system frameworks such as spatial decision support systems [Armstrong, Densham 90]. Based on this study, suggestions for processing spatial knowledge have been worked out, but have not yet been implemented (for further details see [Liske 91]).

### 3.2 Architecture of the NAUDA System

The NAUDA System is a combination of components which were developed by the NAUDA project team itself, and of two components from other research groups, namely LanguageAccess and LEU/2 (both IBM).

LanguageAccess is responsible for analyzing a user query. This includes solving references to the previous discourse. LanguageAccess makes use of a *conceptual schema* which contains information about the domain and the specific vocabulary. As a first result of the analysis, a paraphrase is presented to the user for verification (in the case of ambiguity, several paraphrases are presented for selection).

NAUDA's dialog component is responsible for handling false presuppositions on the conceptual level. It uses the inference engine of LEU/2 to check if the requested objects are legal within the domain. LEU/2 contains a modified version of LanguageAccess' conceptual schema as a model of the domain. If an inconsistency is detected, the constraints of the illegal object description are weakened until it fits into the taxonomy of the domain. The type of error is determined by computing the difference between the most general inconsistent and the most specific consistent object description. This information is the source from which the generation component constructs a natural language response for the user. A correction is provided, indicating both the type of error (intensional or extensional), as well as giving adequate additional information.

If no presupposition failure is detected but the question is over-answered (cf. section above), LanguageAccess is advised to generate an SQL-expression for a wh-question which corresponds to the original yes-no question of the user. Depending on the result of the database query, the generation component decides wheather to answer "Yes", or to provide a sentence with the actual value of the property in question.

If none of the above cases hold, LanguageAccess will query the database with an SQL expression which is constructed from the logical representation of the user's query.

Finally, the generation module decides on the form of the presentation of the database results. In addition, it must adapt the form of expression to the preferences of the user, who has the possibility of choosing between two different levels of granularity (that is, short or more precise).

Most of the components of our current prototype are implemented in PROLOG. LanguageAccess and the SQL-DS database itself are components which run on an IBM Mainframe (IBM9370) under VM while the other components run on a PS/2 under AIX. The communication is realized by three interface processes. The first one provides communication with Language-Access, the second one with the NAUDA components, and the third one with a user interface which has been developed on the basis of X-Windows and Motif.

# 4. FUTURE RESEARCH

## 4.1 Integration of Graphics

The visualization of spatial relationships by means of geographic maps can be seen as a starting point for further work. Currently tables, natural language, and graphics are used as media for the presentation of answers. Using an adequate output medium is a definite improvement in terms of human perception and information processing. Yet, the linking of the different channels remains to be worked out, both on the representational side and on the display side. The principles of connectivity which bind them together and force co-interpretation are well worked out within the different media (e.g. within texts), but the coordination remains a topic for further research (cf. [Schmauks, Reithinger 88]).

In order to achieve coherence within the output, referent specification should be done in a multimodal way (e.g. connecting language and graphics by deictic expressions like *this* and *here* which refer to the visually marked objects shown on the map).

In addition to these issues, the interplay between language and imagery for thinking about spatial relations remains to be investigated. Another open question is whether language captures only binary relationships between features or whether images are required to deal with more complex configurations (as noticed by [McGranaghan 88]).

## 4.2 Additional Information

In the current state of the system, only meta-knowledge resulting from false presuppositions is made explicit. But there are several other kinds of meta-information which could be helpful if presented to the user, e.g. information about the structure of the database and about definitions of concepts.

Especially when dealing with highly complex databases, users may have problems with the types and localizations of the information available. A highly cooperative system could support users in becoming familiar with the contents and structure of the database if it were able to answer questions such as *'Where can I find information about XY?'*.

A system which is capable of referring back to meta-information provided in earlier stages of the current dialog (or in previous sessions) could recognize the case where messages did not come across in the way they were intended and react correspondingly. Moreover, unknown concepts could be explained in terms of relationships with previously introduced ones. For this purpose, a powerful dialog memory and a user model must be established.

Additional information for better readability: one of the problems with traditional database interfaces is the fact that the user must remember too many things [Wong, Kuo 82]. Although LanguageAccess has reduced this memory load for the input side quite well, the output data correspond to the form in which they are represented in the database. Databases might contain data in coded form (like numerical keys representing geographic regions) whose meaning might not be known to certain users. The output should be translated into, or annotated with, the names used in natural language. In a similar way, cryptic column names, acronyms and headings of aggregate functions may be made readable by adding appropriate words.

### 4.3 Supporting Problem Solving

Information systems are usually only one of several sources of knowledge which is used to solve an overall task. For complex databases, users cannot be expected to know which contents of the database can support the solving of their task(s). Because data cannot be exploited unless its existence and relevance for a specific task is known, the benefit of a database may increase if the system helps the user to find relevant data. In this case we expect that a user will start with a (probably incomplete) description of her/his task, rather than asking for concrete data. The system should be capable of processing such descriptions.

Furthermore, it must deduce, verify and update its assumptions about the user's goals in order to provide data which are relevant for her/his specific needs. In addition to a model of the user's goals (which must be built during the dialog with the user), the system requires knowledge of the structure of the domain and database and especially insight into the purpose of the data.

## 5. SUMMARY

We have outlined our approach to increasing the cooperative behavior of a natural language interface to a 'real-life' database (i.e. with a broad spectrum of modelled objects and relations). The system can handle some presupposition failures within the user's query. Corrections, over-answering results and the contents of single values are given in natural language. Output modalities have been extended so that answers containing certain spatial aspects are enriched with topographical maps. To date, a first prototype has been implemented.

## ACKNOWLEDGEMENTS

We would like to thank Joachim Posegga and Rüdiger Wirth for their comments on versions of this paper, Harald Bayer for his work on the communication processes, Michael Horn for the implementation of the user interface, Frank Liske for his ideas on spatial aspects, and Manfred Reichert for his help resulting in many system inprovements (e.g. integration of topographical maps, adaption of a speech recognizer).

**REFERENCES**

[Armstrong, Densham 90] M.P. Armstrong, P.J. Densham: Database organization strategies for spatial decision support systems. In *International Journal of Geographical Information Systems*, 1990, Vol.4, No.1, 3-20.

[Grice 75] H.P. Grice: Logic and conversation. In *Syntax and Semantics Vol. 3: Speech Acts*, P. Cole & J.L. Morgan, eds. Academic Press, N.Y., 1975, 41-58.

[Joshi 83] Aravind Joshi: Varieties of cooperative responses in question-answer-systems. In *Question and Answers*, F. Kiefer, ed. Reidel Publishing Company, Dordrecht, 1983 (=Linguistic Calculation 1) S. 229-240.

[Kaplan 83] S. Jerrold Kaplan: Cooperative responses from a portable natural language database query system. In *Computational Models of Discourse*, Brady & Berwick, eds. MIT Press, Cambridge, Massachusetts, 1983, 167-208.

[Khen 91] M.N. Khenkhar: Object-oriented representation of depictions on the basis of cell matrices. In *Text Understanding in LILOG*, O. Herzog & C.R. Rollinger, eds. Lecture Notes in Artificial Intelligence, No. 546, Springer Verlag, 1990, 645-656.

[Küpper et al. 90] D. Küpper, D. Rösner, A. Striegl-Scherer: Natürlichsprachliche Zugangssysteme mit Deutsch als Interaktionssprache - eine vergleichende Studie -. FAW-TR-89011, FAW Ulm, 10'1990.

[Lehmann et al. 78] H. Lehmann, N. Ott, M. Zoeppritz: User experiments with natural language for data base access. In *Proceedings 7th International Conference of Computational Linguistics*, Bergen, 1978.

[Liske 91] Frank Liske: *Zur Repräsentation von räumlichen Objekten mit natürlichsprachlicher Schnittstelle*. Diploma thesis, University of Ulm, Germany, 1991.

[Marburger 88] Heinz Marburger: *Generierung kooperativer natürlichsprachlicher Antworten in einem Dialogsystem mit Zugang zu relationalen Datenbanken*. Dissertation, Universität des Saarlandes, Saarbrücken, 1988

[Mays 80] E. Mays: Failures in natural language systems: Applications to data base query systems. In *Proceedings of National Conference on Artificial Intelligence*. AAAI-80, 1980, 327-330.

[McDonald 86] N.H. McDonald: Video-graphic query facility for database retrieval. In *The Visual Computer 2(2)*, 1986, 72-77.

[McGranaghan 88] M. McGranaghan: Are mental manipulations of surfaces done in language or image space? In *Cognitive and Linguistic Aspects of Geographic Space: Report on a Workshop*, NCGIA Buffalo, June 11-12, 1988.

[Paivio 71a] A. Paivio: Imagery and Language, Imagery: Current Cognitive Approaches, Holt, Rinehart & Winston Inc., New York, 1971.

[Paivio 71b] A. Paivio: Imagery and Verbal Processes, Holt, Rinehart & Winston Inc., New York, 1971.

[Schmauks, Reithinger 88] D. Schmauks, N. Reithinger: Generating multimodal output - conditions, advantages and problems. Technical Report, SFB 314, FB Informatik, Universität Saarbrücken, 1988.

[Wahlster et al. 83] W. Wahlster, H. Marburger, A. Jameson, S. Busemann: Over-answering YES-NO questions: extended responses in a NL interface to a vision system. In *Proceedings of the 8th IJCAI*, Karlsruhe, FRG, 1983, 643-646.

[Webster 90] C. Webster: Rule-based spatial search. In *International Journal of Geographical Information Systems*, 1990, Vol. 4, No. 3, 241-259.

[Wong, Kuo 82] H.K.T. Wong, I. Kuo, GUIDE: Graphical user interface for database exploration. In *Proceedings of the 8th International Conference on Very Large Data Bases*, VLDB Endowment, Saragora, CA, 1982, 22-32.

Education and Society / R. Aiken (Editor)
Information Processing 92, Volume II
Elsevier Science Publishers B.V. (North-Holland)


# Application of Fourth Generation Prototyping Tools and Methods: A Municipal Industrial Water Quality Monitoring System

C. M. Beise[a] and N. Meeks Griffith[b]

[a]School of Business, West Georgia College, Carrollton, Georgia 30118, USA

[b]Bureau of Pollution Control, City of Atlanta, Atlanta, Georgia 30302, USA

**Abstract**

Recent growing public concern about water quality has increased the need for more stringent monitoring of industrial producers of wastewater, which must be treated by municipal facilities. This paper describes the systems development process used to automate a program of industrial wastewater inspection and monitoring. Systems development tools used to build the system include structure charts, data flow diagrams, E-R diagrams, a custom-built data dictionary, and the relational Ingres DBMS and accompanying tools used to generate menus, screens, reports, and applications. The paper discusses the difficulties and benefits of active participation by end-users in analysis and design of the system. Finally, the paper attempts to place this particular case study within a general framework of current and future models of environmental decision support systems (EDSS).

Keyword Codes: D.2.1; D.2.2; H.4; K.4
Keywords: Software Engineering, Requirements/Specifications; Tools and Techniques; Information Systems Applications; Computers and Society

## 1. INTRODUCTION

Recent growing public concern about water quality has placed increased pressure on municipal wastewater treatment plant administrators to provide accurate and precise testing of pollutant levels in wastewater effluents discharged into water sources. In addition, municipal, state, and federal agencies face greater pressure to monitor industrial wastewater released into city sewage systems. This industrial effluent increases the burden on municipal facilities of providing clean water and of maintaining public confidence in water quality.

The City of Atlanta Bureau of Pollution Control operates four wastewater treatment plants serving a metropolitan area population of about two million as well as 150 industrial users. Recently, the Bureau has developed an automated laboratory information management system (LIMS) for more effective measurement and reporting of wastewater pollutant levels (Beise et al., 1991).

In addition to operating the four treatment plants, the Bureau also has a second major functional responsibility for inspecting and monitoring industrial users of the City's sewage system. The Bureau has thus undertaken design and development of a separate information subsystem, interfaced to the system mentioned above (LIMS). The new subsystem (MIMS - monitoring and inspection management system) is intended to improve the industrial inspection and monitoring task by keeping more accurate, more detailed, and more up-to-date records of regular and random sampling and inspections of industrial sites.

Both systems are part of the Bureau's long-term plan for addressing the changing needs and demands of its constituents. As part of the gradual implementation of this plan, the Bureau has installed automated process control equipment at the plants, a communications network, and a relational database management system (INGRES). The database is intended to provide a repository for most of the Bureau's data, which includes information such as personnel records, plant flow rates, lab test data, industrial discharge limits, equipment maintenance schedules, and industrial inspection permits and histories. All of this data will eventually be available on-line to all authorized employees of the Bureau.

This paper describes the development of the inspection and monitoring sub-system, which has followed a formal System Development Life Cycle phased approach combined with prototyping using the software tools provided with the INGRES DBMS. The following sections describe the background of the project, the systems development process and tools that were used, and the difficulties encountered and benefits anticipated in soliciting the participation of end-users in the development process. Environmental benefits expected from the system will be discussed. Finally, this system and its organizational context will be discussed within the framework of environmental decision support systems (EDSS).

The multiple purposes for the paper are thus: 1) to provide additional case studies for organizations developing similar applications, 2) to share experiences with the use of the methods and tools for such environmental applications, and 3) to contribute toward the development of a broader framework for the study and implementation of EDSS.

## 2. BACKGROUND AND CONTEXT

The Bureau of Pollution Control has responsibility for water protection and for the planning, design, construction, operation, and monitoring of wastewater treatment facilities. In support of this mission are four wastewater treatment plants, two laboratories, a Research and Development (R&D) division, and an Inspection and Monitoring division, focusing on industrial wastewater sources. These entities cooperate in ensuring that wastewater which undergoes treatment by City facilities and is then returned to clean water sources complies with State and Federal discharge permit limits. Management control over the water treatment process is maintained by monitoring water quality before, during, and after treatment.

The primary focus of this paper is on the development of an information system to support the Inspection and Monitoring (I&M) function of the Bureau. However, the relationship of I&M to the other divisions requires interfacing with information systems supporting the other divisions (the plants, the laboratories, and R&D).

The relationship of I&M to the treatment plants is that I&M's purpose is to control the amount of unwanted substances that the plants must remove from wastewater. The laboratories provide test results from water samples which support the I&M function. Finally, R&D may conduct special ad-hoc studies as needed when unexpected events related to industrial users occur (such as chemical spills). The results of such studies also support the I&M function. Thus, users in these other divisions, as well as Bureau administration, external agencies such as EPA (Federal Environmental Protection Agency) and EPD (State Environmental Protection Division), the industries themselves, and finally the general community are all stakeholders which make up part of the organizational context within which the I&M system is being developed (Mitroff, 1983; Mendelow, 1984).

## 3. ANALYSIS OF THE INSPECTION AND MONITORING SYSTEM

This section discusses the process of analyzing the problems and information requirements for the industrial monitoring system (MIMS) that is the focus of this paper.

### 3.1 Problems, Opportunities, and System Requirements

The stated purpose of the I&M division, according to one of the I&M users, is to protect the treatment plants. Industries within the city limits must apply for permission to discharge wastewater into the city sewage system. Permission is granted by the City based on permit applications, baseline monitoring reports, self-monitoring reports, annual inspections, and unscheduled "drive-by" inspections. When an industrial user is found in violation of its permitted limits, that company is subject to fines or other prosecution if the violation is not removed within a given time period. Thus, one of the major requirements for the new system is to track inspections, violations, and followup schedules for compliance. In addition, automatic scheduling and reminders are needed for regular annual inspections of industry sites.

A second major functional requirement is issuing and maintaining the permit information. Permits contain information about the kind of industrial process that a company conducts, according to SIC code. Companies must re-apply for permits on a regular basis, and the system must track the permit schedule as well as keep accurate and up-to-date versions of each permit. The new system must also manage septage discharge permits for companies that truck portable units to dumping sites, as well as handle administration of treated groundwater discharge permits (a new federal requirement).

Finally, a third area which the new system is intended to address is automation of several lengthy reports required by state and federal agencies. These include the NPDES (National Pollutant Discharge Elimination System), the Annual Inspection Form for each company, the Significant Industrial Users' list (SIU), and the Significant Noncompliance Industries' list (SNC). One of the key requirements of the new system is to maintain accurate and up-to-date information on each industrial user, so that all reports reflect consistent and timely information.

The new system will alleviate several current problems, which occur primarily in carrying out inspections and in calculating surcharges. The current inspection process includes three types of inspections of industrial user sites. Regular annual inspections are made of each company. In addition, during each water sampling period, a pre-sampling inspection is conducted. These two types of inspections are expected in advance by each industrial client. Inspectors may take manual notes as they tour the sites, but often rely on their memory of the interview when writing it up later in order to send the write-up back to the industry official for agreement on terms of compliance. This sometimes results in accidentally overlooking some violations.

A third type of inspection, which is intended to monitor user operations without prior notice, is the "drive-by" inspection, which is not scheduled in advance. Each inspector has responsibility for a particular geographic area within which a number of industrial sites operate. The inspector literally drives around the area and drops in on the industrial sites over a period of time. Currently, the frequency and comprehensiveness of drive-by coverage of each inspector is somewhat arbitrary, and the results of drive-by inspections often are not recorded.

The new system can assist the inspectors by providing an easy opportunity to record every drive-by, regardless of the presence or absence of violations. It can also provide the inspector with a current list, at any given time, of prior visits to all companies in the area, thus reducing the difficulty of inspector's task of determining whom to visit next. Triggers in the system can produce a suggested drive-by schedule for each inspector, assisting him or her in making decisions about which sites to visit and how frequently to check back.

Another current problem is the calculation and administration of surcharges that companies must pay to use the City's sewage system. Although calculated by I&M, the actual billing of surcharges is carried out by two other City departments, the Water Bureau and the Finance Department, making it more difficult for I&M to easily obtain up-to-date, accurate information on surcharge payments (or lack of payment). The new system is expected to provide both automatic surcharge calculations and also easy access to current payment dates and amounts.

The sheer volume of information and required reports, and the complexity of scheduling inspections, sampling, and follow-up for violations (which vary according to industry type, prior records, and other factors) inhibit rigorous enforcement of state and federal regulations, and currently expand the amount of time that companies have to address violations. An information system that can store and provide quick access to accurate, up-to-date, consistent, and detailed current and historical information about each industrial site can reduce hardcopy paper flow and handling, which decreases decision time and increases the Bureau's ability to enforce compliance with standards.

### 3.2 User Participation

In the development of MIMS, the primary users of the system, and thus primary sources of requirements information, are industrial waste monitors (who carry out water sampling as part of monitoring industrial wastewater) and industrial waste compliance inspectors (who track compliance and violations by performing inspections). Communication between the systems analyst/designer and these users has consisted of the analyst soliciting whatever documents are relevant to understanding the current processes and information, and thus relevant to the design of a new system which supports these processes. Specific documents which have been helpful include formal job descriptions for both the job types mentioned above, a variety of reports (baseline monitoring, annual inspection, permits), and especially a formal narrative analysis of the current system, problems, and requirements written by one of the key compliance inspectors.

One of the key activities of the analyst has been for her to accompany the inspectors on actual site visits and inspections. This has served the obvious purpose of allowing the analyst to gain a better understanding of exactly what takes place during an inspection, by observing first hand the actions of the inspector, what information is recorded (and what is not), what documents are inputs, work sheets, and outputs of the process, and what jargon (terminology) is used by inspectors in the field.

A less obvious but perhaps more important result of this effort on the analyst's behalf has been to develop rapport with the potential users of the system. This has served to develop a sense of cameraderie between the analyst and users and thus to decrease their hesitancy in expressing what they think the new system should do for them. It also has allowed the analyst to maintain on-going communication on an informal basis as needed throughout the analysis, design, and implementation of the system, increasing the users' commitment, sense of involvement and ownership, and satisfaction with the resulting system. "Rapport" is one of the outcomes of analyst/user communication studied by Guinan (1988).

However, problems can also arise when attempts are made to actively involve users. The analyst received three different descriptions of the procedure for permitting a new industry (allowing a new company to begin using the City sewage system), from three different legitimate sources. Her options were to: 1) to make her own decision about how the system would be designed to handle the task (which would risk implementing the system incorrectly), 2) find a higher level manager to resolve their different perspectives (which would risk alienating important system users and sources of further information), or 3) bring the sources together to resolve their different perspectives, potentially creating a conflict situation. The analyst arranged a meeting between the I&M division manager and the other primary user source, and the conflicting perspectives were amicably resolved, primarily due to the good working relationship among the participants (analyst and users).

Another problem occurred when one of the users who was working closely with the analyst volunteered to redesign better key codes for uniquely identifying industrial sampling points. The current key was cumbersome, limited, and incompatible with the systems with which MIMS needed to interface. After several weeks and several reminders, no list of codes was forthcoming from the user. The analyst finally succeeding in getting feedback about the codes after making available to the users a prototype report that used the codes.

The analyst sincerely valued the user's views on this matter, and the user sincerely wanted to participate. The real problem was simply lack of time on the users' part to spend on defining his own requirements. Users are rarely given any extra time to provide information to analysts, even when assigned formal responsibility for involvement in systems projects. It is left to the analyst to delicately balance extraction of the needed information within a given period of time, while maintaining good relations with users by not interfering with their normal work responsibilities and deadlines.

## 4. SYSTEMS DEVELOPMENT METHODS AND TOOLS

In order to meet the requirements described above, the developers followed formal systems development methods, including the Systems Development Life Cycle (SDLC), structured decomposition tools and methods, and rapid prototyping using Fourth Generation (4GL) tools available with the INGRES DBMS. The combination of these methods was intended to reduce system errors, increase end-user involvement and communication, and thus increase the probability that the system ultimately satisfies its intended requirements.

Specific methods and tools used in the project, and the benefits they provided, include the following:

- A hypertext-based narrative description (built by the systems analyst) of the existing I&M system functions and procedures, which provided a easy-to-retrieve reference during analysis, design, and implementation, as well as a tool for communication with users.
- Structure charts and data flow diagrams (DeMarco, 1978; Gane & Sarson, 1979), which provided system organization, functional decomposition, and graphical documentation. These also served as communication tools with users and among developers.
- Entity-relationship diagrams (Chen, 1977) and relational table designs, which served as the basis for database design and as additional system documentation.
- A custom-built data base design tool which incorporated data dictionary functions, provided data base integrity checking, and assisted in automatically creating application shells.

Both process and data models were necessary to fully understand and represent the system. Although not used in the development of this system due to lack of appropriate tools and knowledge on the part of the developers, object-oriented approaches may offer a better future alternative to integrating process- and data-oriented approaches (cf., Booch, 1991).

Incremental development through prototyping lets users see and use the system in action and may often catch previously unstated requirements or reveal exceptions to rules that users have neglected to mention. Prototyping permits users to enter realistic data early in the cycle, which helps correct errors before they are too deeply embedded in developed code and which provides programmers with better test data.

MIMS was prototyped and is being implemented using the relational data base management system, INGRES and its accompanying prototyping tools, ABF/4GL (proprietary language), Report Generator, and Screen Generator. INGRES runs on a DEC VAX network using VMS. The VAX C compiler was also used for some procedures. GUIDE was the hypertext tool used for narrative description of information gathered during analysis. DrawPerfect was used for DFD's, structure charts, and E-R diagrams. WordPerfect was used for other system documentation including analysis and requirements documents and process narratives.

## 5. IMPLEMENTATION ALTERNATIVES

Field observation and other analysis of the users' needs has led the Bureau to investigate providing the inspectors with notebook computers on which are stored parts of the central database on disk for reference. This scheme has several benefits for the inspectors. By having at their fingertips access to up-to-date permit, violation, reporting, and other historical information about the industrial site, the inspectors will be in a better position to discuss violations and enforcement decisions with the industrial users on the spot. They will also be able to immediately enter and preserve the critical details of their observations. If a printer is available, a hardcopy of their assessment could be printed, reviewed, and signed by the industrial user on the spot as well.

An additional benefit of this approach is that the inspectors will not have to carry with them to the field bulky legal documents, reducing the risk of loss or damage. All of these changes in procedures will result in speedier processing, less paperwork, greater accuracy, fewer errors, and thus more rigorous maintenance of water quality standards.

Also under consideration is the electronic transmittal by companies of self-monitoring data and permit applications. Security considerations and current lack of externally integrated resources will probably results in initially implementing this plan by simply mailing diskettes from companies to the Bureau. If the data is properly formatted, this approach can still save considerable time and money in terms of reduced data entry and paperwork.

## 6. BENEFITS AND CONSEQUENCES

The benefits of the MIMS system and its interfaces to other divisional information systems include:

- more effective monitoring of industrial wastewater producers,
- increased ability of Bureau, plant, and division management a) to make quick decisions and take immediate actions on the basis of unanticipated events (for example, a broken sewage line) and/or b) provide accurate and up-to-date information to the media and public,

- greater integration of information so little or no re-entry of redundant data is needed, for reporting and/or consolidation, and reduction of paper flow,
- better tracking and reporting of historical and current industry status, along a variety of parameters,
- more management control over industrial effluent, indirectly benefiting treatment plant operations by reducing possible excesses of unwanted substances which could adversely affect plant operations,
- increased efficiency of I&M operations, resulting in more effective allocation of personnel and financial resources.

Thus, the use of formal development methods, prototyping tools, and a sophisticated relational database management system has resulted in an information system which will support efforts to maintain a quality environment, specifically water quality, by providing more accurate, more precise, and more complete information to both internal and external constituents. The information will be used to provide more stable plant and industrial operations, more consistent compliance with standards, higher quality effluents, and thus better water quality, not only for recreational use but also for better protection of aquatic life and human health.

## 7. FUTURE DIRECTIONS IN EDSS

Guariso and Werthner (1989) have described environmental decision support systems (EDSS) using the standard DSS elements of database, knowledge base, model base, and user interface. The system described in this paper, although not designed specifically as a DSS, can provide the basis for decision support (as discussed above), partly due to its relational database and Fourth Generation query capabilities and its menu-oriented, windowed, user-friendly interface. Modeling capabilities are included in the flexible reporting system design. A true knowledge base of inspector experience and expertise is not part of the current design but offers potential for more sophisticated decision support as well as for training, and may be added later.

The application described in this paper fits the description of environmental problems characterized by Guariso and Werthner (1989) as dynamic, with cyclical time scales, randomness, complexity, and massive data requirements. An industrial monitoring application is dynamic, in having to accommodate changing requirements, in agency regulations, pollutant levels, industrial site turnover, and unpredictable industrial accidents. The application is cyclical in requiring scheduling and tracking of water sampling, permit applications, and inspections. Complexity arises in the system having to incorporate multiple viewpoints and criteria, and the details of sampling data stored over a period of time will generate a significant volume of data.

Computer applications for environmental problems must be accurate, robust, simple, transparent, and have easy-to-use interfaces (Guariso & Werthner, 1989). All of these characteristics are being incorporated into the the design of the system described in this paper.

Finally, one of the key characteristics of environmental applications which the EDSS described by Guariso and Werthner only indirectly addresses is the need for close cooperation, not only between computer analysts and decision-makers, but also among multiple experts from different environment-related disciplines. A potentially useful emerging technology for improved communication and collaboration among work teams such as these is group decision support systems (GDSS). Other current names for such systems include groupware, computer-supported collaborative work systems (CSCW), and electronic meeting systems (EMS).

Among the many group applications for which these systems are currently being explored is that of joint application design (JAD) and other forms of team requirements definition which facilitate active user participation (Carmel & George, 1991; Daniels et al., 1991). Future research and applications in EDSS should consider the great potential offered by GDSS, in defining more accurately and completely the complex environmental requirements demanded by environmental applications, by facilitating interactive communication and decision-making among multiple experts and multiple constituents, and thus resulting in more effective and satisfactory computer information systems for protecting the environment

## 8. REFERENCES

Beise, C.M., MacDonald, R.N., Griffith, N.M., & Barnes, G.D. (1991) "Development of a Municipal Water Quality Control System: Application of Fourth Generation Prototyping Tools." *Proceedings of the Sixth Symposium in Computer Science for Environmental Protection*, Dec 4-6, Munich, Germany.

Booch, G. (1991) *Object-Oriented Design with Applications*. Redwood City, CA: Benjamin-Cummings.

Carmel, E. & George, J. (1991) "Joint Application Design (JAD) and Electronic Meeting Systems (EMS): Opportunities for the future". University of Arizona Working Paper WPS-91-06.

Chen, P. (1977) *The Entity-Relationship Approach to Logical Data Base Design*. Wellesley, MA: QED Information Sciences.

Daniels, R.M., Dennis, A.R., Hayes, G., Nunamaker, J.F., & Valacich, J. (1991) "Enterprise Analyzer: Electronic support for group requirements elicitation" in *Proceedings of the 24th Hawaii Conference on Systems Science, Vol. 3*, 43-50.

DeMarco, T. (1979) *Structured Analysis and System Specification*. Englewood Cliffs, NJ: Prentice-Hall.

Gane, C. & Sarson, T. (1979) *Structured Systems Analysis: Tools and Techniques.* Englewood Cliffs, NJ: Prentice-Hall.

Guariso, G. & Werthner, H. (1989) *Environmental Decision Support Systems.* Chichester, West Sussex, England: Ellis Horwood Ltd.

Guinan, P.J. (1988) *Patterns of Excellence: An analysis of communication behavior.* Washington, DC: ICIT Press.

Mendelow, A. (1984) "Information systems for organizational effectiveness: The use of the Stakeholder approach" in Bemelmans, T.M.A., Ed., *Beyond Productivity: Information Systems Development for Organizational Effectiveness.* Amsterdam: North-Holland.

Mitroff, I.I. (1983) *Stakeholders of the organizational mind.* San Franciso, CA: Jossey-Bass.

Education and Society / R. Aiken (Editor)
Information Processing 92, Volume II
Elsevier Science Publishers B.V. (North-Holland)
1992 IFIP.

# Integration of GIS into Decision Support Systems for Management of Ground Water

J. Fürst

Institut für Wasserwirtschaft, Hydrologie und konstruktiven Wasserbau, Universität für Bodenkultur, Nußdorfer Lände 11, A-1190 Wien, Austria

**Abstract**

The requirements for Decision Support Systems (DSS) for the management of ground water are derived from a discussion of relevant data and functions. Geographical Information Systems (GIS) evidently can contribute tools for spatial data management and display. The feasibility and technique of the integration of GIS and DSS are demonstrated in two case studies, one using the vector based GIS ARC/INFO, the second using the raster based GIS GRASS.

Keyword Codes: H.5.2; I.3.8; J.6
Keywords: Information Systems, User Interfaces; Computer Graphics, Applications; Computer-Aided Engineering

## 1. INTRODUCTION

Availability of enough water in good quality - which is to a large amount taken from ground water - can no longer be taken as granted. In fact, two developments are forcing us to improve the management of ground water resources. On one side the demand for water is still significantly increasing. Quantity and quality of our ground water resources are on the other side endangered by sealing the ground surfaces, by agricultural soil processing, or by pollution from agriculture and defect waste dump sites. Construction of runoff hydropower schemes often reduces ground water dynamics due to a decoupling of surface water and ground water.

A responsible management of ground water resources requires a comprehensive database and a set of tools to model the system. Data and tools cover more than only the ground water domain to take care for the interactions between ground water and surface water, soil and vegetation as well as ecological aspects.

## 2. MANAGEMENT OF GROUND WATER

Ground water is the water beneath the ground surface that completely fills the pores and the movement of which is mainly determined by gravity and friction. The methodology described in this paper typically refers to alluvial aquifers with an area somewhere between

10 and a few thousands of square kilometers. Groundwater dynamics is influenced by streams and recharge from precipitation as well as human utilization.

Typical actions with impacts on ground water systems and thus requiring ground water management are:

- ❑ discharge in pumping wells for domestic, industrial and agricultural supply
- ❑ hydraulic engineering constructions such as hydro power plants, river regulations, dams, reservoirs
- ❑ other actions influencing the regional water cycle: roads and highways, tunnels, waste dump sites, sewer systems, etc.

### 2.1. Systems approach to the ground water management problem

The objective of management is to improve a ground water system under given criteria by appropriate decisions. Following a systems approach [1], a ground water system is described by its input, state, output, state transition and output function.

*System input* has an uncontrolled component, primarily derived from precipitation. Management decisions like discharges, infiltration and modifications of boundary conditions make up the controllable part.

The *state* of the system at a given time is described by time invariant variables like the hydrogeological parameters and time dependent variables, usually the ground water level as a function of space.

*System output* is characterised by the ground water level, by the flow velocity, possible discharges or subsurface outflow.

*State transition* describes the reaction of the groundwater system to stresses. Typically, this can be explained by the differential equation of ground water flow. Analytical solutions exist for simple cases. For more complex problems numerical ground water models (finite differences, finite elements) are frequently applied.

The *output function* relates system output and taken decisions and thus represents the problem under investigation.

### 2.2. Data

A large amount of different categories of data forms the model of a ground water system in the computer.

*Time invariant spatial data:* Primarily the hydrogeological properties of the aquifer (geological layers, hydraulic conductivity, porosity), but also maps of land use, valuable habitats or regional planning topics fall in this category. Ideally, we need to know all this information as continuous functions of space. However, in most cases only point (e.g., from boreholes) or line related data (e.g., seismic profiles) are available.

*Time series data:* For analysis of the historic behaviour of a ground water system, ground water levels, solute concentrations, discharges and meteorological variables are measured at several observation points. These variables are a function of space and time. The density of observation points varies and is often very low. Also the observation interval is usually not constant and observation times are not the same on different points.

We must distinguish original (observed) data from derived (computed) data. Another important aspect is to account for uncertainty and errors in the data.

## 3. DECISION SUPPORT SYSTEMS

Decision Support Systems (DSS) support decision making for complex, yet weakly structured problems. They couple specialised models for parts of the problem with the database. A friendly, interactive user interface makes it accessible at the level of the decision maker [2,3].

The key term of modern DSS is information management. Their central component is its database. All the functions of the DSS access this database and add and/or retrieve information. This holds for a simple time series plotter as well as for a complex numerical ground water model. So the database is "the model" on which the functions (including numerical ground water "models") provide different views and perform experiments.

### 3.1. Database

The database has to hold time invariant spatial data, time series data and textual information or expertise. The organisation of the spatial data must provide the following access methods:

- ❑ selection of objects by identification, coordinates, and attribute values
- ❑ selection by topological criteria (neighbours, nearest points)
- ❑ interpolation in 3-d surface models, including cross sections

The time series data base must provide selection of observation points by name and position, by time criteria and by value. A special case is the selection of a value at a given time for a set of observation points. This involves interpolation in time. The result of this type of query usually is used to build a 3-d surface of the ground water level. Evidently, a strong connection to the spatial database is required.

Textual information must be incorporated to capture expertise and to document the important steps of analysis.

### 3.2. Functions

The functions of a DSS for ground water management can be grouped in 3 categories: information, scenario generation and decision support.

*Information functions* are the tools for data acquisition, data analysis and display. Data acquisition tools cover the tasks of map digitizing, data entry and conversion and import of external data.

Data analysis functions provide specific views at the state of the ground water system as represented in the database. They include time series analysis, spatial analysis, neighbourhood analysis, area statistics, cluster analysis and others.

*Scenario generation and simulation.* The main goal of building a computer model of a ground water system is to provide a facility for specifying decision alternatives and simulate their impact in the model. Numerical ground water models are frequently applied, powerful tools to study the dynamic behaviour of a regional ground water system under various conditions.

### 3.3. User interface

A large database and an extensive and complex set of tools makes a friendly user interface a precondition for successful use. The users want convenient and safe ways to submit their questions to the DSS and they want fast, intuitive presentation of the results [4]. State of the art technology for this purpose are graphical user interfaces and extensive use of interactive computer graphics.

## 4. ROLE OF GIS

Geographic Information Systems (GIS) became important tools to aid solutions of space related problems. They are designed for acquisition, storage, analysis and display of spatial data. It is obvious, that a GIS can provide many of the capabilities needed in a DSS for ground water management.

### 4.1. Spatial database

The original data usually refer to three types of geometric objects: points, lines or areas (polygons). With any of these geometric primitives we have to associate a number of attributes. Hydrogeologic parameters at boreholes, hydraulic properties of river reaches and land use maps are examples. The final representation of many variables is a continuous function of space (3-D model).

GIS can manage these space related data of ground water systems. To serve as the database management system of a DSS, it is necessary to interface external tools (e.g., a numerical ground water model) with the GIS data. GIS database objects must thus be well documented and accessible to programs not provided with the GIS.

### 4.2. Analysis functions

Many functions of GIS are useful for ground water DSS. A few examples together with typical applications are presented below:

- ❑ spatial interpolation to build 3-d models (e.g., triangulated irregular networks) from point and line data: ground water surfaces generated from water levels at observation wells and rivers, geologic strata from borehole data and seismic profiles.

- ❑ neighbourhood analysis: how many wells are within a certain distance from a river or leaking dump site?

❑ map overlay: which wells are in a forest, how many are at points with a confining layer of less than xx meters, which precious habitats are affected by a groundwater drawdown of more than yy meters?

❑ intersection of surfaces: which area would be flooded after impoundment of a river?

❑ area statistics: distribution of agricultural areas in given classes of depth of ground water.

### 4.3. Map Display

Spatial data are conveniently visualised as maps. Therefore mapping is probably the best known feature of GIS. For a DSS fast, interactive mapping features on high resolution graphics displays are more important than publication quality hardcopy output. The types of maps most frequently needed for ground water management are:

❑ contour maps: Contour maps are the most common type of map to display the elevation of the ground surface, the ground water level, or the relief of geologic strata. In a contour map it is easy to identify magnitude and direction of gradients (which is correlated with flow velocity), or to compare two surfaces with small differences by superimposing two contour maps with different line types.

❑ colour coded maps: When suitable palettes are used, colour coded maps can be very intuitive and striking means to display an important aspect of a spatial phenomenon. As an example, consider the distribution of the concentration of a toxic solute: paint the areas with concentrations in an acceptable range in gradually varying "friendly" colours, and use signal red for areas of dangerous concentration. While still displaying all the information, the user's attention is immediately captured by the part that obviously demands for his decision.

### 4.4. Software architecture

Although practically every GIS has useful functions for a ground water DSS, the integration of GIS and DSS depends on the software architecture of the GIS. To facilitate integration, the GIS must be an open system, i.e. it must

❑ allow access of the data structures to external programs

❑ allow the integration of GIS functions and user developed DSS tools under a common, consistent user interface.

Two different approaches proved to be feasible: In the first, the GIS is "extended" by specific functions to build a ground water DSS. This is done by development of pre- and postprocessors that interface GIS-data and ground water programs and are packed into the GIS by the macro language of the GIS. The user interface of the DSS is also built in the macro language of the GIS that provides access to selected GIS functions as well as to the ground water specific tools. This approach allows rapid prototyping, but being bound to the capabilities of the GIS macro language might become restrictive.

In the second approach the DSS is not "centered" around the GIS, but makes use of data structures, data access libraries and selected GIS functions. This requires a modular structure of the GIS, so a call of a function would not enforce large overhead.

## 5. CASE STUDIES

Two prototypes of DSS for ground water management have been developed to study different approaches, both in terms of the type of GIS and the technique of integration. [5]. The DSS ARCGW is rather an extension of the vector based GIS ARC/INFO, while LGW ("Logical Ground water Workstation") uses parts of the raster based GIS GRASS.

### 5.1. ARCGW

ARCGW is based on ARC/INFO. The spatial database of ARCGW consists of a set of ARC/INFO coverages. All three ARC/INFO topologies (point, line and polygon) as well as triangulated irregular networks (TIN) are used. Original data are distinguished from working data. Fig. 1 illustrates the spatial database of ARCGW. A specific time series database was developed that interfaces with the GIS.

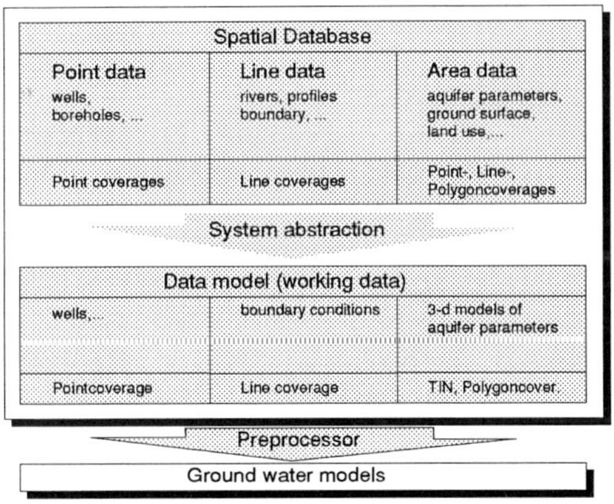


Figure 1. The spatial database of ARCGW

ARC/INFO provides the majority of data acquisition and digitizing functions. The specific strength of the GIS is evident in the data analysis and display functions. Area statistics, map overlays, surface intersections, vertical sections or contour maps are the most significant contributions in this group.

The most important part of the DSS is the generation and simulation of management scenarios. In ARCGW a finite difference ground water model for simulation of transient two-dimensional ground water flow is currently available. This model is integrated into the DSS via pre- and postprocessors.

The preprocessor is the "command board" of the numerical model. Its main features are interactive graphical design of the model grid, definition of boundaries using available maps in the GIS, and automatic interpolation of the aquifer parameters for the designed grid. This required direct access to ARC/INFO coverages using the ARC/INFO object libraries [6].

The postprocessor simply transforms the model's output and passes selected results to the DSS database for further analysis and display. Thus the results of the model can also be compared with other information in the database.

The user interface of ARCGW is developed in the ARC/INFO macro language AML, which allows customization of selected ARC/INFO functionality as well as integration of external programs. Consistent with ARC/INFO, ARCGW functions are accessible as commands and in a menu system.

### 5.2. LGW

LGW (Logical Groundwater Workstation) follows similar design principles. It is based on the raster based GIS GRASS from the U.S. Army Construction Engineering Research Laboratory (USA-CERL). GRASS is a complete GIS with nearly 200 functions, runs on UNIX workstations and is in the public domain, including source code. The software architecture of GRASS harmonises perfectly with the intended structure of LGW. It is a collection of rather independent UNIX command line driven programs that can easily be called from any UNIX process. GRASS data structures are well documented. A library of functions supports convenient access for the programmer.

GRASS data structures are available for point, line and area (polygon) data, although GIS operations can only be performed on raster maps. Point and line maps are used for data import via digitizer or from ARC/INFO maps. They are directly used for the display of background maps and GRASS also has tools for spatial interpolation to generate raster maps. Raster maps are used as the desired 3-D models of aquifer parameters. Additional data objects were defined and are organised in a hierarchical file system, consistent with GRASS data (Fig. 2).

A layered design was selected for the software. The interface between tools and database is built by a library of functions, including the GRASS prgrammer's library and similar functions for DSS specific data objects. These functions are called from command line programs (from GRASS or "new" programs) or highly interactive programs with their own graphical user interface and interactive graphics. Command line programs can be combined for more complex tasks by UNIX shell scripts. The top level of the user interface is realised by the script-driven application generator XGEN [7,8].

All graphics is based on the X Window System. The user interface uses the OSF/Motif toolkit. As an example of the appearance of LGW to a user, fig. 3 shows a screen dump of the postprocessor of a finite difference ground water model.

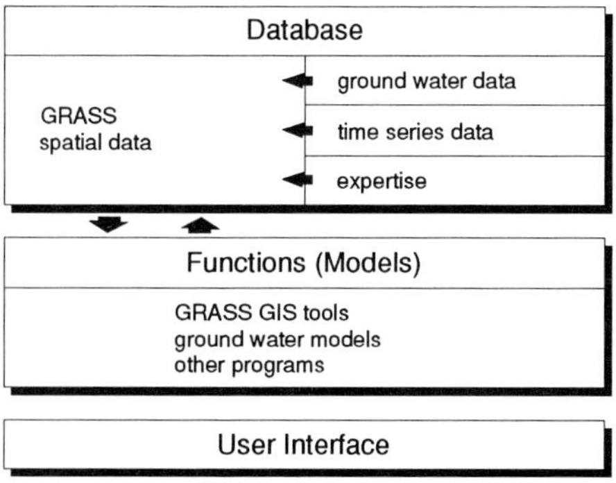


Figure 2. Schematic view of LGW database

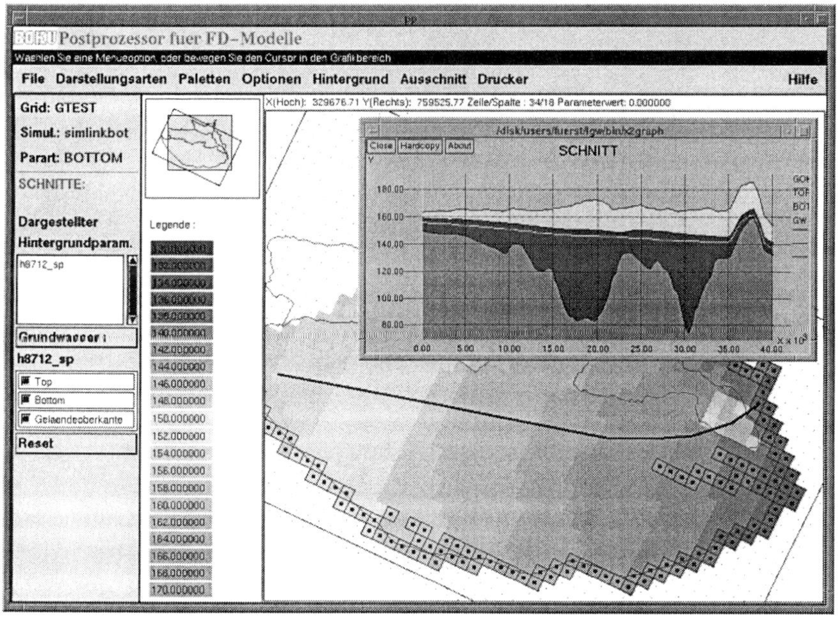


Figure 3. User interface of the postprocessor for a FD ground water model

## 6. CONCLUSIONS

The functionality of GIS provides a considerable part of DSS for ground water management. If the software architecture of the GIS is sufficiently open, integration of GIS into DSS has advantages compared to using less powerful components and tools for the DSS.

The raster based GIS has the disadvantage, that the minimum resolution of a raster map has to be decided when it is created. Thus, if for an area analysis needs to be done in different scales (a regional and a local), we have either huge dimensions of the raster or information might get lost.

GIS operations are performed faster on a raster, which is important for an interactive tool.

The availability of GIS source code, or at least a linkable library for direct data access is essential for a reasonable performance of interactive programs. Interfaces using file export techniques generally have bad performance and are only acceptable for tasks of lower priority.

Support of 3-D data elements is still not satisfactory in both, ARC/INFO and GRASS. Especially, features of digital terrain models like non-convex boundaries and break lines are desirable.

A higher degree of modularity would avoid significant overhead, when only part of the GIS needs to be integrated.

## 7. REFERENCES

1 Wymore, Systems Enginieering Methodology for Interdisciplinary Teams. Wiley Interscience, New York, (1976).
2 Bonczek R.H., C.W. Holsapple & A.B. Whinston, Foundations of Decision Support Systems. Academic Press, New York, (1981).
3 Sol, H.H. (Ed.), Processes and Tools for Decision Support. Proc. of the joint IFIP WG 8.3 / IIASA Working Conference on Processes and Tools for Decision Support, North Holland Publ., Amsterdam, (1983).
4 Loucks, D. P., J. Kindler & K. Fedra, Interactive Water Resources Modeling and Model Use: An Overview. Water Resources Research. Vol. 21, No. 2, (1985), pp. 95-102.
5 Fürst, J., Decision Support Systeme für die Grundwasserwirtschaft unter Verwendung geographischer Informationssysteme. Wiener Mitteilungen. Band 93, Wien, (1990).
6 Fürst, J., S. Haider, H.P. Nachtnebel, ARC/INFO as a Tool in Groundwater Systems Analysis. ESRI European User Conference, Kranzberg, BRD, (1987) pp. 7/1-12.
7 Awaida, A.A., R.D. Logcher, Development of an Application Generator for GRASS. Research Report R89-01, IESL MIT, Cambridge, MA., (1989).
8 Buehler, K. A., Xgen: An Application Interface Generator Program. User's Manual. Purdue University, West Lafayette, USA., (1990).

Education and Society / R. Aiken (Editor)
Information Processing 92, Volume II
Elsevier Science Publishers B.V. (North-Holland) 


# Linking Environmental Studies and IT - a East-West Project in Bulgaria, Germany and the United Kingdom

**U. Bosler (IPN, Kiel), D. Squires (King's College London) & R. Tsankova (Technical University - Sofia), W. Ziebarth (IPN, Kiel)**

The use of information technology (IT) to support teaching and learning is now established at all levels; with claims that IT can improve existing educational practice and introduce exciting new approaches to teaching and learning. Given the needs to develop new environmental education curricula and related teaching practice there is a strong case for investigated the potential of IT to support, enhance and develop work in environmental education. Computer Based Environmental Studies (COBES), a current TEMPUS project based on cooperation between the IPN-Institute for Science Education (Germany), King's College London (UK), and the Technical University, Sofia (Bulgaria), is designed to explore these issues through the development of university level environmental studies curricula which make extensive use of IT.

The structure and tasks of the project are shown in the diagram. Activities are shown on the left, resulting tasks are shown in the centre, and the outputs of the project are shown on the right and on the bottom.

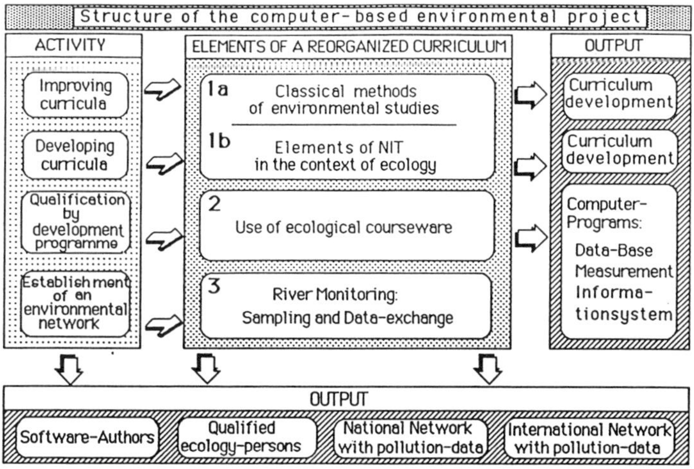

The fundamental aim of COBES is to integrate the revision and development of university level environmental studies curicula with the use of IT (particularly the data logging of water pollution). Existing courses within the Technical University, Sofia are providing a context for this work. These developments are supported by the extensive use of IT to support teaching and learning. IT support is currently focused on the collection and analysis of data to provide illustrative curriculum materials. Data logging equipment is being used to collect data concerned with the levels of pollution in Bulgarian rivers, and information handling software is being used to analyse these data. It is planned to incorporate the use of modelling and simulation software as the project progresses.

•Task 1 consists of two related sub-tasks: (a) to develop or to improve environmental studies curricula and (b) to identify appropriate and relevant uses of IT in these curricula. Two information handling packages have been identified to support the analysis of the river pollution data: *Bioview* and *Umweltatlas* .

•Task 2 is to identify and integrate the use of computer-based learning in the delivery of the curricula developed in Task 1. It is planned to adapt pieces of educational software as an integral part of the project. This idea would be based on the adaptation of existing EC educational software to produce Bulgarian language versions. Bulgarian versions of *Bioview* and *Umweltatlas* are currently being prepared.Simulations and modelling systems will feature prominently in the development programme. It is planned that the training of a number of educational software authors will be a feature of this task.

•Task 3 is to develop a data exchange system concerned with river pollution, with data exchanged between a number of centres located in various parts of Bulgaria. This exchange of data will lead to a national database on river pollution. The curriculum revision in Task 1 will make use of this database to develop exemplar teaching materials. Data are to be collected according to the data collection framework established by the worldwide Global Rivers Environmental Education Network (GREEN). This framework defines nine data collection parameters: dissolved oxygen, fecal coliform, pH, biochemical oxygen demand, temperature, total phosphorous, nitrates, turbidity, and total solids. In addition , the existence of representative micro-organisms are used to give a broad classification of water quality. Data is being collected by the use of self contained purpose designed computer based data logging kits.

# AUTHOR INDEX

* Paper not submitted

# IFIP

*The INTERNATIONAL FEDERATION FOR INFORMATION PROCESSING is a multinational federation of professional and technical organisations (or national groupings of such organisations) concerned with information processing. From any one country, only one such organisation – which must be representative of the national activities in the field of information processing – can be admitted as a Full Member. In addition a regional group of developing countries can be admitted as a Full Member. On 1 October 1991, 46 organisations were Full Members of the Federation, representing 70 countries.*

The aims of IFIP are to promote information science and technology by:

- fostering international co-operation in the field of information processing;
- stimulating research, development and the application of information processing in science and human activity;
- furthering the dissemination and exchange of information about the subject;
- encouraging education in information processing.

IFIP is dedicated to improving worldwide communication and increased understanding among practitioners of all nations about the role information processing can play in all walks of life.

Information technology is a potent instrument in today's world, affecting people in everything from their education and work to their leisure and in their homes. It is a powerful tool in science and engineering, in commerce and industry, in education and adminstration. It is truly international in its scope and offers a significant opportunity for developing countries. IFIP helps to bring together workers at the leading edge of the technology to share their knowledge and experience, and acts as a catalyst to advance the state of the art.

IFIP came into official existence in January, 1960. It was established to meet a need identified at the first International Conference on Information Processing which was held in Paris in June, 1959, under the sponsorship of UNESCO.

**Organisational Structure**
The Federation is governed by a GENERAL ASSEMBLY, which meets once every year and consists of one representative from each Member organisation. The General Assembly decides on all important matters, such as general policy, the programme of activities, admissions, elections and budget.

## IFIP ORGANISATION CHART

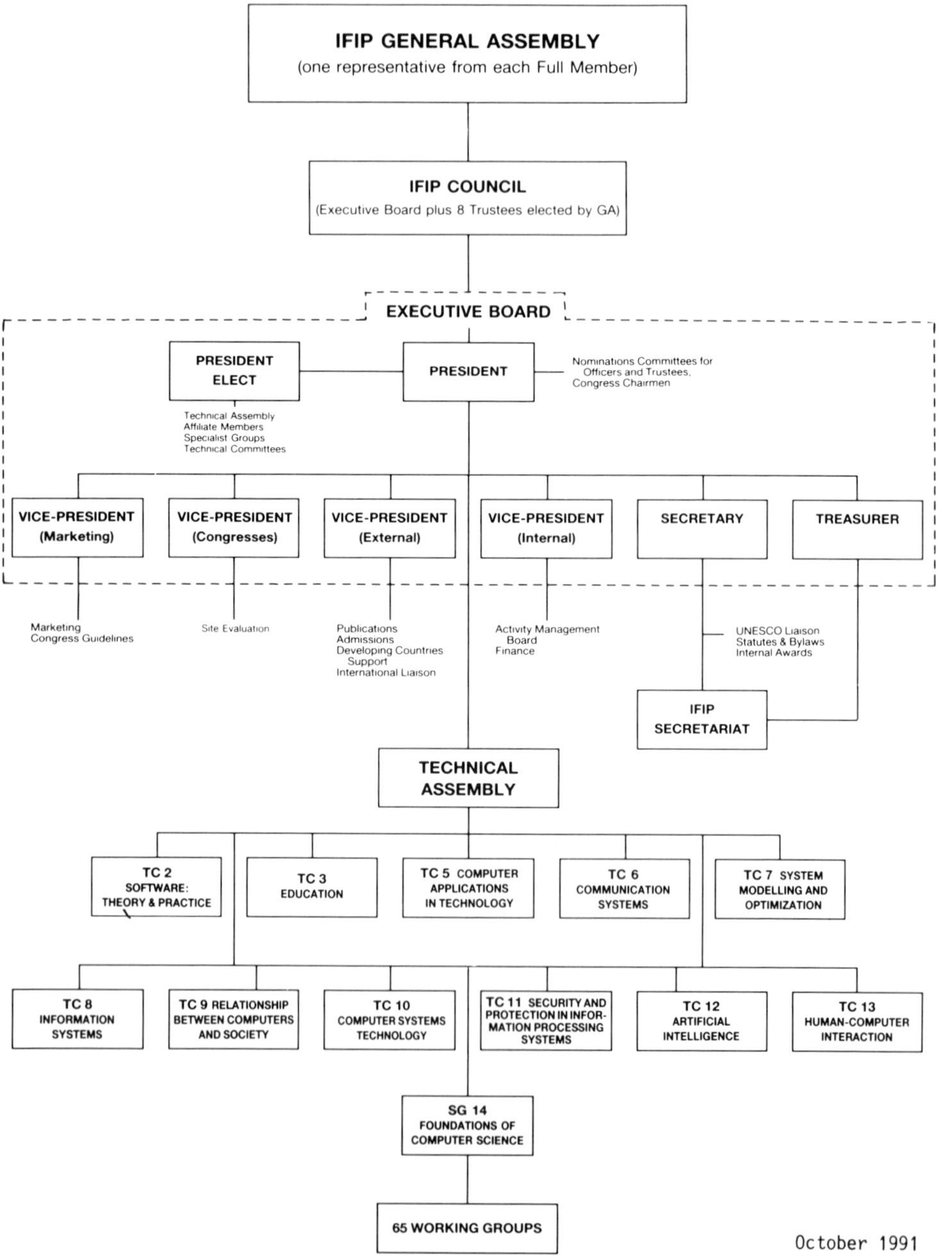


October 1991

The day-to-day work of IFIP is directed by its Officers: the President, Vice-Presidents, Secretary and Treasurer, who are elected by the General Assembly and together constitute the EXECUTIVE BOARD.

The COUNCIL, consisting of the Officers and up to eight Trustees elected from the General Assembly, meets twice a year and takes decisions which become necessary between General Assembly meetings.

The headquarters of the Federation are in Geneva, Switzerland where the IFIP Secretariat administers its affairs.

**For further information please contact:**

**IFIP Secretariat**
attn. Mme. GWYNETH ROBERTS
16 Place Longemalle
CH-1204 Geneva, Switzerland
telephone: 41 (22) 28 26 49
facsimile: 41 (22) 781 23 22
Bitnet: ifip@cgeuge51

# IFIP's MISSION STATEMENT

IFIP's mission is to be the leading, truly international, apolitical organisation which encourages and assists in the development, exploitation and application of Information Technology for the benefit of all people.

**Principal Elements**

1. To stimulate, encourage and participate in research, development and application of Information Technology (IT) and to foster international co-operation in these activities.
2. To provide a meeting place where national IT Societies can discuss and plan courses of action on issues in our field which are of international significance and thereby to forge increasingly strong links between them and with IFIP.
3. To promote internation co-operation directly and through national IT Societies in a free environment between individuals, national and international governmental bodies and kindred scientific and professional organisations.
4. To pay special attention to the needs of developing countries and to assist them in appropriate ways to secure the optimum benefit from the application of IT.
5. To promote professionalism, incorporating high standards of ethics and conduct, among all IT practitioners.
6. To provide a forum for assessing the social consequences of IT applications; to campaign for the safe and beneficial development and use of IT and the protection of people from abuse through its improper application.

7. To foster and facilitate co-operation between academics, the IT industry and governmental bodies and to seek to represent the interest of users.
8. To provide a vehicle for work on the international aspects of IT development and application including the necessary preparatory work for the generation of international standards.
9. To contribute to the formulation of the education and training needed by IT practitioners, users and the public at large.

**Note to Conference Organizers**
Organizers of upcoming IFIP Working Conferences are urged to contact the Publisher. Please send full details of the Conference to:

Mrs. STEPHANIE SMIT
Administrative Editor – IFIP Publications
**ELSEVIER SCIENCE PUBLISHERS**
P.O. Box 103, 1000 AC Amsterdam
The Netherlands
telephone: 31 (20) 5862481
facsimile: 31 (20) 5862616
email: s.smit@elsevier.nl

# IFIP TRANSACTIONS

IFIP TRANSACTIONS is a serial consisting of 15,000 pages of valuable scientific information from leading researchers, published in 35 volumes per year. The serial includes contributed volumes, proceedings of the IFIP World Conferences, and conferences at Technical Committee and Working Group level. Mainstream areas in the IFIP TRANSACTIONS can be found in Computer Science and Technology, Computer Applications in Technology, and Communication Systems.

Please find below a detailed list of topics covered.

IFIP TRANSACTIONS A:
**Computer Science and Technology**
1992: 19 Volumes, US $ 1181.00/Dfl. 2185.00
ISSN 0926-5473

**IFIP Technical Committees**
Software: Theory and Practice (TC2)
Education (TC3)
System Modelling and Optimization (TC7)
Information Systems (TC8)
Relationship Between Computers and Society (TC9)

Computer Systems Technology (TC10)
Security and Protection in Information Processing Systems (TC11)
Artificial Intelligence (TC12)
Human-Computer Interaction (TC13)
Foundations of Computer Science (SG14)

IFIP TRANSACTIONS B:
**Applications in Technology**
1992: 8 Volumes. US $ 497.00/Dfl. 920.00
ISSN 0926-5481

**IFIP Technical Committee**
Computer Applications in Technology (TC5)

IFIP TRANSACTIONS C:
**Communication Systems**
1992: 8 Volumes. US 497.00/Dfl. 920.00
ISSN 0926-549X

**IFIP Technical Committee**
Communication Systems (TC6)

**IFIP TRANSACTIONS FULL SET: A, B & C**
**1992: 35 Volumes. US $ 1892.00/Dfl. 3500.00**

The Dutch Guilder prices (Dfl.) are definitive. The US $ prices mentioned above are for your guidance only and are subject to exchange rate fluctuations. Prices include postage and handling charges.

The volumes are also available separately in book form.

Please address all orders and correspondence to:

**ELSEVIER SCIENCE PUBLISHERS**
attn. PETRA VAN DER MEER
P.O. Box 103, 1000 AC Amsterdam
The Netherlands
telephone: 31 (20) 5862602
facsimile: 31 (20) 5862616
email: m.haccou@elsevier.nl